FIFTH EDITION

Treffpunkt Deutsch

GRUNDSTUFE

E. Rosemarie Widmaier

McMaster University

Fritz T. Widmaier

McMaster University

Margaret Gonglewski

The George Washington University

PEARSON
Prentice Hall

woRLd Languages

Upper Saddle River,
New Jersey 07458

Library of Congress Cataloging-in-Publication Data

Widmaier, E. Rosemarie
   Treffpunkt Deutsch : Grundstufe / E. Rosemarie Widmaier, Fritz T. Widmaier,
Margaret Gonglewski.—5th ed.
      p.   cm.
   Includes index.
   ISBN 0-13-195546-2 (student edition : alk. paper)
1. German language—Grammar.   2. German language—Textbooks for foreign speakers—
English.   I. Widmaier, Fritz T.   II. Gonglewski, Margaret.   III. Title.
   PF3112.W5 2007
   438.2'421—dc22   2006101986

Acquisitions Editor: Rachel McCoy
Director of Marketing: Kristine Suárez
Senior Marketing Manager: Denise Miller
Director of Editorial Development: Julia Caballero
Developmental Editor: Karen Storz
Production Editor: Manuel Echevarria
Project Manager: Semjon Lukashov, Emilcomp/Preparé
Prepress and Manufacturing Buyer: Brian Mackey
Prepress and Manufacturing Assistant Manager:
   Nick Sklitsis
Supplements Editor: Meriel Martinez
Senior Media Editor: Samantha Alducin
Cover and Interior Design: Lisa Delgado

Illustrations: Michael Widmaier
Cover Concept: Sabine Grosser
Cover Images: Christian Ohde and Marian Rene Menges
Editorial Assistant: Alexei Soma
Director, Image Resource Center: Melinda Patelli
Manager, Rights and Permissions: Zina Arabia
Manager, Visual Research: Beth Brenzel
Manager, Cover Visual Research & Permissions:
   Karen Sanatar
Image Permission Coordinator: Angelique Sharps
Marketing Coordinator: William J. Bliss
Publisher: Phil Miller

This book was set in 10/12 New Baskerville by Emilcomp/Prepare and was printed and bound by Courier/Kendallville.
The cover was printed by Phoenix Color/Hagerstown.

Printed in the United States of America
10   9   8   7   6   5   4   3   2

ISBN: 0-13-195546-2   (Student Edition)
         978-0-13-195546-2
ISBN: 0-13-189042-5   (Annotated Instructor's Edition)
         978-0-13-189042-8

Pearson Education LTD., *London*
Pearson Education Australia PTY, Limited, *Sydney*
Pearson Education Singapore, Pte. Ltd
Pearson Education North Asia Ltd., *Hong Kong*
Pearson Education Canada, Ltd., *Toronto*
Pearson Educación de México, S.A. de C.V.
Pearson Education-Japan, *Tokyo*
Pearson Education Malaysia, Pte. Ltd
Pearson Education, *Upper Saddle River*, New Jersey

Brief Contents

Scope & Sequence

Strukturen im Kontext

Wörter: Bedeutung, Form, Aussprache

Kommunikationsziele und Kultur	Sprache im Kontext

x

Kommunikationsziele und Kultur

Sprache im Kontext

Strukturen im Kontext

Wörter: Bedeutung, Form, Aussprache

Kommunikationsziele und Kultur	Sprache im Kontext

Strukturen im Kontext

Wörter: Bedeutung, Form, Aussprache

Kommunikationsziele und Kultur

Sprache im Kontext

Kommunikationsziele und Kultur

Sprache im Kontext

Anhang

Strukturen im Kontext

Wörter: Bedeutung, Form, Aussprache

Preface

We are pleased to present you with the fifth edition of *Treffpunkt Deutsch.* Our introductory German language program has its foundation in a student-centered, communicative approach. Since the first edition nearly two decades ago, *Treffpunkt Deutsch* has been carefully designed to encourage students to interact spontaneously and meaningfully in German. The title itself reflects a major objective of the program: to transform the classroom into a **Treffpunkt,** a *meeting place,* where students will get to know one another better through the German language.

We are indebted to our loyal following of instructors and students over the past four editions. The improvements and additions to the fifth edition of *Treffpunkt Deutsch* are a direct result of the feedback and suggestions they provided, based on their classroom experience with the program. We hope that new users will become equally committed to the pedagogy of *Treffpunkt Deutsch.*

Goals of the *Treffpunkt Deutsch* Program

In *Treffpunkt Deutsch* linguistic competence is developed through skill-chaining, i.e., through cyclical practice in listening, speaking, reading, and writing:

- **Listening comprehension** is an integral part of the text, signaling to students that developing aural skills in the target language is a crucial step for successful communication. We are proud to have been pioneers in introducing in-text listening comprehension materials. The listening activities in *Treffpunkt Deutsch* focus first on global comprehension and then on detailed understanding.

- **Speaking skills** are developed as students progress from controlled dialogue situations to open-ended conversation about topics that involve them personally and address their interests. Speaking skills are further honed through role plays and activities that are spin-offs of the in-text listening and reading material.

- **Reading practice** is introduced from day one. Students are challenged to negotiate with the German language through realia-based activities, poetry, and short literary excerpts. The *Leute* readings at the end of *Kapitel 1* through *Kapitel 9* present both famous and ordinary people in the German-speaking countries. From *Kapitel 10* on, readings are literary texts that challenge but do not overwhelm beginning students. Pre- and post-reading activities help students develop useful reading strategies.

- **Writing skills** are developed through guided writing activities, introduced as early as *Kapitel 1.* Themes for writing activities are centered on students' personal interests and are connected to the in-text listening and reading material. New to the fifth edition are *Schreibtipps* that help students hone their writing skills.

The development of cultural competence continues to be a major goal of *Treffpunkt Deutsch.* The culture of the German-speaking countries pervades all aspects of the text, including the line drawings. Many users have commented on the German "feel" that the artist, who lives in Germany, has projected into his work.

Developing a rich active and passive lexicon is one of the central goals of *Treffpunkt Deutsch.* The two vocabulary lists in each chapter are organized according to parts of speech, and within these sections, in semantic groupings. The lists are followed by exercises *(Wörter im Kontext)* that help students internalize the lexical items. Vocabulary learning is further enhanced by the vocabulary-building activities in the unique *Wort, Sinn und Klang* sections, which conclude with often whimsical pronunciation activities.

Who's Who in *Treffpunkt Deutsch*

Martin Keller
aus Mannheim

Claudia Berger
aus Hamburg

Stephanie Braun
aus Chicago

Peter Ackermann
aus Berlin

Students will meet many characters of various ethnic backgrounds as they progress through *Treffpunkt Deutsch.* However, they will get to know two sets of characters especially well. First, there are four friends who are all studying in Munich: Martin is studying art history; Claudia's focus is mechanical engineering; Stephanie's major is physics; and Peter studies linguistics. As the book progresses, Claudia and Martin, and Stephanie and Peter become romantically involved.

Second, there are the Zieglers from Göttingen: Klaus and Brigitte, their sixteen-year-old daughter Nina, and their fourteen-year-old son Robert. Sibling rivalry plays a role in this family portrait.

New to the *Fifth Edition*

This new edition of *Treffpunkt Deutsch* maintains the solid pedagogical approach that instructors have come to rely upon for the past four editions. The changes in the fifth edition were inspired by their kudos and practical suggestions and by our own experience teaching with this program:

- All *Kultur* and *Infobox* sections have been revised to give the most up-to-date information on the cultures of the German-speaking countries. Wherever appropriate, relevant cross-cultural comparisons to the United States and Canada have been highlighted.

- Expanded cultural sections on Austria and Switzerland feature short literary texts by well-known authors.

- New readings that will appeal to students include a feature on the inventor of the Swiss Army Knife and an excerpt from Jana Hensel's coming-of-age book *Zonenkinder.*

- More realia-based activities promote increased interaction with authentic language.

- Grammar presentations have been improved in several ways:
  - Explanations have been made even more accessible to students. Attention is drawn to similarities or differences between English and German wherever appropriate to help learners use what they already know to connect to the German language.
  - Charts accompanying grammar explanations have been enhanced visually to help students make connections between recurring grammatical themes.
  - The explanation of the position of **nicht** has been clarified and simplified throughout.
- The *Zusammenschau* sections have been streamlined to serve as a thorough review of the chapter theme, vocabulary, and grammar in a unified communicative context. These sections also include a pre-viewing activity for the highly praised *Treffpunkt Deutsch* video.
- Building on the highly praised marginal annotations for teachers in the *Annotated Instructor's Edition,* a new category of annotations *for learners* has been created for the *Student Text.* These notes give additional cultural information, offer useful *Lerntipps,* and encourage students to reflect on the forms and meanings of words and their relationship to other words. New *Schreibtipps* offer explicit strategies that provide targeted guidance for the writing activities.
- Web links, placed at strategic points in each chapter, entice students to explore specific cultural topics via the *Treffpunkt Deutsch Companion Website.*
- As a pronunciation aid to students, the words and phrases in vocabulary lists have been marked to indicate the stressed syllables and to show whether the vowels in these syllables are long or short. This follows the convention of many German-language dictionaries.
- Nearly all photos throughout the book are new, providing fresh views of contemporary culture in the German-speaking countries. Ads and signs highlight vocabulary and structures in a communicative, real-life context.
- The new design accentuates the chapter organization by color-coding each section. In addition, the chapter and section titles are now reflected in the page footers for easier orientation.
- The latest Spelling Reforms (from March 2006) have been incorporated into the text.
- The *Anhang* of the fifth edition includes several new features:
  - Word sets for quick reference to useful word groups have been expanded. A new set of useful classroom expressions includes typical questions, responses, instructions, and grammatical terms.
  - A new *Answer Key* for the *Wörter im Kontext* sections makes it possible to assign the exercises for self study.

Organization of *Treffpunkt Deutsch*

Treffpunkt Deutsch consists of an introduction *(Erste Kontakte)* and twelve chapters. *Erste Kontakte* is the warm-up for the course. Each of the twelve subsequent chapters focuses on a theme and follows a consistent structure, with four main sections: *Vorschau, Kommunikation und Formen, Zusammenschau,* and *Wort, Sinn und Klang.* The "Guided Tour" on the following pages highlights the features of the *Student Text.*

Vorschau: Language models and activities

Language models introduce vocabulary and structures connected to the chapter theme in natural, idiomatic German through a variety of genres such as dialogues, letters, brief narratives, realia pieces, and authentic literature. Follow-up activities check comprehension and encourage immediate use of new vocabulary and forms.

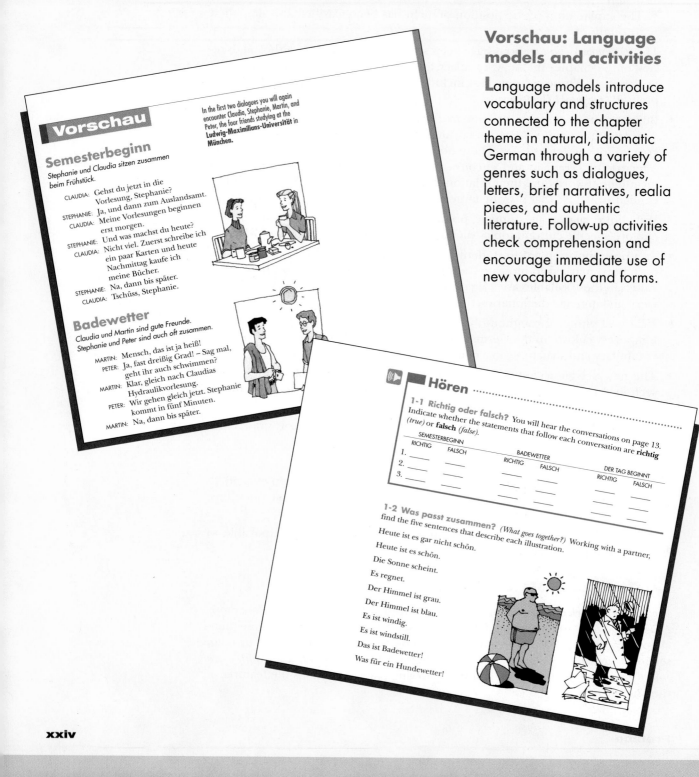

Vorschau

In the first two dialogues you will again encounter Claudia, Stephanie, Martin, and Peter, the four friends studying at the **Ludwig-Maximilians-Universität** in **München.**

Semesterbeginn
Stephanie und Claudia sitzen zusammen beim Frühstück.

CLAUDIA: Gehst du jetzt in die Vorlesung, Stephanie?
STEPHANIE: Ja, und dann zum Auslandsamt.
CLAUDIA: Meine Vorlesungen beginnen erst morgen.
STEPHANIE: Und was machst du heute?
CLAUDIA: Nicht viel. Zuerst schreibe ich ein paar Karten und heute Nachmittag kaufe ich meine Bücher.
STEPHANIE: Na, dann bis später.
CLAUDIA: Tschüss, Stephanie.

Badewetter
Claudia und Martin sind gute Freunde. Stephanie und Peter sind auch oft zusammen.

MARTIN: Mensch, das ist ja heiß!
PETER: Ja, fast dreißig Grad! – Sag mal, geht ihr auch schwimmen?
MARTIN: Klar, gleich nach Claudias Hydraulikvorlesung.
PETER: Wir gehen gleich jetzt. Stephanie kommt in fünf Minuten.
MARTIN: Na, dann bis später.

Hören

1-1 Richtig oder falsch?
You will hear the conversations on page 13. Indicate whether the statements that follow each conversation are **richtig** *(true)* or **falsch** *(false).*

	SEMESTERBEGINN		BADEWETTER		DER TAG BEGINNT	
	RICHTIG	FALSCH	RICHTIG	FALSCH	RICHTIG	FALSCH
1.	___	___				
2.	___	___	___	___		
3.	___	___	___	___	___	___

1-2 Was passt zusammen?
(What goes together?) Working with a partner, find the five sentences that describe each illustration.

Heute ist es gar nicht schön.

Heute ist es schön.

Die Sonne scheint.

Es regnet.

Der Himmel ist grau.

Der Himmel ist blau.

Es ist windig.

Es ist windstill.

Das ist Badewetter!

Was für ein Hundewetter!

Kultur

These sections present a cultural reading related to the chapter theme along with an activity that encourages students to engage with the topic. Many activities are based on authentic materials, ranging from recipes to short literary texts. *Kultur* sections are presented entirely in German in the last four chapters.

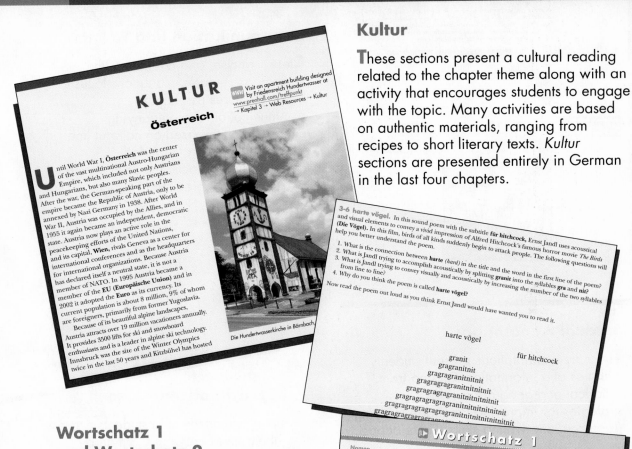

KULTUR

Österreich

Visit an apartment building designed by Friedensreich Hundertwasser at
www.prenhall.com/treffpunkt!
→ Kapitel 3 → Web Resources → Kultur

Until World War I, **Österreich** was the center of the vast multinational Austro-Hungarian Empire, which included not only Austrians and Hungarians, but also many Slavic peoples. After the war, the German-speaking part of the empire became the Republic of Austria, only to be annexed by Nazi Germany in 1938. After World War II, Austria was occupied by the Allies, and in 1955 it again became an independent, democratic state. Austria now plays an active role in the peacekeeping efforts of the United Nations, and its capital, **Wien**, rivals Geneva as a center for international conferences and as the headquarters for international organizations. Because Austria has declared itself a neutral state, it is not a member of NATO. In 1995 Austria became a member of the **EU (Europäische Union)** and in 2002 it adopted the **Euro** as its currency. Its current population is about 8 million, 9% of whom are foreigners, primarily from former Yugoslavia.

Because of its beautiful alpine landscapes, Austria attracts over 19 million vacationers annually. It provides 3500 lifts for ski and snowboard enthusiasts and is a leader in alpine ski technology. Innsbruck was the site of the Winter Olympics twice in the last 50 years and Kitzbühel has hosted

Die Hundertwasserkirche in Bärnbach

3-6 harte vögel. In this sound poem with the subtitle **für hitchcock**, Ernst Jandl uses acoustical and visual elements to convey a vivid impression of Alfred Hitchcock's famous horror movie *The Birds* **(Die Vögel)**. In this film, birds of all kinds suddenly begin to attack people. The following questions will help you better understand the poem.

1. What is the connection between **harte** *(hard)* in the title and the word in the first line of the poem?
2. What is Jandl trying to accomplish acoustically by splitting **granit** into the syllables **gra** and **nit**?
3. What is Jandl trying to convey visually and acoustically by increasing the number of the two syllables from line to line?
4. Why do you think the poem is called **harte vögel**?

Now read the poem out loud as you think Ernst Jandl would have wanted you to read it.

harte vögel

granit   für hitchcock
gragranitnit
gragragranitnitnit
gragragragranitnitnitnit
gragragragragranitnitnitnitnit
gragragragragragranitnitnitnitnitnit
gragragragragragragranitnitnitnitnitnitnit

Wortschatz 1 and Wortschatz 2

Chapter vocabulary appears in two lists containing useful, high-frequency words related to the chapter theme. Diacritical marks under vowels in stressed syllables provide pronunciation guidance for words and phrases. The lists are followed by exercises *(Wörter im Kontext)* that encourage students to use the new words in a variety of contexts.

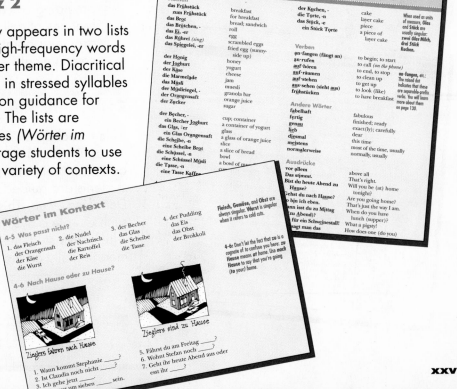

Wortschatz 1

Nomen

das Frühstück	breakfast
zum Frühstück	for breakfast
das Brot	bread; sandwich
das Brötchen, -	roll
das Ei, -er	egg
das Rührei *(sing)*	scrambled eggs
das Spiegelei, -er	fried egg (sunny-side up)
der Honig	honey
der Joghurt	yogurt
der Käse	cheese
die Marmelade	jam
das Müsli	muesli
der Müsliriegel, -	granola bar
der Orangensaft	orange juice
der Zucker	sugar
der Becher, -	cup; container
ein Becher Joghurt	a container of yogurt
das Glas, -er	glass
ein Glas Orangensaft	a glass of orange juice
die Scheibe, -n	slice
eine Scheibe Brot	a slice of bread
die Schüssel, -n	bowl
eine Schüssel Müsli	a bowl of muesli
die Tasse, -n	cup
eine Tasse Kaffee	

der Kuchen, -	cake
die Torte, -n	layer cake
das Stück, -e	piece
ein Stück Torte	a piece of layer cake

When used as units of measure, **Glas** and **Stück** are usually singular: *zwei Glas Milch, drei Stück Kuchen*.

Verben

an·fangen (fängt an)	to begin; to start
an·rufen	to call *(on the phone)*
auf·hören	to end, to stop
auf·räumen	to clean up
auf·stehen	to get up
aus·sehen (sieht aus)	to look (like)
frühstücken	to have breakfast

Andere Wörter

fabelhaft	fabulous
fertig	finished; ready
genau	exact(ly); carefully
lieb	dear
diesmal	this time
meistens	most of the time, usually
normalerweise	normally, usually

an·fangen, etc.: The raised dot indicates that these are separable-prefix verbs. You will learn more about them on page 130.

Ausdrücke

vor allem	above all
Das stimmt.	That's right.
Bist du heute Abend zu Hause?	Will you be (at) home tonight?
Gehst du nach Hause?	Are you going home?
So bin ich eben.	That's just the way I am.
Wann isst du zu Mittag *(zu Abend)*?	When do you have lunch (supper)?
So ein Schweinestall!	What a pigsty!
...sagt man das	How does one (do you)

Wörter im Kontext

4-5 Was passt nicht?

1. das Fleisch
   der Orangensaft
   der Käse
   die Wurst

2. die Nudel
   der Nachtisch
   die Kartoffel
   der Reis

3. der Becher
   das Glas
   die Scheibe
   die Tasse

4. der Pudding
   das Eis
   das Obst
   der Brokkoli

Fleisch, Gemüse, and **Obst** are always singular. **Wurst** is singular when it refers to cold cuts.

4-6 Nach Hause oder zu Hause?

Zieglers fahren nach Hause

Zieglers sind zu Hause

1. Wann kommt Stephanie _____?
2. Ist Claudia noch nicht _____?
3. Ich gehe jetzt _____.
4. Ich muss um sieben _____ sein.

5. Fährst du am Freitag _____?
6. Wohnt Stefan noch _____?
7. Geht ihr heute Abend aus oder esst ihr _____?

4-6: Don't let the fact that **zu** is a cognate of *to* confuse you here: **zu Hause** means *at home*. Use **nach Hause** to say that you're going (to your) home.

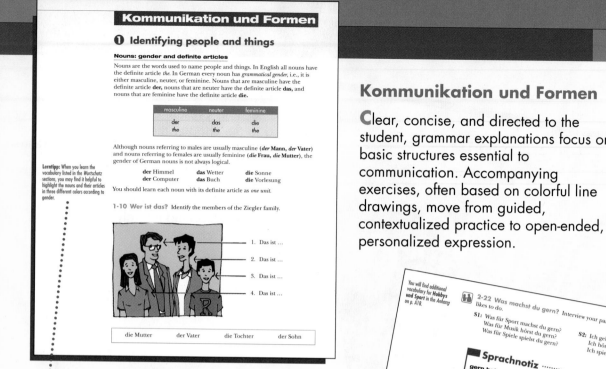

Kommunikation und Formen

① Identifying people and things

Nouns: gender and definite articles

Nouns are the words used to name people and things. In English all nouns have the definite article *the*. In German every noun has *grammatical gender*, i.e., it is either masculine, neuter, or feminine. Nouns that are masculine have the definite article **der**, nouns that are neuter have the definite article **das**, and nouns that are feminine have the definite article **die**.

masculine	neuter	feminine
der	das	die
the	*the*	*the*

Although nouns referring to males are usually masculine (**der** Mann, **der** Vater) and nouns referring to females are usually feminine (**die** Frau, **die** Mutter), the gender of German nouns is not always logical.

der Himmel	**das** Wetter	**die** Sonne
der Computer	**das** Buch	**die** Vorlesung

You should learn each noun with its definite article as *one unit*.

Lerntipp: When you learn the vocabulary listed in the *Wortschatz* sections, you may find it helpful to highlight the nouns and their articles in three different colors according to gender.

1-10 Wer ist das? Identify the members of the Ziegler family.

1. Das ist …
2. Das ist …
3. Das ist …
4. Das ist …

die Mutter	der Vater	die Tochter	der Sohn

Kommunikation und Formen

Clear, concise, and directed to the student, grammar explanations focus on basic structures essential to communication. Accompanying exercises, often based on colorful line drawings, move from guided, contextualized practice to open-ended, personalized expression.

You will find additional vocabulary for *Hobbys und Sport* in the *Anhang* on p. A18.

2-22 Was machst du gern? Interview your partner about what she/he likes to do.

S1: Was für Sport machst du gern?
Was für Musik hörst du gern?
Was für Spiele spielst du gern?

S2: Ich gehe (spiele) gern …
Ich höre gern …
Ich spiele gern …

Sprachnotiz

gern haben

Gern haben is used to express fondness for someone as opposed to being in love with a person.

STEFAN: Liebst du Maria?
LUKAS: Nein, aber ich **habe** sie sehr **gern.**

Are you in love with Maria?
No, but I'm very fond of her.

Student Annotations

These new annotations present students with tips and information ranging from historical and geographical facts to strategies for improving language learning *(Lerntipps)* and writing skills *(Schreibtipps)*.

Sprachnotizen

Sprachnotizen help students express themselves better in German by providing discourse strategies, idiomatic features of colloquial German, and short grammar points relevant to the chapter's communicative goals.

Zwischenspiel

The two soccer teams mentioned are usually front runners in the *Erste Bundesliga (First Federal League)*. The **FC Bayern München** has been **Deutscher Fußball Meister** 20 times in the last 40 years. **FC Schalke 04** was founded in 1904. It was originally a team of coal miners. You will find more information about *Fußball* on page 145.

Zwischenspiel

■ **Hören**

Du musst dein Leben ändern

Kurt Becker is sitting in front of the TV watching the soccer game between **Bayern München** and **Schalke 04**. His wife Petra has just walked in the door.

NEUE VOKABELN			
ändern	*to change*	anders	*different*
du hast recht	*you are right*	bestimmt	*really, for sure*
von Montag ab	*from Monday on*	zu Fuß gehen	*to walk*

4-26 Erstes Verstehen. In what sequence do you hear the following statements?

____ Du stehst jeden Morgen zu spät auf und hast nie Zeit für ein gutes Frühstück.
____ Vielleicht hast du recht, Petra. Aber von Montag ab wird alles anders.
____ Du wirst noch krank, so wie du lebst.
____ Aber ich brauche mein Bier nach so viel Stress im Büro!
____ Und schon heute Abend gehen wir spazieren, Petra, du und ich.
____ Bayern München – Schalke 04! Und da willst du diskutieren?!

4-27 Detailverstehen. Listen to the conversation again and write the responses to the following questions.

1. Warum soll Petra nicht so laut sein?
2. Was isst Kurt im Büro zum Frühstück?
3. Was macht Kurt, wenn er nach Hause kommt?
4. Was darf Kurt nicht mehr?
5. Was muss Kurt mehr tun?
6. Was will Kurt von Montag ab jeden Morgen tun?

This mid-chapter "interlude" synthesizes vocabulary and structures learned so far. It begins with listening comprehension, in which students are guided from *Erstes Verstehen* to *Detailverstehen*. This is followed by activities such as role plays, interviews, and writing tasks, which give students the opportunity to interact meaningfully on the theme of the *Zwischenspiel*.

4-28 Ich will mein Leben ändern. Tell your classmates about three things you want to change in your life.

Ich will nicht mehr so viel
(so oft, so spät, so lange) …

Ich will mehr …

fernsehen	in die Kneipe gehen	Milch trinken
schlafen	Bier trinken	Gemüse und
aufstehen	Junkfood essen	Obst essen
ausgehen	Kaffee trinken	lernen
to smoke rauchen°	ins Bett gehen	Sport machen
…	…	…

Web links

This feature invites students to explore authentic German-language Web pages through the **Treffpunkt Deutsch** *Companion Website* (http://www.prenhall.com/treffpunkt) where students are guided by short, engaging tasks. The *Companion Website* also contains self-correcting vocabulary and grammar exercises for independent language practice.

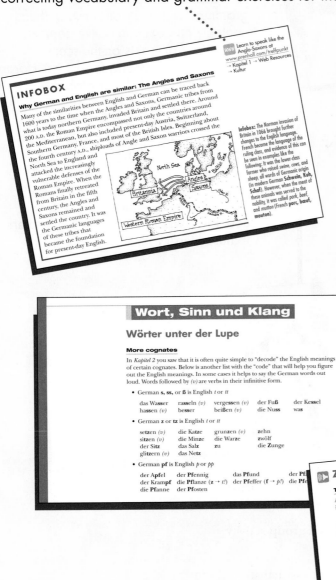

WWW Learn to speak like the Anglo-Saxons at www.prenhall.com/treffpunkt
→ Kapitel 1 → Web Resources
→ Kultur

INFOBOX

Why German and English are similar: The Angles and Saxons

Many of the similarities between English and German can be traced back 1600 years to the time when the Angles and Saxons, Germanic tribes from what is today northern Germany, invaded Britain and settled there. Around 200 A.D. the Roman Empire encompassed not only the countries around the Mediterranean, but also included present-day Austria, Switzerland, Southern Germany, France, and most of the British Isles. Beginning about the fourth century A.D., shiploads of Angle and Saxon warriors crossed the North Sea to England and attacked the increasingly vulnerable defenses of the Roman Empire. When the Romans finally retreated from Britain in the fifth century, the Angles and Saxons remained and settled the country. It was the Germanic languages of these tribes that became the foundation for present-day English.

Infobox: The Norman invasion of Britain in 1066 brought further changes to the English language. French became the language of the ruling class, and evidence of this can be seen in examples like the following: It was the lower-class farmer who raised swine, cows, and sheep, all words of Germanic origin (in modern German **Schwein, Kuh, Schaf**). However, when the meat of these animals was served to the nobility, it was called pork, beef, and mutton (French **porc, bœuf, mouton**).

Infoboxen

Strategically placed throughout the text, *Infoboxen* highlight additional information to enrich students' understanding of the cultures of the German-speaking countries.

Wort, Sinn und Klang

With an eye to enhancing vocabulary learning, *Wörter unter der Lupe* takes a closer look at words by discussing cognates, words that change their meaning in different contexts, word families, compound words, suffixes that signal gender, and idiomatic expressions. *Zur Aussprache* rounds off this section with engaging pronunciation activities.

Wort, Sinn und Klang

Wörter unter der Lupe

More cognates

In *Kapitel 2* you saw that it is often quite simple to "decode" the English meanings of certain cognates. Below is another list with the "code" that will help you figure out the English meanings. In some cases it helps to say the German words out loud. Words followed by (v) are verbs in their infinitive form.

- German **s, ss,** or **ß** is English *t* or *tt*

  das Wasser   rasseln (v)   vergessen (v)   der Fuß   der Kessel
  hassen (v)   besser   beißen (v)   die Nuss   was

- German **z** or **tz** is English *t* or *tt*

  setzen (v)   die Katze   grunzen (v)   zehn
  sitzen (v)   die Minze   die Warze   zwölf
  der Sitz   das Salz   zu   die Zunge
  glitzern (v)   das Netz

- German **pf** is English *p* or *pp*

  der Apfel   der Pfennig   das Pfund   der Pf
  der Krampf   die Pflanze (z → t!)   der Pfeffer (f → p!)   die Pfe
  die Pfanne   der Pfosten

Zur Aussprache

The diphthongs

A diphthong is a combination of two vowel sounds. There are three diphthongs in German.

3-54 Hören Sie gut zu und wiederholen Sie!

The diphthong **ei** (also spelled **ey, ai, ay**) is pronounced like the *i* in *mine*.

eins   zwei   drei
Herr Meyer   Herr Sailer   Herr Bayer

Heike Bayer und Heinz Frey heiraten am zweiten Mai.

The diphthong **au** is pronounced like the *ou* in *house*.

brauchen   laufen   kaufen
blau   braun   grau

Paul, du bist zu laut. Ich glaube, du bist blau.
Brautkleid bleibt Brautkleid und Blaukraut bleibt Blaukraut.

The diphthong **eu** (also spelled **äu**) is pronounced like the *oy* in *boy*.

heute   teuer   neu
Häuser   Mäuse   Verkäufer

Wer ist Frau Bäuerles neuer Freund?
Ein Verkäufer aus Bayreuth.

WIR SUCHEN EINE

freundliche Verkäuferin

bitte im Laden melden

Zusammenschau

Video-Treff

Meine Familie

Maiga, Stefan Meister, Anja Peter, Thomas, André, and Karen talk about their families.

Zum besseren Verstehen

3-44 Was ist das auf Englisch?

1. Meine Eltern leben seit drei Jahren **getrennt.**
2. Mein Bruder geht in **die 11. Klasse.**
3. Mein Vater hat ein **Segelboot.**
4. Ich habe eine **supersüße** Nichte.
5. Meine Eltern haben ein schönes Haus in einer **tollen Gegend.**
6. Sie wohnen jetzt **außerhalb von** Berlin.
7. Meine Schwester **macht** ihre Klamotten **selber.**
8. Ich habe zwei Halbgeschwister; wir haben alle drei **unterschiedliche** Mütter.
9. Ich habe eine **ältere** Schwester.

a. sailboat
b. in a great area
c. different
d. makes ... herself
e. eleventh grade
f. separated
g. older
h. outside of
i. very sweet

Mein Vater hat ein Segelboot.

Now watch the video and complete the post-viewing activities in the *Video-Treff* section of the *Student Activities Manual.*

Schreiben und Sprechen

3-47 Wer ist das? Describe the style and color of a classmate's hair and clothing. Useful descriptive adjectives are given below. Be sure to attach the correct endings. The rest of the class then guesses whom you are describing.

S: Sie hat lange, blonde Haare. Sie trägt ein schönes, gelbes T-Shirt, einen langen, dunkelblauen Rock, weiße Socken und weiße Tennisschuhe. Wer ist das?

HAARE
• lang, kurz, glatt°, lockig°, wellig°
• blond, brünett, rot, schwarz ...

straight / curly / wavy

Sie/Er hat _____e, _____e Haare.

KLEIDER
• lang, kurz, groß, klein, elegant, schick, schön, toll, hübsch
• blau, grün, orangefarben, rot, rosarot, schwarz, hellblau, dunkelrot ...

Sie/Er trägt   einen   _____en, _____en Pullover (Rock, Mantel, Gürtel)
                ein   _____es, _____es Polohemd (T-Shirt, Sweatshirt, Kleid)
                eine   _____e, _____e Hose (Jogginghose, Jacke, Bluse)
                        _____e, _____e Jeans (Shorts, Socken, Schuhe, Sandalen)

3-48 Eine Personenbeschreibung. Use as many adjectives as possible to describe a family member or a friend. Use the questions below and the information in the previous activity to guide you.

Wie heißt die Person?
Wie alt ist sie/er?
Ist sie/er eine Verwandte/ein Verwandter oder eine gute Freundin/ ein guter Freund?
Welche Farbe haben ihre/seine Augen? *Sie/Er hat _____ Augen.*
Was für Haare hat sie/er?
Was für Kleider trägt sie/er gern?

Schreibtipp: This writing task focuses on visual information. Before you write, take the time to form a mental picture of the person you want to describe. You can also use a photo or draw a quick ske... then jot down words and ... describe what you see, la... articles of clothing, color... sizes, etc. Then write com... sentences based on your...

Lesen

Zum besseren Verstehen

3-49 Klassische Musik.

1. Have you ever listened to classical music?
2. Do you have a favorite composer of classical music?
3. What do you know about Mozart?

3-50 Was ist das auf Englisch?

1. Leopold Mozart ist Violinist im Orchester **des Erzbischofs** von Salzburg.
2. Sein Sohn Wolfgang ist ein musikalisches **Wunderkind.**
3. In Salzburg ist Wolfgang nur ein **schlecht bezahlter** Musiker.
4. In Wien verdient Wolfgang viel Geld und lebt **wie ein König.**
5. Er braucht viel **mehr** Geld **als** er verdient.
6. Er macht **Schulden,** denn er braucht viel

a. debts
b. like a king
c. feverishly
d. poorly paid
e. child prodigy
f. of the archbishop
g. more ... than

Mozart „verkauft" Mozartkugeln.

Zusammenschau

Activities in this section synthesize the four skills and the vocabulary and grammar of the chapter in a unified, content-rich communicative context. *Video-Treff* presents on-the-scene interviews with young Germans. *Hören* hones listening skills for global and detailed understanding. *Schreiben und Sprechen* further contextualizes the chapter theme in guided activities to develop solid writing and speaking skills. In the first nine chapters, *Lesen* spotlights both famous and ordinary people in the German-speaking countries, while the last three chapters feature literary texts.

Icons

(((•	listening activity	👥	personalized partner activity
📖	reading activity	👥👥	personalized group activity
✏️	writing activity	*i*	information gap activity
🎭	role play	🖥️	video activity
WWW	Web activity		

Components of the *Treffpunkt Deutsch* Program

For the Student

***Treffpunkt Deutsch* Student Text.** The *Student Text* contains listening, speaking, writing, reading, and culture-focused activities; grammar explanations with contextualized exercises; and helpful appendices, including useful word lists, grammatical tables and comprehensive German-English/English-German vocabularies.

Audio CDs to Accompany Text. This component provides all audio for the listening activities in the *Student Text*, including recordings of material from the *Vorschau, Zwischenspiel, Zusammenschau,* and *Zur Aussprache* sections as well as the vocabulary items in *Wortschatz 1* and *Wortschatz 2* for each chapter of the text-book. The *In-Text Audio* is available both on CD and through the ***Treffpunkt Deutsch*** *Online Resources* (*OneKey with Quia* and the *Companion Website*).

Treffpunkt Deutsch* Video.** Filmed in Germany specifically for ***Treffpunkt Deutsch, the *Video* features clips from unscripted interviews with native speakers on topics relating to the chapter themes. Students hear natural, everyday German from a variety of speakers in the places where they live, work, study, and have fun. In addition to the pre-viewing activity incorporated into each chapter of the *Student Text,* follow-up activities are provided in the *Student Activities Manual.* Students can view the *Video* independently via the online *Student Activities Manual.* It is also available in both DVD and VHS formats.

Student Activities Manual (SAM). Available in print and online versions, the *SAM* gives students extensive practice with the structures and vocabulary intro-duced in the *Student Text.* Beginning with *Kapitel 1,* each chapter of the *SAM* consists of four sections: *Strukturen, Arbeitsbuch, Hören und Sprechen,* and *Video-Treff.*

- The *Strukturen* section presents a concise summary of the chapter's grammati-cal points, cross-referenced throughout the subsequent *Arbeitsbuch* and *Hören und Sprechen* sections. In the online version the *Strukturen* are presented as pop-ups.

- The *Arbeitsbuch* section offers a variety of exercises, including realia-based and picture-cued activities; sentence-building, sentence-completion, fill-in, and matching exercises; and vocabulary-building and reading comprehension activities.

- The *Hören und Sprechen* section, completely rewritten for the fifth edition, offers students listening and speaking practice in real-world communicative tasks, such as gleaning information from a voice-mail or answering questions about anec-dotes. *Hören und Sprechen* exposes students to both paragraph- and sentence-length speech, formal and informal discourse, and task types ranging from multiple choice and true/false to fill-in-the-blank and full-sentence answers.

- In the *Video-Treff* section, students hone their comprehension skills via match-ing, true/false, and multiple-choice activities, as well as personalized writing tasks. All activities are based on the ***Treffpunkt Deutsch*** *Video.*

The *SAM* is available online with *Quia* and *Quia Standalone* (see *Online Resources*).

Audio to Accompany Student Activities Manual. This component contains the audio material needed to complete the *Hören und Sprechen* component of the *SAM*. It is available on CD, on the *Companion Website*, and in the online version of the *SAM* through *OneKey with Quia*. All audio materials are available to language labs and resource centers free of charge.

Answer Key to Accompany the Student Activities Manual. Answers to the exercises of the *SAM* are available in a separate answer key, so that students can check their own work.

For the Instructor

Annotated Instructor's Edition. Based on the experiences of the authors and their teaching assistants over many years of classroom testing, the extensive marginal notes in the *Annotated Instructor's Edition* were written with the novice instructor in mind. They include warm-up activities, resource materials, cultural information, and suggestions for using and expanding the activities and materials in the textbook. They also include the scripts and answer keys for the *Hören* sections as well as the scripts for the narration series *(Bildgeschichten)*. The *Annotated Instructor's Edition* provides the answers to the *Erstes Verstehen* activities in the *Zwischenspiel* and *Zusammenschau* sections as well as the responses from the *Anhang* for the Information Gap activities.

Instructor's Resource Manual with Testing Program. The *Instructor's Resource Manual* includes sample course syllabi, detailed lesson plans for the whole program, a full script for the *SAM* Audio Program and the ***Treffpunkt Deutsch*** *Video,* tips for using video successfully in the foreign language classroom, and strategies for effective integration of Web-based activities in the course. The *Testing Program* offers multiple versions of hour-long tests for each chapter along with mid-term and final examinations. Each test uses a variety of techniques to address the skill areas of listening, reading, writing, and speaking. New to the fifth edition is a culture component. The *Testing Program* is available electronically so that instructors can mix and match material according to their needs. An answer key is provided for all testing materials.

Audio to Accompany Testing Program. These recordings correspond to the listening comprehension activities in the *Testing Program.*

Transparencies. A set of colorful transparencies consisting of maps and illustrations from the text offers the instructor flexibility in creating activities and in presenting vocabulary and cultural information.

Online Resources

QUIA™ Student Activities Manual. An interactive version of the *Student Activities Manual,* including the related audio and video materials, is available in the highly regarded Quia™ platform.

OneKey with Quia. The ***Treffpunkt Deutsch*** *OneKey 2.0 Powered by Quia* is an online resource that provides access to an array of course resources for both instructors and students, organized to match the course syllabus.

- The **Student Activities Manual.** In this online format, the *SAM* offers convenient, self-correcting exercises, giving students immediate feedback and affording instructors more time to focus on assessing open-ended writing tasks.

- The ***Treffpunkt Deutsch* Video.** Through *OneKey*, students can view the *Treffpunkt Deutsch Video* independently at any time from any computer with Internet access.
- All audio resources for ***Treffpunkt Deutsch*.** *OneKey* offers all of the Audio Program for the text and the *SAM* in one online setting.
- *Companion Website* materials (see below). In addition to all *SAM* components, *OneKey* brings all materials from the *Companion Website* into one online location.

OneKey is available in the following Course Management platforms: Blackboard, WebCT, and the nationally hosted CourseCompass.

Companion Website (http://www.prenhall.com/treffpunkt). The *Companion Website* is a robust online resource designed to give students a chance to practice and further explore the vocabulary, structures, and cultural themes introduced in the text. For each chapter, students will find self-grading practice exercises on vocabulary and grammar topics as well as Web-based reading and writing activities. Web links to carefully selected sites in Germany, Austria, Switzerland, Luxemburg, Liechtenstein, and South Tyrol (Italy), accompanied by interesting activities, provide additional interaction with the cultures of these German-speaking areas of Europe. Also available on the Website are the audio components of the *Student Text* and the *SAM*, as well as an interactive vocabulary flashcards tool.

Acknowledgments

We would like to express our gratitude to the many instructors and coordinators who took time from their busy schedules to assist us with comments and suggestions over the course of the development of all five editions of ***Treffpunkt Deutsch*.** We also extend our deepest thanks to the colleagues across North America who have used or reviewed the fourth edition and provided valuable input. We appreciate their participation and candor, and many of their suggestions have been incorporated into the text and annotations of the fifth edition.

Rita Abercrombie, *Baylor University;* Keith Anderson, *St. Olaf College;* Reinhard Andress, *St. Louis University;* William Anthony, *Northwestern University;* John Austin, *Georgia State University;* Linda Austin, *Glendale Community College;* Thomas Bacon, *Texas Tech University;* Linda Daves Baldwin, *Washington College;* Katharina Barbe, *Northern Illinois University;* Gamin Bartle, *University of Alabama;* Gary Bartlett, *Normandale Community College;* Claudia A. Becker, *University of Toronto;* Christel Bell, *University of Alabama;* John M. Brawner, *University of California, Irvine;* Brigitte Breitenbücher, *Elgin Community College;* Johannes Bruestle, *Grossmont College;* Helga Bister-Broosen, *University of North Carolina;* Joan Keck Campbell, *Dartmouth College;* Esther Enns-Connolly, *University of Calgary;* Heidi Crabbes, *Fullerton College;* Rudolph Debernitz, *Golden West College;* Sharon M. DiFino, *University of Florida;* Christopher Dolmetsch, *Marshall University;* Nikolaus Euba, *University of California, Berkeley;* Judith Fogle, *Pasadena City College;* Catherine C. Fraser, *Indiana University;* Jurgen Froehlich, *Pomona College;* Harold P. Fry, *Kent State University;* Henry Fullenwider, *University of Kansas;* Anna Glapa-Grossklag, *College of the Canyons;* Andrea Golato, *University of Illinois at Urbana-Champaign;* Peter Gölz, *University of Victoria;* Anne-Katrin Gramberg, *Auburn University;* Christian Hallstein, *Carnegie Mellon University;*

Barbara Harding, *Georgetown University;* Frauke A. Harvey, *Baylor University;* Elizabeth Hasler, *University of Cincinnati;* Gisela Hoecherl-Alden, *University of Pittsburgh;* Robert G. Hoeing, *SUNY Buffalo;* Deborah L. Horzen, *University of Central Florida;* Charles James, *University of Wisconsin, Madison;* William Keel, *University of Kansas;* George Koenig, *SUNY Oswego;* Richard Alan Korb, *Columbia University;* Arndt A. Krüger, *Trent University;* John A. Lalande II, *University of Illinois;* Alan H. Lareau, *University of Wisconsin, Oshkosh;* Betty Mason, *Valencia Community College;* Dennis R. McCormick, *University of Montana;* Robert Mollenauer, *University of Texas;* Kamakshi P. Murti, *University of Arizona;* Margaret Peischle, *Virginia Commonwealth University;* Manfred Prokop, *University of Alberta;* Robert C. Reimer, *University of North Carolina Charlotte;* Richard C. Reinholdt, *Orange Coast College;* Veronica Richel, *University of Vermont;* Roger Russi, *University of North Carolina Charlotte;* Beverly Harris-Schenz, *University of Pittsburgh;* Gerd Schneider, *Syracuse University;* Carolyn Wolf Spanier, *Mt. San Antonio College;* Gerhard Strasser, *Pennsylvania State University;* Michael L. Thompson, *University of Pennsylvania;* Suzanne Toliver, *University of Cincinnati;* Walter Tschacher, *University of North Dakota;* Hulya Unlu, *Penn State University;* Helga Van Iten, *Iowa State University;* Janet Van Valkenburg, *University of Michigan;* Wilfried Voge, *University of California, Los Angeles;* Morris Vos, *Western Illinois University;* Elizabeth I. Wade, *University of Wisconsin, Oshkosh;* William Garrett Welch, *West Texas A&M University;* Hendrik H. Winterstein, *University of Houston;* Margrit V. Zinggeler, *Eastern Michigan University.*

We are grateful to the many people at Prentice Hall who participated in the development of the fifth edition of ***Treffpunkt Deutsch.*** Special thanks go to Phil Miller, Publisher of World Languages, for his genuine dedication to this project. We consider ourselves fortunate to work with a publisher fluent in German! We are deeply indebted to Karen Storz, our Developmental Editor. Her intelligent editorial comments, her meticulous attention to detail, her knowledge of the production end, her ability to anticipate what's going to happen down the road, along with her infinite patience and good humor were invaluable assets during the revision process. We are grateful also to Karen Hohner for her careful and thorough copyedit of the manuscript. We thank Manuel Echevarria, our Production Editor, for his promptness and efficiency when he came on board. We would also like to thank Julia Caballero, Director of Editorial Development, for her ongoing coordination and support. We are grateful to Rachel McCoy, Senior Acquisitions Editor, for her excitement and commitment to the success of this project, and to Alexei Soma, Editorial Assistant, for his assistance in providing tools for all to help with the promotion of the fifth edition. We also thank Samantha Alducin, Senior Media Editor, for her work in coordinating the revision of the *Video* and the *Companion Website,* and particularly in the development of the new online *Student Activities Manual.* Meriel Martinez, Supplements Editor, deserves our thanks for diligently managing the preparation of ancillary materials and for pushing us firmly but kindly on deadlines. For the colorful interior design we sincerely thank Lisa Delgado. It has been an absolute pleasure working with Semjon Lukashov, Project Manager from Preparé/Emilcomp. He attended carefully, efficiently, and with good humor to every detail in the production process. Without the marketing team and sales staff, led by Kristine Suarez, Director of Marketing; Denise Miller, Senior Marketing Manager; and Bill Bliss, Marketing Coordinator, ***Treffpunkt Deutsch*** would never have attained such a long and distinguished roster of adopters. We thank them for their enthusiasm in promoting the book!

To Sabine Grosser we offer sincere thanks for providing the vibrant and innovative cover concept. A graphic designer by profession, she also helped us immeasurably in readying the many new photos, which we have provided digitally for the first time. We are again indebted to Michael Widmaier, an architect in Berlin, for his willingness to update some of his line drawings. With his outstanding computer expertise, he also gave us invaluable assistance whenever we needed it. *Treffpunkt Deutsch* is dedicated to our fellow German teachers and also to our families, whose unconditional support and enthusiasm made our work not just possible but also enjoyable.

Erste Kontakte

Humboldt-Universität Berlin: Hinterhof

Kommunikationsziele

Greeting someone and
responding to greetings

Introducing yourself

Making phone calls

Addressing letters

Saying good-bye

Strukturen

Du, ihr, and **Sie**

The numbers from 0–1000

The alphabet

Kultur

Studying at a German university

Social implications of **du, ihr,**
and **Sie**

Beim Studentenwerk

*Christian Lohner and Asha Singh meet at the student center at the **Humboldt-Universität** in Berlin. They are checking the bulletin board for rooms.*

— Hallo, ich heiße Christian,
   Christian Lohner.
— Und ich bin Asha Singh. Woher
   kommst du, Christian?
— Ich komme aus Hamburg. Und du,
   woher bist du?
— Ich bin aus Bombay.

In this course you will want to communicate in German with your instructor and your classmates as much as possible. On p. A15 in the *Anhang* at the back of this book, you will find some useful classroom expressions to help you do this.

E-1 Wir lernen einander kennen. *(Getting to know each other.)* Walk around the classroom and get to know as many of your classmates as possible. In the German-speaking countries, it is customary to shake hands when greeting someone.

Student 1: Hallo, ich heiße _____.
Wie heißt du?

Student 2: Ich heiße _____.

Student 1: Ich komme aus _____.
Woher bist du?

Student 2: Ich bin aus _____.
(Ich bin auch° aus _____.)   too

Im Studentenheim

Heike Fischer has already settled into her room in the dorm. Yvonne Harris, her new roommate, has just arrived.

— Entschuldigung, bist du
   Heike Fischer?
— Ja. Und du, wie heißt du?
— Ich bin Yvonne Harris aus Pittsburgh.
— Oh, grüß dich, Yvonne!

E-2 Entschuldigung, bist du ...? Now walk around the classroom again and see how many of your classmates' names you remember.

S1: Entschuldigung, bist du _____?

S2: Ja, ich bin _____. (Nein, ich
bin _____.)
Und du, heißt du _____?

S1: Ja, ich heiße _____. (Nein, ich
heiße _____.)

S2: Oh, grüß dich, _____.

INFOBOX

Studying at a German university

www See what's on the menu at a university **Mensa** at www.prenhall.com/treffpunkt
→ Erste Kontakte → Web Resources
→ Kultur

In ancient Greece, the **Gymnasium** was an institution for the development of the body *and* the mind. In English the word retains only the physical aspect. In German the word stresses the intellectual aspect. **Mensa** is the Latin word for *table*. The noonday meal for students used to be served at the **mensa academica**.

In Germany the percentage of young people attending a **Universität** is much smaller than in North America. In order to be considered for university admission, students must successfully complete the **Abitur,** a series of exams given in the last year of a **Gymnasium,** a college preparatory high school.

Attending a **Uni** is less expensive than in North America, since students pay little or no tuition and the government subsidizes dormitory rooms and meals in the **Mensa.** In Germany the **Bundesländer** *(states)* have jurisdiction over education, and in 2003 six of them challenged a federal law prohibiting tuition fees. In 2005 the Supreme Court overturned the law, causing a storm of protest throughout the country. Opponents argue that tuition fees deny the less affluent segment of society access to higher education.

Berlin: Technische Universität

◀ Im Hörsaal

Peter knows Martin and Claudia, but he hasn't met Claudia's roommate Stephanie yet. Claudia introduces them after class in the lecture hall.

MARTIN: *(to Claudia and Stephanie)* Hallo, ihr zwei! Wie geht's?

CLAUDIA: Super. Du, Peter, das ist Stephanie, meine Mitbewohnerin.

PETER: Grüß dich, Stephanie.

STEPHANIE: Hallo, Peter.

now MARTIN: Geht ihr jetzt° auch in die Mensa?

CLAUDIA: Nein, noch nicht.

MARTIN: Na, dann tschüss, ihr zwei.

STEPHANIE: Ciao!

Im Hörsaal: This is the first introduction to four friends who will reappear throughout the text. They are all students at the **Ludwig-Maximilians-Universität** in **München.** Peter Ackermann (from Berlin) and Martin Keller (from Mannheim) share a room in a private home. Claudia Berger (from Hamburg) and Stephanie Braun (an exchange student from Chicago) are roommates in the student residence. As the book progresses, Martin and Claudia become romantically involved, as do Peter and Stephanie.

▌ Sprachnotiz ······························

Some distinctive features of written German

- In German all nouns are capitalized: **Studentenheim, Mensa, Mitbewohnerin.**
- In addition to the letter **s**, German also uses **ß** (called **Eszett**) to represent the **s**-sound: **Grüß dich!**
- The letter **ä** in **Universität** is called **a-Umlaut.** The letters **o** and **u** can also be umlauted: **Hörsaal, tschüss.**
- German verbs have endings that change, depending on the subject, e.g., **ich komme, du kommst.**

E-3 Grüß dich! Walk up to two classmates and greet one by name. She/He will then introduce the other classmate to you.

S1: Grüß dich, _____, wie geht's?

S2: Super. Du, _____ (name of S1), das ist _____ (name of S3).

S1: (to S3) Grüß dich, _____.
S1: Woher kommst du, _____?

S3: (to S1) Hallo, _____.
S3: Ich bin aus _____. Und du?

S1: Ich komme aus _____.
S1: (to S2 and S3) Geht ihr jetzt auch in die Mensa?
S1: Na, dann tschüss, ihr zwei.

S2: Nein, noch nicht.

S3: Tschüss.
S2: Ciao!

▶ Im Konferenzsaal

Ms. Ziegler and Mr. O'Brien are business associates who have frequently corresponded, but are meeting for the first time at a conference.

— Entschuldigung, mein Name ist O'Brien. Sind Sie Frau Ziegler aus Göttingen?
— Ja. – Ach, Herr O'Brien aus Dublin! Guten Tag! Wie geht es Ihnen?
— Danke, gut.

E-4 Guten Tag! You are meeting a German business associate with whom you have been corresponding. Introduce yourself, using your last name. Address your partner with **Frau** or **Herr** and don't forget to shake hands!

S1: Entschuldigung, mein Name ist
Cadd (your last name). Sind Sie
Frau/Herr _Meier_ aus _~~place~~ münchen_?
S1: Danke, gut.

S2: Ja. – Ach, Frau/Herr _meier or Hüttel_
aus _münchen_ Guten Tag!
Wie geht es Ihnen?

How to say *you* in German

German has more than one way of saying *you*. The familiar **du** is used to address family members, close friends, children, and teenagers up to about age sixteen. It is also used among students, even if they are not close friends. The plural form of **du** is **ihr.**

The formal **Sie** is used for addressing adults who are not close friends. **Sie** is always capitalized and does not change in the plural.

	singular	plural
FAMILIAR	du	ihr y'all
FORMAL	Sie	Sie

If you are in a German-speaking country and are unsure about which form of address to use, it is better to err on the side of caution and use **Sie.**

E-5 *Du, ihr* oder *Sie?* Indicate with a check mark how you would address the following people if you were in a German-speaking setting.

	du	**ihr**	**Sie**
1. your two cousins	___	___	___
2. your grandmother	___	___	___
3. your professor	___	___	___
4. your roommate	___	___	___
5. two classmates	___	___	___
6. your roommate's parents	___	___	___
7. the letter carrier	___	___	___

Greetings and farewells

In the German-speaking countries, there are various ways of saying hello and good-bye. In North America it is customary for people to shake hands when they first meet each other. In the German-speaking countries, people often shake hands whenever they meet or say good-bye.

	FORMAL	LESS FORMAL	
GREETINGS	**Guten Tag!**	**Tag!**	*Hello!*
	Guten Morgen!	**Morgen!**	*Good morning!*
	Guten Abend!	**'n Abend!**	*Good evening!*
		Hallo!	
		Grüß dich!	
		Grüß Gott! *(S. German)*	*Hello! Hi!*
		Grüezi! *(Swiss)*	
		Servus! *(Austrian)*	
FAREWELLS	**Auf Wiedersehen!**	**Wiedersehen!**	*Good-bye!*
		Tschüss!	
		Ciao!	*Bye! So long!*
		Servus! *(Austrian)*	
	Gute Nacht!		*Good night!*

E-6 Grußformeln. Find greetings that are used in the German-speaking countries. If you recognize any other non-English greetings, identify them and say them for your classmates.

((▶ Counting

The numbers from 0 to 1000

0	null						
1	ein**s**	11	elf	21	**ein**un**d**zwanzig	10	zehn
2	zwei	12	zwölf	22	zweiundzwanzig	20	zwanzig
3	drei	13	dreizehn	23	dreiundzwanzig	30	drei**ß**ig
4	vier	14	vierzehn	24	vierundzwanzig	40	vierzig
5	fünf	15	fünfzehn	25	fünfundzwanzig	50	fünfzig
6	sech**s**	16	se**chz**ehn	26	sechsundzwanzig	60	se**chz**ig
7	sieb**en**	17	sie**bz**ehn	27	sieb**en**undzwanzig	70	sie**bz**ig
8	acht	18	achtzehn	28	achtundzwanzig	80	achtzig
9	neun	19	neunzehn	29	neunundzwanzig	90	neunzig
10	zehn	20	zwanzig	30	drei**ß**ig	100	hundert

101	(ein)hunderteins	200	zweihundert	1000	(ein)tausend
102	(ein)hundertzwei	300	dreihundert		
usw.°	(und so weiter)	usw.			*etc.*

Note the following:

1. The **-s** in **eins** is dropped in combination with **zwanzig, dreißig,** etc.: **einundzwanzig, einunddreißig,** etc.
2. The numbers from the twenties through the nineties are "turned around": **vierundzwanzig** (four and twenty), **achtundsechzig** (eight and sixty), etc.
3. **Dreißig** is the only one of the tens that ends in **-ßig** instead of **-zig.**
4. The final **-s** in **sechs** is dropped in **sechzehn** and **sechzig.**
5. The **-en** of **sieben** is dropped in **siebzehn** and **siebzig.**

E-7 Ohne Taschenrechner, bitte! *(Without a calculator, please!)*

▶ $15 + 2$

how much   **S1:** Wie viel° (Was) ist fünfzehn plus zwei?   **S2:** Fünfzehn plus zwei ist siebzehn.

▶ $70 - 10$

S1: Wie viel (Was) ist siebzig minus zehn?   **S2:** Siebzig minus zehn ist sechzig.

1. $2 + 5$	5. $9 + 3$
2. $10 - 4$	6. $20 - 4$
3. $32 - 2$	7. $11 + 7$
4. $50 + 40$	8. $50 - 5$

E-8 Celsius und Fahrenheit.

For an American traveling in Europe, it is important to be familiar with the Celsius scale. With a partner, work on converting Celsius to Fahrenheit.

approximately

S1: Was (Wie viel) ist zwanzig Grad Celsius in Fahrenheit?   **S2:** Zwanzig Grad Celsius ist etwa° achtundsechzig Grad Fahrenheit.

E-8: In the Celsius scale, 0° represents the freezing point of water and 100° the boiling point. In the Fahrenheit scale, 32° represents the freezing point of water and 212° the boiling point.

Making phone calls; addressing letters

Most German telephone numbers are given in pairs of digits (e.g., 86 68 22). The area code is called **die Vorwahl.**

Telephone etiquette requires that the person answering the phone, as well as the caller, give her/his name. To say good-bye on the phone, the phrase **auf Wiederhören** (a variant of **auf Wiedersehen**) is often used. In colloquial German most people say **tschüss.**

In the German-speaking countries, letters are addressed a bit differently than in North America. The house number follows the name of the street (e.g., **Lindenstraße 29**). The postal code **(die Postleitzahl)** precedes the name of the city. It has five digits in Germany and four in Austria and Switzerland.

E-9 Ein Brief von Mutter. Peter has just received a letter from his mother.

1. Peters Familienname ist _____.
2. Peters Hausnummer ist _____.
3. Die Hausnummer von Peters Mutter ist _____.
4. Peters Postleitzahl ist _____.
5. Die Postleitzahl von Peters Mutter ist _____.
6. Ein Brief von Berlin nach München kostet _____ Cent.

E-10 Was ist die Telefonnummer? Listen to the snippets from radio ads and match the numbers with the businesses listed below.

1. Pizzeria Roma   a. 4 30 24
2. Tai Chi Studio   b. 3 08 65
3. Amendt Computersysteme   c. 4 51 13
4. Cinema Metropolis   d. 3 77 10

E-11 Eine SMS an Stephanie. Read Peter's text message to Stephanie on the display of his **Handy** and then mark the correct answers to the questions below.

1. Where will Stephanie be able to find Peter at 10 a.m.?
   a. in lecture hall 9   b. in lecture hall 12   c. in the cafeteria

2. Where will Stephanie be able to find Peter at 12 noon?
   a. in lecture hall 9   b. in lecture hall 10   c. in the cafeteria

3. When did Peter send this text message to Stephanie?
   a. at 8 a.m.   b. at night   c. in the afternoon

Spelling

The alphabet

The name of almost every letter in the German alphabet contains the sound represented by that letter. Learning the alphabet is therefore useful not only for purposes of spelling, but also for your pronunciation. Listen carefully to the recording and to your instructor. Repeat what you hear.

 E-12 Hören Sie gut zu und wiederholen Sie! *(Listen carefully and repeat!)*

a	ah	**g**	geh	**m**	emm	**s**	ess	**y**	üppsilon
b	beh	**h**	hah	**n**	enn	**t**	teh	**z**	tsett
c	tseh	**i**	ee	**o**	oh	**u**	oo		
d	deh	**j**	yott	**p**	peh	**v**	fow		
e	eh	**k**	kah	**q**	coo	**w**	veh		
f	eff	**l**	ell	**r**	airr	**x**	iks		

E-13 Abkürzungen. Your instructor will read the names below. Find the appropriate abbreviations in the illustrations and spell them aloud.

Bundesrepublik Deutschland

Vereinigte Staaten von Amerika

Bayerische Motorenwerke

Volkswagen

Allgemeiner Deutscher Automobilclub

Deutsches Jugendherbergswerk

Christlich-Demokratische Union

 E-14 Adressen. You **(S1)** and a friend **(S2)** are students in Berlin and are updating your address books. The information for **S1** is on this page; the information for **S2** is in the *Anhang* on page A1.

still

S1: Ist Lillis Adresse immer noch° Albrechtstraße 17?

S2: Nein, die Adresse ist jetzt Bismarckstraße 25.

Pardon? / How do you spell that?

S1: Wie bitte?° Wie schreibt man das?°

S2: B-i-s-m-a-r-c-k

S1: Und die neue Telefonnummer?

S2: Die neue Telefonnummer ist 27 30 81 15.

S1: Oh, und was ist die Postleitzahl?

S2: Die Postleitzahl ist jetzt 12169.

NAME	POSTLEITZAHL	ADRESSE	TELEFON
Lilli Sieger	12167	Albrechtstr. 17	35 41 56 03
Asha Singh	10707 ~~12207~~	Bregenzerstr. 44 ~~Bahnhofstr. 28~~	80 49 76 63 ~~68 94 26 38~~
Daniel Sommer	14167	Schuberstr. 57	77 46 33 84
Heather Smith	13355 ~~10405~~	Bergstr. 39 ~~Raabestr. 60~~	13 24 74 66 ~~56 45 32 69~~

E-15 Wir lernen einander besser kennen. Find out the last name, address, and telephone number of two of your classmates.

S1: Was ist dein Familienname?
Wie schreibt man das?
Was ist deine Adresse?
Was ist deine Telefonnummer?

S2: Mein Familienname ist _____.
…
Meine Adresse ist …
Meine Telefonnummer ist _____.

E-16 Eine Jugendherberge. For young people traveling in Europe, youth hostels are a popular and inexpensive place to stay. Find out more about one German hostel by reading the sign and answering the questions.

Jugendherberge
Ostseebad Sellin

Kiefernweg 4 • D - 18586 Ostseebad Sellin
Tel. 038303 95099 • Fax 038303 95098
E-Mail: jh-sellin@djh-mv.de www.djh-mv.de

YOUTH HOSTELLING INTERNATIONAL

Deutsches Jugendherbergswerk

1. What is the **Postleitzahl** of Sellin?
2. What do you think the **D** preceding the **Postleitzahl** stands for?
3. The **seebad** in **Ostseebad** means *seaside resort*. Look at the map **Deutschland Bundesländer** on the third page at the very front of your textbook, find the **Ostsee,** and give the English equivalent.
4. Look at the same map to find out what the **mv** in the e-mail and Web site addresses stands for.

Find out more about youth hostels in **Mecklenburg-Vorpommern** at www.prenhall.com/treffpunkt
→ Erste Kontakte → Web Resources → Kultur

Zur Aussprache

Some sounds and letters that are quite different from those found in English are discussed here. Listen carefully and imitate the sounds that you hear.

The umlauted vowels *ä*, *ö*, and *ü*

The sound represented by the letter **ä** is close to the sound represented by the letter *e* in English *let*.

short *ä*		long *ä*	
Bäcker	Gärtner	Käse	Universität

The sound represented by the letter **ö** has no equivalent in English. To produce this sound, pucker your lips as if to whistle, hold them in this position, and say *eh*.

short *ö*		long *ö*	
zwölf	Göttingen	schön	hören

The sound represented by the letter **ü** also has no equivalent in English. To produce this sound, pucker your lips as if to whistle, hold them in this position, and say *ee*.

short *ü*		long *ü*	
fünf	Tschüss!	grün	Grüß dich!

The *Eszett*

The letter **ß,** which is called **Eszett,** is pronounced like an *s.*

> heiß   heißen   dreißig

German *ch*

After **a, o,** and **u,** the sound represented by **ch** resembles a gentle gargling.

> acht   noch   auch

After **i** and **e,** the sound represented by **ch** is pronounced like a loudly whispered *h* in *huge.*

> ich   nicht   sechzehn

The suffix **-ig** is pronounced as if it were spelled **-ich.**

> windig   zwanzig   dreißig

German *v*

The sound represented by the letter **v** is generally pronounced like English *f.*

> vier   viel   Volkswagen

German *w*

The sound represented by the letter **w** is always pronounced like English *v.*

> woher   Wie geht's?   Wiedersehen!

German *z*

The sound represented by the letter **z** is pronounced like English *ts* in *hits.*

> zwei   zehn   zwanzig

Kind mit Rucksack und Knackwurst

E-17 Deutsch und Englisch. Of the many words you will encounter as you learn German, some will already be familiar to you. This is because languages borrow words from one another.

By matching appropriately in each of the two sets below, you can reconstruct some German words commonly used in English. Compare the difference between the English and German pronunciation as your instructor says the words in German.

1. kinder-	a. sack	6. sauer-	f. land
2. wunder-	b. garten	7. leit-	g. lust
3. knack-	c. geist	8. hinter-	h. heit
4. polter-	d. kind	9. gesund-	i. motiv
5. ruck-	e. wurst	10. wander-	j. kraut

Be sure to learn the numbers listed on page 5.

Informelle Situationen

Morgen!	Good morning!
Tag!	Hello!
'n Abend!	Good evening!
Grüß dich!	Hi! *(to greet one person)*
Hallo!	Hi!
Tschüss!	Bye!
Ciao!	
Entschuldigung!*	Excuse me!
Wie heißt du?	What's your name?
Ich heiße …	My name is . . .
Ich bin …	I'm . . .
Woher kommst (bist) du?	Where are you from?
Ich komme (bin) aus …	I'm from . . .
Wie geht's?	How are you?
Danke, gut.*	Fine, thanks.
Super.	Super.

Formelle Situationen

Guten Morgen!	Good morning!
Guten Tag!	Hello!
Guten Abend!	Good evening!
Auf Wiedersehen!	Good-bye!
Auf Wiederhören!	Good-bye! *(on phone)*
Wie heißen Sie?	What is your name?
Ich heiße …	
Mein Name ist …	My name is . . .
Woher kommen (sind) Sie?	Where are you from? ~Bitte~
Wie geht es Ihnen?	How are you?
Wie bitte?*	Pardon?
Frau	Mrs., Ms.
Herr	Mr.
ja ≠ nein	yes ≠ no

*The words marked with an asterisk can be used formally and informally.

Wörter im Kontext

E-18 Formell oder informell? How could you greet the following people at the times given?

	YOUR PROFESSOR	YOUR FELLOW STUDENTS
9 a.m.	_____	_____
3 p.m.	_____	_____
7 p.m.	_____	_____

E-19 Wie viel ist das? Match each problem with its correct solution.

1. Wie viel ist zwei plus fünf?
2. Was ist elf minus eins?
3. Wie viel ist dreizehn plus vier?
4. Was ist siebzig minus zehn?

a. Das ist zehn.
b. Das ist sechzig.
c. Das ist sieben.
d. Das ist siebzehn.

E-20 Was passt wo? *(What goes where?)* Complete with the appropriate word or expression.

wie geht's / Name / nein / Entschuldigung /
wie geht es Ihnen / super / wie bitte

1.   MARTIN: Grüß dich, Claudia. _____?
    CLAUDIA: _____.
2.   PETER: _____, bist du Asha Singh?
    YVONNE: _____, ich bin Yvonne Harris.
3.   HERR PEERY: Guten Tag. Mein _____ ist Peery.
    FRAU BORG: _____? Wie heißen Sie?
    HERR PEERY: Ich bin Frank Peery.
    FRAU BORG: Oh, Herr Peery aus Iowa! _____?

Jahraus, jahrein

Universitätsstadt Tübingen: Stocherkähne auf dem Neckar

Kommunikationsziele

Talking about . . .

- the weather and the seasons
- student life
- everyday activities and objects
- colors
- nationality

Strukturen

Gender and number of nouns

Ein and **kein**

Word order:

- Position of the verb in questions and statements
- Expressions of time and place
- Position of **nicht**

Personal pronouns

Present tense of **sein**

The verb: infinitive and present tense

Kultur

Landscapes and climate of the German-speaking countries

About university life

Why German and English are similar

Video-Treff: **Das bin ich**

Lesen: **Eine Schweizerin, eine deutsche Familie und zwei Österreicher**

Vorschau

In the first two dialogues you will again encounter Claudia, Stephanie, Martin, and Peter, the four friends studying at the **Ludwig-Maximilians-Universität** in **München.**

Semesterbeginn

Stephanie und Claudia sitzen zusammen beim Frühstück.

CLAUDIA: Gehst du jetzt in die Vorlesung, Stephanie?

STEPHANIE: Ja, und dann zum Auslandsamt.

CLAUDIA: Meine Vorlesungen beginnen erst morgen.

STEPHANIE: Und was machst du heute?

CLAUDIA: Nicht viel. Zuerst schreibe ich ein paar Karten und heute Nachmittag kaufe ich meine Bücher.

STEPHANIE: Na, dann bis später.

CLAUDIA: Tschüss, Stephanie.

Badewetter

Claudia und Martin sind gute Freunde. Stephanie und Peter sind auch oft zusammen.

MARTIN: Mensch, das ist ja heiß!

PETER: Ja, fast dreißig Grad! – Sag mal, geht ihr auch schwimmen?

MARTIN: Klar, gleich nach Claudias Hydraulikvorlesung.

PETER: Wir gehen gleich jetzt. Stephanie kommt in fünf Minuten.

MARTIN: Na, dann bis später.

Der Tag beginnt

Frau Ziegler steht am Fenster. Herr Ziegler ist noch im Bett.

HERR ZIEGLER: Wie ist das Wetter?

FRAU ZIEGLER: Gar nicht schön. Der Himmel ist grau und es regnet.

HERR ZIEGLER: Ist es kalt?

FRAU ZIEGLER: Das Thermometer zeigt zehn Grad.

HERR ZIEGLER: Nur zehn Grad! Was für ein Hundewetter!

1-1 Richtig oder falsch? You will hear the conversations on page 13. Indicate whether the statements that follow each conversation are **richtig** (*true*) or **falsch** (*false*).

	SEMESTERBEGINN		BADEWETTER		DER TAG BEGINNT	
	RICHTIG	FALSCH	RICHTIG	FALSCH	RICHTIG	FALSCH
1.	_____	_____	_____	_____	_____	_____
2.	_____	_____	_____	_____	_____	_____
3.	_____	_____	_____	_____	_____	_____

1-2 Was passt zusammen? (*What goes together?*) Working with a partner, find the five sentences that describe each illustration.

Heute ist es gar nicht schön.

Heute ist es schön.

Die Sonne scheint.

Es regnet.

Der Himmel ist grau.

Der Himmel ist blau.

Es ist windig.

Es ist windstill.

Das ist Badewetter!

Was für ein Hundewetter!

■ Sprachnotiz ··

Flavoring particles and discourse strategies

Speakers of German often use *flavoring particles* to add color to what they are saying. When **ja** is used as a flavoring particle, it often adds emphasis to an exclamation.

> Mensch, das ist **ja** heiß!
> Das ist **ja** Badewetter!

If you use certain words or phrases to influence the direction a conversation is taking, you are employing a *discourse strategy*. For example, when you want to change the subject, you can use a question introduced by **Sag mal.**

> MARTIN: Hallo, Claudia. Kommst du jetzt?
> CLAUDIA: Ja, gleich. – **Sag mal,** regnet es noch?

1-3 Wie ist das Wetter? Working with a partner, read through the following situations. Complete the conversations with appropriate questions and answers from the box.

SITUATION A

When your friend went to the library early this morning, it was pouring rain. When you come to pick your friend up, she/he wants to know whether it's still raining. You tell her/him that it's nice out now. Your friend responds appropriately.

S1: Hallo, _____. Kommst du jetzt?

S2: Ja, gleich. – Sag mal, wie ist das Wetter? … ?

S1: …

S2: …

SITUATION B

When your friend went to the library early this morning, the sun was shining. When you come to pick your friend up, she/he wants to know whether it's still so nice outside. You tell her/him that it's raining now. Your friend responds appropriately.

S1: Grüß dich, _____. Kommst du jetzt?

S2: Klar! – Sag mal, wie ist das Wetter? … ?

S1: …

S2: …

Ist es noch so schön?	Regnet es noch?
Nein, der Himmel ist grau und es regnet.	Nein, die Sonne scheint und der Himmel ist blau.
Toll°, das ist ja Badewetter!	Was für ein Hundewetter!

fantastic

1-4 Drei kleine Gespräche. With a partner, unscramble the exchanges in the following three mini-conversations by numbering appropriately. Then read the conversations for your classmates.

S1:

___ Ja, aber erst heute Nachmittag.

_1_ Gehst du heute schwimmen?

___ Wann° gehst du?

S2:

___ Gleich jetzt. Und du, gehst du auch?

___ Na, dann bis später.

___ Klar, das Thermometer zeigt fast dreißig Grad.

when

S1:

_1_ Was machst du jetzt?

___ Und wann gehst du zum Auslandsamt?

___ Und dann? Gehst du dann gleich zum Auslandsamt?

S2:

___ Das mache ich heute Nachmittag.

___ Nein, zuerst kaufe ich meine Bücher.

___ Ich gehe in die Vorlesung.

S1:

___ Und was machst du heute?

___ Und dann? Was machst du dann?

_1_ Gehst du jetzt in die Vorlesung?

S2:

___ Dann gehe ich schwimmen.

___ Zuerst schreibe ich ein paar Karten.

___ Nein, meine Vorlesungen beginnen erst morgen.

As you read, look at the maps of the German-speaking countries inside the front cover and find the places mentioned.

KULTUR

Landscapes and climate of the German-speaking countries

Located in the center of Europe, the German-speaking countries are only about two-thirds the size of Texas. And yet, the topography and climate of **Deutschland, Österreich,** and the **Schweiz** are enormously varied.

It is about a day's journey from the coast of the **Nordsee** to the peaks of the German, Swiss, and Austrian **Alpen** in the south. The Lowlands of Northern Germany extend from the Dutch border in the west to the border of Poland in the east. Just south of the **Lüneburger Heide,** where you can hike through thousands of acres of purple heather, the Lowlands give way to the mountain ranges of Central Germany. The most famous of these are the **Harz** mountains. To the southwest lies the **Rheintal,** and following the Rhine south, you reach the densely forested mountains of the **Schwarzwald.** From its highest point, you can see the snow-covered peaks of the Swiss **Alpen** to the southwest.

It also takes about a day to drive from **Freiburg,** at the western edge of Southern Germany, to the eastern border of Austria. You can follow the **Donau,** as it flows through a succession of culturally significant towns like **Regensburg, Passau,** and **Linz,** until you reach **Wien,** the capital of Austria.

On the beaches of the North Sea and the Baltic Sea there is often a cool onshore wind. **Strandkörbe** (literally: *beach baskets*) can be rented as shelter from the wind.

Weinberge in Süddeutschland

The German-speaking countries show considerable climatic variation. In the north, the weather is influenced by the cool air currents off the **Nordsee** and the **Ostsee.** The summers are only moderately warm and the winters are mild, but often stormy and very wet.

In the central region, between the Northern Lowlands and the **Alpen** in the south, the summers are usually much warmer and the winters much colder than in the north. The highest summer temperatures occur in the protected valleys of the **Rhein** and **Mosel** rivers, providing perfect growing conditions for the thousands of acres of vineyards that produce the famous white wines of Germany.

To the south, the climate of the Swiss and Austrian **Alpen** is characterized by high precipitation, shorter summers, and longer winters. But even in these small countries, the variation in climate from one area to the next is quite striking. In Switzerland, which is about half the size of the state of Maine, the climate is so varied that a sports enthusiast can go windsurfing and skiing in a single summer's day!

An der Nordsee ist es oft sehr windig.

1-5 Ein bisschen Geografie. Unscramble the following geographical names from the reading and check the appropriate category.

		REGION OR COUNTRY	CITY	RIVER OR SEA
1. ondua	_____	_____	_____	_____
2. wachzwarlds	_____	_____	_____	_____
3. enwi	_____	_____	_____	_____
4. plane	_____	_____	_____	_____
5. sneredo	_____	_____	_____	_____
6. athlerin	_____	_____	_____	_____
7. tesoes	_____	_____	_____	_____
8. terröcheis	_____	_____	_____	_____
9. olems	_____	_____	_____	_____
10. wizechs	_____	_____	_____	_____

Seefeld in Tirol, Österreich

Bauernhäuser im Schwarzwald

In den Schweizer Alpen

Locate the German-speaking countries in the context of Europe on the map inside the back cover. Which countries are the immediate neighbors of each?

Experience Alpine skiing at www.prenhall.com/treffpunkt → Kapitel 1 → Web Resources → Kultur

There are two vocabulary lists per chapter. Organized according to parts of speech, items are also grouped alphabetically by theme wherever possible.

✴ Nomen (Nouns)

der Himmel	sky; heaven
die Sonne	sun
das Wetter	weather
der Freund, die Freunde	friend; boyfriend
die Freundin, die Freundinnen	friend; girlfriend

In German the same word is used for a friend and for someone to whom one is romantically attached.

das Auslandsamt	foreign students office
das Buch, die Bücher	book
die Karte, die Karten	card; postcard; map
die Mensa	university dining hall
die Vorlesung, die Vorlesungen	lecture

STUDENTENWERK LEIPZIG
ZENTRALMENSA
Oberer Speisesaal Cafeterien
Unterer Speisesaal

Verben ✴

beginnen	to begin
gehen	to go
kaufen	to buy
kommen	to come
machen	to do; to make
regnen	to rain
scheinen	to shine
schreiben	to write
studieren	to study

✴ Andere Wörter (Other words)

schön	nice; beautiful
windig	windy
dann	then
gleich	right away
heute	today
heute Nachmittag	this afternoon
jetzt	now
morgen	tomorrow
oft	often
zuerst	first

auch	also
ein paar	a few
fast	almost
nicht	not
gar nicht	not at all
noch	still
noch nicht	not yet
nur	only
viel	much; a lot

Ausdrücke (Expressions)

Bis später!	See you later!
Klar!	Of course!
Mensch!	Wow!
Toll!	Fantastic!
Das Thermometer zeigt zehn Grad.	The thermometer reads ten degrees.
Die Vorlesungen beginnen erst morgen.	(The) lectures don't begin until tomorrow.

✴ Das Gegenteil (Opposites)

bitte ≠ danke	please ≠ thank you
heiß ≠ kalt	hot ≠ cold
richtig ≠ falsch	true; right ≠ false; wrong

✴ Die Farben (Colors)

blau		blue
braun		brown
gelb		yellow
grau		gray
grün		green
rosarot		pink
rot		red
schwarz		black
violett		purple
weiß		white

✴ Leicht zu verstehen (Easy to understand)

das Semester, die Semester
der Student, die Studenten
die Studentin, die Studentinnen
die Universität, die Universitäten
   (die Uni, die Unis)

Lerntipp: Some helpful strategies for learning vocabulary include writing out words, quizzing a partner, and creating your own sentences. You should also listen to and repeat aloud the recorded vocabulary items available on the audio CDs or on the *Treffpunkt Deutsch* Website.

To help you with pronunciation, short stressed vowels are marked with a dot below the vowel and long stressed vowels or vowel combinations are underlined. In phrases or sentences, these markings indicate which vowel in the phrase or sentence is stressed. Note that these markings do not appear in regular written German.

Ländernamen		Die Nationalität	
die Bundesrepublik Deutschland (die BRD)	the Federal Republic of Germany (the FRG)	**Er ist Deutscher.**	He's a German.
		Sie ist Deutsche.	She's a German.
Österreich	Austria	**Er ist Österreicher.**	He's an Austrian.
die Schweiz	Switzerland	**Sie ist Österreicherin.**	She's an Austrian.
die Vereinigten Staaten (die USA)	the United States (the U.S.)	**Er ist Schweizer.**	He's Swiss.
		Sie ist Schweizerin.	She's Swiss.
Kanada	Canada	**Er ist Amerikaner.**	He's an American.
		Sie ist Amerikanerin.	She's an American.
		Er ist Kanadier.	He's a Canadian.
		Sie ist Kanadierin.	She's a Canadian.

The names of most countries are neuter and are not normally preceded by an article (e.g., **England, Dänemark**). When the name of a country is masculine, feminine, or plural, the article must be used (e.g., **der Libanon, die Türkei, die USA**).

Wörter im Kontext

1-6 Fragen und Antworten. Choose the appropriate response to your partner's questions or statements.

S1:
1. Woher kommst du?
2. Was studierst du?
3. Beginnen die Vorlesungen heute?
4. Gehst du in die Mensa?
5. Was machst du heute Nachmittag?
6. Ich gehe nicht oft in die Disco.

S2:
a. Biologie und Chemie.
b. Ich auch nicht.
c. Nicht viel.
d. Nein, erst morgen.
e. Aus Österreich.
f. Nein, noch nicht.

1-7 Fragen und Antworten. Choose the appropriate response to your partner's questions.

S1:
1. Wie ist das Wetter?
2. Regnet es noch?
3. Was zeigt das Thermometer?
4. Ist es heiß?
5. Was machst du morgen?
6. Kommst du jetzt?

S2:
a. Ja, fast dreißig Grad.
b. Nur zehn Grad.
c. Nein, jetzt scheint die Sonne.
d. Gar nicht schön.
e. Ja, gleich.
f. Zuerst schreibe ich ein paar Karten und dann gehe ich schwimmen.

1-8 Was sind die Farben?

1. Schokolade ist _____.
2. Gras ist _____.
3. Milch ist _____.
4. Butter ist _____.
5. Kohle° ist _____.

6. Blut ist _____.
7. Die Sonne scheint und der Himmel ist _____.
8. Der Himmel ist _____ und es regnet.

coal

1-9 Die Nationalität, bitte!

1. Frau Bürgli ist aus Zürich. Sie ist _____.
2. Herr Karlhuber kommt aus Salzburg. Er ist _____.
3. Frau Kröger ist aus Hamburg. Sie ist _____.
4. Herr Chang ist aus San Francisco. Er ist _____.
5. Frau Thomson kommt aus Vancouver. Sie ist _____.

Signs similar to the one depicted here can be found at border points of the European Union member countries (27 as of 2007): Austria, Belgium, Bulgaria, Cyprus, Czech Republic, Denmark, Estonia, Finland, France, Germany, Great Britain, Greece, Hungary, Ireland, Italy, Latvia, Lithuania, Luxemburg, Malta, the Netherlands, Poland, Portugal, Romania, Slovakia, Slovenia, Spain, and Sweden. The blue flag with the 12 gold stars has been used since 1986. Other documents and symbols of the EU include an EU passport for citizens of member countries, an EU driver's license, Europe Day on May 9, and the *Ode to Joy* from Beethoven's Ninth Symphony as the EU anthem. Some EU countries (including Germany) have introduced license plates with the EU flag on the left side.

❶ Identifying people and things

Nouns: gender and definite articles

Nouns are the words used to name people and things. In English all nouns have the definite article *the*. In German every noun has *grammatical gender*, i.e., it is either masculine, neuter, or feminine. Nouns that are masculine have the definite article **der,** nouns that are neuter have the definite article **das,** and nouns that are feminine have the definite article **die.**

masculine	neuter	feminine
der	das	die
the	*the*	*the*

Although nouns referring to males are usually masculine (*der* **Mann,** *der* **Vater**) and nouns referring to females are usually feminine (*die* **Frau,** *die* **Mutter**), the gender of German nouns is not always logical.

der Himmel	**das** Wetter	**die** Sonne
der Computer	**das** Buch	**die** Vorlesung

You should learn each noun with its definite article as *one unit*.

Lerntipp: When you learn the vocabulary listed in the *Wortschatz* sections, you may find it helpful to highlight the nouns and their articles in three different colors according to gender.

1-10 Wer ist das? Identify the members of the Ziegler family.

1. Das ist …

2. Das ist …

3. Das ist …

4. Das ist …

die Mutter	der Vater	die Tochter	der Sohn

1-11 Verwandte Wörter. *(Related words.)* The names of the objects below are very close in form and meaning to their English equivalents. With a partner, read the names of the objects listed in the box, find each one in the illustration, and read the corresponding number.

Words in different languages that are similar or identical in form and meaning are called cognates.

S1: Der Computer ist Bild° Nummer vierzehn. Und der Fußball?
...

S2: Der Fußball ist Bild Nummer siebzehn. Und der Hammer?
...

picture

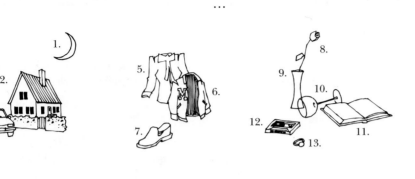

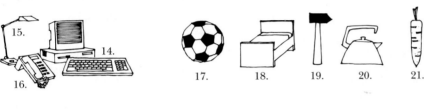

MASCULINE	NEUTER	FEMININE
der Computer	das Auto	die Bluse
der Fußball	das Boot	die Jacke
der Hammer	das Bett	die Karotte
der Mond	das Buch	die Kassette
der Ring	das Weinglas	die Lampe
der Schuh	das Haus	die Rose
der Teekessel	das Telefon	die Vase

Most nouns that end in **-e** are feminine.

Plural forms: definite articles and nouns

All three definite articles (**der, das, die**) have the same plural form: **die.**

singular	plural
der	
das	die
die	

Although a few English nouns have irregular plural forms (e.g., woman, wom*en*; child, child*ren*; mouse, m*ice*), most English nouns form the plural by adding *-s* or *-es* (e.g., student, student*s*; class, class*es*).

The table below shows the five basic plural forms for German nouns. The column *dictionary entry* shows how nouns are presented in vocabulary lists with the abbreviated plural forms. The column *you should learn* shows how a German noun must be learned, i.e., with its definite article and its plural form.

	abbreviation of plural form	dictionary entry	you should learn
1	- ::	der Finger, - die Mutter, ::	der Finger, die Finger die Mutter, die Mütter
2	-e ::e	der Freund, -e die Maus, ::e	der Freund, die Freunde die Maus, die Mäuse*
3	-er ::er	das Kind, -er das Buch, ::er	das Kind, die Kinder das Buch, die Bücher
4	-n -en -nen	die Karte, -n die Vorlesung, -en die Freundin, -nen	die Karte, die Karten die Vorlesung, die Vorlesungen die Freundin, die Freundinnen**
5	-s	das Auto, -s	das Auto, die Autos

* In the diphthong (vowel combination) **au,** it is always the **a** that receives the umlaut in the plural.
** All nouns with the plural ending **-nen** are derived from masculine nouns, e.g., **der Student, die Student*in*, die Student*innen.***

1-12 Was sind die Farben?
The nouns beneath the illustrations are listed as you would find them in a dictionary. Using the plural forms, say what colors the objects or animals are.

S1: Die Tennisbälle sind gelb.
Und die Schuhe?
...

S2: Die Schuhe sind braun.
Und die Äpfel?
...

1.
der Tennisball, ::e

2.
der Schuh, -e

3.
der Apfel, ::

4.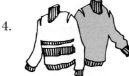
der Pullover, -

5.
das Auto, -s

6.
das Haus, ::er

7.
das Bett, -en

8.
das Buch, ::er

9.
die Banane, -n

10.
die Blume, -n

11.
die Katze, -n

12.
die Maus, ::e

The indefinite articles *ein* and *kein*

The forms of the indefinite article *(a, an)* are **ein** (masculine and neuter) and **eine** (feminine). Just like *a* and *an*, **ein** and **eine** have no plural form.

Das ist **ein** Buch über die EU und hier ist **eine** Karte von Europa.	*This is **a** book about the EU and here is **a** map of Europe.*

	masculine	neuter	feminine
DEFINITE	**der** Student	**das** Buch	**die** Studentin
INDEFINITE	**ein** Student	**ein** Buch	**eine** Studentin

If the numeral *one* (**eins**) precedes a noun, German uses the indefinite article instead.

Stephanie hat heute nur **eine** Vorlesung.	*Stephanie has only **one** lecture today.*

The negative forms of the indefinite article *(not a, not any, not, no)* are **kein** (masculine and neuter) and **keine** (feminine). Note that **kein** has a plural form: **keine.**

Das ist **kein** Restaurant, das ist eine Mensa.	*That's **not a** restaurant, that's a cafeteria.*
Das sind **keine** Amerikaner, das sind Kanadier.	*Those aren't Americans, they're Canadians.*

INFOBOX

About university life

In the German-speaking countries, university students receive much less guidance than in North America. They are not assigned an advisor, and their schedules are rather flexible, as is the number of semesters they spend at the university. Thus, students talk about where they are in their studies according to semesters, e.g., **Ich bin im vierten Semester.**

There are no semester finals in the North American sense of the word. Usually the first set of major exams (**Zwischenprüfungen**) is taken after the fourth semester. In order to qualify for these exams, students must acquire a certain number of **Scheine** *(certificates)* or **Leistungspunkte** *(credit points)*, which varies from university to university. Students must pass the **Zwischenprüfungen** in order to continue their studies.

WWW Take a stroll around a German university at www.prenhall.com/treffpunkt
→ Kapitel 1 → Web Resources
→ Kultur

Leipzig: Universitätsbibliothek

1-13 Was für dumme Fragen! Correct your partner.

▶ Glas (n)

S1: Ist das ein Glas?

S2: Nein, das ist kein Glas. Das ist eine Vase.

▶ Lilien (pl)

S1: Sind das Lilien?

S2: Nein, das sind keine Lilien. Das sind Tulpen.

1. Biergläser (pl)

2. Tennisball (m)

3. Jacke (f)

4. Pullover (m)

5. Barometer (n)

6. Mäuse (pl)

7. Mikroskop (n)

8. Disketten (pl)

| Sweatshirt (n) | Ratten (pl) | Fußball (m) | Teleskop (n) |
| Thermometer (n) | Kassetten (pl) | Weingläser (pl) | Bluse (f) |

❷ Word order

Position of the verb in yes/no questions

In yes/no questions the verb is always the *first element*.

Regnet es noch?   *Is it still **raining?***
Scheint die Sonne heute?   *Is the sun **shining** today?*

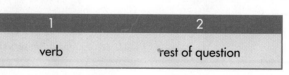

1	2
verb	rest of question

Position of the verb in information questions

In information questions the verb immediately follows a question word or phrase.

Wie **ist** das Wetter heute?	*How **is** the weather today?*
Was **zeigt** das Thermometer?	*What **does** the thermometer **read**?*
Wie kalt **ist** es heute?	*How cold **is** it today?*

Wie ist das Wetter?

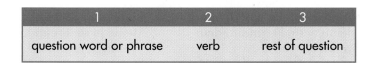

1	2	3
question word or phrase	verb	rest of question

In German all question words begin with the letter **w** (pronounced like English *v*).

wann?	*when?*	**wie viel?**	*how much?*
warum?	*why?*	**wie viele?**	*how many?*
was?	*what?*	**wo?**	*where? (in what place?)*
wer?	*who?*	**woher?**	*where . . . from? (from what place?)*
wie?	*how?*	**wohin?**	*where? (to what place?)*

Be careful to distinguish between **wo** *(where)* and **wer** *(who)*. Don't let the English equivalents confuse you.

Note that German uses three words for the word *where*, according to whether it means *in what place, from what place,* or *to what place.*

Wo ist Graz?	***Where** is Graz?*
Graz ist in Österreich.	*Graz is in Austria.*
Woher ist Martin?	***Where** is Martin **from?***
Ich glaube, er ist aus Mannheim.	*I think he's from Mannheim.*
Wohin gehst du heute Abend?	***Where** are you going tonight?*
Heute Abend gehe ich ins Kino.	*Tonight I'm going to the movies.*

1-14 Fragen und Antworten. Choose the appropriate response to your partner's questions.

S1:

1. Wann beginnt der Winter?
2. Warum gehst du nicht schwimmen?
3. Was macht ihr heute Abend?
4. Wer ist Tom Hanks?
5. Woher kommt Stephanie?
6. Wo ist Chicago?
7. Wohin gehst du?
8. Wie viele Meter hat° ein Kilometer?

S2:

a. In Illinois.
b. Tausend.
c. Ein amerikanischer Filmstar.
d. Wir gehen ins Kino.
e. In die Mensa.
f. Im Dezember.
g. Aus Chicago.
h. Ich finde es zu kalt.

does . . . have

1-15 Smalltalk. Answer your partner's questions appropriately.

S1:	**S2:**
1. Wie heißt du?	Ich heiße …
2. Woher bist du?	Ich bin aus …
3. Wo ist das?	Das ist in …
4. Was ist deine° Telefonnummer?	Meine Telefonnummer ist …
5. Wie viele Vorlesungen hast° du heute?	Heute habe ich …
6. Wie viele Vorlesungen hast du morgen?	Morgen habe ich …
7. Wer ist deine beste Freundin/dein bester Freund?	Meine beste Freundin/Mein bester Freund ist …
8. Woher ist deine beste Freundin/dein bester Freund?	Meine beste Freundin/Mein bester Freund ist aus …

your
do . . . have

1-16 So viele Fragen! Introduce the following questions with **Ist** or a question word. Your partner should know the answers.

▶ _____ Steffi Graf aus Österreich?

S1: Ist Steffi Graf aus Österreich?   **S2:** Nein, Steffi Graf ist aus Deutschland.

1. _____ kommt Neil Young, aus England oder aus Kanada?
2. _____ ist Innsbruck, in Deutschland oder in Österreich?
3. _____ Frankfurt in Österreich?
4. _____ singt besser, Whitney Houston oder Madonna?
5. _____ Sekunden hat eine Minute?
6. _____ ist das Wetter heute?
7. _____ beginnt der Sommer, im Juni oder im Juli?
8. _____ ist einunddreißig plus sechs?
9. _____ sind im Winter so viele Deutsche in Florida?
10. _____ Arnold Schwarzenegger aus Österreich?

Position of the verb in statements

In English statements the verb usually follows the subject. This holds true whether the statement begins with the subject or with another element (e.g., an expression of time or place).

	The thermometer	**reads**	*only ten degrees.*
Today	**the thermometer**	**reads**	*only ten degrees.*

In German statements the verb is *always the second element*. If the statement begins with an element other than the subject, the subject follows the verb.

1	2	3	
subject	verb	rest of statement	
Das Thermometer	**zeigt**	nur zehn Grad.	

1	2	3	4
other element	verb	subject	rest of statement
Heute	**zeigt**	**das Thermometer**	nur zehn Grad.

1-17 Badewetter. Read the following sentences, beginning each one with the expression of place or time given in parentheses.

1. Das Wetter ist heute sehr schön. (in München)
2. Das Thermometer zeigt fast dreißig Grad. (im Moment)
3. Stephanie hat keine Vorlesungen. (heute Nachmittag)
4. Sie geht mit Claudia, Peter und Martin schwimmen. (gleich nach Claudias Hydraulikvorlesung)

Ja, nein, and the conjunctions in the table below do not count as elements in a sentence.

und	and	**aber**	but
oder	or	**sondern**	but, (but) . . . instead, but rather
denn	because		

Ist das Wetter schön?	*Is the weather nice?*
Ja, die Sonne **scheint**	*Yes, the sun is shining*
und der Himmel **ist** blau,	*and the sky is blue,*
aber es **ist** sehr windig.	*but it's very windy.*

Note that **sondern** is always preceded by a negative statement.

Gehst du schwimmen?	*Are you going swimming?*
Nein, ich **gehe** nicht schwimmen,	*No, I'm not going swimming,*
sondern ich **schreibe** Karten.	*(but) I'm writing postcards instead.*

1-18 Und, oder, denn, aber, sondern?

1. Ich gehe heute nicht schwimmen, _____ es ist kalt _____ es regnet.
2. Der Himmel ist grau, _____ es regnet nicht.
3. Dreißig Grad ist nicht warm, _____ es ist sehr heiß.
4. Regnet es _____ scheint die Sonne?

■ Sprachnotiz ·····································

Verb forms in English and German

The three forms of the English present tense have only one equivalent in German, i.e., forms like *it is raining* and *it does rain* do not exist in German.

it rains	
it is raining	**es regnet**
it does rain	

*How often **does it rain** in Hamburg?*	Wie oft **regnet** es in Hamburg?
*In Hamburg it **rains** very often.*	In Hamburg **regnet** es sehr oft.
*It's **raining** today.*	Es **regnet** heute.

1-19: Be sure to read the *Sprachnotiz* on p. 27 before you do the exercise.

1-19 Auf Englisch, bitte!

1. PETER: Kommt Stephanie heute oder kommt sie morgen?
   CLAUDIA: Sie kommt erst morgen.
2. MARTIN: Beginnen die Vorlesungen morgen?
   PETER: Nein, die Vorlesungen beginnen heute.
3. MARTIN: Wie viele Vorlesungen hast du heute?
   PETER: Heute habe ich keine Vorlesungen, aber morgen habe ich fünf.

1-20 Wie ist das Wetter? Answer your partner's questions according to the illustration.

S1: Ist der Himmel blau oder grau?   **S2:** Der Himmel ist grau.

1. Regnet es oder scheint die Sonne?
2. Ist es heiß oder kalt?
3. Ist es windig oder windstill?
4. Zeigt das Thermometer fünf Grad oder zehn Grad?
5. Ist das Regenwetter oder Badewetter?

1-21 Wie ist das Wetter heute? Again, answer your partner's questions according to the illustration. Begin each answer with **heute.**

S1: Ist der Himmel heute grau oder blau?   **S2:** Heute ist der Himmel blau.

1. Ist es heute kalt oder heiß?
2. Zeigt das Thermometer heute zwanzig Grad oder dreißig Grad?
3. Ist es heute windig oder windstill?
4. Scheint die Sonne heute oder regnet es?

1-22 So ist das Wetter heute. Look out the window and write a few lines describing what the weather is like today. Use the questions from the previous exercise and the additional vocabulary below as a guide. Begin your description with **Heute …** Read your weather report to the class.

es nieselt	*it's drizzling*
es schneit	*it's snowing*
es donnert und blitzt	*it's thundering and lightning*
es ist neblig	*it's foggy*
es ist schwül	*it's humid*
es ist heiter	*it's sunny with some clouds*

Expressions of time and place

In German, expressions of time precede expressions of place. In English it is the reverse.

	TIME	PLACE		PLACE	TIME
Gehst du	**jetzt**	**in die Bibliothek?**	*Are you going*	*to the library*	*now?*
Nein, ich gehe	**jetzt**	**in die Kneipe.**	*No, I'm going*	*to the pub*	*now.*

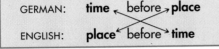

GERMAN: **time** ←before→ **place**

ENGLISH: **place** ←before→ **time**

1-23 Wohin gehst du jetzt?
Your partner isn't going where you expect her/him to go. Use the expressions of place from the box below.

▶ jetzt

S1: Gehst du jetzt in die Bibliothek? **S2:** Nein, ich gehe jetzt in die Kneipe.

1. jetzt

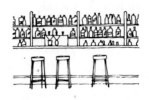

2. heute Abend

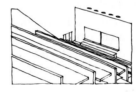

3. morgen Abend

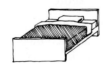

4. am Sonntagabend

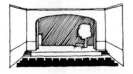

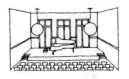

ins Theater	in die Mensa	in die Kneipe	ins Bett
in die Disco	in die Bibliothek	ins Konzert	in die Vorlesung

1-24 Was machst du heute Abend? Walk around the classroom, ask two of your classmates where they are going tonight, and respond to their questions.

S1: Hallo, _____. Wohin gehst du heute Abend?

S1: Ich gehe …

S2: Ich gehe heute Abend … Und du? Wohin gehst du?

Continue by asking two other classmates where they are going **morgen Abend** and **am Sonntagabend.**

Position of *nicht*

You have already learned that you use **kein/keine** to negate a noun preceded by **ein/eine** or a noun without an article.

Not a ✓✓✓

Ist das ein Restaurant oder eine Kneipe?	Das ist **kein** Restaurant und auch **keine** Kneipe. Das ist ein Bistro.
Hast du morgen Vorlesungen?	Nein, morgen habe ich **keine** Vorlesungen.

When you want to negate any other words or expressions, you use **nicht** and place it directly in front of those words or expressions.

Es ist **nicht kalt.**
Es ist **nicht sehr** windig.
Ich gehe **nicht in die Disco.**
Ich gehe **nicht oft** in die Disco.
Ich gehe **nicht mit Bernd** in die Disco. *Box*
Claudia kommt **nicht heute Abend,** sondern morgen Abend.

When you don't want to negate a particular word or expression, you place **nicht** at the end of the sentence.

Claudia kommt heute Abend **nicht.**
Martin kommt auch **nicht.**
Heute scheint die Sonne **nicht.**

Claudia kommt heute Abend nicht: Compare this with the sentence above, where **heute Abend** is specifically negated: **Claudia kommt** *nicht* **heute Abend, sondern morgen Abend.**

Hier bitte nicht parken

1-25 Wer kommt wann? Respond negatively according to the information given in the box. The check mark indicates when the people listed are coming.

	HEUTE ABEND	MORGEN ABEND
Claudia	—	✓
Peter	—	—

S1: Kommt Claudia heute Abend?

Kommt Peter heute Abend?

Kommt er morgen Abend?

S2: Nein, Claudia kommt nicht heute Abend, sondern morgen Abend.

Nein, Peter kommt heute Abend nicht.

Nein, morgen Abend kommt er auch nicht.

	HEUTE ABEND	MORGEN ABEND
Stephanie	—	✓
Martin	✓	—
Sabine	—	—
Tom	—	✓

S1:

1. Kommt Stephanie heute Abend?
2. Kommt Martin morgen Abend?
3. Kommt Sabine heute Abend?
   Kommt sie morgen Abend?
4. Kommt Tom heute Abend?

S2:

Nein, Stephanie …, sondern …

Nein, Martin …, sondern …

Nein, Sabine …

Nein, morgen Abend …

Nein, Tom …, sondern …

1-26 Was für dumme Fragen! Your partner doesn't seem to be very knowledgeable. Use **nicht** or **kein/keine** to answer her/his questions.

1. Regnet es in Israel viel?
2. Regnet es am Südpol°?
3. Ist der Winter in Italien sehr kalt?
4. Beginnt der Sommer im Juli?
5. Donnert und blitzt es am Nordpol?
6. Ist McDonald's ein Supermarkt?
7. Ist fünf plus sechs zwölf?
8. Ist Tiger Woods ein Rockstar?

Nein, in Israel …

Nein, am Südpol … *nicht regnet es nicht viel*

South Pole

Nein, in Italien …

Nein, der Sommer …

Nein, am Nordpol …

Nein, McDonald's … *kein*

Nein, fünf plus sechs …

Nein, Tiger Woods … *kein*

1-27 Was zeigt die Wetterkarte? With a partner look at the weather map. Using the weather symbols on the right and the description of the weather in Hamburg as a model, make up a weather report for another city. Read your reports to the class.

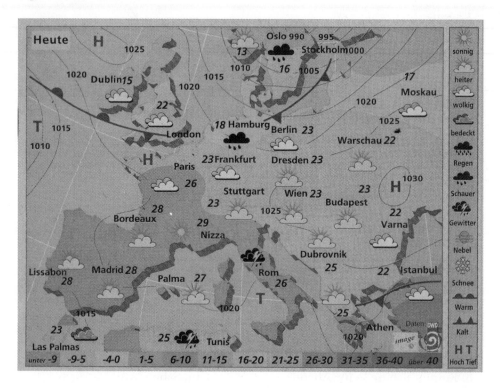

DAS WETTER IN HAMBURG

Heute ist das Wetter in Hamburg nicht sehr schön. Der Himmel ist grau und es regnet. Das Thermometer zeigt 18 Grad. Das ist nicht kalt, aber es ist auch nicht sehr warm.

1-28 Hauptstadtwetter. The electronic billboard on the **Kurfürstendamm** in Berlin shows the temperatures and weather conditions of four European **Hauptstädte.**

1. What do you think the word **Hauptstadt** means?
2. Referring to the key in the weather map above, describe in English the weather for each city on the billboard. (Note: **bewölkt = bedeckt**).

◀) ■ Hören ···

Beim Auslandsamt

Claudia has accompanied Stephanie to a reception organized by the **Auslandsamt** of the **Ludwig-Maximilians-Universität** in **München**.

1-29 Erstes Verstehen. Listen to the conversation and choose the correct responses.

1. How many people are speaking?

   1   2   3   4

2. Which names do you hear?

   Tom   Martin   Stephanie   Claudia

3. Which of the following cities are mentioned in the conversation?

   Hamburg   Toronto   Frankfurt   Chicago

4. How many Americans are among the speakers?

   0   1   2   3

5. How many Canadians are among the speakers?

   0   1   2   3

1-30 Detailverstehen. Listen to the conversation again. Then write the answers to the following questions in German. Note the German spellings of physics and biology: **Physik, Biologie.**

1. Woher kommt Claudia?
2. Was ist Toms Nationalität? Ist er Amerikaner? *Nein, er …*
3. Kommt Tom aus Vancouver? *Nein, er …*
4. Was ist Stephanies Nationalität und woher kommt sie?
5. Was studiert Stephanie?
6. Was studiert Tom?

1-31 Wir lernen einander kennen. You are at a reception organized by the **Auslandsamt.** Walk around and . . .

1. introduce yourself to other students and ask what their names are.
2. say what nationality you are and ask where they come from.
3. say what you are majoring in (**Ich studiere … **). Ask what their major is (**Was studierst du?**).

1-31: Look up the word for your major field of study under **Studienfächer** on page A17 of the *Anhang* before you do the activity.

Photo: The signs point to departments or buildings of the **Freie Universität** in Berlin. The **Silberlaube** is a building with a silvery façade, and the façade of the **Rostlaube** shows corrosion damage (**Rost**). **Laube** means **pergola**. Both names were coined by students.

❸ Talking about people and things without naming them

Personal pronouns: subject forms

When you want to talk about persons without repeating their names, you use personal pronouns. The personal pronouns are categorized under three "persons."

1st person:	I / we *(to talk about oneself)*
2nd person:	you / you *(pl)* *(to talk to a second party)*
3rd person:	he, it, she / they *(to talk about a third party)*

What facility does this sign point to?

	singular		plural	
1ST PERSON	**ich**	*I*	**wir**	*we*
2ND PERSON	**du**	*you (familiar)*	**ihr**	*you (familiar)*
	Sie	*you (formal)*	**Sie**	*you (formal)*
3RD PERSON	**er**	*he, it*		
	es	*it*	**sie**	*they*
	sie	*she, it*		

As you have already learned, German nouns are either masculine, neuter, or feminine. The pronouns in the 3rd person singular (**er, es, sie**) are chosen according to the principle of *grammatical gender,* i.e., **er** for all nouns with the article **der, es** for all nouns with the article **das,** and **sie** for all nouns with the article **die.**

Ist **der** Student intelligent?	Ja, **er** ist sehr intelligent.
Ist **der** Film lang?	Ja, **er** ist sehr lang.
Ist **das** Kind intelligent?	Ja, **es** ist sehr intelligent.
Ist **das** Studentenheim groß°?	Ja, **es** ist sehr groß.
Ist **die** Professorin fair?	Ja, **sie** ist sehr fair.
Ist **die** Vorlesung interessant?	Ja, **sie** ist sehr interessant.

big

In the 3rd person plural, the personal pronoun for all three genders is **sie** *(they).*

Sind **die** Studenten intelligent?	Ja, **sie** sind sehr intelligent.
Sind **die** Vorlesungen gut?	Ja, **sie** sind sehr gut.

singular	plural
der → er	
das → es	die → sie
die → sie	

1-32 Wie ist die Uni? You and your partner know different things about a university you've visited. Find out what your partner knows, and tell her/him what you know. The questions and information for **S2** are in the *Anhang* on page A2.

S1: Ist die Uni gut?
S2: Sind die Computer up to date?
…

S2: Ja, sie ist sehr gut.
S1: Nein, sie sind nicht alle up to date.
…

Ist die Uni gut?	
	Nein, _____ sind nicht alle up to date.
Ist der Campus groß?	
Sind die Vorlesungen interessant?	
	Ja, _____ ist sehr gut.
	Ja, _____ ist gut, aber _____ ist noch nicht sehr gut.
Sind die Professoren fair?	
Ist der Präsident populär?	
	Ja, _____ sind fast alle sehr intelligent.
Ist die Bibliothek groß?	
	Nein, _____ sind nicht sehr modern, aber _____ sind sehr schön.
Ist die Mensa gut?	

1-33 Meine Uni. Using the previous activity as a guide, write a short description of your own university or college.

1-34 Welche Farbe hat Lisas Bluse? Your instructor will ask you the colors of your classmates' clothes. Sometimes you may want to add **hell** or **dunkel** to the basic color, e.g., **hellblau** *(light blue)*, **dunkelblau** *(dark blue)*.

LEHRER(IN): Welche Farbe hat Lisas Bluse?   STUDENT(IN): Sie ist rot.

1. die Jacke
2. der Pullover
3. die Bluse
4. das Hemd

5. die Hose

6. der Rock
7. das Sweatshirt

8. die Jeans

④ Expressing states and actions

The present tense of *sein*

The present-tense forms of **sein** *(to be)* are as frequently used and as irregular as their English counterparts. Be sure to learn them well.

Because the **Sie**-form is both singular and plural, it is generally placed at the bottom of a chart, between the singular and plural forms.

singular		plural	
ich bin	*I am*	**wir sind**	*we are*
du bist	*you are*	**ihr seid**	*you are*
er/es/sie ist	*he/it/she is*	**sie sind**	*they are*
	Sie sind	*you are*	

1-35 Ergänzen Sie! *(Complete!)* With a partner, take on the roles of the people below. Read the conversations, using the proper forms of **sein.**

1. Hallo!

MARTIN: Hallo! Ich _____ Martin und das _____ Peter.
HELGA: _____ ihr Brüder°?
MARTIN: Nein, wir _____ Freunde.
HELGA: Woher _____ ihr?
MARTIN: Ich _____ aus Mannheim und Peter _____ aus Berlin.

brothers

2. Woher sind Stephanie und Tom?

DAVID: _____ Stephanie Amerikanerin?
MARTIN: Ja, sie _____ aus Chicago.
DAVID: Und woher _____ Tom?
MARTIN: Ich glaube°, er _____ aus Kanada.

think

3. Wo sind Herr und Frau Ziegler?

FRAU HOLZ: Entschuldigung, _____ Sie Herr und Frau Ziegler aus Göttingen?
FRAU NAGLER: Nein, wir _____ nicht Herr und Frau Ziegler.
FRAU HOLZ: Sie _____ nicht Herr und Frau Ziegler?
FRAU NAGLER: Nein, und wir _____ auch nicht aus Göttingen.
FRAU HOLZ: Aber wer _____ Sie dann?
FRAU NAGLER: Ich _____ Beate Nagler aus Kassel und das _____ Herr Müger aus Frankfurt.
FRAU HOLZ: Und wo _____ Herr und Frau Ziegler?
FRAU NAGLER: Ich glaube, sie _____ noch im Hotel.

1-36 Kleine Gespräche. In groups of three, take on the roles of the people below. Read the conversations, supplying the correct forms of **sein** and/or the correct personal pronouns.

1. LUKAS: Hier ist ein Bild von Stephanie und Peter.
   ____ ____ gute Freunde.
   JULIA: Wie alt ____ Stephanie?
   LUKAS: ____ ____ neunzehn.
   ERGEM: Und wie alt ____ Peter?
   LUKAS: ____ ____ einundzwanzig.

   Peter   Stephanie
   21 J.   19 J.

2. FRAU ERB: Wie alt ____ ____, Brigitte?
   BRIGITTE: ____ ____ fünf.
   FRAU ERB: Und du, Holger, wie alt ____ ____?
   HOLGER: ____ ____ drei.
   FRAU ERB: Und woher ____ ____ zwei?
   BRIGITTE
   UND HOLGER: ____ ____ aus Stuttgart.

   Holger   Brigitte

3. REPORTER: ____ ____ Amerikaner, Herr Smith?
   HERR SMITH: Nein, ____ ____ Kanadier.
   REPORTER: Und Sie, Frau Jones, ____ ____
   auch Kanadierin?
   FRAU JONES: Nein, ____ ____ Amerikanerin.

   Frau Jones   Herr Smith

The verb: infinitive and present tense

The infinitive

In English the infinitive form of the verb is usually signaled by *to: to ask, to answer, to travel, to do*. German infinitives consist of a *verb stem* plus the ending **-en** or **-n.**

infinitive	stem	ending
fragen *(to ask)*	**frag**	-en
antworten *(to answer)*	**antwort**	-en
reisen *(to travel)*	**reis**	-en
tun *(to do)*	**tu**	-n

The present tense

In English only the 3rd person singular has an ending in the present tense: he ask*s*, she answer*s*, she do*es*, it work*s*. In German *all* the forms of the present tense have endings. These endings are attached to the verb stem.

singular		plural	
ich	frag**e**	wir	frag**en**
du	frag**st**	ihr	frag**t**
er/es/sie	frag**t**	sie	frag**en**
	Sie	frag**en**	

gehen

1-37 Semesterbeginn. On their way to the cafeteria, Claudia and Martin meet Peter and Christo. Supply the appropriate verb endings.

PETER: Grüß dich, Claudia! Tag, Martin! Das ist mein Freund Christo aus Italien.

CLAUDIA: Tag, Christo. Woher in Italien komm__ du?

CHRISTO: Ich komm__ aus Rom. Und ihr, woher komm__ ihr?

CLAUDIA: Ich bin aus Hamburg und Martin komm__ aus Mannheim.

MARTIN: Was studier__ du, Christo?

CHRISTO: Ich studier__ Linguistik.

CLAUDIA: Was mach__ ihr jetzt? Geh__ ihr auch in die Mensa?

our PETER: Nein, wir kauf__ jetzt unsere° Bücher, denn morgen beginn__ ja die Vorlesungen.

to work
to open
If a verb stem ends in **-t** or **-d** (**antwort-en, arbeit-en°, find-en**) or in certain consonant combinations like the **-gn** in **regnen** or the **-ffn** in **öffnen°**, an **-e-** is inserted before the personal endings **-st** and **-t** (**du arbeit*e*st, er find*e*t, es regn*e*t**).

singular		plural	
ich	antworte	wir	antworten
du	antwortest	ihr	antwortet
er/es/sie	antwortet	sie	antworten
	Sie	antworten	

If a verb stem ends in **-s, -ß,** or **-z,** the personal ending in the 2nd person
you sit singular is only a **-t** (not an **-st**): **du reis*t*, du heiß*t*, du sitz*t*°.**

singular		plural	
ich	reise	wir	reis**en**
du	reist	ihr	reist
er/es/sie	reist	sie	reis**en**
	Sie	reis**en**	

Verbs with the infinitive ending **-n** also have the ending **-n** in the 1st and 3rd person plural and in the **Sie**-form: **wir tu*n*, sie tu*n*, Sie tu*n*.**

1-38 Wer macht das? First supply the verb ending that agrees with the subject given. Then replace the subject with the nouns and pronouns in parentheses and change the verb endings accordingly.

1. Warum antwort__ du nicht? (Sie, ihr, Robert)
2. Sitz__ du oft im Park? (ihr, Professor Denner, Sie)
3. Ich find__ die Musik toll. (wir, Thomas, Nina und Alexander)
4. Warum tanz__ ihr nicht? (du, Sabine und Thomas, Robert)
5. Jessica arbeit__ zu viel. (ich, wir, ihr)
nothing 6. Warum tu__ ihr nichts°? (Sie, du, Peter)
to 7. Wann reis__ Herr und Frau Ziegler nach° Spanien? (ihr, du, Sie)

1-39 Kleine Gespräche. Complete the following conversations with the correct forms of the verbs given in parentheses.

Im Garten

FRAU ZIEGLER: Du, Robert, warum _____ du hier und _____ nichts? (stehen, tun)

ROBERT: Warum _____ du? (fragen)

FRAU ZIEGLER: Vater und ich _____ im Garten. (arbeiten)

ROBERT: Ich _____, ihr _____ zu viel. (glauben, arbeiten)

FRAU ZIEGLER: Und du, du _____ zu wenig°. (arbeiten) *little*

Beim Rockfest

SABINE: Ich _____ Sabine. Wie _____ du? (heißen, heißen)

THOMAS: Ich _____ Thomas. Wie _____ du die Band? (heißen, finden)

SABINE: Die Band _____ sehr gut. Sag mal, _____ du? (spielen°, tanzen) *to play*

THOMAS: Klar! Komm, wir _____. (tanzen)

Schulbeginn

HERR ZIEGLER: Am Montag _____ die Schule. (beginnen)

NINA: Ja. Heute Nachmittag _____ ich neue Kleider°. (kaufen) *clothes*

HERR ZIEGLER: Und wie viel _____ das? (kosten)

NINA: Viel. Kleider _____ viel. (kosten)

HERR ZIEGLER: Ja. Kleider und Kinder _____ viel zu viel! (kosten)

Im Winter

FRAU ZIEGLER: Tag, Frau Berg. Das _____ ja kalt! (sein)

FRAU BERG: Ja, das Thermometer _____ minus zehn! (zeigen)

FRAU ZIEGLER: Wann _____ Sie nach Spanien, Ende Dezember? (reisen)

FRAU BERG: Nein, wir _____ erst im Januar, da° _____ es nicht so viel. (reisen, kosten) *then*

1-40 Was für Sport machst du? Interview three classmates about what types of sports they do in the summer and in the winter. Additional ideas are listed under **Hobbys und Sport** in the *Anhang* on page A18.

S1: Was für Sport machst du im Sommer (im Winter)?

S2: Im Sommer … (Im Winter …)

Im Sommer	gehe ich schwimmen (surfen, segeln°, wandern°, …) *sailing / hiking*
	spiele ich Tennis (Fußball, Golf, …)
Im Winter	gehe ich Skilaufen (Schlittschuhlaufen°, …) *ice skating*
	spiele ich Eishockey, …

The present tense to express future time

German uses the present tense to express future time more frequently than English. However, the context must show that one is referring to the future.

Nächstes Jahr **fliege** ich nach Leipzig.	*Next year I'm flying to Leipzig.*
	Next year I'll be flying to Leipzig.
Was **machst** du dort?	*What will you be doing there?*
	What are you going to do there?
Ich **arbeite** bei DHL.	*I'll be working for DHL.*
	I'm going to be working for DHL.

The international courier firm DHL is a subsidiary of Deutsche Post World Net. In 2005 the company decided to move its European Logistics center from Brussels to Leipzig, creating about 10,000 new jobs in the area. DHL stands for the first letter of the last names of Adrian Dalsey, Larry Hillblom, and Robert Lynn, the American founders of the company.

1-41 Klischees. With a partner, match the cities and activities according to the map.

	Berlin	segeln gehen
	Innsbruck	zum Karneval gehen
trade fair	Kiel	auf die Messe° gehen
	Köln	Walzer tanzen
money	Leipzig	viel Geld° investieren
	München	ins Daimler-Benz-Museum gehen
	Norderney	Skilaufen gehen
	Stuttgart	in die Philharmonie gehen
	Wien	aufs Oktoberfest gehen
beach	Zürich	am Strand° sitzen

1-42 Reisepläne (1). You **(S2)** and your friends are going to travel in the German-speaking countries. Your roommate **(S1)** wants to know what you are going to do in the cities you visit.

▶ Juni   Berlin / in die Philharmonie gehen

S1: Wo seid ihr im Juni?   **S2:** Im Juni sind wir in Berlin.
S1: Was macht ihr dort?   **S2:** Wir gehen in die Philharmonie.

1. Juli   Kiel / segeln gehen
2. August   Norderney / am Strand sitzen
3. September   München / aufs Oktoberfest gehen
4. Oktober   Wien / Walzer tanzen

1-43 Reisepläne (2). From January to May you are going to travel by yourself.

▶ Januar   Innsbruck / Skilaufen gehen

S1: Wo bist du im Januar?   **S2:** Im Januar bin ich in Innsbruck.
S1: Was machst du dort?   **S2:** Ich gehe Skilaufen.

1. Februar   Köln / zum Karneval gehen
2. März   Leipzig / auf die Messe gehen
3. April   Zürich / viel Geld investieren
4. Mai   Stuttgart / ins Daimler-Benz-Museum gehen

1-44 Reisepläne (3). Interview your partner about her/his travel plans and report your findings to the class.

> Hast du Reisepläne? Wann reist du? Wohin reist du? Was machst du dort?

WWW Catch a ride to Hamburg at www.prenhall.com/treffpunkt
→ Kapitel 1 → Web Resources → Kultur

INFOBOX

More about university life

At most universities in the German-speaking countries, the **Wintersemester** begins in mid-October and ends in mid-February. The **Sommersemester** begins in mid-April and ends in mid-July. The lengthy breaks between semesters are called **Vorlesungsfreie Zeit.** Students are expected to use this time to read, study, and write papers.

Many students also work or travel during the semester breaks. The Internet offers a wide choice of student discounts on travel. Students who want to visit family or friends out of town often find transportation through a **Mitfahrzentrale,** a ride-sharing service that links drivers and passengers heading to the same destination.

MFZOO.de
Mitfahrzentrale Berlin
19440
8831313
Fax: 8811390
U-Bhf. Zoo Bahnsteig U2 / Rchtg. Pankow

Zusammenschau

■ Video-Treff

Das bin ich

In the *Treffpunkt Deutsch* video, you will get to know some Germans – where they live, study, work, and have fun. Each of the 12 segments contains clips from informal interviews based on the theme of the respective chapter. In this segment the interviewees introduce themselves.

Zum besseren Verstehen

This pre-viewing activity introduces you to some words and expressions you will encounter in the video.

1-45 Was ist das auf Englisch? Find the English equivalents for the German words in boldface.

1. Ich **arbeite als** Radiomoderator.
2. Das **buchstabiert sich** S-o-w-a-d-e.
3. Homburg ist **eine Kleinstadt** nahe der französischen Grenze.
4. Nicolai **ist bald** drei Jahre alt.
5. Brandenburg ist **im Osten von Deutschland.**
6. Ich studiere **an der** Humboldt-Universität.
7. Ich studiere hier **Germanistik** und Sport.
8. Ich **bin** in Mainz **geboren.**
9. Ich **lebe** in Berlin und arbeite auch hier.

a. live
b. at the
c. work as
d. was born
e. is spelled
f. will soon be
g. a small town
h. German Studies
i. in Eastern Germany

Der Löwe ist das Symbol von Leipzig.

Now watch the video and complete the post-viewing activities in the *Video-Treff* section of the *Student Activities Manual.*

Hören

Semesterbeginn in München

Peter Ackermann calls his mother to tell her that he has found a room.

NEUE VOKABELN

das Zimmer	*room*	**wieder**	*again*
übrigens	*by the way*	**Mach's gut!**	*Take care!*

1-46 Erstes Verstehen. Listen to the telephone conversation and choose the correct responses.

1. Who is speaking in this conversation?

   Martin   Peter   Peter's mother

2. What is Martin's last name?

   Ackermann   Zenner   Keller

3. Which cities do you hear?

   Mannheim   Frankfurt   Berlin   München

4. Who is working too much?

   Peter's mother   Martin   Peter's father

5. When will Peter see his family again?

   in mid-October   in mid-November   at the end of November

1-47 Detailverstehen. Listen to the conversation again and write responses to the following questions.

city

1. Wie viel kostet Peters Zimmer?
2. Was ist Peters Adresse? (Straße, Hausnummer, Postleitzahl und Stadt°)
3. Was findet Peter in München so toll? *In München sind …*
4. Was macht Peter am Nachmittag?
5. Woher kommt Martin?
6. Wo in Deutschland ist Peters Mutter?

Schreiben und Sprechen

1-48 Das bin ich. Write about yourself, using the following questions as a guide.

Write your height in meters and centimeters. A height of **ein Meter und siebzig Zentimeter**, for example, is written **1,70 (eins siebzig)**.

Blonde in German is **blond**.

There are lists for fields of study and sports activities in the *Anhang* on pp. A17 and A18.

Wie heißt du und woher kommst du?

tall Wie alt und wie groß° bist du?

Welche Farbe haben deine Haare? *(Meine Haare sind …)*

Was studierst du?

Was für Sport machst du im Sommer? *(Im Sommer …)*

Was für Sport machst du im Winter? *(Im Winter …)*

1-49 Wer ist das? Your instructor will collect and randomly distribute the profiles you and your classmates wrote in the activity above. Read the profile you receive, omitting the name of the writer. The class will guess who the author is.

📖 Lesen ··

Zum besseren Verstehen

1-50 Ein paar Fragen. Look at the title of
the reading and the accompanying photos as
you answer the following questions.

Kathrin Spyri

1. What is Kathrin Spyri's nationality?
   Approximately how old is she? Name one
   sport she likes to do.
2. In which country do the Schürers live?
   What is Mr. Schürer's profession? How old
   do you judge the children to be?
3. The man in the red jacket on the next
   page is Arnold Karlhuber. What is his
   nationality? What is his winter occupation?
   Where do you think this picture was taken?

| LEUTE | Eine Schweizerin, eine deutsche Familie und zwei Österreicher |

Kathrin Spyri ist Schweizerin. Sie
kommt aus Bern und studiert in
Zürich Architektur. Sie ist im zehnten
Semester und nächsten Sommer
macht sie ihr Diplom. Kathrin jobbt
oft für ein Züricher Architekturbüro,
denn ihr Vater und ihre Mutter haben
nicht viel Geld. Kathrin ist nicht sehr
sportlich, aber sie spielt oft Federball,
und im Sommer geht sie in die Alpen
und wandert.

Familie Schürer

Das sind Sybille und Stefan
Schürer aus Dresden. Sie haben zwei
Kinder: Caroline und Moritz. Stefan
ist Arzt[1] und Sybille ist
Programmiererin. Sie arbeitet aber
nur morgens[2], denn Moritz ist nur
morgens im Kindergarten. Jeden[3]
Winter gehen Sybille und Stefan
vierzehn Tage zum Skilaufen in die Schweiz und die Kinder sind dann bei
Oma[4] Schürer in Leipzig. Im Sommer gehen Stefan, Sybille und die
Kinder drei oder vier Wochen[5] nach Österreich. Sie wandern,
schwimmen, surfen und segeln, und sie haben alle viel Spaß[6].

[1]*physician* [2]*in the morning* [3]*every* [4]*grandma* [5]*weeks* [6]*fun*

Arnold Karlhuber

Arnold Karlhuber ist aus Salzburg. Er ist Automechaniker, aber im Winter arbeitet er als Skilehrer[1] in Kitzbühel. Arnolds Vater hat in Salzburg eine Autofirma, und Arnold arbeitet dort von[2] April bis November. Arnolds Frau heißt Christa. Sie ist Buchhalterin[3] und sie arbeitet auch für Arnolds Vater. Christa ist aus München, sie ist aber jetzt Österreicherin. Arnold und Christa haben noch keine Kinder.

[1]*ski instructor* [2]**von ... bis:** *from . . . to* [3]*accountant*

Arbeit mit dem Text

1-51 Ergänzen Sie! Fill in the missing information from the biographical sketches above. You should be able to guess the meanings of **Wohnort** and **Beruf**.

NAME	WOHNORT	BERUF	NATIONALITÄT
	Zürich		
Sybille Schürer	Dresden	Programmiererin	Deutsche
Arnold Karlhuber	Salzburg	Automechaniker	Österreichen
	Leipzig		
Stephan Schürer	Dresden	Arzt	Deutsche
Christa Karlhuber	München	Buchhalterin	Österreicherin

Wort, Sinn und Klang

Wörter unter der Lupe

Cognates

In *Erste Kontakte* and this chapter you have seen that German and English are closely related languages. Many words are so close in sound and spelling to their English equivalents that you can easily guess their meanings. Words in different languages that are identical or similar in form and meaning are called *cognates*.

Some words are identical or almost identical in form, but different in meaning. These are sometimes called "false friends": **arm** (*poor*), **also** (*so*), **fast** (*almost*), **bekommen** (*to receive*).

INFOBOX

Why German and English are similar: The Angles and Saxons

Many of the similarities between English and German can be traced back 1600 years to the time when the Angles and Saxons, Germanic tribes from what is today northern Germany, invaded Britain and settled there. Around 200 A.D. the Roman Empire encompassed not only the countries around the Mediterranean, but also included present-day Austria, Switzerland, Southern Germany, France, and most of the British Isles. Beginning about the fourth century A.D., shiploads of Angle and Saxon warriors crossed the North Sea to England and attacked the increasingly vulnerable defenses of the Roman Empire. When the Romans finally retreated from Britain in the fifth century, the Angles and Saxons remained and settled the country. It was the Germanic languages of these tribes that became the foundation for present-day English.

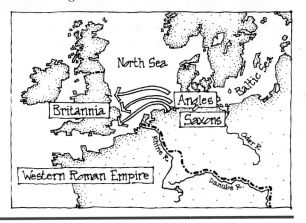

WWW Learn to speak like the Anglo-Saxons at www.prenhall.com/treffpunkt → Kapitel 1 → Web Resources → Kultur

Infobox: The Norman invasion of Britain in 1066 brought further changes to the English language. French became the language of the ruling class, and evidence of this can be seen in examples like the following: It was the lower-class farmer who raised *swine, cows,* and *sheep,* all words of Germanic origin (in modern German **Schwein, Kuh, Schaf**). However, when the meat of these animals was served to the nobility, it was called *pork, beef,* and *mutton* (French **porc, bœuf, mouton**).

1-52 Leicht zu verstehen. Give the English cognates of the following sets of German words.

1. *Family:* die Mutter, der Vater, der Sohn, die Tochter, der Bruder, die Schwester
2. *Parts of the body:* das Haar, die Nase, die Lippe, die Schulter, der Arm, der Ellbogen, die Hand, der Finger, der Fingernagel, das Knie, der Fuß
3. *Descriptive words:* jung, alt, neu, hart, lang, laut, voll, frisch, sauer, dumm, gut, reich
4. *Animals:* der Fisch, die Ratte, die Maus, die Katze, die Laus, der Wurm, der Fuchs, der Bulle, die Kuh
5. *Food and drink:* die Butter, das Brot, der Käse, der Apfel, das Salz, der Pfeffer, das Wasser, das Bier, der Wein, die Milch

1-53 Wie heißt das Restaurant? In the German-speaking countries, many restaurants and hotels have ornate wrought-iron signs. Look at the sampling below and match them with the names in the box.

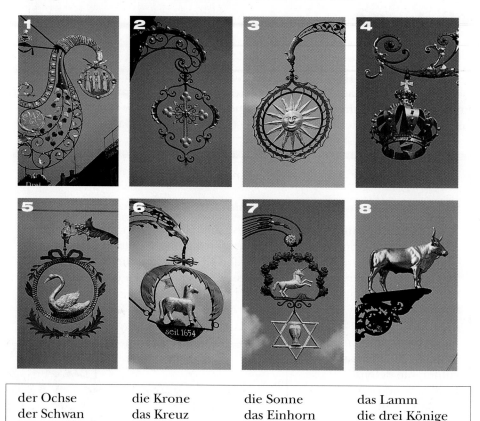

der Ochse	die Krone	die Sonne	das Lamm
der Schwan	das Kreuz	das Einhorn	die drei Könige

Zur Aussprache

German *ei* and *ie*

Because of the inconsistencies of English spelling and pronunciation (e.g., N*ei*ther of my fr*ie*nds rec*ei*ved a p*ie*ce of p*ie*), English-speaking students of German often confuse the pronunciation of the German **ie** and **ei** (e.g., **D*ie* Sonne sch*ei*nt**). When the two vowels appear together, use the second vowel as an indication of how the word is pronounced. To help you keep these two vowel combinations straight, you can also think of "Frankenst*ei*n is a f*ie*nd."

colloquial for:
That's not my problem!

1-54 Hören Sie gut zu und wiederholen Sie!

W**ei**n	W**ie**n	s**ei**n	s**ie**
d**ei**n	d**ie**	b**ei**	B**ie**r

Distinguish between **ei** and **ie** by reading the following sentences aloud.

1. W**ie** v**ie**l ist dr**ei** und v**ie**r?
   Dr**ei** und v**ie**r ist s**ie**ben.
2. W**ie** h**ei**ßen Sie?
   Ich h**ei**ße Z**ie**gler.
3. Das ist nicht m**ei**n B**ie**r.°
4. D**ie** Schw**ei**z ist **ei**ne Demokrat**ie**.
5. D**ie**ter und Melan**ie** r**ei**sen in d**ie** Schw**ei**z.

Nomen

der Tag, -e	day
die Woche, -n	week
der Monat, -e	month
das Jahr, -e	year
die Jahreszeit, -en	season
der Frühling	spring
der Sommer	summer
der Herbst	fall, autumn
der Winter	winter
der Mitbewohner, -	(male) roommate
die Mitbewohnerin, -nen	(female) roommate
das Zimmer, -	room

Verben

arbeiten	to work
finden	to find
fliegen	to fly
glauben	to believe; to think
kosten	to cost
lernen	to learn; to study
reisen	to travel
sitzen	to sit
spielen	to play
stehen	to stand
tanzen	to dance
tun	to do

Konjunktionen

und	and
oder	or
denn	because
aber	but
sondern	but, (but) . . . instead, but rather

Fragewörter

wann?	when?
warum?	why?
was?	what?
wer?	who?
wie?	how?
wie viel?	how much?
wie viele?	how many?
wo?	where? (in what place?)
woher?	where . . . from? (from what place?)
wohin?	where? (to what place?)

Andere Wörter

interessant	interesting
sportlich	athletic
nichts	nothing
sehr	very
übrigens	by the way
von … bis	from . . . to
wieder	again
zusammen	together

Ausdrücke

am Montag	on Monday
Ende Januar	at the end of January
im Januar	in January
im Winter	in the winter
nach Claudias Vorlesung	after Claudia's lecture
ein bisschen	a bit
nach Florida	to Florida
Claudia kommt auch nicht.	Claudia isn't coming either.
Mach's gut!	Take care!
Was für Sport machst du?	What sports do you do?

Das Gegenteil

die Frage, -n ≠ die Antwort, -en	question ≠ answer
fragen ≠ antworten	to ask ≠ to answer
gut ≠ schlecht	good ≠ bad
hell ≠ dunkel	light ≠ dark
hier ≠ dort	here ≠ there
viel ≠ wenig	much ≠ little

Wohin gehst du?

in die Bibliothek	to the library
in die Disco	to the disco
in die Kneipe	to the pub
in die Mensa	to the cafeteria
in die Vorlesung	to the lecture
ins Bett	to bed
ins Kino	to the movies
ins Konzert	to a concert
ins Theater	to the theater

Like the months and the seasons, the days of the week are masculine.

Die Wochentage

der Montag *mon*
der Dienstag *Tue*
der Mittwoch *wed*
der Donnerstag *Thur*
der Freitag *Fri*
der Samstag *Sat*
der Sonntag *Sun*

Die Monate

der Januar	der Juli
der Februar	der August
der März	der September
der April	der Oktober
der Mai	der November
der Juni	der Dezember

Wörter im Kontext

1-55 Konjunktionen, bitte!

1. Claudia _____ Stephanie studieren in München.
2. Kommt Martin aus Berlin _____ aus Mannheim?
3. Martin kommt nicht aus Berlin, _____ aus Mannheim.
4. Ist es kalt?
   Ja, _____ nicht sehr.
5. Heute kaufe ich meine Bücher, _____ morgen beginnen die Vorlesungen.

1-56 Fragen und Antworten. Choose the appropriate response to your partner's questions.

S1:

1. Wann reisen Sie nach Italien, Frau Erb?
2. Wohin fliegen viele Deutsche im Winter?
3. Wie lange seid ihr in Berlin?
4. Wie heißt Claudias Mitbewohnerin?
5. Spielt ihr heute wieder Eishockey?
6. Was tust du heute Abend?

S2:

a. Nach Florida.
b. Ja, gleich nach Peters Vorlesung.
c. Nichts.
d. Von Freitag bis Sonntag.
e. Im Herbst.
f. Stephanie.

1-57 Fragen und Antworten. Choose the appropriate response to your partner's questions.

S1:

1. Wie viele Monate hat ein Jahr?
2. Wie viel kostet Peters Zimmer?
3. Wie viele Tage hat eine Woche?
4. Wo arbeitet Frau Berger?
5. Was macht ihr heute Abend?
6. Wie tanzt Stephanie?

S2:

a. Hundertfünfzig Euro.
✓b. Im Supermarkt.
✓c. Zwölf.
d. Sehr gut.
✓e. Sieben.
✓f. Ich glaube, wir gehen in die Bibliothek und lernen.

> Note the difference between **lernen** and **studieren**. **Thomas studiert Germanistik** = *Thomas is studying German language and literature (as a major).* **Andrea lernt Deutsch** = *Andrea is learning German (she is learning the language, taking a language course).* **Andrea lernt für das Quiz** = *Andrea is studying for the quiz.*

1-58 Was passt nicht? In each group cross out the word that doesn't fit.

1. der Tag
   der Monat
   die Kneipe
   die Woche
   das Jahr

2. interessant
   sportlich
   dunkel
   lernen
   gut

3. sitzen *sit*
   nichts *nothing*
   tun *to do*
   reisen *travel*
   kosten *cost*

1-59 Gegenteile.

1. Der Tag ist _____ und die Nacht ist _____.
2. Der Professor _____ und der Student _____.
3. Fünfhundert Euro sind _____ und fünf Euro sind _____.
4. Ein „A" ist _____ und ein „F" ist _____.

> Letter grades are not used in the German-speaking countries. An A is a **1 (eine Eins)**, a B is a **2 (eine Zwei)**, etc.

1-60 Ergänzen Sie!

1. Heute ist Montag und morgen ist _____.
2. Gestern war° Samstag und heute ist _____.
3. Heute ist Donnerstag und gestern war _____.
4. Heute ist Sonntag und morgen ist _____.
5. Gestern war Donnerstag und morgen ist _____.

was

hours

Fischverkauf
Öffnungszeiten

Sommer   1.5. — 31.10.

Montag	:	9.00 - 18.00 Uhr
Dienstag	:	Ruhetag
Mittwoch	:	9.00 - 18.00 Uhr
Donnerstag	:	9.00 - 18.00 Uhr
Freitag	:	9.00 - 18.00 Uhr
Samstag	:	9.00 - 18.00 Uhr
Sonntag	:	11.00 - 18.00 Uhr

Was ist ein Ruhetag?

Freunde

Freunde

Kommunikationsziele

Talking about . . .
- friends
- leisure activities
- clothing and possessions

Telling time

Expressing likes, dislikes, and preferences

Strukturen

The verb **haben**

Verb + **gern** or **lieber**

Nominative case:
- subject and subject completion
- **der**-words and **ein**-words
- adjective endings

Kultur

The cuckoo clock

Liechtenstein

Ethnic diversity in Germany

English words in German

Video-Treff: **Freunde**

Lesen: **Fatma Yützel erzählt**

Freundschaften

Nina Ziegler sagt: Das ist mein Freund
Alexander. Er ist groß und schlank, tanzt sehr
gut und hat ein tolles Motorrad. Alex hat viele
Hobbys: er spielt sehr gut Basketball und
Eishockey, er schwimmt gern, er spielt ganz
toll Gitarre, er sammelt Briefmarken und er
kocht auch gern und gut. Übrigens ist Alex
auch ein sehr guter Schüler.

Robert Ziegler sagt: Ich finde Alexander doof.
Er telefoniert oft stundenlang mit Nina und
abends ist er oft bis zehn oder elf bei uns und
spielt seine blöde Gitarre. Was findet meine
Schwester denn so toll an Alex? Ich finde nur
sein Motorrad toll!

Freundschaften: These four
narratives feature the Ziegler family
talking about friends. You will hear
from 16-year-old **Nina**, 14-year-old
Robert, and their parents **Frau
und Herr Ziegler.** You will get to
know them better as you progress
through the textbook.

Frau Ziegler sagt: Das ist Beverly Harper. Sie ist
Journalistin und meine beste Freundin. Sie
arbeitet für amerikanische Zeitungen und
schreibt Artikel über die politische Szene in
Europa. Beverly ist nicht nur sehr intelligent,
sondern auch sehr sportlich, und montags
von 19 bis 21 Uhr spielen wir immer Tennis
miteinander. Übrigens ist Beverly auch sehr
elegant und kauft gern schicke Kleider.

Herr Ziegler sagt: Ich spiele nicht gern Tennis
mit Beverly, denn sie spielt viel besser als ich.
Aber sie ist eine gute Journalistin und schreibt
sehr interessante Artikel. Wir trinken oft ein
Glas Wein hier bei uns und haben lange
Diskussionen miteinander.

■ Sprachnotiz

The flavoring particle *denn*

The flavoring particle **denn** is frequently added to questions. It may express
curiosity and interest, but it can also indicate irritation. It does not change
the basic meaning of the question. **Denn** usually follows the subject of the
question.

Was für Artikel schreibt Beverly **denn?**	*What sort of articles does Beverly write?*
Was findet meine Schwester **denn** so toll an Alex?	*What does my sister find so great about Alex?*

Be careful not to confuse the
flavoring particle **denn** with the
conjunction **denn** *(because):* **Ich
spiele nicht gern mit Beverly
Tennis,** *denn* **sie spielt viel
besser als ich.**

2-1 Richtig oder falsch? You will hear the descriptions of Alexander and Beverly Harper. Indicate whether the statements about each set of descriptions are **richtig** or **falsch.**

	ALEXANDER			BEVERLY HARPER	
	RICHTIG	FALSCH		RICHTIG	FALSCH
1.	_____	_____	1.	_____	_____
2.	_____	_____	2.	_____	_____
3.	_____	_____	3.	_____	_____

2-2 Anders gesagt. With a partner, read *Freundschaften* again and find equivalents for the following statements.

▶ Alexander ist sehr musikalisch. = Alexander spielt ganz toll Gitarre.

1. Alexander ist sehr sportlich.
2. Alex ist auch sehr intelligent.
3. Ich finde Alexander gar nicht toll.
4. Alex ist abends oft bis 22 oder 23 Uhr bei Zieglers.
5. Beverly Harper schreibt Zeitungsartikel.
6. Beverly Harper macht viel Sport.
7. Montagabends von sieben bis neun spielen wir immer Tennis miteinander.
8. Wir diskutieren lange miteinander.

> You will find additional vocabulary to describe personal characteristics and personality traits under **Persönliche Merkmale** in the *Anhang* on p. A21.

2-3 Meine beste Freundin/Mein bester Freund. Answer your partner's questions about your best friend.

S1: Wie heißt deine beste Freundin/ dein bester Freund? **S2:** Sie/Er heißt …

S1: Wie alt ist sie/er? **S2:** Sie/Er ist …

S1: Wie ist sie/er? **S2:** Sie/Er ist …

nice	groß	sehr nett°	(nicht) sehr praktisch
short	klein°	sehr intelligent	(nicht) sehr sportlich
	schlank	sehr kreativ	(nicht) sehr musikalisch
plump	mollig°		…

> You will find additional vocabulary for **Hobbys und Sport** and **Musikinstrumente** in the *Anhang* on pp. A18 and A19.

2-4 Hobbys. Now answer questions about your friend's hobbies.

S1: Was für Hobbys hat deine Freundin/dein Freund? **S2:** Sie/Er … gern. Sie/Er spielt gern …

	fotografiert	Tennis
	kocht	Squash
	tanzt	Eishockey
	schwimmt	Gitarre
piano	reist	Klavier°
	…	…

KULTUR
Die Kuckucksuhr

Schwarzwälder Kuckucksuhr

Throughout the world, the **Schwarzwald** is synonymous with clocks, particularly the **Kuckucksuhr.** The first Black Forest clocks appeared in the 1650s. The fact that so many clocks were produced in this region is linked to the way family farms were handed down from one generation to the next. To keep the family farm intact, the entire farm was handed down to the youngest son. All other sons were granted a tiny acreage from the farm on which they could build a small cottage and keep a cow, a pig, some poultry, and a garden. To supplement their meager income, these cottagers began to produce inexpensive wooden clocks that ordinary townsfolk and farmers could afford to buy. Clockmaking was also a popular trade in the harsh, mountainous regions of Austria and Switzerland, but it was the clockmakers of the Black Forest who were the most successful in selling their clocks, particularly the cuckoo clock, around the world. In the mid-nineteenth century, 5000 people in the Black Forest were producing 600,000 clocks annually. For over 170 years the **Kuckucksuhr** has remained one of the most popular and successful timepieces. In Black Forest resorts like **Triberg** and **Titisee,** tens of thousands of cuckoo clocks are purchased annually by tourists from all over the world.

In the **Schwarzwald,** farms were handed down to the youngest instead of the oldest son so that the parents could retain ownership as long as possible.

Triberg is famous for its waterfall. **Titisee** is situated on a lake of the same name. It is one of the few natural lakes in the Black Forest.

2-5 Wann ist das? The German-speaking countries use the 24-hour clock to announce the time of public events. Use North American equivalents to answer the questions.

1. When does the mountain bike club meet?
2. When does a demonstration of musical instruments take place?
3. When does the flamenco workshop take place?
4. At what time does the bird and aquarium club meet?

Heute in Schorndorf

Samstag, 1. Februar:
Vereine / Organisationen

Jugendmusikschule: Instrumentendemonstration , 14 bis 16 Uhr, Gottlieb-Daimler-Realschule im Schulzentrum Grauhalde.
Vogel- und Aquarienverein: Hauptversammlung, 20 Uhr, Vereinsheim.
Radfahrverein „Wanderer": Mountainbiker-Treff 14 Uhr, Gmünder Straße 49.
Kultur

Manufaktur: Flamenco-Workshop, 12 bis 15.30 Uhr; Schwof mit Musik aus den 70ern, ab 22 Uhr; Bilderwand – Neue Arbeiten von Gui Ripper, Foyer, 1. Stock.

Nomen

die Freundschaft, -en	friendship
der Lehrer, -	teacher
die Lehrerin, -nen	
die Schule, -n	school
der Schüler, -	pupil, student in a primary
die Schülerin, -nen	or secondary school
die Briefmarke, -n	postage stamp
die Zeitung, -en	newspaper

Freundschaft, Zeitung: All nouns with the suffix **-schaft** or **-ung** are feminine.

Schüler: German always distinguishes between students at a primary or secondary school (**Schüler**) and university students (**Studenten**).

Verben

haben	to have
kochen	to cook
sagen	to say
sammeln	to collect
telefonieren (mit)	to talk on the phone (with)

Andere Wörter

blöd	stupid, dumb
doof	
nett	nice
bis	until
immer	always
miteinander	with each other; together

Ausdrücke

bei uns	at our house
bei Zieglers	at the Zieglers
Ich koche gern.	I like to cook.

Das Gegenteil

groß ≠ klein	big; tall ≠ little, small; short
intelligent ≠ dumm	intelligent ≠ stupid
mollig ≠ schlank	plump ≠ slim

Zeit

die Zeit, -en	time
die Minute, -n	minute
die Sekunde, -n	second
die Stunde, -n	hour
stundenlang	for hours
die Uhr, -en	clock; watch
zehn Uhr	ten o'clock
um zehn Uhr	at ten o'clock

die Minute, die Sekunde, die Stunde: Remember that most nouns that end in **-e** are feminine.

Getränke

das Getränk, -e	beverage
das Bier	beer
die Cola	cola
der Kaffee	coffee
die Milch	milk
der Tee	tea
das Wasser	water
der Wein	wine

Sport

Sport machen	to do sports
Fitnesstraining machen	to work out
Basketball spielen	to play basketball
Eishockey spielen	to play hockey
Fußball spielen	to play soccer
Golf spielen	to play golf
joggen gehen	to go jogging
schwimmen gehen	to go swimming
snowboarden gehen	to go snowboarding
Tennis spielen	to play tennis
wandern gehen	to go hiking
windsurfen gehen	to go windsurfing

Was machen diese Leute?

Leicht zu verstehen

der Artikel, -	diskutieren
die Diskussion, -en	fotografieren
die Gitarre, -n	amerikanisch
das Hobby, -s	kreativ
der Journalist, -en	modern
die Journalistin, -nen	musikalisch
die Szene, -n	politisch
	praktisch

Which words in the list above are stressed on a different syllable than their English equivalents?

Hobby: Loan words like **Hobby** and **Baby** form the plural simply by adding **-s**.

Wörter im Kontext

2-6 Was passt wo? Complete the sentences with the correct form of the appropriate verb.

kochen / haben / telefonieren / sammeln / sagen

1. Heute Nachmittag _____ wir keine Schule.
2. _____ du Kaffee oder Tee?
3. Robert _____, er findet Alexanders Motorrad toll.
4. Warum _____ du immer so lang, Nina?
5. Alexander _____ Briefmarken.

Photo: This stamp commemorates the World Cup Soccer Games held in Germany in 2006. It is interesting to note that in Germany it is not permitted to depict living persons on stamps (with the exception of the Federal President). This explains the blurred legs of a soccer player.

2-7 Was passt wo? One of the words in the list is to be used twice.

Zeit / stundenlang / Uhr / Stunde

1. Nina telefoniert oft _stunden_ mit Alexander.
2. Für Alexander hat Nina immer _Zeit_.
3. Alexander ist abends oft bis elf _Uhr_ bei Zieglers.
4. Roberts neue Swatch ist eine sehr gute _____.
5. Eine _____ hat sechzig Minuten.

2-8 Was für Getränke passen hier?

1. In _____, in _____ und in _____ ist Koffein.
2. Babys trinken _____.
3. In _____ und _____ ist Alkohol.
4. In allen Getränken ist sehr viel _____.

2-9 Was passt wo? Some of the words in the list are to be used twice.

Photo: Bastelladen = *crafts store*

mollig / schlank / groß / klein

1. Elefanten sind _groß_ und Mäuse sind _klein_.
2. Fotomodelle sind sehr _schlank_ und sehr schick.
3. Balletttänzerinnen sind nicht _mollig_, sondern schlank.
4. Basketballspieler sind oft sehr _schlank und groß_
5. Jockeys sind _klein_

2-10 Getrennte Wörter. Reconstruct the cognates below by matching the parts appropriately.

1. mo-   a. -tisch
2. fotogra-   b. -kalisch
3. ameri-   c. -tieren
4. kre-   d. -dern
5. prak-   e. -nieren
6. po-   f. -litisch
7. telefo-   g. -fieren
8. musi-   h. -kanisch
9. disku-   i. -ativ

Bastelst du gern?

Kommunikation und Formen

① Telling time

In German there are two ways of telling time. The one used in everyday conversation is similar to our system. The other counts the day from 0 to 24 hours and is used for things such as train schedules, public announcements, and TV guides. Because speakers of German see and hear this way of telling time every day, it is common to use the official forms in colloquial German as well.

The expressions **Wie viel Uhr ist es?** or **Wie spät ist es?** are used to ask for the time.

Wie viel Uhr ist es?

Note the position of **Uhr** in writing (e.g., **13.05** *Uhr*) and speaking (e.g., **dreizehn** *Uhr* fünf).

COLLOQUIAL		OFFICIAL	
eins (ein Uhr)		13.00 Uhr	dreizehn Uhr
fünf nach eins		13.05 Uhr	dreizehn Uhr fünf
Viertel nach eins		13.15 Uhr	dreizehn Uhr fünfzehn
zwanzig nach eins		13.20 Uhr	dreizehn Uhr zwanzig
fünf vor halb zwei		13.25 Uhr	dreizehn Uhr fünfundzwanzig
halb zwei		13.30 Uhr	dreizehn Uhr dreißig
fünf nach halb zwei		13.35 Uhr	dreizehn Uhr fünfunddreißig
zwanzig vor zwei		13.40 Uhr	dreizehn Uhr vierzig
Viertel vor zwei		13.45 Uhr	dreizehn Uhr fünfundvierzig
fünf vor zwei		13.55 Uhr	dreizehn Uhr fünfundfünfzig
zwei (zwei Uhr)		14.00 Uhr	vierzehn Uhr

2-11 Wie viel Uhr ist es? Respond to your partner's questions in colloquial time.

S1: Wie viel Uhr ist es?   **S2:** Jetzt ist es Viertel vor acht.

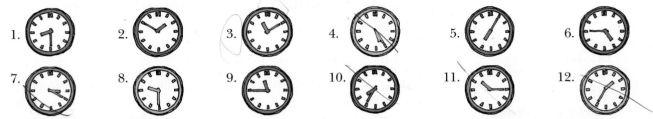

Expressions of time referring to parts of the day

German has no equivalents for the terms *a.m.* and *p.m.* In colloquial German, you use the following adverbs of time to refer to the parts of a day. Note that all of these adverbs of time end in **-s.**

morgens	*in the morning*	**abends**	*in the evening*
vormittags	*in the morning*	**nachts**	*at night*
nachmittags	*in the afternoon*		

Eine 24-Stunden-Uhr

2-12 Wie viel Uhr ist es?

▶ (abends)

S1: Wie viel Uhr ist es?   **S2:** Es ist fünf vor neun.
S1: Wie bitte? Wie spät ist es?   **S2:** Es ist zwanzig Uhr fünfundfünfzig.

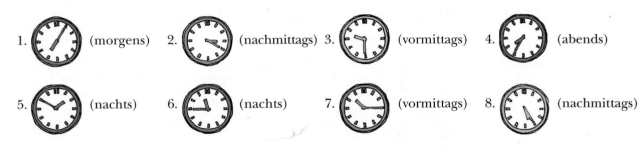

2-13 Wie spät ist es? Respond to your partner's questions in colloquial time. Specify the part of the day.

▶ 13.45 Uhr

S1: Wie spät ist es?   **S2:** Es ist Viertel vor zwei nachmittags.

1. 16.30 Uhr	5. 6.25 Uhr
2. 9.35 Uhr	6. 14.15 Uhr
3. 20.40 Uhr	7. 23.45 Uhr
4. 17.20 Uhr	8. 15.55 Uhr

More on expressions of time

You have just learned that adverbs such as **nachmittags** and **abends** refer to parts of the day. (Remember that they end in **-s.**) You can also use these adverbs to express that something happens *repeatedly* or *regularly*.

Ich habe **nachmittags** Vorlesungen und **abends** gehe ich oft in die Bibliothek.	*I have lectures in the afternoon and in the evening I often go to the library.*

When referring to a part of a *specific* day (e.g., ***this*** *afternoon,* **tomorrow** *evening*), you first state the day (**gestern, heute,** or **morgen**) and then the part of the day.

When you refer to part of a specific day, the part of the day (**Morgen, Abend,** etc.) is capitalized and does not end in **-s**.

The adverb **früh** is used to avoid the awkwardness of **morgen Morgen.** Because **früh** is not a noun, it is not capitalized.

heute Morgen	*this morning*	**morgen früh**	*tomorrow morning*
gestern Nacht	*last night*	**gestern Vormittag**	*yesterday morning*
heute Abend	*tonight*	**morgen Nachmittag**	*tomorrow afternoon*

Ich gehe **heute Abend** ins Kino.	*I'm going to the movies tonight.*

The same distinction is made with days of the week or parts of days of the week.

belegte Brötchen = *sandwich rolls*

REPEATEDLY OR REGULARLY		ON A SPECIFIC DAY	
freitags	*on Fridays*	**am Freitag**	*on Friday*
montagabends	*on Monday evenings*	**am Montagabend**	*on Monday evening*
Ich habe **freitags** nie Zeit.		**Am Freitag** kommt mein Freund!	
I never have time on Fridays.		*On Friday my friend is coming!*	

2-14 Um wie viel Uhr ...? Use colloquial time in the questions and official time in the responses. To find out what time something occurs, you begin your question with **Um wie viel Uhr** or **Wann.** The time given in the response is always preceded by **um.**

▶ 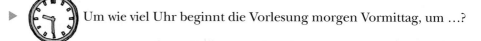 Um wie viel Uhr beginnt die Vorlesung morgen Vormittag, um …?

S1: Um wie viel Uhr beginnt die Vorlesung morgen Vormittag, um halb zehn?
S2: Ja, um neun Uhr dreißig.

1. Um wie viel Uhr spielst du heute Nachmittag Tennis, um …?

2. Wann gehen wir morgen früh joggen, um …?

3. Um wie viel Uhr geht ihr am Samstagabend in die Disco, um …?

over 4. Wann ist die Vorlesung heute Nachmittag zu Ende°, um …?

2-15 Wann ...? Find out a bit about your partner's schedule.

1. Um wie viel Uhr sind deine Vorlesungen heute zu Ende?
2. Wann gehst du normalerweise° in die Mensa?   *usually*
3. Um wie viel Uhr gehst du normalerweise ins Bett?
4. Wann beginnen deine Vorlesungen morgen?

❷ Expressing *to have*

The present tense of *haben*

Like English *to have*, the verb **haben** has many functions. For example, it is used to show possession or relationships, to describe the characteristics of people or things, to state amounts, and to express availability.

Peters Eltern **haben** ein schönes Haus.	*Peter's parents have a beautiful house.*
Hast du eine Freundin, Robert?	*Do you have a girlfriend, Robert?*
Ich **habe** braune Augen.	*I have brown eyes.*
Eine Minute **hat** sechzig Sekunden.	*A minute has sixty seconds.*
Wie viele Vorlesungen **habt** ihr heute?	*How many lectures do you have today?*
Heute **haben** wir viel Zeit.	*Today we have a lot of time.*

singular		plural	
ich	habe	wir	haben
du	**hast**	ihr	habt
er/es/sie	**hat**	sie	haben
	Sie	haben	

Note that the **b** of the verb stem is dropped in the 2nd and 3rd person singular.

2-16 Was passt zusammen?

1. Alexander   d
2. Zieglers   e
3. Du   B
4. Ich   A
5. Ihr   C

a. habe sehr gute Professoren.
b. hast so schöne, braune Augen, Claudia.
c. habt ein schönes, großes Zimmer.
d. hat ein tolles Motorrad.
e. haben viele Freunde.

Ein Briefkasten in Österreich

2-17 Fragen und Antworten. Supply the appropriate forms of **haben.**

S1:

1. _____ du heute Abend Zeit?
2. Habt Claudia blaue Augen?
3. H Peters Eltern ein Haus?
4. bt ihr heute viele Vorlesungen?
5. _____ Sie ein Auto, Herr Berger?
6. Wie viele Stunden _____ ein Tag?
7. Wie viele Kinder _____ Zieglers?
8. _____ du eine Freundin, Robert?
9. Wie viel Geld _____ ihr noch?
10. Was _____ du jetzt, Physik oder Deutsch?

S2:

Nein, heute Abend _____ ich keine Zeit.
Nein, sie Habt braune Augen.
Ja, sie _____ ein sehr schönes Haus.
Nein, heute _____ wir nur zwei Vorlesungen.
Nein, aber ich _____ ein Motorrad.
Ein Tag _____ vierundzwanzig Stunden.
Sie _____ zwei Kinder.
Nein, ich _____ keine Freundin.
Wir _____ nur noch fünfzig Euro.
Zuerst _____ ich Deutsch und dann Physik.

2-18 Günters Stundenplan. With a partner, complete Günter's schedule. Take turns asking your questions. The questions for **S2** are in the *Anhang* on page A2.

*Note that the indefinite article **eine** will only be used when the response contains the word **-übung**.*

math lab

S1: Was hat Günter montags von acht bis zehn?

S2: Was hat Günter montags von fünfzehn bis achtzehn Uhr?

S2: Da hat er eine Matheübung°.

S1: ...

1. Was hat Günter montags von acht bis zehn?
3. Was hat Günter dienstags von zehn bis zwölf?
5. Was macht Günter mittwochs von elf bis dreizehn Uhr?
7. Was hat Günter mittwochs von dreizehn bis fünfzehn Uhr?
9. Was hat Günter donnerstags von fünfzehn bis achtzehn Uhr?
11. Was hat Günter freitags von elf bis zwölf?
13. Wo ist Günter sonntags?

	Mo	Di	Mi	Do	Fr	Sa	So
8.00				Bio- chemie	Genetik		
9.00			Mikro- biologie				
10.00							
11.00							
12.00					mit Tina Tennis	bei Helga	
13.00							
14.00							
15.00	Genetik- übung						
16.00							
17.00							

2-19 Stundenpläne. Write your partner's name on a blank timetable and fill it in according to her/his responses. Follow the model below. Then read your partner's schedule to the class. You can find a list of **Studienfächer** in the *Anhang* on page A17.

S1:

Was für Vorlesungen hast du montags?

Was hast du dienstags?

…

S2:

Von neun bis zehn habe ich Geografie.
Von elf bis zwölf habe ich Deutsch.
Von vierzehn bis sechzehn Uhr habe ich eine Physikübung.
Dienstags habe ich keine Vorlesungen.

…

❸ Expressing likes, dislikes, and preferences

Verb + *gern* or *lieber*

In German the most common way of saying that you like to do something is to use a verb with **gern.** To say that you don't like to do something, you can use a verb with **nicht gern.**

Alexander kocht **gern.**	*Alexander **likes to** cook.*
Helga spielt **gern** Klavier.	*Helga **likes to** play the piano.*
Nina geht **gern** tanzen.	*Nina **likes to** go dancing.*
Robert lernt **nicht gern.**	*Robert doesn**'t** like studying.*

To express a preference, German uses a verb plus **lieber.**

Was spielst du **lieber,** Karten oder Scrabble?

*What do you **prefer to** play, cards or Scrabble?*

Gern, nicht gern, and **lieber** are usually placed directly after the verb.

2-20 Das mache ich gern. Working with a partner, tell each other what you like or don't like to do. Follow the model. You will find additional vocabulary in the *Anhang* on pages A20 and A18 under **Essen und Trinken** and **Hobbys und Sport.**

▶ spielen: Golf / Tennis / Fußball / …

S1: Ich spiele gern Golf.

S2: Ich auch.
Ich nicht, ich spiele lieber Tennis.

1. gehen: ins Konzert / ins Theater / in die Disco / …
2. gehen: schwimmen / windsurfen / tanzen / …
3. spielen: Karten / Scrabble / Billard / …
4. trinken: Kaffee / Tee / Milch / …
5. hören: Rock / Jazz / Mozart / …
6. trinken: Wein / Bier / Cola / …

2-21 Was machen diese Leute gern? The information for **S2** is in the *Anhang* on page A3.

S1: Was für Sport macht Anna gern?
S2: Was für Musik hört Anna gern?
S1: Was für Spiele spielt Anna gern?
...

S2: Sie geht gern schwimmen.
S1: Sie hört gern ...
S2: Sie spielt gern ...
...

	SPORT	MUSIK	SPIELE
Anna		Jazz	
Peter			Karten
Maria	Tischtennis	Country and Western	
Moritz	snowboarden		Monopoly

You will find additional vocabulary for **Hobbys und Sport** in the *Anhang* on p. A18.

2-22 Was machst du gern? Interview your partner about what she/he likes to do.

S1: Was für Sport machst du gern?
Was für Musik hörst du gern?
Was für Spiele spielst du gern?

S2: Ich gehe (spiele) gern ...
Ich höre gern ...
Ich spiele gern ...

▪ Sprachnotiz

gern haben

Gern haben is used to express fondness for someone as opposed to being in love with a person.

STEFAN: Liebst du Maria? *Are you in love with Maria?*
LUKAS: Nein, aber ich **habe** sie sehr **gern.** *No, but I'm very fond of her.*

❹ Answering *who* or *what*

Subject and subject completion

A simple sentence consists of a noun or pronoun *subject* and a *predicate*. The predicate expresses what is said about the subject and consists of a verb or a verb plus other parts of speech.

The boldfaced words in the following examples are the subjects of the verbs.

subject	predicate		
		VERB	OTHER PARTS OF SPEECH
Nina		tanzt	gern.
Nina und Alexander		gehen	oft in die Disco.
Sie		tanzen	dort oft bis zwölf Uhr nachts.

Sometimes the predicate contains a noun that further describes what the subject is or what the subject is called. This noun is called a *subject completion*.

The boldfaced words in the following examples are subject completions. The verbs **heißt** and **ist** function like equal signs, i.e., they show that the subject and the subject completion are one and the same person or thing.

subject	predicate	
	VERB	SUBJECT COMPLETION
Ninas Freund	heißt	**Alexander.**
Er	ist	**ein toller Tänzer.**

2-23 Alexander. Find the subjects and the subject completions. Not every sentence has a subject completion.

Nina sagt:
1. Mein Freund heißt Alexander.
2. Alex tanzt gern und kocht auch gern und gut.
3. Alex ist ein sehr guter Schüler.
4. Alex ist abends oft bei uns.

Robert sagt:
1. Alexander ist Ninas Freund.
2. Nina und Alexander telefonieren oft stundenlang miteinander.
3. Alex ist viel zu oft bei uns.
4. Alexanders Motorrad ist eine Honda.

The nominative case

As you progress through this text, you will learn that German grammar assigns every noun or pronoun to one of four cases. These cases signal the function of the noun or pronoun in a sentence.

In the following examples, the forms of the definite or indefinite articles show that the nouns are in the *nominative case* and that they are subjects or subject completions.

Der Pulli, **das** Hemd, **die** Jacke und **die** Schuhe kosten zusammen fast 300 Euro.	*Altogether the sweater, the shirt, the jacket, and the shoes cost almost 300 euros.*
Ein Magazin ist **keine** Zeitung.	*A magazine is not a newspaper.*

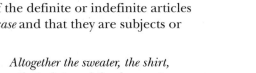

	masculine		neuter		feminine		plural	
NOMINATIVE	der ein kein	} Pulli	das ein kein	} Hemd	die eine keine	} Jacke	die — keine	} Schuhe

Remember:
- Like *a* and *an* in English, **ein** and **eine** have no plural forms.
- **Kein** and **keine** do have a plural form.

2-24 Beverly kauft gern Kleider.

▶ Mantel (m)

coat
S1: Wie viel kostet der Mantel°?
S2: Der Mantel kostet 490 Euro.

skirt   1. Rock° (m)   5. Sweatshirt (n)
belt   2. Bluse (f)   6. Gürtel° (m)
        3. Kleid (n)   7. Socken (pl)
        4. Schuhe (pl)   8. Jacke (f)

 ### 2-25 Wie viel kostet so ein Pulli? Approach three classmates, point to certain articles of clothing they are wearing, and ask how much such items cost. Use **so ein(e)** with singular nouns and **solche** with plural nouns.

such   **S1:** Wie viel kostet so° ein Pulli?   **S2:** So ein Pulli kostet _____ Dollar.
such   Wie viel kosten solche° Schuhe?   Solche Schuhe kosten _____ Dollar.
         …   …

You will find additional articles of clothing under **Kleidungsstücke** in the *Anhang* on p. A19.

Pulli (m)	Jacke (f)	Jeans (pl)	Bluse (f)
Schuhe (pl)	T-Shirt (n)	Mantel (m)	Hose° (f)
Sweatshirt (n)	Rock (m)	Shorts (pl)	Hemd (n)

pants — Hose° (f)

The interrogative pronouns *wer* and *was*

The nominative forms of the interrogative pronouns are **wer** and **was.**

Wer ist Bill Gates?   ***Who** is Bill Gates?*
Was ist Microsoft?   ***What** is Microsoft?*

interrogative pronouns		
	PERSONS	THINGS OR IDEAS
NOMINATIVE	wer?	was?

2-26 Wer oder was? Complete each question with **wer** or **was.** Your partner responds appropriately from the choices given.

▶ _____ ist Pavarotti?   Tenor (m)

S1: Wer ist Pavarotti?   **S2:** Pavarotti ist ein Tenor.

1. _Was_ ist Rotwein?   Insekten (pl) _Rotwein_
2. _____ ist *The New York Times*?   Land (n)
3. _____ ist Hillary Rodham Clinton?   Komponisten (pl)
4. _____ ist Afrika?   Getränk (n)
5. _____ ist Mexiko?   Autorin (f)
6. _Wer_ sind Chopin und Tschaikowski?   Kontinent (m)
7. _____ sind Moskitos?   Zeitung (f)
8. _____ ist J. K. Rowling?   Politikerin (f)

Hören ··

Jazzfans

David and Frank, students at the university in Linz, Austria, are good friends and avid jazz fans. David has just picked up the program for **Das Internationale Jazzhaus-Festival.** Listen as they decide which concerts they are going to attend.

NEUE VOKABELN

das erste Konzert   *the first concert*   **die Karte, -n**   *ticket*
noch mal   *again*

2-27 Erstes Verstehen. Listen to the conversation and choose the correct responses.

1. Which days of the week do you hear?
   Freitag   Samstag   Sonntag   Montag

2. When does Frank work at the Gin Gin?
   freitags   samstags   sonntags

3. What time of day does Frank work?
   vormittags   nachmittags   abends

4. How many artists are mentioned by name?
   1   2   3   4

5. What amounts are mentioned in connection with the tickets?
   10 Euro   15 Euro   20 Euro   25 Euro

2-28 Detailverstehen. Listen to the conversation again and write responses to the following questions.

1. An welchem° Tag und um wie viel Uhr ist das erste Konzert?   *on which*
2. Welche Band spielt im ersten Konzert?
3. Was für eine Arbeit hat Frank im Gin Gin?
4. An welchem Tag arbeitet Frank nicht?
5. An welchem Tag und um wie viel Uhr singt Dianne Reeves?
6. Was kosten die Karten für das Konzert von Dianne Reeves?

INTERNATIONALES JAZZHAUS-FESTIVAL

2-29 Bist du auch Jazzfan? Write down what type of music you like and your favorite performers. Then find other classmates who share your enthusiasm, and ask if they like to listen to the same performers. Use the two models below as a guide.

S1: Ich bin Jazzfan. Bist du auch Jazzfan?

S2: Ja, ich bin auch Jazzfan.

S1: Toll! Hörst du gern Diana Krall?

S2: Ja, sie ist echt cool.
Ja, aber Steve Klink höre ich lieber.

S1: Ich bin Rockfan. Bist du auch Rockfan?

S2: Nein, ich bin kein Rockfan.

S1: Was für Musik hörst du denn gern?

S2: Ich höre gern . . .

2-30 In welches Beisel gehen wir heute? Of the many pubs (**Beisel**) in Linz, David and Frank particularly favor the four that are circled. Study the advertising of these pubs and answer the questions below.

1. Where would David and Frank cap an evening at the theater? In what style is this pub decorated?
2. At which pub can David and Frank join in with the musicians? In which part of town is this pub located?
3. Where can David and Frank hear live jazz performances in a pub located in a cellar? What does the name of the pub have to do with its address?
4. At which pub can David and Frank sit outdoors? Is this pub in the new or old part of town?
5. Of all the pubs listed, choose the one to which you would like to go. What makes this pub appealing to you?

PUBS BEISEL

Nestroy
Traditionslokal seit 33 Jahren, im Herzen von Urfahr, gute Parkmöglichkeiten.
So-Fr 9-24 Uhr
Nestroystr. 4, Tel. 23 22 38 [B6]

Gin Gin
Sehr schön gelegenes Cafe-Pub am Alten Markt in der Altstadt, schöner Gastgarten, beliebter Treffpunkt für jede Altersgruppe
Hahnengasse 7, Tel. 77 41 20 [C11]

S'Kistl
25 verschiedene Biersorten, davon 6 vom Fass, 15 offene Weinspezialitäten, täglich Menüs und Vollwertküche.
Mo-Sa 10-2, So 18-2 Uhr
Altstadt 17, Tel. 78 45 45 [C12]

Musikcafe Cello
Das Musikcafé in zentraler Lage–machen Sie selbst Musik!
Mo-Sa 10-4, So 15-24 Uhr
Graben 17, Tel. 77 32 18 [D11]

PUBS BEISEL

1. Akt
Bar-Restauration in Theaternähe, schöne Bar im Stil der 30er-Jahre, reiche Auswahl an erlesenen Getränken und pikanten Speisen.
So-Fr 17-2 Uhr
Klammstr. 20, Tel. 77 53 31 [B12]

Casino-Treff
Ein Casino-Treffpunkt beim Schillerpark! Angenehme, diskrete Atmosphäre, nette Bedienung, Spiel-Spaß-Unterhaltung durch aktuelle Spielautomaten, lange Öffnungszeiten, für Jugendliche unter 18 Jahren verboten!
Mo-Sa 10-24 Uhr, So ab 16 Uhr
Rainerstr. 12, Tel. 66 24 83 [D15/16]

17er Keller
Gepflegte Drinks, Jazz-Music, Live-Konzerte.
Mo-So 19-2 Uhr
Hauptplatz 17, Tel. 77 90 00 [C11]

⑤ Describing people, places, and things

Der-words in the nominative case

The endings of words like **dieser** *(this)*, **jeder** *(each, every)*, and **welcher** *(which)* correspond closely to the forms of the definite article. For this reason these words, along with the definite article, are called **der**-words.

Welches deutschsprachige Land hat nur 34 000 Einwohner?

Ich glaube, **dieses** Land heißt Liechtenstein.

Diese Briefmarken kommen aus Liechtenstein.

In Liechtenstein kauft fast **jeder** Tourist Briefmarken.

Which German-speaking country has only 34,000 inhabitants?

*I believe **this** country is called Liechtenstein.*

***These** stamps are from Liechtenstein.*

*In Liechtenstein just about **every** tourist buys stamps.*

	masculine	neuter	feminine	plural
NOMINATIVE	dies**er** (der)	dies**es** (das)	dies**e** (die)	dies**e** (die)

INFOBOX
61 square miles = approximately 150 km² (25 km x 6 km).

Liechtenstein

Nestled in the **Alpen** between Austria and Switzerland lies the principality of **Liechtenstein** (capital: **Vaduz**). With an area of only 61 square miles (15.6 miles long and 3.75 miles wide), it is the smallest of the German-speaking countries.

Liechtenstein has its own government and constitution, but since 1920 it has been using Swiss currency and the Swiss postal system.

The 34,000 inhabitants of Liechtenstein enjoy a high standard of living, and taxes are so low that many foreign companies are located there. In fact, there are more companies registered in Liechtenstein than there are inhabitants.

Liechtenstein is well known to anyone who collects **Briefmarken.** Its thriving philatelic industry does over 10 million dollars worth of business annually.

www Plan a weekend with friends in **Liechtenstein** at www.prenhall.com/treffpunkt
→ Kapitel 2 → Web Resources
→ Kultur

Das Wappen von Liechtenstein

Hier residiert der Fürst von Liechtenstein.

2-31 Dies-, jed-, welch-?

smaller than

1. _____ deutschsprachige Land (n) ist kleiner als° die Schweiz?
2. Woher sind _____ Briefmarken (pl)?

so … wie: *as . . . as*

3. Nicht _____ Land (n) hat so° schöne Briefmarken wie Liechtenstein.
4. _____ Bus (m) ist das? Ist es der Bus nach Vaduz?
5. In Vaduz kauft fast _____ Tourist (m) ein paar Briefmarken.
6. Sind _____ Touristen (pl) Amerikaner oder Kanadier?

Ein-words in the nominative case:
ein, kein, and the possessive adjectives

Both **ein** and **kein** belong to a group of words called **ein**-words. Also included in this group are the possessive adjectives, which are used to indicate possession or relationships, e.g., *my* book, *my* friend. The chart below shows the personal pronouns with their corresponding possessive adjectives.

singular				plural			
PERSONAL PRONOUN		**POSSESSIVE ADJECTIVE**		**PERSONAL PRONOUN**		**POSSESSIVE ADJECTIVE**	
ich	*I*	**mein**	*my*	**wir**	*we*	**unser**	*our* 
du	*you*	**dein**	*your*	**ihr**	*you*	**euer**	*your*
Sie	*you*	**Ihr**	*your*	**Sie**	*you*	**Ihr**	*your*
er	*he, it*	**sein**	*his, its*				
es	*it*	**sein**	*its*	**sie**	*they*	**ihr**	*their*
sie	*she, it*	**ihr**	*her, its*				

Like the formal **Sie,** the formal **Ihr** is always capitalized. The possessive adjectives take the same endings as **ein** and **kein.**

Wo leben **deine** beiden Freundinnen jetzt, Kirsten?	*Where do **your** two friends live now, Kirsten?*
Meine Freundin Maria lebt in Hamburg, und **meine** Freundin Anna und **ihr** Mann leben in Düsseldorf.	***My** friend Maria lives in Hamburg and **my** friend Anna and **her** husband live in Düsseldorf.*
Wie alt sind **Ihre** Kinder, Frau Ziegler?	*How old are **your** children, Ms. Ziegler?*
Unsere Tochter ist sechzehn und **unser** Sohn ist vierzehn.	***Our** daughter is sixteen and **our** son is fourteen.*

In the following chart the possessive adjective **mein** is used to show the nominative forms of all possessive adjectives.

	masculine	neuter	feminine	plural
NOMINATIVE	mein Lehrer	mein Auto	mein**e** Freundin	mein**e** Eltern

When an ending is added to **euer,** the **e** before the **r** is dropped.

Ist **eure** Mensa gut?	*Is **your** dining hall good?*

2-32 Günter. Supply the appropriate forms of **mein.**

Ich heiße Günter, bin zwanzig Jahre alt und studiere hier in Leipzig Genetik. _____ Eltern leben auch hier in Leipzig. _____ Vater ist Polizist und _____ Mutter ist Lehrerin. _____ Bruder Stefan ist siebzehn und geht noch in die Schule. _____ Schwester Melanie ist zweiundzwanzig und studiert in Hamburg Biochemie. _____ Freundinnen heißen Helga und Tina und sie studieren auch hier in Leipzig.

2-33 Ich, meine Familie und meine Freunde. Use the previous activity as a model to write a short description of yourself, your family, and your friends. You will find pertinent vocabulary for **Studienfächer** and **Jobs und Berufe** in the *Anhang* on pages A17. In the next class, read your description to your classmates.

2-34 Ein kleines Gespräch. Supply the appropriate forms of **sein, ihr, Ihr,** and **unser.** *our*

FRAU BENN: Wie alt sind _Ihre_ Kinder jetzt, Herr Haag?
HERR HAAG: _Unser_ Tochter ist sechsundzwanzig und _sein_ beiden Söhne sind einundzwanzig und siebzehn.
FRAU BENN: Und wo lebt _Ihre_ Tochter?
HERR HAAG: Laura und _ihr_ Mann leben in Hannover.
FRAU BENN: Und _ihre_ Söhne?
HERR HAAG: Lukas studiert in Münster und _sein_ Bruder Daniel ist noch hier bei uns.

2-35 Wie ist eure Uni? Imagine that you and your partner are studying at different universities. Find out about your partner's school by completing the questions and responses with the appropriate forms of **euer** and **unser.**

M	F	N	PL
er	e	es	e

S1:
1. Wie alt ist _euer_ Uni (f)?
2. Ist _Ihr_ Campus (m) groß?

3. Wie sind _____ Vorlesungen (pl)?

4. Ist _____ Bibliothek (f) gut?
5. Sind _____ Computer (pl) up to date?
6. Wie ist _____ Mensa?

7. Sind _____ Studentenheime (pl) schön?
8. Wie gut ist _____ Footballteam (n)?

S2:
_____ Uni ist fast 200 Jahre alt.
Nein, _____ Campus ist nicht sehr groß.
_____ Vorlesungen sind sehr interessant.
Ja, _____ Bibliothek ist sehr gut.
Ja, _____ Computer sind fast alle up to date.
_____ Mensa ist gut, aber ein bisschen zu teuer°.   *expensive*
Ja, _____ Studentenheime sind sehr modern und sehr schön.
_____ Footballteam ist echt° spitze°.   *really / great*

2-36 Unsere Uni. Gather in groups of four or five. One student plays a reporter who is interested in finding out more about your university or college. The reporter can use the questions in the previous activity as a model. Take turns responding to the reporter's questions.

Nominative endings of adjectives preceded by *der*-words

An adjective takes an ending when it comes directly before the noun it describes.

Diese eleganten Schuhe kosten
nur 50 Euro.

These elegant shoes cost only
50 euros.

	masculine	neuter	feminine	plural
NOMINATIVE	der rote Pulli	das blaue Hemd	die weiße Jacke	die braunen Schuhe

In the nominative, these same endings occur after *all* **der**-words, e.g., **der** rote Pulli, **dieses** blaue Hemd, **jede** weiße Jacke, **welche** braunen Schuhe.

If two or more adjectives come directly before a noun, they all have the same ending.

Wie viel kosten diese beiden
hübschen Blusen?

How much do these two pretty
blouses cost?

An adjective takes an ending even if the noun to which it refers is not repeated.

Die rote Bluse kostet 40 Euro und
die gelbe kostet 55 Euro.

The red blouse costs 40 euros and
the yellow one costs 55 euros.

2-37 Bei Peek und Cloppenburg.

1. **S1:** Wie viel kosten diese beid__ hübsch__ Blusen?
   S2: Die rot__ Bluse kostet 40 Euro und die weiß__ kostet 35 Euro.
2. **S1:** Wie viel kosten diese beid__ schick__ Pullis?
   S2: Der weiß__ Pulli kostet 55 Euro und der rot__ kostet 60 Euro.
3. **S1:** Wie viel kosten diese beid__ toll__ Sweatshirts?
   S2: Das blau__ Sweatshirt kostet 20 Euro und das rot__ kostet 30 Euro.
4. **S1:** Wie viel kosten diese beid__ lang__ Mäntel?
   S2: Der braun__ Mantel kostet 215 Euro und der dunkelblau__ kostet 300 Euro.
sporty 5. **S1:** Wie viel kosten diese beid__ sportlich__° Jacken?
   S2: Die schwarz__ Jacke kostet 110 Euro und die weiß__ kostet 115 Euro.
6. **S1:** Wie viel kosten diese beid__ schön__ T-Shirts?
   S2: Das weiß__ T-Shirt kostet 12 Euro und das hellblau__ kostet 17 Euro.

Nominative endings of adjectives preceded by *ein*-words

	masculine	neuter	feminine	plural
NOMINATIVE	**ein** rot**er** Pulli	**ein** blau**es** Hemd	eine weiß**e** Jacke	keine braun**en** Schuhe

In the chart above, you see that the **ein**-word has no ending in the masculine and neuter. In these two instances, the adjective itself shows the gender and case of the noun by taking the appropriate **der**-word ending: dies**er** Pulli, **ein** rot**er** Pulli; dies**es** Hemd, **ein** blau**es** Hemd.

CLAUDIA:	Dein rot**er** Pullover ist echt toll.	*Your red sweater is really fabulous.*
MARTIN:	Ja, und er war nur halb so teuer wie mein neu**es** blau**es** Hemd.	*Yes, and it was only half as expensive as my new blue shirt.*

2-38 Komplimente. Look at what your classmates are wearing and compliment them on a specific article of clothing.

S: Lisa, dein roter Rock ist sehr schick.
David, deine schwarze Jacke is echt cool.

sehr schick	echt cool	sehr hübsch
sehr schön	echt spitze	sehr elegant
sehr sportlich	echt toll	sehr interessant

2-39 Wir spielen Trivial Pursuit. In each response, use the appropriate form of the indefinite article. The information for **S2** is in the *Anhang* on page A3.

S1: Wer ist Johnny Depp?

S2: Johnny Depp ist ein amerikanischer Filmstar.

… …

LEUTE (WER?)		GETRÄNKE (WAS?)		GEOGRAFIE (WAS?)	
Johnny Depp		Löwenbräu	deutsches Bier	Angola	afrikanisches Land
Margaret Atwood		Chianti		Linz	
Tony Blair	englischer Politiker	Fanta		die Wolga	russischer Fluss
Maria Callas		Budweiser	amerikanisches Bier	Brandenburg	
Felix Mendelssohn	deutscher Komponist	Benedictine		der Vesuv	italienischer Vulkan

Nominative endings of unpreceded adjectives

	masculine	neuter	feminine	plural
NOMINATIVE	gut**er** Kaffee	gut**es** Bier	gut**e** Milch	gut**e** Oliven

Adjectives that are not preceded by a **der**-word or an **ein**-word show the gender, number, and case of the noun by taking the appropriate **der**-word ending.

Warum ist dies**er** Kaffee so teuer? *Why is this coffee so expensive?*
Gut**er** Kaffee ist immer teuer. *Good coffee is always expensive.*

2-40 Herr Ziegler im Feinkostgeschäft°. *gourmet foods store*

▶ dieser Kaffee

S1: Warum ist dieser Kaffee so teuer? **S2:** Guter Kaffee ist immer teuer.

1. diese Salami
2. dieses Bier
3. diese Pistazien (pl)
4. dieser Tee
5. dieser Wein
6. diese Oliven (pl)
7. dieses Olivenöl
8. diese Schokolade

Zusammenschau

🖥️ ▮ Video-Treff ·····················

Freunde

In this video segment Anja Szustak, André, Susann, Thomas, Karen, and Stefan Kuhlmann will introduce good friends.

Zum besseren Verstehen

2-41 Was ist das auf Englisch?

1. Wir haben ein **gemeinsames** Hobby, und das ist Schwimmen.
2. Wir kochen nicht so **häufig** zusammen.
3. Wir **kennen uns** seit zwei Jahren.
4. Wir **sind** zusammen zur Schule **gegangen.**
5. Wir wohnen zusammen in einer **Wohngemeinschaft** in Kreuzberg.
6. Er arbeitet als **Veranstaltungstechniker.**
7. Meine Freundin ist sehr offen und **natürlich.**
8. Er ist jetzt **zirka** sechs Jahre alt.
9. Meine Freundin und ich sind beide sehr **verliebt.**

a. approximately
b. often
c. natural
d. went
e. common
f. event technician
g. have known each other
h. in love
i. shared housing

Now watch the video and complete the post-viewing activities in the *Video-Treff* section of the *Student Activities Manual.*

Hören

Before listening to the narrative, look at the map inside the front cover and locate **Schwerin, Göttingen, die Schweiz, Liechtenstein,** and **Österreich.**

Freundinnen

Listen to what Beate and Sabine will be doing between the completion of their **Abitur** and the beginning of their university studies.

NEUE VOKABELN   The **Abitur** was explained in the cultural note on page 2.

schon	*already*	**bald**	*soon*
seit	*since*	**fahren**	*to travel*
die Radtour	*bicycle trip*	**durch**	*through*
das Geld	*money*	**der Koffer, -**	*suitcase*
suchen	*to look for*	**die Wohnung**	*apartment*

2-42 Erstes Verstehen. Listen to the narrative and choose the correct responses.

1. Which cities are mentioned?
   Köln   Göttingen   Schweinfurt   Schwerin
2. Which months of the year do you hear?
   Juni   Juli   August   September   Oktober
3. What types of stores do you hear?
   Feinkostgeschäft   Fotogeschäft   Schuhgeschäft   Sportgeschäft
4. Which countries are mentioned?
   Dänemark   Deutschland   Österreich   Schweden
   die Schweiz   Liechtenstein

2-43 Detailverstehen. Listen to the narrative again and write the responses to the following questions.

1. Wo leben Beate und Sabine im Juli und wo leben sie im Oktober?
2. Was planen Beate und Sabine für September?
3. Warum suchen sie für August Arbeit?
4. Was ist Beates Hobby?
5. Wer arbeitet im Fotogeschäft und wer im Sportgeschäft?
6. Ende September sind Beate und Sabine wieder in Schwerin. Was machen sie dann?

Das Schloss in Schwerin

Schreibtipp: 2-44: This writing activity divides well into three paragraphs: 1. Who is the person? (name, age, residence, work/study); 2. What does she/he like to do? (hobbies, sports, music); and 3. Why is she/he my best friend? (what she/he is like, what we do together).

2-44 Meine beste Freundin/Mein bester Freund. Write a description of your best friend, using the following questions to guide you. You may want to refer to the lists of **Studienfächer, Jobs und Berufe, Hobbys und Sport, Musikinstrumente,** and **Persönliche Merkmale** (*personal characteristics*) in the *Anhang* on pages A17-A19 and A21.

- Wie heißt deine beste Freundin/dein bester Freund?
- Wie alt ist sie/er?
- *at home* Wo wohnt sie/er? Im Studentenheim oder zu Hause°, oder hat sie/er ein Zimmer oder eine Wohnung?
- Was studiert sie/er oder wo arbeitet sie/er? (*Sie/Er arbeitet bei ...*)
- Was sind ihre/seine Hobbys?
- Was für Sport macht sie/er gern?
- Spielt sie/er ein Instrument?
- Wie ist sie/er?
- Was macht ihr gern zusammen?

2-45 Deine beste Freundin/Dein bester Freund. Using the questions from the previous activity, find out about your partner's best friend. Fill in the information and report your findings to the class.

IHRE/SEINE BESTE FREUNDIN *ODER* IHR/SEIN BESTER FREUND

Name _____

Alter _____

Wohnen _____

subjects Studienfächer°/Arbeit _____

Hobbys _____

Sport _____

Musik/Instrumente _____

Wie sie/er ist _____

common Gemeinsame° Interessen _____

Lesen ···

Zum besseren Verstehen

2-46 Interkulturelle Freundschaften.

- Do you have friends of an ethnic background different from your own?
- Do your friends or their parents view friendship and interpersonal relationships differently than you do? How?

2-47 Was ist das auf Englisch?

1. Ein **Mietshaus** ist ein großes Haus mit vielen Wohnungen.
2. Yützels Wohnung ist die Nummer 15. In Nummer 16 wohnen Herr und Frau Gürlük. Yützels und Gürlüks sind **Nachbarn.**
3. Frau Yützel **besucht** Frau Gürlük fast jeden Tag.
4. In Deutschland **sprechen** viele junge Türken oft besser Deutsch als Türkisch.
5. Morgen **heiraten** Stefan Müller und Tansu Gürlük. Sie sind dann Herr und Frau Müller.

a. speak
b. are marrying
c. apartment building
d. visits
e. neighbors

WWW Learn more about Germany's immigrants at www.prenhall.com/treffpunkt
→ Kapitel 2 → Web Resources → Kultur

LEUTE Freundschaften: Fatma Yützel erzählt[1]

Ich heiße Fatma Yützel, bin fünfzehn Jahre alt und bin in Berlin geboren. Meine Eltern kommen aus einem kleinen Dorf[2] in Anatolien[3] und leben seit zwanzig Jahren in Berlin. Wir wohnen in einem großen Mietshaus und haben dort viele Nachbarn, Türken und Deutsche. Am Abend und am Wochenende besuchen wir oft unsere türkischen Nachbarn, oder die Nachbarn besuchen uns, denn unsere Nachbarn sind auch unsere Freunde. Unsere deutschen Nachbarn besuchen wir nie[4], und die Deutschen besuchen ihre Nachbarn auch fast nie. Deshalb[5] denken[6] meine Eltern, die Deutschen sind unfreundlich und haben keine Freunde. Aber meine Freundin Melanie sagt, das ist gar nicht so. Melanie ist Deutsche und sagt, ihre Eltern haben sehr gute Freunde. Diese Freunde sind aber normalerweise nicht ihre Nachbarn, sondern Freunde aus der Schulzeit oder Arbeitskollegen. Also[7] sind die Deutschen gar nicht unfreundlich, sondern nur anders als[8] wir.

Meine Eltern sprechen nicht gut Deutsch und sie haben auch deshalb nur sehr wenig Kontakt mit Deutschen. Aber wie[9] so viele junge Türken in Deutschland spreche ich besser Deutsch als Türkisch. Ich bin auch sehr gern und sehr oft bei Melanie und ich finde nicht nur sie, sondern auch ihren Bruder David sehr nett. Aber das sage ich meinen Eltern lieber nicht, denn im Heimatdorf[10] von meinen Eltern hat ein ordentliches[11] Mädchen[12] keinen Freund, und die Eltern finden den Mann für ihre Tochter. Aber ich bin hier in Deutschland geboren und vielleicht[13] heirate ich sogar[14] mal einen Deutschen.

[1]*tells her story* [2]*village* [3]*a very poor rural region of Turkey* [4]*never* [5]*therefore* [6]*think* [7]*so*
[8]*different from* [9]*like* [10]*home village* [11]*decent* [12]*girl* [13]*perhaps* [14]*even*

Arbeit mit dem Text

2-48 Wer denkt so? Indicate whether the statements below describe the thinking of **Fatmas Eltern** or **Melanies Eltern** by writing **FE** or **ME.**

1. Unsere Nachbarn sind auch unsere Freunde. _____
2. Unsere Freunde sind Arbeitskollegen oder Freunde aus unserer Schulzeit. _____
3. Bei uns° hat ein ordentliches Mädchen keinen Freund. _____   *where we come from*
4. Bei uns finden die Eltern den Mann für ihre Tochter. _____
5. Unsere Töchter haben nicht nur Freundinnen, sondern auch Freunde. _____
6. Unsere Töchter finden ihre Männer selbst°. _____   *themselves*

www Learn more about becoming a German citizen at www.prenhall.com/treffpunkt → Kapitel 2 → Web Resources → Kultur

Mosques: Germany has approximately 2200 mosques and prayer rooms.

Kebab: Döner Kebab (note the Turkish spelling **Kebap** in the photo) is very popular among Germans. It is pita bread filled with meat roasted on a spit, lettuce, tomatoes, and onions.

Both Zehra Çirak and Feridun Zaimoglu have received prestigious German literary prizes, and their books are widely read in Germany. Fatih Akin's film **Gegen die Wand** (English title: *Head-On*) won the Golden Bear at the 2004 Berlin Film Festival. Aziza A and her band attract enthusiastic audiences in many countries.

INFOBOX

Ethnic diversity in Germany

During the 1950s and 1960s, the period of reconstruction after World War II, the former West Germany experienced a period of economic growth known as the **Wirtschaftswunder** (*economic miracle*). To ease severe labor shortages, workers were recruited from countries such as Italy, Yugoslavia, Greece, and Turkey. Currently the number of **Ausländer** (*foreigners*) living in Germany is between seven and eight million.

Die Sehitlik Moschee in Berlin

The various ethnic groups have influenced the cultural life of Germany in many ways. This is particularly noticeable in the restaurant scene, where Greek, Italian, Turkish, and Asian establishments successfully compete with traditional German restaurants. Turkish markets with colorful displays of fruits and vegetables are a common sight, and a town without a **Kebab** stand is almost unthinkable. Many towns also have Islamic centers of worship or a mosque. Less visible are the important contributions that **Einwanderer** (*immigrants*) make to other sectors of the cultural and economic life of Germany. Many **Einwanderer** and their descendants have become successful doctors, lawyers, writers, journalists, actors, artists, politicians, and entrepreneurs.

It has always been possible for persons of non-German descent to become German citizens. However, the new citizenship law of January 1, 2000, makes this easier. Foreigners who have lawfully lived in Germany for eight years now have a legal claim to German citizenship, provided that they can prove they are self-supporting and have an adequate knowledge of German. Children born in Germany to foreigners who have lived in Germany lawfully for at least eight years automatically have dual citizenship until age 23. They must then choose one citizenship.

The history of immigration in North America has shown that integration into a new society does not always come easily. In Germany the struggles of immigrants have been documented by people such as the writers Zehra Çirak and Feridun Zaimoglu, the actor-director Fatih Akin, and the hip-hop star Aziza A.

While discrimination and even violence against foreigners can still be found in Germany, most Germans acknowledge and value the cultural and economic contributions that immigrants make to the country.

Wort, Sinn und Klang

Wörter unter der Lupe

Words as chameleons: *erst*

Just as a chameleon changes its color according to its environment, certain words change their meaning according to their context. One of these is **erst.**

- As an adverb, **erst** can mean *first, only,* or *not until.*

  Lena trinkt **erst** eine Tasse Kaffee und dann geht sie in die Vorlesung.

  First Lena drinks a cup of coffee and then she goes to her lecture.

  Es ist **erst** zehn Uhr.

  It's only ten o'clock.

  Morgen gehe ich **erst** am Nachmittag zur Uni.

  *Tomorrow I'm **not** going to the university **until** the afternoon.*

- As an adjective, **erst** always means *first.*

  Wie heißt Mozarts **erste** Oper?

  *What is Mozart's **first** opera called?*

Bitte erst zahlen dann fahren

Im Parkhaus

2-49 Was bedeutet° erst?

does . . . mean

1. Das Konzert beginnt **erst** um 21 Uhr. (not until / first)
2. Thomas ist **erst** siebzehn. (only / first)
3. Anita geht morgens **erst** joggen und dann geht sie zur Uni. (not until / first)
4. Martin kommt heute **erst** um zehn. (first / not until)
5. Freitags beginnt meine **erste** Vorlesung schon um acht. (not until / first)

More on cognates

In *Kapitel 1* you saw that you often don't need a dictionary to understand cognates. If you know the "code," you will be able to add many German words to your vocabulary simply by recognizing the patterns they follow. You should have no trouble guessing the meaning of the German words in each category below. Words followed by (v) are the infinitive forms of verbs.

- German **f** or **ff** is English *p*

der A**ff**e	das Schi**ff**
schar**f**	hel**f**en *(v)*
die Har**f**e	o**ff**en
rei**f**	ho**ff**en *(v)*

- German **d, t,** or **tt** is English *th*

das Ba**d**	der Bru**d**er
danken *(v)*	der Va**t**er
das **D**ing	die Mu**tt**er
dick	die Fe**d**er
dünn	das Le**d**er
tausen**d**	das We**tt**er

- German **b** is English *v* or *f*

ha**b**en *(v)*	das Kal**b**
das Gra**b**	une**b**en
hal**b**	das Fie**b**er

The adjective suffixes *-ig*, *-lich*, and *-isch*

German and English create many adjectives by adding suffixes to other words. The German adjectives with the suffixes **-ig, -lich,** and **-isch** often have English equivalents with the suffixes *-y, -ly,* and *-ish.*

2-50 Was ist das auf Englisch?

-ig *(-y)*		**-lich** *(-ly)*	**-isch** *(-ish)*
sonnig	lausig	freundlich	kindisch
schattig	wurmig	mütterlich	dänisch
windig	haarig	väterlich	irisch
eisig	fettig	täglich	polnisch
salzig	stinkig	wöchentlich	türkisch
rostig	sandig	monatlich	schwedisch
schleimig	buschig	jährlich	spanisch

Expose "false friends" at
www.prenhall.com/treffpunkt
→ Kapitel 2 → Web Resources
→ Kultur

INFOBOX

English words in German

Like every language, German is constantly changing, due in part to the influence from other languages and cultures. **Lehnwörter** *(loan words)* entering a language usually reflect a particular area of influence from another culture. For example, words borrowed from English often relate to advertising, business, technology, fashion, and pop culture, e.g., nouns like **der Trend, das Meeting, die Homepage, der Blazer,** and **der DJ,** and verbs like **lunchen, downloaden,** and **stylen.** Even though these words take on German grammatical forms (like gender or verb endings: *das* **Meeting, wir lunch*en***), they usually have the same meaning as in English. However, some English words used in German have a rather unexpected meaning for speakers of English. Match the German loan words below with their English equivalents.

1. der Smoking
2. der Oldtimer
3. der Shootingstar
4. das Set
5. der Dressman

a. suddenly successful person
b. male model
c. tuxedo
d. vintage car
e. place mat

Chicken-Mix-Menü

verschiedene Chicken-Snacks

mit 2 Dips,
Pommes Frites
und 0,3 l Getränk

5,50 €

((▶ Zur Aussprache

In English the spelling of a word does not always indicate how it is pronounced (e.g., pl*ough*, thr*ough*, thor*ough*, en*ough*). English pronunciation is also a poor indicator of spelling (e.g., b*e*, s*ee*, b*elie*ve, r*ecei*ve). In German, spelling and pronunciation are much more consistent. Once you have mastered a few basic principles, you should have no trouble pronouncing and spelling new words.

The vowels *a, e, i, o,* and *u*

In a stressed syllable, each of these five vowels is either long or short. Listen carefully to the pronunciation of the following words and sentences and at the same time note the spelling. You will see that certain letter combinations indicate quite reliably whether a vowel in a stressed syllable is long or short.

- A doubled vowel is always long: **H*aa*r, T*ee*, B*oo*t.**
- A vowel followed by an **h** is always long: **J*ah*r, g*eh*t, S*oh*n, *Uh*r.** Note that the **h** is used as a length marker only and is therefore silent.
- An **i** followed by an **e** is always long: **B*ie*r, s*ie*ben.**
- A vowel followed by one consonant plus another vowel is always long: **N*a*se, w*e*nig, K*i*no, M*o*nat, Min*u*te.**
- A vowel followed by an **ß** is always long: **gr*o*ß, Str*a*ße, F*u*ßball.**
- A vowel followed by a doubled consonant is always short: **W*a*sser, W*e*tter, L*i*ppe, S*o*mmer, S*u*ppe.**
- Usually, a vowel followed by two or more consonants is short: **L*a*nd, M*e*nsa, tr*i*nken, T*o*chter, St*u*nde.**

2-51 Hören Sie gut zu und wiederholen Sie!

Peter geht im Regen segeln.

a (lang)	**a (kurz)**
Haar	hart
lahm	Lampe
Lama	Lamm
Mein Name ist Beate Mahler.	Tanja tanzt gern Tango.
Mein Vater ist aus Saalfeld.	Walter tanzt lieber Walzer.

e (lang)	**e (kurz)**	
Tee	Teddybär	
gehen	gestern	
leben	lernen	
Peter geht im Regen segeln.	Ein Student hat selten° Geld.	*seldom*

i (lang)	**i (kurz)**
Liebe	Lippe
Miete	Mitte
Kino	Kinder
Dieter liebt Lisa.	Fischers Fritz fischt frische Fische.

o (lang)	**o (kurz)**
doof	Donner
Sohn	Sonne
Ton	toll
Warum ist Thomas so doof?	Am Sonntag kommt Onkel Otto.

u (lang)	**u (kurz)**	
Stuhl	Stunde	
Schule	Schulter	
super	Suppe	
Utes Pudel frisst° nur Nudeln.	In Ulm und um Ulm und um Ulm herum.	*eats*

Nomen

die Arbeit	work
das Geld	money
die Radtour, -en	bicycle trip
das Wochenende, -n	weekend
das Haus, ⁻er	house
das Land, ⁻er	country
die Stadt, ⁻e	city; town
die Straße, -n	street
die Wohnung, -en	apartment
der Nachbar, -n	} neighbor
die Nachbarin, -nen	

Universitätsleben

das Fach, ⁻er	} field of study; subject
das Studienfach, ⁻er	
das Studentenheim, -e	student residence, dormitory
der Stundenplan, ⁻e	schedule, timetable
die Übung, -en	exercise; seminar; lab
zur Uni	to the university

Kleidungsstücke

das Kleidungsstück, -e	article of clothing
der Anzug, ⁻e	(men's) suit
die Bluse, -n	blouse
der Gürtel, -	belt
das Hemd, -en	shirt
die Hose, -n	pants
die Jacke, -n	jacket
die Jeans (pl)	jeans
das Kleid, -er	dress
die Kleider (pl)	clothes
der Mantel, ⁻	coat
der Pulli, -s	light sweater
der Pullover, -	sweater
der Rock, ⁻e	skirt
der Schuh, -e	shoe
die Shorts (pl)	shorts
die Socke, -n	sock
das Sweatshirt, -s	sweatshirt
das T-Shirt, -s	T-shirt

Verben

bedeuten	to mean
besuchen	to visit
denken	to think
erzählen	to tell (a story)
hören	to hear
trinken	to drink
leben	to live (in a country or city)
wohnen	to live (in a building or a street)

Andere Wörter

beide	both; two
hübsch	pretty
schick	chic
bald	soon
deshalb	therefore; that's why
erst	first; only; not until
schon	already
vielleicht	perhaps

Ausdrücke

Be sure to learn the expressions of time on pages 57 and 58.

morgen früh	tomorrow morning
Um wie viel Uhr …?	(At) what time …?
Wie spät ist es?	} What time is it?
Wie viel Uhr ist es?	
zu Ende sein	to be over
besser als	better than
echt cool	really cool
echt spitze	really great
so … wie	as . . . as
Heute ist es nicht so kalt wie gestern.	Today it's not as cold as yesterday.

ISFAHAN

SO BUNT WIE DIE WELT

Was bedeutet „bunt"?

Das Gegenteil

der Mann, ¨er ≠ die Frau, -en	husband; man ≠ wife; woman
suchen ≠ finden	to look for ≠ to find
dick ≠ dünn	thick; fat ≠ thin; skinny
lang ≠ kurz	long ≠ short
teuer ≠ billig	expensive ≠ cheap
immer ≠ nie	always ≠ never

Leicht zu verstehen

der Autor, -en	der Euro
die Autorin, -nen	die Olive, -n
das Magazin, -e	das Olivenöl
der Film, -e	die Salami
das Konzert, -e	die Schokolade
die Oper, -n	elegant

Leicht zu verstehen: Which words in this list are stressed on a different syllable than their English equivalents?

Wörter im Kontext

2-52 Was passt nicht?

1.	das Hemd	2.	die Jeans	3.	die Jacke	4.	die Schuhe
	die Hose		der Rock		der Gürtel		der Pullover
	die Bluse		die Hose		der Mantel		das Sweatshirt
	der Pullover		die Bluse		das Kleid		das Hemd

2-53 *Leben oder wohnen?*

1. Stephanie und Claudia _____ beide im Studentenheim.
2. Stephanies Eltern _____ in Chicago.
3. Maria ist aus Salzburg, aber sie _____ jetzt in Wien und _____ dort bei ihrer Großmutter.

Leben and **wohnen**: **Leben** is usually used in connection with the country or city of residence. **Wohnen** is used in connection with a building, street, or family (e.g., **Michael lebt in Berlin und wohnt in der Crellestraße**).

2-54 Was ist die richtige Reihenfolge? What's the proper sequence?
Number the following items from largest to smallest (1 to 5).

_____ das Haus   _____ das Land
_____ die Stadt   _____ die Straße
_____ die Wohnung

2-55 Was passt wo?

dick ≠ dünn / sucht ≠ findet / immer ≠ nie / Mann ≠ Frau / lang ≠ kurz / billig ≠ teuer

1. Im Winter sind die Tage _____ und die Nächte _____.
2. Silber ist nicht _____, aber es ist nicht so _____ wie Gold.
3. Sweatshirts sind _____ und T-Shirts sind _____.
4. Warum hörst du _____ nur Rock und _____ Mozart oder Beethoven?
5. Stefan und Tansu heiraten morgen. Sie sind dann _____ und _____.
6. Lukas _____ eine Frau, aber er _____ keine.

Eine österreichische Familie

Kommunikationsziele

Talking about . . .

- family
- shopping and other activities
- useful everyday objects
- occupations

Expressing preferences and favorites

Describing people, places, and things

Strukturen

Accusative case:

- direct object
- **der**-words and **ein**-words
- adjective endings
- time phrases

Word order: More on the position of **nicht**

Verbs with stem changes in the present tense

Kultur

Austria

Family life in the German-speaking countries

Video-Treff: **Meine Familie**

Lesen: **Eine musikalische Familie und ihr genialer Sohn**

Verwandte

Oma Ziegler sagt: Das ist meine Tochter Bettina. Sie ist nicht verheiratet und hat keine Kinder, aber sie ist eine sehr gute Physiotherapeutin. Bettina kauft gern teure Kleider, sie hat einen viel zu teuren Wagen und sie fährt auch oft zu schnell. Und warum reist Bettina denn immer so viel?

Nina sagt: Tante Bettina ist meine Lieblingstante. Sie hat ein echt tolles Leben: viel Geld, schicke Kleider, große Reisen (auch nach Nordamerika, denn sie spricht sehr gut Englisch) und ein rotes Sportcoupé.

Herr Ziegler sagt: Das ist mein Bruder Alfred. Er ist Bankdirektor, verdient viel Geld und fährt einen großen, grauen Mercedes. Er isst gern gut, trinkt teure Weine und trägt sehr teure, graue Anzüge.

Robert sagt: Onkel Alfred ist nicht mein Lieblingsonkel. Er lacht fast nie und seine Anzüge sind so grau und so langweilig wie sein dicker, grauer Mercedes. Er sitzt den ganzen Tag am Computer oder liest seine blöden Börsenberichte.

Verwandte: The following four narratives again feature members of the Ziegler family.

((( )) ▌ Hören ···

3-1 Richtig oder falsch? You will hear the descriptions of Bettina Ziegler and Alfred Ziegler. Indicate whether the statements following each set of descriptions are **richtig** or **falsch.**

BETTINA ZIEGLER

	RICHTIG	FALSCH		RICHTIG	FALSCH
1.	_____	_____	3.	_____	_____
2.	_____ ✓	_____	4.	_____	_____

ALFRED ZIEGLER

	RICHTIG	FALSCH		RICHTIG	FALSCH
1.	_____	_____	3.	_____	_____
2.	_____	_____	4.	_____	_____

3-2 Anders gesagt. With a partner, read *Verwandte* again, and find equivalents for the following statements.

▶ Oma Ziegler ist Bettinas Mutter.   =   Oma Ziegler sagt: Das ist meine Tochter Bettina.

1. Bettina hat keinen Mann.
2. Bettinas Kleider kosten viel Geld.
3. Bettina macht zu viele Reisen.
4. Bettina hat einen sehr sportlichen Wagen.
5. Onkel Alfred arbeitet bei der Bank.
6. Alfred hat einen teuren Wagen.
7. Alfreds graue Anzüge kosten viel Geld.
8. Alfred hat keinen Humor.
9. Alfreds Anzüge und sein Wagen sind gar nicht sportlich.

3-3 Eine Familie. The following well-known children's rhyme describes one family. Read the poem. Then study the family tree and answer the questions.

Illustration of family: (from left to right) Benjamin, Sebastian, Susanna, Katharin, Daniel, Michael, Regine, Rosine, Johanna, Ottilie, Christian.

Der Vater, der heißt Daniel,
der kleine Sohn heißt Michael,
male cousin *die Mutter heißt Regine,*
die Tochter heißt Rosine,
der Bruder, der heißt Christian,
know *der Onkel heißt Sebastian,*

die Schwester heißt Johanna,
die Tante heißt Susanna,
der Vetter°, der heißt Benjamin,
die Kusine, die heißt Katharin,
die Oma heißt Ottilie –
jetzt kennst° du die Familie.

Ein Stammbaum

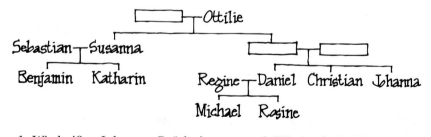

1. Wie heißen Johannas Brüder?
2. Wie heißen Susannas Kinder?
3. Wie heißt Michaels Schwester?
siblings 4. Wie heißen Daniels Geschwister°?
5. Wie heißen Katharins Vettern?

6. Wie heißt Ottilies Tochter?
7. Wie heißt Benjamins Kusine?
8. Wie heißt Rosines Tante?
9. Wie heißt Johannas Großmutter?
10. Wie heißen Katharins Eltern?

■ Sprachnotiz ·······························

Expressing *favorite*

The noun **Liebling** means *darling* or *favorite*. With the addition of an **-s** (**Lieblings-**), it can be prefixed to many nouns to express that someone or something is one's favorite.

Tante Bettina ist meine **Liebling**stante. *Aunt Bettina is my **favorite** aunt.*
Was ist dein **Liebling**sfilm? *What's your **favorite** film?*

3-4 Lieblingsverwandte. Answer your partner's questions about your favorite relative. You will find additional vocabulary to describe personal characteristics and personality traits under **Persönliche Merkmale** in the *Anhang* on page A21.

S1: Wer ist deine Lieblingsverwandte oder dein Lieblingsverwandter?

S2: Das ist meine Oma/Tante/ Kusine (*name of relative*). Das ist mein Opa/Onkel/Vetter (*name of relative*).

S1: Wie alt ist sie/er?

S2: Sie/Er ist …

S1: Warum ist sie/er deine Lieblingsverwandte/dein Lieblingsverwandter?

S2: Sie/Er …

ist immer freundlich	hat viel Fantasie	kocht gut	
ist immer optimistisch	hat viel Humor	bäckt° gut	*bakes*
ist so intelligent	versteht° meine Probleme	…	*understands*
ist so sportlich	lacht viel		

3-5 Lieblingsdinge. What are your partner's favorite things or activities? Write the information in the spaces provided and report your findings to the class.

S1: Was ist deine/dein Lieblings_____?

S2: Meine/Mein Lieblings_____ ist …

Lieblingsmusik (f) _____
Lieblingssport (m) _____
Lieblingssong (m) _____
Lieblingsfilm (m) _____
Lieblingsband (f) _____

Lieblingsfach (n) _____
Lieblingsbuch (n) _____
Lieblingsgetränk (n) _____
Lieblingsauto (n) _____
…

KULTUR

Österreich

WWW Visit an apartment building designed by Friedensreich Hundertwasser at www.prenhall.com/treffpunkt
→ Kapitel 3 → Web Resources → Kultur

Until World War I, **Österreich** was the center of the vast multinational Austro-Hungarian Empire, which included not only Austrians and Hungarians, but also many Slavic peoples. After the war, the German-speaking part of the empire became the Republic of Austria, only to be annexed by Nazi Germany in 1938. After World War II, Austria was occupied by the Allies, and in 1955 it again became an independent, democratic state. Austria now plays an active role in the peacekeeping efforts of the United Nations, and its capital, **Wien,** rivals Geneva as a center for international conferences and as the headquarters for international organizations. Because Austria has declared itself a neutral state, it is not a member of NATO. In 1995 Austria became a member of the **EU (Europäische Union)** and in 2002 it adopted the **Euro** as its currency. Its current population is about 8 million, 9% of whom are foreigners, primarily from former Yugoslavia.

Because of its beautiful alpine landscapes, Austria attracts over 19 million vacationers annually. It provides 3500 lifts for ski and snowboard enthusiasts and is a leader in alpine ski technology. Innsbruck was the site of the Winter Olympics twice in the last 50 years and Kitzbühel has hosted

Die Hundertwasserkirche in Bärnbach, Österreich

Am Grundlsee bei Salzburg

many World Cup ski events. In the summer, thousands of kilometers of trails attract hikers and mountain climbers.

Austria also has a rich cultural tradition. Haydn, Mozart, Schubert, and Johann Strauß were born there. Beethoven, although born in Germany, lived and worked in Vienna until his death. Today Vienna's glittering **Staatsoper** and its **Burgtheater,** and Salzburg's **Festspiele** (an annual summer festival featuring opera, drama, and concerts) and **Mozarteum** (a music and art academy) are synonymous with excellence to music and theater lovers throughout the world. Early twentieth-century Austrian artists such as the painter Gustav Klimt contributed to the **Jugendstil** (art nouveau) movement, which in turn influenced the Austrian artist and architect Friedensreich Hundertwasser.

In addition to creating richly colorful paintings and prints, Hundertwasser, an avid environmentalist, designed buildings that defied more traditional approaches to architecture.

With actors such as Klaus Maria Brandauer and Arnold Schwarzenegger, and directors like Billy Wilder (*Some Like It Hot*, starring Marilyn Monroe), Austrians and Austrian emigrants have made their mark on Hollywood. In Austria, Michael Haneke directed the award-winning film **Die Klavierspielerin** (English title: *The Piano Teacher*), based on a novel by Austrian writer Elfriede Jelinek, who won the Nobel Prize for literature in 2004. Jelinek's highly controversial work is sharply critical of many aspects of contemporary society. Another well-known Austrian author, experimental poet Ernst Jandl, wrote many **Sprechgedichte** (poems meant to be spoken) such as **harte vögel** below.

3-6 harte vögel. In this sound poem with the subtitle **für hitchcock,** Ernst Jandl uses acoustical and visual elements to convey a vivid impression of Alfred Hitchcock's famous horror movie *The Birds* **(Die Vögel).** In this film, birds of all kinds suddenly begin to attack people. The following questions will help you better understand the poem.

1. What is the connection between **harte** *(hard)* in the title and the word in the first line of the poem?
2. What is Jandl trying to accomplish acoustically by splitting **granit** into the syllables **gra** and **nit**?
3. What is Jandl trying to convey visually and acoustically by increasing the number of the two syllables from line to line?
4. Why do you think the poem is called **harte vögel?**

Now read the poem out loud as you think Ernst Jandl would have wanted you to read it.

harte vögel

für hitchcock

granit
gragranitnit
gragragranitnitnit
gragragragranitnitnitnit
gragragragragranitnitnitnitnit
gragragragragragranitnitnitnitnitnit
gragragragragragragranitnitnitnitnitnitnit
gragragragragragragragranitnitnitnitnitnitnitnit

Nomen

das Ding, -e	thing
die Fantasie	imagination
das Leben	life
der Liebling, -e	darling; favorite
die Reise, -n	trip

die Fantasie: Most nouns that end in **-ie** are feminine.

das Leben: This is an infinitive of a verb used as a noun. Such nouns are always neuter.

Die Familie

die Familie, -n	family
die Eltern (pl)	parents
die Mutter, ⸚	mother
die Stiefmutter, ⸚	stepmother
der Vater, ⸚	father
der Stiefvater, ⸚	stepfather
das Kind, -er	child
das Einzelkind, -er	only child
die Tochter, ⸚	daughter
der Sohn, ⸚e	son
die Schwester, -n	sister
der Bruder, ⸚	brother
die Geschwister (pl)	sisters and brothers, siblings
der/die Verwandte, -n	relative
die Großeltern (pl)	grandparents
die Großmutter, ⸚	grandmother
die Oma, -s	grandma
der Großvater, ⸚	grandfather
der Opa, -s	grandpa
der Enkel, -	grandson; grandchild
die Enkelin, -nen	granddaughter
die Tante, -n	aunt
der Onkel, -	uncle
die Kusine, -n	(female) cousin
der Vetter, -n	(male) cousin
die Nichte, -n	niece
der Neffe, -n	nephew

Stiefvater: How would you say *stepbrother* and *stepsister*?

Fahrzeuge

das Haustier, -e	pet
der Hund, -e	dog
die Katze, -n	cat
das Fahrzeug, -e	vehicle
das Auto, -s	} car
der Wagen, -	
der Bus, -se	bus
das Fahrrad, ⸚er	bicycle
das Rad, ⸚er	bike; wheel
das Motorrad, ⸚er	motorcycle
der Zug, ⸚e	train

Haustier: Tier is related to English *deer*. In Anglo-Saxon, the word for *beast* was **deor**. In German this meaning has been retained (**Tier** = *animal*). In English it has come to refer to a species of animal.

Der Computer

der Computer, -	computer
der Bildschirm, -e	monitor; screen
das CD-ROM-Laufwerk, -e	CD-ROM drive
der Drucker, -	printer
das DVD-Laufwerk, -e	DVD drive
die E-Mail, -s	} e-mail
die Mail, -s	
die E-Mail-Adresse, -n	e-mail address
die Festplatte, -n	hard drive
die Maus	mouse
das Notebook, -s	notebook (computer)
der Scanner, -	scanner
die Tastatur, -en	keyboard

Computer, E-Mail, Mail, Notebook, and **Scanner** are all pronounced as in English.

Verben

kennen	to know; to be acquainted with
lachen	to laugh
verdienen	to earn
verstehen	to understand

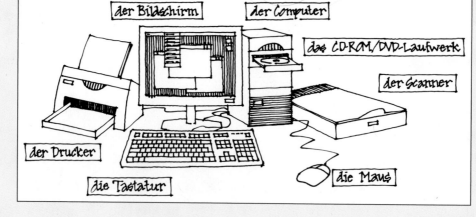

der Bildschirm   der Computer
das CD-ROM/DVD-Laufwerk
der Scanner
der Drucker
die Tastatur   die Maus

Computer: Another commonly used word for computer is **der Rechner, -.**

Andere Wörter

freundlich   friendly
geschieden   divorced

freundlich: As in English, the opposites of adjectives are sometimes formed by adding the prefix **un-**. What is the opposite of this adjective?

Das Gegenteil

interessant ≠ langweilig   interesting ≠ boring
schnell ≠ langsam   fast ≠ slow(ly)
verheiratet ≠ ledig   married ≠ single

Ausdrücke

viel zu viel   far too much
Was ist dein Lieblingsbuch?   What's your favorite book?

Leicht zu verstehen

die Bank, -en   **das Problem, -e**
der Direktor, -en   **klicken**
die Direktorin, -nen   **optimistisch**
der Humor   **pessimistisch**
der Partner, -
die Partnerin, -nen

Wörter im Kontext

3-7 Die Familie. What are the male or female counterparts?

1. die Kusine
2. die Schwester
3. die Großmutter
4. der Onkel
5. der Opa
6. der Vater
7. die Tochter
8. die Enkelin
9. der Neffe

3-8 Was passt wo?

Zug / Fahrräder / Fahrzeug / Motorräder / Wagen

1. Der BMW 735i ist ein sehr guter und sehr teurer _____.
2. _____ und _____ haben nur zwei Räder.
3. Ein Bus ist nicht so lang wie ein _____.
4. Welches _____ hat keinen Motor?

Wagen or **Auto** is used when talking about a personal vehicle. When referring to vehicles in general, **Pkw (Personenkraftwagen)** for a car and **Lkw (Lastkraftwagen)** for a truck are also common.

3-9 Das neue Notebook. Match the questions and responses appropriately.

1. Hast du jetzt auch ein Notebook?
2. Ist der Bildschirm gut?
3. Wie groß ist deine Festplatte?
4. Ist dein Notebook schnell?
5. Warum hast du denn ein DVD-Laufwerk?
6. Hast du einen guten Drucker?
7. Warum hast du einen Scanner?
8. Was ist deine E-Mail-Adresse?

a. Ja, sehr. Es hat 3,6 Gigahertz.
b. Ich scanne alle meine Fotos ein.
c. Ja, ich habe einen Laserdrucker.
d. Sie hat 400 Gigabyte.
e. Ja, und ich nehme es auch immer in die Vorlesungen.
f. Sie ist e.c.gruber@mdx.de
g. Ja, er ist sehr scharf und klar.
h. Meine Filme sind jetzt fast alle auf DVD.

3-9, f: Speakers of German jokingly refer to the @-sign (spoken like English *at*) as **Klammeraffe** (*spider monkey*). The tail of this monkey is longer than its body.

3-10 Was passt wo?

interessant / langweilig / schnell / langsam / optimistisch / pessimistisch

1. Daniel ist immer sehr _pessimistisch_ und hat oft Depressionen.
2. Laura lacht gern und ist immer _optimistisch_
3. _Langsam_, bitte! Ich verstehe noch nicht so gut Deutsch.
4. Ist das Buch _interessant_
   Nein, ich finde es sehr _langweilig_
5. Fahrräder fahren nicht so _schnell_ wie Motorräder.

nom der/das/die die
AKK

Kommunikation und Formen

❶ Answering *whom* or *what*

The direct object

You already know that a simple sentence consists of a noun or pronoun *subject* and a *predicate*. You also know that the predicate is whatever is said about the subject and that it consists of a verb or a verb plus other parts of speech.

One of the "other parts of speech" is often a noun or pronoun that is the target of what is expressed by the verb. This noun or pronoun is called the *direct object*. It answers the question *whom?* or *what?*

The boldfaced words in the following examples are the direct objects of the verbs.

subject	predicate		
	VERB	OTHER PARTS OF SPEECH	
Aunt Bettina	travels	a lot.	
She	visits	**exotic countries.**	(**What** does she visit?)
She	meets	**interesting people** there.	(**Whom** does she meet?)
Uncle Alfred	travels	very rarely.	
He	reads	only **the Financial Times.**	(**What** does he read?)
Nina and Robert	find	**him** awfully boring.	(**Whom** do they find boring?)

3-11 Onkel Alfred. Find the subjects and direct objects. Not every sentence has a direct object.

SUBJECT		DIRECT OBJECT
Mein Bruder Alfred	verdient	viel Geld.

Herr Ziegler sagt:
1. Kennen Sie meinen Bruder Alfred?
2. Er fährt einen großen Mercedes.
3. Er trägt teure Anzüge und er trinkt teure Weine.
4. Aber warum lacht mein Bruder fast nie?

Robert sagt:
1. Onkel Alfred hat keine Familie und keine Freunde.
2. Er liest immer Börsenberichte.
3. Er macht keinen Sport und macht auch keine Reisen.
4. Ich finde Onkel Alfred doof und sein Leben stinklangweilig.

The accusative case

The masculine forms of both the definite article (**der**) and the indefinite article (**ein**) change depending on whether the nouns they precede are the subject or the direct object of the verb.

SUBJECT FORMS

Der Pullover ist schön.
Ein Pullover ist teuer.

DIRECT OBJECT FORMS

Ich kaufe **den** Pullover.
Ich brauche° **einen** Pullover.   *need*

The neuter and feminine forms of the definite article (**das, die**) and of the indefinite article (**ein, eine**) remain unchanged, regardless of whether the nouns they precede are subjects or direct objects.

Das Sweatshirt ist schön.
Ein Sweatshirt ist teuer.

Ich kaufe **das** Sweatshirt.
Ich brauche **ein** Sweatshirt.

Die Jacke ist schön.
Eine Jacke ist teuer.

Ich kaufe **die** Jacke.
Ich brauche **eine** Jacke.

The plural form of the definite article (**die**) also remains unchanged.

Die Schuhe sind schön.

Ich kaufe **die** Schuhe.

You already know that subjects and subject completions are in the *nominative case*. Direct objects are in the *accusative case*.

nominative case	=	subject and subject completion
accusative case	=	direct object

	masculine	neuter	feminine	plural
NOMINATIVE	der ein }Rock kein	das ein }Kleid kein	die eine }Jacke keine	die — }Schuhe keine
ACCUSATIVE	den einen }Rock keinen	das ein }Kleid kein	die eine }Jacke keine	die — }Schuhe keine

Note that the only accusative forms that differ from the nominative are the masculine (**den, einen,** and **keinen**).

3-12 Karstadt oder C&A? Frau Ziegler needs the items listed on the next page but wants to save money. You know Karstadt's prices and your partner knows C&A's prices. Compare the prices for each item listed and decide where Frau Ziegler will get the better buy. The information for **S2** is in the *Anhang* on page A4.

S1: Wie viel kostet der Rock bei C&A?
S2: Wie viel kostet der Rock bei Karstadt?
S2: Wo kauft Frau Ziegler den Rock?
S2: Wie viel kostet das Kleid …

S2: Bei C&A kostet der Rock 90 Euro.
S1: Bei Karstadt kostet der Rock 80 Euro.
S1: Frau Ziegler kauft den Rock bei Karstadt.

KLEIDUNGSSTÜCK	PREIS BEI C&A	WAS KAUFT FRAU ZIEGLER WO?
der Rock		den Rock bei _____
das Kleid		das Kleid bei _____
die Jacke		die Jacke bei _____
die Bluse		die Bluse bei _____
der Mantel		den Mantel bei _____
das Sweatshirt		das Sweatshirt bei _____
die Schuhe		die Schuhe bei _____
der Gürtel		den Gürtel bei _____
die Socken		die Socken bei _____

 **3-13 Brauchst du das?**

▶

S1: Brauchst du einen Pullover?　　　**S2:** Ja, ich brauche einen Pullover.
　　　　　　　　　　　　　　　　　　　　　Nein, ich brauche keinen Pullover.

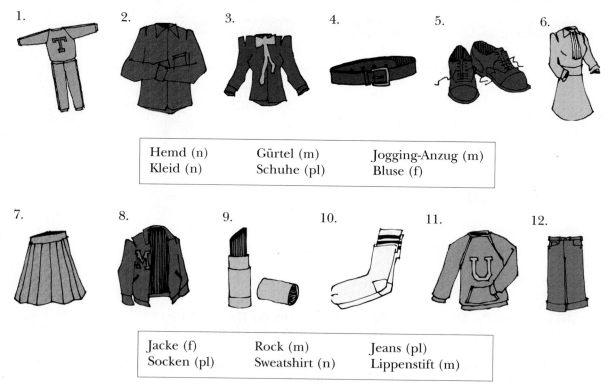

Hemd (n)	Gürtel (m)	Jogging-Anzug (m)
Kleid (n)	Schuhe (pl)	Bluse (f)

Jacke (f)	Rock (m)	Jeans (pl)
Socken (pl)	Sweatshirt (n)	Lippenstift (m)

3-14 Was für Klamotten° brauchst du und wo kaufst du sie?

Respond to your classmates' questions according to the model.

S1: Was für Klamotten brauchst du? **S2:** Ich brauche eine Jacke.
S1: Und wo kaufst du die Jacke? **S2:** Ich kaufe die Jacke bei Gap.
S2: Was für Klamotten brauchst du? **S3:** Ich brauche …

clothes

Klamotten: This is an informal expression originally used to describe shabby clothes. It is commonly used among students instead of **Kleider.**

The interrogative pronouns *wen* and *was*

The accusative forms of the interrogative pronouns are **wen** and **was.**

Wen besuchst du heute Abend? ***Whom*** *are you going to visit tonight?*
Was macht ihr heute Abend? ***What*** *are you doing tonight?*

	interrogative pronouns	
	PERSONS	THINGS OR IDEAS
NOMINATIVE	wer?	was?
ACCUSATIVE	wen?	was?

3-15 Was machst du? Complete each question with **wen** or **was.**

Your partner must choose an appropriate response.

S1:
1. _____ machst du am Wochenende?
   _____ besuchst du da?
   _____? Deine Freundin Maria?
   _____ macht Maria in Salzburg?

2. _____ machst du jetzt?
   _____ für eine Vorlesung? Biologie?
   Und _____ hast du für Physik?

S2:
Eine gute Freundin.
Ich fahre nach Salzburg.
Sie studiert dort am Mozarteum.
Ja, Maria Schneider.

Nein, Physik.
Den alten Professor Seidlmeyer.
Ich habe jetzt eine Vorlesung.

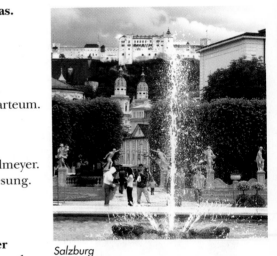

Salzburg

Der-words in the accusative case

In the accusative case, as in the nominative, the endings of **dieser** *(this)*, **jeder** *(each, every)*, and **welcher** *(which)* correspond closely to the forms of the definite article.

Ich verstehe **diesen** Satz nicht. *I don't understand **this** sentence.*
Welchen Satz meinst du? ***Which*** *sentence do you mean?*
Diesen Satz. Ich verstehe ***This*** *sentence. I understand*
   jedes Wort, aber nicht den Satz. ***every*** *word, but not the sentence.*

	masculine	neuter	feminine	plural
NOMINATIVE	dieser	dieses	diese	diese
ACCUSATIVE	diesen	dieses	diese	diese

Lerntipp: The only accusative form that differs from the nominative is **diesen (jeden, welchen).**

Jeden
Montag
neu!

Expressing time with the accusative case

To express definite points in time or duration of time, German often uses time phrases in the accusative case.

Ich fliege **diesen Freitag** nach Kanada.   *I'm flying to Canada this Friday.*
Ich bleibe **einen Monat** dort.   *I'll stay there for a month.*

3-16 Das Familienalbum. Nina and a friend are looking at the Ziegler family photo album. Supply the appropriate nominative or accusative endings.

SABINE: Wer ist denn dies___ elegante Frau?
NINA: Das ist meine Tante Bettina.
SABINE: Fährt sie dies___ tolle, rote Sportcoupé (n)?
NINA: Ja. – Hier ist sie in Australien. Sie macht jed___ Sommer (m) so eine
große Reise. – Dies___ Foto (n) zeigt° meine ganze Familie.
SABINE: Ist dies___ Mann hier dein Vater?
NINA: Nein, das ist mein langweiliger Onkel Alfred. Er liest jed___ Morgen (m)
dies___ blöden Börsenberichte (pl) und kauft fast jed___ Jahr (n) einen
neuen grauen Mercedes.
SABINE: Welch___ Mann ist dann dein Vater?
NINA: Dies___ große Mann hier.

shows

3-17 Meine Familie. Bring a family photo to class. Discuss your photo with a partner, using the previous activity as a guide.

Ein-words in the accusative case

You already know that the **ein**-words are **ein, kein,** and the possessive adjectives, and that all **ein**-words take the same endings. The chart below reviews the possessive adjectives.

possessive adjectives			
mein	my	**unser**	our
dein	your	**euer**	your
sein	his, its		
ihr	her, its	**ihr**	their
	Ihr	your	

Remember that just like the formal **Sie,** the formal **Ihr** is always capitalized.

Warum verkaufen Sie denn **Ihren**   *Why are you selling your*
Wagen, Herr Ziegler?   *car, Mr. Ziegler?*
Ich brauche **meinen** Wagen nicht   *I don't need my car any more.*
mehr. Ich nehme jetzt den Bus.   *I take the bus now.*

In the chart below, **mein** shows the nominative and accusative forms of *all* possessive adjectives.

	masculine	neuter	feminine	plural
NOMINATIVE	mein Freund	mein Auto	meine Freundin	meine Eltern
ACCUSATIVE	meinen Freund	mein Auto	meine Freundin	meine Eltern

Lerntipp: The only accusative form that differs from the nominative is **meinen (deinen, seinen, ihren, unseren, euren, ihren, Ihren)**

Remember that when an ending is added to **euer** *(your)*, the **e** before the **r** is dropped: **eure, euren.**

Warum verkauft ihr **euren** Wagen?   *Why are you selling **your** car?*

3-18 Besuche. Complete the sentences with the proper forms of **sein, ihr,** and **unser** and the appropriate forms of **machen** and **besuchen.**

▶ … Frau Ziegler heute?   Sie … Schwester.

S1: Was macht Frau Ziegler heute?   **S2:** Sie besucht ihre Schwester.

1. … Nina heute Abend?   Sie … Lieblingstante.
2. … Robert morgen Nachmittag?   Er … langweiligen Onkel Alfred.
3. … Oma Ziegler am Wochenende?   Sie … Sohn Klaus.
4. … Alexander heute Abend?   Er … Freundin Nina.
5. … Bergers nächstes Wochenende?   Sie … Tochter Claudia in München.
6. … ihr am Sonntag?   Wir … Großmutter.
7. … Zieglers im August?   Sie … Freunde in Amerika.
8. … ihr im Sommer?   Wir … Onkel Karl.

3-19 Wen besuchst du? Ask whether your partner is planning to visit someone.

S1: Besuchst du heute Abend jemand°?

S2: Ja, ich besuche mein__ …
(Nein, ich besuche niemand°.)
Und du? Besuchst du heute Abend jemand?

someone / no one

am Wochenende / an Thanksgiving / nächsten Sommer

3-20 Warum denn? Why are these people selling the things mentioned? **S1** completes the questions with the proper forms of **dein, euer,** or **Ihr. S2** responds appropriately.

S1:

1. Warum verkaufen Sie denn _____ Kamera (f)?
2. Warum verkauft ihr denn _____ Fahrräder (pl)?
3. Warum verkaufst du denn _____ Keyboard (n)?
4. Warum verkaufen Sie denn _____ Wagen (m)?
5. Warum verkauft ihr denn _____ Haus (n)?
6. Warum verkaufst du denn _____ Videokassettenrecorder (m)?

S2:

Ich spiele viel lieber Gitarre.
Ich kaufe nächste Woche einen DVD-Recorder.
Ich nehme jetzt immer den Bus.
Wir haben jetzt einen Wagen.
Ich mache jetzt nur noch Videos.
Es ist viel zu klein für unsere große Familie.

Warum sind Häuser „Immobilien"?

Haben versus sein

      Müllers haben **einen** Esel.   *The Müllers have a donkey.*

In the example above, the noun **Esel** answers the question *What do the Müllers have?* **Esel** is the direct object and is therefore in the accusative case. The verb **haben** always takes an accusative object.

      Günter ist **ein** Esel.   *Günter is a nitwit.*

In this example, **Esel** also answers the question *what?* But here **Esel** is used to describe *what Günter is* and is therefore a subject completion that appears in the nominative case after the verb **sein.**

Der Citroën 2CV heißt auch „Ente".

dummy

3-21 Immer negativ.

   ▶   haben / du / Wagen (m)

S1: Hast du einen Wagen?   **S2:** Nein, ich habe keinen Wagen.

1. sein / Daniel / guter Student (m)
2. haben / Monika / Freund (m)
3. sein / Daniel / Dummkopf° (m)
4. haben / Müllers / Kinder (pl)
5. sein / Herr Müller / guter Automechaniker (m)
6. haben / Müllers / Mercedes (m)
7. sein / Frau Müller / gute Hausfrau (f)
8. haben / du / Motorrad (n)
9. sein / Müllers Hund / Foxterrier (m)
10. haben / ihr / Hund (m)

3-22 Was hast du alles? Ask each other questions as in the example.

S1: Hast du einen Wagen?

S1: Was für einen Wagen hast du?
S1: Hast du ein Motorrad (ein Fahrrad, einen Hund, eine Katze)?

S2: Ja, ich habe einen Wagen.
(Nein, ich habe keinen Wagen.)
Ich habe einen . . .

■ Sprachnotiz ·····································

Omission of articles

Omission of the indefinite article

When stating someone's membership in a specific group (e.g., nationality, place of residence, occupation, or religious affiliation), German does not use the indefinite article.

    Maria ist **Österreicherin.**   *Maria is **an** Austrian.*
    Ich bin **Berliner.**   *I am **a** Berliner.*
    Kurt ist **Koch.**   *Kurt is **a** cook.*
    Melanie ist **Methodistin.**   *Melanie is **a** Methodist.*

Remember that **die Deutsche** is one of the few designations of nationality for a female that is not formed by adding **-in.** Another is **die Israeli** (masculine: **der Israeli**).

Omission of the definite article

When naming a musical instrument after **spielen,** German does not use the definite article before the name of the instrument.

    Ich spiele **Klavier** und **Flöte.**   *I play **the** piano and **the** flute.*

Hören

Jennifer Winklers Familie

Jennifer Winkler is an American student studying at the **Christian-Albrechts-Universität** in Kiel. She is being interviewed by a student reporter for the newsletter published by the **Auslandsamt** of the university.

NEUE VOKABELN

Norddeutschland	*Northern Germany*
mütterlicherseits	*on my mother's side*
Er ist Koch von Beruf.	*He is a cook by trade.*
Er wird Koch.	*He is going to be a cook.*

3-23 Erstes Verstehen. Listen to the interview and choose the correct responses.

1. Which names are mentioned?
   Karl   Oliver   Thomas   Kurt   Jennifer   Erika

2. What cities are mentioned?
   Salzburg   Flensburg   Kiel   Köln   East Lansing

3. Which words describing family relationships do you hear?
   Verwandte   Eltern   Mutter   Vater   Großeltern   Großmutter
   Geschwister   Schwester   Bruder   Onkel

4. How many grandparents does Jennifer still have in Germany?
   1   2   3   4

5. How many children do Jennifer's parents have?
   1   2   3   4

3-24 Detailverstehen. Listen to the interview again and write answers to the following questions.

1. Warum studiert Jennifer in Kiel?
2. Wo in Deutschland ist Flensburg?
3. Was machen Jennifers Eltern in Amerika?
4. Was wird Jennifers Bruder Kurt und wo lernt er das?
5. Wer sind die drei Köche in Jennifers Familie?
6. Was macht Jennifers Bruder Thomas?

Before you begin listening, locate Kiel and Flensburg on the map inside the front cover. Kiel (pop. 250,000) is an important port on the **Ostsee,** and the site of the **Kieler Woche,** a week of regattas and sailing competitions. The **Christian-Albrechts-Universität zu Kiel,** which has about 23,000 students, takes its name from **Herzog** (*Duke)* **Christian Albrecht von Schleswig-Holstein-Gottorf,** who founded it in 1665, just seven years after the end of the Thirty Years War. The seal of the university (below) symbolizes peace, as does the motto **Pax optima rerum** (*Peace is the best of all things).* The woman on the seal is nicknamed **Christine** (a feminine form of **Christian**) by students. Note the Latin equivalent of **Kiel** (here in the genitive case).

You can write about cousins, aunts, and uncles if you have no **Geschwister.**

 **3-25 Meine Familie.** Describe your family using the following questions as a guide. You will find vocabulary for **Jobs und Berufe** and **Hobbys und Sport** in the *Anhang* on pages A17 and A18.

1 sis 1 Bro

Wie heißen deine Eltern? Sam und Deb   Wie viele Geschwister hast du?

Wie alt sind sie?   Wie heißen sie?

Wo wohnen sie?   engineer Wie alt sind sie?

Was sind sie von Beruf? Vater ist   Wo wohnen sie?

home   Was machen sie?

Remember: In German the names of cars are masculine.

Was für Hobbys haben sie? maker

Was für einen Wagen fahren sie?   …

Haben sie einen Hund oder eine Katze? ✓

…

Again, you can substitute cousins, aunts, and uncles if you have no **Schwestern** or **Brüder.**

3-26 Deine Familie. Using the questions from the activity above, find out about your partner's family. Write the information in the chart and report your findings to the class.

	NAME UND ALTER	WOHNORT	BERUF	HOBBYS
Vater	_____	_____	_____	_____
Mutter	_____	_____	_____	_____
Schwestern	_____	_____	_____	_____
	_____	_____	_____	_____
Brüder	_____	_____	_____	_____
	_____	_____	_____	_____

❷ Describing people, places, and things

Accusative endings of adjectives preceded by *der*-words

	masculine	neuter	feminine	plural
NOMINATIVE	der neue Drucker	das teure Notebook	die große Festplatte	die tollen CDs
ACCUSATIVE	den neuen Drucker	das teure Notebook	die große Festplatte	die tollen CDs

- In the masculine accusative singular, the ending of an adjective preceded by a **der**-word is **-en**.

- The other accusative endings are identical to those in the nominative.

- Adjectives that end in **-er** or **-el** drop the **e** when they take an ending (**teu*er***: **den teu*ren* Drucker; dunk*el*: das dunk*le* Sofa).

CHRISTA:	Welch**en** Drucker kaufst du, **den** teur**en** oder **den** billig**en**?	*Which printer are you going to buy, the expensive one or the cheap one?*
ANNA:	Ich glaube, ich kaufe **den** billig**en**.	*I think I'm going to buy the cheap one.*

3-27 Im Kaufhaus.

▶ das Sofa, hell, dunkel

S1: Welches Sofa kaufst du, das helle oder das dunkle?

S2: Ich glaube, ich kaufe das dunkle.

1. die Schuhe (pl), braun, schwarz
2. das Armband°, golden, silbern   *bracelet*
3. der iPod, teuer, billig
4. der CD-Spieler, japanisch, deutsch
5. die Weingläser (pl), billig, teuer
6. der Teppich°, dunkel, hell   *carpet*
7. das Fahrrad, deutsch, italienisch

3-28 Im Kleidergeschäft. You need a few new items in your wardrobe, but you don't have a lot of money.

▶ der Rock, die Röcke

S1: Wie viel kosten diese beiden Röcke?

S1: Ja, dann nehme ich den blauen.

S2: Der blaue Rock kostet vierzig Euro und der rote fünfundfünfzig.

1. die Jacke, die Jacken

2. der Mantel, die Mäntel

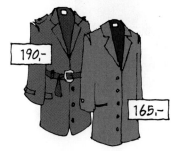

3. das Sweatshirt, die Sweatshirts

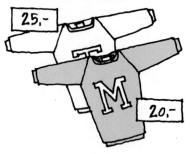

4. der Pullover, die Pullover

5. das Hemd, die Hemden

6. die Hose, die Hosen

Accusative endings of adjectives preceded by *ein*-words

	masculine	neuter	feminine	plural
NOMINATIVE	ein neuer Drucker	ein teures Notebook	eine große Festplatte	meine tollen CDs
ACCUSATIVE	einen neuen Drucker	ein teures Notebook	eine große Festplatte	meine tollen CDs

- In the masculine accusative singular, the ending of an adjective preceded by an **ein**-word is **-en.**

- The other accusative endings are identical to those in the nominative.

- Remember that wherever the **ein**-word has no ending, the adjective itself shows the gender and case of the noun by taking the appropriate **der**-word ending: dies**er** Drucker, **ein** neu**er** Drucker; dies**es** Notebook, **ein** teur**es** Notebook.

VERKÄUFER:	Möchten Sie ein**en** teur**en** oder ein**en** preisgünstig**en** Drucker?	*Would you like an expensive or an inexpensive printer?*
HERR KUHN:	Ich möchte ein**en** preisgünstig**en.**	*I would like an inexpensive one.*

3-29 Im Elektronikgeschäft.

▶ das Handy, grau, schwarz

S1: Möchten Sie ein graues oder ein schwarzes Handy? **S2:** Ich möchte ein graues.

1. die Kamera, professionell, semiprofessionell
2. der DVD-Spieler, schwarz, silbergrau
3. das Notebook, teuer, preisgünstig
4. die Tastatur, deutsch, englisch
5. der Bildschirm, groß, klein
6. die Computerspiele (pl), kompliziert, einfach°   *easy*
7. DVD-Laufwerk, intern, extern

@ NOTEBOOKS
@ LASERDRUCKER
SERVER
MARKEN-PC'S
AN-
VERKAUF
@ MONITORE
@ SOFTWARE

3-30 Im Kleidergeschäft. You are in a clothing store and the salesperson keeps showing you things in colors you don't want.

▶ das T-Shirt, preisgünstig, blau   blau, rot

S1: Hier ist ein preisgünstiges blaues T-Shirt. **S2:** Aber ich möchte kein blaues T-Shirt, ich möchte ein rotes.

1. die Jacke, schön, braun   braun, grau
2. der Mantel, toll, schwarz   schwarz, dunkelblau
3. das Polohemd, sportlich, blau   blau, weiß
4. der Pullover, elegant, schwarz   schwarz, grau
5. das Sweatshirt, praktisch, grün   grün, weinrot
6. die Hose, schick, braun   braun, schwarz

3-31 Was trägt Lisa? Using adjectives from each of the two groups below, write descriptions of what two of your classmates are wearing today. Then read your descriptions to the class. Express shades of color by adding **dunkel-** or **hell-** . You will find a list of **Kleidungsstücke** in the *Anhang* on page A19.

S: Lisa trägt einen wunderschönen dunkelroten Pulli und einen langen schwarzen Rock. David trägt …

cool	praktisch	blau	rosarot
elegant	schick	braun	rot
interessant	schön	gelb	schwarz
kurz	toll	grau	violett
lang	sportlich	grün	weiß

Accusative endings of unpreceded adjectives

	masculine	neuter	feminine	plural
NOMINATIVE	guter Kaffee	gutes Bier	gute Salami	gute Oliven
ACCUSATIVE	gut**en** Kaffee	gutes Bier	gute Salami	gute Oliven

- In the masculine accusative singular, the ending of an unpreceded adjective is **-en.**
- The other accusative endings are identical to those in the nominative.

server KELLNER°: Möchten Sie lieber schottisch**en** oder kanadisch**en** Lachs?

Would you rather have Scottish or Canadian salmon?

guest GAST°: Heute esse ich mal kanadisch**en** Lachs.

Today I'm going to eat Canadian salmon for a change.

3-32 Im Hotel. Use **essen** or **trinken** in the responses to the server's questions.

▶ Wein (m), italienisch, spanisch

KELLNERIN: Möchten Sie lieber italienischen oder spanischen Wein?

GAST: Heute trinke ich mal spanischen Wein.

1. Oliven (pl), griechisch, türkisch
2. Salami (f), italienisch, ungarisch
3. Bier (n), bayrisch, australisch
4. Käse (m), holländisch, französisch
5. Mineralwasser (n), deutsch, italienisch
6. Tee (m), chinesisch, indisch
7. Kaffee (m), arabisch, kolumbianisch

Seit 1989

LIBERTY PIZZA®

Original amerikanische Pizza

❸ Word order

More on the position of *nicht*

Nicht usually follows the direct object.

> Mein Freund kennt den Film *Good Bye, Lenin!* **nicht.**
> Warum verstehen meine Eltern meine Probleme **nicht?**
> Ich glaube, ich kaufe den Scanner **nicht.**

Remember that nouns preceded by the indefinite article **ein** or nouns without an article are negated with **kein.**

Hast du **einen** Bruder?	Nein, ich habe **keinen** Bruder.
Hast du Geschwister?	Nein, ich habe **keine** Geschwister.

Remember, when you want to negate a particular word or expression, you place **nicht** directly before this word or expression.

adjectives	Ich finde diesen Artikel **nicht interessant.**
	Meine Tante ist **nicht verheiratet.**
adverbs	Mein Onkel lacht **nicht oft.**
	Ich koche **nicht gern.**
prepositional phrases	Meine Eltern fliegen diesen Sommer **nicht nach Europa.**
	Heute Abend gehen wir mal **nicht in die Disco,** sondern ins Kino.
subject completions	Rot ist **nicht meine Lieblingsfarbe.**
	Ich heiße **nicht Müller.**
direct objects	Ich kaufe den Computer, aber **nicht den Scanner.**

3-33 Immer negativ!

S1: Kennst du diese Familie?   **S2:** Nein, ich kenne diese Familie nicht.

1. Kaufen Zieglers dieses Haus?   Nein, sie …
2. Ist Roberts Schwester immer so optimistisch?   Nein, sie …
3. Hat Roberts Kusine Geschwister?   Nein, sie …
4. Reist Ninas Tante diesen Sommer nach Japan?   Nein, sie …, sondern nach China.
5. Kaufen Zieglers diesen Hund?   Nein, sie …
6. Verdient Jennifers Vater viel Geld?   Nein, er …
7. Haben Jennifers Verwandte ein großes Haus?   Nein, sie …
8. Kennst du Jennifers Vetter?   Nein, ich …
9. Verstehen Jennifers Eltern ihre Probleme?   Nein, sie …
10. Gehst du heute Abend ins Kino?   Nein, ich …, sondern ins Konzert.

3-34 Ja oder nein? Be sure to answer your partner's questions in complete sentences.

1. Hast du viele Geschwister?
2. Leben deine Eltern hier in *(name of college town)?*
3. Wohnst du im Studentenheim?
4. Hast du einen Wagen?
5. Schreibst du viele E-Mails?
6. Kochst du gern?
7. Sammelst du Briefmarken?
8. Gehst du oft ins Konzert?
9. Gehst du heute Abend ins Kino?
10. Kennst du den Film *Lola rennt?*
...

❹ Expressing actions in the present and future

Verbs with stem-vowel changes in the present tense

Some German verbs have a stem-vowel change in the **du**-form and in the **er/es/sie**-form of the present tense. Note that the stem vowel changes *only* in the **du**-form and in the **er/es/sie**-form.

e → i	e → ie	a → ä	au → äu
SPRECHEN	LESEN	FAHREN	LAUFEN
ich spreche	ich lese	ich fahre	ich laufe
du sprichst	du liest	du fährst	du läufst
er/es/sie spricht	er/es/sie liest	er/es/sie fährt	er/es/sie läuft
wir sprechen	wir lesen	wir fahren	wir laufen
ihr sprecht	ihr lest	ihr fahrt	ihr lauft
sie/Sie sprechen	sie/Sie lesen	sie/Sie fahren	sie/Sie laufen

In vocabularies, verbs with these stem vowel changes are usually listed as follows:

sprechen (spricht)	*to speak*
fahren (fährt)	*to drive*

Verbs with stem-vowel change from e → i or ie

essen	*to eat*	ich esse	du **isst**	er **isst**
geben	*to give*	ich gebe	du **gibst**	er **gibt**
lesen	*to read*	ich lese	du **liest**	er **liest**
nehmen	*to take*	ich nehme	du **nimmst**	er **nimmt**
sehen	*to see*	ich sehe	du **siehst**	er **sieht**
sprechen	*to speak*	ich spreche	du **sprichst**	er **spricht**
versprechen	*to promise*	ich verspreche	du **versprichst**	er **verspricht**
werden	*to become; to get; to be*	ich werde	du **wirst**	er **wird**

3-35 Was passt? In the chart on the previous page, find the appropriate verb for each sentence. Insert it in the correct form. Then substitute the subjects in parentheses, changing the verb form accordingly.

1. Peter _____ morgen zweiundzwanzig. (ich, du, meine Mitbewohnerin)
2. Stephanie _____ sehr gut Deutsch. (ihr, Sie, du)
3. _____ du immer den Bus zur Uni? (ihr, Stephanie, Sie)
4. Ich _____ viel zu viel Schokolade. (du, ihr, Nina)
5. Mein Vater _____ jeden Morgen die Zeitung. (ich, wir, Frau Ziegler)
6. Welchen Film _____ ihr heute Abend? (wir, du, Martin und Claudia)
7. Claudia und Stephanie _____ morgen Abend eine Party. (ich, Günter, wir)
8. _____ ihr, zu kommen? (du, Sie)

■ Sprachnotiz ·····························

The expression *es gibt*

From the verb **geben** comes the expression **es gibt**. Its English equivalent is *there is* or *there are*. **Es gibt** always has an accusative object.

Heute **gibt es** keinen Pudding zum Nachtisch.	*Today **there is** no pudding for dessert.*
Wie viele McDonald's **gibt es** in Hamburg?	*How many McDonald's **are there** in Hamburg?*

Two common expressions using **es gibt: Was gibt's?** *(What's up?)* and **Was gibt's Neues?** *(What's new?)*

3-36 Was für eine Touristenattraktion gibt es in ...? Match the locations with the appropriate attractions.

1. In San Francisco gibt es
2. In Arizona gibt es
3. In Japan gibt es
4. In Wyoming gibt es
5. In Ägypten gibt es
6. In Paris gibt es
7. In Indien gibt es

a. den Fudschijama
b. die Pyramiden
c. den Eiffelturm
d. die Golden Gate Brücke
e. das Taj Mahal
f. den Yellowstone Nationalpark
g. den Grand Canyon

3-37 Hier gibt es ... Working in small groups, make a list of at least five attractions in your university/college town. Then present your list to the class, and include appropriate adjectives to describe the attraction, e.g., **In** *(name of town)* **gibt es ein tolles chinesisches Restaurant, einen fantastichen Zoo, ein erstklassiges Sinfonieorchester,** etc.

Es gibt
sie noch,
die guten
Dinge.

Verbs with stem-vowel change from *a* → *ä* or *au* → *äu*

backen	to bake	ich backe	du **bäckst**	er **bäckt**
fahren	to drive	ich fahre	du **fährst**	er **fährt**
halten	to hold; to stop; to keep	ich halte	du **hältst**	er **hält**
lassen	to let; to leave	ich lasse	du **lässt**	er **lässt**
schlafen	to sleep	ich schlafe	du **schläfst**	er **schläft**
tragen	to wear	ich trage	du **trägst**	er **trägt**
waschen	to wash	ich wasche	du **wäschst**	er **wäscht**
laufen	to run	ich laufe	du **läufst**	er **läuft**

3-38 Was passt? In the chart above, find the appropriate verb for each sentence. Insert it in the correct form. Then substitute the subjects in parentheses, changing the verb form accordingly.

1. Was für einen Wagen _____ du? (Sie, dein Vater, ihr)
2. In wie viel Sekunden _____ du die hundert Meter? (ihr, Sie, Alexander)
3. Warum _____ Müllers den Hund nicht ins Haus? (du, ihr, Sie)
4. Oma Ziegler _____ echt gute Kuchen°. (ihr, du, ich) — *cakes*
5. _____ du jeden Sonntagmorgen bis halb zwölf? (ihr, Sie, Robert)
6. Warum _____ du denn schon wieder die Haare? (Nina, Sie, ihr)
7. _____ Sie lieber Pullover oder Sweatshirts? (du, ihr, Peter)
8. Warum _____ der Bus hier? (du, ihr, der Zug)

3-39 Ein Samstagnachmittag bei Zieglers. Complete the sentences with the appropriate words from the list.

backen / fahren / waschen / essen / werden / schlafen / lesen / halten

1. Nina *isst* einen Apfel und *liest* ein Buch.
2. Oma Ziegler *backt* einen Kuchen, denn Nina _____ morgen siebzehn.
3. Frau Ziegler ist im Bett und *schläft*
4. Dann geht Frau Ziegler joggen, denn Joggen *halten* fit.
5. Herr Ziegler und Robert *waschen* den Wagen.
6. Dann *fährt* Herr Ziegler in die Stadt.

3-40 Herr Ziegler kritisiert heute alles!

sprechen / laufen / halten / nehmen / geben / versprechen / lassen / tragen

1. Warum _____ du denn keine Brokkoli, Robert?
2. Warum _____ es denn heute keinen Nachtisch?
3. Warum _____ ihr denn nicht ein bisschen lauter, Kinder?
4. Warum _____ denn das Wasser im Badezimmer°? — *bathroom*
5. Warum _____ du denn immer dieses blöde T-Shirt, Nina?
6. Warum _____ ihr denn mitten im Winter das Fenster° offen, Kinder? — *window*
7. Warum _____ Politiker so viel und _____ es fast nie?

Photo: **Händler** = *dealer*

3-41 Was machen diese Leute?

S1: Was macht Tanja?   **S2:** Sie läuft Ski.

▶ … Ski.

1. Was macht Helga?

… ein Bad.

2. Was macht Ralf?

… sein Motorrad.

3. Was macht Frau Schneider?

… ein Buch.

4. Was macht Charlyce?

… mit Bernd.

5. Was macht Günter?

… alles doppelt.

6. Was macht Herr Lukasik?

… seinen Wagen.

7. Was macht Tina?

… einen Apfel.

8. Was macht Monika?

…

3-42 Was machen diese Leute gern? Was machen sie lieber? The information for **S2** is in the *Anhang* on page A5.

S1: Isst Maria gern Spaghetti?
S2: Isst Thomas gern Nudeln?
S1: Essen Tina und Lisa gern Hotdogs?

S2: Nein, sie isst lieber Makkaroni.
S1: Ja, er isst sehr gern Nudeln.
S2: Nein, sie essen lieber Pizza.

		MARIA	THOMAS	TINA UND LISA
ESSEN		Spaghetti?		Hotdogs?
			Ja, …	
LESEN			Zeitungen?	
		Nein, … Krimis.		Ja, …
SEHEN			Dokumentarfilme?	Sportreportagen?
		Nein, … Komödien.		
SPRECHEN		Spanisch?		Deutsch?
			Nein, … Englisch.	
FAHREN			Auto?	
		Ja, …		Ja, …
TRAGEN		Jeans?		
			Nein, … Sweatshirts.	Nein, … lange Hosen.

3-43 Ein Interview. Interview your partner and report your findings to the class.

Was isst du gern?

Was liest du gern?

TV programs Welche Fernsehprogramme° siehst du gern?

languages Wie viele Sprachen° sprichst du? Welche?

Was für einen Wagen fährst du?

Was für Kleider trägst du gern?

Wie lange schläfst du denn am Wochenende?

MO 6. März
20.40 ARTE

Good bye, Lenin!
TRAGIKOMÖDIE
(D, 2002) mit Daniel Brühl –
Alex' Mutter fällt kurz vor
der Wende ins Koma.
Um ihr schwaches Herz
nach dem Erwachen zu
schonen, gaukelt er ihr
eine real existierende
DDR vor.

DI 7. März
20.15 SAT 1

**UEFA
Champions-League**
FUSSBALL
Achtelfinale – Rückspiel:
Juventus Turin – Werder
Bremen. SAT 1 entscheidet
kurzfristig, ob das heutige
Spiel oder die Partie der
Bayern morgen übertragen
wird.

DO 9. März
20.15 VOX

The Beach
ABENTEUER
(USA, 1999) mit Leonardo
DiCaprio – Rucksack-Tourist
Richard sucht mit dem
Pärchen Etienne und
Françoise eine abgelegene
thailändische Insel auf.
Das vermeintliche Paradies
wird zur Hölle auf Erden …

Average births per woman between 1995–2000: Germany, 1.3; Austria, 1.4; Switzerland, 1.5; Canada, 1.6; U.S., 2.0. Why do you think governments would be concerned about low birthrates?

www Find out more about the **Bundesministerium für Familie, Senioren, Frauen und Jugend** at www.prenhall.com/treffpunkt
→ Kapitel 3 → Web Resources
→ Kultur

INFOBOX

Deutschland wird familienfreundlich

Recent statistics show that 80 percent of young people in Germany would like to have children, yet Germany has the lowest birthrate in Europe and the highest percentage of childlessness in the world. In response, the government has passed legislation to make it easier for couples to start a family and have more children. Parents receive support to help ease the financial burden of raising children (**Kindergeld** and **Erziehungsgeld**), and both parents can take leave from their jobs or reduce their working hours without fear of being fired (**Elternzeit**). While the number of fathers taking leave has increased over the past several years, the onus of child-rearing still rests primarily on mothers. Women are increasingly unwilling to forfeit their career aspirations in order to have a family. The **Bundesministerium für Familie, Senioren, Frauen und Jugend** therefore launched an extensive campaign to provide even more support to working parents. One goal is to increase the quantity and quality of day care facilities. Another is to make industry more **familienfreundlich.** In the program **Allianz für die Familie,** government, business, and research organizations are working together to develop models like flexible work schedules, in-house day care facilities, and vacation day camps.

Zusammenschau

🖥 Video-Treff ·····································

Meine Familie

Maiga, Stefan Meister, Anja Peter, Thomas, André, and Karen talk about their families.

Zum besseren Verstehen

3-44 Was ist das auf Englisch?

1. Meine Eltern leben seit drei Jahren **getrennt.**
2. Mein Bruder geht in **die 11. Klasse.**
3. Mein Vater hat ein **Segelboot.**
4. Ich habe eine **supersüße** Nichte.
5. Meine Eltern haben ein schönes Haus **in einer tollen Gegend.**
6. Sie wohnen jetzt **außerhalb von** Berlin.
7. Meine Schwester **macht** ihre Klamotten **selber.**
8. Ich habe zwei Halbgeschwister; wir haben alle drei **unterschiedliche** Mütter.
9. Ich habe eine **ältere** Schwester.

a. sailboat
b. in a great area
c. different
d. makes … herself
e. eleventh grade
f. separated
g. older
h. outside of
i. very sweet

Mein Vater hat ein Segelboot.

Now watch the video and complete the post-viewing activities in the *Video-Treff* section of the *Student Activities Manual.*

Be sure to read the statements in
3-45 before you begin listening.

Wie erkennen wir einander?

Before Stephanie arrived in **München** in mid-October, she spent two weeks
visiting relatives in **Köln**. In the conversation you are about to hear,
Stephanie is calling from Chicago to make arrangements to have her
cousins Michael and Martina, whom she has never met, pick her up at the
international airport in **Düsseldorf**.

NEUE VOKABELN

mich	*me*	**die Flugnummer**	*flight number*
das Flugzeug	*airplane*	**ganz kurz**	*very short*
zum Flughafen	*to the airport*	**erkennen**	*to recognize*
übermorgen	*the day after tomorrow*		

3-45 Erstes Verstehen. In which sequence do you hear the following
statements and questions?

_____ Nein, meine Haare sind jetzt kurz und blond.
_____ Na, dann tschüss bis übermorgen, Stephanie, und gute Reise.
_____ Dann bist du übermorgen in Deutschland.
_____ Martina! Was trägst du übermorgen?
_____ Hier spricht deine Kusine Stephanie aus Chicago.
_____ Ja, wie erkennen wir einander dann?

3-46 Detailverstehen. Listen to the telephone conversation again and
write responses to the following questions.

1. Was ist Michaels Familienname?
2. Wann fahren Stephanie und ihr Vater zum Flughafen?
3. Wie kommen Michael und Martina zum Flughafen in Düsseldorf?
4. Wer ist blond und wer ist brünett?
5. Wer hat ganz kurze Haare und wer hat lange Haare?
6. Wer kommt übermorgen in Blau, wer in Weiß und wer in Schwarz?

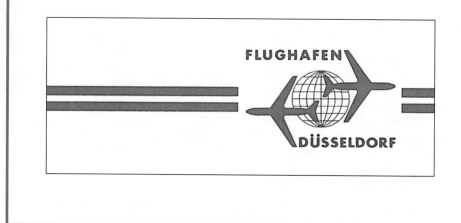

■ Schreiben und Sprechen ·······················

3-47 Wer ist das? Describe the style and color of a classmate's hair and clothing. Useful descriptive adjectives are given below. Be sure to attach the correct endings. The rest of the class then guesses whom you are describing.

S: Sie hat lange, blonde Haare. Sie trägt ein schönes, gelbes T-Shirt, einen langen, dunkelblauen Rock, weiße Socken und weiße Tennisschuhe. Wer ist das?

HAARE
- lang, kurz, glatt°, lockig°, wellig°   *straight / curly / wavy*
- blond, brünett, rot, schwarz …

Sie/Er hat _____e, _____e Haare.

KLEIDER
- lang, kurz, groß, klein, elegant, schick, schön, toll, hübsch
- blau, grün, orangefarben, rot, rosarot, schwarz, hellblau, dunkelrot …

Sie/Er trägt   einen   _____en, _____en Pullover (Rock, Mantel, Gürtel)

            ein   _____es, _____es Polohemd (T-Shirt, Sweatshirt, Kleid)

            eine   _____e, _____e Hose (Jogginghose, Jacke, Bluse)

                     _____e, _____e Jeans (Shorts, Socken, Schuhe, Sandalen)

3-48 Eine Personenbeschreibung. Use as many adjectives as possible to describe a family member or a friend. Use the questions below and the information in the previous activity to guide you.

Wie heißt die Person?
Wie alt ist sie/er?
Ist sie/er eine Verwandte/ein Verwandter oder eine gute Freundin/ ein guter Freund?
Welche Farbe haben ihre/seine Augen? *Sie/Er hat _____ Augen.*
Was für Haare hat sie/er?
Was für Kleider trägt sie/er gern?

Schreibtipp: This writing task focuses on visual information. Before you write, take the time to form a mental picture of the person you want to describe. You can also use a photo or draw a quick sketch, and then jot down words and phrases that describe what you see, labeling articles of clothing, colors, lengths, sizes, etc. Then write complete sentences based on your notes.

Eine Berliner Familie

📖 Lesen ···

Zum besseren Verstehen

3-49 Klassische Musik.

1. Have you ever listened to classical music?
2. Do you have a favorite composer of classical music?
3. What do you know about Mozart?

3-50 Was ist das auf Englisch?

1. Leopold Mozart ist Violinist im Orchester **des Erzbischofs** von Salzburg.
2. Sein Sohn Wolfgang ist ein musikalisches **Wunderkind.**
3. In Salzburg ist Wolfgang nur ein **schlecht bezahlter** Musiker.
4. In Wien verdient Wolfgang viel Geld und lebt **wie ein König.**
5. Er braucht viel **mehr** Geld **als** er verdient.
6. Er macht **Schulden,** denn er braucht viel mehr Geld als er verdient.
7. Mozart arbeitet **fieberhaft** und verdient jedes Jahr mehr.

   a. debts
   b. like a king
   c. feverishly
   d. poorly paid
   e. child prodigy
   f. of the archbishop
   g. more . . . than

Note that **genial** does not mean *genial*. It is the adjective form of the noun **Genie** (*genius*).

Mozart „verkauft" Mozartkugeln.

LEUTE   **Eine musikalische Familie und ihr genialer[1] Sohn**

In diesem Haus in Salzburg, Österreich, wohnt im achtzehnten Jahrhundert Leopold Mozart mit seiner Familie. Er ist Violinist im Orchester des Erzbischofs und auch Musiklehrer und Komponist. Seine Tochter Nannerl ist eine ausgezeichnete[2] Pianistin und sein Sohn Wolfgang schreibt schon mit vier Jahren die ersten Kompositionen. Im Jahr 1762 reist die ganze[3] Familie nach Wien. Dort spielen die beiden Wunderkinder – Nannerl ist jetzt elf und Wolfgang sechs – für die Kaiserin[4] und sie bekommen[5] schöne Kleider und viel Geld. Von 1763 bis 1767 – fast vier Jahre lang – reisen Mozarts dann in ihrer Kutsche[6] Tausende von Kilometern durch Deutschland, Belgien, Frankreich, England und Holland. Oft ist das Wetter schlecht und die Kinder sind oft sehr krank[7], aber sie geben Hunderte von Konzerten. 1769 reist der jetzt 13-jährige Wolfgang mit seinem Vater nach Italien. Fünfzehn Monate lang ist der junge Pianist und Komponist auch

dort die große Sensation. Dann ist Wolfgang wieder in Salzburg und wird sechzehn Jahre alt. Aber jetzt ist er kein Wunderkind und keine Sensation mehr, sondern nur ein schlecht bezahlter Musiker im Orchester des Erzbischofs.

1781 geht Mozart nach Wien und verdient dort als Pianist und Komponist viel Geld. 1782 heiratet er die Wienerin Konstanze Weber, lebt mit seiner Frau wie ein König und braucht viel mehr Geld als er verdient. Er macht Schulden und bezahlt[8] diese Schulden mit immer neuen Schulden. Er arbeitet fieberhaft und verdient jedes Jahr mehr. Im Jahr 1791, seinem letzten[9] Lebensjahr, schreibt Mozart zwei Opern, ein Klavierkonzert, ein Klarinettenkonzert, ein Quintett und eine Kantate und arbeitet an einem Requiem. Aber im November wird er sehr krank und kann nicht mehr arbeiten. Am fünften Dezember ist Mozart tot[10]. Er ist erst fünfunddreißig Jahre alt.

Familie Mozart

This famous painting by Johann Nepomuk della Croce shows Wolfgang and his sister Nannerl at the harpsichord and father Leopold with his violin. The mother, who died before the portrait was painted, is included by means of the painting on the wall. Leopold and his wife Anna had seven children, but only two survived.

[1]*genius* [2]*excellent* [3]*whole* [4]*empress* [5]*receive* [6]*carriage* [7]*ill* [8]*pays for* [9]*last* [10]*dead*

www Enjoy some of Mozart's music at www.prenhall.com/treffpunkt
→ Kapitel 3 → Web Resources → Kultur

Arbeit mit dem Text

3-51 Daten. In what year did the following events take place?

_____ Konstanze Weber wird Mozarts Frau.
_____ Die große Konzertreise durch halb Europa beginnt.
_____ Mozarts kurzes Leben ist zu Ende.
_____ Leopold Mozart fährt mit Wolfgang nach Italien.
_____ Wolfgang lebt jetzt nicht mehr in Salzburg, sondern in Wien.
_____ Nach fast vier Jahren ist Familie Mozart wieder in Salzburg.
_____ Wolfgang und Nannerl spielen für die Kaiserin in Wien.

3-52 Familie Mozart. Your instructor will read eight questions about *Eine musikalische Familie und ihr genialer Sohn.* Check the correct response for each.

1. _____ Erzbischof.
   _____ Musiker.
2. _____ Klavier.
   _____ Violine.
3. _____ Für die Kaiserin.
   _____ Für den Erzbischof.
4. _____ Sie sind in Italien.
   _____ Sie reisen durch halb Europa.

5. _____ Er spielt nicht mehr so gut.
   _____ Er ist keine Sensation mehr.
6. _____ In Salzburg.
   _____ In Wien.
7. _____ Er lebt wie ein König.
   _____ Er verdient nicht viel.
8. _____ 53.
   _____ 35.

Wort, Sinn und Klang

Wörter unter der Lupe

More cognates

In *Kapitel 2* you saw that it is often quite simple to "decode" the English meanings of certain cognates. Below is another list with the "code" that will help you figure out the English meanings. In some cases it helps to say the German words out loud. Words followed by *(v)* are verbs in their infinitive form.

- German **s, ss,** or **ß** is English *t* or *tt*

das Wasser	rasseln *(v)*	vergessen *(v)*	der Fuß	der Kessel
hassen *(v)*	besser	beißen *(v)*	die Nuss	was

- German **z** or **tz** is English *t* or *tt*

setzen *(v)*	die Katze	grunzen *(v)*	zehn
sitzen *(v)*	die Minze	die Warze	zwölf
der Sitz	das Salz	zu	die Zunge
glitzern *(v)*	das Netz		

- German **pf** is English *p* or *pp*

der Apfel	der Pfennig	das Pfund	der Pfad (**d** → *th!*)
der Krampf	die Pflanze (**z** → *t!*)	der Pfeffer (**f** → *p!*)	die Pfeife (**f** → *p!*)
die Pfanne	der Pfosten		

Words as chameleons: *wie*

In different contexts, the word **wie** can take on a number of different meanings.

- **Wie** can mean *how:*

Wie alt sind Sie?	*How old are you?*
Wie geht's?	*How are you?*

- **Wie** can mean *what:*

Wie ist Ihr Name und Ihre Adresse?	*What is your name and your address?*
Wie heißt du?	*What is your name?*

- **Wie** can mean *what . . . like:*

Wie ist Ihre neue Wohnung?	*What is your new apartment **like?***

- **Wie** can mean *like:*

Eine Wohnung **wie** meine kostet viel Geld.	*An apartment **like** mine costs a lot of money.*

- **Wie** means *as* in the expression **so ... wie:**

Meine Wohnung kostet nicht so viel **wie** deine.	*My apartment doesn't cost as much **as** yours.*

3-53 Was bedeutet wie? Write the number given after each occurrence of **wie** beside the appropriate English equivalent.

1. LAURA: **Wie** (1) heißt Lenas neuer Freund und **wie** (2) alt ist er?
   MARIA: Er heißt Florian und er ist 22 Jahre alt.
   LAURA: Und **wie** (3) ist er? Ist er so doof **wie** (4) ihr letzter Freund?

   how _____   what _____   what . . . like _____   as _____

2. JULIA: **Wie** (1) ist das Wetter? Ist es immer noch so schön **wie** (2) heute Morgen?
   LUKAS: Nein, jetzt regnet es **wie** (3) verrückt°.   *crazy*

   what . . . like _____   like _____   as _____

3. PETER: **Wie** (1) geht's, Claudia? **Wie** (2) ist deine neue Mitbewohnerin? Ist sie so nett **wie** (3) die letzte?
   CLAUDIA: Klar. Stephanie und ich sind schon fast **wie** (4) gute, alte Freundinnen.

   how _____   what . . . like _____   like _____   as _____

((► Zur Aussprache

The diphthongs

A diphthong is a combination of two vowel sounds. There are three diphthongs in German.

3-54 Hören Sie gut zu und wiederholen Sie!

The diphthong **ei** (also spelled **ey, ai, ay**) is pronounced like the *i* in *mine*.

eins	zwei	drei
Herr M**ey**er	Herr S**ai**ler	Herr B**ay**er

H**ei**ke B**ay**er und H**ei**nz Fr**ey** h**ei**raten am zw**ei**ten M**ai**.

The diphthong **au** is pronounced like the *ou* in *house*.

br**au**chen	l**au**fen	k**au**fen
bl**au**	br**au**n	gr**au**

P**au**l, du bist zu l**au**t. Ich gl**au**be, du bist bl**au**.
Br**au**tkleid bleibt Br**au**tkleid und Bl**au**kraut bleibt Bl**au**kraut.

The diphthong **eu** (also spelled **äu**) is pronounced like the *oy* in *boy*.

h**eu**te	t**eu**er	n**eu**
H**äu**ser	M**äu**se	Verk**äu**fer

Wer ist Frau B**äu**erles n**eu**er Fr**eu**nd?
Ein Verk**äu**fer aus Bayr**eu**th.

WIR SUCHEN EINE

freundliche Verkäuferin

bitte im Laden melden

Nomen

der Familienname, -n	last name
der Vorname, -n	first name
der Flug, ⸚e	flight
der Flughafen, ⸚	airport
die Flugnummer, -n	flight number
das Flugzeug, -e	airplane
das Geschäft, -e	store; business
das Feinkostgeschäft, -e	gourmet foods store
das Kleidergeschäft, -e	clothing store
die Klamotten (pl)	clothes
das Kaufhaus, ⸚er	department store
der Verkäufer, -	sales clerk
die Verkäuferin, -nen	
das Handy, -s	cell phone
die Kaffeemaschine, -n	coffee maker
die Schulden (pl)	debts
die Sprache, -n	language

Verben

bekommen	to get; to receive
bezahlen	to pay
brauchen	to need
erkennen	to recognize
heiraten	to marry

Bekommen: is a "false friend."

Wir haben alles, was keiner braucht!

backen (bäckt)	to bake
fahren (fährt)	to drive
halten (hält)	to hold; to stop; to keep
lassen (lässt)	to let; to leave
laufen (läuft)	to run
schlafen (schläft)	to sleep
tragen (trägt)	to wear
waschen (wäscht)	to wash
essen (isst)	to eat
geben (gibt)	to give
lesen (liest)	to read
nehmen (nimmt)	to take
sehen (sieht)	to see

Flugzeug: Das **Zeug** means *thing.* What is the literal meaning of **Flugzeug?** Can you guess the meaning of **Werkzeug, Spielzeug, Schreibzeug, Bettzeug?**

sprechen (spricht)	to speak
versprechen (verspricht)	to promise
werden (wird)	to become; to get; to be

Andere Wörter

ausgezeichnet	excellent
laut	loud
offen	open
preisgünstig	inexpensive
tot	dead
wunderbar	wonderful
wunderschön	very beautiful
blond	blonde
brünett	brunette
glatt	straight (of hair)
lockig	curly
gestern	yesterday
mehr	more

Ausdrücke

es gibt (+ acc)	there is, there are
ganz kurz	very short
die ganze Familie	the whole family
nächstes Jahr	next year
Er arbeitet nicht mehr.	He's not working any more.
Sie wird zwanzig.	She is going to be twenty.
Was sind Sie von Beruf?	What is your occupation?

Das Gegenteil

die Hausfrau, -en ≠ der Hausmann, ⸚er	housewife ≠ househusband
kaufen ≠ verkaufen	to buy ≠ to sell
erst ≠ letzt	first ≠ last
krank ≠ gesund	sick ≠ healthy
neu ≠ alt	new ≠ old
alles ≠ nichts	all ≠ nothing
jemand ≠ niemand	somebody ≠ nobody
vorgestern ≠ übermorgen	the day before yesterday ≠ the day after tomorrow

Leicht zu verstehen

die CD, -s	das Mineralwasser
der CD-Spieler, -	das Mountainbike, -s
das Interview, -s	die Person, -en
der iPod, -s	der Preis, -e
die Kamera, -s	die Sandale, -n
die Klasse, -n	kritisieren

Person: Although this noun can refer to males or females, it is always feminine.

Wörter im Kontext

3-55 Jennifers Familie. Complete with words from the list.

nimmt / wird / von Beruf / nächste / niemand / Flughafen /
gibt es / bekommt / offen / Flugzeug / übermorgen

1. Jennifers Vater und ihr Bruder Kurt sind beide Koch _____.
2. Im Restaurant von Jennifers Eltern _____ oft deutsche
   Spezialitäten.
3. Montags ist das Restaurant nicht _____, denn montags isst
   fast _____ im Restaurant.
4. _____ fliegt Jennifers Mutter nach Deutschland, denn Jennifer
   _____ _____ Woche einundzwanzig.
5. Ihr _____ landet auf dem Hamburger _____, und von dort _____
   sie dann den Zug nach Kiel.
6. Jennifer _____ von ihren Eltern dreihundert Euro zum Geburtstag.

3-56 Was passt zusammen? For each sentence in the first column, find
the most appropriate statement in the second column and complete it with the
correct form of a suitable verb from the following list.

essen / tragen / schlafen / waschen / sehen / fahren / lesen

1. Er ist Polizist.
2. Sie ist Studentin.
3. Er ist Bankdirektor.
4. Er ist ein Gourmet.
5. Das ist ein Bär.
6. Das ist eine Katze.
7. Er ist Hausmann.

a. Er kocht und bäckt und _____.
b. Er _____ fast den ganzen Winter.
c. Sie _____ jeden Morgen zur Uni.
d. Er _____ eine Uniform.
e. Er _____ oft Börsenberichte.
f. Er _____ gern Kaviar.
g. Sie _____ auch bei Nacht sehr gut.

3-57 Anders gesagt. Decide which two sentences in each group have
approximately the same meaning.

1. a. Anna ist Verkäuferin.
   b. Anna kauft Klamotten.
   c. Anna verkauft Klamotten.

2. a. Wie viel Geld verdienst du?
   b. Wie viel Geld bekommst du?
   c. Wie viel Geld brauchst du?

3. a. Tom und Maria heiraten
      morgen.
   b. Maria wird morgen Toms
      Frau.
   c. Maria und Tom sind nicht
      mehr verheiratet.

4. a. Tom spricht viele Sprachen.
   b. Toms Muttersprache ist Englisch.
   c. Toms Englisch ist ausgezeichnet.

5. a. Mein Familienname ist Müller.
   b. Ich heiße Stefan Müller.
   c. Ich heiße Müller.

6. a. Morgen habe ich keine
      Schulden mehr.
   b. Morgen habe ich wieder viel
      mehr Geld.
   c. Morgen bezahle ich alle meine
      Schulden.

Alltagsleben

Obst- und Gemüsemarkt in Biel, Schweiz

Kommunikationsziele

Talking about . . .

- daily routines
- food and meals
- abilities, necessities, and obligations

Expressing permission, wishes, and likes

Telling someone what to do

Making requests

Giving advice

Giving reasons and conditions

Strukturen

Modal verbs

Separable-prefix verbs

The imperative

Word order: Position of the verb in dependent clauses

Kultur

Switzerland

Railways in the German-speaking countries

Soccer

Video-Treff: **Ein typischer Tag**

Lesen: **Karl Elsener und das Schweizeroffiziersmesser**

So bin ich eben

MARTIN: *(steht auf und gähnt)* Was?! Du bist schon auf? Wie spät ist es denn?

PETER: Fast acht Uhr. Ich muss mein Referat für Professor Weber fertig schreiben. Das Seminar fängt schon um elf an.

MARTIN: *(lacht)* Ja ja, du und deine Referate: viel Stress, viel Kaffee, kein Frühstück. Iss doch eine Scheibe Brot. Und hier ist auch Butter, Wurst und Käse dazu.

PETER: Ich kann jetzt nicht aufhören, ich muss das Ding fertig schreiben.

MARTIN: Du bist echt doof, Peter. Warum fängst du immer so spät an?

PETER: Ich brauche den Stress, Martin. So bin ich eben.

Morgen, morgen, nur nicht heute ...

STEPHANIE: Unser Zimmer sieht ja wie ein Schweinestall aus! Kannst du nicht mal ein bisschen aufräumen, Claudia?

CLAUDIA: Klar! Nur nicht heute. Heute habe ich viel zu viel zu tun.

STEPHANIE: Das sagst du immer und dann muss *ich* aufräumen.

CLAUDIA: Das musst du gar nicht. Morgen habe ich viel Zeit.

STEPHANIE: Das sagst du auch immer.

CLAUDIA: Ja, aber diesmal stimmt's. Ich bin morgen den ganzen Vormittag zu Hause, stehe früh auf und um zwölf ist hier alles tipptopp.

STEPHANIE: Na ja, mal sehen.

Stephanie schreibt eine E-Mail nach Hause

Von: Stephanie Braun <sbraun@mdx.de>
Betreff: Hallo aus München!
Datum: 23. November 2006 19:12:48 MEZ
An: Thomas Braun <tbraun@golden.nit>

Hallo ihr Lieben,

hier ist alles immer noch echt super: die Uni, die Stadt und vor allem meine neuen Freunde. Claudia ist immer noch meine beste Freundin. Übrigens kocht sie ganz fabelhaft und macht echt leckere Gerichte mit viel Gemüse und Salat und wenig Fleisch. Sie mag aber auch meine Tomatensoße mit Nudeln oder Spaghetti. Zum Frühstück isst man hier übrigens oft Wurst und Käse. Ich esse aber meistens eine Schüssel Cornflakes, genau wie zu Hause, und manchmal mache ich auch mein Lieblingsfrühstück, meine Pancakes. Peter, ein Freund von Claudias Freund Martin, findet sie echt spitze. Peter ist übrigens sehr nett. Er ist oft bei uns und er ruft auch oft an.
Liebe Grüße
Stephanie

Hören

4-1 Richtig oder falsch. You will hear the conversations and the text of the e-mail on pages 119 and 120. Indicate whether the statements that follow each conversation and the e-mail are **richtig** or **falsch.**

SO BIN ICH EBEN

	RICHTIG	FALSCH		RICHTIG	FALSCH		RICHTIG	FALSCH
1.	_____	_____	2.	_____	_____	3.	_____	_____

MORGEN, MORGEN, NUR NICHT HEUTE …

	RICHTIG	FALSCH		RICHTIG	FALSCH		RICHTIG	FALSCH
1.	_____	_____	2.	_____	_____	3.	_____	_____

STEPHANIE SCHREIBT EINE E-MAIL NACH HAUSE

	RICHTIG	FALSCH		RICHTIG	FALSCH		RICHTIG	FALSCH
1.	_____	_____	2.	_____	_____	3.	_____	_____

4-2 Was passt zusammen?

1. Warum ist Peter schon so früh auf?
2. Warum fängt Peter immer so spät an?
3. Was sieht wie ein Schweinestall aus?
4. Warum kann Claudia heute nicht aufräumen?
5. Wer mag Stephanies Tomatensoße?
6. Wer mag Stephanies Pancakes?

a. Claudia.
b. Sie hat zu viel zu tun.
c. Stephanies und Claudias Zimmer.
d. Peter.
e. Er braucht den Stress.
f. Er muss sein Referat fertig schreiben.

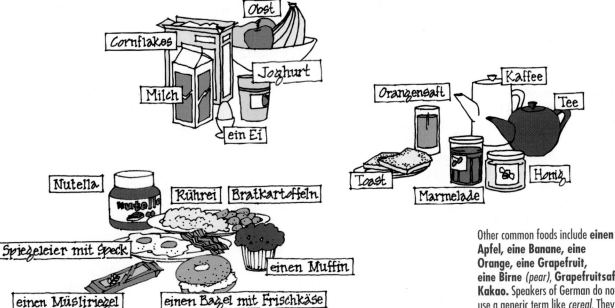

Other common foods include **einen Apfel, eine Banane, eine Orange, eine Grapefruit, eine Birne** (*pear*)**, Grapefruitsaft, Kakao.** Speakers of German do not use a generic term like *cereal*. They refer to cereals by name, e.g., **Rice Krispies.** In the German-speaking countries **Bratkartoffeln** are not a breakfast food, but are often served with other meals. **Bagel, Grapefruit, Muffin,** and **Toast** are pronounced as in English.

S1:

Wann stehst du an Wochentagen auf?

Was isst und trinkst du an Wochentagen zum Frühstück?

Wann stehst du am Wochenende auf?

Und was isst und trinkst du dann zum Frühstück?

S2:

An Wochentagen stehe ich normalerweise um _____ auf.

Ich esse … und ich trinke …

Am Wochenende stehe ich meistens erst um _____ auf.

Ich esse … und ich trinke …

Record what you find out and report your findings to the rest of the class.

S: An Wochentagen steht [*Name*] normalerweise um _____ auf.
Am Wochenende steht sie/er meistens um _____ auf.
An Wochentagen isst sie/er … zum Frühstück und trinkt …
Am Wochenende isst sie/er … zum Frühstück und trinkt …

Sprachnotiz: Remember that for English *man* the German equivalent is **der Mann.**

■ Sprachnotiz ······························

The pronoun *man*

The pronoun **man** is used to make generalizations and is the equivalent of *one, you, they,* or *people.* **Man** is always singular.

Wie sagt **man** das auf Deutsch?

In Deutschland isst **man** oft Wurst und Käse zum Frühstück.

How does one (do you) say that in German?

In Germany they (people) often eat cold cuts and cheese for breakfast.

KULTUR

WWW Listen to **Schweizerdeutsch** at
www.prenhall.com/treffpunkt
→ Kapitel 4 → Web Resources
→ Kultur

Die Schweiz

Die Schweiz is a country of four distinct cultures and four official languages: **Deutsch, Französisch, Italienisch,** and **Rätoromanisch.** Of a population of about 7.4 million, 64% speak German, 20% speak French, 6% speak Italian, and about 1% speak Rhaeto-Romanic. Switzerland has one of the highest standards of living in the world, even though over 70 percent of this tiny country consists of rugged mountains and has no natural resources apart from hydroelectric power. In order to survive, the Swiss have had to be very inventive. They have built a prosperous food industry on milk, the only product that mountain pastures have enabled them to produce in large quantities. Swiss cheeses, milk chocolate, and baby foods are known the world over through brand names like Emmi, Lindt, and Nestlé. Switzerland also has a highly sophisticated machine industry that produces everything from enormous diesel engines to watches and other precision instruments. The Swiss are leaders in pharmaceuticals and high-fashion textiles as well, and they also provide world-wide services in the banking and insurance industries. While Switzerland is not a member of the EU, many of its most important trading partners are EU countries like Germany.

The Swiss country code **CH** stands for **Confoederatio Helvetica,** and many Swiss Web addresses end in **.ch.** The **Confoederatio Helvetica** originated in 1291 when the peasants in the cantons **Schwyz, Uri,** and **Unterwalden** united against their oppressors, the Habsburgs, the dynasty that later ruled the Austrian empire. Now a federation of 26 **Kantone,** Switzerland requires

Museum Rotes Kreuz/Roter Halbmond in Genf

in its constitution that all important decisions be reached by plebiscite; for example, all changes to the Constitution are subject to a compulsory referendum. However, the (male) electorate did not give women the right to vote in federal elections until 1971, and at the local level, women in the **Kanton Appenzell** could still not vote until the end of the 1980s.

Since 1815, Switzerland has been internationally recognized as a permanently neutral country. Although military service is compulsory for all males, the military's sole mission is to defend the country and assist in peace-keeping and humanitarian activities. The country's neutral status allows it to play a unique role in international politics. Geneva **(Genf)** has long been the headquarters for many international organizations and has also been the neutral site for dialogue between nations with opposing ideologies.

Das Internationale Rote Kreuz was founded in Geneva in 1863 to implement ideas put forward by Henry Dunant, a Swiss citizen. As a young man, Dunant witnessed the aftermath of the bloody Battle of Solferino in northern Italy in 1859. For three days and nights he helped local women care for the wounded and dying and recounted the horrors of what he saw in *A Memory of Solferino.* The book was translated into many languages, and the questions he raised in it led to the founding of the International Committee of the Red Cross and the adoption of the first Geneva Convention. In 1901, he received the first Nobel Peace Prize for his work. The symbol of the Red Cross, a red cross on a white background, is the Swiss flag reversed. In Muslim countries, the equivalent symbol is a red crescent on a white background.

The natural beauty and recreational opportunities of this mountainous country are the basis for its flourishing tourist trade. The magnificent **Schweizer Alpen** provided the setting

Die Kapellbrücke in Luzern

Schweizer Alpen: Lidernenhütte

Switzerland is the world's second largest producer of watches. What do you think the company name **Swatch** stands for?

for Johanna Spyri's classic 19th-century children's novel *Heidi*. Swiss landscapes also figure prominently in many of the poems, novels, and **Kleine Prosa** of modernist writer Robert Walser (1878-1956). The excerpt below is the beginning of one of his short writings, entitled **Schneien**.

4-4 Schneien.

1. As the title indicates, this text is about snowing. What kind of snowing do you think Walser is describing? Support your answer with words or phrases from the text.

2. What descriptive words would you use to express the feeling that this text evokes?

> Es schneit, schneit, was vom Himmel herunter[1] mag[2], und es mag Erkleckliches[3] herunter. Das hört nicht auf, hat nicht Anfang und nicht Ende. Einen Himmel gibt es nicht mehr, alles ist ein graues weißes Schneien. Eine Luft[4] gibt es auch nicht mehr, sie ist voll von Schnee. Eine Erde[5] gibt es auch nicht mehr, sie ist mit Schnee und wieder mit Schnee zugedeckt[6].
>
> [1]*down* [2]= möchte [3]*a lot* [4]*air* [5]*earth* [6]*covered up*

Nomen

das Frühstück	breakfast
zum Frühstück	for breakfast
das Brot	bread; sandwich
das Brötchen, -	roll
das Ei, -er	egg
das Rührei (*sing*)	scrambled eggs
das Spiegelei, -er	fried egg (sunny-side up)
der Honig	honey
der Joghurt	yogurt
der Käse	cheese
die Marmelade	jam
das Müsli	muesli
der Müsliriegel, -	granola bar
der Orangensaft	orange juice
der Zucker	sugar
der Becher, -	cup; container
ein Becher Joghurt	a container of yogurt
das Glas, ⸚er	glass
ein Glas Orangensaft	a glass of orange juice
die Scheibe, -n	slice
eine Scheibe Brot	a slice of bread
die Schüssel, -n	bowl
eine Schüssel Müsli	a bowl of muesli
die Tasse, -n	cup
eine Tasse Kaffee	a cup of coffee
das Mittagessen	noon meal; lunch
zum Mittagessen	for lunch
das Abendessen	evening meal
zum Abendessen	for supper; for dinner
das Fleisch (*sing*)	meat
das Gemüse (*sing*)	vegetables
die Kartoffel, -n	potato
die Bratkartoffeln (*pl*)	fried potatoes
die Pommes frites	} French fries
die Pommes	
die Wurst, ⸚e	sausage; cold cuts
der Nachtisch	dessert
zum Nachtisch	for dessert
das Eis	ice cream; ice
das Obst (*sing*)	fruit
der Nachmittagskaffee	afternoon coffee
zum Nachmittagskaffee	for afternoon coffee

Pommes frites is pronounced as in French, i.e., **-es** is not pronounced. However, when it is shortened to **Pommes, -es** is pronounced.

On Sunday afternoons, family and friends often meet for **Kaffee und Kuchen.** Many pastry shops open for a few hours on Sunday to sell fresh pastries and cakes.

der Kuchen, -	cake
die Torte, -n	layer cake
das Stück, -e	piece
ein Stück Torte	a piece of layer cake

When used as units of measure, **Glas** and **Stück** are usually singular: zwei *Glas* Milch, drei *Stück* Kuchen.

Verben

an·fangen (fängt an)	to begin; to start
an·rufen	to call (*on the phone*)
auf·hören	to end, to stop
auf·räumen	to clean up
auf·stehen	to get up
aus·sehen (sieht aus)	to look (like)
frühstücken	to have breakfast

an·fangen, etc.: The raised dot indicates that these are separable-prefix verbs. You will learn more about them on page 130.

Andere Wörter

fabelhaft	fabulous
fertig	finished; ready
genau	exact(ly); carefully
lieb	dear
diesmal	this time
meistens	most of the time, usually
normalerweise	normally, usually

Ausdrücke

vor allem	above all
Das stimmt.	That's right.
Bist du heute Abend zu Hause?	Will you be (at) home tonight?
Gehst du nach Hause?	Are you going home?
So bin ich eben.	That's just the way I am.
Wann isst du zu Mittag (zu Abend)?	When do you have lunch (supper)?
Was für ein Schweinestall!	What a pigsty!
Wie sagt man das auf Deutsch?	How does one (do you) say that in German?

Das Gegenteil

früh ≠ spät	early ≠ late
manchmal ≠ oft	sometimes ≠ often

Leicht zu verstehen

der Bagel, -s	die Nudel, -n
die Banane, -n	die Orange, -n
der Brokkoli	der Pudding
die Butter	der Reis
der Fisch, -e	der Salat, -e
die Grapefruit, -s	das Sauerkraut
der Muffin, -s	der Toast

Wörter im Kontext

4-5 Was passt nicht?

1. das Fleisch	2. die Nudel	3. der Becher	4. der Pudding
der Orangensaft	der Nachtisch	das Glas	das Eis
der Käse	die Kartoffel	die Scheibe	das Obst
die Wurst	der Reis	die Tasse	der Brokkoli

Fleisch, Gemüse, and **Obst** are always singular. **Wurst** is singular when it refers to cold cuts.

4-6 *Nach Hause* oder *zu Hause?*

Zieglers fahren nach Hause

Zieglers sind zu Hause

4-6: Don't let the fact that **zu** is a cognate of *to* confuse you here: **zu Hause** means *at home.* Use **nach Hause** to say that you're going *(to your) home.*

1. Wann kommt Stephanie _____?
2. Ist Claudia noch nicht _____?
3. Ich gehe jetzt _____.
4. Ich muss um sieben _____ sein.

5. Fährst du am Freitag _____?
6. Wohnt Stefan noch _____?
7. Geht ihr heute Abend aus oder esst ihr _____?

4-7 Was passt wo?

diesmal / manchmal / meistens

1. Müllers essen sonntags oft im Restaurant. Sie essen sehr gern italienisch und gehen deshalb _____ ins Ristorante Napoli. _____ essen sie aber auch gern chinesisch. Heute ist wieder Sonntag, aber _____ möchte Frau Müller nicht italienisch und auch nicht chinesisch essen, sondern türkisch.

Mittagessen: In the German-speaking countries this is often the main meal of the day.

zum Mittagessen / zum Frühstück / zum Nachtisch

2. _____ esse ich Obst oder italienisches Eis.
   _____ esse ich Brötchen oder eine Schüssel Müsli.
   _____ esse ich Fleisch und Gemüse.

Joghurt / Pommes frites / Käse / Chips / Butter

3. _____, _____ und _____ macht man aus Milch.
   _____ und _____ macht man aus Kartoffeln.

eine Scheibe / eine Tasse / einen Becher / ein Glas / ein Stück

4. Zum Frühstück trinke ich normalerweise _____ eiskalten Orangensaft und _____ schwarzen Kaffee und esse _____ Toast dazu. Zum Nachmittagskaffee esse ich _____ Torte und abends esse ich zum Nachtisch oft _____ Fruchtjoghurt.

❶ Modifying the meaning of verbs: modal verbs

Wir müssen leider draußen bleiben.

Meaning and position of modal verbs

Verbs like English *can* and *must* are called modal verbs. They modify the meaning of other verbs (*I **can** go now; I **must** go now*).

In German there are six modal verbs. The verbs modified by the modals appear in the infinitive form at the very end of the sentence.

Ich **kann** gleich anfangen.	*I **can** begin right away.*
Ich **muss** gleich anfangen.	*I **must** begin right away.*
Ich **will** gleich anfangen.	*I **want to** begin right away.*

The modals *können*, *müssen*, and *wollen*

Below are the present tense forms of **können** (*to be able to, to know how to, can*), **müssen** (*to have to, must*), and **wollen** (*to want to*).

können		müssen		wollen	
ich	kann	ich	muss	ich	will
du	kannst	du	musst	du	willst
er/es/sie	kann	er/es/sie	muss	er/es/sie	will
wir	können	wir	müssen	wir	wollen
ihr	könnt	ihr	müsst	ihr	wollt
sie/Sie	können	sie/Sie	müssen	sie/Sie	wollen

Note:

Lerntipp: For modal verbs the **ich**- and **er/sie/es**-forms are always identical.

- These modals have a stem-vowel change in the **ich-, du-,** and **er/es/sie-** forms.
- Modals have no personal endings in the **ich**-form and the **er/es/sie**-form.
- When **können** is used to express mastery of a foreign language, it is not followed by an infinitive.

> **Können** Sie Deutsch?   ***Can** you speak German?*

especially   **4-8 Wer kann was besonders° gut?**

1. Herr und Frau Ziegler _____ sehr gut Spanisch.
2. Nina _____ ausgezeichnet Klavier spielen.
3. Alexander _____ ganz fabelhaft kochen.

LEHRER/IN: Und Sie? Was können Sie besonders gut?
STUDENT/IN: Ich _____ sehr gut (ausgezeichnet, ganz fabelhaft) …

4-9 Was müssen Zieglers alles tun?

1. Herr und Frau Ziegler _____ beide arbeiten und Geld verdienen.
2. Nina und Robert _____ jeden Morgen in die Schule gehen und jeden Abend _____ sie ihre Hausaufgaben° machen. *homework*
3. Herr Ziegler _____ jeden Morgen das Frühstück machen und jeden Samstag das Haus putzen°. *clean*
4. Frau Ziegler _____ jeden Abend kochen und jeden Samstag waschen.

LEHRER/IN: Und Sie? Was müssen Sie alles tun?
STUDENT/IN: Ich _____ …

4-10 Was wollen Nina, Robert und Alexander werden?

1. Nina _____ Journalistin werden.
2. Robert _____ Fußballprofi° werden. **Profi:** *pro*
3. Alexander _____ Ingenieur werden.

LEHRER/IN: Und Sie? Was wollen Sie werden?
STUDENT/IN: Ich _____ …
LEHRER/IN: Und warum wollen Sie … werden?
STUDENT/IN: Ich finde diesen Beruf sehr interessant.
Ich arbeite gern mit Kindern / mit alten Leuten / mit Tieren° / … *animals*
Ich kann sehr gut schreiben / fotografieren / …
Ich will viel Geld verdienen.

4-11 Mal ganz ehrlich. *(Let's be honest.)* Ask your partner what she/he is not so good at. Report your findings to the class.

S1: Was kannst du nicht so gut? **S2:** Ich kann nicht so gut (gar nicht gut) …

The modals *dürfen, sollen,* and *mögen*

Below are the present tense forms of **dürfen** *(to be allowed to, to be permitted to, may)*, **sollen** *(to be supposed to, should)*, and **mögen** *(to like)*.

dürfen		sollen		mögen	
ich	darf	ich	soll	ich	mag
du	darfst	du	sollst	du	magst
er/es/sie	darf	er/es/sie	soll	er/es/sie	mag
wir	dürfen	wir	sollen	wir	mögen
ihr	dürft	ihr	sollt	ihr	mögt
sie/Sie	dürfen	sie/Sie	sollen	sie/Sie	mögen

Note:

- **Sollen** is the only modal that does not have a stem-vowel change in the **ich-, du-,** and **er/es/sie-**forms.

- **Mögen** is usually used without an infinitive.

Ich **mag** Stephanie. *I like Stephanie.*
Warum **mögt** ihr kein Gemüse? *Why don't you like vegetables?*

Ich darf hier nicht hinein !

4-12 Was dürfen Zieglers alles nicht tun?

1. Herr und Frau Ziegler _____ keinen Kaffee trinken.
2. Ihre Tochter Nina ist erst sechzehn und _____ noch nicht Auto fahren.
3. Ihr Sohn Robert ist vierzehn und _____ nicht nach Mitternacht nach Hause kommen.

LEHRER/IN: Und Sie? Was dürfen Sie alles nicht tun?
STUDENT/IN: Ich _____ nicht …

4-13 Was sollen Zieglers nächsten Samstag alles tun?

1. Frau Ziegler und Nina _____ nächsten Samstag Oma Ziegler besuchen.
2. Robert _____ nächsten Samstag Vaters Wagen waschen.
3. Herr Ziegler _____ nächsten Samstag die Waschmaschine reparieren.

LEHRER/IN: Und Sie? Was sollen Sie nächsten Samstag alles tun?
STUDENT/IN: Ich _____ nächsten Samstag …

4-14 Was mögen Zieglers alles nicht?

1. Herr Ziegler _____ keine Kartoffeln und keine Nudeln.
2. Die beiden Teenager _____ kein Gemüse und keinen Salat.
3. Frau Ziegler _____ kein Fleisch.

LEHRER/IN: Und Sie? Was mögen Sie alles nicht?
STUDENT/IN: Ich _____ kein__ …

 4-15 Was magst du und was magst du nicht? You and your partner ask each other what you especially like to eat and what you don't like at all. You will find additional food items under **Essen und Trinken** in the *Anhang* on p. A20.

S1: Was magst du besonders gern?
Was magst du gar nicht?

S2: … mag ich besonders gern.
… mag ich gar nicht.

Möchte versus *mögen*

Although the modal **möchte** is derived from **mögen,** it is not used to express what one likes or dislikes, but what one *would like* to have or to do. **Ich möchte** is therefore a more polite way of saying **ich will.**

Ich **mag** Käsekuchen.   *I like cheesecake.*
Ich **möchte** ein Stück Käsekuchen.   *I would like a piece of cheesecake.*

It would be impolite to say:

Ich **will** ein Stück Käsekuchen.   *I want a piece of cheesecake.*

singular		plural	
ich	möchte	wir	möchten
du	möchtest	ihr	möchtet
er/es/sie	möchte	sie	möchten
	Sie	möchten	

4-16 Wer möchte was?

1. Frau Ziegler _____ eine Weltreise° machen.
2. Herr Ziegler _____ einen Porsche.
3. Robert _____ ein neues Mountainbike.
4. Nina _____ ein Jahr in Amerika studieren.

LEHRER/IN: Und Sie? Was möchten Sie?
STUDENT/IN: Ich _____ …

trip around the world

Omission of the infinitive after modal verbs

If the meaning of a sentence containing a modal is clear without an infinitive, the infinitive is often omitted.

Ich muss jetzt nach Hause.　　　*I have to **go** home now.*

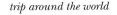
4-17 Welcher Infinitiv passt?

trinken / gehen / essen / fliegen / sprechen

1. Wir müssen jetzt in die Vorlesung.
2. Können deine Eltern Deutsch?
3. Möchten Sie ein Stück Kuchen?
4. Darf deine kleine Schwester immer noch nicht in die Disco?
5. Möchtest du auch nach Australien?
6. Wollt ihr lieber Bier oder Wein?
7. Im Winter mag ich kein Eis.
8. Warum willst du denn nicht ins Kino?

Position of *nicht* in sentences with modal verbs

You know how to negate a particular word or expression with **nicht**: Put **nicht** directly before it. The same rule applies when a modal is present.

Ich muss **nicht** jede Woche so viel lesen.
I don't have to read so much every week.

Ich muss **nicht** beide Artikel lesen.
I don't have to read both articles.

However, when you don't want to negate a particular word or expression, **nicht** is the second-to-last element. It comes directly before the infinitive.

Professor Raabe kann morgen **nicht** kommen.
Professor Raabe can't come tomorrow.

Toll! Dann muss ich seinen Artikel **nicht** lesen.
Great! Then I don't have to read his article.

You can review the rules for the position of **nicht** on pages 30 and 103.

4-18 Immer negativ.

S1: Kannst du kochen?　　　**S2:** Nein, ich kann nicht kochen.

1. Kann Martin gut kochen?　　　　　　　Nein, er kann …
2. Dürfen wir diesen Apfelkuchen essen?　　Nein, ihr dürft …
3. Darf ich den ganzen Kuchen essen?　　　Nein du darfst …
4. Muss ich dieses langweilige Buch lesen?　Nein, du musst …
5. Kannst du Peter nach Hause fahren?　　　Nein, ich kann …
6. Will Claudia den ganzen Abend zu Hause bleiben°?　　　　　　　Nein, sie will …
7. Soll ich beide Artikel lesen?　　　　　　Nein, du sollst …
8. Möchtest du mein Referat lesen?　　　　Nein, ich möchte …

stay

4-19 So bin ich eben. Write about yourself, using the modal verbs in the questions to guide you.

Was kannst du besonders gut?
Was kannst du gar nicht gut?
Wen magst du besonders gern? Warum?
Was magst du besonders gern?
Was magst du gar nicht?

anyway Was willst du nicht tun und musst es trotzdem° tun?
Was möchtest du gern tun und darfst es nicht?
Was sollst du tun und tust es nicht?

Photo: Felgen = *tire rims*

❷ Modifying the meaning of verbs: prefixes

Meaning of separable-prefix verbs

In English the meaning of certain verbs is modified or changed when you add a preposition or an adverb after the verb. In German the same effect is achieved by adding a prefix to the verb.

*to go **out***	**aus**gehen	*to try **out***	**aus**probieren
*to go **away***	**weg**gehen	*to clean **up***	**auf**räumen
*to come **back***	**zurück**kommen	*to wake **up***	**auf**wachen
*to come **home***	**heim**kommen	*to stand **up**;*	**auf**stehen
*to try **on***	**an**probieren	*to get **up***	

Note: In pronunciation the stress always falls on the separable prefix.

Separable-prefix verbs are not usually as similar to their English equivalents as in the examples given above.

abfahren	*to depart, to leave*	**an**rufen	*to call (on the phone)*
ankommen	*to arrive*	**ein**schlafen	*to fall asleep*
anfangen	*to begin, to start*	**fern**sehen	*to watch TV*
aufhören	*to end, to stop*	**vor**haben	*to plan, to have planned*
anhören	*to listen to*		

▮ Sprachnotiz ···················

More about separable prefixes

By combining prefixes with verbs, German creates a host of new verbs. In each set below, look at the first example and its English equivalent. Then figure out the meaning of the other verbs.

mitkommen *(to come **along**):* mitbringen, mitnehmen, mitlesen, mitsingen
weggehen *(to go **away**):* wegfahren, wegsehen, weglaufen, wegnehmen
weiterlesen *(to **continue** reading):* weiterarbeiten, weiteressen, weiterfahren
zurückrufen *(to call **back**):* zurückbringen, zurückfahren, zurückgeben

Position of the separable prefix

In the infinitive form, the prefix is attached to the front of the verb (**aus**gehen, **heim**kommen, etc.). In the present tense, the prefix is separated from the verb and is placed at the end of the sentence.

Ich **gehe** jetzt **aus**.
Ich **komme** sehr spät **heim**.

I'm going out now.
I'm coming home very late.

4-20 Was machst du heute Nachmittag?

▶ du heute Nachmittag

meine neue CD anhören

S1: Was machst du heute Nachmittag?

S2: Da höre ich meine neue CD an.

1. du am Samstagmorgen

2. du am Samstagabend

3. du morgen Abend

4. ihr am Sonntagabend

fernsehen	mit Claudia ausgehen
erst um elf aufstehen	mein Zimmer aufräumen

5. du heute Abend

6. ihr bei Karstadt

7. du am Starnberger See°

8. ihr am Freitagabend

lake south of Munich

noch nichts vorhaben	mein Surfbrett ausprobieren
meine Eltern anrufen	ein paar Kleider anprobieren

Position of separable-prefix verbs with modals

When used with a modal, the separable-prefix verb appears in its infinitive form at the end of the sentence.

Du **musst** jetzt **aufstehen.**   *You **have to get up** now.*

4-21 Kleine Gespräche.

▶ aufstehen
Warum _____ du denn so
früh _____?

S1: Warum stehst du denn so
früh auf?

anrufen
Ich will meine Kusine in
Deutschland _____.

S2: Ich will meine Kusine in
Deutschland anrufen.

1. ausgehen
_____ du heute Abend mit
uns _____?

   aufräumen
Nein, heute Abend muss ich endlich°
mal mein Zimmer _____.

finally

2. anhören
Möchtest du meine neue
CD _____?

   ausprobieren
Nein, ich möchte lieber deinen
neuen Computer _____.

3. vorhaben
Was _____ du heute Nachmittag
_____?

   anprobieren
Heute Nachmittag will ich bei
Karstadt Kleider _____.

4. anrufen
Kann ich Frau Müller abends um
zehn noch _____?

   fernsehen
Klar! Sie _____ jeden Abend bis
nach Mitternacht _____.

5. heimgehen
Können wir jetzt endlich _____?

   aufhören
Nein, erst muss der Regen _____.

▮ Sprachnotiz ·······························

Position of *nicht* with separable-prefix verbs

When you don't want to negate a particular word or expression, you place **nicht** directly before the separable prefix. **Nicht** is then the second-to-last element. When you add a modal to the sentence, **nicht** stands directly before the infinitive, again as the second-to-last element.

Ich gehe heute **nicht** aus.   *I'm **not** going out today.*
Ich will heute **nicht** ausgehen.   *I don't want to go out today.*

4-22 Was machst du den ganzen Tag?

S1:

Wann stehst du morgens auf?
Wann fangen deine
    Vorlesungen an?
Wann kommst du heim?
Gehst du abends oft aus?

rarely

S2:

Ich _____ meistens um … _____.
Meine Vorlesungen _____ meistens
    um … _____.
Ich _____ meistens um … _____.
Ja, ich _____ abends oft _____. /
    Nein, ich _____ abends nur sehr
    selten° _____.

4-23 Verkehrszeichen. Ask each other what these German traffic signs mean. The information for **S2** is in the *Anhang* on page A6.

S1: Was bedeutet Verkehrszeichen Nummer 1?

S2: Hier kommt gleich eine scharfe Rechtskurve.

1

2 Hier fängt die Autobahn an.

3

4

5 Hier geht es zur Autobahn nach Berlin.

6 Hier darf man nur nach rechts fahren.

7

8 Hier darf man nicht halten.

9

10 Autos und Motorräder dürfen hier nicht hineinfahren.

11 Hier darf man nur drei Minuten halten.

12

Verb-noun and verb-verb combinations

Some verbs are so closely associated with a noun or another verb that they function like separable-prefix verbs.

With nouns this happens most frequently with the verbs **spielen, laufen,** and **fahren.**

Im Sommer **fährt** David fast jeden Nachmittag **Rad.**

In the summer David goes cycling almost every afternoon.

Im Winter **läuft** er fast jedes Wochenende **Ski.**

In the winter he skis almost every weekend.

With verbs this happens most frequently with the verb **gehen.**

Ich **gehe** jeden Tag **joggen.**

I go jogging every day.

If a modal is present, these combinations again function like separable-prefix verbs, although they are written as separate words.

Dein Opa **kann** noch **Auto fahren?!**   *Your grandpa can still drive?!*
Ich **möchte** deinen Opa **kennen lernen.**   *I'd like to get to know your grandpa.*

As is the case with separable-prefix verbs, **nicht** precedes the noun or verb that stands at the end of the sentence. If a modal is present, **nicht** precedes the entire combination.

Claudia spielt heute **nicht Tennis.**   *Claudia isn't playing tennis today.*
Sie **will** auch **nicht spazieren gehen.**   *She doesn't want to go for a walk either.*

4-24 Was Tanja, Dieter und Laura können oder nicht können.

	TANJA	DIETER	LAURA
Motorrad fahren	sehr gut	nein	sehr gut
Gitarre spielen	nein	sehr gut	sehr gut
Ski laufen	sehr gut	sehr gut	nein

1. Tanja fährt … und sie läuft auch …, aber sie kann …
2. Dieter spielt … und er läuft auch …, aber er kann …
3. Laura fährt … und sie spielt auch …, aber sie kann …

 4-25 Frau Ziegler studiert den Fahrplan. Frau Ziegler war zwei Tage in Berlin. Es ist schon 13.30 Uhr, und sie möchte nicht nach 18.30 in Göttingen ankommen. Sie möchte aber auch nicht gleich abfahren, denn sie möchte noch

things ein paar Sachen° für Nina und Robert kaufen. Übrigens möchte Frau Ziegler direkt nach Göttingen durchfahren.

1. Wie viele Züge fahren nach 13 Uhr von Berlin Zoologischer Garten ab und kommen vor 18.30 Uhr in Göttingen an?
2. Mit wie vielen von diesen Zügen muss man in Hannover umsteigen?
3. Wann fährt der ICE 693 von Berlin ab und wann kommt er in Göttingen an?
4. Wann fährt der ICE 846 von Berlin ab und wann kommt er in Göttingen an?
5. Welchen Zug nimmt Frau Ziegler?

Berlin Zoolg. Garten → **Göttingen**

ab	Zug		Umsteigen	an	ab	Zug	an
12.56	ICE	558 ✘	Hannover	14.28	14.41	ICE 577	15.16
13.40	ICE	691 ✘					15.54
13.57	ICE	848 ✘	Hannover	15.28	15.41	ICE 579	16.16
14.39	ICE	879 ✘					16.54
14.56	ICE	546 ✘	Hannover	16.28	16.41	ICE 671	17.16
15.40	ICE	693 ✘					17.54
15.57	ICE	846 ✘	Hannover	17.28	17.41	ICE 673	18.16
16.41	ICE	977 ✘					18.54

Der ICE: dritte Generation

INFOBOX

Die Bahn

In the German-speaking countries, train travel is a vital part of **Alltagsleben**, for both business and pleasure. The railway systems of these countries are renowned for their fast, efficient, and punctual passenger service.

The fastest trains of the **Deutsche Bahn** are the **ICE (InterCityExpress)** and the **ICE International,** connecting major German cities to each other and to other cities in Europe at speeds up to 300 km/h (about 186 mph). Even the **RE (RegionalExpress)** trains, which connect to both long-distance trains and rapid transit trains within large urban areas, are capable of speeds up to 160 km/h (100 mph). Germany has approximately 5,400 **Bahnhöfe,** including Berlin's new **Hauptbahnhof,** Europe's largest railway station.

Der neue Hauptbahnhof in Berlin

The mountainous terrain of **Österreich** and **die Schweiz** did not stop those countries from building thriving rail systems. Every year, over 250 million people travel with the **Schweizerische Bundesbahnen (SBB)**, and two-thirds of all freight passing through the Swiss Alps is transported by train. To get trains through the Alps, the Swiss have constructed some of the world's highest bridges and longest tunnels. The **Österreichische Bundesbahnen (ÖBB)** connect Austrian cities to European destinations through their **EuroCity** trains. Both Austria and Switzerland have capitalized on the mountain rail system: Apart from connecting skiers to the alpine slopes, train companies offer scenic route trips such as the Swiss **Glacier Express,** a day-long ride traveling across 291 bridges, through 91 tunnels, and over the 2033-meter-high (6670 feet) Oberalp Pass.

WWW Travel with **Deutsche Bahn** at www.prenhall.com/treffpunkt
→ Kapitel 4 → Web Resources → Kultur

What do the meanings of German **Pendler** and English *pendulum* have in common?

While train travel is not always cheap, rail companies offer discounts for nearly every kind of traveler, e.g., commuters **(Pendler)**, travelers under 26, groups, and **Senioren. Passagiere** can book online and print out tickets at home. On most long-distance trains, you can purchase a ticket directly from the **Schaffner** *(conductor).* But be sure to buy a ticket before you get on a local train, since traveling without one **(Schwarzfahren)** can incur a hefty fine.

For North American students, one of the most popular ways of experiencing Europe is with the Eurail Pass, which provides unlimited travel on a total of 280,000 kilometers (174,000 miles) of track through 17 European countries.

Der Glacier Express

The two soccer teams mentioned are usually front runners in the **Erste Bundesliga** (*First Federal League*). The **FC Bayern München** has been **Deutscher Fußball Meister** 20 times in the last 40 years. **FC Schalke 04** was founded in 1904. It was originally a team of coal miners. You will find more information about **Fußball** on page 145.

Hören ······························

Du musst dein Leben ändern

Kurt Becker is sitting in front of the TV watching the soccer game between **Bayern München** and **Schalke 04.** His wife Petra has just walked in the door.

NEUE VOKABELN

ändern	*to change*	**anders**	*different*
du hast recht	*you are right*	**bestimmt**	*really, for sure*
von Montag ab	*from Monday on*	**zu Fuß gehen**	*to walk*

4-26 Erstes Verstehen. In what sequence do you hear the following statements?

_____ Du stehst jeden Morgen zu spät auf und hast nie Zeit für ein gutes Frühstück.

_____ Vielleicht hast du recht, Petra. Aber von Montag ab wird alles anders.

_____ Du wirst noch krank, so wie du lebst.

_____ Aber ich brauche mein Bier nach so viel Stress im Büro!

_____ Und schon heute Abend gehen wir spazieren, Petra, du und ich.

_____ Bayern München – Schalke 04! Und da willst du diskutieren?!

4-27 Detailverstehen. Listen to the conversation again and write the responses to the following questions.

1. Warum soll Petra nicht so laut sein?
2. Was isst Kurt im Büro zum Frühstück?
3. Was macht Kurt, wenn er nach Hause kommt?
4. Was darf Kurt nicht mehr?
5. Was muss Kurt mehr tun?
6. Was will Kurt von Montag ab jeden Morgen tun?

4-28 Ich will mein Leben ändern. Tell your classmates about three things you want to change in your life.

Ich will nicht mehr so viel
   (so oft, so spät, so lange) …

fernsehen	in die Kneipe gehen
schlafen	Bier trinken
aufstehen	Junkfood essen
ausgehen	Kaffee trinken
to smoke rauchen°	ins Bett gehen
…	…

Ich will mehr …

Milch trinken
Gemüse und
   Obst essen
lernen
Sport machen
…

❸ Expressing commands and requests, and giving advice

Imperatives

You can use the imperative form of a verb to express a command, make a request, or give advice. Since English has only one form of address *(you)*, it has only one imperative form. German has three forms of address **(du, ihr,** and **Sie),** and so it has three imperative forms. In written German, imperative sentences often end with an exclamation mark.

> **Komm!**
> **Kommt!**   } *Come!*
> **Kommen Sie!**

The *du*-imperative

The **du**-imperative is simply the stem of the verb.

Komm schnell, Martin! Das Konzert fängt in fünf Minuten an.	*Hurry up, Martin! The concert starts in five minutes.*
Fahr doch bitte nicht so schnell!	*Please don't drive so fast!*
Lass mich in Ruhe!	*Stop bothering me!*
Sei doch nicht immer so unordentlich, Peter!	*Don't always be so sloppy, Peter!*

Verbs that have a stem-vowel change from **e** to **i** or **ie** in the 2nd and 3rd person singular of the present tense (e.g., **ich lese, du l**i**est, er l**i**est**) use the changed stem in the **du**-imperative.

Nimm doch nicht so viel Fleisch, Robert!	*Don't take so much meat, Robert!*
Iss ja nicht wieder den ganzen Kuchen!	*Don't eat all the cake again!*

Verbs with stems ending in **-d** or **-t** add an **-e** in the **du**-imperative.

Rede doch nicht so viel!	*Don't talk so much.*
Antworte bitte so bald wie möglich!	*Please answer as soon as possible.*

The prefix of a separable verb appears at the end of the imperative sentence.

Komm ja nicht wieder so spät **heim!**	*Don't come home so late again!*

Again, verb-noun and verb-verb combinations function like separable-prefix verbs.

Spiel doch mit uns **Volleyball!**	*Play volleyball with us.*
Geh ja nicht allein **schwimmen!**	*Don't go swimming alone.*

Sprachnotiz ···

Flavoring particles and *bitte* in imperative sentences

Imperative sentences frequently contain the flavoring particles **doch** and/or **mal.** Depending on your tone of voice they can help to express either well-meant advice or strong irritation.

Gehen Sie **doch mal** zum Arzt.	*You should really go to the doctor.*
Lass mich **doch** in Ruhe!	*Why don't you leave me alone!*

The particle **ja,** strongly stressed, gives a command an almost threatening note, as if you were adding the words *or else!*

Trink **ja** nicht wieder zu viel!	*Don't drink too much again!*

The addition of **bitte** to an imperative sentence can transform it into a request, but it can also intensify a command.

Ruf mich **bitte** morgen an.	*Please call me tomorrow.*
Mach **bitte,** was ich sage!	*Please do as I say!*

vor dem Fernseher: *in front of the TV*

4-29 Mach bitte, was ich sage! You and your partner are siblings. One tries to lord it over the other, but it isn't working.

▶ _____ doch endlich _____! (auf·stehen)

    S1: Steh doch endlich auf!

1. _____ doch endlich mal deine Cornflakes! (essen)

2. _____ doch nicht immer nur vor dem Fernseher°! (sitzen)

3. _____ bitte gleich dein Zimmer _____! (auf·räumen)

4. _____ deinen Freund doch nicht schon wieder _____! (an·rufen)

5. _____ ja nur ein Stück Kuchen! (nehmen)

6. _____ bitte gleich meinen Wagen! (waschen)

    yourself

▶ _____ still und _____ mich schlafen! (sein, lassen)

    S2: Sei still und lass mich schlafen!

_____ still und _____ deinen Kaffee! (sein, trinken)

_____ mich in Ruhe und _____ deine Vokabeln! (lassen, lernen)

_____ still und _____ dein Referat fertig! (sein, schreiben)

_____ mich in Ruhe und _____ dein Müsli! (lassen, essen)

_____ still und _____ dein Buch! (sein, lesen)

_____ deinen Wagen doch selbst°! (waschen)

4-30 Du nervst mich! Using the suggestions below, tell your roommate or a family member to stop doing things that get on your nerves.

▶ doch nicht immer den Hund auf mein Bett lassen

S: Lass doch nicht immer den Hund auf mein Bett!

to snore

doch nicht so schnell/langsam fahren
doch nicht so laut schnarchen°
doch nicht immer nur Junkfood essen
doch nicht immer so lange telefonieren
doch nicht so schnell/langsam essen
doch nicht immer so viel reden

doch nicht so schnell/langsam sprechen
doch nicht immer nur deine doofen Comics lesen
doch nicht immer nur vor dem Fernseher sitzen

The *ihr*-imperative

The **ihr**-imperative is the **ihr**-form of the verb without the pronoun.

Kommt, Kinder! Wir gehen schwimmen.
Come on, children! We're going swimming.

Nehmt eure Badeanzüge **mit!**
Take your bathing suits along.

Seid doch bitte nicht so laut!
Please don't be so noisy.

4-31 Ein Picknick. You and your friends are going on a picnic. Your mother gives last-minute instructions.

1. _____ genug° Getränke _____! (mit·nehmen)   *enough*
2. _____ das Frisbee nicht! (vergessen°)   *to forget*
3. _____ auch eure Badeanzüge _____! (ein·packen)
4. _____ genug Sonnencreme _____! (mit·nehmen)
5. _____ auch ein paar schöne Fotos! (machen)
6. _____ genug Brote _____! (ein·packen)
7. _____ bitte nicht zu schnell! (fahren)
8. _____ bitte nicht zu viel! (trinken)
9. _____ bitte vor neun wieder zurück! (sein)
10. _____ doch endlich _____! (ab·fahren)

The *Sie*-imperative

The **Sie**-imperative is the infinitive of the verb followed directly by **Sie.**

Wiederholen Sie bitte, was ich sage!
Please repeat what I say.

Hören Sie bitte gut **zu!**
Please listen carefully.

The verb **sein** is slightly irregular in the **Sie**-imperative.

Seien Sie doch nicht so nervös!
Don't be so nervous.

4-32 In Professor Kuhls Deutschkurs.

1. _____ dieses Wort bitte, Kevin! (buchstabieren°)   *to spell*
2. _____ es jetzt bitte an die Tafel°! (schreiben)   *board*
3. _____ bitte _____, Andrea! (weiter·lesen)
4. _____ doch bitte ein bisschen lauter! (sprechen)
5. _____ doch nicht so nervös! (sein)
6. _____ jetzt bitte gut _____! (zu·hören)
7. _____ diese Übung bitte schriftlich°! (machen)   *in writing*
8. _____ bitte _____, Michael! (auf·wachen)
9. _____ diesen Dialog bitte zu Hause _____! (an·hören)
10. Michael! _____ doch nicht schon wieder _____! (ein·schlafen)

4-33 Guter Rat. One of you (**S1**) assumes the role of the person(s) asking for advice. The other (**S2**) gives the advice in the **du-, ihr-,** or **Sie**-imperative.

▶ einen Audi

FRAU FISCHER:	Was soll ich kaufen, einen VW oder einen Audi?	**S2:** Kaufen Sie lieber einen Audi.
1. EVA UND TANJA:	Wo sollen wir studieren, in Freiburg oder in Berlin?	in Freiburg
2. FRAU BRAUN:	Wann soll ich fliegen, am Donnerstag oder am Freitag?	am Donnerstag
3. BERND:	Was soll ich lesen, ein Buch oder die Zeitung?	ein Buch
4. TIM UND SILKE:	Wann sollen wir kommen, um zwei oder um drei?	schon um zwei
5. RALF:	Was soll ich trinken, Bier oder Wein?	ein Glas Wein
6. KURT UND JAN:	Wann sollen wir morgen aufstehen, um sieben oder um acht?	schon um sieben
7. FRAU SPOHN:	Wen soll ich anrufen, die Polizei oder einen Arzt°?	einen Arzt
8. TOURIST:	Wo soll ich essen, im Wienerwald° oder bei McDonald's?	im Wienerwald

doctor

a restaurant chain specializing in chicken

❹ Word order

Position of the verb in independent and dependent clauses

You already know the following conjunctions:

und	*and*	**aber**	*but*
denn	*because, for*	**sondern**	*but, (but) . . . instead, but rather*
oder	*or*		

These conjunctions are called coordinating conjunctions. They connect independent clauses, i.e., clauses that can stand alone as complete sentences. Coordinating conjunctions do not affect the position of the verb.

independent clause	conjunction	independent clause
Bernd hat endlich ein Zimmer	**und**	es kostet nur 150 Euro im Monat.
Es ist nur ein kleines Zimmer,	**aber**	es ist groß genug für Bernd.
Bernd geht nicht zu Fuß zur Uni,	**sondern**	er nimmt den Bus.

- The conjunctions **aber** and **sondern** are always preceded by a comma.
- The clause preceding **sondern** states what is *not* happening. The clause following **sondern** states what is happening *instead*.

4-34 Bernd hat ein Problem. Make Bernd's story read more smoothly. Using the appropriate coordinating conjunctions, connect the sentences in the left column with those directly opposite in the right column.

1. Ich habe endlich ein Zimmer!   Es kostet nur 150 Euro im Monat!
2. Das Zimmer ist sehr schön.   Von hier zur Uni ist es sehr weit°.   *far*
3. Der Bus braucht nicht nur ein   Er braucht eine volle Stunde.
   paar Minuten.
4. Ich brauche also einen Wagen.   Ich muss jeden Tag zur Uni.
5. Soll ich jetzt einen Wagen kaufen?   Soll ich ein anderes Zimmer suchen?

The following conjunctions are called subordinating conjunctions:

bis	*until*	**sobald**	*as soon as*
bevor	*before*	**weil**	*because*
damit	*so that*	**wenn**	*if; when*
obwohl	*although; even though*		

Subordinating conjunctions introduce dependent clauses, i.e., clauses that make sense only in connection with an independent clause. Subordinating conjunctions affect the position of the verb: the verb stands at the end of the clause. A dependent clause is *always* separated from the independent clause by a comma, and the comma directly precedes the subordinating conjunction.

independent clause	dependent clause
Bernd möchte das Zimmer,	**weil** es sehr schön und sehr preisgünstig ist.
Er möchte das Zimmer,	**obwohl** es von dort zur Uni sehr weit ist.

4-35 Wie löst Bernd sein Problem? Describe how Bernd solves his problem. Using the subordinating conjunctions provided, connect the sentences in the left column with those directly opposite in the right column.

1. Bernd ruft seine Eltern an.   bevor   Er nimmt das Zimmer.
2. Er möchte einen Wagen.   damit   Er kommt schneller° zur Uni.   *faster*
3. Er ruft seine Eltern an.   weil   Er braucht Geld für einen
                                                    Wagen.
4. Es braucht fast eine halbe   bis   Seine Eltern sagen endlich
   Stunde.   ja.
5. Bernd geht zu Auto-Müller.   sobald   Er hat das Geld.
6. Er möchte gern ein Sportcoupé.   wenn   Es kostet nicht zu viel.
7. Aber dann kauft er einen alten   obwohl   Dieser Wagen ist gar nicht
   VW Polo.   sehr sportlich.

In clauses introduced by a subordinating conjunction, modal verbs appear at the end of the clause and separable-prefix verbs are not separated.

independent clause	dependent clause
Peter steht früh auf,	**weil** er sein Referat fertig schreiben **muss.**
Claudia steht früh auf,	**weil** ihre erste Vorlesung um halb neun **anfängt.**

4-36 Warum steht Peter heute so früh auf? Describe Peter's morning. Using the conjunctions provided, connect the sentences in the left column with those directly opposite in the right column.

1. Peter steht heute schon um fünf auf.	weil	Er muss sein Referat fertig schreiben.
2. Es sind nur noch wenige Stunden.	bis	Das Seminar bei Professor Weber fängt an.
3. Martin macht heute das Frühstück.	damit	Peter kann länger schreiben.
4. Um halb neun muss Martin weg.	weil	Seine Vorlesungen fangen um neun an.
5. Peter will das Referat noch genau durchlesen.	bevor	Er muss wegfahren.
6. Aber er kommt zu spät zur Uni.	wenn	Er liest es zu Hause durch.
7. Peter nimmt ein Taxi.	obwohl	Das kostet viel Geld.
8. Er nimmt das Taxi.	damit	Er kann das Referat im Taxi noch schnell durchlesen.

i **4-37 Fragen, Fragen, Fragen.** You and your partner are sharing information about Kathrin, Florian, and Frau Özal. Begin the responses to your partner's requests for information with the conjunctions provided. The questions and responses for **S2** are in the *Anhang* on page A7.

S1: Warum geht Florian nicht ins Kino?

S2: Warum geht Kathrin nicht ins Kino?

S2: Weil er ein Referat schreiben muss.

S1: Weil …

		KATHRIN	FLORIAN	FRAU ÖZAL
Warum geht … nicht ins Kino?	weil	Sie muss Briefe schreiben.		Sie kann keine Babysitterin finden.
Geht … heute schwimmen?	wenn		Es wird sehr heiß.	
Wann geht … nach Hause?	sobald	Der Regen hört auf.	Seine Vorlesungen sind zu Ende.	
Wie lange schläft … sonntags?	bis			Ihre Kinder wachen auf.
Wann sieht … gern fern?	bevor	Sie steht auf.		
Warum arbeitet …?	damit	Sie kann weiterstudieren.	Er kann einen Wagen kaufen.	

4-38 Lebst du gesund oder ungesund? Choose responses to your partner's questions that reflect your lifestyle.

S1: Trinkst du Kaffee?

S2: Nein, ich trinke keinen Kaffee. / Ja, ich trinke Kaffee.

S1: Warum nicht? / Warum?

S2: Weil …

1. Trinkst du Kaffee?
2. Trinkst du Alkohol?
3. Rauchst du?
4. Trinkst du viel Milch?
5. Frühstückst du jeden Morgen?
6. Isst du viel Fleisch?
7. Machst du Sport?
8. Nimmst du Vitamine?
…

Ich will fit bleiben°.   *stay*
Ich bin sowieso° viel zu nervös.   *anyway*
Ich will nicht krank werden.
Ich kann dann besser denken.
Ich habe keine Zeit.
Ich kann ohne° Kaffee/Zigaretten nicht leben.   *without*
Ich bin Vegetarier(in).
…

4-39 Martin hat Geburtstag. Tell the story of Martin's birthday party. Using the coordinating or subordinating conjunctions provided, connect the sentences in the left column with those directly opposite in the right column.

1. Martin lädt° meistens viele Freunde ein.	wenn	Er hat Geburtstag.	**lädt … ein:** *invites*
2. Heute ist Freitag, der siebte Juli.	und	Martin wird heute einundzwanzig.	
3. Das ist ein wichtiger° Geburtstag.	aber	Martin lädt diesmal nur Claudia und Stephanie ein.	*important*
4. Peter muss er nicht extra einladen.	denn	Peter ist ja sein Mitbewohner.	
5. Heute geht Martin gleich nach Hause.	sobald	Seine letzte Vorlesung ist zu Ende.	
6. Zu Hause bäckt er dann einen Apfelkuchen.	weil	Claudia mag seinen Apfelkuchen so gern.	
7. Peter räumt das Zimmer auf.	bevor	Claudia und Stephanie kommen.	
8. Dann hören Martin und Peter eine CD an.	bis	Claudia und Stephanie kommen endlich.	
9. Stephanie kommt zuerst.	und	Sie muss dann gleich Kaffee kochen.	
10. Claudia kommt zuletzt°.	weil	Sie muss freitags immer bis siebzehn Uhr arbeiten.	*last*

„Warum haben die Franzosen so lange Brote?"

„Damit Sie die französische Käsevielfalt genießen können!"

Dependent clause before independent clause

If the dependent clause precedes the independent clause, the entire dependent clause becomes the first element in the sentence. The independent clause then begins with the conjugated verb (i.e., the verb with personal endings). The conjugated verbs of both clauses thus appear side by side, separated by a comma.

dependent clause	independent clause
Bevor ich **aufstehe**,	**sehe** ich meistens eine halbe Stunde **fern.**
Wenn du fit bleiben **willst**,	**musst** du viel mehr Sport machen.

4-40 Lauras Tag. In each set, combine the dependent clauses with the independent clauses so that the resulting sentences make good sense.

S: Bevor Laura frühstückt, geht sie eine halbe Stunde joggen.

1. Bevor Laura frühstückt,
   Bevor Laura joggen geht,

   Sie trinkt ein Glas Milch.
   Sie geht eine halbe Stunde joggen.

2. Bis Laura zurückkommt,
   Bis Laura zur Uni muss,

   Ihre Mutter macht das Frühstück.
   Sie liest dann noch die Zeitung.

3. Sobald Lauras letzte Vorlesung
      zu Ende ist,
   Sobald Laura zu Hause ist,

   Sie macht das Abendessen.
   Sie fährt nach Hause.

4. Weil ihre Mutter oft sehr lange
      arbeiten muss,
   Weil Laura oft noch
      Hausaufgaben machen muss,

   Laura macht meistens das
      Abendessen.
   Ihre Mutter wäscht° dann ab.

wäscht ... ab: *does the dishes*

5. Wenn Laura ihre Hausaufgaben
      fertig hat,
   Wenn Laura im Bett ist,

   Sie schläft immer gleich ein.
   Sie geht meistens bald ins Bett.

4-41 Was machst du, ...?

S1:

Was machst du, bevor du zur Uni
   gehst?

Was machst du, sobald deine letzte
   Vorlesung zu Ende ist?

Was machst du, wenn du deine
   Hausaufgaben fertig hast?

S2:

Bevor ich zur Uni gehe, ...

Sobald meine letzte Vorlesung zu
   Ende ist, ...

Wenn ich meine Hausaufgaben
   fertig habe, ...

WWW See which **Bundesliga** team is currently number one at www.prenhall.com/treffpunkt
→ Kapitel 4 → Web Resources → Kultur

INFOBOX

Fußball: King of sports in Germany

Fußball is so much a part of German sports culture that it's hard to imagine it hasn't always been that way. Before World War II, Germany had only a lackluster national team, especially compared to its successful competitors in Austria, Hungary, and England. It was not until 1954, when the national team won its first World Cup in Bern, Switzerland, that **Fußball** really came into its own in Germany. Nine years after the end of World War II, Germany's unexpected win over Hungary went a long way toward giving Germans the feeling that they were once again a part of the world community.

Today **Fußball** is a multimillion-euro business. Top **Fußballspieler** enjoy celebrity status and earn large salaries. Many players are from other countries. On soccer season weekends, about 300,000 fans flock to the stadiums to cheer on their favorite teams in the **Bundesliga.** With 6 to 7 million viewers, televised games pull in huge advertising revenues. Once considered a working-class sport, **Fußball** has become a national passion.

While not as lucrative as men's soccer, professional women's soccer holds its own: the German national team has won many European and World tournaments as well as bronze medals at the Olympic games in 2000 and 2004.

Fußball is more than just a spectator sport in Germany. The game is played by young and old, male and female, mostly as a leisure-time activity. Just about every town has an amateur soccer team and each team belongs to the **Deutscher Fußball-Bund.** With 6.2 million members, this umbrella organization is the largest sporting association in the country.

Frauenfußballweltmeisterschaft 2003: Deutschland vs. USA

Germany won the World Cup again in 1974 and 1990. Germany hosted the games in 1974 and 2006. The U.S. was host in 1994.

A **Bundesliga** team can hire five **Nichteuropäer.** There is no limit to the number of players from other EU countries, as long as there are 12 German members on the team.

Zusammenschau

▣ ■ Video-Treff ·······

Ein typischer Tag

Christina, Ursula, André, Maiga, and Stefan Kuhlmann talk about their daily routines.

Zum besseren Verstehen

4-42 Was ist das auf Englisch?

1. Ich **bringe** dann die Wohnung **in Ordnung.**
2. Ich habe eine Vorlesung in **Sinologie** und lerne chinesische Aussprache.
3. Ich esse **entweder** ein Brot von zu Hause **oder** ich gehe in die Mensa.
4. Wenn ich **großen Hunger habe,** dann gehe ich in die Mensa.
5. Ich gehe um eins oder zwei ins Bett. Ich bin **ein Nachtmensch.**
6. Ein typischer Tag fängt **ohne** Frühstück an, weil ich nicht gern frühstücke.
7. Danach fahre ich mit dem Fahrrad in die Uni, meistens **etwas knapp.**

a. either . . . or
b. without
c. a night person
d. Chinese Studies
e. just barely in time
f. am really hungry
g. tidy up

Now watch the video and complete the post-viewing activities in the *Video-Treff* section of the *Student Activities Manual.*

🔊 ■ Hören

Ein typischer Tag in Lisas Leben

Listen as Lisa describes a typical day in her life.

NEUE VOKABELN

Punkt halb sieben	*six-thirty on the dot*	**eineinhalb**	*one and a half*
die Dusche	*shower*	**auf·passen**	*to pay attention*
dazu	*with it*	**mit·schreiben**	*to take notes*

4-43 Erstes Verstehen. Check off which words or expressions you hear in the three categories.

ESSEN UND TRINKEN	AKTIVITÄTEN	TAGESZEITEN
_____ Müsli	_____ ausgehen	_____ Viertel vor acht
_____ Joghurt	_____ aufstehen	_____ halb acht
_____ Milch	_____ mitgehen	_____ Viertel nach acht
_____ Kaffee	_____ mitschreiben	_____ halb elf
_____ Apfel	_____ lesen	_____ Viertel vor zwölf
_____ Käse	_____ kochen	_____ halb fünf

4-44 Detailverstehen. Listen to the narrative again and write responses to the following questions.

1. Warum geht Lisa jeden Morgen um halb sieben joggen? *Weil …*
2. Was isst und trinkt Lisa zum Frühstück?
3. Wann fängt Lisas erste Vorlesung an?
4. Wann geht Lisa in die Cafeteria? *Sobald …*
5. Warum geht Lisa um halb elf eine Stunde schwimmen? *Damit …*
6. Was macht Lisa, bevor sie zu Mittag isst?
7. Warum kommt Lisa erst um fünf nach Hause?
8. Warum kocht Lisa ein gutes Abendessen, bevor sie ihre Hausaufgaben macht? *Weil …*

4-44: Lisa's narrative is in the 1st person singular. Remember to write your responses in the 3rd person singular.

■ Schreiben und Sprechen

4-45 Ein Interview. You and your partner take on the roles of an interviewer and Lisa. The illustrations show Lisa how to respond to the interviewer's questions.

1. Wann stehst du morgens auf, Lisa, und was machst du dann zuerst?

2. Joggen, das macht hungrig. Was isst und trinkst du zum Frühstück?

3. Wann beginnt deine erste
   Vorlesung und wann ist sie
   zu Ende?

4. Was machst du dann?

5. Was isst und trinkst du dort?

6. Hast du dann wieder eine
   Vorlesung?

7. Joggen um halb sieben,
   Schwimmen um halb elf. Warum
   machst du denn so viel Sport?

8. Gehst du dann zum
   Mittagessen?

9. Von wann bis wann hast du
   nachmittags Vorlesungen?

10. Um wie viel Uhr kommst du
    nach Hause?

4-46 Das ist mein Tag. Using the questions below to guide you, describe a
typical day in your life. To answer the question **Warum?,** use a dependent clause
introduced by **weil** or **damit.**

Wann stehst du auf? Warum so früh/so spät?
Was isst und trinkst du zum Frühstück?
Wann musst du zur Uni?
Was sind deine Lieblingsvorlesungen? Warum?
Wann und was isst du zu Mittag?
Machst du Sport? Warum?/Warum nicht? Wann machst du das?
Hast du einen Job? Wann und wo arbeitest du?
Wann und wo lernst du?
Gehst du abends oft aus? Wohin gehst du?

Schreibtipp: By using the questions
to guide you, you will include both
modal verbs and separable-prefix
verbs in your description. To make
your writing more interesting, you
could divide your description into
three paragraphs, i.e., what you do
in the morning, the afternoon, and
the evening. Try to start some of
your sentences with elements other
than the subject: **Weil ich schon
um acht eine Vorlesung habe,
..., Meistens ..., Zum
Frühstück esse ich ..., Von 10
bis 12 habe ich ...,** etc.

Lesen ·······································

Zum besseren Verstehen

There is a Swiss cross on the handle of an original Swiss Army Knife. On the base of the main blade are the words "VICTORINOX, SWITZERLAND, STAINLESS, ROSTFREI."

4-47 The Swiss Army Knife.

1. Do you own an original Swiss Army Knife?
2. How many blades and what other tools does your knife have?
3. Do you know why this knife is called a Swiss Army Knife?

4-48 Was ist das auf Englisch?

1. Das *Swiss Army Knife* ist ein **Taschenmesser.**
2. Ein **Messerschmied** macht nicht nur Taschenmesser, sondern auch andere Messer.
3. In jeder Armee gibt es **Soldaten** und Offiziere.
4. 1891 bekommt der Schweizerische Messerschmiedverband den **Auftrag** für die Produktion von Soldatenmessern.
5. Ein Jahr später **entwickelt** Karl Elsener das Schweizer „Offiziersmesser".
6. 1909 **stirbt** Karl Elseners Mutter im Alter von 73 Jahren.
7. 1945 ist der **Zweite Weltkrieg** zu Ende.
8. Das *Swiss Army Knife* wird jetzt ein ganz großer **Erfolg.**

a. contract
b. develops
c. soldiers
d. success
e. pocket knife
f. Second World War
g. knifesmith
h. dies

Karl Elsener

www Check out the latest Victorinox innovations at
www.prenhall.com/treffpunkt
→ Kapitel 4 → Web Resources
→ Kultur

| **LEUTE** | **Karl Elsener und das Schweizer Offiziersmesser** |

Als[1] Karl Elsener im Jahr 1884 in Ibach im Kanton Schwyz eine kleine Messerwerkstatt[2] eröffnet[3], haben viele Schweizer Messerschmiede nicht genug Arbeit. Die Schweizer Armee aber kauft die Taschenmesser für ihre Soldaten bei einer großen Firma in Deutschland, denn in der Schweiz gibt es noch keine industrielle Massenproduktion. Karl Elsener möchte die „Soldatenmesser" in der Schweiz produzieren. Er gründet[4] deshalb mit fünfundzwanzig Kollegen den Schweizerischen Messerschmiedverband[5] und 1891 bekommt dieser Verband den Auftrag für die Soldatenmesser. Aber schon nach einem Jahr findet die Armee die Schweizer Messer zu teuer und kauft sie wieder in Deutschland. Da denkt Karl Elsener, die Offiziere möchten vielleicht ein besseres Taschenmesser als die Soldaten, und er entwickelt das hübsche und elegante „Offiziersmesser". Die Offiziere müssen dieses Taschenmesser selbst bezahlen, aber weil es so schön ist, kaufen sie es trotzdem[6], und bald kaufen es auch viele andere Leute. Als dann aus Deutschland die ersten Imitationen kommen, darf Karl Elsener im Jahr 1909 sein Offiziersmesser mit dem Schweizer Kreuz[7] schützen[8]. In diesem Jahr stirbt auch seine Mutter Victoria, und er nennt[9] seine Firma „Victoria". 1923 sind die Messer dann aus dem rostfreien Stahl[10] Inox, und die Firma heißt jetzt „Victorinox".

International erfolgreich[11] wird das Schweizer Offiziersmesser aber erst nach dem Ende des Zweiten Weltkriegs. Die *PX Stores* verkaufen es als *Swiss Army Knife* an die amerikanischen Soldaten und der Export nach Amerika und in viele andere Länder beginnt. Heute gibt es über hundert Modelle und

Victorinox produziert neben[12] vielen anderen Produkten täglich 34 000 *Swiss Army Knives* und exportiert sie in über hundert Länder. Die amerikanischen Präsidenten Lyndon B. Johnson, Ronald Reagan und George H.W. Bush bestellen[13] Tausende von Spezialmodellen mit ihrer Signatur und dem Präsidenten-Siegel[14] für Besucher im Weißen Haus. *Swiss Army Knives* sind heute nicht nur in Millionen Hosentaschen, bei jeder Expedition und sogar bei den Spaceshuttle-Flügen der NASA, sondern auch in der MoMa Design Kollektion in New York.

Soldatenmesser von 1891

Victorinox kennt aber nicht nur Erfolge, sondern auch Krisen. Nach dem 11. September 2001 darf man die *Swiss Army Knives* nicht mehr ins Flugzeug nehmen, und dazuhin[15] kommen aus China Hunderttausende von billigen Imitationen. Victorinox, jetzt unter Carl Elsener IV., entlässt[16] aber keine Mitarbeiter, sondern reagiert mit immer neuen innovativen Produkten wie zum Beispiel[17] dem „Swiss Bit Schweizer Offiziersmesser mit Memory Stick".

[1]*when* [2]*knifesmith's shop* [3]*sets up* [4]*founds* [5]*knifesmiths' association* [6]*anyway*
[7]*cross* [8]*protect (against imitation)* [9]*names* [10]**rostfreien Stahl:** *stainless steel* [11]*successful*
[12]*in addition to* [13]*order* [14]*seal* [15]*additionally* [16]*lets go* [17]*for example*

Arbeit mit dem Text

4-49 Wer oder was ist das? Match the following items from the story of the Swiss Army Knife appropriately.

1. Victoria Elsener
2. Soldatenmesser
3. Inox
4. Carl Elsener IV.
5. *PX Store*
6. Schweizer Kreuz

a. Geschäft für amerikanische Soldaten
b. Schweizer nationales Symbol
c. Karl Elseners Mutter
d. rostfreier Stahl
e. jetziger Direktor von Victorinox
f. Taschenmesser für Schweizer Soldaten

4-50 Das Schweizer Offiziersmesser. Find the appropriate response for each question.

1. Wo kauft die Schweizer Armee ihre Soldatenmesser vor 1891?
2. Warum will Karl Elsener die Soldatenmesser in der Schweiz produzieren?
3. Warum darf Karl Elsener sein Offiziersmesser 1909 mit dem Schweizer Kreuz schützen?
4. Woher kommt der Name „Victorinox"?
5. Wie heißt das Schweizer Offiziersmesser in den *PX Stores*?
6. Warum verkauft Victorinox nach dem 11. September nicht mehr so viele *Swiss Army Knives*?
7. Wie reagiert die Firma Victorinox auf die billigen Imitationen aus China?

a. *Swiss Army Knife.*
b. Damit die Leute sehen können, welche Messer original Schweizer Produkte sind.
c. Weil man sie nicht mehr ins Flugzeug nehmen darf.
d. In Deutschland.
e. Sie entwickelt immer neue innovative Produkte.
f. Weil er nicht genug Arbeit hat.
g. „Victoria" ist der Name von Karl Elseners Mutter und „Inox" steht für „rostfreier Stahl".

Modernes Offiziersmesser

Wort, Sinn und Klang

Wörter unter der Lupe

Denn versus *dann*

The words **denn** and **dann** occur very frequently in German. Because these words are so similar in sound and appearance and because **denn** has two very different meanings, they deserve a closer look.

- The flavoring particle **denn** occurs only in questions. It expresses curiosity and interest, and sometimes irritation.

  Wann stehst du **denn** endlich auf?   *When are you finally going to get up?*

- The coordinating conjunction **denn** introduces a clause that states the reason for something. Its English equivalents are *because* and *for.* Like **und, oder, aber,** and **sondern,** this **denn** does not count as an element in the sentence and therefore does not affect the position of the verb.

  Frau Berger fährt oft nach   *Mrs. Berger often goes to*
      Leipzig, **denn** sie hat dort   *Leipzig, **because** she has*
      viele Freunde und Verwandte.   *many friends and relatives there.*

- The adverb **dann** is an equivalent of English *then.* It expresses that a certain thing or action follows another thing or action. **Dann** does count as an element in the sentence and therefore affects the position of the verb.

  Zuerst sind wir ein paar Tage   *First we'll be in Paris for a few*
      in Paris und **dann** fliegen   *days and **then** we're flying*
      wir nach Berlin.   *to Berlin.*

Airport Express Schönefeld

Hier kurz warten und dann
nur 31 Minuten
bis Schönefeld.
Von da in alle Welt.

4-51 *Denn* or *dann*?

1. HEIKE: Was schreibst du _____ da?
   SYLVIA: Einen Brief an meine Eltern.
   HEIKE: Und _____? Was machst du _____?
   SYLVIA: _____ rufe ich Holger an, _____ wir wollen heute Abend zusammen ins Kino gehen.
2. MARTIN: Was möchtest du _____ essen, Claudia?
   CLAUDIA: Lasagne. Im Ristorante Napoli esse ich immer Lasagne, _____ hier ist sie am besten.
3. SONJA: Wann rufst du _____ endlich deine Eltern an?
   LAURA: Erst heute Abend, _____ _____ sind sie bestimmt zu Hause.

🔊 Zur Aussprache

The vowels *ä, ö,* and *ü*

The vowels **a, o,** and **u** can be umlauted: **ä, ö,** and **ü.** These umlauted vowels can be long or short. Listen carefully and you will hear the difference between **a, o, u** and their umlauted equivalents.

4-52 Hören Sie gut zu und wiederholen Sie!

a (lang)	ä (lang)	a (kurz)	ä (kurz)
Glas	Gläser	alt	älter
Rad	Räder	kalt	kälter
Vater	Väter	lang	länger

o (lang)	ö (lang)	o (kurz)	ö (kurz)
Brot	Brötchen	oft	öfter
Sohn	Söhne	Tochter	Töchter
groß	größer	Wort	Wörter

If you have trouble producing the sound **ö,** pucker your lips as if to whistle, hold them in this position, and say *eh*.

u (lang)	ü (lang)	u (kurz)	ü (kurz)
Buch	Bücher	Mutter	Mütter
Bruder	Brüder	jung	jünger
Fuß	Füße	dumm	dümmer

If you have trouble producing the sound **ü,** pucker your lips as if to whistle, hold them in this position, and say *ee*.

Brötchen: The **ö** and the suffix **-chen** signal that this is the diminutive form of **Brot** (compare English *manikin* and *man, piglet* and *pig*). The diminutive forms of nouns with **a, o, u,** and **au** add an umlaut. What are the diminutive forms of **Haus, Bett, Hund,** and **Sohn**? You will encounter more diminutive forms in the story below.

4-53 Das Rübenziehen.

In the following story about pulling out a turnip, long and short vowels, including umlauts, stand in sharp contrast to one another. Listen carefully and try to imitate the speaker.

Väterchen hat Rüben gesät°. Er will eine dicke Rübe herausziehen; er packt° sie beim Schopf°, er zieht und zieht und kann sie nicht herausziehen. Väterchen ruft Mütterchen: Mütterchen zieht Väterchen, Väterchen zieht die Rübe, sie ziehen und ziehen und können sie nicht herausziehen.

hat ... gesät: *has sown / grabs by the top*

Kommt das Söhnchen: Söhnchen zieht Mütterchen, Mütterchen zieht Väterchen, Väterchen zieht die Rübe, sie ziehen und ziehen und können sie nicht herausziehen.

Kommt das Hündchen: Hündchen zieht Söhnchen, Söhnchen zieht Mütterchen, Mütterchen zieht Väterchen, Väterchen zieht die Rübe, sie ziehen und ziehen und können sie nicht herausziehen.

Kommt das Hühnchen: Hühnchen zieht Hündchen, Hündchen zieht Söhnchen, Söhnchen zieht Mütterchen, Mütterchen zieht Väterchen, Väterchen zieht die Rübe, sie ziehen und ziehen und können sie nicht herausziehen.

Kommt das Hähnchen: Hähnchen zieht Hühnchen, Hühnchen zieht Hündchen, Hündchen zieht Söhnchen, Söhnchen zieht Mütterchen, Mütterchen zieht Väterchen, Väterchen zieht die Rübe: sie ziehen und ziehen – schwupps°, ist die Rübe heraus, und das Märchen° ist aus.

whoops
fairy tale

Nomen

die Autobahn, -en	freeway
der Bahnhof, ̈-e	train station
der Fahrplan, ̈-e	train or bus schedule
die Hausaufgabe, -n	homework (assignment)
das Referat, -e	(oral) report; paper
das Seminar, -e	seminar
die Tafel, -n	(black)board
der Erfolg, -e	success
der Fernseher, -	television set
der Geburtstag, -e	birthday
der Schnee	snow
die Tasche, -n	pocket; bag
das Taschenmesser, -	pocket knife

Verben

bleiben	to stay, to remain
buchstabieren	to spell
rauchen	to smoke
reden	to talk, to speak
schneien	to snow
vergessen (vergisst)	to forget
ab·fahren (fährt ab)	to leave, to depart
an·kommen	to arrive
an·hören	to listen to
an·probieren	to try on
aus·probieren	to try out
aus·gehen	to go out
auf·passen	to pay attention
auf·wachen	to wake up
durch·lesen (liest durch)	to read through
ein·laden (lädt ein)	to invite
ein·schlafen (schläft ein)	to fall asleep
fern·sehen (sieht fern)	to watch TV
heim·kommen	to come home
mit·kommen	to come along
vor·haben	to plan, to have planned
weg·fahren (fährt weg)	to drive away
weiter·lesen (liest weiter)	to continue reading
zurück·kommen	to come back
kennen lernen	to get to know
spazieren gehen	to go for a walk
Rad fahren (fährt Rad)	to ride a bike, to go cycling

Konjunktionen

bevor	before
bis	until
damit	so that
obwohl	although, even though
sobald	as soon as
weil	because
wenn	if; when

Andere Wörter

erfolgreich	successful(ly)
anders	different(ly)
besonders	especially
endlich	finally, at last
genug	enough
schriftlich	in writing; written
selbst	myself, yourself, herself, etc.

Ausdrücke

du hast recht	you're right
nach Mitternacht	after midnight
von Montag ab	from Monday on
vor dem Fernseher	in front of the TV
zu Fuß gehen	to walk
Lass mich in Ruhe!	Stop bothering me!

Das Gegenteil

der Anfang, ̈-e ≠ das Ende, -n	beginning ≠ end
gesund ≠ ungesund	healthy ≠ unhealthy
möglich ≠ unmöglich	possible ≠ impossible
ordentlich ≠ unordentlich	neat, tidy ≠ messy, sloppy
oft ≠ selten	often ≠ seldom, rarely
rechts ≠ links	right, to the right ≠ left, to the left
zuerst ≠ zuletzt	first ≠ last

Leicht zu verstehen

der Alkohol	die Zigarette, -n
die Firma, Firmen	joggen
das Foto, -s	nervös
der Stress	typisch

Autobahn, Bahnhof: The literal meaning of **Bahn** is *path* or *track*. By itself, **die Bahn** is now used to refer to the whole German railway system.

A **Referat** is usually presented orally in a seminar and then handed in in written form for final grading.

Linkshändler **photo:** Note the play on words here between **-händler** (*dealer*) and **-händer** (*-handed*).

Wörter im Kontext

4-54 Welches Präfix passt hier?

weg / auf / ein / vor / heim

1. Wachst du immer so früh _____?
2. Wann fährst du morgens _____ und wann kommst du abends _____?
3. Was hast du heute Nachmittag _____?
4. Schläfst du in Professor Altmanns Vorlesung auch immer _____?

fern / an / mit / weiter / aus / ab

5. Heute Abend gehen wir alle _____. Kommst du _____?
6. Siehst du immer so viel _____?
7. Warum hörst du denn auf, Matthias? Lies doch _____.
8. Wann fährt euer Zug in Frankfurt _____ und wann kommt er in Hannover _____?

4-55 Was macht hier Sinn? Match the dependent and independent clauses appropriately.

1. Bevor du das Kleid kaufst,
2. Bevor du wegfährst,
3. Obwohl Karl Asthma hat,
4. Obwohl Bergers nie genug Geld haben,
5. Sobald ich mein neues Taschenmesser habe,
6. Sobald seine Eltern weg sind,
7. Wenn Maria Geburtstag hat,
8. Wenn du Professor Ports Vorlesungen verstehen willst,

   a. gehen sie sehr oft aus.
   b. musst du es anprobieren.
   c. sitzt Robert vor dem Fernseher.
   d. lädt sie immer alle ihre Freunde ein.
   e. musst du mein Referat durchlesen.
   f. musst du sehr gut aufpassen.
   g. darfst du es auch ausprobieren.
   h. raucht er jeden Tag ein paar Zigaretten.

> **Fernseher:** The prefix *tele-* in *television* is derived from Greek and means *far* in English and **fern** in German. Can you guess the meanings of **Fernost, Fernkurs, Fernglas, Ferngespräch, Fernfahrer?**
>
> **Zigarette:** All nouns that end in -ette are feminine (**Operette, Schlaftablette, Kassette, Klarinette**).

4-56 Was passt wo?

unordentlich / in Ruhe / endlich / genug / zu Fuß / besonders / anders

1. Schweizer Schokolade mag ich _____ gern.
2. Hast du noch _____ Geld?
3. Bist du immer so _____? Dein Zimmer sieht ja wie ein Schweinestall aus!
4. Von Montag ab wird alles _____.
5. Wann bist du denn _____ fertig? Der Bus kommt in fünf Minuten!
6. Warum kannst du mich denn nicht endlich _____ lassen?
7. Nehmt ihr den Bus oder geht ihr_____?

4-57 Gegenteile.

selten / ungesund / möglich / rechts / oft / links / gesund / unmöglich

1. Sport machen ist _____. Rauchen ist _____.
2. In Finnland schneit es _____. In Sizilien schneit es nur sehr _____.
3. In England fährt man _____. In Nordamerika fährt man _____.
4. Ich fahre so schnell wie _____, aber ich kann _____ in zehn Minuten zu Hause sein.

Wir sind ein rauchfreies Krankenhaus und setzen uns aktiv für den Schutz von Nichtrauchern ein.

Liebe Raucherinnen und Raucher! Wir bitten um Ihr Verständnis.

Vielen Dank!

Freizeit – Ferienzeit

Kajaker auf der Müritz-Elde-Wasserstraße

Kommunikationsziele

Making plans . . .

- for a day off
- for a vacation

Expressing personal opinions and tastes

Comparing qualities and characteristics

Talking about . . .

- whom and what you know
- events in the past

Strukturen

More on the accusative:

- personal pronouns
- prepositions

Dafür and **dagegen**

The comparative and superlative

Word order: Position of the verb in object clauses

Wissen and **kennen**

Simple past tense of **haben, sein,** and the modal verbs

Kultur

Munich

Vacationing on a shoestring

Paid vacations in North America and Europe

South Tyrol

Video-Treff: **Ferienzeit**

Lesen: **Ludwig II. von Bayern**

Morgen haben wir keine Vorlesungen

Claudia erzählt Stephanie, was sie morgen vorhat.

STEPHANIE: Was machst du morgen, Claudia?

CLAUDIA: Zuerst schlafe ich mal bis elf oder halb zwölf und dann rufe ich Martin an.

STEPHANIE: Und er holt dich ab und schleppt dich wieder in die Alte Pinakothek.

CLAUDIA: Ja denkste! Dort waren wir jetzt oft genug. Morgen machen wir mal, was ich will.

STEPHANIE: Und das ist?

CLAUDIA: Erst gehen wir Weißwürste essen beim Donisl am Marienplatz …

STEPHANIE: Mmm, die sind echt lecker dort.

CLAUDIA: Dann gehen wir ins Deutsche Museum und schauen historische Maschinen an.

STEPHANIE: Armer Martin!

CLAUDIA: Und dann fahren wir zum Englischen Garten.

STEPHANIE: Geht ihr dort baden?

CLAUDIA: Nein, wir gehen spazieren. Der Eisbach ist noch viel zu kalt.

STEPHANIE: Und wo esst ihr zu Abend?

CLAUDIA: Morgen geben wir mal viel Geld aus und gehen ins Mövenpick.

Ferienpläne

Frau Ziegler will nicht, was ihre Kinder wollen, aber Herr Ziegler findet eine gute Lösung.

NINA: Mitte Juli beginnen die Sommerferien, Vati. Fahren wir wieder zum Grundlsee? Der Campingplatz dort war echt spitze.

VATER: Aber du weißt doch, dass Mutti nicht dafür ist. Sie wollte schon letztes Jahr nicht mehr campen gehen.

ROBERT: Aber wir hatten doch so viel Spaß dort.

MUTTER: Spaß? Fast jeden Tag Regen und alles nass im Zelt. Und diese primitive Kocherei! Weißt du, Robert, das ist kein Urlaub für mich.

NINA: Aber wir hatten so gute Freunde, Robert und ich. Sie sind dieses Jahr bestimmt wieder dort.

MUTTER: Ich weiß, ich weiß, aber ich brauche auch mal Urlaub und möchte am liebsten in ein Hotel. Und bitte nicht in das billigste, Klaus.

VATER: Auch am Grundlsee?

MUTTER: Wenn es schön ist, habe ich nichts dagegen.

VATER: Ich kenne da nämlich ein kleines, aber sehr komfortables Hotel, nicht weiter als einen halben Kilometer vom Campingplatz. Dann haben die Kinder ihre Freunde, ich kann zum See und angeln gehen …

MUTTER: Und ich kann endlich auch mal ein bisschen ausspannen.

Der Grundlsee in Österreich

Hören

5-1 Richtig oder falsch? You will hear the conversations on page 155. Indicate whether the statements that follow each conversation are **richtig** or **falsch.**

	MORGEN HABEN WIR KEINE VORLESUNGEN			FERIENPLÄNE	
	RICHTIG	FALSCH		RICHTIG	FALSCH
1.	_____	_____	1.	_____	_____
2.	_____	_____	2.	_____	_____
3.	_____	_____	3.	_____	_____
4.	_____	_____	4.	_____	_____

The **Alte Pinakothek** houses art from the 14th to the 18th century; the **Neue Pinakothek** displays art from the 18th to the beginning of the 20th century; the **Pinakothek der Moderne** is home to 20th- and 21st-century art. The **Deutsche Museum** is so large that viewing all the exhibits requires a ten-mile walk.

München: Deutsches Museum

Oktoberfest: The world's largest **Volksfest** employs 12,000 people. In 2005, 6.1 million visitors drank 6.1 million **Maß Bier (die Maß = 1 Liter),** and consumed 479,616 grilled chickens and 359,114 sausages. The 14 beer tents provide seating capacity for 100,000 people.

www Visit the **Münchner Oktoberfest** at www.prenhall.com/treffpunkt
→ Kapitel 5 → Web Resources
→ Kultur

INFOBOX

München

München, the capital of **Bayern** *(Bavaria),* is one of Germany's major cultural centers. It boasts over 60 theaters and six orchestras. The most famous of its many art museums are the **Alte Pinakothek,** the **Neue Pinakothek,** and the **Pinakothek der Moderne. München** is also the home of the largest technical museum in the world, the **Deutsche Museum.**

With close to 60,000 students, the **Ludwig-Maximilians-Universität** in **München** is the largest university in the Federal Republic. Adjoining the university is the **Englische Garten,** a 925-acre park in the heart of the city. The park is a favorite playground for students, who spend their leisure time strolling, cycling, sunbathing, or swimming in the chilly waters of the **Eisbach.**

München, the home of **BMW (Bayerische Motorenwerke)** and **Siemens,** is also an important industrial and high tech center.

The end of September marks the beginning of **München**'s 16-day **Oktoberfest,** which each year attracts about six million visitors from all over the world.

5-2 Fragen und Antworten. Choose the appropriate response to your partner's questions.

1. Warum will Claudia beim Donisl zu Mittag essen?
2. Warum will sie nicht im Eisbach baden gehen?
3. Warum will Claudia ins Deutsche Museum?
4. Warum will sie nicht in die Alte Pinakothek?

a. Weil sie schon viel zu oft dort war.
b. Weil sie gern historische Maschinen anschaut.
c. Weil das Wasser noch viel zu kalt ist.
d. Weil die Weißwürste dort so lecker sind.

■ **Sprachnotiz** ·······························

The flavoring particles *mal* and *doch*

Mal is the shortened form of **einmal** *(once)* and is often used in colloquial German to make a statement or question sound more casual. This usage has no equivalent in English.

Wann besuchst du uns **mal** wieder?   *When are you going to visit us again?*

Mal can also mean *for a change* or *for once.*

Morgen machen wir **mal,** was   *Tomorrow we're doing what I*
    ich will.   *want for a change.*

Doch is often used as an intensifier. It has no English equivalent.

Aber wir hatten **doch** so viel   *But we had so much fun at Grundl*
    Spaß am Grundlsee.   *Lake.*

5-3 Was ist die richtige Antwort? Indicate whether the responses below answer question 1 or question 2 by writing the appropriate number in the spaces provided.

1. Warum wollen Nina und Robert diesen Sommer wieder zum Grundlsee?
2. Warum will Frau Ziegler nicht mehr campen gehen?

_____ Weil sie die primitive Kocherei nicht mag.

_____ Weil der Campingplatz dort echt spitze war.

_____ Weil sie dort so gute Freunde hatten.

_____ Weil im Zelt alles nass wird, wenn es zu viel regnet.

_____ Weil das für sie kein Urlaub ist.

_____ Weil sie dort so viel Spaß hatten.

5-4 Eine Umfrage. Walk around the classroom and survey three or four classmates about their vacation preferences. Fill in the questionnaire as you do so. Then report to the class.

S1: Wann machst du am liebsten   **S2:** Ich mache am liebsten … Ferien.
    Ferien?
Wo machst du am liebsten Ferien?   Ich mache am liebsten … Ferien.
Warum machst du dort am   Weil …
    liebsten Ferien?

PERSON	WANN?	WO?	WARUM?
Lisa	*im Winter*	*in Whistler, B.C.*	*Weil sie gern Ski läuft.*
_____	_____	_____	_____
_____	_____	_____	_____
_____	_____	_____	_____

WWW Plan a trip with **Deutsche Jugendherbergen** at www.prenhall.com/treffpunkt
→ Kapitel 5 → Web Resources
→ Kultur

KULTUR

Vacationing on a shoestring

Many young people experience the landscapes of the German-speaking countries by hiking or biking; hiking trails and bike paths can be found everywhere. A network of over 700 **Jugendherbergen** *(youth hostels)* in Germany, Austria, and Switzerland provides reasonably priced, clean overnight accommodations and meals. Accommodations are dorm-like but much cheaper than a room in a hotel, and some **Jugendherbergen** are housed in interesting old buildings such as medieval castles. They are a good place to get to know other young people from all over the world.

There are also thousands of **Campingplätze** *(campgrounds)* in the German-speaking countries. As in North America, they are usually situated in areas that offer lots of recreational activities. **Campen** is a favorite way of vacationing for families with children.

Die Jugendherberge in Windischleuba, Thüringen

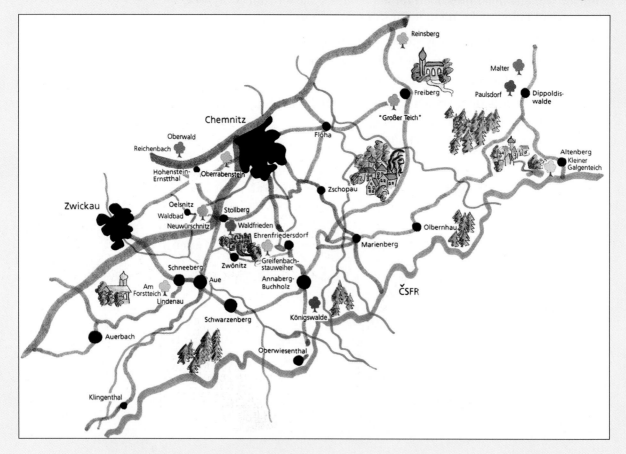

5-5 Campen im Erzgebirge.

Lisa und Ralf leben in Zwickau in Sachsen. Sie haben bald vierzehn Tage Urlaub, wollen campen gehen und studieren deshalb eine Broschüre von Campingplätzen im Erzgebirge. Sie gehen beide gern baden und sie möchten auch ein paar kleine Radtouren machen. Ralf ist ein Fitnessfreak und denkt, dass er auch beim Campen ohne Fitnesscenter und ohne Sauna nicht leben kann. Lisas Lieblingssport ist Segeln, und weil Lisa und Ralf passionierte Angler sind, suchen sie einen Campingplatz, wo sie auch angeln gehen können.

Finden Sie den idealen Campingplatz für Lisa und Ralf!

- Suchen Sie zuerst die vier Campingplätze, wo die beiden angeln gehen können, und schreiben Sie die Namen von diesen Campingplätzen in die ersten vier Lücken[1].
- Haken[2] Sie dann ab, welche von diesen vier Campingplätzen auch Bademöglichkeit[3], Fahrradverleih[4], Fitnesscenter, Sauna und Segeln haben.

[1]spaces [2]check . . . off [3]swimming [4]bike rental

	1.	2.	3.	4.
Angeln	_____	_____	_____	_____
Bademöglichkeit	_____	_____	_____	_____
Fahrradverleih	_____	_____	_____	_____
Fitnesscenter	_____	_____	_____	_____
Sauna	_____	_____	_____	_____
Segeln	_____	_____	_____	_____

	Bademöglichkeit	Tankstelle	Einkaufsmöglichkeit	Fahrradverleih	Bootsverleih	Haustiere	Gaststätte	Surfen/Segeln	Waschautomat	Fitnesscenter	Sauna	Duschen/WC	Kinderspielplatz	Angeln	Behinderte
Altenberg	●	●	●		●		●	●	●	●		●	●		
Freiberg	●	●	●		●		●				●	●			●
Königswalde		●	●	●								●	●		
Lindenau	●		●		●										
Malter	●	●	●	●			●	●	●	●	●	●	●	●	
Oberrabenstein	●	●	●	●	●			●				●			
Paulsdorf	●		●	●					●			●	●	●	
Reichenbach	●	●	●	●	●			●				●	●		
Stollberg	●			●	●		●		●			●	●		

Legende:
- Bademöglichkeit
- Tankstelle
- Einkaufsmöglichkeit
- Sportgeräteausleih/Fahrradverleih
- Bootsverleih
- Haustiere möglich
- Gaststätte
- Surfen/Segeln
- Wasch-, Trockenautomat
- Fitnesscenter
- Sauna
- Duschen, Waschraum, WC
- Kinderspielplatz
- Angeln
- Einrichtungen für Behinderte

Nomen

die Freizeit	leisure time
die Ferien *(pl)*	vacation *(generally of students)*
der Urlaub	vacation *(generally of people in the workforce)*
die Bademöglichkeit, -en	(place to go) swimming; swimming facility
der Campingplatz, ⸚e	campground; campsite
der Fahrradverleih, -e	bike rental
die Jugendherberge, -n	youth hostel
das Zelt, -e	tent
der Baum, ⸚e	tree
der Berg, -e	mountain
das Dorf, ⸚er	village
das Feld, -er	field
der Fluss, ⸚e	river
das Gebirge, -	mountain range
die Insel, -n	island
die Landschaft, -en	landscape
der Regen	rain
das Schloss, ⸚er	castle
der See, -n	lake
der Strand, ⸚e	beach
das Tal, ⸚er	valley
der Wald, ⸚er	woods; forest
die Wolke, -n	cloud

Verben

ab·holen	to pick up
angeln	to fish
an·schauen	to look at
aus·geben (gibt aus)	to spend *(money)*
aus·spannen	to relax
baden	to swim; to bathe
fließen	to flow
schleppen	to drag
wissen (weiß)	to know

In Latin fließen is fluere. What is the English equivalent of Ich spreche fließend Deutsch?

Andere Wörter

bestimmt	definite(ly); for sure
frei	free *(of time)*
lecker	delicious

Bademöglichkeit: Möglichkeit actually means *possibility* or *opportunity*. What is the literal meaning of **Einkaufsmöglichkeit, Kochmöglichkeit, Parkmöglichkeit,** and **Schlafmöglichkeit?** What do you think their English equivalents might be?

Campingplatz: The basic meaning of **Platz** is *place*. What are the English equivalents in the following combinations: **Parkplatz, Marktplatz, Tennisplatz, Golfplatz?**

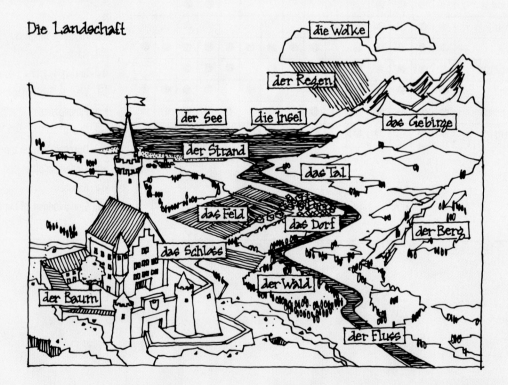

Die Landschaft

Ausdrücke

Anfang Juli	(at) the beginning of July
Ende Juli	(at) the end of July
Mitte Juli	(in) mid-July
eine Reise machen	to go on a trip, to take a trip
Ferien (Urlaub) machen	to go on vacation
Wo machst du am liebsten Ferien?	Where's your favorite vacation spot?
Spaß haben	to have fun
vierzehn Tage	two weeks

Das Gegenteil

das Problem, -e ≠ die Lösung, -en	problem ≠ solution

alt ≠ jung	old ≠ young
arm ≠ reich	poor ≠ rich
nass ≠ trocken	wet ≠ dry
weit ≠ nah	far ≠ near

Leicht zu verstehen

der Angler, -	**der Plan, ⸚e**
die Anglerin, -nen	**die Sauna, -s**
die Broschüre, -n	**campen**
das Campen	**historisch**
das Fitnesscenter, -s	**ideal**
der Garten, ⸚	**komfortabel**
das Hotel, -s	**passioniert**
die Maschine, -n	**primitiv**
das Museum, Museen	

Museum, Museen: Nouns that end in **-um** are almost always neuter, and many form the plural this way. What are the singular forms for **Alben, Zentren, Daten?** To find out how other noun endings signal gender, see p. 188.

Wörter im Kontext

5-6 Was passt zusammen? Match appropriately in each set.

1. Schlösser
2. Lösungen
3. Fische
4. Geld
5. Hotelzimmer

a. angelt man.
b. reserviert man.
c. schaut man an.
d. sucht man.
e. gibt man aus.

6. Wenn man Urlaub macht,
7. Wenn man im Regen steht,
8. Wenn die Sonne scheint,
9. Wenn man viel Geld hat,
10. Wenn man wenig Geld hat,

f. ist man arm.
g. ist man reich.
h. wird man nass.
i. bleibt man trocken.
j. will man ausspannen.

5-7 Was passt zusammen?

1. Obwohl Martin am liebsten in die Alte Pinakothek geht,
2. Claudia will morgen mal viel Geld ausgeben
3. Herr und Frau Ziegler machen immer dann Urlaub,
4. Weil es im Zelt so primitiv war,
5. Nina und Robert möchten wieder zum Grundlsee,
6. Herr Ziegler braucht einen See,
7. Wenn man eine Radtour machen will und kein Rad hat,

a. möchte Frau Ziegler diesen Sommer mal in ein komfortables Hotel.
b. weil sie dort so viel Spaß hatten.
c. weil er ein passionierter Angler ist.
d. will Claudia ihn morgen ins Deutsche Museum schleppen.
e. geht man zum Fahrradverleih.
f. wenn ihre Kinder Schulferien haben.
g. und im Mövenpick zu Abend essen.

Schleppen has come into English via Yiddish.

5-8 Was passt wo? Complete the description of the illustration on the preceding page.

Wolken / Tal / Strand / Berg / fließt / Dorf / Insel / Schloss / Felder / Gebirge / baden

Links im Bild ist ein altes _____, in der Mitte sind ein kleiner Wald und ein Fluss und rechts ist ein _____. Der Fluss _____ durch ein schönes _____ in einen großen See. Direkt am Fluss ist ein kleines _____ und links von dort sind ein paar _____. Im See ist eine kleine _____. Oft _____ auch viele Leute an dem sandigen _____. Am Himmel sind zwei _____, und im _____ regnet es schon.

Kommunikation und Formen

❶ Talking about persons or things without naming them

Personal pronouns in the accusative case

In English the object forms of the personal pronouns are often different from the subject forms, e.g., *I love **him** and he loves **me** too.*

The same is true in German, where the accusative (object) forms of the personal pronouns are often different from the nominative (subject) forms.

> Ich liebe **ihn** und er liebt **mich** auch.   *I love **him** and he loves **me** too.*

Remember that *things* also have gender in German and that this is reflected in the pronoun forms.

> Warum liest du **den Roman** nicht fertig?   *Why don't you finish reading **the novel?***
> Ich finde **ihn** langweilig.   *I find **it** boring.*

personal pronouns							
SINGULAR				**PLURAL**			
NOMINATIVE		ACCUSATIVE		NOMINATIVE		ACCUSATIVE	
ich	*I*	**mich**	*me*	**wir**	*we*	**uns**	*us*
du	*you*	**dich**	*you*	**ihr**	*you*	**euch**	*you*
er	*he, it*	**ihn**	*him, it*				
es	*it*	**es**	*it*	**sie**	*they*	**sie**	*them*
sie	*she, it*	**sie**	*her, it*				
Sie	*you*	**Sie**	*you*	**Sie**	*you*	**Sie**	*you*

5-9 Reisepläne. You and your partner are making plans for a trip. Respond to your partner's questions using the appropriate pronouns.

> **S1:** Kennst du den Grundlsee?   **S2:** Ja, ich kenne ihn.

1. Kennst du den Campingplatz? (die Jugendherberge, den Strand, das Schloss)
2. Nehmen wir das Zelt mit? (die Wanderschuhe, die Fahrräder, den Kajak)
3. Hast du die Kreditkarten? (den Fahrplan, die Kamera, das Handy)
4. Nehmen wir Sylvia mit? (Thomas, Maria und ihren Freund Daniel)

5-10 *Lieben* und *mögen*. Supply the appropriate personal pronouns.

1. Philipp loves Vanessa but, although she is fond of him, Vanessa doesn't love Philipp.

> PHILIPP: Ich liebe dich, Vanessa, liebst du _____ auch?
> VANESSA: Ich mag _____, Philipp, aber ich liebe _____ nicht.

2. Sarah quizzes Philipp about his feelings for Vanessa.

SARAH: Liebst du Vanessa?
PHILIPP: Ja, ich liebe _____, ich liebe _____ sehr.
SARAH: Und Vanessa? Liebt sie _____ auch?
PHILIPP: Sie sagt, sie mag _____, aber sie liebt _____ nicht.

3. Sarah quizzes Vanessa about her feelings for Philipp.

SARAH: Liebst du Philipp?
VANESSA: Ich mag _____, aber ich liebe _____ nicht.
SARAH: Und Philipp? Liebt er _____?
VANESSA: Er sagt, er liebt _____ sehr.

5-11 Wie findest du Davids Pullover? Look at your fellow students. How do you like their clothes, their hairdos, their beards, their glasses, their jewelry?

S1: Wie findest du Davids Pullover?   **S2:** Ich finde ihn echt spitze.
S2: Wie findest du …?   **S3:** Ich finde …
    …

der Pulli	sehr schön
der Pullover	sehr elegant
das Sweatshirt	echt spitze
das T-Shirt	sehr schick
das Hemd	echt toll
die Jeans	sehr hübsch
die Hose	echt cool
der Rock	sehr geschmackvoll° *tasteful*
die Schuhe	gar nicht schlecht

die Frisur

der Ohrring, -e

das Armband, ¨er

die Tätowierung, -en

der Ring, -e

die Halskette, -n

die Brille

der Nasenstecker, -

der Haarschnitt

der Bart

der Schnurrbart

die Baseballkappe, -n

❷ Expressing direction, destination, time, manner, and place

Accusative prepositions

A preposition is a word that combines with a noun or pronoun to form a phrase.

> *For whom* are you printing out this train schedule, *for David* or *for me?*

The noun or pronoun in the prepositional phrase is called the object of the preposition. After the following German prepositions, the noun or pronoun object appears in the accusative case.

durch	*through*	Nächsten Sommer möchte ich mit David **durch die Schweiz** reisen.
für	*for*	**Für wen** druckst du diesen Fahrplan aus, **für mich?**
gegen	*against*	Meine Eltern haben nichts **gegen diese Reise.**
	around	Morgen planen wir die Reise. Ich komme **gegen zwei.**
ohne	*without*	Mach ja keine Pläne **ohne mich!**
um	*at*	**Um acht** läuft beim Studentenwerk ein Dokumentarfilm über° die Schweiz.
	around	Das Studentenwerk ist **um die nächste Ecke°.**

about

corner

In the examples above there are two German equivalents for *around.*

gegen	*around (in a temporal sense)*	**gegen** zwei
um	*around (in a spatial sense)*	**um** die Ecke

Briefkasten links um die Ecke

In colloquial German the prepositions **durch, für,** and **um** are often contracted with the article **das: durchs, fürs, ums.**

Buchst du den Flug **durchs** Reisebüro im Studentenwerk?

Are you booking your flight through the travel agency in the student center?

In deutschen Hotels muss man **fürs** Frühstück nicht extra bezahlen.

In German hotels you don't have to pay extra for breakfast.

Ums Parkhotel stehen viele alte Bäume.

There are many old trees around the Park Hotel.

5-12 Durch, für, gegen, ohne, um? Supply the appropriate prepositions.

1. Sind deine Eltern _____ oder _____ diese Reise?
2. Wie willst du in Deutschland Arbeit finden? _____ deinen Onkel?
3. Hier ist ein Brief _____ dich.
4. Heute müsst ihr mal _____ mich baden gehen.
5. Wohnt Bernd immer noch _____ die nächste Ecke?
6. Trinkst du deinen Kaffee immer _____ Milch und Zucker?
7. _____ dich mache ich diese Radtour nicht.
8. Spielt Schalke 04 morgen _____ Hansa Rostock oder _____ Mainz?
9. Fährt der Zug nach München _____ 17.35 Uhr oder _____ 18.35 Uhr?
10. _____ sieben ist nicht Punkt° sieben. Es ist ein bisschen vor oder nach sieben.

on the dot

5-13 Kleine Gespräche.

▶ Für wen sind diese Fotos?   dein__ Schwester
Für mein__ Bruder?

S1: Für wen sind diese Fotos?   **S2:** Nein, für deine Schwester.
Für meinen Bruder?

1. Durch wen bekommen wir die   eur__ Professor
Theaterkarten? Durch d__
Sekretärin?
2. Für wen holen Sie das Flugticket   sein__ Frau
ab? Für Ihr__ Chef°?   *boss*
3. Gegen wen spielt Kaiserslautern   d__ Stuttgarter Kickers (pl)
nächsten Samstag? Gegen
d__ VfB (m)?
4. Durch wen bekommst du den   mein__ Vetter
Ferienjob? Durch dein__
Onkel?
5. Für wen ist diese Broschüre? Für   dein__ Freund
mein__ Mitbewohnerin?

5-14 Ich reise nie ohne ... What would you never travel without? Check off some items in the list below and add some of your own. Tell your classmates one item that is important to you and then call on another student. Follow the example.

S1: Ich reise nie ohne ein gutes   **S2:** Ich reise nie ohne …
Buch. Und du, David?

☑ eine Packung Aspirin   ❑ meinen Pass
❑ meinen Regenmantel   ❑ meine Zahnbürste°   *toothbrush*
❑ meine ATM Karte   ❑ meinen Regenschirm°   *umbrella*
❑ meine Kreditkarte   ❑ eine Flasche° Wasser   *bottle*
❑ eine warme Jacke   ❑ meinen Studentenausweis°   *student I.D.*
❑ meinen iPod   ❑ mein Handy
❑ _____   ❑ _____

Dafür and *dagegen*

The German equivalents of the prepositional phrases *for it* and *against it* are **dafür** and **dagegen**.

Ist Frau Ziegler für den Campingurlaub am Grundlsee?	*Is Ms. Ziegler for the camping vacation at the Grundlsee?*
Nein, sie ist nicht **dafür**.	*No, she isn't **for it**.*
Hat sie etwas gegen einen Urlaub im Hotel?	*Does she have anything against a vacation in a hotel?*
Nein, sie hat nichts **dagegen**.	*No, she has nothing **against it**.*

5-15 Urlaub am Grundlsee. Complete the following questions and responses with **dafür** or **dagegen**.

S1:

1. Ist Frau Ziegler für den Campingurlaub am Grundlsee?
2. Warum ist sie _____?

3. Ist Herr Ziegler auch gegen einen Campingurlaub?
4. Und warum ist er nicht so sehr _____?

of course 5. Sind die Kinder _____ oder _____?

6. Warum sind sie so sehr _____?

7. Und wenn Herr Ziegler ein komfortables Hotel am Grundlsee findet? Ist seine Frau dann immer noch gegen diesen Urlaub?

S2:

Nein, sie ist nicht _____, sie ist _____.

Sie ist _____, weil Campen für sie kein Urlaub ist.

Nein, er ist nicht so sehr _____.

Weil er ein passionierter Angler ist.

Die Kinder sind natürlich° sehr _____.

Weil sie dort immer so gute Freunde und so viel Spaß haben.

Nein, dann ist sie natürlich auch _____.

❸ Making comparisons

The comparative of adjectives and adverbs

You can compare characteristics and qualities by using the comparative forms of adjectives and adverbs. In contrast to English, German has only one way of forming the comparative: by adding **-er** to the adjective or adverb, e.g., **klein*er*, schnell*er*, schön*er*, primitiv*er*.** Note that the German equivalent of *than* is **als**.

Vom Hotel ist es ein bisschen **weiter** zum See **als** vom Campingplatz.	*From the hotel it's a bit **farther** to the lake **than** from the campground.*
Robert und Nina finden den Campingplatz **interessanter als** ein Hotel.	*Robert and Nina find the campground **more interesting than** a hotel.*

Most German one-syllable adjectives or adverbs with the vowels **a, o,** or **u** are umlauted in the comparative.

a → ä	**o → ö**	**u → ü**
nah – näher	oft – öfter	jung – jünger
warm – wärmer	groß – größer	kurz – kürzer

Die Sommerferien sind viel **länger als** die Weihnachtsferien.

Summer vacation is much longer than Christmas vacation.

Unsere Nachbarn machen **öfter** Urlaub **als** wir.

Our neighbors go on vacation more often than we do.

As in English, a few adjectives and adverbs have irregular comparative forms.

gut – **besser**	hoch° – **höher**
viel – **mehr**	gern – **lieber**

high

Ich übernachte **lieber** in Jugendherbergen **als** in Hotels.

I would rather stay in youth hostels than in hotels.

In Österreich sind die Berge **höher als** in Deutschland.

In Austria the mountains are higher than in Germany.

Adjectives that end in **-er** or **-el** drop the **e** in the comparative.

teuer – **teurer**   dunkel – **dunkler**

Ein gutes Hotel ist **komfortabler als** eine Jugendherberge.

A good hotel is more comfortable than a youth hostel.

■ Sprachnotiz ·······································

Immer and the comparative

Immer is used with the comparative form of adjectives and adverbs to express ideas like *more and more, better and better.*

Ich lerne **immer mehr** Deutsch.

I'm learning more and more German.

Meine Zensuren werden **immer besser.**

My grades are getting better and better.

5-16 Wie alt und wie groß bist du? Walk around the classroom and find out the age and height of your classmates. Use the scale to convert feet and inches to metric measure.

S1: Wie alt bist du?   **S2:** Ich bin …

S1: Dann bist du | so alt wie ich.
| älter als ich.
| jünger als ich.

S1: Und wie groß bist du?   **S2:** Ich bin …

S1: Dann bist du | so groß wie ich.
| größer als ich.
| kleiner als ich.

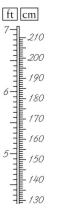

Remember how heights are read: **1,68 = eins achtundsechzig (ein Meter und achtundsechzig Zentimeter).** Note that a comma is used where English would use a decimal point.

5-17 Weißt du das? You and your partner are sharing general knowledge. Use the comparative forms for the adjectives given. **S2**'s questions are in the *Anhang* on page A7.

S1: Ist der Rhein länger als die Donau?

S2: Nein, der Rhein ist kürzer als die Donau.

FRAGEN	ANTWORTEN
lang: Ist der Rhein _____ als die Donau?	
	warm: Nein, in Island ist es _____ als in Grönland.
groß: Ist Deutschland _____ als Kalifornien?	
wenig: Leben in Deutschland _____ Menschen° als in Kalifornien?	
	dunkel: Nein, der Mars ist _____ als die Venus.
	nah: Nein, zum Mars ist es _____ als zum Jupiter.

people

 5-18 Wie heißt die Stadt? Think of a large American or Canadian city. Take turns asking the following questions to find out which city each of you has in mind. Use the comparative forms of the adjectives and adverbs.

1. Ist die Stadt in Amerika oder in Kanada?
2. Ist die Stadt im Norden, im Süden, im Osten oder im Westen von Amerika/Kanada?
3. Ist die Stadt _____ oder _____ als (*name of your college or university town*)? (groß, klein)
4. Ist der Sommer dort _____ oder _____ als der Sommer hier? (heiß, kühl)
5. Ist der Winter dort _____ oder _____ als der Winter hier? (kalt, warm)
6. Regnet es dort _____ oder _____ als hier? (viel, wenig)
7. Schneit es dort _____ oder _____ als hier? (viel, wenig)
8. Heißt die Stadt _____?

kühl: The word **cool** in the sense of *hip* is an "in" word among young people in the German-speaking countries. However, you use **kühl** to describe temperature.

An adjective in the comparative before a noun

When you put an adjective in the comparative before a noun, you add an adjective ending to the comparative form. Remember to add the adjective ending even if you don't repeat the noun to which it refers.

Wer hat das größer**e** Zimmer, Laura oder Maria?
Laura hat ein klein**es** Zimmer und möchte ein größer**es**.

5-19 Entscheidungen. The arrows show **S2** which decision to make.

▶ Welches Fahrrad kaufst du,
das teurer___ oder das billiger___?

S1: Welches Fahrrad kaufst du,
das teurere oder das billigere?

S2: Ich kaufe das teurere Fahrrad.

1. Welchen Apfel möchtest du,
den kleiner__ oder den größer__?

2. Welche Wurst möchtest du,
die dicker__ oder die dünner__?

3. Welches Stück Torte möchtest du,
das kleiner__ oder das größer__?

4. Welchen Wagen kaufst du,
den älter__ oder den neuer__?

5. Welchen Mantel nimmst du,
den heller__ oder den dunkler__?

6. Welche Jacke nimmst du,
die länger__ oder die kürzer__?

7. Welche Wanderschuhe kaufst du,
die leichter__° oder die schwerer__°?

lighter / heavier

8. Welchen ICE nimmst du,
den früher__ oder den später__?

Ab   Zug
9.43 ICE 591 ⬅
9.50 IR 2475
10.43 ICE 791

The superlative

When you want to compare the qualities, characteristics, or capabilities of more than two persons or things, you use the superlative forms of adjectives and adverbs. Unless the superlative precedes a noun (see page 171), you form it by using the pattern **am _____sten** (e.g., **am** schnell**sten**).

Maria spricht schnell, Anna spricht schneller als Maria, aber Tina spricht **am schnellsten.**	*Maria talks fast, Anna talks faster than Maria, but Tina talks **the fastest.***

If the adjective or adverb ends in **-d, -t,** an **s**-sound, or a vowel, you add an **e** before the **st** (e.g., **am leicht*e*sten, am heiß*e*sten, am neu*e*sten**). In contrast to English, German uses the pattern **am _____(e)sten** with all adverbs and adjectives, regardless of their length (e.g., **am interessantesten**).

Evas Referat war interessant, Davids Referat war noch interessanter, aber Lauras Referat war **am interessantesten.**	*Eva's report was interesting, David's report was even more interesting, but Laura's report was **the most** interesting.*

Most one-syllable adjectives or adverbs with the stem vowels **a, o,** or **u** are umlauted in the superlative, just as they are in the comparative (e.g., **am k*ä*ltesten, am w*ä*rmsten, am j*ü*ngsten**).

Im Juli und im August ist es hier **am wärmsten.**	*In July and in August it's **warmest** here.*

A few adjectives and adverbs have irregular superlative forms.

gut	besser	**am besten**
viel	mehr	**am meisten**
groß	größer	**am größten**
gern	lieber	**am liebsten**
hoch	höher	**am höchsten**
nah	näher	**am nächsten**

5-20 Stephanie. In the questions and responses, use the superlative forms of the words provided.

1. MARTIN: Welches Fach findet Stephanie am _____? (interessant)
   CLAUDIA: Sie findet Physik am _____.

2. MARTIN: Für welches Fach muss sie am _____ lernen? (viel)
   CLAUDIA: Für Mathematik muss sie am _____ lernen.

3. MARTIN: Was macht Stephanie an freien Tagen am _____? (gern)
   CLAUDIA: An freien Tagen geht sie am _____ mit Peter in den Englischen Garten.

4. MARTIN: Was für Musik findet sie am _____? (schön)
   CLAUDIA: Sie findet Rock am _____.

5. MARTIN: Welche Sprache spricht Stephanie am _____? (gut)
   CLAUDIA: Sie spricht natürlich Englisch am _____.

5-21 Ein paar persönliche Fragen. Using the superlative forms of the words provided, ask each other the following questions.

1. Welche Sprache sprichst du am _____? (gut)
2. Welches Fach findest du am _____? (interessant)
3. Für welches Fach musst du am _____ lernen? (viel)
4. Was für einen Wagen möchtest du am _____? (gern)
5. Was isst und trinkst du am _____? (gern)
6. Was für Musik findest du am _____? (schön)

An adjective in the superlative before a noun

If an adjective in the superlative precedes a noun, you don't use the pattern **am _____(e)sten.** Instead, you add **-(e)st** plus an adjective ending. Remember that you add the adjective ending even if you don't repeat the noun to which it refers.

David hat jetzt das neu**este** Notebook, aber es ist natürlich auch das teuer**ste**.

David now has the newest notebook, but of course it's also the most expensive one.

Learn about German holidays at www.prenhall.com/treffpunkt → Kapitel 5 → Web Resources → Kultur

INFOBOX

Freizeit: Europe and North America

European workers generally have a greater number of paid **Urlaubstage** per year than their North American counterparts. **Die Schweiz** and the member countries of the **EU** have a legally mandated minimum number of paid vacation days **(gesetzlicher Mindesturlaub).** However, most European employers offer more than this minimum number **(tariflicher Urlaub).** Workers are also paid for national and religious **Feiertage** *(holidays)*, which vary from country to country and often from state to state as well. With 44 days off per year, **Schweden** was **Freizeitweltmeister** in 2004. **Österreich** was in fourth place, **Deutschland** in fifth, and **die Schweiz** in twelfth.

In North America, **Kanada** also has a legally mandated minimum number of paid vacation days. In contrast, the U.S. Fair Labor Standards Act makes no such provision. Aside from federal holidays, the number of paid **Urlaubstage** enjoyed by American workers is typically based on the length of time they have worked for an employer.

FREIZEITWELTMEISTER SCHWEDEN

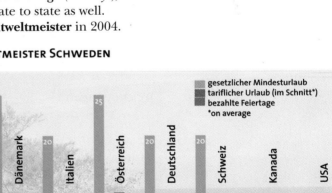

5-22 Superlative. Supply the appropriate superlatives with the proper endings.

▶ teuer   klein

Welche Vase ist die _____?   Die ...

S1: Welche Vase ist die   **S2:** Die kleinste Vase.
teuerste?

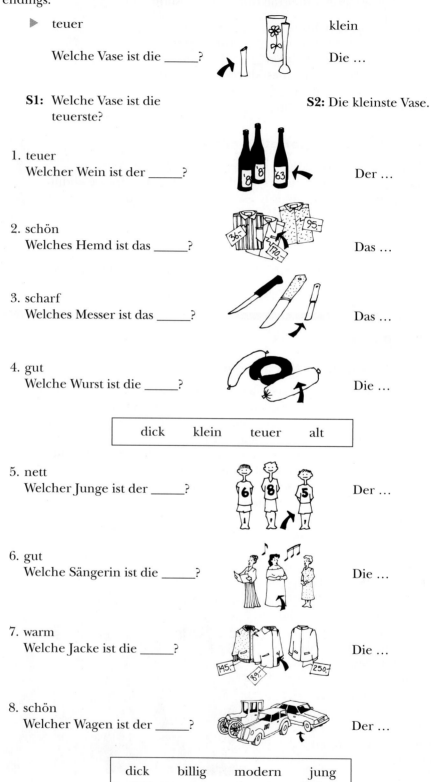

1. teuer
   Welcher Wein ist der _____?   Der ...

2. schön
   Welches Hemd ist das _____?   Das ...

3. scharf
   Welches Messer ist das _____?   Das ...

4. gut
   Welche Wurst ist die _____?   Die ...

dick	klein	teuer	alt

5. nett
   Welcher Junge ist der _____?   Der ...

6. gut
   Welche Sängerin ist die _____?   Die ...

7. warm
   Welche Jacke ist die _____?   Die ...

8. schön
   Welcher Wagen ist der _____?   Der ...

dick	billig	modern	jung

		Frankfurt	München	Düsseldorf	Berlin-Tegel	Hamburg	Köln/Bonn	Berlin-Schönefeld	Dresden	Bremen	Leipzig-Halle
Entfernung zur City (in km)		15	35	8	8	13	K 15 B 22	18	9	4,5	L 18 H 23
Fahrtdauer (in Minuten)	U-Bahn S-Bahn	12	45	12	–	–	–	35	20	17	L 14 H 16
	Bus	–	45	30	20	30	K 20 B 30	–	30	–	L 30 H 35
	Taxi	20	45	30	20	30	K 20 B 30	35	30	15	L 30 H 40
Taxipreis (in Euro)		25	50	20	20	20	K 30 B 35	30	20	12	L 30 H 40
Parkpreis (pro Stunde)		3	3	2	4	2	3	2	3	2	1,50

5-23 Deutsche Flughäfen im Vergleich. The chart compares ten German airports in the following categories: distance from the airport to the city, time it takes to drive this distance with different means of transportation, price charged by taxis, and price for parking. Study the chart with your partner and answer the questions below.

1. Welche Stadt hat die meisten Flughäfen?
2. Wo ist ein Taxi zur City am teuersten?
3. Wo ist ein Taxi zur City am billigsten?
4. Wo ist der Parkpreis pro Stunde am höchsten?
5. Welcher Flughafen hat die kürzeste Entfernung° zur City?   *distance*
6. Von wo ist es weiter zum Flughafen, von Leipzig oder von Halle?
7. Wie kommt man von Düsseldorf schneller zum Flughafen, per Taxi oder per S-Bahn°?   *rapid transit train*

Flughafen Leipzig-Halle

▶ Hören

Auch Martin macht Pläne

Martin's plans for his day off are quite different from Claudia's. Listen as he discusses them with Peter.

Imbiss means *snack*.

NEUE VOKABELN

der Schnellimbiss	*fast-food stand*	**verrückt**	*crazy*
das Bild, -er	*picture; painting*		

5-24 Erstes Verstehen. In which sequence do you hear the following statements and questions?

_____ Dann fahren wir zum Englischen Garten und gehen baden.
_____ Glaubst du, dass sie die alten Bilder dort interessant findet?
_____ Und zuletzt will Claudia bestimmt noch tanzen gehen.
_____ Esst doch mal wieder beim Donisl!
_____ Was machst du morgen den ganzen Tag?
_____ Claudia geht bestimmt gern ins Mövenpick.
_____ Wir essen beim Schnellimbiss eine Knackwurst und gehen dann gleich in die Alte Pinakothek.

Knackwurst: The name of this sausage stems from the cracking sound it makes when you bite into its firm skin: **Knack!**

5-25 Detailverstehen. Listen to the conversation again and write responses to the following questions.

1. Wie lange will Martin morgen schlafen?
2. Warum will er nicht beim Donisl zu Mittag essen?
3. Wo will er mit Claudia eine Knackwurst essen?
4. Warum geht Claudia nicht gern in die Alte Pinakothek?
5. Warum denkt Peter, dass Martin verrückt ist, wenn er im Englischen Garten baden gehen will?
6. Warum will Martin zu Hause zu Abend essen?
7. Was will Martin zuletzt noch machen?

◢ Sprachnotiz

Discourse strategies

When you want to find out more about the plans of the person you are talking to, you can use the question **Und dann?** to elicit more information. You can use it by itself or as an introduction to a more exact question.

Und dann? Was machst du **dann?**
Und dann? Wohin geht ihr **dann?**

5-26 Morgen machen wir mal, was ich will. With a partner, look at the drawings and then take turns narrating what Claudia and Martin have planned for tomorrow.

Claudias Pläne

Martins Pläne

5-27 Heute habe ich frei. Write about your plans for a day off. You could begin your first sentence with **Zuerst …** and the last one with **Zuletzt …**

bis _____ Uhr schlafen
ein gutes Buch lesen
meine Lieblings-CDs anhören
E-Mails schreiben
Freunde besuchen
mein Zimmer aufräumen
meine Wäsche waschen
Muffins backen

fernsehen (Meine Lieblingsprogramme
   sind …)
einkaufen gehen°
Seifenopern° anschauen
Tennis (Computerspiele, Karten, …)
   spielen
ins Kino (ins Konzert, …) gehen

Schreibtipp: When writing about a sequence of events, try to avoid beginning each sentence with **Dann …** Use expressions like **Am Vormittag …, Am Nachmittag …, Um 13 Uhr …,** etc.

to go shopping
soap operas

Seifenoper is a loan translation from American English.

5-28 Freizeitpläne. Now that you have written about your plans for a day off, tell your classmates about them.

❹ Word order

Object clauses introduced by *dass*

Sometimes the object of a verb is not a noun or a pronoun, but a clause. When you introduce this object clause with the conjunction **dass** *(that)*, it becomes a dependent clause. You must therefore put the conjugated verb at the end of the clause.

	verb	object clause	verb	object clause introduced by *dass*
hope	Ich hoffe°,	ihr **habt** immer schönes Wetter.	Ich hoffe,	**dass** ihr immer schönes Wetter **habt.**
	Ich hoffe,	ihr **könnt** mal richtig ausspannen.	Ich hoffe,	**dass** ihr mal richtig ausspannen **könnt.**
	Ich hoffe,	ihr **kommt** total fit **zurück.**	Ich hoffe,	**dass** ihr total fit **zurückkommt.**

Remember that **doch** and **mal** are often used when giving advice.

5-29 Meine überkritische Freundin. Using clauses with **dass,** talk about your friend's criticisms. Your partner responds with advice.

▶ Ich arbeite zu lange.　　　　　　　gehen / doch mal ein bisschen früher nach Hause

S1: Meine Freundin denkt, dass ich zu lange arbeite.

S2: Dann geh doch mal ein bisschen früher nach Hause.

1. Ich bin zu dünn.
2. Ich kann nicht gut tanzen.
3. Meine Haare sind zu lang.
4. Ich kann nicht gut kochen.
5. Ich schaue zu viele Seifenopern an.
6. Ich bin zu nervös.

hair stylist

essen / doch mal ein bisschen mehr
nehmen / doch mal einen Tanzkurs
gehen / doch mal zum Friseur°
nehmen / doch mal einen Kochkurs
lesen / doch mal einen guten Roman
trinken / doch mal weniger Kaffee

5-30 Ratschläge geben. Tell your classmates about something you do that annoys members of your family or your friends. Your classmates should have some advice for you.

S1: Meine Eltern denken, dass ich zu viel fernsehe.

S2: Dann lies doch mal ein gutes Buch.

S3: Dann mach doch mal ein bisschen mehr Sport.

S4: Mein Bruder denkt, dass …

S5: …

Information questions as object clauses

You can introduce information questions with phrases like **Weißt du, …** or **Könnten Sie mir bitte sagen, …** *(Could you please tell me . . .)*. The information questions then become object clauses. These object clauses are dependent clauses, and you must therefore put the conjugated verb at the end of the clause.

information question	introductory phrase + object clause	
Wie viel Uhr **ist** es?	Weißt du,	wie viel Uhr es **ist?**
Wann **fängt** das Konzert **an?**	Weißt du,	wann das Konzert **anfängt?**
Wo **kann** man Karten bekommen?	Weißt du,	wo man Karten bekommen **kann?**

5-31 Höfliche Fragen. You are a stranger in town. Politely ask a passerby for directions and information.

▶ Wie komme ich zum Fußballstadion?

nehmen / am besten ein Taxi

S1: Könnten Sie mir bitte sagen, wie ich zum Fußballstadion komme?

S2: Da nehmen Sie am besten ein Taxi.

1. Wann fängt das Fußballspiel an?
2. Wo kann man hier gut und billig essen?
3. Wo kann man hier billig übernachten°?
4. Wie komme ich zur Jugendherberge?
5. Wie komme ich zum Bahnhof?

fragen / am besten den Taxifahrer
gehen / am besten ins Ristorante Napoli
gehen / am besten in die Jugendherberge
nehmen / am besten die S-Bahn
nehmen / am besten die Buslinie 10

spend the night

Yes/no questions as object clauses

You can also introduce a yes/no question with phrases like **Weißt du, ...** or **Könnten Sie mir bitte sagen, ...** When a yes/no question is the object of an introductory phrase, it begins with the conjunction **ob** *(whether)*, and you must put the conjugated verb at the end of the clause.

yes/no question	introductory phrase + object clause	
Ist Claudia zu Hause?	Weißt du,	**ob** Claudia zu Hause **ist?**
Hat sie heute Abend etwas **vor?**	Weißt du,	**ob** sie heute Abend etwas **vorhat?**
Möchte sie mit uns ausgehen?	Weißt du,	**ob** sie mit uns ausgehen **möchte?**

5-32 Weißt du das?

▶ Ist Professor Weber noch hier?

Ja, er ...

S1: Weißt du, ob Professor Weber noch hier ist?

S2: Ja, er ist noch hier.

1. Müssen wir diese Wörter lernen?
2. Ist die Bibliothek noch offen?
3. Ist dieser Film interessant?
4. Hat Florian einen Wagen?
5. Geht Maria heute Abend aus?

Nein, wir ...
Ja, sie ...
Nein, er ...
Ja, er ...
Nein, sie ...

Nimm Deine Organe nicht mit in den Himmel, denn der Himmel weiß, wir brauchen sie hier!

Eine Initiative der 1. Steirischen Interessengemeinschaft
der Dialysepatienten und Nierentransplantierten

5-33 Höfliche Fragen.

▶ Fährt dieser Bus zum Bahnhof?

Nein, er fährt zum …

S1: Könnten Sie mir bitte sagen, ob dieser Bus zum Bahnhof fährt?

S2: Nein, er fährt zum Englischen Garten.

1. Wohin fährt dieser Bus?

Er fährt zum …

2. Ist das die Alte Pinakothek?

Nein, das ist …

Das Deutsche Museum

3. Wann fängt das Konzert heute Abend an?

W.A.MOZART
Violinkonzert Nr.1

Konzertbeginn: 20.30

Ich glaube, es beginnt …

4. Ist das das Deutsche Museum?

Nein, das ist …

Die Alte Pinakothek

5. Wohin fährt dieser Zug?

Gleis 1 IC 522 Hannover
Abfahrt 15 20

Das ist der Intercity …

6. Wann fährt der Intercity nach Hannover ab?

Um …

7. Ist der Intercity nach Hannover schon weg?

Nein, es ist doch erst …

track 8. Von wo fährt der Intercity nach Hannover ab?

Ich glaube, von Gleis° …

⑤ Talking about what and whom you know

The verb *wissen*

The present tense of **wissen** *(to know)* is irregular in the singular.

singular	plural
ich **weiß**	wir wissen
du **weißt**	ihr wisst
er/es/sie **weiß**	sie wissen
	Sie wissen

As you have already seen, the object of the verb **wissen** can be a dependent clause. It can also be a pronoun like **das, es, alles,** or **nichts.**

Weißt du, **ob wir morgen eine Klausur schreiben?**

Nein, **das** weiß ich nicht.

*Do you know **whether we have a test tomorrow?***

*No, I don't know **(that).***

5-34 Wer weiß das? Supply the appropriate forms of **wissen.**

1. KURT: _____ deine Eltern, dass du so schlechte Zensuren° hast?   *grades*
   GÜNTER: Meine Mutter _____ es, aber mein Vater _____ es noch nicht.

2. TOURISTIN: Entschuldigung, _____ Sie vielleicht, wohin dieser Bus fährt?
   TOURIST: Nein, das _____ ich leider° auch nicht.   *unfortunately*

3. BERND: _____ ihr vielleicht, wo Peter ist?
   MARTIN: Nein, das _____ wir auch nicht.
   CLAUDIA: Frag doch Stephanie! Sie _____ es bestimmt.

4. FRAU KOHL: Warum _____ du denn nicht, wie man Sauerkraut kocht?
   HERR KOHL: Ich kann doch nicht alles _____.

Wissen versus *kennen*

Whereas **wissen** means *to know something as a fact,* **kennen** means *to know* in the sense of *to be acquainted with someone* or *to be familiar with something.* **Kennen** is always followed by a direct object. It cannot be followed by an object clause.

Kennst du Günters neue Freundin?

Ja, ich **kenne** sie sehr gut.

Weißt du, wie alt sie ist?

Nein, das **weiß** ich nicht.

*Do you **know** Günter's new girlfriend?*

*Yes, I **know** her very well.*

*Do you **know** how old she is?*

*No, that I don't **know.***

5-35 Wissen oder kennen?

1. FRAU LANG: _____ Sie Frau Ziegler?
    FRAU KUNZ: Ja, ich _____ sie sehr gut.

2. FRAU HOFER: _____ Sie vielleicht, wie viel Uhr es ist?
    FRAU KUHN: Genau _____ ich es nicht, aber ich glaube, es ist fast fünf.

3. GÜNTER: _____ du Monika?
    ANNA: Ja, natürlich _____ ich sie.
    GÜNTER: Und _____ du, wo sie wohnt?
    ANNA: Nein, das _____ ich nicht.

4. TOURISTIN: _____ Sie Berlin?
    FRAU GÜRLÜK: Ja, ich _____ Berlin sehr gut.
    I'm sure   TOURISTIN: Dann _____ Sie doch sicher°, wo die Grimmstraße ist.
    FRAU GÜRLÜK: Nein, das _____ ich leider nicht.

5. DAVID: _____ du den Mann dort?
    TOM: Ja, ich _____ ihn, aber ich _____ nicht, wie er heißt.

6. SYLVIA: _____ ihr, wo Günter ist?
    MARKUS: Ich glaube, er ist bei Eva.
    SYLVIA: Bei Eva?! Ja, woher _____ er sie denn?
    THOMAS: Das _____ wir auch nicht.

❻ Talking about events in the past

The simple past of *sein, haben,* and the modal verbs

In conversational situations, speakers of German refer to events in the past by using the perfect tense. You will learn how to use this tense in the next chapter.

Gestern Nachmittag **habe** ich mit Lisa Tennis **gespielt.**

*Yesterday afternoon I **played** tennis with Lisa.*

However, with **sein, haben,** and the modal verbs (**dürfen, können, mögen, müssen, sollen, wollen),** most speakers of German use the simple past tense.

Warum **warst** du gestern Abend nicht auf Lisas Party?

*Why **weren't** you at Lisa's party last night?*

Ich **hatte** keine Zeit. Ich **musste** für eine Klausur lernen.

*I **didn't have** time. I **had to** study for a test.*

The simple past of *sein*

The simple past stem of **sein** is **war.** Note that there are no personal endings in the 1st and 3rd person singular.

singular	plural
ich war	wir waren
du warst	ihr wart
er/es/sie war	sie waren
Sie waren	

5-36 Kleine Gespräche. Use the simple past of **sein** in the following mini-conversations.

▶ Wo _____ ihr gestern Abend? im Kino

_____ der Film gut? Nein, ... viel zu sentimental.

S1: Wo wart ihr gestern Abend? **S2:** Wir waren im Kino.
War der Film gut? Nein, er war viel zu sentimental.

1. Wo _____ ihr letztes Wochenende?

_____ das Wasser warm? Nein, ... noch ziemlich° kalt. *quite*

2. Wo _____ Sie letzten Sommer?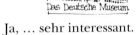

_____ es heiß? Ja, ... sehr heiß.

3. Wo _____ du am Sonntagnachmittag?

_____ es interessant? Ja, ... sehr interessant.

4. Wo _____ ihr am Samstagnachmittag?

_____ das Bier gut? Ja, ... sehr gut.

5. Wo _____ du am Sonntagabend?

_____ der Geiger° gut? Ja, ... ganz fabelhaft. *violinist*

6. Wo _____ Sie letzten Sommer?

_____ das Wetter schön? Ja, ... fast immer warm und schön.

im Biergarten	im Konzert	am Starnberger See
in Österreich	in Italien	im Deutschen Museum

The simple past of *haben*

The simple past stem of **haben** is **hatt-**.

singular	plural
ich hatte	wir hatten
du hattest	ihr hattet
er/es/sie hatte	sie hatten
Sie hatten	

5-37 Warum? In the questions use the simple past of **sein**, and in the responses the simple past of **haben**.

▶ ihr nicht auf Lisas Party   wir / zu viel zu tun

S1: Warum wart ihr nicht auf Lisas Party?   **S2:** Wir hatten zu viel zu tun.

1. du gestern Nachmittag nicht zu Hause   ich / Vorlesungen
2. ihr am Samstag nicht beim Fußballspiel   wir / zu viele Hausaufgaben
3. Martin nicht beim Mittagessen   er / keinen Hunger
4. ihr gestern Nachmittag nicht im Biergarten   wir / keine Zeit
5. Stephanie nicht mit euch am Starnberger See   sie / eine Klausur
6. Meyers letzten Sommer nicht in Italien   sie / kein Geld

The simple past of modal verbs

You form the simple past of modal verbs by adding the past tense marker **-t-** to the verb stem and then adding the personal endings. When a modal has an umlaut in the infinitive form, you drop the umlaut in the simple past. Note that the **g** of **mögen** becomes **ch.**

dürfen	können	mögen	müssen	sollen	wollen
ich durfte	ich konnte	ich mochte	ich musste	ich sollte	ich wollte

In the simple past, all modals follow the pattern shown in the table below.

Lerntipp: The personal endings for modal verbs in the simple past tense are the same as those for the simple past tense of **haben.**

singular	plural
ich konnte	wir konnten
du konntest	ihr konntet
er/es/sie konnte	sie konnten
Sie konnten	

5-38 Ich wollte, aber ich konnte oder durfte nicht.

▶ wollen / können: Ich _____ letzten Sommer nach Europa,
   aber ich _____ nicht.
könne: Warum _____ du denn nicht?
müssen: Ich _____ arbeiten und Geld verdienen.

S1: Ich wollte letzten Sommer nach Europa, aber ich konnte nicht.
S2: Warum konntest du denn nicht?
S1: Ich musste arbeiten und Geld verdienen.

1. wollen / können: Wir _____ gestern Abend in die Disco,
   aber wir _____ nicht.
können: Warum _____ ihr denn nicht?
müssen: Wir _____ unsere deutschen Vokabeln lernen.

2. wollen / dürfen: Meine kleine Schwester _____ gestern Abend tanzen gehen,
   aber sie _____ nicht.
dürfen: Warum _____ sie denn nicht?
müssen: Sie _____ ihr Zimmer aufräumen und ihre Hausaufgaben machen.

3. wollen / können: Wir _____ letztes Wochenende zum Starnberger See,
   aber wir _____ nicht.
können: Warum _____ ihr denn nicht?
müssen: Wir _____ unser Projekt für Biologie fertig machen.

4. wollen / dürfen: Mein kleiner Bruder _____ letzten Samstag Fußball spielen,
   aber er _____ nicht.
dürfen: Warum _____ er denn nicht?
müssen: Er _____ im Garten arbeiten.

5. wollen / können: Peter _____ gestern Abend mit uns ins Kino,
   aber er _____ nicht.
können: Warum _____ er denn nicht?
müssen: Er _____ einen wichtigen° Brief schreiben.   *important*

6. wollen / können: Ich _____ gestern Nachmittag mit Martin baden gehen,
   aber ich _____ nicht.
können: Warum _____ du denn nicht?
müssen: Ich _____ meine Wäsche waschen.

5-39 Weißt du das noch? Ask each other about childhood memories and note down your partner's responses. Then report your findings to the class. You will find vocabulary to describe **Jobs und Berufe** and **Essen und Trinken** in the *Anhang* on pages A17 and A20.

S1:

1. Was wolltest du als Kind werden?
2. Was durftest du als Kind nicht?
3. Was konntest du als Kind besser als andere Kinder?
4. Was mochtest du als Kind nicht essen?
5. Musstest du das dann trotzdem° essen?

S2:

Ich wollte … werden.
Ich durfte nicht …
Ich konnte besser …

Ich mochte kein__ …
Ja, das musste ich. / Nein, das   *anyway*
   musste ich nicht.

 Go sightseeing in **Südtirol** at
www.prenhall.com/treffpunkt
→ Kapitel 5 → Web Resources
→ Kultur

Ladin: A Rhaeto-Romance **(rätoromanisch)** dialect spoken in several valleys of the Dolomites in northeast Italy. It is similar to the Rhaeto-Romance dialect spoken in Switzerland. You can find **Südtirol** on the map of **Österreich** inside the front cover.

The photo shows Schloss Tirol.

INFOBOX

Südtirol

The northern Italian province of **Südtirol** (**Alto Adige** in Italian), with its spectacular mountains and its valleys of orchards and vineyards, is a mecca for tourists. However, this area has had a turbulent history. At the beginning of the twentieth century it was part of the Austrian province of **Tirol.** In 1919 **Südtirol** was ceded to Italy, and the Italian government prohibited the use of German in public life and worked to attract Italian-speaking settlers to the region. In 1939, Hitler and Mussolini signed an agreement to resettle the population of **Südtirol** in German territory. Because of World War II, the resettlement never came about.

After 1945, **Südtirol** became an autonomous Italian province with three official languages. Of a population of 463,000, 69 percent speak German, 26 percent speak Italian, and 4 percent speak Ladin. In **Südtirol** all laws are published in German and Italian, and civil servants must be competent in both languages.

The autonomy of **Südtirol** has been hailed as an outstanding example of the protection of ethnic minorities.

Südtirol is situated in the **Alpen,** and tourism employs over half of the work force. Of the 4 million tourists who visit annually, most come from Germany. The top quality fruit and wine from **Südtirol** is found in markets throughout Europe.

Zusammenschau

🖥 ▮ Video-Treff ·······································

Ferienzeit

Christoph and Christina Brieger, Stefan Meister, André, and Stefan Kuhlmann talk about their vacation preferences.

Zum besseren Verstehen

5-40 Was ist das auf Englisch?

1. Wir machen **zweimal** im Jahr Urlaub.
2. Wir fahren **ans Meer** und sind viel am Strand.
3. Englisch ist die Fremdsprache, die ich am besten **beherrsche.**
4. Man kann im **Mittelmeer** schwimmen.
5. Das war unser **Mietwagen:** der Ford Ka.
6. Ich **habe mich** in die Frau und in das Land **verliebt.**
7. Australien ist das schönste Land **der Welt.**

a. Mediterranean Sea
b. know
c. in the world
d. rental car
e. fell in love
f. to the ocean
g. twice

Now watch the video and complete the post-viewing activities in the *Video-Treff* section of the *Student Activities Manual.*

◀)) ■ Hören ···

Zwei Telefongespräche

It's Sunday afternoon, and Monika Pohl receives two phone calls within a few minutes of one another. The first is from Günter, who wants to go to the movie *Lola rennt* with her tomorrow. The second is from Patrick, who would like her to go sailing on Lake Constance tomorrow.

NEUE VOKABELN

die Wahrheit   *truth*   **die Chorprobe**   *choir practice*
die Ausrede   *excuse*   **der Bodensee**   *Lake Constance*

5-41 Erstes Verstehen. As you listen to the first telephone conversation, compare what you hear with the entries in Monika's calendar. Check off for which days she is telling the truth and for which she is making excuses.

Juli	196.–202. Tag 29. Woche
15	Montag 19.30 Chorprobe
16	Dienstag 10.30 H 303 Klausur in Physik
17	Mittwoch 19.00 Tennis mit Sylvia
18	Donnerstag 20.00 Kino mit David „Lola rennt"
19	Freitag 21.30 Disco mit David
20	Samstag nach Hause fahren
21	Sonntag

Wahrheit   Ausrede

____   ____   Mo
____   ____   Di
____   ____   Mi
____   ____   Do
____   ____   Fr

Lola rennt *(Run Lola Run)* stars Franka Potente and was written and directed by Tom Tykwer. **Der Bodensee:** Lake Constance is the largest lake in the German-speaking area of Europe, and its English name comes from the city of **Konstanz.** Germany, Switzerland, and Austria all have jurisdiction over certain areas of the lake. It is situated in one of the oldest and richest cultural regions in the German-speaking countries.

5-42 Detailverstehen. Listen to the second telephone conversation and write responses to the following questions.

1. Was machen Patrick und Thomas morgen?
2. Was für ein Wochentag ist heute?
3. Warum konnten Patrick und Thomas heute nicht segeln gehen?
4. Warum will Monika nicht mitgehen?
5. Wann will Patrick morgen Abend wieder zurück sein?
6. Warum denkt er, dass Monika morgen Abend noch für ihre Klausur lernen kann? *Er weiß nicht, dass …*
7. Wer holt morgen wen ab?

■ Schreiben und Sprechen ·····················

5-43 Mein Kalender. Draw up your calendar for this week, listing the days and times of some activities you plan to do, following the example.

Montag   9–10   Cafeteria: mit Lisa deutsche Vokabeln lernen
            10–11   Deutsch (Wortschatzquiz!)
            19–?   Kino + Kneipe
Dienstag   …

5-44 Gehst du mit? Using your calendar entries from **5-43,** find a good time for going out, say for a movie and a beer. Then call up a friend and ask whether she/he can join you. You may want to use phrases like the ones below.

dials   **S1:** *(wählt°)*   **S2:** _____ hier.

S1: Ich bin's, _____. Du, _____, ich   **S2:** Ich auch. Wann hast du Zeit?
möchte mal wieder ins Kino
afterward   und nachher° in die Kneipe.

S1: Für heute Abend habe ich nichts   **S2:** Heute kann ich leider nicht. Ich
im Kalender. Geht das?   muss …

S1: Und wie ist's mit Mittwoch?   **S2:** Am Mittwoch habe ich … Aber
Freitag ist gut.

S1: Super! Da habe ich auch nichts vor.   **S2:** …

▌ Lesen ···

Zum besseren Verstehen

5-45 Touristenattraktionen.

1. Have you ever visited a castle? Tell your classmates what you found interesting.
2. Can you give examples of extravagant buildings or monuments that have become major tourist attractions?

5-46 Was ist das auf Englisch?

1. Kinder hören gern **Märchen.**
2. *Hänsel und Gretel* ist ein **berühmtes** deutsches Märchen.
3. **Könige** leben in Schlössern.
4. Könige **bauen** gern Schlösser.
5. Weißt du **etwas** von König Ludwigs Schlössern?
6. Neuschwanstein ist ein **märchenhaftes** Schloss.
7. München ist die **Hauptstadt** von Bayern.

a. famous
b. fairy-tale
c. something
d. capital
e. fairy tales
f. build
g. kings

LEUTE   **Ludwig II. von Bayern und seine Märchenschlösser**

Die größte Touristenattraktion in Bayern sind die märchenhaften Schlösser von König Ludwig (1845–1886). Jedes Jahr kommen Tausende von Touristen aus aller Welt, marschieren in Gruppen durch eine fantastische Märchenwelt und hören von Ludwigs extravagantem Lebensstil und von seinem mysteriösen Tod.

In seiner Jugend ist Ludwig am liebsten auf Schloss Hohenschwangau in den bayerischen Bergen, wo er durch die wundervolle Bergwelt wandert. Er liebt Kunst[1], Musik und Literatur, aber von Finanzen und Politik versteht er fast nichts.

Im Jahr 1864 wird der 18-jährige Ludwig König. Er hat große Pläne für seine Hauptstadt: München soll ein Zentrum für Kunst und Musik werden. Und weil er die romantischen Opern von Richard Wagner so liebt, holt[2] er den berühmten Komponisten nach München und finanziert Wagners verschwenderischen[3] Lebensstil.

Für Ludwigs konservative Minister[4] ist Richard Wagner nicht die richtige Gesellschaft[5] für den jungen König. Der Komponist muss gehen, und Ludwig ist so verbittert, dass er immer weniger in München ist und immer mehr in seinen geliebten bayerischen Bergen. Wenn er aus München keine Märchenstadt machen darf, so will er jetzt hier eine Märchenwelt bauen: die Schlösser Neuschwanstein, Linderhof und Herrenchiemsee.

Schlösser kosten Geld, viel Geld, und im Jahr 1886 hat der König so viel Schulden, dass die Minister in München etwas dagegen tun müssen. Vier Ärzte[6] müssen den König für verrückt erklären[7], und am 12. Juni 1886 bringt man ihn ins Schloss Berg am Starnberger See. Dort gehen Ludwig und ein Arzt am nächsten Abend spazieren, und wenige Stunden später findet man sie beide tot im See.

[1] *art* [2] *summons* [3] *lavish* [4] *government ministers* [5] *company* [6] *physicians* [7] *declare insane*

Neuschwanstein

WWW Take a look around **Neuschwanstein** at www.prenhall.com/treffpunkt → Kapitel 5 → Web Resources → Kultur

Arbeit mit dem Text

5-47 Anders gesagt. Find equivalents for these statements in the reading.

1. Schlösser sind sehr teuer.
2. Ludwig ist kein guter Finanzier und kein guter Politiker.
3. Richard Wagner darf nicht in München bleiben.
4. Vier Ärzte müssen sagen, dass Ludwig nicht normal ist.
5. Ludwig schaut gern schöne Bilder an, hört gern Musik und liest gern.
6. In Bayern schauen die meisten Touristen die Schlösser von König Ludwig an.
7. Ludwig bezahlt für Wagners extravagantes Leben.
8. Ludwig will, dass München eine berühmte Kunst- und Musikstadt wird.

5-48 Was ist die richtige Antwort? Your instructor will read six questions about *Ludwig II. von Bayern.* Check off the correct answers.

1. _____ Mysteriös.
   _____ Extravagant.
2. _____ Auf Schloss Hohenschwangau.
   _____ In München.
3. _____ Von Finanzen und von Politik.
   _____ Von Kunst und von Literatur.
4. _____ Romantisch.
   _____ Konservativ.
5. _____ In den bayerischen Bergen.
   _____ In München.
6. _____ Seine Minister.
   _____ Vier Ärzte.

Wörter unter der Lupe

Predicting gender

The gender of many German nouns is indicated by their suffixes. Here are some examples.

- Nouns with the suffixes **-or** and **-ent** are masculine.

  der Profess**or**   **der** Stud**ent**

- Nouns with the suffix **-er** that are derived from verbs are always masculine. These nouns can refer to people as well as things.

  arbeiten   **der** Arbeit**er**   fernsehen   **der** Fernseh**er**

- Nouns with the suffix **-in** added to a masculine noun are feminine.

  die Professor**in**   **die** Arbeiter**in**

- Nouns with the suffix **-ur** are almost always feminine.

  die Temperat**ur**   **die** Zens**ur**   **die** Klaus**ur**

- Nouns with the suffix **-ment** are almost always neuter.

  das Instru**ment**   **das** Experi**ment**   **das** Argu**ment**

- Nouns with the suffix **-(i)um** are almost always neuter.

  das For**um**   **das** Gymnas**ium**

- Nouns with the diminutive suffixes **-chen** and **-lein** are always neuter. These two suffixes (compare English *-kin* in mani*kin* and lamb*kin*, or *-let* in star*let*, book*let*, and pig*let*) can be affixed to virtually every German noun to express smallness. This also explains why both **Mädchen** *(girl)* and **Fräulein** *(Miss; young lady)* are neuter. The vowels **a, o, u,** and the diphthong **au** are umlauted when a diminutive suffix is added to the noun. Remember that with the diphthong **au** it is the **a** that is umlauted.

  die Stadt   **das** Städt**chen**   **der** Bruder   **das** Brüder**lein**
  die Tochter   **das** Töchter**lein**   **das** Haus   **das** Häus**chen**

5-49 *Der, das* oder *die*? Say the following nouns with their definite articles. If a noun has a corresponding feminine form, give that form and the corresponding article as well.

1. Präsident	7. Frisur	13. Kätzchen	19. Projektor
2. Element	8. Assistent	14. Besucher	20. Patient
3. Mäuschen	9. Fahrer	15. Dokument	21. Ornament
4. Motor	10. Kompliment	16. Agent	22. Medium
5. Verkäufer	11. Fischlein	17. Autor	23. Lautsprecher
6. Aquarium	12. Mentor	18. Individuum	24. Diktatur

Suffix -er: English also derives many so-called agent nouns from verbs. As in German, they do not always refer to people: *to work/worker; to serve/server; to wash/washer; to dry/dryer.*

Suffix -ur: *das Abitur* is an exception.

Fräulein: Before the feminist movement exerted its influence on gender-related vocabulary, this word referred to unmarried women of any age. Now the term has become archaic.

Words as chameleons: *ganz*

The word **ganz** occurs very frequently, especially in conversational German. Depending on the context, it can have any one of the following meanings: *all, all of, whole, very, quite,* or *completely.*

5-50 Was bedeutet *ganz*? What is the correct English equivalent of **ganz** in each of the sentences below?

1. Meine Eltern haben nur ein ganz kleines Haus. *(whole / very / all)*
2. Ich glaube, du musst diesen Mann ganz vergessen. *(all of / very / completely)*
3. Nächsten Sommer reise ich durch ganz Europa. *(all of / quite / very)*
4. Machst du diese Reise ganz allein? *(quite / all / whole)*
5. Keinen Zucker, bitte, und nur ganz wenig Milch. *(completely / all / very)*
6. Ich glaube, du verstehst das nicht ganz. *(quite / very / whole)*
7. Iss bitte nicht wieder den ganzen Kuchen. *(completely / whole / quite)*
8. Ralf spricht viel zu viel, aber sonst ist er ganz nett. *(all / quite / completely)*
9. Die Suppe ist schon ganz kalt. *(whole / all of / completely)*

((▶ Zur Aussprache

German *ch*

German **ch** is one of the few consonant sounds that has no equivalent in English.

- **ch** after **a, o, u,** and **au**

  When **ch** follows the vowels **a, o, u,** or **au**, it resembles the sound of a gentle gargling.

  > Frau Ba**ch** kommt Punkt a**ch**t.
  > Am Wo**ch**enende ko**ch**t immer meine To**ch**ter.
  > Warum su**ch**st du denn das Ko**ch**bu**ch**?
  > Ich will versu**ch**en°, einen Ku**ch**en zu backen.   *try*
  > Hat Herr Rau**ch** au**ch** so einen Bierbau**ch**° wie Herr Strau**ch**?   *beer belly*

- **ch** after all other vowels and after consonants

  The sound of **ch** after all other vowels (including the umlauted vowels) and after consonants is similar to the sound of a loudly whispered *h* in *huge* or *Hugh.*

  > Mi**ch**aels Kät**zch**en mö**ch**te ein Teller**ch**en° Mil**ch**.   *little dish*

  The ending **-ig** is pronounced as if it were spelled **-ich,** unless it is followed by a vowel.

  > Es ist sonn**ig**, aber sehr wind**ig**.

- The two types of **ch** sounds are often found in the singular and plural forms of the same noun.

die Na**ch**t	die Nä**ch**te	das Bu**ch**	die Bü**ch**er
die To**ch**ter	die Tö**ch**ter	der Bierbau**ch**	die Bierbäu**ch**e

- The combination **-chs** is pronounced like English *x.*

  > das Wa**chs**   se**chs**   der **Ochs**e   der Fu**chs**

▶ Wortschatz 2

Nomen

die Hauptstadt, ̈e	capital city
der Pass, ̈e	passport
das Reisebüro, -s	travel agency
der Studentenausweis, -e	student ID
die Welt, -en	world

Hauptstadt: Haupt- prefixed to a noun indicates *main* or *major*. What are the English equivalents of **Hauptfach, Hauptstraße, Hauptbahnhof?**

das Bild, -er	picture; painting
die Kunst, ̈e	art
das Märchen, -	fairy tale
der Roman, -e	novel
die Seifenoper, -n	soap opera

der Arzt, ̈e die Ärztin, -nen	physician; doctor
der Chef, -s die Chefin, -nen	boss
die Jugend (sing)	youth
der Mensch, -en	human being; person; (pl) people

Chef: What is the German equivalent of English *chef?*

der Bart, ̈e	beard
der Schnurrbart, ̈e	mustache
der Friseur, -e die Friseurin, -nen	hair stylist; hairdresser
die Frisur, -en	hair style; hairdo
der Haarschnitt, -e	haircut

die Brille, -n	(eye)glasses
die Kontaktlinse, -n	contact lens

Brille: Brille is used in the plural only when it refers to more than one pair.

das Armband, ̈er	bracelet
die Halskette, -n	necklace
der Nasenstecker, -	nose stud
der Ohrring, -e	earring

die Ausrede, -n	excuse
die Wahrheit, -en	truth

die Klausur, -en	test
das Quiz, -	quiz
die Zensur, -en	grade

Quiz: Note that there is no ending in the plural.

die Ecke, -n	corner
die Flasche, -n	bottle
der Schnellimbiss, -e	fast-food stand

Verben

buchen	to book
ein·kaufen	to shop
hoffen	to hope
lieben	to love
übernachten	to spend the night; to stay overnight

Andere Wörter

berühmt	famous
hoch	high
kühl	cool (of weather)
märchenhaft	fairy-tale, fantastic
müde	tired
verrückt	crazy; insane
wahr	true
wichtig	important
leider	unfortunately
natürlich	of course
trotzdem	anyway; nevertheless
ziemlich	quite; rather

Ausdrücke

als Kind	as a child
Punkt halb zwei	at one-thirty on the dot
Ich bin's.	It's me.
Ich habe Durst.	I'm thirsty.
Ich habe Hunger.	I'm hungry.

Das Gegenteil

der Junge, -n ≠ das Mädchen, -	boy ≠ girl

altmodisch ≠
    modern
	old-fashioned ≠
	    modern

geschmackvoll ≠
    geschmacklos
	tasteful ≠
	    tasteless

dafür ≠ dagegen	for it ≠ against it
etwas ≠ nichts	something ≠ nothing
mit ≠ ohne	with ≠ without

Leicht zu verstehen

das Argument, -e	die Literatur, -en
die ATM Karte, -n	der Tourist, -en
die Baseballkappe, -n	die Touristin, -nen
das Experiment, -e	finanzieren
der Job, -s	arrogant
der Kalender, -	fantastisch
das Kompliment, -e	konservativ
die Kreditkarte, -n	romantisch
der Kurs, -e	sentimental

Which words in this list are stressed on a different syllable than their English equivalents?

Wörter im Kontext

5-51 Was passt zusammen?

1. Wenn man einen Haarschnitt braucht,
2. Wenn man sehr teure Ohrringe kaufen will,
3. Wenn man eine ATM Karte braucht,
4. Wenn man krank ist,
5. Wenn man eine Reise buchen will,
6. Wenn man wenig Zeit zum Essen hat,
7. Wenn man billig übernachten will,
8. Wenn man eine Brille oder Kontaktlinsen braucht,

a. geht man zum Reisebüro.
b. geht man in die Jugendherberge.
c. geht man zum Optiker.
d. geht man zum Juwelier.
e. geht man zum Friseur.
f. geht man zum Arzt.
g. geht man zur Bank.
h. geht man zum Schnellimbiss.

5-52 Was passt zusammen?

1. Wenn ich kein Geld habe,
2. Wenn ich jemand ein Kompliment mache,
3. Wenn ich sehr müde bin,
4. Wenn ich in München berühmte Bilder anschauen will,
5. Wenn ich eine Klausur nicht schreiben will,
6. Wenn ich für eine Konzertkarte weniger bezahlen will,
7. Wenn ich gute Zensuren will,

a. sage ich manchmal nicht die ganze Wahrheit.
b. kann ich nicht einkaufen gehen.
c. brauche ich einen Studentenausweis.
d. muss ich eine gute Ausrede finden.
e. muss ich viel lernen.
f. gehe ich ins Bett.
g. gehe ich in die Alte Pinakothek.

The German equivalent of *to take a test* or *to have a test* is **eine Klausur schreiben.**

5-53 Was passt zusammen? Match appropriately in each set.

1. die ATM Karte
2. die Seifenoper
3. die Kunst
4. die Flasche

a. die Galerie
b. der Wein
c. das Geld
d. der Fernseher

5. der Pass
6. der Kurs
7. die Literatur
8. der Kalender

e. das Jahr
f. der Roman
g. die Klausur
h. die Weltreise

Flasche: By analogy to **ein Glas Milch,** what is the German equivalent of *a bottle of wine?*

5-54 Kleine Gespräche.

leider / wichtig / Durst / trotzdem / ziemlich / etwas / wahr

1. STEFAN: Ich habe _____. Hast du _____ zu trinken für mich?
   HORST: Nein, _____ nicht.
2. ANNA: Ist es _____, dass Ludwig II. verrückt war?
   JULIA: Ja, aber seine Schlösser sind _____ schön.
3. MARIA: Für Laura sind schöne Kleider sehr _____.
   LUKAS: Ich finde Lauras Kleider trotzdem _____ geschmacklos.

geschmacklos: Many words form their opposites in meaning by adding the suffix **-voll** or **-los.** What are the English equivalents of the following sets of opposites: **liebevoll ≠ lieblos; humorvoll ≠ humorlos; taktvoll ≠ taktlos; respektvoll ≠ respektlos?**

KAPITEL 6

Ein Blick zurück

1924: Einwandererkinder auf Ellis Island

Kommunikationsziele

Describing past events . . .

- in conversational situations
- in personal narratives

Writing personal letters

Talking about . . .

- one's ancestors
- education and job qualifications

Describing someone's appearance

Strukturen

The perfect tense

Ordinal numbers

Hin and **her**

Kultur

Immigration to North America

The German language in North America

The educational systems in the German-speaking countries

Video-Treff: **Mein erster Job**

Lesen: **Aus Christian Köchlings Tagebuch**

Ein deutscher Auswanderer

Hans Keilhau ist im Sommer 1930 nach Amerika ausgewandert und hat kurz vorher diesen Pass bekommen. Schauen Sie den Pass genau an.

1. Wann hat Herr Keilhau diesen Pass bekommen?
2. Was war Hans Keilhau von Beruf?
3. Wo ist er geboren?
4. Wann ist er geboren?
5. Wo in Deutschland hat Herr Keilhau im Juni 1930 gewohnt?
6. Ist er groß, klein oder mittelgroß?
7. Welche Form hat sein Gesicht? *Es ist …*
8. Welche Farbe haben seine Augen? *Sie sind …*
9. Welche Farbe hat sein Haar? *Es ist …*
10. Wie heißt der Ringfinger in Hans Keilhaus Pass?
11. Wie weiß man, dass Hans Keilhau nicht verheiratet ist?

Ein bisschen Familiengeschichte

Es ist Anfang Oktober, Stephanie ist gestern in München angekommen und Claudia möchte wissen, warum ihre amerikanische Mitbewohnerin einen deutschen Namen hat.

CLAUDIA: *(schreibt und liest)* „… Brief folgt bald. Liebe Grüße, Claudia" – So! Fertig ist die Postkarte! – Sag mal, Stephanie, hast du schon nach Hause geschrieben?

STEPHANIE: Aber Claudia, ich habe ja noch nicht mal meine Koffer ausgepackt!

CLAUDIA: Eine Postkarte mit „Bin gut angekommen, Brief folgt bald" braucht doch keine fünf Minuten.

STEPHANIE: Meine Eltern wollen keine Postkarte, sondern einen langen Brief. Sie wollen wissen, wo und wie ich wohne, wie meine Mitbewohnerin heißt und wie alt, woher und wie sie ist. Und vieles weiß ich ja noch gar nicht.

CLAUDIA: Kein Problem, Stephanie. Du weißt, ich heiße Claudia, Claudia Maria Berger. Ich komme aus Hamburg und bin sehr, sehr nett. – Weißt du, du bist eigentlich viel interessanter, Stephanie: Amerikanerin aus Chicago, jung, schön, intelligent …

STEPHANIE: Ach Quatsch!

CLAUDIA: Und dann dieser Name, „Stephanie Braun"! *(lacht)* So typisch amerikanisch! – Sag mal, ist dein Vater Deutscher? Ist er ausgewandert?

STEPHANIE: Nein, mein Vater ist in Amerika geboren. Aber mein Großvater ist aus Deutschland und ist 1950 nach Amerika ausgewandert.

◉▶ ▮ Hören ···

6-1 Richtig oder falsch? You will hear the conversation between Stephanie and Claudia. Indicate whether the statements that follow this conversation are **richtig** or **falsch.**

	RICHTIG	FALSCH		RICHTIG	FALSCH
1.	_____	_____	4.	_____	_____
2.	_____	_____	5.	_____	_____
3.	_____	_____	6.	_____	_____

6-2 Stephanies Stammbaum.

1. Wo ist Stephanies Mutter geboren?
2. Wie heißt Stephanies Großvater mütterlicherseits?
3. Wo ist er geboren?
4. Wie heißt Stephanies Großmutter mütterlicherseits?
5. Woher kommen Sophia Castellos Eltern?
6. Wie heißt Stephanies Großmutter väterlicherseits?
7. Woher sind Christa Bauers Eltern?

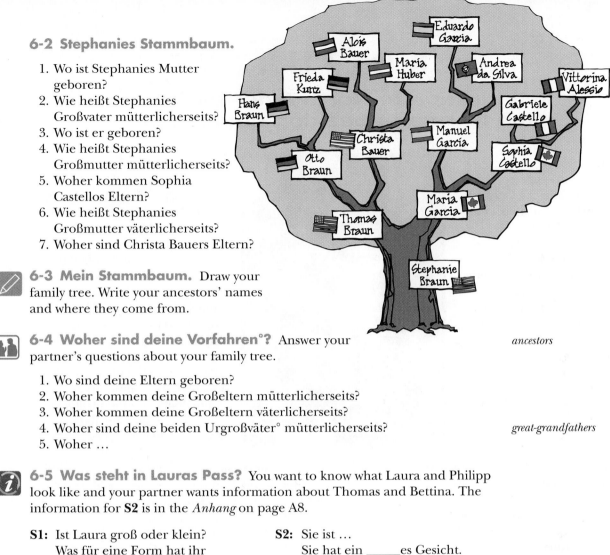

6-3 Mein Stammbaum. Draw your family tree. Write your ancestors' names and where they come from.

6-4 Woher sind deine Vorfahren°? Answer your partner's questions about your family tree.   *ancestors*

1. Wo sind deine Eltern geboren?
2. Woher kommen deine Großeltern mütterlicherseits?
3. Woher kommen deine Großeltern väterlicherseits?
4. Woher sind deine beiden Urgroßväter° mütterlicherseits?   *great-grandfathers*
5. Woher …

6-5 Was steht in Lauras Pass? You want to know what Laura and Philipp look like and your partner wants information about Thomas and Bettina. The information for **S2** is in the *Anhang* on page A8.

S1: Ist Laura groß oder klein?
Was für eine Form hat ihr Gesicht?
Was für Augen hat sie?
Was für Haar hat sie?

S2: Sie ist …
Sie hat ein _____es Gesicht.

Sie hat _____e Augen.
Sie hat _____es, _____es Haar.

	LAURA	THOMAS	BETTINA	PHILIPP
Größe		ziemlich groß	ziemlich klein	
Gesichtsform		schmal°	rund	
Augen		dunkelbraun	blau	
Haar		hellbraun, kurz	blond, lockig	

thin

6-6 Wer ist das? In small groups, take turns describing someone in the class. The rest of the group guesses who that person is.

Größe: Sie/Er ist …
Gesichtsform: Sie/Er hat ein _____es Gesicht.
Augen: Sie/Er hat _____e Augen.
Haar: Sie/Er hat _____es, _____es Haar.
Kleidung: Sie/Er trägt heute (oft, gern) …

KULTUR

WWW Learn about ship travel from Germany to the United States in the 19th century at
www.prenhall.com/treffpunkt
→ Kapitel 6 → Web Resources → Kultur

Immigration to North America from the German-speaking countries

Hundreds of towns in North America are named after the German, Swiss, or Austrian birthplaces of their founders. The United States has 26 Berlins, and place names like Baden, Frankfort, Hamburg, Hanover, Heidelberg, Saltsburg, or Zurich can be found across the continent. The first German settlers, 13 Pietist families from Northern Germany, came to America in 1683 seeking freedom from religious persecution. They came at the invitation of William Penn, the Quaker who had founded Pennsylvania. These first settlers built a community that they named Germantown. Other such immigrants followed, among them the Mennonites, who also settled in Pennsylvania and later branched out into other states and Canada. From these beginnings to the end of the nineteenth century, over seven million immigrants from the German-speaking countries reached the shores of North America.

Good Bye Bayern / Grüß Gott America

Auswanderung aus Bayern nach Amerika seit 1683

Ausstellung

Nördlingen im Ries
Alte Schranne
25. Juni bis
26. September
2004
täglich
10 bis 18 Uhr

The twentieth century saw far fewer immigrants from the German-speaking countries. In the 1920s and 1930s quotas were established. Many of the people who immigrated in the 1930s were fleeing Hitler's totalitarian and anti-Semitic regime, and their emigration was an immeasurable loss to Germany and Austria. From 1933 to 1938 approximately 130,000 German Jews fled to North America, among them the physicist **Albert Einstein,** the composers **Arnold Schoenberg** and **Paul Hindemith,** and the film director **Billy Wilder.** Others who came to North America include the writers **Thomas Mann** and **Bertolt Brecht,** and the architects **Walter Gropius** and **Ludwig Mies van der Rohe,** whose work influenced a whole generation of architects.

The last big wave of immigration came after World War II, when over 800,000 refugees from former German territories in eastern Europe and other disillusioned Germans crossed the Atlantic.

Deutsche Presse

THE LARGEST GERMAN LANGUAGE WEEKLY NEWSPAPER ABROAD

SERVING A COMMUNITY OF OVER
438,000 GERMAN-SPEAKING CANADIANS

GERMAN • SWISS • AUSTRIAN
GERMAN PRESS
A Weekly Publication
Canadian Publications
S.A. No. 229989

95 ¢

Arnold Schoenberg developed the 12-tone technique. **Paul Hindemith** also worked with the 12-tone technique. Among his best-known works is the opera *Mathis der Maler*. **Billy Wilder** wrote and directed such Hollywood classics as *Some Like It Hot* and *Sunset Boulevard*. Two of **Thomas Mann**'s best-known works are *Der Zauberberg* and *Buddenbrooks*. **Bertolt Brecht**'s *Dreigroschenoper* and *Mutter Courage und ihre Kinder* continue to be performed worldwide. **Walter Gropius** (profiled in *Kapitel 8*) designed the Harvard Graduate Center and New York's Pan Am Building (now the MetLife Building). The postage stamp featuring **Mies van der Rohe** shows his **Neue Nationalgalerie** in Berlin. He also designed the Chicago Federal Center and the Toronto Dominion Center. The other stamp depicts **Carl Schurz,** who emigrated to the U.S. in 1852. He went on to become a general of the Northern States in the Civil War, and from 1877–91 he was Secretary of the Interior. The **Carl Schurz Society,** which fosters German-American relations, was founded in 1930.

Immigranten in den USA 1850–1980

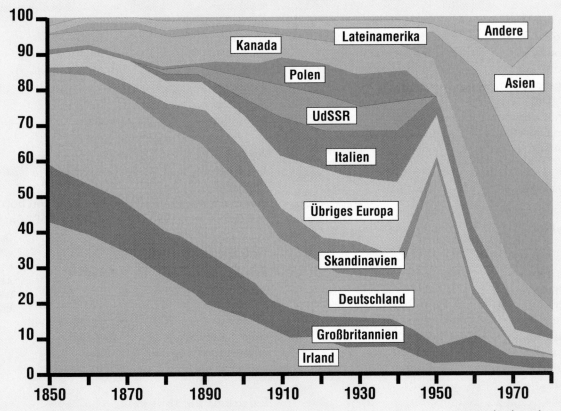

Chart labels: Kanada, Lateinamerika, Andere, Polen, UdSSR, Asien, Italien, Übriges Europa, Skandinavien, Deutschland, Großbritannien, Irland

Y-axis: 0, 10, 20, 30, 40, 50, 60, 70, 80, 90, 100

X-axis: 1850, 1870, 1890, 1910, 1930, 1950, 1970

6-7 Einwanderung in die USA von 1850 bis 1980.

1. Aus welchen zwei Ländern kommen im Jahr 1850 die meisten Einwanderer?
2. Woher kommen zwischen° 1945 und 1960 die meisten Einwanderer?
3. Von welchen zwei Regionen kommen im Jahr 1980 die meisten Einwanderer?

Assuming that the total number of immigrants per year is 100%, the 12 strata show the make-up, by nationality, of immigrants to America in a given year.

between

BUILT 1770

HISTORIC GERMANTOWN MENNONITE **MEETINGHOUSE**

Last wave of immigration: These were the so-called "Displaced Persons." By 1949 Germany had 9,400,000 refugees, most of whom had been expelled from German-speaking areas in Poland, Romania, and what was then Czechoslovakia. There were also many fugitives from the Soviet zone of Germany. Germany was very grateful that the U.S. and Canada were willing to receive so many of the displaced persons.

Nomen

der Geburtsort, -e	place of birth
der Wohnort, -e	place of residence
die Geschichte, -n	history; story
das Land, ̈er	country; state
der Stammbaum, ̈-e	family tree
die Urgroßeltern (pl)	great-grandparents
die Urgroßmutter, ̈	great-grandmother
der Urgroßvater, ̈	great-grandfather
die Vorfahren (pl)	ancestors
der Brief, -e	letter
die Postkarte, -n	postcard
die Größe, -n	height; size
der Koffer, -	suitcase

Land: Within Germany and Austria the states are called **Länder** or **Bundesländer.** In Switzerland they are called **Kantone.**

Das Gesicht

das Gesicht, -er	face
das Haar, -e	hair
die Stirn	forehead
das Auge, -n	eye
das Ohr, -en	ear
die Nase, -n	nose
der Mund, ̈er	mouth
der Zahn, ̈e	tooth
das Kinn	chin

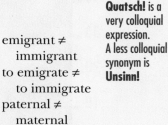

Der Körper

der Körper, -	body
der Kopf, ̈e	head
der Hals, ̈e	neck; throat
die Schulter, -n	shoulder
die Brust, ̈e	chest; breast
der Bauch, ̈e	stomach; belly
der Rücken, -	back
der Arm, -e	arm
die Hand, ̈e	hand
der Daumen, -	thumb
der Finger, -	finger
das Knie, -	knee
das Bein, -e	leg
der Fuß, ̈e	foot
die Zehe, -n	toe

Verben

aus·packen	to unpack
folgen	to follow
packen	to pack
zeichnen	to draw (a picture)

Andere Wörter

eigentlich	actually

Ausdrücke

Liebe Grüße	Love (closing in a letter)
Quatsch!	Nonsense!
Wann bist du geboren?	When were you born?
Am ersten Juni 1990.	On the first of June 1990.

Quatsch! is a very colloquial expression. A less colloquial synonym is **Unsinn!**

Das Gegenteil

der Auswanderer, - ≠	emigrant ≠
der Einwanderer, -	immigrant
aus·wandern ≠	to emigrate ≠
ein·wandern	to immigrate
väterlicherseits ≠	paternal ≠
mütterlicherseits	maternal
vorher ≠ nachher	before ≠ after

Leicht zu verstehen

der Emigrant, -en	die Form, -en
die Emigrantin, -nen	die Region, -en
der Immigrant, -en	exotisch
die Immigrantin, -nen	

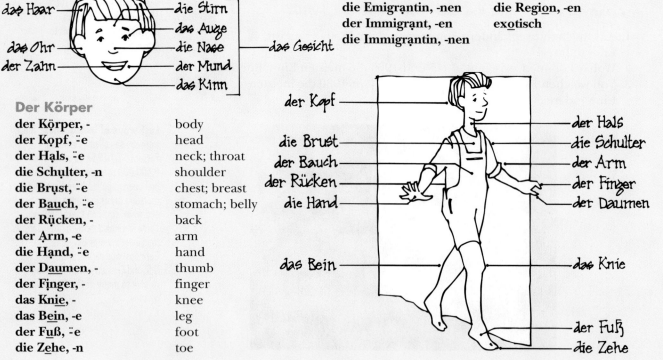

Wörter im Kontext

6-8 Sylvias Vorfahren.

ausgewandert / Stammbaum / eigentlich / Vorfahren / Familiengeschichte / väterlicherseits

Sylvia schreibt ihre _____ und als Illustration zeichnet sie einen schönen, großen _____. Ihre _____ mütterlicherseits kommen aus Italien. Ihre Vorfahren _____ sind im neunzehnten Jahrhundert aus Russland nach Amerika _____, waren aber _____ Deutsche.

> **Aus-** and **einwandern** are constructed just like their Latin-based English equivalents, which are made up of the prefixes *e-* and *im-* (from the Latin *ex-* and *in-*) and the verb *to migrate.*

6-9 Was passt wo?

Koffer / Postkarte / Emigrantin / Geburtsort / Wohnort / Emigrant

1. Wenn ich in ein anderes Land auswandere, bin ich ein _____ oder eine _____.
2. Wenn ich eine Reise machen und viele Kleider mitnehmen will, brauche ich einen _____.
3. Wenn ich in Boston geboren bin, dann ist Boston mein _____.
4. Wenn ich in Hamburg lebe und wohne, dann ist diese Stadt mein _____.
5. Wenn ich keine Zeit für einen Brief habe, schreibe ich eine _____.

6-10 Was passt zusammen? Match appropriately in each set.

1. der Kopf	a. sehen	7. der Fuß	g. die Brille
2. das Auge	b. denken	8. der Finger	h. die Zahnbürste
3. das Ohr	c. schreiben	9. der Hals	i. die Frisur
4. die Hand	d. hören	10. die Augen	j. der Schuh
5. das Bein	e. sprechen	11. das Haar	k. die Halskette
6. der Mund	f. gehen	12. die Zähne	l. der Ring

6-11 Was steht in Hans Keilhaus Pass? What does it say in Hans Keilhau's passport on page 193?

wohnt / Beruf / Haar / Augen / geboren / Gesicht

In Hans Keilhaus Pass steht, …

1. was er von _____ ist.
2. wo und wann er _____ ist und wo er _____.
3. wie groß er ist und was für eine Form sein _____ hat.
4. was für eine Farbe seine _____ und sein _____ haben.

① Talking about events in the past

The perfect tense

The perfect tense is sometimes referred to as the present perfect tense or the conversational past.

To talk about past events in conversational situations, you use the perfect tense in German. In English we generally use the simple past for this purpose.

Was **hast** du gestern **gemacht?**	*What **did** you **do** yesterday?*
Ich **habe** mit Peter Tennis **gespielt.**	*I **played** tennis with Peter.*

The auxiliary verb is sometimes called the helping verb. Why do you think this is so?

The perfect tense consists of an auxiliary verb (usually **haben**) that takes personal endings and a past participle that remains unchanged.

singular	plural
ich habe gespielt	wir haben gespielt
du hast gespielt	ihr habt gespielt
er/es/sie hat gespielt	sie haben gespielt
Sie haben gespielt	

Depending on the context, the German perfect tense can correspond to any of the following English verb forms.

ich habe gespielt {
I played
I have played
I have been playing
I was playing
I did play
}

Position of auxiliary verb and past participle

The auxiliary verb takes the regular position of the verb and the past participle stands at the end of the sentence.

EVA:	**Hast** du deinen Flug schon **gebucht?**	*Have you **booked** your flight yet?*
ANN:	Ja, ich **habe** ihn gestern Nachmittag **gebucht.**	*Yes, I **booked** it yesterday afternoon.*
EVA:	Und was **hast** du gestern Nachmittag noch **gemacht?**	*And what else **did** you **do** yesterday afternoon?*
ANN:	Ich **habe** einen schönen, großen Koffer **gekauft.**	*I **bought** a beautiful, big suitcase.*

The past participle of regular verbs

Most German verbs form the past participle by adding the prefix **ge-** and the ending **-t** or **-et** to the verb stem. The ending **-et** is used if the verb stem ends in **-d, -t,** or certain consonant combinations.

	prefix	verb stem	ending
machen	ge	mach	t
arbeiten	ge	arbeit	et
baden	ge	bad	et
zeichnen	ge	zeichn	et

Past participles of verbs ending in **-ieren** do not have the prefix **ge-**.

	prefix	verb stem	ending
reparieren		reparier	t

6-12 Was haben Yusuf, Maria und Jennifer gestern gemacht?
The information for **S2** is in the *Anhang* on page A8.

S1: Was hat Yusuf gestern Vormittag gemacht?

S2: Gestern Vormittag hat er seinen Wagen repariert.

	MARIA	YUSUF	JENNIFER
gestern Vormittag	stundenlang mit Julia telefoniert		ihren Flug nach Deutschland gebucht
gestern Nachmittag			einen großen Koffer gekauft
gestern Abend	im Internet gesurft	bei McDonald's gearbeitet	

Position of auxiliary verb and past participle in a dependent clause

In a dependent clause, the auxiliary verb stands at the end of the clause, and the past participle precedes it.

Gestern habe ich meine Hausaufgaben erst spät abends gemacht, **weil** ich den ganzen Nachmittag im Supermarkt **gearbeitet habe.**

*Yesterday I didn't do my homework until late in the evening, **because** I **worked** at the supermarket all afternoon.*

Position of *nicht* in sentences in the perfect tense

The rules you learned about the position of **nicht** on pages 30 and 103 still apply. Unless a particular word or expression is negated, **nicht** is placed directly before the past participle.

Du **hast** doch **nicht** den ganzen Nachmittag **gearbeitet,** David. Warum **hast** du denn deine Hausaufgaben **nicht gemacht?**	*You **didn't work** all afternoon, David. Why **didn't** you **do** your homework?*

6-13 Warum hast du das nicht gemacht?

deinen Koffer packen   mit Monika telefonieren

S1: Warum hast du deinen Koffer nicht gepackt?

S2: Weil ich mit Monika telefoniert habe.

1.

2.

3.

Radio hören	frühstücken	deine Vokabeln lernen
den Hund füttern	Karten spielen	Tennis spielen

4.

5.

6.

lawn

Klavier üben	den Rasen° mähen	die Fenster putzen
Gitarre spielen	Fußball spielen	dein Fahrrad reparieren

6-14 Was hast du gestern gemacht? Use a few of the following expressions to tell each other some of the things you did yesterday.

Gestern habe ich …

Karten (Fußball, …) gespielt
für eine Klausur (ein Quiz)
  in _____ gelernt
im Supermarkt gearbeitet
mein Fahrrad repariert
CDs (MP3s, Radio, …) gehört

mit _____ telefoniert
im Internet gesurft
Hausaufgaben gemacht
Klamotten gekauft
stundenlang gebloggt
für ein Referat recherchiert

The past participle of irregular verbs

Irregular verbs are a small but frequently used group of verbs. The past participles of these verbs end in **-en.** The verb stem often undergoes a vowel change and sometimes consonant changes as well.

	prefix	verb stem	ending
finden	ge	f**u**nd	en
nehmen	ge	n**o**mm	en
schlafen	ge	schlaf	en

The list below shows the past participles of some common irregular verbs. Be sure to learn them.

backen	**gebacken**	nehmen	**genommen**	sitzen	**gesessen**	
essen	**gegessen**	schlafen	**geschlafen**	sprechen	**gesprochen**	
finden	**gefunden**	schneiden°	**geschnitten**	stehen	**gestanden**	*to cut*
gießen°	**gegossen**	schreiben	**geschrieben**	streichen°	**gestrichen**	*to water / to paint*
lesen	**gelesen**	sehen	**gesehen**	trinken	**getrunken**	
liegen°	**gelegen**	singen	**gesungen**	waschen	**gewaschen**	*to lie*

6-15 Was haben Julia, Moritz und Lisa gestern gemacht? The information for **S2** is in the *Anhang* on page A8.

S1: Was hat Julia gestern Vormittag gemacht?

S2: Gestern Vormittag hat sie eine Torte gebacken.

	JULIA	MORITZ	LISA
gestern Vormittag			Bernds Haare geschnitten
gestern Nachmittag	mit Sophia Kaffee getrunken	Briefe geschrieben	
gestern Abend			ein heißes Bad genommen

6-16 Morgen, morgen, nur nicht heute ...

▶

die Zimmerpflanzen gießen

mit Eva vor dem Fernseher sitzen

S1: Hast du die Zimmerpflanzen gegossen?

Was hast du denn gemacht?

S2: Nein, noch nicht.

Ich habe mit Eva vor dem Fernseher gesessen.

1.

2.

3.

| dein Referat schreiben | die Zeitung lesen | ein Stück Torte essen |
| mit Professor Berg sprechen | deinen Wagen waschen | mit Eva Kaffee trinken |

4.

5.

6.

| den Zaun streichen | ein Bad nehmen | die Hecke schneiden |
| ein Buch lesen | einen Kuchen backen | ein bisschen schlafen |

6-17 Was Eva gestern alles gemacht hat.

Listen as your instructor narrates what Eva did yesterday. Then take turns telling the story with a partner. Begin the sentences as indicated and use the verbs provided.

1. Um halb sieben hat Eva noch im Bett gelegen und geschlafen.
2. Um … (nehmen)
3. Um … (trinken, lesen)
4. Dann … (gießen)
5. Später … (schreiben)
6. Um … (sprechen)
7. Um … (essen)
8. Am Nachmittag …
   (Wäsche [f] waschen)
9. Nachher …
   (Pizza [f] backen)
10. Später … (sitzen)
11. Und am Abend … (singen)

6-18 Ein paar persönliche Fragen.

Respond to your partner's questions, using the perfect tense.

Bis wann hast du heute Morgen geschlafen?
Was hast du zum Frühstück (zum Mittagessen) gegessen und getrunken?
Welche interessanten Bücher hast du in letzter Zeit° gelesen?   **in letzter Zeit:** *recently*
Was hast du in letzter Zeit im Fernsehen gesehen?
Wie viele Klausuren hast du letzte Woche geschrieben?

The verb *sein* as auxiliary in the perfect tense

In English you always use the verb *to have* as the auxiliary in the perfect tense. In German you usually use **haben,** but for verbs that express a change of location or a change of condition, you use **sein.** These verbs can be regular or irregular.

singular	plural
ich bin gekommen	wir sind gekommen
du bist gekommen	ihr seid gekommen
er/es/sie ist gekommen	sie sind gekommen
Sie sind gekommen	

Change of location:

Ist Eva ins Kino **gegangen?**   *Has Eva gone to the movies?*

Some common verbs that express a change of location:

fahren	**ist gefahren**	kommen	**ist gekommen**
fliegen	**ist geflogen**	reisen	**ist gereist**
gehen	**ist gegangen**	wandern	**ist gewandert**

Change of condition:

Opa Ziegler **ist** plötzlich sehr krank **geworden** und **gestorben.**   *Grandpa Ziegler suddenly **became** very ill and **died.***

Wann **ist** das **passiert?**   *When **did** that **happen?***

Some common verbs that express a change of condition:

werden	**ist geworden**	*to become*
sterben	**ist gestorben**	*to die*
passieren	**ist passiert**	*to happen*

Two very common verbs use **sein** as an auxiliary although they express neither a change of location nor a change of condition:

bleiben	**ist geblieben**	*to stay; to remain*
sein	**ist gewesen**	*to be*

Warum **ist** Sylvia zu Hause **geblieben?**   *Why **did** Sylvia **stay** home?*

Wo **bist** du **gewesen,** Sylvia?   *Where **have** you **been,** Sylvia?*

The list below shows the past participles of some common irregular verbs that use **sein** as an auxiliary. Be sure to learn them.

bleiben	**ist geblieben**	kommen	**ist gekommen**
fahren	**ist gefahren**	sein	**ist gewesen**
fliegen	**ist geflogen**	sterben	**ist gestorben**
gehen	**ist gegangen**	werden	**ist geworden**

6-19 Opa Ziegler ist gestorben. Brigitte Ziegler calls her friend Beverly and tells her why she and Klaus can't come for dinner tonight. Supply the appropriate perfect forms.

ist ... geworden / ist ... passiert / ist ... gefahren / ist ... gestorben /
ist ... gekommen

1. BRIGITTE: Du Beverly, wir können leider nicht zum Abendessen kommen.
   Klaus musste ganz schnell zu seinen Eltern nach Hamburg.
   BEVERLY: Was _____ denn _____?
2. BRIGITTE: Opa Ziegler _____ plötzlich° sehr krank _____.   *suddenly*
   BEVERLY: Ist er im Krankenhaus?
3. BRIGITTE: Ja, und dort _____ er heute Morgen um zehn _____.
   BEVERLY: Hoffentlich° _____ Klaus nicht zu spät _____.   *I hope*
4. BRIGITTE: Nein. Er _____ vom Bahnhof direkt ins Krankenhaus _____ und
   konnte noch ein paar Worte mit Opa sprechen.

■ Sprachnotiz ··

The perfect tense of sein and haben

In Austria, Southern Germany, and Switzerland, the perfect tense of **sein**
and **haben** is used quite frequently in conversational situations.

Wo **bist** du gestern **gewesen?**	*Where **were** you yesterday?*
Wie viele Vorlesungen **hast** du gestern **gehabt?**	*How many lectures **did** you **have** yesterday?*

But remember that most speakers of German use the simple past of these verbs.

Ich **war** den ganzen Tag zu Hause.	*I **was** home all day.*
Ich **hatte** nur eine Vorlesung.	*I **had** only one lecture.*

6-20 Eine Urlaubsreise nach Spanien. Beverly Harper asks Brigitte
Ziegler about the vacation Brigitte and Klaus had last summer at the Costa
Brava in Spain. Supply the appropriate forms of **haben** or **sein.**

1. BEVERLY: _____ Klaus und die Kinder dich letzten Sommer wieder zum
   Grundlsee geschleppt?
   BRIGITTE: Nein, letzten Sommer _____ wir mal ohne Kinder an die Costa
   Brava gereist.
2. BEVERLY: _____ ihr gefahren oder geflogen?
   BRIGITTE: Wir _____ von Frankfurt direkt nach Barcelona geflogen.
3. BEVERLY: Wie lang _____ ihr in Barcelona geblieben?
   BRIGITTE: Nur einen Tag. Aber wir _____ trotzdem viel gesehen.
4. BEVERLY: Wie _____ ihr zur Costa Brava gekommen?
   BRIGITTE: Wir _____ einen Wagen gemietet°.   *rented*
5. BEVERLY: Was _____ ihr denn den ganzen Tag gemacht?
   BRIGITTE: Wir _____ jeden Tag zweimal° schwimmen gegangen, _____viel   *twice*
   Tennis gespielt und sehr gut gegessen.

6-21 Auch das kann im Urlaub passieren. **S1** has all kinds of aches and pains. **S2** seems to know the reason for each one of them.

pains ▶ Schmerzen° im rechten Arm — Du hast bestimmt zu viel Tennis _____.

spielen

S1: Warum habe ich denn solche Schmerzen im rechten Arm?

S2: Du hast bestimmt zu viel Tennis gespielt.

1. Zahnschmerzen — Du hast bestimmt zu viele Süßigkeiten° _____.

sweets

2. Kopfschmerzen — Du hast bestimmt zu viel Bier _____.

3. Schmerzen im Knie — Du hast bestimmt zu viel Beachvolleyball _____.

4. Hals- und Ohrenschmerzen — Du bist bestimmt zu lang im Wasser _____.

5. Bauchschmerzen — Du hast bestimmt zu viel Eis _____.

6. Rückenschmerzen — Du hast bestimmt zu viele schwere Koffer _____.

| trinken | bleiben | essen (2x) | spielen | schleppen |

6-22 Meine letzte Reise. Respond to your partner's questions using the perfect tense.

Wann hast du deine letzte Reise gemacht?
Wohin bist du gereist? Bist du geflogen oder gefahren?
Wie lang bist du geblieben und was hast du dort gemacht?
Bist du mit Schmerzen nach Hause gekommen? Wenn ja, was für Schmerzen und warum?

INFOBOX

The German language in North America

Like many immigrant groups, German-speaking **Einwanderer** continued to use their native language long after they arrived in **Nordamerika.** Even today, with about 1.4 million speakers, German ranks fourth among foreign languages spoken at home in the United States, following Spanish, Chinese, and French (including Cajun French). In Canada, about 438,000 people speak German at home on a regular basis. German-language newspapers were published in the United States as far back as the eighteenth century. In fact, North America's first German-language newspaper, the *Philadelphische Zeitung*, was published by Benjamin Franklin in 1732.

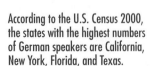

Die deutsche Zeitung für Amerika

AMERIKA WOCHE

www Read a German-language newspaper published in the U.S. at www.prenhall.com/treffpunkt → Kapitel 6 → Web Resources → Kultur

According to the U.S. Census 2000, the states with the highest numbers of German speakers are California, New York, Florida, and Texas.

6-23 „Claudias Mittwoch" oder „Das Studentenleben ist schwer°!" *hard*

Listen as your instructor tells what Claudia did on Wednesday. Then, taking turns with a partner, retell the story. Begin the sentences as indicated and use the verbs provided.

1. Am Mittwoch hat Claudia bis neun geschlafen.
2. Dann … (nehmen)
3. Ein bisschen später … (frühstücken)
4. Dann … (telefonieren)
5. Dann … (fahren)
6. Von … bis … (haben)
7. Um … (essen)
8. Dann … (spielen)
9. Um … (gehen, lernen)
10. Um … (gehen)
11. Nachher … (gehen)
12. Später … (gehen, tanzen)
13. Dann … (fahren)
14. Zu Hause … (gehen, lesen)
15. Um … (schlafen)

Hören

Ein deutscher Einwanderer sucht Arbeit

Hans Keilhau ist 1930 nach Amerika ausgewandert. Sein Freund Paul kommt auch aus Deutschland. Er arbeitet bei *Hutton Machine and Tool* und er erzählt Hans, dass seine Firma einen Schlosser sucht. Weil der Personalchef dort aus Österreich kommt, spricht er Deutsch. Hören Sie, was der Personalchef und Hans Keilhau miteinander sprechen.

NEUE VOKABELN

der Personalchef	*personnel manager*	**der Gärtner**	*gardener*
Aufträge	*orders*	**schicken**	*to send*
arbeitslos	*unemployed*		

Hans Keilhau ist Schlosser von Beruf.

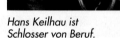

6-24 Erstes Verstehen. In what order do you hear the following questions and statements?

_____ Haben Sie hier Arbeit gefunden?
_____ Wenn Paul Richter Sie geschickt hat, sind Sie bestimmt auch gut.
_____ Wer hat Sie zu *Hutton Machine and Tool* geschickt?
_____ Und wo haben Sie zuletzt gearbeitet?
_____ Warum sind Sie Schlosser geworden?
_____ Escher hatte immer weniger Aufträge.

6-25 Detailverstehen. Listen to the conversation again and write responses to the following questions.

1. Was ist Hans Keilhau von Beruf?
2. Wo hat er seinen Beruf gelernt?
3. Warum ist Hans Keilhau arbeitslos geworden?
4. Warum ist er nach Amerika ausgewandert?
5. Wo und als was arbeitet Hans Keilhau jetzt?
6. Warum hat er Schlosser gelernt?
7. Warum denkt der Personalchef, dass Hans Keilhau ein guter Arbeiter ist? *Weil …*

Map: Sachsen is located in the former **Deutsche Demokratische Republik (DDR)**, i.e., the former German Democratic Republic (GDR, also known as East Germany). Locate it on the map of the **Bundesländer** at the front of your book. **Dresden,** the capital of **Sachsen,** is once again becoming the "pearl of Baroque architecture" that it was before it was completely destroyed by Allied bombs in 1945. **Leipzig** is famous for its industrial fair **(Mustermesse)** and was also the center of non-violent resistance to the Communist regime in the **DDR. Chemnitz,** a center for industrial research and microelectronics, has its original name again after being called **Karl-Marx-Stadt** during the period of the **DDR. Zwickau** is the birthplace of the composer Robert Schumann. The **Trabi,** a smelly two-cycle engine car, was produced here before reunification; now it's the VW. **Meißen** is the home of the world-famous **Meissener Porzellan,** which has been produced here since 1710.

6-26 Das deutsche Schulsystem. Look at the information and the illustration in the *Infobox* below. Then complete the following statements with the appropriate items from the list provided.

einen Hauptschulabschluss / Abitur / zehn / Uni / Schuljahren / Grundschule / die Mittlere Reife / Fachhochschule

1. Alle Kinder müssen vier Jahre in die _____.
2. Den Hauptschulabschluss bekommt man nach neun oder zehn _____.
3. Die mittlere Reife bekommt man nach _____ Schuljahren.
4. Das Abitur braucht man, wenn man zur _____ oder zur _____ will.
5. Wenn man eine Lehre machen will, braucht man mindestens° _____ oder _____.

Wir suchen Dich als freundlichen Azubi
für die Berufe

Bäcker / in
Konditor / in
Konditorei-Fachverkäufer / in

at least

INFOBOX

Vocational training and the school systems in the German-speaking countries

Skilled tradespeople from the German-speaking countries played an important role in the development of industry and technology in North America. This was largely due to the quality of the training they received. Today vocational training is still very important in the educational systems of the German-speaking countries.

School attendance is compulsory from age 6 to 15. Up to age 10 all students go to the **Grundschule.** At age 11, they move on to one of three types of schools, depending on their abilities and their career plans.

A **Hauptschule** provides basic education, and the **Hauptschulabschluss** (diploma) is the minimum requirement for an apprenticeship **(Lehre)** in a trade. For three years, an apprentice **(der Lehrling, der/die Auszubildende)** alternates on-the-job training with classes in a vocational school **(Berufsschule).** This is called **das duale System.**

Students attending a **Realschule** graduate with the **mittlere Reife.** They may decide on an apprenticeship in a trade, but their more demanding education also qualifies them for an apprenticeship at a bank, a dental lab, etc. They attend more specialized **Berufsschulen.** Graduates from a **Realschule** can also opt to go to a **Fachoberschule** to obtain the **Abitur** (**Matura** in Austria and Switzerland). This allows them to study at a **Fachhochschule** (technical college) or a **Universität.** Students who acquire their **Abitur** at a **Gymnasium** are aiming from the outset to study at a **Universität** or a **Fachhochschule.** (Only a **Universität** can grant a doctorate.)

In recent years, **Gesamtschulen,** where academic *and* vocational subjects are taught, have been introduced. These schools also offer an **Abitur.**

www Visit a **Berufsschule** at www.prenhall.com/treffpunkt
→ Kapitel 6 → Web Resources
→ Kultur

der/die Auszubildende: This designation is usually shortened to **Azubi.**

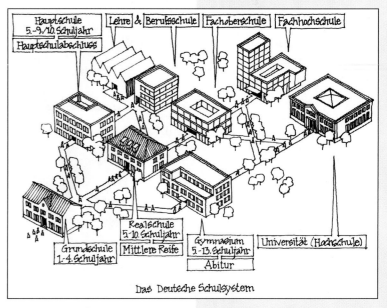

Das Deutsche Schulsystem

➋ More on the past

The past participle of verbs with separable prefixes

To form the past participle of separable-prefix verbs, you simply attach the prefix to the past participle of the base verb. Separable-prefix verbs can be regular or irregular.

regular verbs		irregular verbs	
INFINITIVE	PERFECT TENSE	INFINITIVE	PERFECT TENSE
anhören	hat **an**gehört	**fern**sehen	hat **fern**gesehen
abreisen	ist **ab**gereist	**mit**singen	hat **mit**gesungen
ausprobieren	hat **aus**probiert	**auf**stehen	ist **auf**gestanden

Remember:

- Verbs that express a change of location or condition use **sein** as an auxiliary.
- Past participles of regular verbs ending in **-ieren** do not add **ge-** to the verb stem.

6-27 Was hast du letzte Woche gemacht?

▶

du am Samstag

mein neues Surfbrett ausprobiert

S1: Was hast du am Samstag gemacht?

S2: Ich habe mein neues Surfbrett ausprobiert.

1. du am Sonntagvormittag

3. ihr am Sonntagabend

2. ihr am Sonntagnachmittag

4. du am Montag früh

bis nachts um eins ferngesehen erst um elf aufgestanden	Bilder von Rembrandt angeschaut mein Zimmer aufgeräumt

5. ihr am Dienstagabend

7. du am Donnerstagabend

6. ihr am Mittwochnachmittag

8. ihr am Freitagabend

alle zusammen ausgegangen	im Studentenchor mitgesungen
bei Karstadt Kleider anprobiert	meine neuen CDs angehört

The past participle of verbs with inseparable prefixes

Many regular and irregular verbs have inseparable prefixes. The three most common inseparable prefixes are **be-, er-,** and **ver-.** The past participles of verbs with inseparable prefixes do not add **ge-.** Whereas separable prefixes are *stressed* in pronunciation, inseparable prefixes are *unstressed.*

regular verbs		irregular verbs	
INFINITIVE	PERFECT TENSE	INFINITIVE	PERFECT TENSE
besuchen	hat **besucht**	bekommen	hat **bekommen**
erzählen	hat **erzählt**	ertrinken	ist **ertrunken**
verkaufen	hat **verkauft**	verstehen	hat **verstanden**

6-28 Kleine Gespräche. Complete the mini-dialogues with the perfect tense of the verbs given in parentheses.

1. STEFAN: _____ Professor Kluge die Relativitätstheorie gut _____?
   (erklären°)   *to explain*

   MATTHIAS: Ja, aber ich _____ trotzdem nicht alles _____. (verstehen)

2. MICHAEL: _____ du letzten Sommer gut _____? (verdienen)

   VERONIKA: Ja, meine Chefin _____ mich sehr gut _____. (bezahlen)

3. FRAU FELL: Für wie viel _____ Bergers ihr Haus _____? (verkaufen)

   FRAU HOLZ: Ich glaube, sie _____ fast eine halbe Million Euro
   dafür _____. (bekommen)

4. KATHRIN: Was _____ euer Reiseleiter° von König Ludwig _____?   *tour guide*
   (erzählen)

   SYLVIA: Dass er im Starnberger See _____ _____. (ertrinken°)   *to drown*

5. HORST: _____ du in Berlin auch deine Kusine Sophia _____? (besuchen)

   INGRID: Ich _____ es _____. Aber sie war nie zu Hause. (versuchen°) *to try*

The past participle of mixed verbs

There is a small group of verbs that have characteristics of regular *and* irregular verbs. The past participle of these mixed verbs has a stem change like an irregular verb and ends in **-t** like a regular verb. Be sure to learn these common verbs.

infinitive	perfect tense	
bringen	hat **gebracht**	*to bring*
denken	hat **gedacht**	*to think*
kennen	hat **gekannt**	*to know (be acquainted with)*
nennen	hat **genannt**	*to name, to call*
rennen	ist **gerannt**	*to run*
wissen	hat **gewusst**	*to know (a fact)*

6-29 Der falsche Monat. Complete with the appropriate past participles.

gedacht / gekannt / gebracht / genannt / gewusst / gerannt

Tina und ich haben einander schon im Gymnasium gut _____ und ich habe
her / flowers ihr° oft Blumen° zum Geburtstag _____.
    Heute Morgen habe ich beim Frühstück meinen Kalender angeschaut und
gesehen, dass heute der erste Juni ist. „Der erste Juni?!" habe ich _____, „das ist
immediately doch Tinas Geburtstag!" Ich bin sofort° zum nächsten Blumengeschäft _____,
und weil Tina dieses Jahr einundzwanzig wird, habe ich einundzwanzig rosarote
carnations / astonished Nelken° gekauft. Tina hat die einundzwanzig Nelken zuerst nur verwundert°
guy angeschaut. Dann hat sie gelacht, mich einen lieben Kerl° _____ und gesagt:
„Den Tag hast du richtig _____, aber der Monat ist falsch. Mein Geburtstag ist
nicht am ersten Juni, sondern am ersten Juli."

6-30 Kleine Gespräche. Complete the mini-dialogues with the perfect tense of the verbs given in parentheses.

1.   HOLGER: Warum _____ Paul denn plötzlich _____? (wegrennen)
      KARL: Weil du ihn einen Esel _____ _____. (nennen)

2.   KATHRIN: Warum _____ du Tina Blumen _____? (bringen)
    GERHARD: Ich _____ _____, sie hat heute Geburtstag. (denken)

3. HERR KRUG: _____ Sie Frau Merck gut _____? (kennen)
   FRAU FELL: Ja, aber dass sie so plötzlich gestorben ist, _____ ich nicht _____.
     (wissen)

6-31 Aus meinem Tagebuch. Write a diary entry about what you did last Saturday. The expressions below will give you some ideas. Writing diaries is considered a conversational situation, so remember to use the perfect tense. Avoid beginning each sentence with **Dann …** by using expressions like **Am Nachmittag …, Nachher …, Später …, Um _____ Uhr …, Am Abend …**

erst/schon um _____ Uhr aufstehen
zum Frühstück … essen und … trinken
mein Zimmer aufräumen
in den Waschsalon° gehen und meine Wäsche waschen   *laundromat*
für die ganze nächste Woche einkaufen
mein Fahrrad (mein Auto) putzen (reparieren)
meine Eltern (meine Freundin, meinen Freund) besuchen (anrufen)
im Fernsehen ein Eishockeymatch (Basketballmatch) anschauen
ins Fitnesscenter gehen
mit _____ ins Kino (ins Konzert, in die Disco, auf eine Party) gehen
…

6-32 Das habe ich letzten Samstag gemacht. For homework you wrote about what you did last Saturday. Now share your experiences with your classmates.

❸ Ranking people and things

Ordinal numbers

Ordinal numbers indicate the position of people and things in a sequence (e.g., the first, the second).

Der **erste** Zug fährt um sieben.	*The **first** train leaves at seven.*
Dann nehme ich lieber den **zweiten.**	*Then I'd rather take the **second** one.*

For the numbers 1 through 19, you form the ordinal numbers by adding **-t-** and an adjective ending to the cardinal number. The few irregular forms are indicated below in boldface.

der **erst**e	der **siebt**e	der dreizehnte
der zweite	der **acht**e	der vierzehnte
der **dritt**e	der neunte	der fünfzehnte
der vierte	der zehnte	der sechzehnte
der fünfte	der elfte	der siebzehnte
der sechste	der zwölfte	der achtzehnte
		der neunzehnte

From the number 20 on, you form the ordinal numbers by adding **-st-** and an adjective ending to the cardinal number.

der zwanzigste
der einundzwanzigste
der zweiundzwanzigste
der dreißigste
etc.

DAS SCHÖNSTE AM 20. GEBURTSTAGSFEST
…SIND KORKEN DIE MAN KNALLEN LÄSST !!!

Die größte
BEACH PARTY

Fr. 8.7. bis Sa. 16.7.

K7 ✲✲✲

Eckernförde

Mi. - Fr. - Sa.

www.disco-k7.de

Dates

To ask for and give the date, you use the following expressions.

Der Wievielte ist heute?	*What's the date today?*
Heute ist der Fünfzehnte.	*Today is the fifteenth.*

Den Wievielten haben wir heute?	*What's the date today?*
Heute haben wir den Fünfzehnten.	*Today is the fifteenth.*

Note that **Wievielt-** and ordinal numbers are capitalized unless they are followed by a noun.

When written as a numeral, an ordinal number is indicated by a period. Note that the day always precedes the month.

WRITTEN: Heute ist der 23. Mai.
SPOKEN: Heute ist der dreiundzwanzigste Mai.

The month is also frequently written as an ordinal number.

WRITTEN: Lisa ist am 23. 5.1988 geboren.
SPOKEN: Lisa ist am dreiundzwanzigsten Fünften
  neunzehnhundertachtundachtzig geboren.

Der Wievielte ist heute? and **Den Wievielten haben wir heute?** and their respective responses are synonymous.

6-33 Daten. You and your partner take turns asking each other and responding to the following questions.

S1:	**S2:**
1. Den Wievielten haben wir heute?	Heute haben wir den _____.
2. Der Wievielte ist morgen?	Morgen ist der _____.
3. Der Wievielte ist nächsten Sonntag?	Nächsten Sonntag ist der _____.
4. Den Wievielten hatten wir letzten Sonntag?	Letzten Sonntag hatten wir den _____.
5. Wann ist Valentinstag?	Valentinstag ist am _____ _____.
6. Wann ist Halloween?	Halloween ist am _____ _____.
7. Wann ist Neujahr?	Neujahr ist am _____ _____.

6-34 Wann hast du Geburtstag? Draw a grid showing the months of the year. Walk around the classroom, tell your classmates when your birthday is, ask for theirs, and record them on the grid.

S1: Ich habe am zehnten Juli Geburtstag. Wann ist dein Geburtstag?
S2: Mein Geburtstag ist am einundzwanzigsten Mai.
  …

❹ Writing personal letters

There are certain conventions in writing letters. In German, you write dates as follows: **München, den 5. Oktober 2007.** Note that the article appears in the accusative case and that there is no comma between the month and the year.

  Writing a personal letter is considered a conversational situation. You can therefore use the perfect tense to relate past events. (But remember that the modals and **haben** and **sein** are typically used in the simple past tense.)

6-35 Stephanie schreibt nach Hause. Complete Stephanie's letter using participles and the simple past forms of **haben, sein, können,** and **müssen.**

München, den 5. Oktober 2007

Liebe Eltern und lieber Opa,

gestern kurz vor acht ist mein Flugzeug in München
_____ (landen). Ich _____ (müssen) nur wenige
Minuten auf meine Koffer warten°, aber weil ich nicht gleich ein
Taxi bekommen _____ (können), _____ (sein) ich erst
kurz nach zehn im Studentenheim. Meine Mitbewohnerin heißt
Claudia. Sie ist vier Jahre älter als ich, kommt aus Hamburg und
ist sehr nett. Sie hat viel _____ (fragen) und ich habe
meine Koffer _____ (auspacken) und _____
(erzählen). Um eins _____ (haben) wir beide Hunger und sind
in die Stadt _____ (gehen). Wir haben gut zu Mittag
_____ (essen) und sind erst am späten Nachmittag ins
Studentenheim _____ (zurückkommen). München ist eine
tolle Stadt und es gibt schon so viel zu erzählen. Aber jetzt
müssen wir zum Abendessen in die Cafeteria, denn wir haben noch
gar nichts _____ (einkaufen). Morgen oder übermorgen
bekommt ihr einen viel längeren Brief und du, Mutti, bekommst
einen Extrabrief auf Englisch.

Viele liebe Grüße
Stephanie

wait

❺ Indicating direction away from and toward

Hin and *her* as directional suffixes and prefixes

You already know that **hin** and **her** are used as suffixes with the question word **wo.**

Wo bist du?	*Where are you?*
Wo**hin** gehst du?	*Where are you going (to)?*
Wo**her** kommst du?	*Where are you coming from?*

> **Hin** indicates motion or direction *away from* the speaker.
> **Her** indicates motion or direction *toward* the speaker.

The question words **wohin** and **woher** are often split. The question then begins with **wo** and ends with **hin** or **her.**

Wo gehst du **hin?**　　　　　　**Wo** kommst du **her?**

Hin and **her** are also used as separable prefixes or as parts of separable prefixes.

RALF: Arbeitest du immer noch in Bernau?

Do you still work in Bernau?

LISA: Ja, ich **fahre** immer noch jeden Tag **hin** und **her.**

*Yes, I still **drive there** and **back** every day.*

KURT: Sollen wir **hineingehen?**

*Should we **go in?***

EVA: Nein, wir warten lieber, bis Frau Borg **herauskommt.**

*No, we'd better wait until Ms. Borg **comes out.***

6-36 Was sagen diese Leute? Look at the drawings and complete the sentences for each speech bubble with the appropriate prefix.

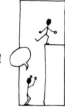

▶ hinunter / herunter
Passen Sie auf, dass Sie nicht _____fallen!
Passen Sie auf, dass Sie nicht herunterfallen!

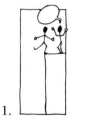

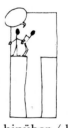

1. hinunter / herunter
Passen Sie auf, dass Sie nicht _____fallen!

2. hinauf / herauf
Keine Angst! Wir ziehen Sie gleich _____.

3. hinüber / herüber
Warum springen Sie denn nicht _____?

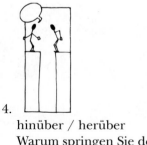

4. hinüber / herüber
Warum springen Sie denn nicht _____?

5. hinein / herein
Kommen Sie doch _____, bitte!

6. hinaus / heraus
Gehen Sie sofort _____!

7. hinein / herein
Sollen wir _____ gehen?

8. hinaus / heraus
Kommen Sie sofort _____!

Sprachnotiz

Away from and *toward* in colloquial German

In colloquial German, prefixes like **hinaus-, herein-, hinauf-,** and **herunter-** are (somewhat illogically) abbreviated to **raus-, rein-, rauf-, runter-.**

Gehen wir **hinein** oder warten wir, bis Dieter **herauskommt?**
Gehen wir **rein** oder warten wir, bis Dieter **rauskommt?**

Zusammenschau

 ## Video-Treff

Mein erster Job

Susann, Thomas, Stefan Meister, and Stefan Kuhlmann talk about their first jobs.

Zum besseren Verstehen

6-37 Was ist das auf Englisch?

1. Ich habe in einem Restaurant **gekellnert.**
2. **Während** der Schulzeit habe ich oft dort gearbeitet.
3. Ich habe 10 Mark **pro Stunde** verdient.
4. Das war **damals** noch die D-Mark Zeit.
5. Ich habe den Job durch eine **Empfehlung** von Freunden bekommen.
6. Die Nachbarn wollten, dass es im Garten kein **Unkraut** gibt.
7. Als Kellner kann man viel **Trinkgeld** verdienen.
8. Ich musste im Supermarkt die **Regale** mit Hundefutter auffüllen.
9. Das war eine Menge Geld für einen **Zwölfjährigen.**

a. recommendation
b. waited tables
c. 12-year-old
d. shelves
e. weeds
f. back then
g. during
h. tips
i. per hour

Now watch the video and complete the post-viewing activities in the *Video-Treff* section of the *Student Activities Manual.*

This interview begins with Martin knocking on Ms. Borg's door. In the German-speaking countries, office doors are generally closed.

Martin sucht einen Ferienjob

Es ist Mitte Juli. Martin hat heute Vormittag seine letzte Klausur geschrieben und sucht jetzt einen Ferienjob. Er geht deshalb zum Studentenwerk und spricht dort mit Frau Borg.

NEUE VOKABELN

zum Beispiel	*for example*	**die Hecke schneiden**	*to clip the hedge*
den Rasen mähen	*to mow the lawn*	**die Arbeitserfahrung**	*work experience*
den Zaun streichen	*to paint the fence*	**der Maler**	*painter*

6-38 Erstes Verstehen. Who says the following? Write M for Martin and B for Frau Borg.

_____ Interessiert Sie das?
_____ Ich habe heute Vormittag noch meine letzte Klausur geschrieben.
_____ Ich fahre dann gleich hin.
_____ Vielleicht können Sie mich dann jeden Tag kurz anrufen, ja?
_____ Was für Arbeitserfahrung haben Sie?
_____ Auch keine Tagesjobs?

6-39 Detailverstehen. Listen to the conversation again and write responses to the following questions.

1. Warum ist Martin nicht früher zum Studentenwerk gegangen?
2. Was für eine Arbeit hat Frau Borg für Donnerstag und Freitag? Was muss Martin alles tun?
3. Wie viel kann er verdienen?
4. Was ist Frau Fischers Adresse? Wann will Martin hinfahren?
5. Warum findet Frau Borg es so gut, dass Martin schon als Maler gearbeitet hat?
6. Was soll Martin von jetzt ab jeden Tag tun? *Er soll …*

Sprachnotiz ··································

The expression *Bitte schön!*

You can use **Bitte schön!** or just **Bitte!** as a response to **Danke, Danke schön,** or **Vielen Dank** to mean *You're welcome!* or *Don't mention it!*

Vielen Dank für Ihre Hilfe!   *Thanks a lot for your help!*
Bitte schön!   *You're welcome!*

■ Schreiben und Sprechen ·············

6-40 Mein erster Job. In this chapter's video segment, you heard four people describe their first job. Write a letter to a good friend describing *your* first job. Use the questions below to give you ideas and add any information you think might be particularly interesting. Follow the format of Stephanie's letter on page 217.

Wie hast du deinen ersten Job gefunden?
* durch eine Freundin / einen Freund / deine Mutter / deinen Vater?
* am Schwarzen Brett°?
* in der Zeitung?

Was für ein Job war das?
Wo war der Job?
Was musstest du tun?
Wie viele Stunden am Tag hast du gearbeitet?
Wie viel hast du verdient?
…

6-41 Was für Arbeitserfahrung haben Sie? You work at the **Studentenwerk** as a job counselor and are interviewing a student looking for a summer job. Find out about her/his work experience. You will find a list of **Jobs und Berufe** in the *Anhang* on page A17. The following questions will help you get started.

Was für Arbeitserfahrung haben Sie? *Ich habe als _____ gearbeitet. Und auch als _____* …
Was mussten Sie alles tun?
Was haben Sie am liebsten gemacht? Warum?
Was haben Sie nicht so gern gemacht? Warum?
Wo haben Sie am meisten gelernt?
Was sind Ihre Stärken° und Schwächen°?
…

Schreibtipp: Using the perfect tense to relate past events lends warmth and familiarity to a personal letter. But remember to use the simple past for **haben, sein,** and the modal verbs.

bulletin board

das Schwarze Brett: So-called because bulletin boards are often black in the German-speaking countries. Don't confuse it with *blackboard,* which is **die Tafel.**

strengths / weaknesses

Als Statue kann man gut verdienen.

Photos: Students in the German-speaking countries can often be seen in pedestrian malls earning money as "statues." They assume a slightly different position each time a passerby drops money into the pail. The less money, the more strenuous the job!

 **Lesen** ···

Zum besseren Verstehen

Do you know any immigrants who have come to this country recently? What sorts of hardships are they encountering?

6-42 Auswanderer.

1. Many immigrants to North America began their lives here doing hard physical labor. What is the occupation of the men in the photo? Describe how you imagine life was like in such a camp.
2. If you were to emigrate, where would you want to go? Why? What sorts of hardships can you imagine encountering?

6-43 Wo war Christian Köchling am ...? Scan the reading text, find out where each diary entry was written, and number the locations accordingly.

S1: Wo war Christian Köchling am achtundzwanzigsten Sechsten neunzehnhundertdreißig?

S2: Da war er …

1. 28. 6. 1930
2. 4. 7. 1930
3. 16. 7. 1930
4. 7. 8. 1930
5. 15. 12. 1930

_____ in Watford.
_____ an Bord der Karlsruhe.
_____ in Bremen.
_____ in Kenora.
_____ im Zug von Montreal nach Toronto.

6-44 Was ist das auf Englisch?

1. Wir lesen nicht das ganze Tagebuch von Christian Köchling, sondern nur ein paar **Auszüge.**
2. Christian ist **über** Hannover nach Bremen gefahren.
3. Die **Bahnfahrt** war sehr schön.
4. In Bremen waren Auswanderer aus ganz Europa, aber die **Mehrzahl** waren Deutsche.
5. Ein **Holzfäller** arbeitet im Wald und fällt dort Bäume.
6. Wenn Christian jeden Tag einen Dollar **spart,** hat er bis zum Frühling hundert Dollar.
7. Er kann dann in Toronto ein kleines Zimmer **mieten.**

a. via
b. lumberjack
c. train trip
d. rent
e. saves
f. excerpts
g. majority

Christian Köchling (ganz rechts) als Holzfäller

Christian Köchling, ein junger deutscher Goldschmied, ist im Sommer 1930 nach Kanada ausgewandert. Die folgenden Auszüge aus Christians Tagebuch zeigen[1], was für ein schweres Leben viele Auswanderer hatten.

Bremen, den 28. 6. 1930

Nach einer langen, schönen Bahnfahrt durch den Harz[2] und über Hannover bin ich endlich in Bremen angekommen. Ganz Europa ist hier vertreten[3], doch die Mehrzahl sind Deutsche.

An Bord der Karlsruhe[4], den 4. 7. 1930

Am 1. 7. sind wir in Bremerhaven aufs Schiff gegangen. Zuerst hatten wir wunderbares Wetter, aber im Englischen Kanal ist es stürmisch geworden. Wir waren alle seekrank.

Im Zug von Montreal nach Toronto, den 16. 7. 1930

Am 11. 7. sind wir in Halifax angekommen und nach 29-stündiger Bahnfahrt waren wir in Montreal. Wir haben da aber nur gehört: „Was wollt ihr denn hier? Wir haben doch selbst keine Arbeit!" Deshalb sind wir heute weitergefahren. Ich habe nur noch 25 Dollar, denn Montreal war sehr teuer: $1,– für eine Übernachtung mit Frühstück!

Watford, den 7. 8. 1930, bei Farmer Robertson

Ich war fast zwei Wochen in Toronto, habe aber keine Arbeit gefunden. Ich habe gehört, dass Farmer im Sommer Hilfe brauchen. Deshalb bin ich hierher gefahren und habe sofort Arbeit gefunden. Aber was für eine Arbeit für einen Goldschmied! Mist laden[5] von morgens bis abends, und nur fürs Essen und ein schlechtes Bett!

Kenora, den 15. 12. 1930

Ich bin jetzt Holzfäller hier im Norden von Kanada. Es ist sehr kalt und die Arbeit ist schwer, aber ich verdiene endlich ein bisschen Geld. Und wenn die anderen abends Karten spielen, wasche ich ihre Socken (10 Cent für ein Paar Socken). Bis zum Frühling möchte ich so viel sparen, dass ich in Toronto eine kleine Werkstatt[6] mieten und endlich wieder als Goldschmied arbeiten kann.

[1]*show* [2]*the Harz mountains* [3]*represented* [4]*name of the ship* [5]*loading manure* [6]*workshop*

www Meet a German immigrant who became one of Washington D.C.'s most important architects at www.prenhall.com/treffpunkt
→ Kapitel 6 → Web Resources → Kultur

Arbeit mit dem Text

6-45 Anders gesagt. Find the equivalents for the following statements in *Aus Christian Köchlings Tagebuch*.

1. Hier sind Menschen aus ganz Europa, aber die meisten kommen aus Deutschland.
2. Am Anfang war das Wetter sehr schön …
3. Am 11.7. ist unser Schiff in Halifax gelandet …
4. … und haben dann bis Montreal noch 29 Stunden im Zug gesessen.
5. Wir sind doch auch alle arbeitslos!
6. … dass es auf Farmen im Juli und im August Arbeit gibt.
7. … und ich bekomme kein Geld dafür, aber darf hier essen und schlafen.

Wort, Sinn und Klang

Wörter unter der Lupe

Predicting gender

All nouns with the suffix **-ung** are feminine. Like most English nouns with the suffix *-ing*, most of these nouns are derived from verbs. Note that the plural forms always end in **-en**.

warnen	*to warn*	**die** Warn**ung, -en**	*warning*
landen	*to land*	**die** Land**ung, -en**	*landing*

However, many English equivalents of German nouns with the suffix **-ung** do not have the suffix *-ing*.

üben	*to practice*	**die** Üb**ung, -en**	*exercise*
wohnen	*to live*	**die** Wohn**ung, -en**	*apartment*
erzählen	*to tell*	**die** Erzähl**ung, -en**	*story*
ausstellen	*to exhibit*	**die** Ausstell**ung, -en**	*exhibition*

6-46 Was ist das? Form nouns from the following verbs and give their English equivalents.

1. erklären	*to explain*		6. übersetzen	*to translate*
2. bestellen	*to order*		7. bedeuten	*to mean*
3. beschreiben	*to describe*		8. verbessern	*to correct*
4. lösen	*to solve*		9. einladen	*to invite*
5. bezahlen	*to pay*		10. übernachten	*to stay overnight*

Giving language color

Like other languages, German uses the names of parts of the body in many colorful expressions. Below is a sampling.

Er ist nicht auf den Kopf gefallen.	*He's no fool.*
Ich habe die ganze Nacht kein Auge zugetan.	*I didn't sleep a wink all night.*
Er hat wieder mal die Nase zu tief ins Glas gesteckt.	*He drank too much again.*
Nimm doch den Mund nicht immer so voll!	*Don't always talk so big!*
Hals- und Beinbruch!	*Good luck!*
Das hat Hand und Fuß.	*That makes sense.*

Hals- und Beinbruch: This expression stems from Hebrew and entered the German language through Yiddish. After a successful business transaction, Yiddish-speaking Jews wished each other **hazloche und broche** *(success and blessings)*. Speakers of German understood this as **Hals- und Beinbruch.** The English equivalent *Break a leg!* is often used in theatrical circles to wish an actor luck. It entered the English language in the 1920s and some sources surmise that it also has its roots in Yiddish, since many German Jews worked in the theater at this time.

6-47 Was passt zusammen?

1. Warum magst du Günter nicht?
2. Warum lässt du mich denn nicht fahren?
3. Warum bist du denn so müde?
4. Warum bekommt Maria für ihre Referate immer so gute Zensuren?
5. Ich muss jetzt gehen. Wir schreiben gleich eine Klausur.
6. Ist es wirklich° wahr, dass Paul die Lösung für dieses Problem gefunden hat?

a. Na, dann Hals- und Beinbruch!
b. Weil alles, was sie schreibt, Hand und Fuß hat.
c. Klar. Er ist doch nicht auf den Kopf gefallen.
d. Weil du wieder mal die Nase zu tief ins Glas gesteckt hast.
e. Weil er den Mund immer so voll nimmt.
f. Weil ich die ganze Nacht kein Auge zugetan habe.

really

Zur Aussprache

German *l*

In English the sound represented by the letter *l* varies according to the vowels and consonants surrounding it. (Compare the *l* sound in *leaf* and *feel*.) In German the sound represented by the letter **l** never varies and is very close to the *l* in English *leaf*. Try to maintain the sound quality of the *l* in *leaf* throughout the exercise below.

6-48 Hören Sie gut zu und wiederholen Sie!

Lilo lernt Latein°.   *Latin*

Latein ist manchmal langweilig.

Lilo lernt Philipp kennen.

Philipp hilft° Lilo Latein lernen.   *helps*

Philipp bleibt lange bei Lilo.

Lilo lernt viel.

Lilo lernt Philipp lieben.

Nomen

die Arbeitserfahrung, -en	work experience
die Bezahlung	pay; wages
der Ferienjob, -s	summer job
der Maler, -	painter; artist
die Malerin, -nen	
der Personalchef, -s	personnel manager
die Personalchefin, -nen	
das Studentenwerk	student center
die Grundschule, -n	elementary school; primary school
das Gymnasium, die Gymnasien	(academic) high school
die Hochschule, -n	university
die Fachhochschule, -n	technical college

Krankenhaus!
Bitte
langsam fahren

das Krankenhaus, ⸚er	hospital
der Schmerz, -en	ache; pain
die Blume, -n	flower
die Hecke, -n	hedge
der Rasen, -	lawn
der Zaun, ⸚e	fence
die Zimmerpflanze, -n	house plant
das Tagebuch, ⸚er	diary
der Waschsalon, -s	laundromat

Verben

Past participles are listed in vocabularies only for irregular and mixed verbs. The auxiliary verb is provided only when it is **sein**.

bringen, gebracht	to bring
erklären	to explain
füttern	to feed
gießen, gegossen	to water
liegen, gelegen	to lie; to be situated
mähen	to mow
malen	to paint (a picture)
mieten	to rent
passieren, ist passiert	to happen
putzen	to clean
recherchieren	to do research

Recherchieren derives from French, so **ch** is pronounced **sch**.

rennen, ist gerannt	to run
schicken	to send
schneiden, geschnitten	to cut
sparen	to save
stehen, gestanden	to stand; to say
sterben (stirbt), ist gestorben	to die
streichen, gestrichen	to paint (e.g., a fence, a house)
üben	to practice
übersetzen	to translate
verbessern	to correct
warten	to wait

Stehen means *to say* in expressions like **Am Schwarzen Brett steht …, Im Pass steht …,** etc.

Andere Wörter

arbeitslos	unemployed
hoffentlich	hopefully, I hope (so)
mindestens	at least
plötzlich	suddenly
sofort	immediately
zweimal	twice

Ausdrücke

Am Schwarzen Brett steht …	On the bulletin board it says . . .
Danke schön!	Thank you!
Vielen Dank!	Many thanks!
Bitte schön!	You're welcome!
in letzter Zeit	recently
die Wäsche waschen	to do the laundry
Den Wievielten haben wir heute?	What's the date today?
Der Wievielte ist heute?	
Hals- und Beinbruch!	Break a leg! Good luck!
zum Beispiel (z.B.)	for example (e.g.)

Das Gegenteil

starten, ist gestartet ≠ landen, ist gelandet	to take off ≠ to land
starten ≠ stoppen	to start (something) ≠ to stop (something)
schwer ≠ leicht	difficult; heavy ≠ easy; light
stark ≠ schwach	strong ≠ weak
die Stärke, -n ≠ die Schwäche, -n	strength ≠ weakness

Leicht zu verstehen

das System, -e	warnen	
die Warnung, -en	an Bord	
bloggen		

Wörter im Kontext

6-49 Was passt zusammen?

1. Hast du die Zimmerpflanzen
2. Hast du den Zaun
3. Hast du die Hecke
4. Hast du die Wohnung
5. Hast du den Rasen
6. Hast du den Hund
7. Hast du die Postkarte

a. weggeschickt?
b. gemietet?
c. gemäht?
d. geschnitten?
e. gegossen?
f. gestrichen?
g. gefüttert?

Zaun: You have learned that a German **z** is often a *t* in the related English word: **zehn** – *ten*, **zwölf** – *twelve*, **Zunge** – *tongue*. Applying this principle to **Zaun** gives you *town*. How do you think these two words are related in meaning?

People in the German-speaking countries treasure their privacy, and most yards are enclosed by fences or hedges.

6-50 Warum David so spät nach Hause gekommen ist.

gelegen / erklärt / gewartet / gerannt / hereingerannt / warten / passiert / starten

Gestern Nacht habe ich stundenlang auf David _____. Als ich dann schon im Bett _____ habe, ist er plötzlich zur Tür _____. „Was ist denn _____, David?" habe ich gefragt, und er hat _____, dass er seinen Wagen nicht _____ konnte, dass er viel zu lange auf den ADAC° _____ musste und dass er dann den ganzen langen Weg nach Hause _____ ist.

Allgemeiner Deutscher Automobil-Club

ADAC: North American equivalents are the *AAA* (U.S.) and the *CAA* (Canada).

Plötzlich ist alles möglich. **Lotto** Lotto Brandenburg

6-51 Was ist hier identisch? Read the following sets of sentences aloud and decide which two in each set convey approximately the same meaning.

1. Was bedeutet dieses Wort?
   Ich verstehe dieses Wort nicht.
   Hast du dieses Wort verbessert?

2. Opa Ziegler ist im Krankenhaus.
   Opa Ziegler lebt nicht mehr.
   Opa Ziegler ist gestorben.

3. Eva ist plötzlich arbeitslos geworden.
   Eva hat seit gestern keine Arbeit mehr.
   Eva hat sehr viel Arbeitserfahrung.

4. Wie ist die Bezahlung?
   Wie viel musst du bezahlen?
   Wie viel verdienst du?

arbeitslos: Remember that the suffix **-los** indicates the lack of something. What are the English equivalents of **endlos, farblos, fleischlos,** and **harmlos?**

Martin-Luther-Gymnasium: This school was designed by an architect you read about in *Kapitel 3*. Do you remember his name?

6-52 Der ideale Ferienjob.

schwer / sparen / hoffentlich / Tagebuch / sofort / mindestens

Aus Annas _____:

Mein idealer Ferienjob muss _____ am ersten Ferientag beginnen und ich möchte bis zum letzten Ferientag arbeiten. Die Firma muss _____ acht Euro die Stunde bezahlen, damit ich viel Geld _____ kann und mein nächstes Studienjahr fast ganz selbst bezahlen kann. Die Arbeit soll interessant und nicht zu _____ sein.
_____ kann ich bald so einen Job finden.

Das Martin-Luther-Gymnasium in Wittenberg

Feste und Feiertage

Fasnacht in Basel, Schweiz

Kommunikationsziele

Talking about . . .

- birthdays and holidays
- buying and giving gifts
- personal tastes and opinions

Purchasing and returning merchandise

Expressing congratulations, best wishes, and thanks

Strukturen

The dative case:

- indirect object
- personal pronouns
- dative verbs
- dative prepositions
- **da**-compounds
- adjective endings

Word order: Sequence of objects

Kultur

Berlin

Holidays and celebrations in the German-speaking countries

Mitbringsel

Video-Treff: **Mein bestes Geschenk**

Lesen: **Margarete Steiff und der Teddybär**

Das Geburtstagsgeschenk

NICOLE: Du, Maria, was soll ich denn meinem kleinen Bruder zum Geburtstag schenken?

MARIA: Schenk ihm doch eine Armbanduhr. Oder eine CD. Was hört er denn gern? Oder kauf ihm ein Computerspiel. Ja! Einem Dreizehnjährigen schenkt man heutzutage sowieso Computerspiele!

NICOLE: Das hat David alles schon und außerdem ist mir ein gutes Computerspiel viel zu teuer.

MARIA: Dann fahren wir doch zum KaDeWe! Wenn wir sehen, was es alles gibt, fällt uns bestimmt etwas ein.

NICOLE: Gute Idee, Maria!

Beim KaDeWe

Beim KaDeWe hat gerade der Winterschlussverkauf begonnen und alle Preise sind stark reduziert. Die beiden Freundinnen gehen deshalb noch schnell in die Damenabteilung, bevor sie ein Geschenk für David suchen. Maria kauft dort eine schicke, warme Winterjacke und Nicole gibt fast ihr ganzes Geld für einen eleganten, schwarzen Pulli aus. Dann schaut sie ein bisschen beschämt auf die paar Euro in ihrer Geldtasche und sagt: „Wie soll ich denn damit meinem Bruder ein Geburtstagsgeschenk kaufen?" Aber Maria hat eine gute Idee: „Kauf ihm doch eine lustige Geburtstagskarte, und zusammen mit dieser Karte schickst du ihm einen Schuldschein mit den Worten: ‚Lieber David, ich schulde dir ein Geburtstagsgeschenk. Du bekommst es, sobald ich wieder Geld habe.'"

((•)) Hören ·····································

7-1 Richtig oder falsch? Sie hören die beiden Texte und nach jedem Text ein paar Aussagen°. Sind diese Aussagen **richtig** oder **falsch?**

statements

DAS GEBURTSTAGSGESCHENK		BEIM KADEWE	
RICHTIG	FALSCH	RICHTIG	FALSCH
1. _____	_____	1. _____	_____
2. _____	_____	2. _____	_____
3. _____	_____	3. _____	_____
4. _____	_____	4. _____	_____

Beginning in this chapter, all directions for exercises except those in the *Wort, Sinn und Klang* sections are in German.

Die Reichstagskuppel in Berlin

INFOBOX

Berlin

Berlin, the capital of Germany, was reduced to a heap of rubble by the end of World War II. Like the rest of Germany, it was divided into four occupation zones (**Besatzungszonen**) under American, British, French, and Soviet control. From 1949 to 1990, only **Ostberlin** had capital city status – as capital of the former **Deutsche Demokratische Republik (DDR)**. In 1961, the communist government of the **DDR** built the Berlin Wall (**die Berliner Mauer**) to stop the mass exodus of its citizens to the West. On November 9, 1989, the city was again the center of world attention when the Wall came down and shortly thereafter, the Soviet empire.

Berlin became the capital of Germany again, and in 1999 the German Parliament (**der Bundestag**) officially moved from Bonn to the Berlin **Reichstag** building.

WWW Explore the city of Berlin at www.prenhall.com/treffpunkt
→ Kapitel 7 → Web Resources
→ Kultur

Designed by the renowned British architect Lord Norman Foster, the glass cupola of the **Reichstag** is a major tourist attraction. Two spiral ramps take visitors to a viewing platform high above the plenary chamber of parliament, symbolically raising them above the heads of the elected representatives. The core of the cupola is a concave cone-like structure, which uses angled mirrors to reflect outside light into the chamber. At night the process is reversed and artificial light in the chamber is reflected outwards.

Heimtrainer: Note that the **ai** in **-trainer** is pronounced as in English.

7-2 Was kann man dir zum Geburtstag schenken?

S1: Ich trinke viel Kaffee.
S2: Dann kann man dir eine Kaffeemaschine schenken.

1. Ich fahre immer mit dem Rad zur Uni.
2. Mein Zimmer muss wie ein Garten aussehen.
3. Ich möchte nächsten Sommer durch den Schwarzwald wandern.
4. Ich komme morgens oft zu spät zur Vorlesung.
5. Ich kann nicht kochen.
6. Die UV-Strahlen machen meine Augen kaputt.
7. Ich möchte mein Deutsch verbessern.
8. Ich möchte fit werden.
9. Ich höre gern Musik.

der Heimtrainer

die Kaffeemaschine

die Zimmerpflanze

der Rucksack

das Wörterbuch

der Fahrradhelm

der CD-Spieler

das Kochbuch

der Wecker

die Sonnenbrille

fellow students **7-3 Geburtstagsgeschenke.** Sagen Sie, was Sie Ihren Mitstudenten° zum Geburtstag schenken wollen und warum.

S: Ich schenke David ein italienisches Kochbuch, weil er so gern Pasta und Pizza isst.

7-4 Helfen statt° Kaufen. Schauen Sie die Geburtstagskarte an und beantworten Sie die Fragen.

instead of

1. Wer hat diese Geburtstagskarte geschrieben?
2. Wer hat Geburtstag?
3. Wann hat Peter diese Karte geschrieben?

4. Wann hilft Peter seiner Mutter?
5. Was tut er alles für sie?

zum **GEBURTSTAG** eine **ÜBERRASCHUNG**

GUTSCHEIN für meine Mutter:

Ich übernehme am __3. 4.__

und am __3.5.__ oder am __8.6.__

⊗ Kochen
○ Frühstück
○ Tisch decken
⊗ Abwasch
○ Schuhe putzen
○ Großeinkauf
⊗ Betten machen
○ Mülleimer leeren
⊗ Fenster putzen
○ _____

Datum __2.4.__

Unterschrift __Peter__

7-5 Warum machen Sie's nicht mal wie Peter? Denken Sie an drei Personen aus Ihrer Familie oder aus Ihrem Freundeskreis°. Fragen Sie einander, wer die drei Personen sind und was Sie zum Geburtstag für sie tun.

circle of friends

S1: Wer sind deine drei Personen?

S2: Mein(e) _____, mein(e) _____ und mein(e) _____.

S1: Was tust du für deine(n) _____?
...

S2: Für meine(n) …
...

- eine Woche lang das Frühstück machen
- eine Woche lang das Mittagessen (das Abendessen) kochen
- eine Woche lang den Tisch decken°
- eine Woche lang den Abwasch° (die Betten) machen
- eine Woche lang den Mülleimer leeren°
- das ganze Haus (die ganze Wohnung, alle Fenster) putzen
- die Wäsche (den Wagen) waschen
- die Garage aufräumen
- den Rasen mähen
- …

set the table
dishes
empty the garbage can

KULTUR
Feste und Feiertage

WWW Learn more about **Karneval** in Germany at www.prenhall.com/treffpunkt
→ Kapitel 7 → Web Resources → Kultur

The German-speaking countries enjoy a wider array of public holidays than the United States or Canada. Many of these holidays have their roots in Christian traditions, although an increasingly secular society celebrates them without giving much thought to their religious origin. As in North America, **Weihnachten** is still the biggest and most important holiday, and preparation begins four weeks in advance. Beginning on December 1, many children count down the 24 days to Christmas Eve **(der Heilige Abend)** with the help of an **Adventskalender.** Each day they open a door or window on the calendar and find motifs related to **Weihnachten** or a small gift.

Weihnachtsmarkt in Berlin

On the eve of **Nikolaustag** (December 6), children put their shoes outside their bedroom door for **Sankt Nikolaus** (the patron saint of children) to fill with candy, chocolate, fruit, and nuts. As in other countries, **Weihnachten** is associated with a Christmas tree **(der Weihnachtsbaum)** and gift-giving **(die Bescherung).** In the German-speaking countries the **Weihnachtsbaum** is frequently not put up until December 24, **am Heiligen Abend,** which is also when the **Bescherung** takes place. On December 25 **(der erste Weihnachtsfeiertag),** families gather for a traditional dinner that often centers around a Christmas goose **(die Weihnachtsgans).** On December 26 **(der zweite Weihnachtsfeiertag),** it is customary to visit relatives and friends. New Year's Eve **(Silvester)** is an evening of parties and revelry culminating at midnight with spectacular displays of fireworks even in smaller towns.

In the time between New Year's and Lent, people in the German-speaking countries celebrate **Karneval** (as it is called in the **Rheinland**) or **Fastnacht / Fasching** (as it is called in Southern Germany, Austria, and Switzerland). **Karneval** celebrations include huge parades with marching bands, elaborate costumes, and huge floats. These floats often depict in satirical fashion scenes critical of politicians and unpopular government policies.

Spring brings Easter **(Ostern).** Businesses are closed on Good Friday **(Karfreitag)** and on **Ostermontag.** On **Ostersonntag** children receive colored eggs and chocolate goodies from the **Osterhase.** The week before and after **Ostern** are school holidays. Pentecost or Whitsun **(Pfingsten)** is celebrated on the seventh Sunday and Monday after **Ostern** and brings with it another week of vacation from school.

Secular holidays in the German-speaking countries include the **Tag der Arbeit** or **Maifeiertag** on May 1 as well as national holidays for each country. On October 3, Germany celebrates the **Tag der deutschen Einheit** to commemorate the reunification in 1990 of the **BRD** and the former **DDR.** Austria has set aside October 26 **(Tag der Fahne)** to celebrate the day in 1955 when it became a neutral state. On August 1, Switzerland celebrates the beginning of the Swiss confederation **(Confoederatio Helvetica),** which took place in 1291.

7-6 Was sind Ihre Feste und Feiertage?

1. Feiern Sie Weihnachten? Wenn ja, wann ist die Bescherung? Wenn nein, wie heißt Ihr wichtigster Feiertag und wie feiern Sie ihn?
2. Wie feiert man in Ihrer Familie Geburtstage?
3. Wann ist der Tag der Arbeit in Ihrem Land?
4. Wie heißt Ihr Nationalfeiertag? Wann ist er und wie feiern Sie ihn?

7-7 Wie Familie Zillich Pfingsten feiert.
Herr und Frau Zillich, ihre Tochter Heike (9) und ihr Sohn Lukas (7) verbringen° die beiden Pfingstfeiertage im Residence Hotel in Potsdam.

1. Wie viel bezahlen Zillichs für den Familienbrunch am Pfingstsonntag?
2. Heike hat schon zwei Jahre lang Flötenstunden°. Was möchte sie deshalb hören? An welchem Tag, wo und um wie viel Uhr ist das?
3. Zillichs essen alle gern Kuchen, haben aber am Montagnachmittag einen Spaziergang nach Schloss Sanssouci geplant. An welchem Tag und ab° wie viel Uhr können sie trotzdem Kuchen im Residence Hotel essen?
4. Wie wissen Zillichs, dass es da viele verschiedene° Kuchen gibt?

Schloss Sanssouci in Potsdam

Note that the stem of the word **Bescherung** (-scher-) is related to English *share*. German equivalents of *Merry Christmas!* are **Frohe Weihnachten! Fröhliche Weihnachten! Frohes Fest!**

spend

flute lessons

ab wie viel Uhr: *from what time on*

different

Silvester, the German equivalent of New Year's Eve, is the name day of Saint Sylvester I, who was pope from 314–355 A.D.

Liturgical Christian churches mark the 40 days before Easter as Lent, a time of prayer and penance. **Karneval,** celebrated in other cultures as *Mardi Gras, Carnival,* etc., was traditionally the last chance for revelry and overindulgence before Lent began.

Pfingsten is a Christian festival that commemorates the descent of the Holy Spirit on Christ's apostles. In the German-speaking countries it has become less a Christian festival than a spring festival, since it comes at a time of year when the whole countryside is in bloom.

Nomen

der Feiertag, -e	holiday
das Fest, -e	celebration; festival
Ostern	Easter
der Osterhase, -n	Easter bunny
Silvester	New Year's Eve
Weihnachten	Christmas
der Weihnachtsbaum, ⁻e	Christmas tree
das Geschenk, -e	present
die Überraschung, -en	surprise

Weihnachten, Ostern, and **Silvester** are used without an article. In greetings **Weihnachten** and **Ostern** are generally regarded as plural nouns.

die Abteilung, -en	department
die Damenabteilung	women's department
die Herrenabteilung	men's department
der Sommerschluss-verkauf, ⁻e	summer clearance sale
der Winterschluss-verkauf, ⁻e	winter clearance sale

die Armbanduhr, -en	wristwatch
der Fahrradhelm, -e	bicycle helmet
die Geldtasche, -n	wallet
der Gutschein, -e	voucher
der Schuldschein, -e	IOU
der Heimtrainer, -	exercise bike
der Rucksack, ⁻e	backpack
die Sonnenbrille, -n	sunglasses
der Wecker, -	alarm clock

Verben

feiern	to celebrate
kaputt machen	to ruin; to break
schauen (auf)	to look (at)
schenken	to give (a gift)
schulden	to owe
verbringen, verbracht	to spend (time)

Why does the past participle of **verbringen** have no **ge-**? Why does it have a stem change, but end in **-t**?

Andere Wörter

lustig	funny, humorous; happy
verschieden	different
außerdem	besides; in addition
gerade	just, just now
heutzutage	nowadays

Ausdrücke

den Abwasch machen	to do the dishes
den Mülleimer leeren	to empty the garbage can
den Tisch decken	to set the table
zum Geburtstag	for one's birthday
Herzliche Glückwünsche zum Geburtstag!	Happy Birthday!
zu Weihnachten	for Christmas
Frohe Weihnachten!	Merry Christmas!
Ein gutes neues Jahr! (Einen) guten Rutsch!	} Happy New Year!
eine Frage beantworten	to answer a question
stark reduziert	sharply reduced

Einen guten Rutsch: Although most speakers of German understand **Rutsch** as coming from **rutschen** (to slide), it probably stems from the Hebrew word **rosh** (head, beginning) as in Rosh Hashanah, the Jewish New Year. It is thought that the word **rosh** came into German via Yiddish.

Das Gegenteil

leer ≠ voll	empty ≠ full

Leicht zu verstehen

der Brunch, -es	das Kochbuch, ⁻er
das Computerspiel, -e	das Wort, ⁻er
die Idee, -n	das Wörterbuch, ⁻er

Beim Cannstatter Volksfest

Wörter im Kontext

7-8 Was ist die richtige Reihenfolge°?

°sequence

_____ das Essen kochen   _____ den Abwasch machen   _____ einkaufen

_____ essen   _____ den Tisch decken

7-9 Was passt zusammen?

1. Wenn es dunkel ist,
2. Wenn man von selbst aufwacht,
3. Wenn man fit ist,
4. Wenn man immer nur Auto fährt,
5. Wenn man immer in der Mensa isst,
6. Wenn man nicht gern Musik hört,

a. braucht man keinen Wecker.
b. braucht man keinen Fahrradhelm.
c. braucht man kein Kochbuch.
d. braucht man keine Sonnenbrille.
e. braucht man keinen CD-Spieler.
f. braucht man keinen Heimtrainer.

7-10 Was ich tue, wenn ...

1. Wenn meine Geldtasche leer ist,
2. Wenn ich nicht weiß, wie spät es ist,
3. Wenn der Mülleimer voll ist,
4. Wenn ich eine Bluse kaufen will,
5. Wenn ich einen warmen Pullover kaufen und nicht viel Geld ausgeben will,

a. muss ich ihn leeren.
b. gehe ich zum Winterschlussverkauf.
c. gehe ich in die Damenabteilung.
d. bezahle ich mit meiner Kreditkarte.
e. schaue ich auf meine Armbanduhr.

7-11 Was brauche ich da? Beginnen Sie alle Antworten mit

Da brauche ich ...

1. Ich möchte wandern gehen.
2. Ich muss das Frühstück machen.
3. Ich verbringe meine Ferien in Australien.
4. Ich weiß nicht, wie man Wiener Schnitzel macht.
5. Meine beste Freundin hat Geburtstag.
6. Ich weiß nicht, wie man auf Deutsch _Happy Birthday!_ sagt.

a. ein Wörterbuch
b. ein Geschenk
c. eine Sonnenbrille
d. eine Kaffeemaschine
e. einen Rucksack
f. ein Kochbuch

verbringen: Be careful to distinguish between **verbringen** (to spend time) and **ausgeben** (to spend money), which you learned in _Kapitel 5._

7-12 Bettina Zieglers Geburtstag.

gerade / Überraschung / lustig / feiert / außerdem / Fest / geschenkt

Bettina Ziegler _____ heute ihren dreißigsten Geburtstag und hat zu diesem _____ die ganze Familie und alle ihre Freunde eingeladen. Sie haben _____ ein paar Flaschen Champagner getrunken und sind deshalb alle sehr _____. Als _____ haben Bettinas Freunde ihr eine Reise nach Kalifornien _____ und von ihrer Familie hat sie _____ dreihundert Euro bekommen.

Kommunikation und Formen

❶ Indicating the person *to whom* or *for whom* something is done

The dative case: the indirect object

In *Kapitel 3* you learned that many verbs take direct objects and that the direct object is signaled by the accusative case.

Klaus möchte **einen Heimtrainer.**   *Klaus would like **an exercise bike.***

Some verbs take not only a direct object, but an *indirect object* as well. The indirect object indicates *to whom* or *for whom* something is done and is therefore almost always a *person.* In German the indirect object is signaled by the *dative case.*

Brigitte kauft **ihrem Mann**
  einen Heimtrainer.

*Brigitte buys **her husband**
  an exercise bike.*
*(Brigitte buys an exercise bike
  for her husband.)*

Sie schenkt **ihrem Mann** den
  Heimtrainer zum Geburtstag.

*She gives **her husband** the exercise
  bike for his birthday.*
*(She gives the exercise bike **to her
  husband** for his birthday.)*

It is important to remember that German signals the indirect object with the dative case, never with the preposition **zu** *(to).*

	masculine		neuter		feminine		plural	
NOMINATIVE	der mein	Vater	das mein	Kind	die meine	Mutter	die meine	Kinder
ACCUSATIVE	den meinen	Vater	das mein	Kind	die meine	Mutter	die meine	Kinder
DATIVE	**dem meinem**	Vater	**dem meinem**	Kind	**der meiner**	Mutter	**den meinen**	Kinde**n**

- The other possessive adjectives (**dein, sein, ihr, unser, euer, ihr, Ihr**) and **ein** and **kein** take the same endings as **mein.**
- In the dative plural, all nouns take the ending **-n** unless the plural form already ends in **-n** (**die Freundinnen, den Freundinnen**) or if it ends in **-s** (**die Chefs, den Chefs**).

7-13 Ein bisschen Grammatik. Sagen Sie, welche von den unterstrichenen° ___underlined___
Wörtern Subjekte, direkte Objekte oder indirekte Objekte sind!

▶ Brigitte Ziegler schenkt ihrem Mann einen Heimtrainer.

S: Brigitte Ziegler ist das Subjekt, einen Heimtrainer ist das direkte
Objekt und ihrem Mann ist das indirekte Objekt.

1. Stephanie feiert dieses Jahr Weihnachten nicht zu Hause in Chicago,
sondern in München, und sie schickt deshalb ihrer Familie ein großes Paket.
Sie schickt ihrem Großvater ein gutes Buch, ihrem Vater ein schönes Bierglas
und ihrer Mutter einen Kalender mit Bildern von München.

2. Und was schenkt Stephanie ihren Freunden in München? Sie schenkt
ihrem Freund Peter ein Sweatshirt, ihrer Mitbewohnerin Claudia
ein Paar Ohrringe und Claudias Freund Martin eine tolle CD.

7-14 Geschenke. Die Information für **S2** ist im _Anhang_ auf Seite A9.

S1: Was schenkt Laura ihren
Eltern?

S2: Was schenkt Florian seinen
Eltern?

S2: Laura schenkt ihren Eltern
ein schönes Bild.

S1: Florian schenkt seinen Eltern
eine neue Kaffeemaschine.

	LAURA	FLORIAN
ihren/seinen Eltern		eine neue Kaffeemaschine
ihrer/seiner Schwester		eine coole Sonnenbrille
ihrem/seinem Bruder	ein warmes Sweatshirt	
ihrer/seiner Freundin	einen neuen Fahrradhelm	

7-15 Was schenkst du …?

S1: Was schenkst du deinen Eltern
(deiner Schwester, deinem
Bruder, …) zu Weihnachten
(zu Chanukka, …)?

S2: Ich schenke meinen
Eltern (meiner Schwester,
meinem Bruder, …) …

The interrogative pronoun in the dative case

The dative form of the interrogative pronoun **wer** has the same ending as the
dative form of the _masculine_ definite article.

	interrogative pronoun	masculine definite article
NOMINATIVE	wer	der
ACCUSATIVE	wen	den
DATIVE	**wem**	**dem**

Wer ist der Mann dort?
Der Briefträger.
Wen hat Ihr Hund gebissen?
Den Briefträger.
Wem schenken Sie den Wein?
Dem Briefträger.

Who is that man there?
The letter carrier.
Whom did your dog bite?
The letter carrier.
To whom _are you giving the wine?_
To the _letter carrier._

7-16 Wem schenkst du das alles? Ihre Partnerin/Ihr Partner hat schon
things alle Weihnachtsgeschenke gekauft. Fragen Sie, wem sie/er diese Sachen° schenkt.

▶   sie mein__ Mutter

S1: Wem schenkst du die   **S2:** Ich schenke sie meiner
     Weingläser?   Mutter.

1.   sie mein__ Vater

2.   es mein__ Schwester

3.   sie mein__ beiden Brüder__

4.   ihn mein__ Großmutter

---

das Armband	den Teekessel	die Geldtasche	die zwei Armbanduhren

---

5.   es mein__ Kusine

6.   sie mein__ Onkel

7.   sie mein__ Tante

8.   sie mein__ beiden Vettern

---

die Gießkanne	das Parfüm	die Krawatte	die zwei Tennisschläger

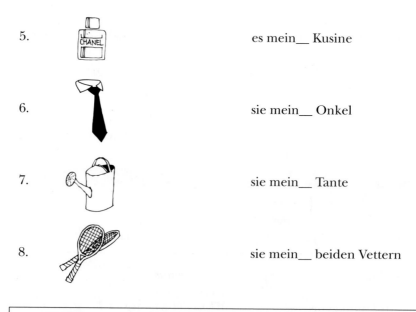

Personal pronouns in the dative case

In English, personal pronouns have only one object form. This one form can function as a direct object and as an indirect object. In German, personal pronouns have two object forms. You are familiar with the accusative form, which is used for the direct object.

Warum habt ihr **mich** nicht eingeladen?

*Why didn't you invite **me**?*

The dative form is used for the indirect object.

Kannst du **mir** deinen iPod leihen?

*Can you lend **me** your iPod?*
*(Can you lend your iPod **to me**?)*

Kannst du **mir** eine Tasse Kaffee machen?

*Can you make **me** a cup of coffee?*
*(Can you make a cup of coffee **for me**?)*

das **Lakritz** = *licorice*

nominative	accusative	dative
ich	mich	**mir**
du	dich	**dir**
er	ihn	**ihm**
es	es	**ihm**
sie	sie	**ihr**
wir	uns	**uns**
ihr	euch	**euch**
sie	sie	**ihnen**
Sie	Sie	**Ihnen**

7-17 Geschenke. Die Information für **S2** ist im *Anhang* auf Seite A9.

S1: Weißt du, was Sophia ihren Eltern schenkt?
S2: Weißt du, was Daniel seinen Eltern schenkt?

S2: Ich glaube, sie schenkt ihnen einen neuen Toaster.
S1: Ich glaube, …

	SOPHIA	DANIEL
ihren/seinen Eltern		ihnen einen ganz teuren Heimtrainer
ihrer/seiner Schwester	ihr ein Paar goldene Ohrringe	
ihrem/seinem Bruder		ihm seinen alten Computer

7-18 Was soll ich diesen Leuten schenken?

▶ mein__ Mutter

S1: Was soll ich meiner Mutter schenken?

S2: Schenk ihr doch ein Paar warme Hausschuhe.

1. mein__ Vater

2. mein__ Großeltern

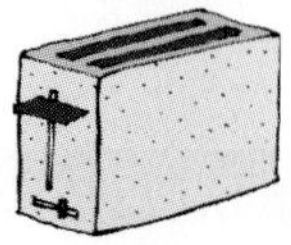

3. mein__ besten Freundin

4. mein__ kleinen Bruder

| einen Hockeyschläger | ein Paar Ohrringe |
| einen schönen Pullover | einen neuen Toaster |

5. mein__ besten Freund

6. mein__ alten Klavierlehrer

7. unser__ neuen Nachbarn (pl)

8. unser__ Briefträgerin

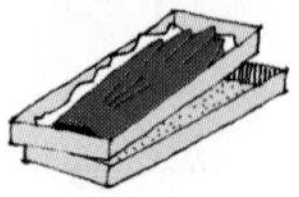

| ein paar Flaschen Wein | eine Flasche Kognak |
| ein Paar Handschuhe | einen schönen Kugelschreiber |

7-19 Vorschläge. Sagen Sie einander, was Ihre Freunde und Verwandten gern tun, und machen Sie einander dann Vorschläge° für passende° Geschenke.

suggestions / appropriate

S1: Meine Freundin spielt gern Tennis.

S2: Dann schenk ihr doch einen Tennisschläger.

Mein Freund (Mein Bruder, Meine Schwester, Meine Kusine, Mein Vetter …)

hört gern Rapmusik
sammelt Stofftiere°
spielt gern Computerspiele
liest gern Comics

trägt gern Schmuck°
reist gern
liebt Süßigkeiten°
…

jewelry
stuffed animals
sweets

Word order: sequence of objects

The dative object (the indirect object) precedes the accusative object (the direct object) *unless the accusative object is a pronoun.*

	DATIVE	ACCUSATIVE	
Maria schenkt	**ihrem Vater**	**ein Buch**	zum Vatertag.
Sie schenkt	**ihm**	**ein Kochbuch.**	
	ACCUSATIVE	DATIVE	
Sie kann	**es**	**ihrem Vater**	nicht persönlich geben.
Sie muss	**es**	**ihm**	schicken.

The examples above also show that regardless of case, pronoun objects precede noun objects.

Sprachnotiz

Ein Paar and *ein paar*

Ein Paar means *a pair*, i.e., *two* of something.

Robert schenkt seinem Vater **ein Paar** Socken.

Robert is giving his father a pair of socks.

Ein paar means *a couple of* in the sense of *a few.*

Robert muss noch **ein paar** Geschenke kaufen.

Robert still has to buy a couple of presents.

Lerntipp: Remember: The dative object comes first unless the accusative object is a pronoun.

supply

sequence

7-20 Kleine Gespräche. Ergänzen° Sie die Akkusativobjekte und Dativobjekte in der richtigen Reihenfolge°.

1. KIND: Kaufst du _____ _____, Vati?

   VATER: Ja, ich kaufe _____ _____.

   das Fahrrad, mir
   dir, es

2. MUTTER: Kaufen wir _____ _____?

   VATER: Ja, ich glaube, wir kaufen _____ _____.

   unserem Sohn, die Kamera
   ihm, sie

shown

3. FLORIAN: Hast du _____ _____ gezeigt°?

   ROBERT: Nein, ich zeige _____ immer nur _____.

   deine Zensuren, deinem Vater
   meiner Mutter, sie

lend

4. BERND: Kannst du _____ _____ leihen°, Eva?

   EVA: Wenn du _____ _____ morgen früh zurückgibst.

   dein Chemiebuch, mir
   es, mir

5. PETER: Hat Bernd _____ _____ zurückgegeben?

   MARTIN: Nein, er schuldet _____ _____ immer noch.

   die hundert Euro, dir
   mir, sie

6. ERGÜN: Hast du _____ _____ geschenkt?

   ANNE: Nein, ich habe _____ _____ geschenkt.

   den Toaster, deinen Eltern
   meinen Großeltern, ihn

noch einmal: *again*

7. TOM: Kannst du _____ _____ bitte noch einmal° erklären?

   VANJA: Nein, jetzt habe ich _____ _____ oft genug erklärt.

   den Dativ, mir
   dir, ihn

8. LENA: Wann gibst du _____ _____?

   STEFAN: Ich glaube, ich gebe _____ _____ an Silvester.

   deiner Freundin, den Ring
   ihr, ihn

Dative verbs

There are a few German verbs that take only a dative object.

antworten	Warum antwortest du **mir** nicht?	*Why don't you answer **me?***
danken	Ich danke **dir** für deine Hilfe.	*I thank **you** for your help.*
folgen	Folg **mir** doch. Ich kenne den Weg.	*Follow **me**. I know the way.*
gehören	Gehört dieser Wagen **dir**?	*Does this car belong **to you?***
gratulieren	Ich gratuliere **Ihnen** zu Ihrem Erfolg!	*I congratulate **you** on your success!*
helfen	Kannst du **mir** bitte helfen?	*Can you help **me** please?*

Note that **gratulieren** is also used to wish someone a Happy Birthday: **Ich möchte dir zum Geburtstag gratulieren.**

7-21 Kleine Gespräche. Ergänzen Sie passende Dativverben.

1. ALEXANDER: Wem _____ denn dieser tolle Wagen?
   SEBASTIAN: Meiner Freundin.

2. MARIA: Warum schreibst du denn deinem Bruder nie?
   NICOLE: Weil er mir ja doch nicht _____.

3. STEFAN: Warum kommst du nicht zu unserer Party?
   ROBERT: Weil ich meinem Vater _____ muss.

4. HELGA: Warum rufst du Claudia an?
   SABINE: Sie hat heute Geburtstag und ich möchte ihr _____.

5. FRAU BERG: Aber Frau Kuhn! Warum bringen Sie mir denn Blumen?
   FRAU KUHN: Weil ich Ihnen für Ihre Hilfe _____ möchte.

6. TOURIST: Wie komme ich zum Stadion?
   POLIZIST: _____ Sie doch einfach° den Fans.   *simply*

7-22 Kleine Gespräche. Ergänzen Sie **mir, mich, dir** oder **dich.**

1. LUKAS: Warum antwortest du _____ nicht?
   HORST: Du hast _____ doch gar nichts gefragt.

2. BEATE: Heute früh hat Markus _____ besucht. Er hat _____ zum Geburtstag gratuliert und hat _____ diese wunderschönen roten Rosen gebracht. Glaubst du, dass er _____ liebt?
   SOPHIA: Wenn er _____ rote Rosen bringt, liebt er _____ bestimmt.

3. PAUL: Gehört dieses tolle Fahrrad _____?
   LISA: Ja, meine Eltern haben es _____ gekauft.

4. STEFAN: Ich danke _____, dass du _____ bei° meinem Referat so viel geholfen hast.   *with*
   MARIA: Wenn du _____ jetzt zum Essen einlädst, helfe ich _____ das nächste Mal° gern wieder.   *time*

The dative case with adjectives

The dative case is often used with adjectives to express a personal opinion, taste, or conviction.

Das ist **mir** sehr wichtig.   *That's very important **to me.***
Rockmusik ist **meiner Oma** zu laut.   *Rock music is too loud **for my grandma.***

7-23 Warum? Ergänzen Sie passende Personalpronomen im Dativ.

▶ Sie ist _____ zu laut.

S1: Warum mögen deine Großeltern keine Rockmusik?   S2: Sie ist ihnen zu laut.

1. Warum liest du den Roman nicht fertig?   Er ist _____ zu langweilig.
2. Warum kaufen Müllers das Haus nicht?   Es ist _____ zu klein.
3. Warum trinkt Ingrid ihren Wein nicht?   Er ist _____ zu sauer.
4. Warum geht Robert nicht schwimmen?   Es ist _____ zu kalt.
5. Warum mag Maria diesen Film nicht?   Er ist _____ zu sentimental.
6. Warum nehmt ihr die Wohnung nicht?   Sie ist _____ zu dunkel.
7. Warum kauft Peter den Wagen nicht?   Er ist _____ zu teuer.

7-24 Die Geschmäcker sind verschieden. Schauen Sie Ihre Mitstudenten an und sagen Sie, was für ein Kleidungsstück Sie ihnen zum Geburtstag schenken wollen, und warum.

S1: Lisa schenke ich ein Sweatshirt. Ihr Sweatshirt ist mir ein bisschen zu verrückt.

S2: David schenke ich …

ein bisschen zu verrückt	ein bisschen zu trendy
ein bisschen zu konservativ	ein bisschen zu altmodisch
nicht sportlich genug	nicht hip genug

The dative case in idiomatic expressions

The dative case also appears in the following common expressions:

Wie geht es **Ihnen**?	*How are you?*
(Es) tut **mir** leid.	*I'm sorry.*
Das ist **mir** egal.	*I don't care.*
Mir fällt nichts ein.	*I can't think of anything.*
Wie gefällt **dir** mein Mantel?	*How do you like my coat?*
Diese Jacke steht **dir**.	*This jacket looks good on you.*

7-25 Was passt zusammen?

1. Wie gefällt dir meine neue Jacke?
2. Kennst du die Frau dort?
3. Ist Lisa immer noch so krank?
4. Warum schreibst du den Brief denn nicht fertig?
5. Mir geht es heute gar nicht gut.
6. Weiß Florian, dass du einen neuen Freund hast?
7. Die Jacke steht dir. Warum nimmst du sie denn nicht?

a. Ja, aber ihr Name fällt mir nicht ein.
b. Ja, aber ich glaube, es ist ihm egal.
c. Weil sie mir zu teuer ist.
d. Sie steht dir sehr gut.
e. Nein, es geht ihr schon wieder viel besser.
f. Weil mir nichts mehr einfällt.
g. Das tut mir aber leid.

7-26 Was gefällt Ihnen an Ihren Mitstudenten?

about **S1:** An° Lisa gefällt mir, dass sie so freundlich ist.

S2: An David gefällt mir, dass …

You will find additional vocabulary to describe personal characteristics and personality traits under **Persönliche Merkmale** in the *Anhang* on p. A21.

witty	freundlich	lustig	pünktlich	witzig°
natural	natürlich°	optimistisch	ordentlich	sportlich
polite	höflich°	spontan	praktisch	…

▬ Sprachnotiz ··

The flavoring particle *aber*

In colloquial German, **aber** is often used to add emphasis to a statement.

Das tut mir **aber** leid!	*I'm **so** sorry.*
Jetzt habe ich **aber** Hunger!	*I'm **really** hungry now.*

Hören

Blumen zum Geburtstag

Stephanie hat morgen Geburtstag. Peter möchte ihr Blumen schenken und ist deshalb im Blumengeschäft.

NEUE VOKABELN

Sie wünschen?   *May I help you?*
drei Euro das Stück   *three euros apiece*
ein·schlagen   *to wrap*

7-27 Erstes Verstehen. Hören Sie, was Peter und die Verkäuferin miteinander sprechen. Haken Sie die richtigen Antworten ab.

1. Welche Farben hören Sie?

_____ gelb   _____ rosarot
_____ blau   _____ rot
_____ weiß   _____ violett

2. Welche Zahlen hören Sie?

_____ 2   _____ 3
_____ 15   _____ 5
_____ 4   _____ 10
_____ 20   _____ 30

3. Welche Imperativformen hören Sie?

_____ Kommen Sie!   _____ Geben Sie …!
_____ Zeigen Sie …!   _____ Schicken Sie …!
_____ Schenken Sie …!   _____ Warten Sie!

7-28 Detailverstehen. Hören Sie Peters Gespräch mit der Verkäuferin noch einmal und schreiben Sie Antworten zu den folgenden Fragen.

1. Warum möchte Peter seiner Freundin Blumen schenken?
2. Warum sagt die Verkäuferin, Peter soll seiner Freundin Rosen schenken?
3. Was für Rosen will Peter seiner Freundin schenken?
4. Was kosten die roten Rosen?
5. Warum schenkt Peter seiner Freundin nicht zehn oder fünfzehn Rosen?
6. Wie viele rote Rosen kauft er?
7. Warum soll die Verkäuferin Peters Freundin die Rosen nicht schicken?
8. Warum soll Peter noch einen Moment warten?

You can further vary the skit by changing the roles to a **Verkäufer** and a **Studentin.** The names for some flowers in German are **Nelken** *(carnations),* **Osterglocken** *(daffodils),* **Rosen, Tulpen, Lilien, Gladiolen.** And remember that flowers come in different colors.

Take some time to prepare your skit before you present it to the class. Some of the phrases and sentences listed here may help you in creating your skit. Don't forget to use the **Sie**-form throughout.

Die sehen ..., die gefallen mir: In colloquial German definite articles are often used as pronouns. Here **die** could translate as *they* or *those.*

7-29 Im Blumengeschäft. Ein Student möchte seiner Freundin zum Geburtstag Blumen schenken. Die Verkäuferin versucht, ihm zu helfen.

VARIATIONEN

seiner Freundin zum Valentinstag
seiner Mutter zum Muttertag
seiner Kusine zum Abitur

seinen Freunden zur neuen Wohnung
seinen Freunden zum neuen Baby
…

VERKÄUFERIN

- Guten Tag! Sie wünschen? / Guten Tag! Darf ich Ihnen helfen?

- Dann schenken Sie ihr doch …

- Ja, heute haben wir … / Nein, heute haben wir leider keine … Wir haben aber …
- Wir haben auch …

- Sie kosten … Euro das Stück.
- Die … sind preisgünstiger und auch sehr schön.
- Darf ich sie Ihrer Freundin schicken?

- Ja, natürlich.

STUDENT

- Guten Tag! Ich möchte meiner Freundin zum Geburtstag Blumen schenken.
- Was für … haben Sie? / Haben Sie vielleicht …?
- Die sehen aber nicht sehr frisch aus.

- Oh, die gefallen mir! Was kosten sie denn?
- Das ist mir zu teuer.
- Gut, dann geben Sie mir mal …

- Ja, bitte. / Nein, ich gebe sie ihr lieber selbst.
- Können Sie die … bitte noch schön einschlagen?
- Danke schön. / Vielen Dank.

Shop for a **Mitbringsel** at www.prenhall.com/treffpunkt
→ Kapitel 7 → Web Resources → Kultur

In the German-speaking countries it is common for families to go for a walk on a Sunday afternoon and to follow this up with **Kaffee und Kuchen,** either at home or in a **Café** along the way.

INFOBOX

Mitbringsel

If you are invited for a meal (**zum Essen**) or **zu Kaffee und Kuchen** in a German-speaking country, it is customary to bring a small gift (**ein Mitbringsel**) for your hostess or host. The most common gifts are chocolates, a bottle of wine, or flowers. A small bouquet should contain an odd number of flowers because this is considered more pleasing to the eye.

In the German-speaking countries, the person celebrating a birthday is expected to organize and host the party (**die Fete, die Party**). The invited guests of course bring gifts.

Baby showers are unknown; in fact, it is considered unlucky to give an expectant mother a gift before the baby is born.

Kaffee und Kuchen

7-30 Aus der Zeitung. Schauen Sie die Glückwunschanzeigen° an und beantworten Sie die folgenden Fragen.

1. Wie nennt Jörg seine Freundin? Was wünscht er ihr vor allem?
2. Wann wird die Mutter von Maja und Waltraut achtzig? Wann feiert die Familie ihren Geburtstag?
3. Warum bekommen Erich und Toni Glückwünsche?
4. Wer hat auch nicht Geburtstag und bekommt trotzdem Glückwünsche? Warum?

Hallo, Häschen!
Die besten Glückwünsche zu Deinem Geburtstag und alles Liebe, Gute, vor allem Gesundheit und viel, viel Glück wünscht Dir von ganzem Herzen
Jörg

Lieber Marco!
Herzliche Glückwünsche zum bestandenen **Abitur** wünschen Dir Papa, Mama, Ralf, Jürgen, Heike, Florian und Elena

Liebe Leute, es ist wahr, unsere Mutter wird heute **80 Jahr** Wir wünschen Dir zu diesem Feste, Gesundheit, Glück und nur das Beste. Und bleib uns noch lange erhalten, Du zählst für uns nicht zu den Alten. Am Sonntag trifft sich die ganze Schar, um zu feiern mit dem Jubilar. Es grüßen Dich ganz herzlich
Maja + Waltraut

Morgen, genau vor 40 Jahren ist es gewesen, da haben sich der **Erich und die Toni** das Ja-Wort gegeben. Wir wünschen Euch weiterhin alles Gute und macht weiter so!
Eure 7 Zwerge mit Familien

7-31 Für die Zeitung. Schreiben Sie eine kleine Glückwunschanzeige für jemand aus Ihrer Familie oder für eine Freundin/einen Freund. Nehmen Sie als Modell die Anzeigen in **7-30**.

▇ Sprachnotiz ·······························

Adjectives after *alles, etwas,* and *nichts*

Adjectives following **alles, etwas,** and **nichts** are capitalized and take the endings shown here.

Alles Gute zum Geburtstag!	*Happy Birthday!*
Ich muss dir **etwas Wichtiges** sagen.	*I have to tell you something important.*
Weißt du denn gar **nichts Neues**?	*Don't you know anything new at all?*

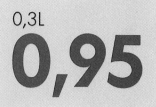

GETRÄNK ZU JEDEM SNACK

0,3L

0,95

❷ Expressing origin, destination, time, manner, and place

The dative prepositions

In *Kapitel 5* you learned the prepositions that are followed by an object in the accusative case: **durch, für, gegen, ohne, um.** The prepositions that are always followed by an object in the *dative case* are **aus, außer, bei, mit, nach, seit, von, zu.**

refrigerator	**aus**	*out of* *from*	Nimm den Weißwein **aus dem Kühlschrank°**! Der Wein ist **aus dem Rheintal.**
	außer	*except for*	**Außer meinem Bruder** sind alle hier.
railway	**bei**	*for*	Mein Bruder arbeitet **bei der Bahn°** und konnte nicht kommen.
		at, at the *home of*	Diesmal feiern wir Muttis Geburtstag **bei** **meiner Schwester** in Potsdam.
		near	Potsdam ist **bei Berlin.**
candles	**mit**	*with*	Der Kuchen **mit den 50 Kerzen°** ist von Tante Anna.
		by	Ich bin **mit dem Zug** nach Potsdam gekommen.
	nach	*after*	**Nach dem Geburtstagsessen** haben wir einen Spaziergang gemacht.
		to	Ich fahre morgen **nach Bonn** zurück.
	seit	*since*	Ich lebe **seit dem letzten Sommer** in Bonn.
		for	Meine Schwester lebt **seit zehn Jahren** in Potsdam.
	von	*from*	**Von meiner Schwester** hat Mutti ein schönes Bild bekommen.
		of	Eine Freundin **von Mutti** hat ihr ein goldenes Armband geschickt.
		about	Mutti hat uns oft **von dieser Freundin** erzählt.
	zu	*to*	Wir kommen alle sehr gern **zu meiner Schwester.**
		for	**Zu ihrem 50. Geburtstag** hat Mutti von uns allen eine Reise nach Hawaii bekommen.
		with	**Zu dem leckeren Geburtstagskuchen** haben wir Muttis Lieblingstee getrunken.

7-32 Was weißt du von diesen Leuten? Sie stellen Fragen° über Sabine und Osman, und Ihre Partnerin/Ihr Partner möchte Information über Wendy und Jan. Die Information für **S2** ist im *Anhang* auf Seite A10.

stellen Fragen: *ask questions*

S1: Woher ist Sabine?
Wo arbeitet sie?

S2: Aus der Schweiz.
…

	SABINE	WENDY	OSMAN	JAN
Woher ist _____?		Aus den USA.		Aus den Niederlanden.
Wo arbeitet sie/er?		Bei einer Computerfirma.		Bei einem Gärtner.
Seit wann arbeitet sie/er dort?		Seit drei Jahren.		Seit einem Dreivierteljahr.
Wie kommt sie/er zur Arbeit?		Mit ihrem neuen BMW.		Mit der S-Bahn.
Wohin geht sie/er im nächsten Urlaub?		Zu ihren Eltern nach New York.		Zu seiner Freundin nach Amsterdam.
Woher weißt du das alles?		Von ihrem Freund.		Von seinem Chef.

7-33 Erzähl mir etwas von deinen Eltern! Stellen Sie einander die ersten fünf Fragen aus **7-32.**

S1: Woher ist deine Mutter/dein Vater?

Wo arbeitet sie/er?

…

S2: Aus …

Bei …

Albrecht Hoch
seit 1893
Importeur von Pflanzen aus der ganzen Welt
Wir beraten Sie gern
Der Blumenzwiebelspezialist

◼ Sprachnotiz

Word order: time/manner/place

You have already learned that expressions of time precede expressions of place.

Claudia und Stephanie fahren **morgen nach Hamburg.**

When an expression of manner is added (i.e., when you want to say how something is done) the order is *time / **manner** / place.*

Claudia und Stephanie fahren **morgen** *mit dem Zug* **nach Hamburg.**

7-34 Ein Brief aus Hamburg. Ergänzen Sie **aus, außer, bei, mit** oder **nach**.

Hamburg, den 24. Dezember 2007

Liebe Eltern und lieber Opa,
herzliche Grüße _____ der Hansestadt Hamburg. Claudias Eltern
wollten, dass ich an Weihnachten _____ Hamburg komme, damit
ich mal sehe, wie man _____ ihnen Weihnachten feiert.
Die ganze Familie ist hier _____ Claudias Schwester Maria.
Sie studiert in Berkeley und verbringt Weihnachten _____ Freunden
in San Francisco. Heute Abend gibt es _____ Bergers wie _____ den
meisten deutschen Familien nur ein ganz einfaches° Essen, und
_____ dem Essen ist dann gleich die Bescherung. Ich schenke
Claudias Eltern einen Kalender _____ vielen schönen Farbfotos von
Amerika. Ich habe euch _____ München ein Paket _____ ein paar
Geschenken geschickt. Für Opa sind übrigens auch ein paar
Münchener Zeitungen im Paket.

Euch allen einen guten Rutsch ins neue Jahr!

Stephanie

°simple

7-35 Meine Winterferien. Stellen Sie einander die folgenden Fragen.

S1: Bei wem verbringst du die
Winterferien?
S1: Was machst du da?
S2: Bei wem …
S2: …

S2: Bei …
S2: Ich …
S3: Bei …

Contractions

The following contractions of dative prepositions and definite articles are commonly used.

bei + dem	=	**beim**	Brigitte ist heute Vormittag **beim** Zahnarzt.
von + dem	=	**vom**	Dieses Brot ist **vom** Öko-Bäcker.
zu + dem	=	**zum**	Fährt dieser Bus **zum** Bahnhof?
zu + der	=	**zur**	Seit wann fährst du denn mit dem Fahrrad **zur** Uni?

Bioland - Brot
ökologisch gut
vom Bioland® - Bäcker

7-36 Wo? Woher? Wohin? Ergänzen° Sie die Antworten mit **beim, vom,** *complete*
zum oder **zur.**

▶ Wohin gehst du?

S1: Wohin gehst du?   **S2:** Zur Bäckerei.

1. Wo ist Brigitte?

5. Wohin rennst du?

2. Woher kommst du?

6. Woher kommt ihr?

3. Wohin fährst du?

7. Wohin gehst du?

4. Wo ist Silke?

8. Wo sind Bernd und Sabine?

| Zahnarzt (m) | Supermarkt (m) | Arzt (m) | Friseur (m) |
| Fleischerei (f) | Bus (m) | Baden (n) | Mittagessen (n) |

Da-compounds

In German, personal pronouns that are objects of prepositions can refer only to people.

Was weißt du **von Lisas neuem Freund?**
Ich weiß sehr wenig **von ihm.**

*What do you know **about Lisa's new boyfriend?***
*I know very little **about him.***

For things or ideas, **da**-compounds must be used. In *Kapitel 5* you were introduced to **da**-compounds with the accusative prepositions **für** and **gegen**: **dafür** *(for it)* and **dagegen** *(against it)*. The **da**-compounds with dative prepositions are **daraus, dabei, damit, danach, davon,** and **dazu.** Note that an **r** is added to **da** if the preposition begins with a vowel: **da**r**aus.**

Was weißt du **von deutschen Festen und Feiertagen?**	*What do you know **about German celebrations and holidays?***
Jetzt weiß ich sehr viel **davon.**	*Now I know a lot **about them.***

object of preposition refers to person	→	preposition + pronoun
object of preposition refers to thing or idea	→	**da**-compound

7-37 *Präposition + Pronomen oder da-Form?* Ergänzen Sie!

S1:

dabei / bei ihr
1. Warst du bei Sabines Geburtstagsfeier?
2. Warst du heute schon bei Sabine?

daraus / aus ihm
   rhubarb 3. Was soll ich aus dem Rhabarber° machen?
   pass 4. Hat Bernd das Abitur bestanden°?

damit / mit ihr
5. Gehst du oft mit Anna in die Mensa?
6. Hat Anna ein neues Fahrrad?

davon / von ihm
7. Hat Maria schon wieder einen neuen Freund?
8. Maria hatte gestern Geburtstag.

dazu / zu dir
9. Wann besuchst du mich mal wieder?
10. Unser Festessen ist gleich fertig.

danach / nach ihm
11. Was habt ihr nach dem Abendessen gemacht?
   approximately 12. Bist du vor oder nach Bernd nach Hause gekommen?

S2:

Nein, dieses Jahr war ich nicht
_____.
Nein, heute war ich noch nicht
_____.

Mach doch einen guten
Nachtisch _____.
Ja, vielleicht wird jetzt doch
noch etwas _____.

Ja, ich esse fast jeden Tag dort
_____ zu Mittag.
Ja, sie fährt jetzt jeden Tag
_____ zur Uni.

Ja, und sie hat mir schon viel
_____ erzählt.
Warum hast du mir denn nichts
_____ gesagt?

Wenn du nichts dagegen hast,
komme ich gleich jetzt _____.
Gut, und was für einen Wein
trinken wir _____?

Wir sind gleich _____
heimgegangen.
Ich bin etwa° eine halbe Stunde
_____ heimgekommen.

Nach versus zu

When **nach** and **zu** indicate a point of destination, they both mean *to*. Which one you use depends on the type of destination.

nach		zu	
to a city	nach Leipzig	to a building	zum Bahnhof
to a state	nach Sachsen	to an institution	zur Uni
to a country	nach Luxemburg	to a place of business	zum Supermarkt
to a continent	nach Europa	to someone's residence	zu Zieglers

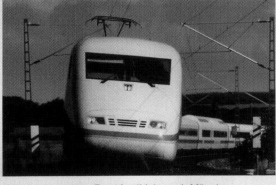

Von Hamburg über Frankfurt/Main nach München und zurück. Der ICE mit Technik von AEG. Schnell, sicher und komfortabel.

7-38 Kleine Gespräche. Ergänzen Sie **nach, zu, zum** oder **zur.**

1. HERR BERG: Wie weit ist es von hier _____ Ihrem Ferienhaus bei Salzburg?
    FRAU KOCH: Von hier _____ Salzburg sind es etwa 500 Kilometer und von dort _____ Ferienhaus fährt man eine halbe Stunde.

2. FRAU ROTH: Was soll ich denn tun, Frau Klein? Ich habe solche Zahnschmerzen und unser Zahnarzt ist über Weihnachten _____ Spanien geflogen.
    FRAU KLEIN: Gehen Sie doch _____ unserem Zahnarzt.

3. FRAU WOLF: Warum fliegt Herr Meyer denn _____ Detroit?
    FRAU KUNZ: Ich glaube, er geht dort _____ Internationalen Auto Show (f).

4. CLAUDIA: Fährst du in den Semesterferien wieder _____ Köln _____ deinem Onkel?
    STEPHANIE: Nein, diesmal fahre ich mit Peter _____ Berlin.

Aus versus von

When **aus** and **von** indicate a point of origin, they both mean *from*.

aus		von	
from a city	aus Leipzig	from a building	vom Bahnhof
from a state	aus Sachsen	from an institution	von der Uni
from a country	aus Luxemburg	from a person	von meinem Freund
from a continent	aus Europa	from a point of departure	von Berlin nach Potsdam

7-39 Kleine Gespräche. Ergänzen Sie **aus** oder **von**.

1. SEBASTIAN: Weißt du vielleicht, wie lang der Bus _____ New York nach San Francisco braucht?

   PETER: Frag doch Stephanie. Sie ist _____ den USA und weiß es bestimmt.

2. CLAUDIA: Hier ist ein Brief _____ Chicago, Stephanie.

   STEPHANIE: _____ meinen Eltern?

   CLAUDIA: Nein, ich glaube, er ist _____ deiner Uni.

3. ANNETTE: _____ wem hast du diese Armbanduhr?

   CHRISTINE: _____ meinem Freund. Er hat sie mir _____ der Schweiz mitgebracht.

7-40 Von wem hast du das? Schauen Sie, welche von Ihren Mitstudenten etwas besonders Schönes tragen, und fragen Sie, von wem sie es haben.

S1: Von wem hast du den interessanten Ring, Lisa?

S2: Von wem hast du …?

S2: Von … / Ich habe ihn selbst gekauft.

S3: …

das schöne Armband
die sportliche Armbanduhr
…

die tollen Ohrringe
die coole Lederjacke

7-41 Eine Platzreservierung. Herr und Frau Baumeister haben für eine Reise mit dem ICE zwei Sitzplätze reserviert. Beantworten Sie mit Ihrer Partnerin/Ihrem Partner die Fragen zu dieser Reservierung.

1. Wohin reisen Baumeisters?
2. Von welchem Bahnhof fahren sie ab?
3. Wann fährt der ICE von Berlin ab und wann kommt er in Stuttgart an? (Datum und Uhrzeit)
4. Welche Zugnummer hat der ICE?
5. In welchem Wagen sind die reservierten Plätze? Finden Sie die Wagennummer!
6. Welche beiden Sitzplätze sind für Baumeisters reserviert?
7. Wie viel haben Baumeisters für diese Reservierung bezahlt?
8. Wann haben Baumeisters diese Reservierung beim Reisebüro Südstern gekauft? (Datum und Uhrzeit)
9. Was dürfen Baumeisters in diesem Wagen nicht tun?

```
DB          Reservierung
CIV 80
            InterCityExpress                    2 Sitzplätze

 🚋  🕐  VON              NACH                🚋    🕐   KI/CI

29.03 11:39 BERLIN ZOO      ->STUTTGRT HBF    29.03  17:08  2

ZUG 797   ICE   Wagen   4   Sitzplätze   51      53

Großraumwagen                        1 Fenster, 1 Mitte
Nichtraucher

                                              PREIS   EUR ****5,20

754585860
 75458586-75          800990116216
                      DB 99 BERLIN 536813 004
                      RB SUEDSTERN 04.03.07    14:42   RECHNUNG
```

The preposition *seit*

When **seit** refers to a *point in time*, its English equivalent is *since;* when it refers to *a period of time*, its English equivalent is *for*. Note that German uses the present tense in such contexts, whereas English uses the perfect tense.

Herr Braun lebt **seit** Anfang
  Januar in Kiel.
Lisa wohnt **seit** einem Jahr
  bei ihrer Freundin.

Mr. Braun has been living in Kiel
  since *the beginning of January.*
Lisa has been living with her friend
  for *a year.*

7-42 Seit wann?

▶ haben / du dieses tolle
  Fahrrad   mein__ Geburtstag (m)

S1: Seit wann hast du dieses tolle   **S2:** Seit meinem Geburtstag.
  Fahrrad?

1. sein / Sandra und Holger so gute   d__ Silvesterparty (f) bei Sylvia
   Freunde
2. trinken / Stephanie so gern   ihr__ Jahr (n) in München
   deutsches Bier
3. haben / du einen Scanner   vierzehn Tage__ (pl)
4. spielen / du Saxofon   meine__ Schulzeit (f)
5. sein / Karin und Kurt verheiratet   eine__ Woche (f)

7-43 Seit wann hast du oder machst du das? Stellen Sie einander die
folgenden Fragen und berichten° Sie dann, was Sie herausgefunden haben.   *report*

Hast du einen Job? Wo? Seit wann?
Hast du einen Hund/eine Katze? Seit wann? Wie heißt er/sie?
Hast du ein Handy? Was für ein Handy? Seit wann hast du es?
Hast du einen Wagen? Was für einen? Seit wann?
Spielst du ein Instrument? Was für ein Instrument? Seit wann?
Bist du verlobt°/verheiratet? Seit wann?   *engaged*

7-44 Immer negativ. Ergänzen Sie in den Fragen aus, außer, bei, mit, nach,
seit, von oder zu. Ergänzen Sie in den Antworten auch die Dativendungen.

S1:   **S2:**

1. Fährt dieser Zug _____ Bremen?   Nein, er fährt _____ Hamburg.
2. Ist Stephanie _____ Kanada?   Nein, sie ist _____ d__ USA.
3. _____ wem hast du diese schönen   Nein, _____ mein__ Eltern.
   Ohrringe? _____ deinem Freund?
4. Wo verbringst du diesmal die   Nein, _____ mein__ Großeltern.
   Feiertage? _____ deinen Eltern?
5. _____ wem gehst du heute Abend   Nein, _____ ein paar Freunde__.
   ins Kino? _____ deinem Bruder?
6. _____ wann hast du dieses schöne   Nein, schon _____ ein__ Jahr.
   Fahrrad? _____ deinem Geburtstag?
7. _____ welchem Zahnarzt gehst   Nein, ich gehe _____ Dr. Meyer.
   du? _____ Dr. Haag?
8. Sind _____ David alle hier?   Nein, alle _____ David und Florian!

Die kleine Kneipe
mit den großen Bieren
DAMPFROSS

❸ Describing people, places, and things

Dative endings of preceded adjectives

Adjectives that are preceded by a **der**-word or an **ein**-word in the dative case always take the ending **-en**.

Wer ist der Typ mit dem golden**en**
Ohrring und den lang**en** Haaren?

*Who's the guy with the gold
earring and the long hair?*

	masculine	neuter	feminine	plural
DATIVE	dem einem jung**en** Mann	dem einem klein**en** Kind	der einer jung**en** Frau	den keinen klein**en** Kindern

7-45 Wer ist auf diesem Familienbild? Ergänzen Sie die passenden Farben.

▶ die Frau mit dem _____ Kleid
und den _____ Haaren

Das ist …

S1: Wer ist die Frau mit dem
grünen Kleid und den
braunen Haaren?

S2: Das ist meine Mutter.

1. der Mann mit der _____ Jacke und der _____ Krawatte
2. der Junge mit den _____ Haaren und dem _____ Hemd
3. die Frau mit der _____ Hose und der _____ Bluse
4. der Mann mit der _____ Brille und dem _____ Pullover
5. das Mädchen mit dem _____ Kleid und den _____ Schuhen
6. die Frau mit dem _____ Hut und dem _____ Kleid

similar
guess

7-46 Wer ist das? Folgen Sie dem Beispiel. Stellen Sie ähnliche° Fragen über Ihre Mitstudenten. Die anderen raten°, wer das ist.

S: Wer ist die Person mit der coolen Brille und der blauen Bluse?

Dative endings of unpreceded adjectives

You will remember that adjectives not preceded by a **der**-word or an **ein**-word show the gender, number, and case of the noun by taking the appropriate **der**-word ending. This also holds true for the dative case.

Zu französisch**em** Camembert trinkt Onkel Alfred immer kanadischen Eiswein.

With French camembert Uncle Alfred always drinks Canadian ice wine.

Hornbrooker Hof
Freilandeier aus Schleswig-Holstein

	masculine	neuter	feminine	plural
NOMINATIVE	gut**er** Kaffee	gut**es** Bier	gut**e** Salami	gut**e** Äpfel
ACCUSATIVE	gut**en** Kaffee	gut**es** Bier	gut**e** Salami	gut**e** Äpfel
DATIVE	gut**em** Kaffee	gut**em** Bier	gut**er** Salami	gut**en** Äpfeln

7-47 Ein Gourmet. Onkel Alfred isst gern international.

1. Zu französisch__ Weißbrot (n) isst er nur holländisch__ Käse (m).
2. Zu italienisch__ Lasagne (f) trinkt er nur griechisch__ Wein (m).
3. Zu polnisch__ Wurst (f) isst er nur französisch__ Senf° (m).   *mustard*
4. Zu englisch__ Cheddar (m) isst er nur neuseeländisch__ Äpfel (pl).
5. Zu deutsch__ Schwarzbrot (n) isst er nur irisch__ Butter (f).
6. Zu italienisch__ Eis (n) trinkt er nur türkisch__ Kaffee (m).
7. Zu belgisch__ Schokolade (f) isst er nur israelisch__ Mandarinen (pl).
8. Zu amerikanisch__ Kartoffelchips (pl) trinkt er nur deutsch__ Bier (n).

Zusammenschau

Video-Treff ·············

Mein bestes Geschenk

Stefan Kuhlmann, Stefan Meister, Ursula und André erzählen von ihrem besten Geschenk.

Zum besseren Verstehen

7-48 Was ist das auf Englisch?

1. Das ist das Cover der Comic-**Ausgabe** von *Der kleine Hobbit.*
2. Das beste Geschenk ist ein **selbstgemachtes** T-Shirt.
3. Ich habe dieses Geschenk von meiner **damaligen** Freundin bekommen.
4. Termiten haben diesen Baum **ausgehöhlt.**
5. Ich habe dann selber **daran** gearbeitet.
6. Ich habe Inlineskates. Meine Freundin hat auch **welche.**
7. Sie sagte, dass ihre Familie diese Instrumente selber **herstellt.**
8. Madame Sec hat von **sich** erzählt.

a. herself
b. some
c. on it
d. former
e. hollowed out
f. produces
g. edition
h. homemade

Schauen Sie jetzt das Video an und machen Sie die Übungen im *Video-Treff*-Teil des *Student Activities Manual.*

Im Kaufhaus ist der Kunde König

Claudia hat im Winterschlussverkauf bei Karstadt einen Pullover gekauft. Am nächsten Tag ist sie schon wieder bei Karstadt und spricht dort mit der Verkäuferin. Hören Sie, warum Claudia zu Karstadt zurückgegangen ist.

NEUE VOKABELN

der Kunde	*customer*	**der Ärmel**	*sleeve*
zum ersten Mal	*for the first time*	**das Loch**	*hole*
an·ziehen,	*to put on*	**flicken**	*to mend*
angezogen			

7-49 Erstes Verstehen. In welcher Reihenfolge hören Sie das?

_____ Zwanzig Euro. Das ist nicht schlecht!
_____ Aber sagen Sie, können Sie flicken?
_____ So einen schönen Pullover für nur vierzig Euro!
_____ Welche Größe war das doch wieder?
_____ Das tut mir aber leid.
_____ Nur zehn Euro? Na, hören Sie mal!

7-50 Detailverstehen. Hören Sie Claudias Gespräch mit der Verkäuferin noch einmal und schreiben Sie Antworten zu den folgenden Fragen.

1. Wann hat Claudia den Pullover gekauft und wann hat sie ihn zum ersten Mal angezogen?
2. Warum ist Claudia zu Karstadt zurückgegangen?
3. Was für eine Größe braucht Claudia?
4. In welchen Farben gibt es diesen Pullover noch?
5. Wie viel hat Claudia gestern für den Pullover bezahlt?
6. Was muss sie tun, damit sie den Pullover billiger bekommt?
7. Wie viel billiger bekommt Claudia den Pullover?

Sprachnotiz

Expressing congratulations, best wishes, or toasts with *zu*

When congratulating someone or wishing someone the best for a special occasion, you can use **zu** or its contractions **zum** or **zur** to mention the occasion.

Wir wünschen dir alles Liebe **zur Erstkommunion.**
Zu deiner Bar-Mizwa wünsche ich dir alles Gute.
Alles Gute **zum neuen Lebensjahr!**
Alles Gute **zum Uni-Abschluss°!**   *graduation*
Ich gratuliere dir **zum neuen Job!**
Die besten Glückwünsche **zur goldenen Hochzeit°!**   *wedding anniversary*

To express *Cheers!* or *To your health!* when raising or clinking glasses, you can say **Zum Wohl!**

Another popular toast is **Prost!** or **Prosit!**

■ Schreiben und Sprechen ·············

7-51 Bei Peek & Cloppenburg. Eine Studentin hat zum Geburtstag ein ziemlich altmodisches Kleidungsstück bekommen. Es gefällt ihr natürlich gar nicht und sie geht deshalb damit und mit dem Kassenzettel° zu Peek & Cloppenburg und möchte es umtauschen°.

sales slip
exchange

VERKÄUFERIN

- Guten Tag! Sie wünschen? / Darf ich Ihnen helfen?

- Was ist denn das Problem?

- Haben Sie den Kassenzettel?

- Danke. Welche Größe haben Sie denn?

- *(sucht)* Größe … und in … Na, wie gefällt Ihnen dies__ … hier?

- Und dies__?

- Ja, natürlich. … steht Ihnen sehr gut.

- … ist ziemlich teuer. … kostet …

STUDENTIN

- Guten Tag! Ich möchte … umtauschen.

- … ist mir zu altmodisch / … gefällt mir nicht.

- Ja, natürlich. Hier, bitte.

- Größe … Meine Lieblingsfarbe ist übrigens …

- … ist mir immer noch zu konservativ.

- … ist mir nicht hip genug. / … ist mir ein bisschen zu verrückt. / … ist echt cool. / … gefällt mir echt gut. Darf ich … anprobieren?

- Das finde ich auch. Wie viel kostet … denn?

- Das ist mir egal. Ich nehme … trotzdem. / So viel Geld habe ich nicht. Tut mir leid.

You can vary the skit by choosing different articles of clothing and by changing the roles to a **Verkäufer** and a **Student.** Take some time to prepare your skit before you present it to the class. Some of the phrases and sentences listed here may help you in creating your skit. Don't forget to use the **Sie**-form throughout. You can use the following conversion charts for clothing sizes.

Damengrößen:

US/CA	DE/AT/CH
6	34
8	36
10	38
12	40
14	42

Herrengrößen:

US/CA	DE/AT/CH
34	44
36	46
38	48
40	50
42	52

See p. 216 to review how to write dates in a letter.

Schreibtipp: Remember that the salutation ends with a comma and that the letter proper begins in lower case. There is no punctuation after the closing (e.g., **Herzliche Grüße**).

at the moment

eine Freude machen: *to make happy*

7-52 Mein bestes Geschenk. Von wem haben Sie Ihr bestes Geschenk bekommen? Schreiben Sie einen Dankesbrief an diese Person oder Personen. Die folgenden Ausdrücke können Ihnen dabei helfen.

(Ihre Stadt), den …

Liebe / Lieber …,

ZUM GESCHENK

- vielen herzlichen Dank für …
- er/es/sie ist genau mein Geschmack
- du hast mir mit diesem Geschenk eine große Freude gemacht° …
- er/es/sie gefällt mir so gut, weil …
- er ist ein gutes Geschenk für mich, weil …

- Herzliche Grüße
- Mit lieben Grüßen

PERSÖNLICHES

- mir geht es gut
- mir geht es zurzeit° nicht so gut, weil …
- hoffentlich geht es dir gut
- ich denke oft an dich

📖 ■ **Lesen** ···

Zum besseren Verstehen

7-53 Spekulieren Sie! Schauen Sie die beiden Fotos an und lesen Sie den Titel. Beantworten Sie dann die folgenden Fragen.

1. Aus welchem Jahr ist das Foto von Margarete Steiff, 1567, 1898 oder 1950?
2. Frau Steiff sitzt in einem Rollstuhl, weil sie als Kind sehr krank war. Was für eine Krankheit hat sie wohl° gehabt?

probably

3. Was könnten Frau Steiff und der Teddybär miteinander zu tun haben?

7-54 Was ist das auf Englisch?

1. Kinder mögen Teddybären, weil sie so **kuschelig** sind.
2. Teddybären sind **Stofftiere.**
3. Wenn Kinder Teddybären bekommen, sind sie **glücklich.**
4. Margarete hatte **Kinderlähmung** und sitzt jetzt im Rollstuhl.
5. Als Margarete stirbt, **hinterlässt** sie eine Weltfirma.
6. **Schneiderinnen** machen Kleider.
7. Mit einer Pistole **schießt** man.
8. **Jäger** schießen auf Tiere.

a. happy
b. seamstresses
c. polio
d. hunters
e. cuddly
f. shoots
g. leaves behind
h. stuffed animals

LEUTE **Margarete Steiff und der Teddybär**

Im Jahr 2003 ist der Teddybär hundert Jahre alt geworden. Sein Geburtsort ist die kleine süddeutsche Stadt Giengen und seine Vorfahren sind Tausende von Stofftieren aus der Spielwarenfabrik[1] von Margarete Steiff.

Margarete Steiff ist 1847 geboren, hat mit achtzehn Monaten Kinderlähmung und muss ihr ganzes Leben im Rollstuhl verbringen. Sie lernt Schneiderin, und weil sie ihre kleinen Nichten und Neffen sehr mag, macht sie ihnen oft hübsche, kleine Stofftiere. Die kuscheligen Tierchen gefallen auch anderen Kindern, und Margarete beginnt, ihre Stofftiere zu verkaufen. Nach ein paar Jahren baut sie eine kleine Spielwarenfabrik und ihre Stoffbären erobern[2] als „Teddybären" bald die ganze Welt. Allein[3] im Jahr 1907 kommen aus Margarete Steiffs neuer und viel größerer Spielwarenfabrik 975 000 Bären, und die Frau im Rollstuhl ist jetzt Chefin von über 2000 Arbeiterinnen und Arbeitern.

Aber woher haben die kleinen deutschen Bären den Namen „Teddybär"? – Der amerikanische Präsident Theodore Roosevelt war ein passionierter, aber humaner Jäger, und im November 1902 zeigt eine Karikatur von Clifford Berryman in der *Washington Post,* wie Roosevelt es ablehnt[4], auf einen hilflosen Bären zu schießen. Die Karikatur gefällt den Lesern so gut, dass Berryman von jetzt ab alle seine Karikaturen von „Teddy" Roosevelt mit einem kleinen Bären signiert. Und als dann die ersten Importe von Margarete Steiffs Stoffbären in amerikanischen Spielwarengeschäften zu sehen sind, nennen die Leute sie sofort *„Teddy's bears".* Ein Teddybär-Fieber erfasst[5] die USA und sogar der Präsident selbst schenkt seinen Gästen manchmal deutsche Teddybären.

Als Margarete Steiff 1909 im Alter von 62 Jahren stirbt, hinterlässt sie eine Weltfirma mit Arbeitsplätzen für Tausende von Menschen, und ihre Teddys haben Millionen von Kindern glücklich gemacht. Aber vielleicht das Wichtigste: sie hat der Welt gezeigt, was eine Frau im Rollstuhl alles leisten[6] kann.

[1]*toy factory*   [2]*conquer*   [3]*alone*   [4]*refuses*   [5]*grips*   [6]*achieve*

WWW Create your own **Teddybär** at
www.prenhall.com/treffpunkt
→ Kapitel 7 → Web Resources
→ Kultur

Arbeit mit dem Text

7-55 Die Frau im Rollstuhl. Was passt zusammen?

1. Margarete Steiff ist als Kind so krank,
2. Weil sie ihre Nichten und Neffen so gern hat,
3. Bald möchten viele Eltern ihren Kindern die kuscheligen Tierchen schenken,
4. Sie verkauft bald so viele Stofftiere,
5. Nach ein paar Jahren muss sie eine viel größere Fabrik bauen,
6. Obwohl Margarete Steiff ihr ganzes Leben im Rollstuhl verbringen musste,

a. dass sie eine kleine Fabrik bauen muss.
b. und Margarete beginnt, ihre Stofftiere auch zu verkaufen.
c. hat sie Millionen Kinder glücklich gemacht.
d. dass sie ihr ganzes Leben lang nicht mehr gehen kann.
e. macht sie ihnen oft kleine Stofftiere.
f. weil jetzt Kinder aus aller Welt ihre Stofftiere haben möchten.

7-56 Warum man Stoffbären „Teddybären" nennt. Finden Sie die richtigen Verben.

verkaufen / schenken / zeigt / assoziieren / nennt / gefällt

1. Clifford Berrymans Karikatur in der *Washington Post* _____, dass der amerikanische Präsident Theodore Roosevelt nicht auf hilflose Bären schießt.
2. Berrymans Karikatur _____ den *Washington Post*-Lesern so gut, dass Berryman alle seine Roosevelt-Karikaturen mit einem kleinen Bären signiert.
3. Bald _____ amerikanische Spielwarengeschäfte die ersten Stoffbären von Margarete Steiff.
4. Die Amerikaner _____ die deutschen Stoffbären mit den kleinen Bären von Clifford Berrymans Karikaturen und nennen sie „*Teddy's bears*".
5. Tausende von amerikanischen Eltern _____ ihren Kindern Teddybären von Margarete Steiff.
6. Heute _____ man alle Stoffbären Teddybären.

7-57 Meine Stofftiere. Stellen Sie einander die folgenden Fragen und berichten Sie, was Sie herausgefunden haben.

Hattest du als Kind Stofftiere? Was für Tiere waren das? Was war dein Lieblingsstofftier und wie hat es geheißen?

Wort, Sinn und Klang

Wörter unter der Lupe

Predicting gender

Infinitive forms of verbs are often used as nouns. Such nouns are always *neuter* and they are capitalized, of course. Their English equivalents usually end in *-ing*.

Wann gibst du endlich **das Rauchen** auf?

*When are you finally going to give up **smoking**?*

When the contraction **beim** is followed by such a noun, it often means *while*.

Opa ist **beim Fernsehen** eingeschlafen.

*Grandpa fell asleep **while watching TV**.*

7-58 Was passt?

Schwimmen / Wissen / Leben / Einkaufen / Trinken / Schreiben

1. _____ ist sehr gesund.
2. Gestern haben wir beim _____ fast zweihundert Euro ausgegeben.
3. Fang doch endlich mit deinem Referat an! Vielleicht fällt dir beim _____ etwas ein.
4. Das viele _____ hat diesen Mann krank gemacht.
5. Helga ist gestern Abend ohne Günters _____ mit Holger ausgegangen.

lazy 6. Dieses faule° _____ gefällt mir.

Giving language color

In *Kapitel 6* you saw how the names of body parts can be used metaphorically. As the expressions below show, the names of common food items can also be

Ich mag meine Brille außer beim Skifahren Joggen Tanzen Tauchen Biken

used in this way. The expressions with an asterisk are quite informal and should only be used with family or friends.

Es ist alles in Butter.*	*Everything's going smoothly.*
Das ist mir wurst.*	*I couldn't care less.*
Er will immer eine Extrawurst.*	*He always wants special treatment.*
Das ist doch alles Käse.*	*That's all bunk!*
Der Apfel fällt nicht weit vom Stamm.	*Like father, like son.*
Er gleicht seinem Bruder wie ein Ei dem anderen.	*He and his brother are as alike as two peas in a pod.*

7-59 Was passt zusammen?

1. Wie sieht Claudias Schwester aus?
2. Hast du immer noch Probleme mit deinem Freund?
3. Deine neue Jacke gefällt mir gar nicht.
4. Günter sagt, dass du ihn liebst.
5. Alle anderen kommen zu Fuß, aber Lisa sollen wir mit dem Auto abholen.
6. Ralf ist wie sein Vater. Er fängt alles an und macht nichts fertig.

a. Das ist doch alles Käse, was er sagt.
b. Das ist mir wurst.
c. Sie will doch immer eine Extrawurst.
d. Der Apfel fällt nicht weit vom Stamm.
e. Sie gleicht ihr wie ein Ei dem anderen.
f. Nein, jetzt ist alles wieder in Butter.

Zur Aussprache

German r

Good pronunciation of the German **r** will go a long way toward making you sound like a native speaker. Don't let the tip of the tongue curl upward and backward as it does when pronouncing an English *r*, but keep it down behind the lower teeth. When followed by a vowel, the German **r** is much like the sound of **ch** in **auch.** When it is not followed by a vowel, the German **r** takes on a vowel-like quality.

7-60 Hören Sie gut zu und wiederholen Sie!

1. **R**ita und **R**ichard sitzen immer im Zimme**r**.
   Rita und **R**ichard sehen gern fern.

2. **R**obert und **R**osi spielen Karten im Garten.
   Robert und **R**osi trinken Bier für vie**r**.

3. Gestern war **R**alf hier und dort,
   morgen fährt er wieder fort.

4. Horst ist hie**r**,
   Horst will Wurst,
   Horst will Bier
   für seinen Durst.

Nomen

das Fieber	fever
die Hilfe	help
die Krankheit, -en	illness
der Rollstuhl, ⸚e	wheelchair
der Zahnarzt, ⸚e	} dentist
die Zahnärztin, -nen	
die Zahnschmerzen (pl)	toothache

die Krankheit: All words with the suffix **-heit** are feminine.

die Fete, -n	party
der Gast, ⸚e	guest
das Mitbringsel, -	small gift (for a host)
die Süßigkeiten (pl)	sweets; candy

der Handschuh, -e	glove
der Hausschuh, -e	slipper
der Hut, ⸚e	hat
die Krawatte, -n	tie
der Schmuck	jewelry

Krawatte: What is the English cognate of this word?

die Anzeige, -n	announcement; ad
der Briefträger, -	} letter carrier
die Briefträgerin, -nen	
die Fabrik, -en	factory
das Ferienhaus, ⸚er	vacation home
die Gießkanne, -n	watering can
der Hockeyschläger, -	hockey stick
die Kerze, -n	candle
der Kugelschreiber, -	ballpoint pen
das Loch, ⸚er	hole
das Paket, -e	package, parcel
die Sache, -n	thing
der Tennisschläger, -	tennis racquet
das Tier, -e	animal
das Stofftier, -e	stuffed animal
der Typ, -en	guy

Kugelschreiber: This word is often shortened to **Kuli.**

Verben

danken (+ dat)	to thank
gehören (+ dat)	to belong to
gratulieren (+ dat)	to congratulate
helfen (hilft), geholfen (+ dat)	to help
an·ziehen, angezogen	to put on
berichten	to report
flicken	to mend
leihen, geliehen	to lend
um·tauschen	to exchange
wünschen	to wish
zeigen	to show

Andere Wörter

einfach	simple; simply
kuschelig	cuddly
witzig	witty; funny
allein	alone
einmal	once
noch einmal, noch mal	once more; (over) again
etwa	approximately
sogar	even
wohl	probably; perhaps
zurzeit	at the moment

Ausdrücke

eine Frage stellen	to ask a question
zum Geburtstag gratulieren	to wish a Happy Birthday
Zum Wohl!	} Cheers! To your health!
Prost!	
Das ist mir egal.	I don't care.
Diese Jacke gefällt mir.	I like this jacket.
Diese Jacke steht dir.	This jacket looks good on you.
Du hast mir eine Freude gemacht.	You've made me happy.
Es tut mir leid.	I'm sorry.
Mir fällt nichts ein.	I can't think of anything.
Sie wünschen?	May I help you?

This expression is used to say that something a person has done for you or given you has made you happy.

Das Gegenteil

faul ≠ fleißig	lazy ≠ hard-working
glücklich ≠ unglücklich	happy ≠ unhappy
höflich ≠ unhöflich	polite ≠ impolite
zum ersten Mal ≠ zum letzten Mal	for the first time ≠ for the last time

Leicht zu verstehen

die Bäckerei, -en
die Kartoffelchips
der Muttertag, -e
der Valentinstag, -e
der Vatertag, -e
das Parfüm, -s
die Party, -s
der Ring, -e
die Rose, -n
der Supermarkt, ⸚e
der Teekessel, -
der Titel, -
schockiert

Bäckerei & Konditorei
Backmännchen

Wörter im Kontext

7-61 Was schenkst du diesen Leuten? Antworten Sie mit „Ich schenke ihr/ihm …"

1. Maria hat immer kalte Hände.
2. Stefan hat viele Zimmerpflanzen.
3. Melanie hat viele Brieffreunde.
4. Paul trägt immer nur Anzüge.
5. Laura hat nur sehr wenig Schmuck.
6. Kurt macht viel Sport.
7. Meine Nichte Anna wird morgen ein Jahr alt.
8. Meine Oma hat immer kalte Füße.

a. eine schicke Krawatte
b. ein Paar warme Hausschuhe
c. ein goldenes Armband
d. ein kuscheliges Stofftier
e. einen guten Kugelschreiber
f. ein Paar warme Handschuhe
g. eine hübsche, kleine Gießkanne
h. einen Tennisschläger und einen Hockeyschläger

Hockeyschläger, Tennisschläger: These are agent nouns derived from the verb **schlagen** *to hit.*

7-62 Was ich für Leah alles tue.

1. Wenn Leah Geburtstag hat,
2. Wenn Leah zu viel zu tun hat,
3. Wenn Leah etwas für mich getan hat,
4. Wenn Leah Zahnschmerzen hat,
5. Wenn Leahs Pullover ein Loch hat,
6. Wenn ich bei Leah eingeladen bin,
7. Wenn Leah bankrott ist,
8. Wenn Leah wieder einmal das Falsche gekauft hat,

a. schicke ich sie zum Zahnarzt.
b. leihe ich ihr sogar Geld.
c. tausche ich es für sie um.
d. helfe ich ihr.
e. danke ich ihr.
f. flicke ich ihn für sie.
g. kaufe ich als Mitbringsel immer Blumen.
h. gratuliere ich ihr.

7-63 Mit anderen Worten. Welche Sätze° bedeuten etwa dasselbe°?   *sentences / the same*

1. Diese Jacke gefällt mir.
2. Diese Jacke steht mir.
3. Sie wünschen?
4. Diese Jacke gehört mir nicht.
5. Sind Sie immer so faul?
6. Tun Sie das zum ersten Mal?
7. Ich habe das ganz allein gemacht.
8. Ich habe zurzeit wenig Geld.

a. Ich bin im Moment ziemlich arm.
b. Das ist nicht meine Jacke.
c. Ich finde diese Jacke schön.
d. Haben Sie das noch nie gemacht?
e. Niemand hat mir dabei geholfen.
f. Was kann ich für Sie tun?
g. In dieser Jacke sehe ich gut aus.
h. Tun Sie immer so wenig?

■ Sprachnotiz ·····················

Derselbe, dasselbe, dieselbe

The English equivalent of **derselbe, dasselbe,** and **dieselbe** is *the same.* Note that both parts of this German compound word take case endings.

Ich wohne in **derselben** Straße wie Peter.

*I live on **the same** street as Peter.*

Sag doch nicht immer **dasselbe**!

*Don't always say **the same** thing!*

Hat Ann immer noch **denselben** Freund?

*Does Ann still have **the same** boyfriend?*

KAPITEL
8
Wohnen

Ein Reihenhaus in Norddeutschland

Die möblierte Wohnung

Frau Wild fliegt für ein Jahr zu ihrem Sohn nach Texas. Martin und Peter haben ihre Wohnung gemietet und sind gerade eingezogen. Claudia kommt zu Besuch, um zu sehen, wie die beiden Freunde jetzt wohnen.

MARTIN: Nun, Claudia, wie gefällt dir die Wohnung? Vollständig möbliert für nur 450 Euro im Monat!

CLAUDIA: Nicht schlecht, nur – die Möbel stehen alle am falschen Platz.

MARTIN: Tut mir leid, aber wir haben versprochen, sie nicht umzustellen.

CLAUDIA: Ist Frau Wild nicht schon weggeflogen?

PETER: Ja, ich glaube, gestern Nachmittag um halb drei.

CLAUDIA: Na, dann können wir ja anfangen. Ihr dürft nur nicht vergessen, wie alles gestanden hat.

PETER: Kein Problem, ich vergesse sowieso nie etwas.

CLAUDIA: Dann nimm doch mal die Stehlampe neben dem Sessel, Peter, und stell sie dahinter. Und du Martin, du nimmst den Teppich hier und legst ihn vor die Couch! Und die hässliche alte Uhr dort auf dem Schreibtisch, die trägst du in die Küche, Peter, und stellst sie auf den Kühlschrank. – So, das sieht schon viel besser aus.

MARTIN: Komm, jetzt gehen wir mal auf unseren Balkon raus, Claudia.

CLAUDIA: *(auf dem Balkon)* Das sind ja tolle Geranien!

PETER: Ja, wir müssen sie auch jeden zweiten Tag gießen.

MARTIN: Du Peter, wer ist denn die Frau dort unten? Sie sieht fast wie Frau Wild aus.

PETER: Das kann doch nicht wahr sein! Das *ist* Frau Wild und sie kommt zu uns! Stellt schnell die Uhr wieder auf den Schreibtisch und die Stehlampe neben den Sessel! Und ich lege den Teppich wieder ...

Das sind ja tolle Geranien!

8-1 Richtig oder falsch? Sie hören das Gespräch auf Seite 267 und nach diesem Gespräch ein paar Aussagen. Sind diese Aussagen **richtig** oder **falsch?**

	RICHTIG	FALSCH		RICHTIG	FALSCH
1.	_____	_____	4.	_____	_____
2.	_____	_____	5.	_____	_____
3.	_____	_____	6.	_____	_____

INFOBOX

Student housing

Finding a place to live in a **Universitätsstadt** in the German-speaking countries is always a challenge. Very few universities are situated on a campus. University buildings are scattered all over town, and the few **Studentenwohnheime** that do exist do not come close to meeting students' housing needs. Occasionally students have to withdraw from their studies because they cannot find a place to live.

Wohngemeinschaften or **WGs** are a popular and economical type of living accommodation: students rent an apartment jointly and share responsibility for meals and household chores. Others rent a room in a **Privathaus,** with or without **Küchenbenutzung** (kitchen privileges).

Look at the excerpt from the Web site of the **Studentenhaus Salzburg.** How do the room prices compare to your university dorms? How do the amenities compare?

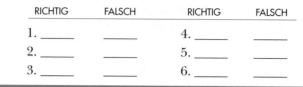

Ein Studentenwohnheim in Berlin

In the German-speaking countries, the term **Wohngemeinschaft** normally refers to an apartment rather than a whole house. If **Gemeinschaft** means *community*, what is the literal meaning of **Wohngemeinschaft?**

[www] Check out a **Studentenwohnheim** in Germany at www.prenhall.com/treffpunkt
→ Kapitel 8 → Web Resources → Kultur

Studentenhaus Salzburg
Tel.: 0662 / 716391 - 40
E-mail: hausmeister@shsb.at

Zimmerangebot:	Einzelzimmer und Doppelzimmer, pro Person monatlich € 160,– bis € 255,–
Lage:	Zentrumsnähe, 15 Gehminuten zum Bahnhof, sehr gute Einkaufsmöglichkeiten.
Ausstattung:	Alle Zimmer mit WC, Dusche, Telefon, u. Internet-Anschlüssen. Auch Zimmer mit Balkon.
Sonstiges:	TV-Räume mit Satelliten-TV, Studierraum, Musikzimmer, Clubraum, Sauna, Tischtennis, Tischfußball, großer Garten, Fahrradabstellplatz, Garagen. Abends Studentenkneipe.

Wo und wie wohnen diese Studenten? Die Information für **S2** ist im *Anhang* auf Seite A10.

S1: Wo wohnt Magda?
Wie gefällt es ihr dort?

S2: Sie wohnt im Studentenheim.
…

	MAGDA	CINDY	PIETRO	KEVIN
Wo wohnt _____?		Sie wohnt in einer WG.		Er hat ein Zimmer in einem Privathaus.
Wie gefällt es ihr/ihm dort?		Es gefällt ihr sehr gut.		Nicht so besonders.
Warum gefällt es ihr/ihm dort (nicht)?		Weil dort alle so nett sind.		Weil er keine Küchenbenutzung hat.
Wie kommt sie/er zur Uni?		Mit dem Bus.		Zu Fuß oder mit dem Fahrrad.

8-3 Wo und wie wohnst du? Stellen Sie einander die folgenden Fragen und berichten Sie, was Sie herausgefunden haben.

S1:

S2:

Wo wohnst du?

Ich wohne
☐ im Studentenheim.
☐ noch zu Hause.
☐ mit ein paar anderen Studenten zusammen in einem Haus/einer WG.

Ich habe
☐ ein Zimmer in einem Privathaus.
☐ (mit einer Freundin/einem Freund zusammen) eine kleine Wohnung.

Gefällt es dir dort?

Ja, weil
☐ meine Mitbewohner sehr nett sind.
☐ es dort sehr ruhig° ist.
☐ das Zimmer (die Wohnung) groß und hell ist.
☐ ich dort kochen kann.
☐ …

Nein, weil
☐ meine Mitbewohner so unordentlich sind.
☐ es mir dort zu laut ist.
☐ ich keine Freunde einladen darf.
☐ ich keine Küchenbenutzung habe.
☐ …

Wie kommst du zur Uni?

Ich
☐ gehe zu Fuß.
☐ fahre mit
  ☐ dem Fahrrad.
  ☐ dem Wagen.
  ☐ dem Bus.
  ☐ …

Zimmer: You have learned that a German **z** is often a *t* in the related English word: **zehn** – *ten,* **Zunge** – *tongue.* German **Zimmer** is related to English *timber.* In this context, what do *quiet* you think a **Zimmermann** is?

KULTUR

Owning a home in the German-speaking countries

Together, the German-speaking countries almost fit into the state of California, but their total population (close to 100 million) is more than three times that of this most populous state in the United States. Owning a home with a yard is the dream of many families, but all too often it remains just that. The density of the population coupled with strict laws for the preservation of green space put real estate at a premium. Because houses are much more solidly constructed than in North America, construction costs are very high. The combination of these factors makes owning a house (**ein Einfamilienhaus**) or a condominium apartment (**eine Eigentumswohnung**) impossible

for about 70 percent of the population. There is a saying in Swabian (a Southern German dialect) that aptly expresses the hardship involved in acquiring a home: **Schaffe, spare, Häusle baue – verrecke!** *(Work, save, build your house – croak!)*.

For many apartment dwellers in Germany, Austria, and Switzerland, the longing for some private green space is fulfilled by buying or leasing a **Schrebergarten,** a small plot of land at the edge of town where they can grow a few flowers or vegetables, or just relax on the weekends. The concept of **Schrebergärten** dates back to the nineteenth century. **Daniel Schreber,** a doctor and professor from **Leipzig,** was concerned that the children of factory workers living in the polluted cities weren't getting enough fresh air and sunshine. On the outskirts of Leipzig he created playgrounds for these children with adjoining garden plots for their parents. Today there are **Schrebergärten,** each with a little **Gartenhäuschen,** on the outskirts of almost every town. By law these little cottages can be no larger than 24m^2 (258 sq. ft.) and can be connected to water and electric mains, but not to gas or sewage. They cannot be used as permanent residences, and staying overnight is only permitted in the summer or on weekends. Long considered uncool and tacky, **Schrebergärten** are again becoming popular among young families.

In dieser alten Villa wohnen jetzt sechs Parteien.

Schaffe, spare, Häusle baue …: In the Swabian dialect (**Schwäbisch**), the **-n** at the end of infinitive forms is routinely dropped. **Häusle** is Swabian for the diminutive form **Häuslein.**

Schrebergärten in Dresden

8-4 Ein Neubau-Einfamilienhaus. Schauen Sie die Reklametafel° für ein *billboard*
neues Einfamilienhaus genau an und beantworten Sie die folgenden Fragen.

1. Welche Wörter auf dieser Reklametafel sind gleich° oder fast gleich wie *the same*
   ihre englischen Äquivalente?
2. Welches Wort sagt uns, dass das Wohn-/Esszimmer ziemlich groß ist?
3. Welches Wort sagt uns, dass die Gartenterrasse auf der Südseite vom
   Haus ist?
4. Wo ist die Garage und was ist zwischen der Garage und dem Wohnhaus?
5. Welcher Architekt hat das Haus geplant und entworfen°? *designed*
6. Welche Firma hat das Haus gebaut?
7. Welche Nummer rufen Sie an, wenn Sie dieses Haus vielleicht kaufen
   wollen?
8. Welche zwei Personen können Ihre Fragen am besten beantworten?

WWW Look for a house
in Germany at
www.prenhall.com/treffpunkt
→ Kapitel 8 → Web Resources
→ Kultur

»Einhundertsechsundfünfzig Quadratmeter Eleganz!«

Freistehendes Neubau-
Einfamilienhaus

Mit 7 1/2 Zimmern,
moderne, fortschrittliche Architektur,
variable Grundrissgestaltung.

Geräumiger Wohn-/Essbereich, sonnige
Gartenterrasse, 2 Bäder, Dachgeschoß
als Atelier oder Kaminzimmer.

Garage und Carport neben dem Wohnhaus.

Bauträger:	Planung/Entwurf:	Projektbetreuung:	Verkauf:	Ihre persönlichen Berater:
Fa. Leibbrand Wohnbau Amselweg 4 7060 Schorndorf Tel. 07181/22306	Freier Architekt C. Stammler Kaspar Kurrer Weg 8/1 7060 Schorndorf Tel. 07181/21096	Planungsgruppe S Gmünder Str. 95 7060 Schorndorf Tel. 07181/61033	RIKO° Immobilien · Schlichtener Str. 17 7060 Schorndorf Tel. 07181/21045	Thomas Haupt Burkhardt Widlicky

Nomen

der Flur, -e	hall
die Garderobe, -n	front hall closet
die Möbel (*pl*)	furniture
die Treppe, -n	staircase
die Tür, -en	door

Möbel is always plural. A single piece of furniture is **das Möbelstück.**

das Bad, ̈er	bath; bathroom
das Badezimmer, -	bathroom
die Badewanne, -n	bathtub
die Dusche, -n	shower
das Klo, -s	toilet
die Toilette, -n	lavatory
das Waschbecken, -	(bathroom) sink

Klo is short for **Wasserklosett (WC).**

die Küche, -n	kitchen
die Geschirrspül-maschine, -n	dishwasher
der Herd, -e	stove
der Kühlschrank, ̈e	refrigerator
die Mikrowelle, -n	microwave
das Spülbecken, -	sink
der Stuhl, ̈e	chair
der Tisch, -e	table

Herd: Replace the **d** of **Herd** with *th* to find out the English cognate.

das Schlafzimmer, -	bedroom
das Bett, -en	bed
die Kommode, -n	dresser
der Nachttisch, -e	night table
der Schrank, ̈e	wardrobe
der Teppich, -e	carpet, rug

das Esszimmer, -	dining room
das Wohnzimmer, -	living room
das Bücherregal, -e	bookcase
der Couchtisch, -e	coffee table
der Fernseher, -	television set
der Papierkorb, ̈e	wastepaper basket
der Schreibtisch, -e	desk
der Sessel, -	armchair
die Stehlampe, -n	floor lamp
die Stereoanlage, -n	stereo

die Decke, -n	ceiling
der Fußboden, ̈	floor
das Fenster, -	window
die Wand, ̈e	wall

Fußboden: Figure out the English cognate of **-boden** by completing the following translations: **bodenlos** = ____ *less;* **Meeresboden** = ____ *of the ocean.*

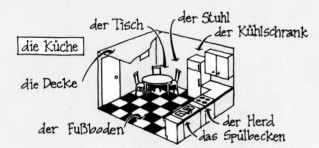

die Küche

der Tisch · der Stuhl · der Kühlschrank
die Decke · der Fußboden · der Herd · das Spülbecken

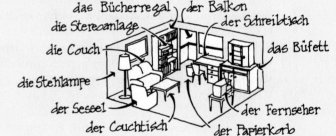

das Wohnzimmer

das Bücherregal · der Balkon · die Stereoanlage · der Schreibtisch · die Couch · das Büfett · die Stehlampe · der Sessel · der Couchtisch · der Fernseher · der Papierkorb

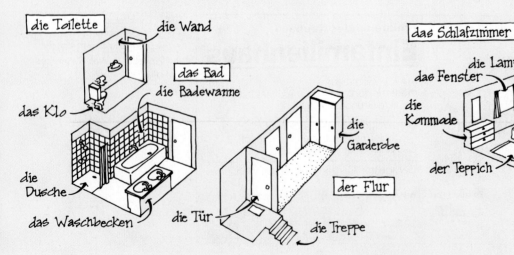

die Toilette · die Wand · das Bad · die Badewanne · das Klo · die Garderobe · die Dusche · das Waschbecken · die Tür · der Flur · die Treppe

das Schlafzimmer

die Lampe · das Bett · das Fenster · das Bild · die Kommode · der Schrank · der Teppich · die Zimmerpflanze

Verben

aus·ziehen, ist **ausgezogen**	to move out
ein·ziehen, ist **eingezogen**	to move in
um·ziehen, ist **umgezogen**	to move (*change residence*)
bauen	to build
legen	to lay (*down*)
stellen	to put (*in an upright position*)
um·stellen	to rearrange

WIR SIND UMGEZOGEN

Neu : Hegauer Weg 35 · 14163 Berlin

Andere Wörter

gleich	same; the same; right, directly
möbliert	furnished
sowieso	anyway

Ausdrücke

zu Besuch kommen	to visit

Das Gegenteil

hässlich ≠ schön	ugly ≠ beautiful
ruhig ≠ laut	quiet ≠ loud

Leicht zu verstehen

der Balkon, -e	**die Lampe, -n**
das Büfett, -s	**die Terrasse, -n**
die Couch, -es	**planen**
die Garage, -n	**Couch** is pronounced as in English.

Wörter im Kontext

8-5 Wie heißen diese Räume?

1. Hier duscht und badet man.
2. Hier kocht und bäckt man.
3. Hier sitzt man am Abend und sieht fern.
4. Hier schläft man.
5. Von hier geht man in alle Zimmer.
6. Hier isst man, wenn man Besuch hat.

> **Räume (rooms, spaces):** This word is used here because **Flur** and **Küche** are not considered **Zimmer**.

> **Badezimmer, Toilette:** In many homes in the German-speaking countries the tub, shower, and sink are in one room (**das Badezimmer**) and the toilet (with a very small sink) is in another (**die Toilette**).

8-6 Was passt in jeder Gruppe zusammen?

1. die Küche	a. die Garderobe	9. der Fußboden	i. das Bild
2. die Toilette	b. die Kommode	10. die Wand	j. der Teppich
3. der Flur	c. der Herd	11. die Badewanne	k. Jacken und Mäntel
4. das Schlafzimmer	d. das Klo	12. die Garderobe	l. das Wasser
5. der Stuhl	e. gießen	13. die Stereoanlage	m. schnell
6. das Bett	f. kochen	14. die Lampe	n. kalt
7. der Herd	g. liegen	15. der Kühlschrank	o. laut
8. die Zimmerpflanze	h. sitzen	16. die Mikrowelle	p. hell

8-7 Was passt wo?

Spülbecken / möblierte / eingezogen / umgezogen / ausgezogen / ruhig / Nachttisch / hässlich / Dusche / Geschirrspülmaschine

1. Ich finde diesen Teppich ziemlich _____.
2. Eine Wohnung mit Möbeln ist eine _____ Wohnung.
3. Wenn man eine _____ hat, muss man den Abwasch nicht am _____ machen.
4. Neben meinem Bett steht ein _____.
5. Unsere neuen Nachbarn sind sehr nett und sehr _____.
6. Nach dem Joggen gehe ich gleich unter die _____.
7. Martin und Peter sind _____. Sie sind aus ihrem Zimmer in der Zennerstraße _____ und in die Wohnung von Frau Wild _____.

❶ Talking about destination and location

Wohin and wo: a review

In *Kapitel 1* you learned that the English question word *where* has three equivalents in German: **wohin** (*to what place*), **wo** (*in what place*), and **woher** (*from what place*). Since **wohin** and **wo** will play an important role in subsequent sections of this chapter, you will have to fine-tune your feeling for the difference between them.

The use of **wohin** or **wo** is obvious in the following questions.

Wohin gehst du?	***Where*** *are you going?* (***to*** *what place?*)
Wohin geht diese Straße?	***Where*** *does this street go?* (***to*** *what place?*)
Wo ist mein Mantel?	***Where*** *is my coat?* (***in*** *what place?*)

For speakers of English it is less obvious whether to use **wohin** or **wo** in the following example.

Where should I hang my coat?	(*to* what place? or *in* what place?)

Here a speaker of German thinks in terms of moving the coat from point A to point B. The German equivalent for *where* is therefore **wohin.**

Wohin soll ich meinen Mantel hängen?	***Where*** (***to*** *what place*) *should I hang my coat?*

Wohin geht es nach rechts, nach links und geradeaus?

8-8 *Wohin* oder *wo*?

1. _____ gehst du?
2. _____ wohnst du?
3. _____ sind denn meine Handschuhe?
4. _____ habe ich denn meine Handschuhe gelegt?
5. _____ soll ich die E-Mail schicken?
6. _____ hast du dieses schöne Sweatshirt gekauft?
7. _____ arbeitet Tina?
8. _____ geht diese Tür?
9. _____ soll ich meine Jacke hängen?
10. _____ fährt dieser Bus?

Two-case prepositions

You have already learned that there are prepositions followed by the accusative and prepositions followed by the dative.

accusative prepositions		dative prepositions	
durch	ohne	aus	nach
für	um	außer	seit
gegen		bei	von
		mit	zu

A third group of prepositions may be followed by either the accusative case or the dative case: When one of these two-case prepositions is used with a verb signaling *movement toward a destination*, the preposition answers the question **wohin?** and is followed by the accusative case. When a two-case preposition is used with a verb signaling a *fixed location*, the preposition answers the question **wo?** and is followed by the dative case.

		wohin?	wo?
		TOWARD A DESTINATION PREPOSITION + ACCUSATIVE	FIXED LOCATION PREPOSITION + DATIVE
an	on *(a vertical surface)*	Lisa hängt das Bild **an die** Wand.	Das Bild hängt **an der** Wand.
	to	Kurt geht **an die** Tür.	
	at		Kurt steht **an der** Tür.
auf	on *(a horizontal surface)*	Lisa legt das Buch **auf den** Tisch.	Das Buch liegt **auf dem** Tisch.
	to	Kurt geht **auf den** Markt.	
	at		Kurt ist **auf dem** Markt.
hinter	behind	Die Kinder laufen **hinter das** Haus.	Die Kinder sind **hinter dem** Haus.
in	in, into, to	Kurt geht **in die** Küche.	Kurt ist **in der** Küche.
neben	beside	Kurt stellt den Sessel **neben die** Couch.	Der Sessel steht **neben der** Couch.
über	over, above	Kurt hängt die Lampe **über den** Tisch.	Die Lampe hängt **über dem** Tisch.
unter	under, below	Lisa stellt die Hausschuhe **unter das** Bett.	Die Hausschuhe stehen **unter dem** Bett.
vor	in front of	Kurt stellt den Wagen **vor die** Garage.	Der Wagen steht **vor der** Garage.
zwischen	between	Lisa stellt die Stehlampe **zwischen die** Couch und **den** Sessel.	Die Stehlampe steht **zwischen der** Couch und **dem** Sessel.

8-9 In der neuen Wohnung (1). Ergänzen Sie die Präpositionen **an, auf, hinter, in, neben, über, unter, vor** und **zwischen.**

1. Der Picasso hängt _____ der Couch.
2. Uli hängt das Landschaftsbild _____ den Schreibtisch.
3. Der Kalender hängt jetzt _____ dem Landschaftsbild und dem Picasso.
4. Der Ball liegt _____ dem Schreibtisch.

crawls 5. Das Baby will den Ball und krabbelt° _____ den Schreibtisch.
6. Helga stellt den Papierkorb _____ den Schreibtisch.
7. Kurt legt den Teppich _____ die Couch.
8. Das Radio und die Zimmerpflanze stehen _____ dem Bücherregal.
9. Thomas stellt die Vase _____ das Radio und die Zimmerpflanze.
10. Die offene Tür geht _____ die Küche.
11. Antje hängt das Poster _____ die Küchentür.
12. Der Herd steht _____ der Küche.
13. Der Karton mit den Büchern steht _____ dem Bücherregal.
14. Die Stehlampe steht _____ dem Sessel.
15. Die Katze springt _____ die Couch.
16. Die Maus läuft _____ die Couch.

8-10 In der neuen Wohnung (2). Ergänzen Sie die Fragen mit **wohin** oder **wo** und die Antworten mit passenden Präpositionen und mit Akkusativ- oder Dativendungen.

▶ _____ steht die Zimmerpflanze?   _____ d__ Bücherregal. (m)
   _____ springt die Katze?   _____ d__ Couch. (f)

S1: Wo steht die Zimmerpflanze?   S2: Auf dem Bücherregal.
    Wohin springt die Katze?   Auf die Couch.

1. _____ hängt Antje das Poster?   _____ d__ Küchentür. (f)
2. _____ steht der Herd?   _____ d__ Küche. (f)
3. _____ geht die offene Tür?   _____ d__ Küche.
4. _____ steht der Karton mit den   _____ d__ Bücherregal. (n)
   Büchern?

5. _____ legt Kurt den Teppich?   _____ d__ Couch. (f)

6. _____ läuft die Maus?   _____ d__ Couch.

7. _____ steht die Stehlampe?   _____ d__ Sessel. (m)

8. _____ hängt der Picasso?   _____ d__ Couch.

9. _____ hängt Uli das Landschaftsbild?   _____ d__ Schreibtisch. (m)

10. _____ hängt der Kalender?   _____ d__ Picasso (m) und d__ Landschaftsbild. (n)

11. _____ liegt der Ball?   _____ d__ Schreibtisch.

12. _____ krabbelt das Baby?   _____ d__ Schreibtisch.

13. _____ stellt Helga den Papierkorb?   _____ d__ Schreibtisch.

14. _____ stellt Thomas die Vase?   _____ d__ Zimmerpflanze (f) und d__ Radio. (n)

Contractions

The prepositions **an** and **in** normally contract with the articles **das** and **dem.**

an + das	=	ans	Hast du unser Poster **ans** Schwarze Brett gehängt?
an + dem	=	am	Hängt unser Poster **am** Schwarzen Brett?
in + das	=	ins	Heute Abend gehen wir **ins** Konzert.
in + dem	=	im	Gestern Abend waren wir **im** Kino.

In colloquial German the article **das** also contracts with other two-case prepositions: **aufs, hinters, übers, unters, vors.**

8-11 *Am, ans, im* oder *ins*? Beginnen Sie die Fragen mit **wohin** oder **wo.**

▶ _____ geht diese Tür?   Sie geht _____ Schlafzimmer.

S1: Wohin geht diese Tür?   **S2:** Sie geht ins Schlafzimmer.

1. _____ soll ich die Zimmerpflanze stellen?   Stell sie _____ Fenster.

2. _____ ist Claudia?   Sie ist _____ Telefon.

3. _____ wart ihr gestern Abend?   Wir waren _____ Kino.

4. _____ gehst du heute Abend?   Heute Abend gehe ich mal ganz früh _____ Bett.

5. _____ soll ich dieses Poster hängen?   Häng es bitte gleich _____ Schwarze Brett.

6. _____ ist Andrea?   Sie sitzt _____ Klavier und übt.

7. _____ essen wir heute, bei dir?   Nein, heute gehen wir mal _____ Restaurant.

8. _____ ist Peter?   Ich glaube, er liegt noch _____ Bett.

PARKHAUS AM HOLSTENTOR

Geöffnet

| • Mo.-Fr.7-22h | • Sa. 7-21 h |
| • Feiertg. 10-19h | • So. 10-19h |

jede angefangene Std. € 1,00
Tageshöchstsatz € 5,00

2m   10 km   2,5t

The verbs *stellen, legen,* and *hängen*

In English the verb *to put* can mean *to put something in a vertical, horizontal,* or *hanging position.*

Put the wine glasses on the table.
Put your coats on the bed.
Put your jacket in the closet.

German uses three different verbs to describe the different actions conveyed by the English *to put*.

stellen	*to put in an upright position*	**Stell** die Weingläser auf **den** Tisch!
legen	*to put in a horizontal position, to lay (down)*	**Legt** eure Mäntel auf**s** Bett!
hängen	*to hang (up)*	**Häng** deine Jacke in **die** Garderobe!

When the verbs above are followed by a two-case preposition, the object of the preposition appears in the *accusative case*.

8-12 Wohin soll ich diese Sachen *stellen, legen* oder *hängen?*

▶ die Stehlampe   der Sessel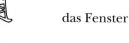

S1: Wohin soll ich die Stehlampe stellen?   **S2:** Stell sie hinter den Sessel!

1. der Kalender   der Schreibtisch

2. der Schaukelstuhl   das Fenster

3. der Teppich   die Couch

4. der Papierkorb   der Schreibtisch

5. die Zimmerpflanze   die Ecke

6. das Landschaftsbild   die beiden Fenster

7. der Beistelltisch   der Sessel

8. der Fernseher   das Bücherregal

The verbs *stehen*, *liegen*, and *hängen*

German also tends to be more exact than English when describing the location of things.

stehen	*to be standing*	Die Weingläser **stehen** auf **dem** Tisch.
liegen	*to be lying*	Eure Mäntel **liegen** auf **dem** Bett.
hängen	*to be hanging*	Deine Jacke **hängt** in **der** Garderobe.

When the verbs above are followed by a two-case preposition, the object of the preposition appears in the *dative case.*

8-13 Wo *stehen, liegen* oder *hängen* diese Sachen?

► die Stehlampe   der Sessel

S1: Wo steht die Stehlampe?   **S2:** Sie steht hinter dem Sessel.

What is the English cognate of **Stuhl?**

1. der Kalender   der Schreibtisch

2. der Schaukelstuhl   das Fenster

3. der Teppich   die Couch

4. der Papierkorb   der Schreibtisch

5. die Zimmerpflanze   die Ecke

6. das Landschaftsbild   die beiden Fenster

7. der Beistelltisch   der Sessel

8. der Fernseher   das Bücherregal

Dies ist ein GARAGENTOR nur ein TROTTEL parkt davor!

Ein Trottel ist ein Dummkopf.

More *da*-compounds

You will remember that personal pronouns that are objects of prepositions can only refer to people and that **da**-compounds are used for things or ideas. Remember that an **r** is added to **da** if the preposition begins with a vowel.

Dort drüben sitzt Moritz und **neben ihm** steht sein Freund Sven.

*That's Moritz sitting over there and his friend Sven is standing **beside him**.*

Das ist mein VW und der Wagen **daneben** gehört meiner Freundin.

*That's my VW and the car **beside it** belongs to my girlfriend.*

8-14 David beschreibt sein möbliertes Zimmer. Ergänzen Sie passende **da**-Formen.

davor / darauf / daneben / dahinter / darüber / darunter

1. Wenn man in mein Zimmer kommt, steht gleich links mein Bett und _____ ein Nachttisch mit einer Nachttischlampe _____.
2. Mitten im Zimmer hängt eine Lampe. Ich habe den Tisch direkt _____ gestellt, weil ich gutes Licht brauche, wenn ich abends meine Hausaufgaben mache.
3. An der rechten Wand steht eine Couch mit einem altmodischen Bild _____ und einem Couchtisch _____.
4. In einer Ecke steht noch ein alter Sessel mit einer hässlichen Stehlampe _____. Hoffentlich finde ich bald ein schöneres Zimmer!

skeleton sentences

8-15 Ich und mein Zimmer. Zeichnen Sie einen Plan von Ihrem Zimmer mit allen Möbeln, Türen und Fenstern. Beschreiben Sie das Zimmer dann in Worten. Die Ausdrücke in Übung **8-14** und die folgenden Skelettsätze° könnten Ihnen dabei helfen.

Salvation Army / flea market

8-15. Schreibtipp: You can make purely descriptive writing more interesting by adding commentary that personalizes the description. Here, for example, you can say what you like (or don't like) about your room, why you put things where you did, etc.

Mein Zimmer ist ziemlich groß (klein, dunkel, hell) …
Die Möbel sind modern (alt, neu, von der Heilsarmee°, vom Flohmarkt°,) …
An der Nordwand (der Südwand, der Ostwand, der Westwand) steht (hängt) …
Links neben … steht …
Rechts daneben steht …
Zwischen … und … steht …
…
Was gefällt Ihnen an Ihrem Zimmer besonders gut (nicht so gut)? Was gibt Ihrem Zimmer eine persönliche Note? Haben Sie ein Lieblingsposter, ein Lieblingsbild …?

German *an, auf, in*, and English *to*

In *Kapitel 7* you learned that both **zu** and **nach** can mean *to*. The prepositions **an**, **auf**, and **in** can also mean *to* if they answer the question **wohin.**

- **An** is used to indicate that your point of destination is *next to* something, such as a door, a telephone, or a body of water.

Geh bitte **an** die Tür.

*Go **to** the door, please.*

Warum gehst du denn nicht **ans** Telefon?

*Why don't you go **to** the phone?*

Wir fahren jeden Sommer **ans** Meer.

*We go **to** the ocean every summer.*

- **In** is generally used if your point of destination is *within* a place, such as a room, a concert hall, or a mountain range.

Geht doch bitte **ins** Wohnzimmer.   *Please go **to** the living room.*
Heute Abend gehen wir **in** die Oper.   *Tonight we're going **to** the opera.*
Warum fahren wir nicht mal **in**   *Why don't we go **to** the mountains*
    die Berge?   *for a change?*

- **In** is used instead of **nach** to express that you are going to a country if the name of the country is masculine, feminine, or plural (e.g., **der Libanon, die Schweiz, die USA**).

Morgen fliegen wir **in** die USA.   *Tomorrow we're flying **to** the U.S.*

- **Auf** can be used instead of **zu** to express that you are going to a building or an institution like the bank, the post office, or the city hall, especially to do business.

Ich muss heute Nachmittag **aufs**   *I have to go **to** the city hall this*
   Rathaus.   *afternoon.*

You have been using **in** in this sense since *Kapitel 1* in phrases like **ins Kino, in die Kneipe, ins Bett.**

Other expressions where **auf** means *to:* **auf eine Party, aufs Klo, auf die Toilette.**

8-16 Was passt in jeder Gruppe zusammen? Verwenden° Sie **ans,** auf, in oder **ins** in den Antworten.   *use*

▶   Man will Schwyzerdütsch hören.   die Schweiz

S1: Wohin geht man, wenn man   **S2:** Man geht in die Schweiz.
     Schwyzerdütsch hören will?

1. Man braucht Geld.   a. das Meer
2. Man möchte schlafen.   b. das Konzert
3. Man will eine Sinfonie hören.   c. die Bank
4. Man braucht Briefmarken.   d. das Bett
5. Man schwimmt gern in Salzwasser.   e. die Post

6. Man will *Hamlet* sehen.   f. das Gasthaus°   *restaurant*
7. Man möchte *Carmen* sehen.   g. der Wochenmarkt
8. Man kocht nicht gern.   h. die Oper
9. Man isst gern frisches Obst.   i. die Alpen
10. Man möchte Ski laufen.   j. das Theater

8-17 Eine Umfrage. Stellen Sie zwei Mitstudentinnen/Mitstudenten die folgenden Fragen. Machen Sie Notizen und berichten Sie dann, was Sie herausgefunden haben.

- Gehst du oft ins Theater (ins Konzert, in die Oper, ins Kino, ins Kunstmuseum, ins Gasthaus)?
- Was ist dein Lieblingstheaterstück (deine Lieblingsmusik, deine Lieblingsoper, dein Lieblingsfilm, dein Lieblingsbild, dein Lieblingsessen)?
- Fährst du lieber in die Berge, ans Meer oder an einen See? Warum? Was machst du dort?

Hören ···

Zimmersuche

landlady

Stephanie findet es im Studentenheim oft zu laut zum Lernen und sucht fürs Sommersemester ein Zimmer in einem Privathaus. Sie hat in der Zeitung ein Zimmer gefunden und hat gleich angerufen. Sie ist dann in die Ebersbergerstraße gefahren und spricht jetzt mit der Vermieterin°. Hören Sie, was Stephanie und Frau Kuhn miteinander sprechen.

NEUE VOKABELN

benutzen	*to use*	**wirklich**	*really*
gegenüber	*across (the hall)*	**stören**	*to disturb*

8-18 Erstes Verstehen. Was ist die richtige Antwort?

1. Was ist groß und hell?   das Zimmer / der Balkon
2. Wo kann Stephanie Kaffee oder   in der Küche / in der Mikrowelle
   Tee machen?
3. Wo ist die Mikrowelle?   in der Küche / in dem freien Zimmer
4. Was benutzt Frau Kuhn im Bad?   die Badewanne / die Dusche
5. Wie viele Personen wohnen   eine / zwei
   jetzt in diesem Haus?
6. Nimmt Stephanie das Zimmer?   ja / vielleicht / nein

8-19 Detailverstehen. Hören Sie das Gespräch noch einmal und schreiben Sie Antworten zu den folgenden Fragen.

1. Warum gefällt Stephanie das Zimmer so gut?
2. Was darf Stephanie bei Frau Kuhn nicht?
3. Für wen ist die Badewanne und für wen ist die Dusche?
4. Wie viel kostet das Zimmer?
5. Wie findet Stephanie diesen Preis?
6. Warum fragt Stephanie, ob es hier auch wirklich ruhig ist?
7. Wann möchte Frau Kuhn wissen, ob Stephanie das Zimmer nimmt?

Ich muss sehr viel lernen.

8-20 Aus der Zeitung. Berlin hat drei Universitäten: die Humboldt-Universität in Mitte, die Freie Universität in Zehlendorf und die Technische Universität in Charlottenburg.

- Suchen Sie Mitte, Zehlendorf und Charlottenburg auf dem Stadtplan.

- Die Anzeigen sprechen auch von den Stadtteilen° Prenzlauer Berg, Friedrichshain und Steglitz. Suchen Sie auch diese drei Stadtteile.

  districts

- Suchen Sie in den Anzeigen passende Unterkünfte° für die folgenden drei Studenten. Alle drei möchten in der Nähe ihrer Uni wohnen.

  accommodations

  1. Studentin an der Freien Universität, mag Kinder und Garten, aber ist allergisch gegen Katzen. Preis bis € 300,– warm.

  2. Amerikanischer Student an der Humboldt-Universität braucht Ruhe zum Lernen, hat nicht viel Geld, kann aber mit wenig Luxus leben.

  3. Architekturstudentin an der Technischen Universität, Individualistin, braucht großes, helles Zimmer. Preis maximal € 250,– warm.

Friedrichshain *Wohnung, 38 m², 1 Zimmer, Küche, WC, kein Bad, Gasheizung, €100,– kalt. Chiffre 11/236*

Prenzl. Berg *Zimmer, 30 m², Kü- Badbenutzung, hell u. ruhig, nur € 150,– Aber: suche Amerikaner/in, um aktiv Englisch lernen zu können. Anna, Tel. 86 79 20 43.*

FU-Nähe *Zimmer (20 m²), Tel., Kabel, Garten, eig. Dusche/WC, bei F (35) + K (7) + Katze. € 300,– warm. Chiffre 11/321*

WG in Steglitz *3 Stud. (1 F, 2 M) + 1 K (2 J.) sucht nette Studentin für helles Zi., 12 m², € 250,– warm. Chiffre 11/377*

Nähe TU *F (30) ernst, depressiv, sucht ruhige Studentin f. gr. Zimmer (ca. 25 m²), hell, m. Balkon, Kü-Benutz., € 220,– warm. Chiffre 11/79*

WG Charlottenbg *4 nette TU-Stud. (2 F, 2 M) bieten Student/in kleines, aber schönes Zi. + Benutzung von groß. gemeinschaftl. Arbeitsraum. € 250,– warm. Tel. 75 88 34 09*

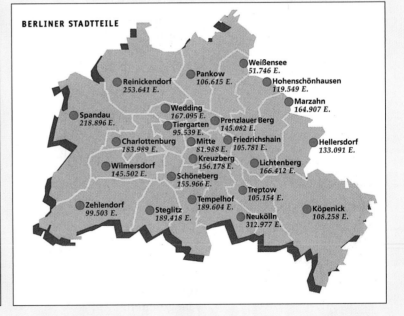

BERLINER STADTTEILE

Weißensee 51.746 E.

Reinickendorf 253.641 E.

Pankow 106.615 E.

Hohenschönhausen 119.549 E.

Marzahn 164.907 E.

Spandau 218.896 E.

Wedding 167.095 E.

Tiergarten 95.539 E.

Prenzlauer Berg 145.082 E.

Charlottenburg 183.989 E.

Mitte 81.988 E.

Friedrichshain 105.781 E.

Hellersdorf 133.091 E.

Kreuzberg 156.178 E.

Wilmersdorf 145.502 E.

Lichtenberg 166.412 E.

Schöneberg 155.966 E.

Treptow 105.154 E.

Zehlendorf 99.503 E.

Steglitz 189.418 E.

Tempelhof 189.604 E.

Köpenick 108.258 E.

Neukölln 312.977 E.

8-21 Mein Zimmer. Zeichnen Sie einen Plan von Ihrem Zimmer mit allen Türen und Fenstern, aber ohne Möbel. Vergessen Sie nicht, zu zeigen, wo Norden, Süden, Osten und Westen sind. Geben Sie Ihrer Partnerin/Ihrem Partner diesen Plan und beschreiben Sie, wo Ihre Sachen stehen, liegen oder hängen. Ihre Partnerin/Ihr Partner zeichnet dann alles ein.

❷ Saying when something occurs

The two-case prepositions *an, in, vor,* and *zwischen* in time phrases

Phrases with the prepositions **an, in, vor,** and **zwischen** are often used to answer the question **wann.** In such time expressions, the objects of the prepositions are always in the dative case.

SVEN: Wann bist du in Freiburg angekommen?	*When did you arrive in Freiburg?*
EVA: **Am** zehnten September.	*On the tenth of September.*
SVEN: Wann beginnt das Wintersemester?	*When does the winter semester begin?*
EVA: **Im** Oktober.	*In October.*
SVEN: Wann gehst du aufs Auslandsamt?	*When are you going to the foreign students office?*
EVA: Morgen Vormittag kurz **vor dem** Mittagessen.	*Tomorrow morning shortly before lunch.*
SVEN: Warst du früher schon mal in Deutschland?	*Have you been in Germany before?*
EVA: Ja, **vor** drei Jahren.	*Yes, three years ago.*
SVEN: Kommen deine Eltern bald mal zu Besuch?	*Are your parents coming to visit you sometime soon?*
EVA: Ja, irgendwann **zwischen dem** ersten und **dem** zehnten März.	*Yes, sometime between the first and the tenth of March.*

Note that in time expressions, **vor** can mean *before* or *ago.*

8-22 Wann ...?

▶ Wann warst du in Berlin?   Vor ein__ Jahr (n).

S1: Wann warst du in Berlin?   **S2:** Vor einem Jahr.

1. Wann hast du die Mikrowelle gekauft?   Vor ein__ Woche (f).

2. Wann beginnt das Wintersemester in Deutschland?   I__ Oktober (m).

3. Wann besuchst du deine Eltern?   A__ Wochenende (n).

4. Wann gehst du auf den Markt?   Vor d__ Mittagessen (n).

5. Wann hast du Petra zum letzten Mal gesehen?   An ihr__ neunzehnten Geburtstag (m).

6. Wann gehst du in die Bibliothek?   Zwischen d__ Mathevorlesung (f) und d__ Mittagessen (n).

7. Wann fliegst du nach Europa?   In d__ Sommerferien (pl).

8. Wann kommst du wieder zurück?   Irgendwann zwischen d__ ersten und d__ siebten September (m).

- Wo waren Sie vor dieser Deutschstunde? *Vor dieser Deutschstunde …*
- Wo waren Sie gestern in der Mittagspause?
- Was haben Sie gestern zwischen dem Mittagessen und dem Abendessen gemacht?
- Wo waren Sie heute vor einer Woche?
- Was haben Sie am vergangenen° Wochenende gemacht? *past*
- …

❸ Word order

Infinitive phrases

Infinitive phrases are phrases that contain an infinitive preceded by **zu.** Some verbs or expressions that may be followed by an infinitive phrase are **versuchen, vergessen, versprechen, anfangen, vorhaben, Zeit haben.**

Ich habe versprochen, **Tim zum Bahnhof** *zu fahren.*	*I promised **to drive** Tim to the train station.*
Vergiss aber diesmal nicht, **einen Parkschein** *zu lösen.*	*But don't forget **to buy** a parking pass this time.*

- In German, **zu** and the infinitive stand at the end of the phrase. (In English, *to* and the infinitive stand at the beginning of the phrase.)
- The German infinitive phrase is often set off with a comma.

With separable-prefix verbs, **zu** is inserted between the prefix and the verb.

Hast du wirklich vor, **bald** *umzuziehen?*	*Are you really planning **to move** soon?*
Ja, ich habe schon angefangen, **meine Bücher** *einzupacken.*	*Yes, I've already started **to pack** my books.*

If a phrase ends with more than one infinitive, **zu** precedes the last one.

Hast du Zeit, **am Wochenende mit uns** *campen zu gehen?*	*Do you have time **to go camping** with us on the weekend?*

Bitte
vergessen Sie nicht
den Parkschein
zu lösen

Parkscheinautomat

is missing **8-24 Was fehlt° hier?** Ergänzen Sie **zu**-Infinitive.

1. Peter hat versprochen, mir beim Umziehen _____. (helfen)
2. Hast du versucht, mit Professor Weber_____? (sprechen)
3. Hat Frau Wild wieder angefangen, von ihrer Amerikareise _____? (erzählen)
4. Wann hast du mal Zeit, die Fotos von meiner Europareise _____? (anschauen)
5. Vergiss nicht, Ella und Florian _____. (einladen)
6. Habt ihr vor, am Sonntag _____? (segeln gehen)

When the **zu**-infinitive follows expressions like **es macht mir Spaß, ich habe es satt,** or **ich habe Lust,** its English equivalent is the *-ing* form of the verb.

Macht es dir Spaß, **Deutsch *zu* lernen?**	*Do you enjoy **learning German?***
Ich habe es satt, **dauernd umzuziehen.**	*I'm sick of **constantly** moving.*
Hast du Lust, *tanzen zu gehen?*	*Do you feel like **going dancing?***

8-25 Kleine Gespräche. Ergänzen Sie **zu**-Infinitive.

1. JUTTA: Macht es dir Spaß, jeden Morgen drei Kilometer _____? (joggen)
   SYLVIA: Nicht immer, aber es hilft mir, fit _____. (bleiben)

2. LAURA: Hast du wirklich vor, einen Wagen _____? (kaufen)
   MARKUS: Klar! Ich habe es satt, immer mit dem Bus _____. (fahren)

3. JENS: Hast du vergessen, Günter _____? (anrufen)
   JULIA: Nein, ich hatte heute keine Lust, mit ihm _____. (sprechen)

4. LUKAS: Habt ihr Lust, heute Abend mit uns _____? (tanzen gehen)
   BERND: Nein, wir haben vor, einen guten Film _____ und nachher noch in die Kneipe _____. (anschauen / gehen)

 8-26 Ein paar persönliche Fragen. Stellen Sie einander die folgenden Fragen. Berichten Sie, was Sie herausgefunden haben.

S1: Was hast du heute Abend vor?
Was hast du am Wochenende vor?
Was macht dir am meisten Spaß?
Hast du mal vergessen, etwas Wichtiges zu tun?

S2: Heute Abend habe ich vor, …
Am Wochenende habe ich vor, …
Am meisten Spaß macht mir, …
Ich habe mal vergessen, …

Infinitive phrases introduced by *um*

To express the purpose of an action, you can use an infinitive phrase intoduced with **um**. The English equivalent of **um … zu** is *in order to*. English often uses only *to* instead of *in order to*. In German the word **um** is rarely omitted.

Morgen früh kommt Pietro, **um** mir beim Umziehen **zu helfen.**	*Tomorrow morning Pietro is coming **(in order) to help** me move.*
Ich brauche ein paar Nägel, **um** meine Bilder **aufzuhängen.**	*I need a few nails **(in order) to hang up** my pictures.*

8-27 In der WG. Sie wohnen in einer WG und fragen einander, was Ihre Mitbewohner mit diesen Geräten° machen wollen. Die Information für **S2** ist im *Anhang* auf Seite A11.

appliances; utensils

S1: Wozu° braucht Benedikt den Staubsauger?

S2: Um in unserem Wohnzimmer den Fußboden sauber° zu halten.

what . . . for
clean

		SABRINA	BENEDIKT
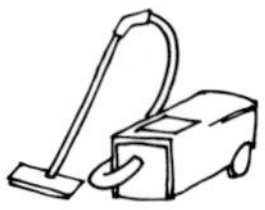	der Staubsauger	ihr Zimmer putzen	
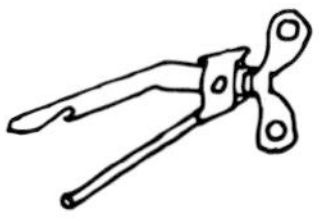	der Dosenöffner		eine Dose Sardinen aufmachen°
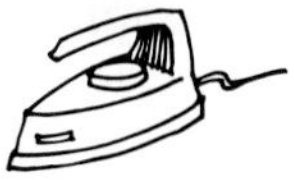	das Bügeleisen		seine schwarze Hose bügeln
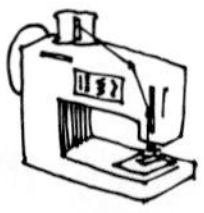	die Nähmaschine	ihren neuen Rock kürzer machen	
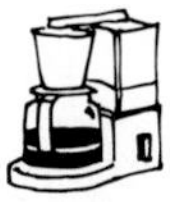	die Kaffeemaschine	für ihre Freundinnen Kaffee kochen	
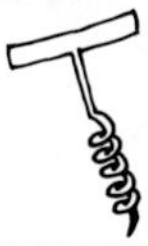	der Korkenzieher		eine Flasche Sherry aufmachen
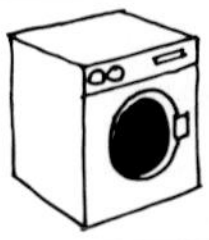	die Waschmaschine		seine vielen T-Shirts waschen

to open

Sprachnotiz

Infinitive phrases introduced by *ohne* and *(an)statt*

When an infinitive phrase begins with **ohne** *(without)* or **(an)statt** *(instead of)*, its English equivalent uses a verb form ending in *-ing*.

Wie kannst du meine Nähmaschine benutzen, **ohne** mich **zu fragen?** — *How can you use my sewing machine* ***without asking*** *me?*

Statt seine Hausaufgaben **zu machen,** hat Florian den ganzen Abend vor dem Fernseher gesessen. — ***Instead of doing*** *his homework, Florian sat in front of the TV all evening.*

④ Indicating possession or relationships

The genitive case

The genitive case is used to express the idea of possession or belonging together. You are already familiar with the **-s** genitive, which is used in German only with proper names. The ending **-s** is not preceded by an apostrophe.

> Claudia**s** Schreibtisch   *Claudia's desk*

For nouns other than proper names you must use a different form of the genitive. Note that this form of the genitive follows the noun it modifies.

> das Büro **des** Professor**s**   *the professor's office*
> das Zimmer mein**er** Schwester   *my sister's room*
> der Teddybär dies**es** Kind**es**   *this child's teddy bear*
> die Wohnung unser**er** Eltern   *our parents' apartment*

In German this form of the genitive is used for persons, animals, and things. In English the possessive *'s* is generally used for persons and animals, while the preposition *of* is used to show that *things* belong together.

> das Dach dies**es** Haus**es**   *the roof **of** this house*
> die Wände unser**er** Wohnung   *the walls **of** our apartment*

	masculine		neuter		feminine		plural	
NOMINATIVE	der mein	Vater	das mein	Kind	die meine	Mutter	die meine	Kinder
ACCUSATIVE	den meinen	Vater	das mein	Kind	die meine	Mutter	die meine	Kinder
DATIVE	dem meinem	Vater	dem meinem	Kind	der meiner	Mutter	den meinen	Kindern
GENITIVE	**des** **meines**	Vater**s**	**des** **meines**	Kind**es**	**der** **meiner**	Mutter	**der** **meiner**	Kinder

- Most one-syllable masculine and neuter nouns add **-es** in the genitive singular (**Kindes**), while masculine and neuter nouns with more than one syllable add **-s** in the genitive singular (**Vaters**).
- Feminine nouns and the plural forms of all nouns have no genitive ending.

The interrogative pronoun *wessen*

The genitive form of the interrogative pronoun is **wessen.**

> **Wessen** Jacke ist das?   *Whose jacket is that?*

	nominative	accusative	dative	genitive
for people	wer	wen	wem	**wessen**
for things or ideas	was	was	—	—

8-28 Wessen Handschuhe sind das?

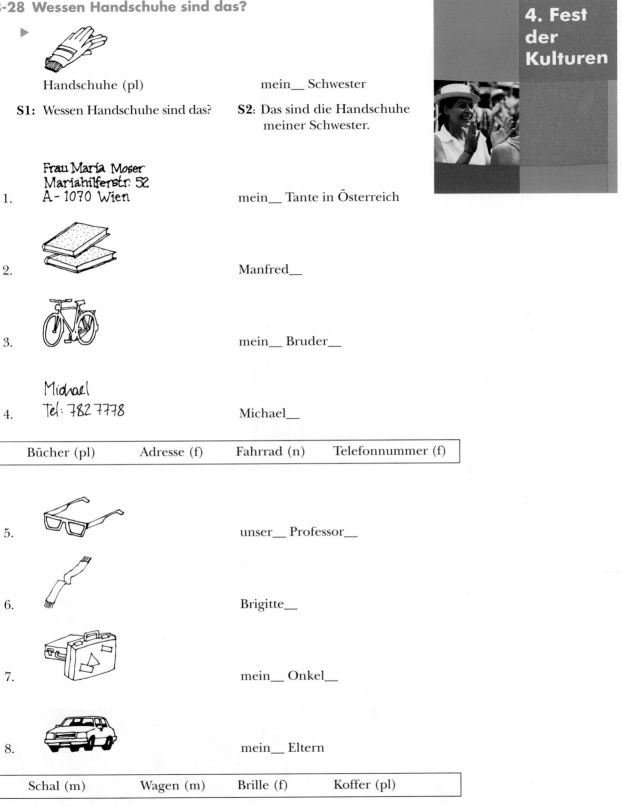

▶ Handschuhe (pl)   mein__ Schwester

S1: Wessen Handschuhe sind das?   **S2:** Das sind die Handschuhe
                                                meiner Schwester.

4. Fest der Kulturen

1. Frau María Moser
    Mariahilferstr. 52
    A- 1070 Wien   mein__ Tante in Österreich

2.   Manfred__

3.   mein__ Bruder__

4. Michael
    Tel: 782 7778   Michael__

Bücher (pl)	Adresse (f)	Fahrrad (n)	Telefonnummer (f)

5.   unser__ Professor__

6.   Brigitte__

7.   mein__ Onkel__

8.   mein__ Eltern

Schal (m)	Wagen (m)	Brille (f)	Koffer (pl)

8-29 Das Familienalbum. Sie und Ihre Partnerin/Ihr Partner sind Frau Kuhn und Frau Stolz. Frau Kuhn zeigt Frau Stolz ihr Familienalbum.

▶ mein Großvater
mein__ Vater__

der Vater Ihr__ Mutter?

FRAU KUHN: Das ist mein Großvater. Nein, der Vater meines Vaters.

FRAU STOLZ: Der Vater Ihrer Mutter?

1. meine Tante
mein__ Mutter

die Schwester Ihr__ Vater__?

2. mein Neffe
mein__ Bruder__

der Sohn Ihr__ Schwester?

3. mein Onkel
mein__ Vater__

der Bruder Ihr__ Mutter?

4. meine Nichte
mein__ Schwester

die Tochter Ihr__ Bruder__?

5. meine Enkelkinder
mein__ Sohn__

die Kinder Ihr__ Tochter?

acquaintances **8-30 Beruf und Wohnung.** Erzählen Sie Ihren Mitstudenten, was zwei oder drei von Ihren Verwandten oder Bekannten° tun und wo und wie sie wohnen.

S: Die Schwester meines Vaters ist Lehrerin und wohnt in Miami in einer Eigentumswohnung.
Der Bruder meiner Freundin ist Student und wohnt in Toronto in einem Studentenheim.

■ Sprachnotiz ··

Using *von* + dative instead of the genitive

In colloquial German the idea of possession or of belonging together is often expressed by **von** with a dative object instead of the genitive case.

Ist das der neue Wagen **von** deinem Bruder?	=	Ist das der neue Wagen deines Bruders?
Herr Koch ist ein Freund **von** meinem Vater.	=	Herr Koch ist ein Freund meines Vaters.

❺ Describing people, places, and things

Genitive endings of preceded adjectives

Adjectives that are preceded by a **der**-word or an **ein**-word in the genitive case always take the ending **-en**.

	masculine		neuter		feminine		plural	
GENITIVE	des eines	jung**en** Mannes	des eines	klein**en** Kindes	der einer	jung**en** Frau	der meiner	klein**en** Kinder

8-31 Nicht alle Maler sind berühmt. Ergänzen Sie die Genitivendungen in dieser Erzählung eines nicht so berühmten Malers.

1. Ich bin diese Woche in der Wohnung einer prominent__ Familie unserer Stadt, um dort die Fenster frisch zu streichen.
2. Die Wohnung liegt direkt im Zentrum des historisch__, alt__ Teil__° der Stadt im fünften Stock° eines wunderschön__, alt__ Haus__. *part* / *floor*
3. Die Fenster der drei groß__, hell__ Schlafzimmer, der beid__ schön__ Bäder und der modern__ und sehr praktisch__ Küche gehen direkt auf den Marienplatz.
4. Trotzdem ist es hier sehr ruhig, denn der Marienplatz ist Teil einer groß__ Fußgängerzone°. *pedestrian zone*
5. Die Fenster der hinter__° Zimmer gehen auf einen Park mit vielen Bäumen. *back*
6. Aber auch in diesen Zimmern ist es sehr hell, denn die Fenster liegen über den Kronen der groß__, alt__ Bäume.
7. An einer Wand des riesig__° Wohnzimmer__ hängt über der teuren Couch ein Bild des berühmt__ französisch__ Maler__ Renoir. *huge*
8. An den anderen Wänden dieses Zimmer__ und an den Wänden des groß__ Esszimmer__ hängen moderne Bilder.
9. Ich kann übrigens fast nicht glauben, dass der Renoir echt ist, denn wer hat schon das Geld, um ein Original dieses groß__ Künstler__° zu kaufen? *artist*
10. Mit dem Lohn° eines klein__ Maler__, wie ich einer bin, kann man die Bilder der berühmt__ Maler sowieso nur im Museum anschauen. *wages*

Zusammenschau

 ## Video-Treff ··············

Mein Zuhause

Christoph und Christina Brieger, Ursula, Karen, André, Maiga und Stefan Kuhlmann erzählen, wo und wie sie wohnen.

Zum besseren Verstehen

8-32 Was ist das auf Englisch?

1. Wir wohnen in einem sehr schönen **Wohnviertel.**
2. Wir **wohnen** hier **zur Miete.**
3. Es gibt viele Geschäfte in den **umliegenden** Straßen.
4. Hier kann man sehr schöne Abende **verbringen.**
5. Ich **fühle mich sehr wohl** hier.
6. Ich muss immer **Kohlen** in den 4. Stock tragen.
7. Ich habe keine **Wanne.**
8. Ich finde es sehr gut, wie die Wohnung **aufgeteilt** ist.
9. Wir wohnen hier **zu fünft.**
10. Man braucht eine große Couch, **falls** Freunde zu Besuch kommen.

Mein Zuhause

a. surrounding
b. in case
c. coal
d. really feel at home
e. tub
f. rent
g. residential area
h. spend
i. divided up
j. five of us

Schauen Sie jetzt das Video an und machen Sie die Übungen im *Video-Treff*-Teil des *Student Activities Manual.*

As you listen, you will notice that the dialogue between Stephanie and Claudia follows in part from the dialogue between Stephanie and Frau Kuhn in the *Zwischenspiel.*

))) Hören ···

Privathaus oder WG?

Im ersten Semester hatten Stephanie und Claudia im Studentenheim viele Feten und nie genug Zeit zum Lernen. Sie sind deshalb beide auf Zimmersuche und sie finden auch beide etwas, was ihnen gefällt. Hören Sie, was Stephanie und Claudia miteinander sprechen.

NEUE VOKABELN

Was ist denn los?	*What's up?*	**sicher**	*sure*
aufgeregt	*excited*	**wenigstens**	*at least*
eigen	*own*	**nur zu viert**	*just the four of us*

8-33 Erstes Verstehen. In welcher Reihenfolge hören Sie das?

_____ Hast du wenigstens Küchenbenutzung?
_____ Nur drei. Na, das geht ja noch.
_____ Aber wir haben da jede unser eigenes Zimmer.
_____ Du bist ja ganz aufgeregt.
_____ Da kommst du doch lieber zu uns.
_____ Aber vielleicht nehme ich doch lieber das Zimmer bei Frau Kuhn.

8-34 Detailverstehen. Hören Sie das Gespräch zwischen Claudia und Stephanie noch einmal und beantworten Sie die folgenden Fragen.

1. Warum ist Claudia so aufgeregt?
2. Was hat Stephanie gegen WGs?
3. Wo können die Studenten in dieser WG ihre Wäsche waschen?
4. Was kostet ein Zimmer in der WG und was kostet das Zimmer bei Frau Kuhn?
5. Was kann Stephanie nicht riskieren?
6. Warum soll Stephanie lieber in Claudias WG kommen?

■ Schreiben und Sprechen ·······················

8-35 Vorteile und Nachteile meiner Unterkunft. _(Advantages and disadvantages of my accommodations.)_ Beschreiben Sie, wo und wie Sie wohnen und was Sie dort gut oder nicht so gut finden. Die folgenden Wörter und Ausdrücke könnten Ihnen dabei helfen.

VORTEILE	NACHTEILE
in der Nähe der Uni (wie nah?)	weit weg von der Uni (wie weit?)
billig / groß / hell / ruhig	teuer / klein / dunkel / laut
kann dort selbst kochen	kann dort nicht kochen
die Möbel sind schön	die Möbel sind alt und hässlich
kann dort tolle Feten geben	darf dort keine Feten geben
…	…

Schreibtipp: Pro and con lists can help you sort out your ideas when you write. In this assignment your introductory paragraph could be a description of the type and location of your accommodations, how long you have lived there, etc. The second and third paragraphs would then address the **Vorteile** and **Nachteile.** A concluding paragraph could express whether you like or dislike your living arrangements, whether you would prefer to move, etc.

8-36 Verschiedene Unterkünfte. Diskutieren Sie in kleinen Gruppen die Vorteile und Nachteile der folgenden Unterkünfte.

	STUDENTENHEIM	WG	WOHNUNG	ZIMMER	ZU HAUSE
VORTEILE	_____	_____	_____	_____	_____
	_____	_____	_____	_____	_____
NACHTEILE	_____	_____	_____	_____	_____
	_____	_____	_____	_____	_____

Zum besseren Verstehen

buildings **8-37 Gebäude° und Architekten.**

Gropius House: Walter Gropius built this house as his family home when he came to teach at Harvard, and he lived there until his death. It is now a National Historic Landmark.

1. Welches Gebäude auf Ihrem Campus oder in Ihrer Stadt gefällt Ihnen am besten? Warum?
2. Gefallen Ihnen das Bauhaus in Dessau und das Gropius House in Lincoln, Massachusetts (siehe Fotos)? Warum oder warum nicht?
3. Kennen Sie den Namen eines berühmten Architekten/einer berühmten Architektin? Was hat er/sie gebaut und was wissen Sie sonst° *else* von ihm/ihr?

Das Gropius House in Lincoln, Massachusetts

Das Bauhaus in Dessau

8-38 Was ist das auf Englisch?

1. Musiker, Balletttänzer, Filmstars usw. sind **Künstler.**
2. Auf einer **Ausstellung** zeigt man Bilder, Skulpturen, Fotografien usw.
3. Der Architekt Walter Gropius hat das Schulgebäude in Dessau selbst **entworfen.**
4. Die Fassaden von modernen Gebäuden sind oft ganz aus **Stahl** und Glas.
5. Die Ideen des Bauhauses hatten einen enormen **Einfluss** auf nordamerikanische Architekten und Designer.
6. Nach 1933 **verlassen** Gropius und viele andere Bauhauslehrer und -schüler das nationalsozialistische Deutschland.
7. Die meisten Bauhauslehrer finden in den USA eine neue **Heimat.**

a. designed
b. influence
c. artists
d. home
e. leave
f. exhibition
g. steel

Im Jahr 1919 gründet[1] der Architekt Walter Gropius in Weimar das Bauhaus, eine Schule, wo Künstler, Architekten, Handwerker[2] und Studenten zusammen leben und lernen und zusammen versuchen, für eine industrialisierte Welt neue Formen zu finden. Auf dem Lehrplan[3] stehen Malerei[4], Skulptur, Architektur, Theater, Fotografie und das Design von Handwerks- und Industrieprodukten. Typisch für die neuen Formen – von der Teekanne bis zum größten Gebäude – sind klare geometrische Linien. Auf der großen Bauhaus-Ausstellung von 1923 charakterisiert Gropius den Bauhausstil mit den folgenden Worten: Kunst und Technik – eine neue Einheit.[5]

1925 zieht das Bauhaus von Weimar nach Dessau. Das Schulgebäude, das berühmte Dessauer Bauhaus, hat Walter Gropius selbst entworfen und seine Stahl- und Glasfassade wird zur Ikone der Architektur des 20. Jahrhunderts. Aber schon 1933 kommt mit Adolf Hitler das Ende des Bauhauses, denn Gropius' Ideen sind für die Nazis „undeutsch" und zu international. 1934 geht Gropius nach England und arbeitet dort als Architekt und Designer. 1937 emigriert er dann in die USA und wird dort an der Harvard Universität *Chairman* des *Department of Architecture*. Seine größten Projekte in den USA sind das Harvard Graduate Center, das Pan Am Building (MetLife Building) in New York und das John F. Kennedy Federal Building in Boston.

Der enorme Einfluss des Bauhauses auf nordamerikanische Architekten und Designer geht aber nicht nur auf Walter Gropius zurück, denn auch viele andere Bauhauslehrer und -schüler verlassen damals[6] Hitler-Deutschland und finden in den USA eine neue Heimat: László Moholy-Nagy gründet 1937 das *New Bauhaus* in Chicago, Josef Albers lehrt am Black Mountain College in North Carolina und später an der Yale Universität, und Ludwig Mies van der Rohe lehrt am Illinois Institute of Technology in Chicago.

[1]*founds* [2]*craftsmen and -women* [3]*curriculum* [4]*painting* [5]*art and technology — a new unity* [6]*at that time*

Walter Gropius

WWW View a **Bauhaus** building at www.prenhall.com/treffpunkt → Kapitel 8 → Web Resources → Kultur

Mies van der Rohe also designed the **Neue Nationalgalerie** in Berlin. You can see it in the background of the postage stamp featuring the architect in *Kapitel 6*, p. 196.

Arbeit mit dem Text

8-39 Wann war das? Finden Sie im Text die richtigen Jahreszahlen.

_____ Der Bauhauslehrer László Moholy-Nagy gründet in Chicago das *New Bauhaus*.

_____ Auf einer großen Ausstellung präsentiert das Weimarer Bauhaus seine Ideen und seine Produkte.

_____ Walter Gropius geht nach England und arbeitet dort als Architekt und Designer.

_____ Walter Gropius gründet in Weimar eine Schule für Architektur, Kunst und Handwerk und nennt sie Bauhaus.

_____ Ende des Dessauer Bauhauses, weil die Nazis die Bauhausideen undeutsch und zu international finden.

_____ Das Bauhaus zieht von Weimar in das neue Schulgebäude in Dessau.

Wort, Sinn und Klang

Wörter unter der Lupe

Compound nouns

A compound noun can be a combination of:

- two or more nouns (**der Nachttisch, die Nachttischlampe**).
- an adjective and a noun (**der Kühlschrank**).
- a verb and a noun (**der Schreibtisch**).
- a preposition and a noun (**der Nachtisch**).

In German these combinations are almost always written as one word. The last element of a compound noun is the base word and determines the gender of the compound noun. All preceding elements are modifiers that define the base word more closely.

die Stadt + **der** Plan = **der** Stadtplan
der Fuß + der Ball + **das** Spiel = **das** Fußballspiel

8-40 Was passt zusammen? Ergänzen Sie auch die bestimmten Artikel.

1. _____ Wochenendhaus	a.	family doctor
2. _____ Hausschuh	b.	househusband
3. _____ Krankenhaus	c.	cottage
4. _____ Hausmeister	d.	single-family dwelling
5. _____ Hochhaus	e.	janitor
6. _____ Hausarzt	f.	department store
7. _____ Reformhaus	g.	hospital
8. _____ Hausmann	h.	slipper
9. _____ Einfamilienhaus	i.	high-rise
10. _____ Kaufhaus	j.	health food store

Giving language color

In this chapter you have learned vocabulary that deals with housing and furnishings. This vocabulary is a source of many idiomatic expressions. The expressions marked with an asterisk are very informal and should only be used with family and friends.

Lena ist ganz aus dem Häuschen.	*Lena is all excited.*
Du hast wohl nicht alle Tassen im Schrank!*	*You must be crazy!*
Setz ihm doch den Stuhl vor die Tür!	*Throw him out!*
Mal den Teufel nicht an die Wand!	*Don't tempt fate!*
Lukas hat vom Chef eins aufs Dach gekriegt.*	*Lukas was bawled out by his boss.*
Auf Robert kannst du Häuser bauen.	*Robert is absolutely dependable.*

8-41 Was passt zusammen?

1. Unser Sohn will einfach keine Arbeit suchen.
2. Hat Anne eine Reise nach Hawaii gewonnen?
3. Gott sei Dank° hatten wir diesen Winter noch keinen Eisregen.
4. Warum ist Kurt denn plötzlich so fleißig?
5. Ist Sven ein guter Babysitter?
6. Ich habe mir gestern einen Porsche gekauft.

a. Ich glaube, er hat vom Chef eins aufs Dach gekriegt.
b. Aber natürlich. Auf ihn können Sie Häuser bauen.
c. Dann setzen Sie ihm doch den Stuhl vor die Tür!
d. Du hast wohl nicht alle Tassen im Schrank!
e. Ja, sie ist ganz aus dem Häuschen.
f. Mal bitte den Teufel nicht an die Wand!

Thank God!

Zur Aussprache

German s-sounds: *st* and *sp*

At the beginning of a word or word stem, **s** in the combinations **st** and **sp** is pronounced like English *sh*. Otherwise it is pronounced like English *s* in *list* and *lisp*.

8-42 Hören Sie gut zu und wiederholen Sie!

1. **St**efan ist **St**udent.
   Stefan **st**udiert in **St**uttgart.
   Stefan findet das **St**udentenleben **st**ressig.
2. Ha**st** du Lu**st** auf eine Wur**st**
   und auf Most° für deinen Dur**st**?
3. Herr **Sp**ielberg **sp**richt gut **Sp**anisch.
4. Worauf° **sp**art Frau **Sp**ohn?
   Auf einen **Sp**ortwagen.
   Die **sp**innt° ja!
5. Unser Ka**sp**ar li**sp**elt ein bisschen.

👑 Hier ist die Königin der Würste !			
Bockwurst	1,80 €	Schaschlik	3,20 €
Bratwurst	2,30 €	Frikadelle 200g	1,80 €
Curry–Bratwurst	2,40 €	Pommes Frites	1,30 €
Schinkenwurst	2,30 €	Hamburger	2,50 €
Riesen–Hot Dog	3,70 €	La Flüte	3,40 €

cider

what . . . for

is crazy

Nomen

das Dach, ⸚er	roof
die Eigentumswohnung, -en	condominium apartment
das Einfamilienhaus, ⸚er	single-family dwelling
die Fußgängerzone, -n	pedestrian zone
das Gebäude, -	building
das Hochhaus, ⸚er	high-rise
der Keller, -	basement; cellar
die Post	post office; mail
das Rathaus, ⸚er	town hall; city hall
der Stadtplan, ⸚e	map of the city/town
der Stadtteil, -e	district, part of the city/town
der Teil, -e	part
der Wochenmarkt, ⸚e	open air market

Gebäude: What verb is the core of this noun?

und auf dem Mexikoplatz ist Wochenmarkt...

immer samstags von 9 bis 15 Uhr

die Küchenbenutzung	kitchen privileges
der Mitstudent, -en	classmate; fellow
die Mitstudentin, -nen	student
die Wohngemeinschaft, -en	shared housing
die WG, -s	

die Wohngemeinschaft: All words with the suffix -schaft are feminine.

das Bügeleisen, -	iron
die Dose, -n	can
der Dosenöffner, -	can opener
das Gerät, -e	appliance; utensil
der Korkenzieher, -	corkscrew
die Nähmaschine, -n	sewing machine
der Schaukelstuhl, ⸚e	rocking chair
der Staubsauger, -	vacuum cleaner

die Ausstellung, -en	exhibition; exhibit
der Künstler, -	artist
die Künstlerin, -nen	

die/der Bekannte, -n	acquaintance
die Heimat	home (country)
die Mittagspause, -n	lunch break

Verben

auf·machen	to open
benutzen	to use
bügeln	to iron
klingeln	to ring
stören	to disturb
versuchen	to try
wiederholen	to repeat

Andere Wörter

aufgeregt	excited
eigen	own
sicher	sure
statt, anstatt	instead of
wenigstens	at least
wirklich	really
wozu	what . . . for

Ausdrücke

in der Nähe der Uni	near the university
Es macht mir Spaß, …	I enjoy . . .
Ich habe es satt, …	I'm sick of . . . , I'm fed up with . . .
Ich habe keine Lust, …	I don't feel like . . .
usw. (und so weiter)	etc. (et cetera, and so on)
Was ist denn los?	What's up?

satt means *full* or *satiated*. If you say **Ich bin satt,** you are indicating that you can't eat another bite.

Das Gegenteil

der Vorteil, -e ≠ der Nachteil, -e	advantage ≠ disadvantage
mieten ≠ vermieten	to rent ≠ to rent (out)
sauber ≠ schmutzig	clean ≠ dirty

mieten ≠ vermieten: Another verb that forms its opposite this way: **kaufen ≠ verkaufen.**

Leicht zu verstehen

der Architekt, -en	das Poster, -
die Architektin, -nen	die Skulptur, -en
der Designer, -	die Technik
die Designerin, -nen	enorm
der Luxus	maximal

Wörter im Kontext

8-43 Was passt in jeder Gruppe zusammen?

1. die Post	a. die Mitbewohner	5. der Staubsauger	e. sitzen
2. die WG	b. der Brief	6. das Telefon	f. einkaufen
3. der Keller	c. die Skulptur	7. der Schaukelstuhl	g. putzen
4. die Künstlerin	d. der Wein	8. der Wochenmarkt	h. klingeln

Staubsauger: This word describes literally the function of a vacuum cleaner: **der Staub** = *dust;* **saugen** = *to suck*

8-44 Was ist die richtige Antwort?

1. Warum bist du denn so aufgeregt?
2. Warum stehst du denn vor dem Schwarzen Brett?
3. Warum suchst du ein Zimmer mit Küchenbenutzung?
4. Warum gehst du heute Abend nicht mit uns tanzen?
5. Warum gehst du auf die Post?

a. Weil ich Briefmarken brauche.
b. Weil ich es satt habe, immer in der Mensa zu essen.
c. Weil ich ein Zimmer in der Nähe der Uni suche.
d. Weil ich ein Zimmer in einer ganz tollen WG gefunden habe.
e. Weil ich keine Lust habe.

8-45 Wozu brauchst du das alles?

1. Wozu brauchst du einen Staubsauger?
2. Wozu brauchst du eine Nähmaschine?
3. Wozu brauchst du einen Korkenzieher?
4. Wozu brauchst du einen Dosenöffner?
5. Wozu brauchst du ein Bügeleisen?
6. Wozu brauchst du denn einen Stadtplan?

a. Um diese Weinflasche aufzumachen.
b. Um mein Kleid zu bügeln.
c. Um mein Zimmer sauber zu machen.
d. Um zu sehen, wo die Kleiststraße ist.
e. Um diesen Rock kürzer zu machen.
f. Um diese Sardinen essen zu können.

Korkenzieher: What is the literal meaning of this word?

Dosenöffner, Flaschenöffner, Korkenzieher, Staubsauger: Remember that agent nouns are always derived from verbs and can refer to things as well as people.

8-46 Was passt zusammen?

1. Herr Ertem ist ein guter Bekannter von mir.
2. Frau Berg hat eine große Eigentumswohnung in einem Hochhaus.
3. Ich habe mir einen Schaukelstuhl gekauft.
4. Im Keller von unserem Einfamilienhaus machen wir oft laute Musik.
5. Ich schaue gern Bilder und Skulpturen an.
6. Stefan gefällt es sehr gut in seiner WG.
7. Frau Otto is Stadtarchitektin in Leipzig.

a. Ich sitze dort immer, wenn ich lese.
b. Ein Nachteil ist aber, dass seine Mitbewohner oft sehr laut sind.
c. Ich kenne ihn seit vielen Jahren.
d. Ich gehe deshalb oft auf Kunstausstellungen.
e. Ihr Büro ist im Rathaus.
f. Sie vermietet zwei von ihren Zimmern an Studenten.
g. Ein großer Vorteil ist, dass wir dort niemand stören.

Rathaus, Keller: The **Ratskeller** was originally an eating establishment in the basement of the **Rathaus,** specifically for the use of the town or city officials. Many North American restaurants with this name are situated below ground level.

Das Rathaus in Leipzig

Andere Länder, andere Sitten

In den Hamburger Alsterarkaden isst man gut.

Kommunikationsziele

Talking about . . .

- cultural differences
- grocery shopping
- personal grooming

Ordering a meal in a restaurant

Describing people, places, and things

Strukturen

Relative clauses and relative pronouns

N-nouns

Reflexive pronouns and reflexive verbs

Kultur

Im Gasthaus

Beim Schnellimbiss

Einkaufsgewohnheiten

Luxemburg

Video-Treff: **Was ich gern esse und trinke**

Lesen: **Robert Kalina und der Euro**

Vorschau

Im Gasthaus

Beverly Harpers Nichte Shauna ist Austauschschülerin und wohnt bei Zieglers. Shauna und Nina stehen vor einem Gasthaus und schauen sich die Speisekarte an, die außen in einem kleinen Kasten hängt.

SHAUNA: Ich habe Lust auf etwas typisch Deutsches. Hier, Sauerbraten mit Rotkohl und Kartoffelknödeln. Das bestelle ich.

NINA: Gut, dann gehen wir hinein.

SHAUNA: Du, das ist ja ganz voll. Da ist kein einziger Tisch mehr frei.

NINA: Bei dem Ehepaar dort mit dem kleinen Jungen und dem Hund sind noch zwei freie Plätze.

SHAUNA: Kennst du die Leute?

NINA: Nein, aber das macht doch nichts. Komm, sonst setzt sich jemand anders dorthin. – Entschuldigung, sind diese beiden Plätze noch frei?

HERR: Ja, bitte, setzen Sie sich nur zu uns. Unser Hund tut Ihnen nichts.

FRAU: Hier ist auch gleich die Speisekarte. Dann können Sie sich schon etwas Gutes aussuchen, bis der Kellner kommt.

Im Supermarkt

Nach dem Essen müssen Nina und Shauna noch ein paar Lebensmittel kaufen.

NINA: Hol doch mal einen von den Einkaufswagen, die dort drüben stehen. *(Liest ihre Einkaufsliste)* Milch, Kartoffeln, Kopfsalat, Tomaten.

SHAUNA: Warum hast du eigentlich diese Einkaufstasche mitgebracht, Nina?

NINA: Weil ich nicht für eine Plastiktasche bezahlen will.

SHAUNA: Was?! Ihr müsst für die Plastiktaschen bezahlen?

NINA: Klar. Die Plastiktaschen, die man im Supermarkt bekommt, kosten fünfzehn Cent das Stück, und diese hier kann ich immer wieder verwenden. – Hier sind die Kartoffeln, der Salat und die Tomaten. So, jetzt brauchen wir nur noch zwei Liter Milch.

SHAUNA: *(an der Kasse)* Oh, eure Kassiererinnen haben es gut, sie dürfen sitzen. – Aber warum packst du denn alles selbst ein? Bei uns macht das die Kassiererin.

NINA: Andere Länder, andere Sitten.

9-1 Richtig oder falsch? Sie hören die Gespräche auf Seite 301 und nach jedem Gespräch ein paar Aussagen. Sind diese Aussagen **richtig** oder **falsch?**

IM GASTHAUS

	RICHTIG	FALSCH		RICHTIG	FALSCH
1.	_____	_____	3.	_____	_____
2.	_____	_____	4.	_____	_____

IM SUPERMARKT

	RICHTIG	FALSCH		RICHTIG	FALSCH
1.	_____	_____	3.	_____	_____
2.	_____	_____	4.	_____	_____

9-2 Im Gasthaus. Lesen Sie die folgenden Sätze in der richtigen Reihenfolge.

_____ Aber Nina sieht zwei freie Plätze und fragt, ob sie sich da hinsetzen dürfen.

_____ Weil Shauna Lust auf etwas typisch Deutsches hat und weil es hier Sauerbraten gibt, gehen sie hinein.

_____ Bevor Nina und Shauna in das Gasthaus gehen, schauen sie sich die Speisekarte an, die außen in einem kleinen Kasten hängt.

_____ Weil kein einziger Tisch mehr frei ist, will Shauna gleich wieder gehen.

9-3 Im Supermarkt. Was passt zusammen?

while   1. Während° Shauna den Einkaufswagen holt,
2. Weil Nina kein Geld für eine Plastiktasche ausgeben will,
3. Weil deutsche Kassiererinnen sitzen dürfen,
customers   4. Weil deutsche Kassiererinnen für die Kunden° nichts einpacken,

a. muss Nina das selbst tun.
b. haben sie es besser als ihre Kolleginnen in Amerika.
c. hat sie eine Einkaufstasche mitgebracht.
d. liest Nina ihre Einkaufsliste.

9-4 Andere Länder, andere Sitten. Finden Sie heraus, wer von Ihren Mitstudenten aus einem anderen Land (einem anderen Staat, einer anderen Provinz) kommt, oder wer schon mal eine Reise in ein anderes Land (einen anderen Staat, eine andere Provinz) gemacht hat. Stellen Sie dann passende Fragen.

STUDENTEN, DIE NICHT VON HIER SIND

- Woher bist du?
- Seit wann bist du hier?
- Was ist hier anders als zu Hause?
- Was gefällt dir hier besonders gut (nicht so gut)?
- Was hat dir zu Hause besser gefallen?

STUDENTEN, DIE EINE REISE GEMACHT HABEN

- Wo warst du?
- Wann war das?
- Wie lange warst du dort?
- Was war dort anders als hier?
- Was hat dir dort besonders gut (nicht so gut) gefallen?

Kultur. Dining photo: The photo shows how people in the German-speaking countries hold silverware when eating. Between bites the lower arms (just above the wrist) rest on the table.

KULTUR

WWW **Whet your appetite at a German Gasthaus at** www.prenhall.com/treffpunkt
→ Kapitel 9 → Web Resources
→ Kultur

Im Gasthaus

In den deutschsprachigen Ländern ist die Gastronomie sehr international und die Gasthäuser gehören oft Italienern, Griechen, Türken und vielen anderen Nationalitäten. Bevor man in ein Gasthaus hineingeht, kann man sich die Speisekarte anschauen, die außen in einem kleinen Kasten hängt.

Eiswasser bekommt man im Gasthaus fast nie und auch Softdrinks trinkt man fast nie mit Eis. Wenn man Wasser trinken will, bestellt man Mineralwasser und bezahlt etwa € 1,50 für ein Glas oder ein kleines Fläschchen. Auch Brötchen und Butter muss man oft extra bestellen und bezahlen. Eine Tasse Kaffee kostet etwa € 2,00 und wenn sie leer ist, füllt der Kellner sie nicht nach[1]. Wenn man mehr als nur eine Tasse Kaffee trinken will, bestellt man für etwa € 3,50 ein Kännchen (das sind zwei bis zweieinhalb Tassen). Die Preise sind alle inklusive Bedienungsgeld[2]. Wenn man die Rechnung[3] bezahlt, gibt man aber trotzdem noch etwa 10 Prozent Trinkgeld[4].

Bevor man in den deutschsprachigen Ländern zu essen beginnt, sagt man meistens „Guten Appetit!" Beim Essen hat man das Messer[5] immer in der rechten und die Gabel[6] in der linken Hand und es gilt[7] als unkultiviert, das Messer auf den Tisch und eine Hand in den Schoß[8] zu legen.

[1] **füllt nach:** *refills*   [2] *service charge*   [3] *bill*   [4] *tip*
[5] *knife*   [6] *fork*   [7] *is considered*   [8] *lap*

9-5 Aus dem Kochbuch. Lesen Sie das Rezept für die Apfelringe in Bierteig. Das nächste Mal, wenn Sie Gäste einladen, können Sie ihnen diese Apfelringe servieren.

Versuchen Sie, die englischen Äquivalente für die folgenden Wörter und Ausdrücke zu erraten°.   *guess*

EL (Esslöffel)	_____
TL (Teelöffel)	_____
Zucker und Zimt	_____
Mehl	_____
mit Zucker bestreuen	_____
mit Rum beträufeln	_____
Eiweiß steif schlagen	_____
in den Teig eintauchen	_____

(200 Gramm = ca. 1 ⅓ cups; ¼ Liter = ca. 1 cup)

Apfelringe in Bierteig

5 bis 6 Äpfel
ein bisschen Zucker
3 EL Rum

3 EL Zucker und Zimt

Teig: 200 Gr. Mehl
3 EL Zucker
¼ L helles Bier
2 TL Öl
2 Eiweiß

Die Äpfel in dicke Ringe schneiden. Die Ringe mit Zucker bestreuen und mit Rum beträufeln.

Aus Mehl, Zucker, Bier und Öl einen dünnen Teig machen. Eiweiß steif schlagen und in den Teig geben.

Die Apfelringe in den Teig eintauchen und in sehr heißem Fett auf beiden Seiten hellgelb backen. Mit Zucker und Zimt bestreuen und mit Vanillesoße oder Vanilleeis servieren.

Nomen

das Gasthaus, ¨er	restaurant
der Kellner, -	server, waiter
die Kellnerin, -nen	server, waitress
die Rechnung, -en	bill
die Speisekarte, -n	menu
das Trinkgeld, -er	tip

The form **Speisenkarte** is also very common.

die Einkaufsliste, -n	shopping list
die Einkaufstasche, -n	shopping bag
der Einkaufswagen, -	shopping cart
die Kasse, -n	checkout
der Kassierer, -	} cashier
die Kassiererin, -nen	
die Lebensmittel *(pl)*	food; groceries

If **Mittel** are *resources* or *means*, what is the literal meaning of **Lebensmittel?**

das Geschirr *(sing)*	dishes
das Glas, ¨er	glass
die Kaffeekanne, -n	coffeepot
die Pfanne, -n	pan
die Schüssel, -n	bowl
die Tasse, -n	cup
die Untertasse, -n	saucer
die Teekanne, -n	teapot
der Teller, -	plate
der Topf, ¨e	pot

das Besteck	cutlery, silverware
die Gabel, -n	fork
der Löffel, -	spoon

der Esslöffel, -	tablespoon
der Teelöffel, -	teaspoon
das Messer, -	knife
die Serviette, -n	napkin, serviette

der Braten, -	roast
der Knödel, -	dumpling
das Mehl	flour
das Rezept, -e	recipe
die Soße, -n	sauce
der Teig	dough; batter

Can you guess the English cognate for **Mehl?** Hint: You can use it to complete the following words: *corn____; ____y potatoes.*

der Austauschschüler, -	} exchange student *(high school)*
die Austauschschülerin, -nen	
das Ehepaar, -e	married couple
der Platz, ¨e	place; seat

Verben

aus·suchen	to choose; to pick out
bedienen	to serve *(guests in a restaurant)*
bestellen	to order
holen	to get; to fetch
verwenden	to use

bedienen: Note the difference between **bedienen** *to serve guests in a restaurant* and **servieren** *to serve a dish.*

Andere Wörter

deutschsprachig	German-speaking
einzig	single; only
steif	stiff

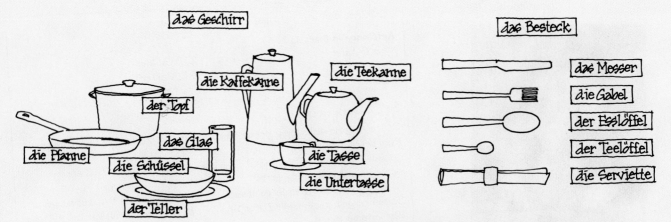

das Geschirr — die Kaffeekanne — die Teekanne — der Topf — das Glas — die Tasse — die Pfanne — die Schüssel — die Untertasse — der Teller

das Besteck — das Messer — die Gabel — der Esslöffel — der Teelöffel — die Serviette

Parents often admonish small children with the saying **Messer, Gabel, Schere** (*scissors*), **Licht** (i.e., *matches*), **sind für kleine Kinder nicht.**

Ausdrücke

dort drüben	over there
immer wieder	again and again
jemand anders	someone else
Das macht doch nichts.	That doesn't matter.
Er tut dir nichts.	He won't hurt you.
Guten Appetit!	Enjoy your meal!

Das Gegenteil

füllen ≠ leeren	to fill ≠ to empty
außen ≠ innen	outside ≠ inside

Leicht zu verstehen

die Gastronomie	der Rum
das Gramm	der Softdrink, -s
der Liter, -	servieren
das Plastik	international

füllen, bestellen: For these verbs the prefix nach is the equivalent of the English prefix re-: nachbestellen *to reorder*, nachfüllen *to refill*.

Wörter im Kontext

9-6 Was brauche ich? Beginnen Sie alle Antworten mit „Ich brauche …"

1. Ich möchte nicht vergessen, was ich im Supermarkt alles kaufen soll.
2. Ich bin im Supermarkt und möchte die Sachen, die ich kaufe, nicht tragen.
3. Ich bin im Gasthaus und möchte etwas zu essen bestellen.
4. Ich möchte die Suppe essen, die der Kellner mir gebracht hat.
5. Ich möchte wissen, wie man Apfelringe in Bierteig macht.
6. Ich will die Apfelringe jetzt backen.
7. Ich möchte das Sauerkraut, das ich gekocht habe, nicht im Topf auf den Tisch stellen.
8. Ich möchte mein Steak essen.

Kellner: Originally, each Wirtshaus had its own Weinkeller. Among his other duties, the Kellner had to go to the Keller to get wine for his guests. Hence his name.

eine Schüssel	eine Einkaufsliste
eine Pfanne	eine Speisekarte
ein Rezept	einen Einkaufswagen
einen Löffel	ein Messer und eine Gabel

9-7 Was passt in jeder Gruppe zusammen?

1. der Softdrink	a. der Kellner	5. das Trinkgeld	e. servieren
2. die Pfanne	b. die Lebensmittel	6. das Essen	f. geben
3. das Gasthaus	c. das Glas	7. die Gäste	g. füllen
4. der Supermarkt	d. das Steak	8. die Gläser	h. bedienen

Other words for Gasthaus are die Gaststätte, das Wirtshaus, das Restaurant, die Raststätte (on the Autobahn).

9-8 Was ist hier identisch? Welche zwei Sätze in jeder Gruppe bedeuten etwa dasselbe?

1. Das mag ich.
   Das ist lecker.
   Guten Appetit!

2. Der Hund tut dir nichts.
   Der Hund tut mir leid.
   Der Hund beißt nicht.

3. Diese Jacke gehört mir.
   Diese Jacke gehört jemand anders.
   Diese Jacke gehört mir nicht.

4. Kein einziger von meinen Freunden war da.
   Keiner von meinen Freunden war da.
   Nur ein einziger von meinen Freunden war da.

Kommunikation und Formen

❶ Describing people, places, and things

Relative clauses and relative pronouns

Like adjectives, relative clauses are used to describe people, places, and things.

	ADJECTIVE	NOUN	
This	*expensive*	wine	is not very good.

	NOUN	RELATIVE CLAUSE	
The	wine	*that cost you so much*	is not very good.

Relative clauses are introduced by relative pronouns. A relative pronoun refers back to a noun, which is called its *antecedent.*

	RELATIVE CLAUSE		
ANTECEDENT	RELATIVE PRONOUN		
The wine	*that*	*you bought*	is not very good.
The friend	*to whom*	*you want to give it*	is a wine connoisseur.

Relative clauses and relative pronouns in German

	RELATIVE CLAUSE		
ANTECEDENT	REL. PRON.		
Der Wein,	**der**	**dich so viel gekostet hat,**	ist nicht sehr gut.
Der Wein,	**den**	**du gekauft hast,**	ist nicht sehr gut.
Der Freund,	**dem**	**du ihn schenken willst,**	ist ein Weinkenner.
Die Freunde,	**die**	**uns eingeladen haben,**	sind Weinkenner.

The relative pronoun has the same *gender* (masculine, neuter, or feminine) and *number* (singular or plural) as its antecedent. Its *case* (nominative, accusative, or dative) is determined by its function within the relative clause.

> Der Wein, **den** du gekauft hast, ist nicht sehr gut.
>
> *The wine **that** you bought is not very good.*

The relative pronoun **den,** like its antecedent **Wein,** is masculine and singular. It is in the accusative case because it is the direct object of the verb within the relative clause.

Note:

- Relative clauses are dependent clauses. They are marked off by commas, and the conjugated verb appears at the end of the clause.
- In contrast to English, the German relative pronoun can never be omitted.

> Der Wein, **den** du gekauft hast, ist nicht sehr gut.
>
> *The wine you bought is not very good.*

EUROCARD.
Für Leute, die auch sonst gute Karten haben.

EUROCARD   MasterCard

Lerntipp: The graphic below may help you remember how to determine the gender, number, and case of a relative pronoun.

antecedent   *rel. clause*

m., n., or f.   nom., acc., or dat.

rel. pron.

sing. or pl.

---

forms of the relative pronoun				
	MASCULINE	NEUTER	FEMININE	PLURAL
NOMINATIVE	der	das	die	die
ACCUSATIVE	den	das	die	die
DATIVE	dem	dem	der	**denen**

Note that except for **denen,** the forms in the chart are identical to those of the definite article.

> Die Freunde, **denen** ich den Wein schenken will, sind Weinkenner.

> *The friends **to whom** I want to give the wine are wine connoisseurs.*

9-9 Der erste Tag. Heute ist Ihr erster Tag als Kellnerin/Kellner und Sie sind oft noch ein bisschen verwirrt°. Ergänzen Sie die Relativpronomen.

confused

1. Wo ist denn der Mann, d__ dieses Bier bestellt hat?
2. Wo ist denn das Ehepaar, d__ dieses Gulasch bestellt hat?
3. Wo ist denn die Frau, d__ diese Tasse Kaffee bestellt hat?
4. Wo sind denn die Leute, d__ diese Suppe bestellt haben?

5. Wo ist denn der Mann, d__ ich so schnell bedienen soll?
6. Wo ist denn das Ehepaar, d__ ich so schnell bedienen soll?
7. Wo ist denn die Frau, d__ ich so schnell bedienen soll?
8. Wo sind denn die Leute, d__ ich so schnell bedienen soll?

9. Wo ist denn der Mann, d__ ich dieses Schnitzel bringen soll?
10. Wo ist denn das Ehepaar, d__ ich diesen Rotwein bringen soll?
11. Wo ist denn die Frau, d__ ich die Speisekarte bringen soll?
12. Wo sind denn die Leute, d__ ich diesen Nachtisch bringen soll?

9-10 Wer ist das? Was für Leute gehören zu den Namensschildern° an diesem Mietshaus°? Die Information für **S2** ist im *Anhang* auf Seite A12.

name plates
apartment building

S1: Wer ist denn dieser Ergül Ertem?

S2: Wer sind denn diese Paul und Lisa Borg?

S2: Das ist der Mann, dem der Schnellimbiss beim Bahnhof gehört.

S1: Das sind die Leute, …

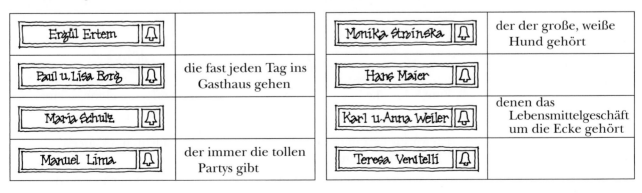

Ergül Ertem 🔔	
Paul u. Lisa Borg 🔔	die fast jeden Tag ins Gasthaus gehen
Maria Schulz 🔔	
Manuel Lima 🔔	der immer die tollen Partys gibt

Monika Stroinska 🔔	der der große, weiße Hund gehört
Hans Maier 🔔	
Karl u. Anna Weiler 🔔	denen das Lebensmittelgeschäft um die Ecke gehört
Teresa Venitelli 🔔	

9-11 Definitionen.

▶ Eine Ärztin ist eine Frau, …

die kranke Menschen wieder gesund macht.

Eine Ärztin ist eine Frau, die kranke Menschen wieder gesund macht.

1. Ein Kellner ist ein Mann, …

3. Ein Automechaniker ist ein Handwerker, …

2. Ein Psychiater ist ein Arzt, …

4. Eine Marktfrau ist eine Frau, …

den man braucht, wenn das Auto kaputt ist.	die auf dem Wochenmarkt Obst und Gemüse verkauft.
der im Gasthaus das Essen serviert.	dem man alles erzählen kann.

bird 5. Eine Fleischerei ist ein Geschäft, …

7. Ein Huhn ist ein Vogel° (m), …

6. Eine Schnecke ist ein Tier (n), …

8. Eine Kaffeemaschine ist eine Maschine, …

den wir für Eier und für Fleisch brauchen.	die man braucht, um Kaffee zu machen.
das Fleisch und Wurst verkauft.	das man in Frankreich gern isst.

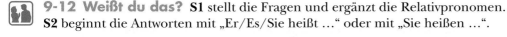

9-12 Weißt du das? **S1** stellt die Fragen und ergänzt die Relativpronomen. **S2** beginnt die Antworten mit „Er/Es/Sie heißt ..." oder mit „Sie heißen ...".

1. Wie heißt der Fluss, d__ bei New Orleans in den Golf von Mexiko fließt°?   *flows*
2. Wie heißt das berühmte Schiff, d__ auf einen Eisberg gefahren und gesunken ist?
3. Wie heißt die europäische Hauptstadt, d__ an der Themse liegt?
4. Wie heißen die Wasserfälle, d__ zwischen dem Eriesee und dem Ontariosee liegen?
5. Wie heißt der Turm° in Paris, d__ der Ingenieur Gustave Eiffel gebaut hat?   *tower*
6. Wie heißt das berühmteste Schloss, d__ König Ludwig II. gebaut hat?
7. Wie heißt die Statue im Hafen° von New York, d__ Frankreich 1886 den USA geschenkt hat?   *harbor*
8. Wie heißt der Mann, d__ viele Millionen Anteile° von Microsoft gehören?   *shares*
9. Wie heißt die Königin, d__ in England sehr viel Land und ein paar Schlösser gehören?

② *N-nouns*

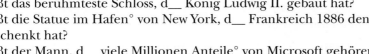

N-nouns are a group of masculine nouns that take the ending **-n** or **-en** in all cases except the nominative singular.

	singular	plural
NOMINATIVE	der Student	die Studenten
ACCUSATIVE	den Studenten	die Studenten
DATIVE	dem Studenten	den Studenten
GENITIVE	des Studenten	der Studenten

Most German dictionaries show the nominative singular of a noun followed by any changes that occur in the genitive singular and in the plural.

nominative singular	genitive singular	plural
der Mann	-es	⸚er
die Frau	-	-en

This convention clearly identifies **n**-nouns: If the genitive singular ending is **-en** or **-n**, the noun is an **n**-noun.

nominative singular	genitive singular	plural
der Student	**-en**	**-en**
der Kunde	**-n**	**-n**

Some common **n**-nouns:

der **Bär**, -en, -en	der **Junge**, -n -n	der **Patient**, -en, -en
der **Elefant**, -en, -en	der **Kollege**, -n, -n	der **Polizist**, -en, -en
der **Hase**, -n, -n	der **Kunde**, -n, -n	der **Präsident**, -en, -en
der **Athlet**, -en, -en	der **Mensch**, -en, -en	der **Tourist**, -en, -en
der **Herr**, -n, -en	der **Nachbar**, -n, -n	

Note that the singular forms of **Herr** end in **-n** (except for the nominative), while the plural forms end in **-en.**

9-13 Kleine Gespräche. Ergänzen Sie die Endungen. Nicht alle Nomen brauchen eine Endung.

1. PROFESSOR: Warum soll ich denn mit meinen Student__ nicht mehr Fußball spielen?
   ARZT: Weil Sie eben kein junger Athlet__ mehr sind.

2. DR. JOOS: Wer war denn dieser Patient__?
   DR. HERZ: Das war der Professor, der mit seinen Student__ so gern Fußball gespielt hat.

3. FRAU KRÜGER: Kennen Sie unseren neuen Nachbar__?
   FRAU SCHLICK: Ja, er ist ein Kollege__ von meinem Mann.

strange 4. FRAU SCHLICK: Sehen Sie den seltsamen° Herr__ dort drüben? Er war gestern auch schon hier.
   HERR ÖZDEMIR: Aber Frau Schlick. Das ist doch nur ein harmloser Tourist__.

5. HERR HOLZER: Was denken Sie von diesem Präsident__?
   HERR SILVA: Er ist eben auch nur ein Mensch__.

9-14 Was ist das? Achtung: Die Nase eines Elefanten heißt Rüssel, die Füße eines Bären heißen Pfoten und ein Kamel hat zwei Höcker auf dem Rücken.

▶

die Ohren / ein Hase

S1: Weißt du, was das ist?   **S2:** Das sind die Ohren eines Hasen.

1.   2.   3.   4.

das Dach / ein Haus	der Henkel / eine Tasse
der Rüssel / ein Elefant	die Pfoten / ein Bär

5.   6.   7.   8.

der Hals / eine Giraffe	der Bizeps / ein Athlet
der Hals / eine Flasche	die Höcker / ein Kamel

■ Hören ···

Wandern macht hungrig

Martin und Peter sind übers Wochenende in die Alpen gefahren, sind seit dem frühen Morgen gewandert und sitzen jetzt im Gasthof Fraundorfer in Garmisch-Partenkirchen. Hören Sie, was Peter, Martin und der Kellner miteinander sprechen.

NEUE VOKABELN

Kassler	*smoked pork chop*	**Die Kartoffeln sind nicht gar.**	*The potatoes are not done.*
Alles in Ordnung?	*Is everything OK?*	**getrennt**	*separate*
		Schon gut.	*It's all right.*

9-15 Erstes Verstehen. In welcher Reihenfolge hören Sie das?

_____ Alles in Ordnung, meine Herren?

_____ Sollen wir etwas sagen?

_____ Die Speisekarte, bitte.

_____ Möchten Sie vielleicht ein paar Knödel?

_____ Machen Sie's sechsundzwanzig Euro.

_____ Du, was machen wir denn nach dem Essen?

_____ Und zu trinken?

9-16 Detailverstehen. Hören Sie das Gespräch noch einmal und schreiben Sie Antworten zu den folgenden Fragen.

1. Warum essen Martin und Peter beide Kassler?
2. Was trinken die beiden?
3. Was machen Martin und Peter nach dem Essen?
4. Was ist mit den Kartoffeln, die der Kellner gebracht hat, nicht in Ordnung?
5. Warum will Peter nichts sagen?
6. Wie viel kostet alles zusammen und auf wie viel rundet Peter auf?

More on restaurant etiquette: In the German-speaking countries, customers often pay the server directly at the table, especially in a pub when only drinks are ordered. The server carries a special purse from which to give change. Leaving money on the table for the bill or a tip is not a common practice.

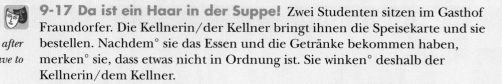

after
notice / wave to

WAS ALLES NICHT IN ORDNUNG
SEIN KÖNNTE

- Da ist ein Haar in der Suppe.
- Die Suppe (die Soße, das Gemüse) ist versalzen°.
- Das Bier (der Weißwein) ist zu warm.
- Der Kaffee (der Tee) ist ganz kalt.
- Da ist Lippenstift an der Tasse.
- Diese Gabel (dieser Löffel, dieses Messer) ist nicht sauber.
  …

too salty

WIE DER KELLNER/DIE KELLNERIN
REAGIEREN KÖNNTE

- Das tut mir aber leid!
- Das ist doch nicht möglich!
- Ich bringe Ihnen gleich ein__ …
- Möchten Sie vielleicht etwas anderes bestellen?
- Soll ich Ihnen die Speisekarte noch einmal bringen?
  …

Tagesmenü: Note that **Menü** and *menu* are not equivalents. How would you translate **Tagesmenü?**

In restaurants beverages are served in glasses with a line and number **(der Eichstrich)** showing how much liquid is in the glass (0,2 l; 0,25 l; 0,33 l). In a glass of beer, the foam starts at this line.

SPEISEKARTE

TAGESMENÜ I	€ 12,20
Tagessuppe	
Wiener Schnitzel mit Kartoffelsalat	
Vanilleeis	
TAGESMENÜ II	€ 12,70
Tagessuppe	
Sauerbraten mit Kartoffelpüree und Salat	
Vanilleeis	

SUPPEN

Tagessuppe	€ 2,00
Nudelsuppe	€ 2,60

HAUPTGERICHTE

1. Bratwurst mit Sauerkraut und Bratkartoffeln	€ 8,50
2. Ungarisches Gulasch, Eiernudeln und gemischter Salat	€ 9,00
3. Schweinebraten mit Rotkraut und Salzkartoffeln	€ 9,50
4. Hühnchen mit Weinsoße, Reis und Tomatensalat	€ 10,00
5. Filetsteak gegrillt mit Champignons, Pommes frites und Gurkensalat	€ 14,60

ZUM NACHTISCH

Schokoladenpudding	€ 1,50
Fruchtsalat mit frischen Früchten	€ 3,00
Apfelstrudel	€ 4,00
Schwarzwälder Kirschtorte	€ 4,00

GETRÄNKE

Cola (0,2 l)	€ 1,60
Apfelsaft (0,2 l)	€ 1,80
Kaffee, Tasse	€ 1,80
Kaffee, Kännchen	€ 3,50
Tee, Kännchen	€ 3,00
Bier, vom Fass (0,33 l)	€ 2,00
Weißwein, Mosel (0,2 l)	€ 3,50
Rotwein, Lemberger (0,2 l)	€ 3,50

9-18 Essen Sie gern international? Was für ethnische Restaurants gibt es in Ihrer Nähe? Welche sind die besten? Warum essen Sie dort so gern?

Ich esse gern   chinesisch   deutsch   französisch
                 griechisch   indisch   italienisch
                 japanisch   mexikanisch   …

Das beste chinesische (deutsche usw.) Restaurant in meiner Nähe heißt …
Ich esse dort so gern, weil …

- der Nachtisch so gut ist.
- alles immer so frisch ist.
- das Essen so billig ist.
- ich scharfe° Sachen mag.

- der Koch mit viel Fantasie kocht.
- die Portionen so groß sind.
- die Bedienung so freundlich ist.
- …

spicy

INFOBOX

Beim Schnellimbiss

Für Leute, die wenig Zeit haben, gibt es verschiedene Möglichkeiten, schnell im Stehen etwas zu essen:

- Würstchenstände verkaufen Bockwurst, Knackwurst oder Currywurst mit Senf[1] und Brötchen,
- beim Schnellimbiss gibt es außer Wurst mit Brötchen auch noch Hamburger und heiße Gulaschsuppe,
- beim Kebabstand kaufen nicht nur türkische Mitbürger[2] ihren Döner Kebab, sondern auch viele Deutsche. Für Vegetarier gibt es hier auch oft Falafel oder türkische Pizza.

Wenn man lieber sitzen möchte, geht man in eine der vielen Pizzerias, zu McDonald's oder Burger King, oder wenn man gern Fisch isst, zu Nordsee.

[1]*mustard*   [2]*fellow citizens*

Discover what's different about a German McDonald's at www.prenhall.com/treffpunkt
→ Kapitel 9 → Web Resources → Kultur

Ein Berliner Schnellimbiss

...wer sich gut anzieht, zieht andere an!

❸ Talking about actions one does to or for oneself

Reflexive pronouns

To express the idea that one does an action *to oneself* or *for oneself*, English and German use reflexive pronouns. In German the reflexive pronoun can be in the accusative or the dative case, depending on its function.

ACCUSATIVE:	Ich habe **mich** geschnitten.	*I cut **myself**.*
DATIVE:	Ich hole **mir** ein Pflaster.	*I'm getting **myself** a Band-Aid.*

Reflexive pronouns in the accusative case

Ich habe **mich** geschnitten.	*I cut myself.*
Tina hat **sich** geschnitten.	*Tina cut herself.*
Haben **Sie sich** geschnitten?	*Did you cut yourself?*

The accusative reflexive pronoun differs from the accusative personal pronoun only in the 3rd person singular and plural and in the **Sie**-form, where it is **sich.** Note that in the **Sie**-form **sich** is not capitalized.

personal pronouns		reflexive pronouns
NOMINATIVE	ACCUSATIVE	ACCUSATIVE
ich	mich	**mich**
du	dich	**dich**
er	ihn	
es	es	*sich*
sie	sie	
wir	uns	**uns**
ihr	euch	**euch**
sie	sie	*sich*
Sie	Sie	*sich*

Reflexive pronouns are used much more frequently in German than in English. Compare the following examples, where the English equivalents do not use reflexive pronouns at all.

Ich habe **mich** noch nicht rasiert.	*I haven't shaved yet.*
Kurt muss **sich** noch duschen.	*Kurt still has to shower.*

If a sentence starts with the subject, the reflexive pronoun follows the conjugated verb directly.

Holger hat **sich** heute nicht rasiert.	*Holger didn't shave today.*

In sentences and clauses that do not begin with the subject, the reflexive pronoun usually precedes noun subjects, but *always* follows pronoun subjects.

Warum hat **sich Holger** denn nicht rasiert?

Why didn't Holger shave?

Ich verstehe nicht, warum **er sich** nicht rasiert hat.

I don't understand why he didn't shave.

Below are some verbs that use reflexive pronouns in the accusative case. Note that the infinitive forms are preceded by **sich.**

sich waschen	*to wash*	**sich schminken**	*to put on makeup*
sich baden	*to take a bath*	**sich anziehen**	*to get dressed*
sich duschen	*to take a shower*	**sich ausziehen**	*to get undressed*
sich kämmen	*to comb one's hair*	**sich umziehen**	*to change (one's clothes)*
sich rasieren	*to shave*		

Lerntipp: To help you remember that these verbs are reflexive, you should always learn them together with the reflexive pronoun, e.g., *sich* **waschen.**

9-19 Was macht Otilia um sieben Uhr zehn? Die Information für **S2** ist im *Anhang* auf Seite A12.

S1: Was macht Otilia um sieben Uhr zehn? **S2:** Sie schminkt sich.

	OTILIA	BERND	MORITZ UND JENS
7.10		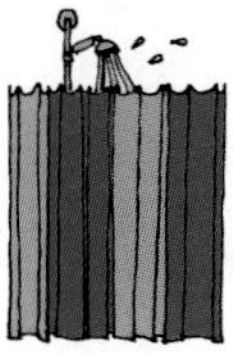 Er duscht sich.	
7.25	 Sie kämmt sich.		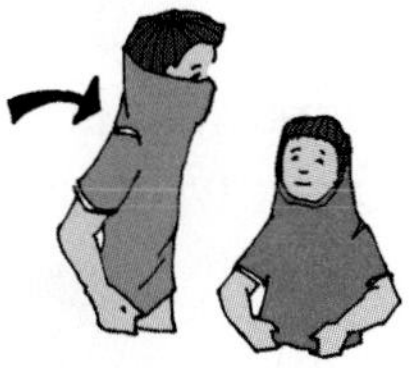 Sie ziehen sich an.
20.30	 Sie zieht sich um.		

9-20 Kannst du nicht ein bisschen schneller machen?

▶

FRANK: Warum duschst du dich nicht endlich?

BERND: Ich muss mich doch erst rasieren.

1.

2.

3.

9-21 Wir sind schneller, als du denkst!

▶

MUTTER: Warum duscht ihr euch nicht endlich?

KINDER: Wir haben uns doch schon geduscht.

1.

2.

3.

4.

5.

6.

9-22 Was ich alles mache, bevor ich zur Uni gehe.
Verwenden Sie so viele reflexive Verben wie möglich.

Ich stehe meistens um _____ auf. Vor dem Frühstück … Nach dem
Frühstück …

joggen gehen
sich duschen/baden
sich anziehen
frühstücken
CNN anschauen
schnell meine Hausaufgaben
machen
nach E-Mails schauen

sich rasieren
sich schminken
sich kämmen
Radio hören
mein Bett machen
meine Freundin/
meinen Freund anrufen
…

9-23 Bevor ich zur Uni gehe, … Erzählen Sie Ihren
Mitstudenten, was Sie alles machen, bevor Sie zur Uni gehen.

Reflexive pronouns in the dative case

In the examples below, the reflexive pronouns are indirect objects and are
therefore in the dative case.

> **Ich** kaufe **mir** ein neues Kochbuch
> zum Geburtstag.

> *I'm going to buy **myself** a new
> cookbook for my birthday.*

Note the difference in the way German and English refer to actions that involve
one's own body.

> **Oliver** wäscht **sich** jeden Tag
> **die** Haare.

> *Oliver washes **his** hair every day.*

Where English uses the possessive adjective (*his hair*), German uses the dative
reflexive pronoun and the definite article (**sich die Haare**).

The dative reflexive pronoun differs from the dative personal pronoun only in
the 3rd person singular and plural and in the **Sie**-form, where it is **sich**.

personal pronouns		reflexive pronouns
NOMINATIVE	DATIVE	DATIVE
ich	mir	**mir**
du	dir	**dir**
er	ihm	
es	ihm	*sich*
sie	ihr	
wir	uns	**uns**
ihr	euch	**euch**
sie	ihnen	*sich*
Sie	Ihnen	*sich*

9-24 Was machen diese Leute?

▶ Anita  sich die Haare bürsten

Anita bürstet sich die Haare.

1. Peter

2. Stephanie

3. ich

4. wir

5. ich

6. Martin und Claudia

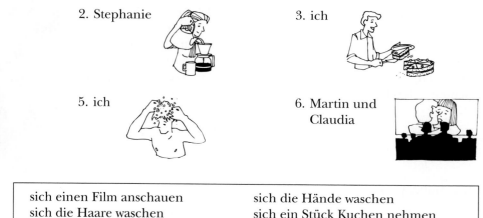

sich einen Film anschauen	sich die Hände waschen
sich die Haare waschen	sich ein Stück Kuchen nehmen
sich eine Tasse Kaffee machen	sich die Zähne putzen

9-25 Kleine Gespräche. Ergänzen Sie die Reflexivpronomen.

1. CLAUDIA: Warum nimmst du _____ nicht ein Stück von meinem Kuchen, bevor du ins Bett gehst?

   STEPHANIE: Weil ich _____ die Zähne schon geputzt habe.

2. CLAUDIA: Warum sucht ihr _____ denn kein größeres Zimmer?

   MARTIN: Weil wir _____ nichts mehr zu essen kaufen können, wenn wir noch mehr Miete zahlen müssen.

3. HERR KOCH: Warum kaufen _____ Müllers denn keinen zweiten Wagen?

   FRAU KOCH: Ich glaube, sie wollen _____ zuerst ein Haus kaufen.

4. FRAU HAAG: Warum soll ich _____ denn einen DVD-Spieler kaufen?

   HERR MERZ: Weil Sie _____ dann zu Hause Filme anschauen können.

9-26 Was kaufst du dir mit diesem Geld? Sie haben 500 Dollar gewonnen und sollen sich damit drei Dinge kaufen. Fragen Sie einander, wie Sie das Geld ausgeben wollen. Berichten Sie, was Sie herausgefunden haben.

S1: Was kaufst du dir zuerst?

Was kaufst du dir dann?
Und was kaufst du dir zuletzt?

S2: Zuerst kaufe ich mir für etwa _____ Dollar …
Dann kaufe ich mir für …
Zuletzt kaufe ich mir für …

S1: Zuerst kauft sich Lisa/David für etwa _____ Dollar …
Dann kauft sie/er sich für etwa _____ Dollar …
Und zuletzt kauft sie/er sich für etwa _____ Dollar …

9-27 Wir machen Marktforschung°. Stellen Sie einander Fragen über   *market research*
Ihre Lieblingsprodukte.

1. Wie oft wäschst du dir die Haare?
2. Mit was für einem Shampoo wäschst du dir die Haare?
3. Wie oft am Tag putzt du dir die Zähne?
4. Mit was für einer Zahnpasta putzt du dir die Zähne?
5. Färbst du dir die Haare? Wenn ja, mit was für einem Produkt?
6. Wie oft rasierst du dich?
7. Mit was für einem Rasierapparat rasierst du dich?
8. Verwendest du Rasierwasser°, nachdem du dich rasiert hast? Wenn ja,   *aftershave*
   welches Produkt verwendest du?
9. Verwendest du Seife° oder ein Dusch- und Badegel, wenn du dich duschst   *soap*
   oder badest? Welches Produkt verwendest du?
10. Schminkst du dich? Wenn ja, was sind deine Lieblingsprodukte?

Reflexive pronouns used to express *each other*

In German you can use the plural reflexive pronoun as a reciprocal pronoun
meaning *each other*. Note that the pronoun is not always expressed in English.

Wie habt ihr **euch** kennen gelernt?   *How did you get to know **each other?***
Wo sollen wir **uns** treffen?   *Where should we meet?*

9-28 Was passt zusammen? Ergänzen Sie die Reflexivpronomen in den
Fragen und beantworten Sie die Fragen. Ein paar Antworten passen mehr als
einmal.

S1:   **S2:**

1. Seit wann kennen _____ Claudia   Durch Freunde.
   und Martin?   Hoffentlich sehr bald.
2. Wie haben sie _____ kennen   Um acht.
   gelernt?   Am besten wieder bei mir.
3. Wie oft rufen _____ die beiden an?   Seit einem halben Jahr.
4. Wann trefft ihr _____ heute   Fast jeden Tag.
   Abend?
5. Wo sollen wir _____ morgen
   Abend treffen?
6. Wann sehen wir _____ wieder?
7. Wie oft schreibt ihr _____ ?
8. Seit wann grüßen _____ Müllers
   und Maiers nicht mehr?

BITTE nicht so nahe!

Wir kennen uns ja kaum!

9-29 Freundschaften. Stellen Sie einander die folgenden Fragen.

Hast du eine gute Freundin/einen guten Freund?
Seit wann kennt ihr euch?
Wo und wie habt ihr euch kennen gelernt?

Reflexive verbs

Lerntipp: To help you remember that these verbs are reflexive, you should always learn them together with the reflexive pronoun, e.g., *sich verspäten.*

Many German verbs are always or almost always accompanied by a reflexive pronoun even though their English equivalents are rarely reflexive. Here are some important ones. The reflexive pronoun for these verbs is in the accusative case.

sich verspäten	*to be late*
sich beeilen	*to hurry (up)*
sich auf·regen	*to get worked up; to get upset*
sich benehmen	*to behave*
sich entschuldigen	*to apologize*
sich erkälten	*to catch a cold*
sich wohl fühlen	*to feel well*
sich setzen	*to sit down*

speech bubbles ## 9-30 Was passt in die Sprechblasen°?

1.

2.

3.

4.

Ich habe mich erkältet.   Reg dich doch nicht so auf!
Sie haben sich verspätet.   Beeil dich doch ein bisschen!

5.

6.

7.

8.

Komm, setz dich zu mir!   Du benimmst dich schlecht.
Ich fühle mich nicht wohl.   Können Sie sich nicht wenigstens
entschuldigen?

9-31 Was passt? Finden Sie zu jeder Situation die passende Reaktion.

Situationen

1. Im Gasthaus „Krone" hat der Kellner Soße auf Herrn Merkels Jacke geschüttet°. Der Kellner sagt kein Wort, sondern versucht, die Jacke mit einer Serviette sauber zu machen. Herr Merkel sagt: *spilled*
2. Monika will ausgehen und mal richtig elegant sein und holt deshalb die neue Jacke ihrer Schwester Bettina aus dem Schrank. Als° sie die Jacke anzieht, kommt Bettina plötzlich zur Tür herein. Da sagt Monika: *when*
3. Holger ist mit Anna auf einer Party. Er isst und trinkt zu viel, steht dann plötzlich auf und will gehen. Anna fragt, warum er denn schon gehen will. Holger antwortet:
4. Günter ist mit Tina auf einer Party. Er trinkt zu viel und fängt an, ziemlich laut zu werden. Tina sagt:

Reaktionen

a. Benimm dich doch nicht so schlecht!
b. Bitte, reg dich nicht auf!
c. Können Sie sich denn nicht wenigstens entschuldigen?
d. Ich fühle mich gar nicht wohl.

9-32 Was passt? Finden Sie zu jeder Situation die passende Reaktion.

Situationen

1. Frau Gürlük ist Kellnerin und liest in der Zeitung, dass das Hotel „Vier Jahreszeiten" Kellnerinnen sucht. Als sie in die Personalabteilung kommt, sagt die Personalchefin:
2. Reichmanns sind bei Frau Reichmanns Chefin zum Abendessen eingeladen. Frau Reichmann hat sich gerade fertig geschminkt, aber ihr Mann steht immer noch unter der Dusche. Frau Reichmann ruft:
3. Patrick ist gestern schwimmen gegangen, obwohl das Wasser noch eiskalt war. Heute Morgen fühlt er sich gar nicht wohl und denkt:
4. Anne fragt Eva, warum Daniel nicht in der Vorlesung war. Eva antwortet:

Reaktionen

a. Beeil dich doch bitte, Dieter! Wir dürfen uns doch nicht verspäten.
b. Ich glaube, ich habe mich gestern erkältet.
c. Guten Tag! Bitte setzen Sie sich!
d. Er ist bestimmt krank. Er hat sich gestern schon nicht wohl gefühlt.

9-33 Persönliche Fragen. Stellen Sie einander die folgenden Fragen.

- Was machst du, wenn du dich erkältet hast?

  Wenn ich mich erkältet habe, …

- In was für Situationen regst du dich auf?

  Ich rege mich auf, wenn …

- Verspätest du dich manchmal? Warum?

  Ich verspäte mich manchmal, weil …

WWW Window-shop at a German **Bäckerei** at www.prenhall.com/treffpunkt
→ Kapitel 9 → Web Resources
→ Kultur

rezeptpflichtig: You know the meaning of **Rezept.** How can you connect it to *prescription?*

INFOBOX

Einkaufsgewohnheiten[1]

In den deutschsprachigen Ländern gibt es in jeder Stadt viele Bäcker und Fleischer, obwohl man Brot, Brötchen, Fleisch und Wurst auch im Supermarkt kaufen kann. Viele Leute kaufen ihr Brot und ihre Wurst aber immer noch bei ihrem Lieblingsbäcker oder -fleischer, weil sie glauben, dass kein anderer Bäcker oder Fleischer so gut ist wie ihrer.

Reformhäuser[2] gibt es in den deutschsprachigen Ländern schon viel länger als in Nordamerika und viele Leute kaufen dort chemiefreie Lebensmittel, Vitamine und viele andere Dinge, die besonders gesund sein sollen.

Eine Drogerie ist nicht ganz dasselbe wie ein nordamerikanischer *drugstore,* denn rezeptpflichtige[3] Medikamente und sogar rezeptfreie Medikamente wie Aspirin kann man in den deutschsprachigen Ländern nur in der Apotheke kaufen.

[1]*shopping habits*   [2]*health food stores*   [3]*prescription*

Zusammenschau

🖥 ▮ Video-Treff ··

Was ich gern esse und trinke

Anja Szustak, Maiga, Thomas, Karen, Stefan Meister, Stefan Kuhlmann, Ursula und Øcsi erzählen, was sie gern essen und trinken.

Zum besseren Verstehen

9-34 Was ist das auf Englisch?

1. Mein Lieblingsgericht sind **Dampfnudeln.**
2. Am liebsten esse ich Salate mit **Putenfleisch.**
3. Ich esse lieber im Restaurant, weil ich da **bedient werde.**
4. Das ist eine **Frage des Geldes.**
5. Mir gefällt die italienische **Küche** so gut, weil sie so einfach ist.
6. Jetzt **schäle** ich die Karotten.
7. Ich werde das Gericht dann scharf **würzen.**

a. peel
b. turkey
c. dumplings
d. cuisine
e. get waited on
f. season
g. question of money

Schauen Sie jetzt das Video an und machen Sie die Übungen im *Video-Treff*-Teil des *Student Activities Manual.*

Einkaufsprobleme

Von Montag bis Freitag machen kleinere Geschäfte um 18.30 Uhr zu.
Weil Herr und Frau Ziegler erst um sieben von der Arbeit kommen und
weil Brot, Wurst, Obst und Gemüse nur wenige Tage frisch bleiben, müssen
Nina oder Robert jeden Mittwochnachmittag ein paar Einkäufe machen.
Hören Sie, was Zieglers beim Frühstück miteinander sprechen.

NEUE VOKABELN

der Fleischer	*butcher*	**Kommt gar**	*That's out of*
Heute bist	*Today it's*	**nicht in**	*the question!*
du dran.	*your turn.*	**Frage!**	
die Schinkenwurst	*ham sausage*	**genauso gut**	*just as good*
die Brezel, -n	*(soft) pretzel*	**schmecken**	*to taste*

9-35 Erstes Verstehen. Wer sagt das? Schreiben Sie HZ (Herr Ziegler),
FZ (Frau Ziegler), N (Nina) oder R (Robert).

_____ Nina! Warum kommst du denn nicht zum Frühstück?
_____ Du musst zum Supermarkt, zum Bäcker und zum Fleischer.
_____ Ich hab' doch letzten Mittwoch eingekauft.
_____ Na, dann gib mir eben die Liste.
_____ Kommt gar nicht in Frage, Nina!
_____ Im Supermarkt ist doch alles genauso gut.
_____ Ja, besonders die Brezeln.

9-36 Detailverstehen. Hören Sie das Gespräch noch einmal und
schreiben Sie Antworten zu den folgenden Fragen.

1. Warum kommt Robert ungekämmt zum Frühstück?
2. Warum will Robert heute nicht einkaufen gehen?
3. Warum will Nina alles im Supermarkt kaufen?
4. Wo soll Nina das Brot, die Brezeln und die Wurst kaufen?
5. Warum soll Nina das Brot, die Brezeln und die Wurst nicht im
   Supermarkt kaufen?
6. Was soll Nina nicht vergessen?

⬛ **Schreiben und Sprechen** ·····························

✏️ **9-37 Mein Lieblingsgericht.** Erzählen Sie von einem Gericht°, das
Ihnen das Wasser im Mund zusammenlaufen lässt.

- Wie heißt dieses Gericht und warum finden Sie es so lecker? *Weil ich gern
  scharfe / süße / saure Sachen esse. Weil ich gern Gemüse / Fleisch / Fisch / Pasta esse.*
- Kochen Sie es selbst oder essen Sie es im Restaurant / bei Ihren Eltern /
  bei Freunden / …?
- Ist das Rezept einfach oder kompliziert? Welche Zutaten° braucht man dazu?
- Was trinken Sie am liebsten dazu?

das Gericht: *dish*

ingredients

Store hours: In 1996 Germany changed
its fairly restrictive laws regarding store
hours. Before 1996 stores had to close at
6:30 p.m. from Monday to Friday and at
2 p.m. on Saturday; now they are allowed
to remain open until 8 p.m. (On Sundays
all stores are closed except flower shops
and bakeries, and these are permitted to
open for only a few hours.) The new law
was very controversial, and it is only in
larger supermarkets and department
stores that the new hours have really
taken hold. In smaller towns many stores
have gone back to the pre-1996 hours
after complaining that the longer hours
weren't drawing customers.

If you know how to cook your favorite
dish, try writing the recipe, using the
one on p. 303 as a guide.

hors d'œuvre
main course

9-38 Freunde kommen zu Besuch.
Planen Sie zusammen ein Essen für acht Personen. Machen Sie eine Einkaufsliste für eine kleine Vorspeise°, ein Hauptgericht° und einen guten Nachtisch. Vergessen Sie nicht, dass Sie auch Getränke kaufen müssen, und schreiben Sie genau auf, wie viel Gramm, Scheiben, Flaschen, Dosen, Becher, Stück oder Packungen Sie bei Bolle kaufen wollen.

9-38: 500 Gramm = approx. 1.1 lb; **1 Liter** = approx. 1 quart. Cold cuts and cheese are often priced per **100 Gramm.**

In the German-speaking countries people tend to shop for groceries more frequently than in North America. One reason for this is that they prefer to buy very fresh products from the local butcher or baker. Another reason is that most refrigerators are fairly small by North American standards.

INFOBOX

Die Altstadt von Luxemburg

Luxemburg

Das Großherzogtum[1] Luxemburg ist ein kleines Land: von Norden nach Süden sind es nur 82 km und von Osten nach Westen sogar nur 52. Von den fast 451 000 Einwohnern sind etwa 174 000 Ausländer, d.h.[2] etwa 39 Prozent der Gesamtbevölkerung[3]. Damit hält Luxemburg den absoluten Rekord unter den Ländern der Europäischen Union. Dazu kommen noch über 105 000 Pendler[4], die täglich aus den Nachbarländern Deutschland, Frankreich und Belgien nach Luxemburg zur Arbeit kommen. Es ist deshalb kein Wunder, dass in dieser multikulturellen Gesellschaft[5] Sprachkompetenz eine enorme Rolle spielt. Luxemburgs offizielle Sprachen sind Luxemburgisch (eine Sprache, die dem Deutschen sehr ähnlich[6] ist), Deutsch und Französisch. Schon in der Grundschule lernen die Kinder alle drei offiziellen Sprachen und alle Grundschullehrer müssen dreisprachig sein. Anders als in der Schweiz sprechen deshalb in Luxemburg viele Menschen nicht nur eine, sondern alle offiziellen Sprachen.

Luxemburg ist ein hoch industrialisiertes Land, doch der dynamischste Sektor der Luxemburger Wirtschaft[7] sind die Banken mit fast 22 000 Beschäftigten[8]. In Luxemburg sind auch drei Institutionen der Europäischen Union mit über 7 000 „Eurokraten" aus allen Ländern der EU. In der Hauptstadt – auch sie heißt Luxemburg – kontrastieren die modernen Gebäude der Banken und der EU mit der historischen Altstadt, die seit 1994 zum Weltkulturerbe[9] der UNESCO gehört. Über 50 Prozent von den etwa 82 000 Einwohnern sind Ausländer und Luxemburg ist deshalb eine Hauptstadt mit besonders internationalem Flair.

Dass Luxemburgisch dem Deutschen sehr ähnlich ist, können Sie an den folgenden Beispielen sehen. Finden Sie die deutschen Äquivalente.

1. Kënne mir eis?
2. Mir schwätze Lëtzebuergesch.
3. Mir léiere Lëtzebuergesch.
4. Wéivill Auer ass et?
5. Wéivill kascht dat?
6. Wéi geet et Iech?
7. Et geet mir gutt.

a. Wie viel Uhr ist es?
b. Wie geht es Ihnen?
c. Wie viel kostet das?
d. Es geht mir gut.
e. Wir lernen Luxemburgisch.
f. Kennen wir uns?
g. Wir sprechen Luxemburgisch.

[1] *grand duchy*   [2] *i.e.*   [3] *total population*   [4] *commuters*   [5] *society*
[6] *similar*   [7] *economy*   [8] *employees*   [9] *world cultural heritage*

---

82 km = 51 miles; 52 km = 32 miles

In contrast to Luxemburg, Switzerland is divided into distinct linguistic regions, i.e., **die deutsche Schweiz, die französische Schweiz, die italienische Schweiz.**

drei Institutionen der EU: These are the Court of Justice, the Court of Auditors, and the European Parliament. The latter is split between Luxemburg, Brussels, and Strasbourg. The parliament does not sit in Luxemburg, but its secretariat is based there. The parliament sits for one week a month in Strasbourg, and parliamentary committees spend two weeks a month in Brussels.

WWW Learn more about **Luxemburg**'s many cultural treasures at www.prenhall.com/treffpunkt
→ Kapitel 9 → Web Resources → Kultur

Das Sekretariat des Europaparlaments in Luxemburg

Lesen

Zum besseren Verstehen

banknotes, bills **9-39 Geldscheine°.**

1. Kennen Sie Geldscheine von anderen Ländern? Wenn ja, von welchen?
2. Was gefällt Ihnen an diesen Geldscheinen nicht so gut wie oder besser als an den Geldscheinen Ihres Landes?

9-40 Was ist das auf Englisch?

1. Geldscheine sind aus Papier und **Münzen** sind aus Metall.
2. **Vorderseite** ist das Gegenteil von Rückseite.
3. Durch einen **Wettbewerb** findet man heraus, wer etwas am besten kann.
4. Felix studiert Musik und **nimmt** oft **an** Wettbewerben **teil.**
5. Mit dem Computer hat ein neues **Zeitalter** begonnen.
6. In seinem Charakter hat Daniel große **Ähnlichkeit** mit seinem Vater.
7. Ein Banknoten-Designer **entwirft** Banknoten.
8. Was ein Designer entwirft, ist ein **Entwurf.**
9. Über eine **Brücke** kommt man von einer Seite eines Flusses auf die andere.
10. Geldscheine und Münzen sind **Bargeld.**

a. design
b. epoch
c. cash
d. similarity
e. front
f. takes part in
g. competition
h. bridge
i. coins
j. designs

www Check out the security features of the **Euro** at www.prenhall.com/treffpunkt
→ Kapitel 9 → Web Resources
→ Kultur

LEUTE **Robert Kalina und der Euro**

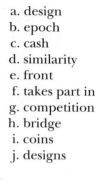

Seit dem 1. Januar 2002 bezahlen die Europäer ihre Einkäufe nicht mehr mit Mark, Schilling, Franken, Lire, Peseten, Gulden, Drachmen usw., sondern mit Euros. Die Euro-Münzen haben eine „europäische" Vorderseite – sie ist das Werk des belgischen Münzen-Designers Luc Luycx – und eine „nationale" Rückseite, die in jedem Land anders aussieht. Bei den Euro-Scheinen dagegen[1] sind beide Seiten „europäisch" und alle sieben Scheine (5, 10, 20, 50, 100, 200 und 500 Euro) sind das Werk des österreichischen Banknoten-Designers Robert Kalina.

Robert Kalina ist Banknoten-Designer bei der Österreichischen Nationalbank. Als die EZB (Europäische Zentralbank) im Februar 1996 zu einem Wettbewerb für das Design des Euro einlädt, nimmt auch Robert Kalina daran teil und wählt[2] das Thema „Zeitalter und Stile Europas". Mögliche Motive sind Porträts und Architektur, aber ohne Ähnlichkeit mit wirklichen Personen oder realen Gebäuden. Porträts von imaginären Europäern, denkt

Robert Kalina, machen wenig Sinn[3]. Er entwirft deshalb imaginäre Gebäude in den Baustilen verschiedener europäischer Epochen: von der griechisch-römischen Antike auf dem Fünf-Euro-Schein bis zum Ende des zwanzigsten Jahrhunderts auf dem Fünfhunderter. Auf der Vorderseite zeigen Kalinas Scheine Tore[4] und Fenster und auf der Rückseite Brücken, alles Symbole für den Weg[5] der europäischen Staaten zueinander. Die verschiedenen Größen und Farben der Scheine sind übrigens von der EZB vorgegeben[6]. Man soll daran sofort erkennen, welchen Schein man in der Hand hält.

Im September 1996 wählt eine Experten-Jury die fünf besten Entwürfe und Robert Kalinas Entwurf ist einer davon. Danach prüft[7] die EZB die Akzeptanz dieser Entwürfe durch eine Umfrage[8] unter 2 000 Europäern, die viel mit Bargeld zu tun haben, d.h. unter Taxifahrern, Verkäufern, Kassierern usw. Robert Kalinas Designs gefallen diesen Leuten am besten und im Juli 1999 beginnt in zwölf europäischen Ländern die Produktion von 16 Milliarden[9] Scheinen.

[1] on the other hand   [2] selects   [3] sense   [4] gates   [5] path   [6] set   [7] tests   [8] poll   [9] billion

Arbeit mit dem Text

9-41 Richtig oder falsch?

1. _____ Bei den Euro-Münzen ist nur eine Seite „europäisch".
2. _____ Die Euro-Scheine haben eine „nationale" Rückseite.
3. _____ Imaginäre europäische Personen und Gebäude sind mögliche Motive für das Design der Euro-Scheine.
4. _____ Für den Fünf-Euro-Schein wählt Robert Kalina den Baustil der griechisch-römischen Antike.
5. _____ Fenster, Tore und Brücken sollen symbolisieren, dass die europäischen Staaten einander immer näher kommen.
6. _____ Robert Kalina wählt für seine Scheine verschiedene Größen und Farben.
7. _____ Die Jury will durch eine Umfrage herausfinden, welches Design der EZB am besten gefällt.

Wort, Sinn und Klang

Wörter unter der Lupe

Predicting gender

In German and in English the suffix **-er** is used to form *agent nouns*, i.e., nouns that show who or what does the action described by a given verb. Agent nouns with the suffix **-er** are always masculine and can refer to things as well as people. Some of these nouns take an umlaut.

| kaufen | *to buy* | **der** Käuf**er**, - | *buyer* |
| wecken | *to wake (someone) up* | **der** Weck**er**, - | *alarm clock* |

If an agent noun refers to a female, the suffix **-in** is added to the masculine suffix **-er.**

| der Käuf**er** | *(male) buyer* | **die** Käuf**erin**, **-nen** | *(female) buyer* |

9-42 Was passt wo?   Choosing appropriate infinitives, create German equivalents of the English nouns listed below. The articles indicate whether the nouns are to refer to a male or a thing (**der**) or to a female (**die**). Note that there are three compound nouns.

vermieten / einwandern / verkaufen / kennen / übersetzen / Korken + ziehen / anfangen (Umlaut!) / besuchen / Arbeit + geben / Anruf + beantworten

1. beginner   der _____
2. translator   die _____
3. corkscrew   der _____
4. immigrant   der _____
5. answering   der _____
   machine

6. visitor   die _____
7. sales clerk   der _____
8. employer   der _____
9. landlady   die _____
10. connoisseur   der _____

Giving language color

There are so many expressions based on the names of the parts of the body that another sampling is in order!

Mir raucht der Kopf.	*I can't think straight anymore.*
Sie findet immer ein Haar in der Suppe.	*She finds fault with everything.*
Ich muss mit dir unter vier Augen sprechen.	*I have to talk to you in private.*
Sie tanzen ihr auf der Nase herum.	*They walk all over her.*
hit **Er hat mich übers Ohr gehauen°.**	*He pulled a fast one on me.*
Wir haben uns die Beine in den Bauch gestanden.	*We stood until we were ready to drop.*
Ich drücke dir die Daumen.	*I'll keep my fingers crossed for you.*

9-43 Was passt zusammen?

1. Warum hörst du denn schon auf, zu lernen?
2. Warum soll ich denn nicht Lehrerin werden?
3. Warum soll ich weggehen, wenn Günter kommt?
4. Warum kaufst du Ulis Wagen nicht?
5. Warum willst du mich dein Referat nicht lesen lassen?
6. Warum soll *ich* denn die Karten für das Fußballspiel kaufen?
7. Warum hast du in dieser Klausur nur eine Drei bekommen?

a. Weil ich mit ihm unter vier Augen sprechen muss.
b. Weil du immer ein Haar in der Suppe findest.
c. Weil mir der Kopf raucht.
d. Weil du dir auch mal die Beine in den Bauch stehen kannst.
e. Weil dir die Schüler bestimmt alle auf der Nase herumtanzen.
f. Weil du mir die Daumen nicht gedrückt hast.
g. Weil ich Angst habe°, dass er mich übers Ohr haut.

Angst habe: *am afraid*

Zur Aussprache

German *s*-sounds: voiced *s* and voiceless *s*

Before vowels the sound represented by the letter **s** is *voiced*, i.e., it is pronounced like English *z* in **zip**.

1. Wohin reisen Suse und Sabine? – Auf eine sonnige Südseeinsel.
2. So ein Sauwetter! Seit Sonntag keine Sonne!

Before consonants and at the end of a word, the sound represented by the letter **s** is *voiceless*, i.e., it is pronounced like English *s* in **sip**. The sounds represented by **ss** and **ß** (**Eszett**) are also *voiceless*.

1. Der Mensch ist, was er isst.
2. Ist das alles, was du weißt?
3. Wo ist hier das beste Gasthaus?

The sound represented by the letter **z** is pronounced like English *ts* in **hits**.

1. Der Zug nach Zürich fährt um zehn.
2. Wann kommt Heinz aus Graz zurück?
3. Zahnärzte ziehen Zähne.

Schloss Eggenberg in Graz, Österreich

Contrasting German *s*-sounds

so	Zoo	Gras	Graz	
seit	Zeit	Schweiß°	Schweiz	*sweat*
Saal	Zahl	Kurs	kurz	
selten	zelten	heißen	heizen°	*to heat*
Sieh!	Zieh!	beißen	beizen°	*to stain (wood)*

Remember that at the beginning of a word or word stem, **s** in the combinations **st** and **sp** is pronounced like English *sh*.

Liechtenstein	Österreich	Speisekarte	Aspik	
Stadt	Gast	Spende°	Wespe°	*donation / wasp*
Student	Assistent	Aussprache	Aspirin	
Besteck	Fest	spielen	lispeln	
Lippenstift	Liste	versprechen	vespern°	*to have a snack*

Nomen

der Föhn, -e	blow-dryer
die Haarbürste, -n	hairbrush
das Handtuch, ⸚er	towel
der Kamm, ⸚e	comb
der Lippenstift, -e	lipstick
der Rasierapparat, -e	shaver, electric razor
das Rasierwasser	aftershave
die Seife, -n	soap
das Shampoo, -s	shampoo
der Spiegel, -	mirror
der Waschlappen, -	washcloth
die Zahnbürste, -n	toothbrush
die Zahnpasta	toothpaste
die Apotheke, -n	pharmacy
die Drogerie, -n	drugstore
das Reformhaus, ⸚er	health food store
das Bargeld	cash
der Geldschein, -e	} banknote, bill (*money*)
der Schein, -e	
die Münze, -n	coin
die Vorspeise, -n	hors d'oeuvre
das Gericht, -e	dish (*food*)
das Hauptgericht, -e	main course
der Essig	vinegar
das Öl	oil
der Pfeffer	pepper
das Salz	salt
der Senf	mustard
der Herr, -n, -en	gentleman; Mr.
der Kollege, -n, -n	} colleague
die Kollegin, -nen	
der Kunde, -n, -n	} customer
die Kundin, -nen	
der Mitbürger, -	} fellow citizen
die Mitbürgerin, -nen	
der Polizist, -en, -en	} police officer
die Polizistin, -nen	

die Drogerie: Remember that most nouns that end in **-ie** are feminine (**Soziologie, Biologie, Allergie**).

Gericht: What are the English equivalents for **Nebengericht** and **Fleischgericht?**

Herr, Kollege, Kunde, Polizist: Remember that the genitive singular ending is added before the plural ending to show that these are **n**-nouns. Find the **n**-nouns under *Leicht zu verstehen.*

Verben

sich an·ziehen, angezogen	to dress, to get dressed
sich aus·ziehen, ausgezogen	to undress, to get undressed
sich um·ziehen, umgezogen	to change one's clothes
sich baden	to take a bath
sich duschen	to take a shower
sich die Haare föhnen/ trocknen	to blow-dry/dry one's hair
sich kämmen	to comb one's hair
sich rasieren	to shave
sich schminken	to put on make-up
sich auf·regen	to get worked up; to get upset
sich beeilen	to hurry
sich benehmen (benimmt), benommen	to behave
sich entschuldigen	to apologize
sich erkälten	to catch a cold
sich setzen	to sit down
sich verspäten	to be late
sich wohl fühlen	to feel well
fühlen	to feel
schmecken	to taste; to taste good
treffen (trifft), getroffen	to meet

schmecken: Note the relationship between **schmecken** and *to smack* in a sentence like *His promotion smacks of favoritism.* The meaning *to taste good* is used in **9-46, #1: Diese Suppe schmeckt mir nicht.**

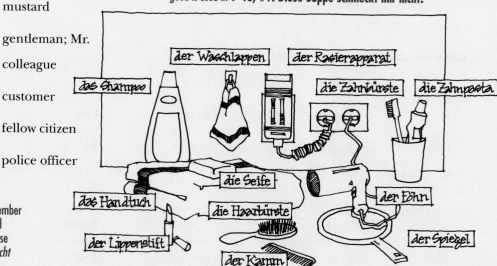

Andere Wörter

ähnlich	similar
derselbe, dasselbe, dieselbe	the same
versalzen	too salty

Ausdrücke

Angst haben	to be afraid
das heißt (d.h.)	that is (i.e.)
genauso gut	just as good (well)
Alles in Ordnung?	Is everything okay?
Das kommt nicht in Frage!	That's out of the question!
Jetzt bist du dran.	Now it's your turn.

Das Gegenteil

bevor ≠ nachdem   before ≠ after *(conj)*

Leicht zu verstehen

der Athlet, -en, -en	die Patientin, -nen
die Athletin, -nen	der Präsident, -en, -en
der Bär, -en, -en	die Präsidentin, -nen
der Elefant, -en, -en	der Vegetarier, -
das Kamel, -e	die Vegetarierin, -nen
der Patient, -en, -en	vegetarisch

Leicht zu verstehen: Which words in this list are stressed on a different syllable than their English equivalents?

Wörter im Kontext

9-44 Was passt zusammen? Beginnen Sie jede Frage mit

Was brauche ich, …

1. um mir die Haare zu waschen?
2. um mir die Haare zu trocknen?
3. um mir die Zähne zu putzen?
4. um mir die Hände zu waschen?
5. um mich zu kämmen?
6. um mich zu schminken?
7. um mich zu rasieren?

a. Einen Lippenstift.
b. Einen Kamm und einen Spiegel.
c. Einen Rasierapparat.
d. Wasser und Seife.
e. Ein Handtuch und einen Föhn.
f. Wasser und Shampoo.
g. Eine Zahnbürste und Zahnpasta.

Frisch vom Fass füllen wir für Sie ab:

-Essig + Öl
-Wein   -Cognac
-Likör   -Edelbrand
-Whisky -Grappa

Was gibt es hier außer Essig und Öl?

9-45 Was passt?

sich umziehen / sich anziehen / sich ausziehen / sich beeilen
sich erkälten / sich wohl fühlen / sich entschuldigen

1. Bevor man sich duscht oder sich badet, _____ man _____.
2. Nachdem man sich geduscht oder sich gebadet hat, _____ man _____ wieder _____.
3. Bevor man in die Oper geht, _____ man _____ _____.
4. Wenn man im Winter mit nassen Haaren aus dem Haus geht, kann man _____ _____.
5. Wenn man morgens zu spät aufgestanden ist, sollte man _____ _____.
6. Wenn man sich verspätet hat oder wenn man sich schlecht benommen hat, sollte man _____ _____.
7. Wenn man _____ nicht _____ _____, sollte man zu Hause bleiben.

9-46 Was ist hier identisch? Welche zwei Sätze in jeder Gruppe

bedeuten etwa dasselbe?

1. Diese Suppe schmeckt mir nicht.
   Ich mag diese Suppe nicht.
   Ich habe keine Lust auf Suppe.

2. Jetzt bist du dran.
   Das darfst du nicht.
   Das kommt nicht in Frage!

3. Ich fühle mich nicht wohl.
   Es tut mir leid.
   Mir geht es nicht gut.

4. Kommt ja rechtzeitig!
   Verspätet euch nicht!
   Regt euch nicht auf!

Und jeder Tag schmeckt wie Sonntag.

Orang
100%

Aus Büchern und Zeitungen

Büchermarkt vor der Humboldt-Universität

Kommunikationsziele

Telling stories

Contradicting negative statements or questions

Giving opinions

Describing people, places, and things

Strukturen

Simple past tense

Principal parts of verbs

Wann, als, wenn

More on relative pronouns

Summary of adjective endings

Kultur

Der Beginn des Informationszeitalters

Zeitungen und Magazine

Die Brüder Grimm

Video-Treff: **Meine Lieblingslektüre**

Lesen: **Der Hase und der Igel**

Der schlaue Student vom Paradies

nach Hans Sachs

Im sechzehnten Jahrhundert studierte einmal ein deutscher Student in
Paris. Im Juli war das Sommersemester zu Ende und der Student wollte
zu seinen Eltern nach Deutschland zurück. Weil er aber sehr arm war,
konnte er kein Pferd kaufen, sondern musste zu Fuß nach Deutschland
5   wandern. (Busse und Züge gab es damals natürlich noch nicht.)

Als der Student nach einer Woche zum ersten deutschen Dorf kam,
war es gerade Mittag, und weil er heute noch nichts gegessen hatte,
war er sehr hungrig. Er blieb deshalb bei einer Bäuerin stehen, die
vor ihrem Haus im Garten arbeitete, und sagte: „Guten Tag, liebe
10   Frau. Haben Sie vielleicht etwas zu essen für mich? Ich bin heute
schon weit gewandert und habe noch nicht mal gefrühstückt."

Die Bäuerin schaute von ihrer Arbeit auf und fragte: „Wer sind Sie
denn und woher kommen Sie?"

„Ich bin ein armer Student," antwortete er, „und ich komme von Paris."

15   Nun war die gute Frau zwar sehr fromm, aber nicht sehr intelligent.
Sie ging jeden Sonntag in die Kirche und sie hörte dort viel vom
Paradies, aber von Paris hatte sie noch nie etwas gehört. Und so
verstand sie nicht *Paris,* sondern *Paradies* und rief: „Was, Sie kommen
vom Paradies?! Ja, dann kennen Sie doch sicher meinen ersten Mann.
20   Er war gut und fromm und ist jetzt bestimmt im Paradies."

„Wie heißt er denn?" fragte der schlaue Student.

„Hans," antwortete die Bäuerin, „Hans Krüger."

„Oh, der Hans!" rief der Student. „Aber natürlich kenne ich ihn.
Er ist sogar ein guter Freund von mir und ich habe erst kürzlich mit
25   ihm gesprochen."

„Wie geht es ihm denn im Paradies?" fragte die Frau.

„Leider nicht sehr gut," antwortete der Student. „Hans ist sehr arm.
Er hat kein Geld, ist in Lumpen gekleidet und hat oft nicht mal genug
zu essen."

30   „Oh, du mein armer Hans," weinte da die gute Frau, „du hast kein Geld
und keine Kleider und musst oft hungern und frieren. Mein zweiter
Mann ist so reich und so gut, und ich möchte dir so gern helfen."

Schließlich sagte sie zu dem Studenten: „Sie gehen wohl nie wieder
ins Paradies zurück, junger Mann?"

Da rief der Bauer: „Oh, Frau!"

35 „Doch," sagte er, „meine Ferien sind fast zu Ende und ich gehe schon übermorgen wieder zurück."

„Könnten Sie vielleicht für meinen armen Hans ein bisschen Geld und ein paar gute Kleider mitnehmen?" fragte die Frau.

„Aber natürlich," antwortete der Student, „das mache ich gern. Holen
40 Sie nur das Geld und die Kleider, dann muss Ihr Hans bald nicht mehr hungern und frieren."

Da war die gute Frau sehr glücklich. Sie lief ins Haus und bald kam sie mit einem Bündel Kleider, mit zehn Goldstücken und mit einem großen Stück Brot wieder zurück. Das Brot gab sie dem Studenten
45 und die Goldstücke steckte sie in das Bündel. „Bitte, geben Sie meinem Hans dieses Bündel," sagte sie, „und grüßen Sie ihn von mir. Ich habe zwar wieder geheiratet, aber meinen Hans vergesse ich nie."

Der Student dankte der Bäuerin für das Brot, nahm das Bündel und wanderte so schnell wie möglich weiter.

50 Nach einer halben Stunde kam der Bauer vom Feld und die glückliche Frau erzählte ihm alles. Da rief er: „Oh, Frau!", lief schnell in den Stall, sattelte sein Pferd und galoppierte dem Studenten nach.

Der Student war mit seinem Bündel schon weit gewandert. Als er plötzlich ein Pferd galoppieren hörte, nahm er das Bündel schnell
55 vom Rücken und versteckte es in einem Busch.

Der Bauer kam, hielt sein Pferd an und fragte: „Haben Sie vielleicht einen Studenten mit einem Bündel auf dem Rücken gesehen?"

„Ja," log der schlaue Student, „das ist sicher der Mann, mit dem ich gerade gewandert bin. Als er Ihr Pferd hörte, hat er Angst gekriegt
60 und ist schnell in den Wald gerannt."

„Halten Sie doch bitte mein Pferd!" rief da der Bauer. „Ich muss diesen Studenten fangen." Er stieg schnell vom Pferd und lief in den Wald. Der Student aber holte das Bündel aus dem Busch, stieg auf das Pferd und ritt schnell weg.

65 Der Bauer fand niemand im Wald, und als er wieder zurückkam, fand er auch den Studenten und das Pferd nicht mehr. Da wurde ihm alles klar und er ging langsam zu Fuß nach Hause zurück.

Zu Hause fragte ihn seine Frau: „Warum kommst du zu Fuß zurück? Wo ist denn dein Pferd?"

70 „Ich habe es dem Studenten gegeben," antwortete der Bauer. „Mit dem Pferd kommt er schneller ins Paradies."

10-1 Wahrheit oder Lüge°? Sie hören *Der schlaue Student vom Paradies*   *lie*
und dann acht Aussagen. Haken Sie nach jeder Aussage ab,

a. wer das sagt (der Student, die Bäuerin, der Bauer)
b. ob diese Leute glauben, was sie sagen (Wahrheit), oder ob sie lügen (Lüge).

A. DER STUDENT	DIE BÄUERIN	DER BAUER	B. WAHRHEIT	LÜGE
1. _____	_____	_____	_____	_____
2. _____	_____	_____	_____	_____
3. _____	_____	_____	_____	_____
4. _____	_____	_____	_____	_____
5. _____	_____	_____	_____	_____
6. _____	_____	_____	_____	_____
7. _____	_____	_____	_____	_____
8. _____	_____	_____	_____	_____

10-2 Was passt wo?

arbeitete / kam / sah

1. Als der Student durch das erste deutsche Dorf _____, _____ er dort eine
   Bäuerin, die vor ihrem Haus im Garten _____.

hatte / fragte / war / sagte

2. Weil es gerade Mittag _____ und weil er Hunger _____, _____ er „Guten
   Tag!" und _____: „Haben Sie vielleicht etwas zu essen für mich?"

hörte / fragte / verstand / antwortete

3. Die Frau _____: „Woher kommen Sie?" und der Student _____: „Von
   Paris." Weil die Frau aber jeden Sonntag vom Paradies _____, _____
   sie nicht Paris, sondern Paradies.

hörte / holte / zurückging / war

4. Als die Frau _____, dass der Student übermorgen wieder ins Paradies
   _____, _____ sie ganz glücklich und _____ Geld, Kleider und ein
   Stück Brot.

galoppierte / sattelte / erzählte / lief

5. Als die Frau dem Bauern später von dem Studenten und dem Bündel
   _____, _____ er schnell in den Stall, _____ sein Pferd und _____ dem
   Studenten nach.

fragte / hörte / schickte / versteckte

6. Als der Student ein Pferd galoppieren _____, _____ er das Bündel schnell
   in einem Busch. Als der Bauer ihn nach° dem Studenten _____, _____ er   *about*
   ihn in den Wald.

stieg / fand / ritt / holte

7. Der Bauer _____ natürlich niemand. Der Student aber _____ das Bündel
   aus dem Busch, _____ auf das Pferd und _____ schnell weg.

10-3 Der schlaue Student vom Paradies. Bilden Sie Dreiergruppen. Jede Gruppe bringt die Fragen und Aussagen in einer Szene in die richtige Reihenfolge. Dann spielen alle zusammen den ganzen Sketch.

Szene 1: Erzähler(in), Bäuerin, Student

Ein deutscher Student wanderte einmal in den Ferien von Paris nach Deutschland zurück. Als er durch das erste deutsche Dorf kam, sah er vor einem großen Bauernhaus eine Frau im Garten arbeiten. Weil er heute noch nichts gegessen hatte, blieb er stehen und sagte:

___1___ Guten Tag, liebe Frau. Haben Sie vielleicht etwas zu essen für mich?

_____ Hans heißt er, Hans Krüger.

_____ Ich bin ein armer Student und komme von Paris.

_____ Etwas zu essen? Ja, wer sind Sie denn und woher kommen Sie?

_____ Was?! Vom Paradies?! Ja, dann kennen Sie doch sicher meinen ersten Mann!

_____ Oh, der Hans! Ja, natürlich kenne ich ihn. Er ist sogar ein guter Freund von mir.

_____ Wie heißt er denn?

Szene 2: Erzähler(in), Bäuerin, Student

Als die Frau hörte, dass der Student ihren ersten Mann so gut kannte, war sie ganz glücklich und fragte:

___1___ Wie geht es meinem Hans im Paradies?

_____ Doch, ich gehe schon übermorgen wieder zurück.

_____ Aber natürlich, das mache ich sehr gern.

_____ Leider nicht sehr gut. Er hat kein Geld und keine Kleider.

_____ Könnten Sie meinem Hans vielleicht ein bisschen Geld und ein paar Kleider bringen?

_____ Ach, du armer Hans! Ich möchte dir so gern helfen. Sie gehen aber wohl nie wieder ins Paradies zurück, junger Mann?

Szene 3: Erzähler(in), Bäuerin, Student

Die Bäuerin lief ins Haus, und als sie wieder zurückkam, sagte sie:

___1___ Also, hier ist erst mal ein großes Stück Brot für Sie.

_____ Grüßen Sie meinen Hans von mir und sagen Sie ihm, dass ich ihn nie vergesse.

_____ Und das hier sind die Sachen für meinen Hans.

_____ Oh, vielen Dank, liebe Frau.

_____ Das mache ich gern. Und noch mal vielen Dank für das Brot, liebe Frau. Auf Wiedersehen!

_____ Mm, was für ein großes Bündel! Was schicken Sie ihm denn alles?

_____ Zehn Goldstücke! Damit kann er sich viel zu essen kaufen, der gute Hans!

_____ Schöne warme Kleider, und in die Hosentaschen habe ich zehn Goldstücke gesteckt.

Szene 4: Erzähler(in), Bäuerin, Bauer

Nach einer halben Stunde kam der Bauer vom Feld, und weil die Frau so glücklich war, begann sie gleich zu erzählen:

___1___ Oh, Hermann, ich bin ja so glücklich!

_____ Ja, weißt du, da war dieser Student vom Paradies ...

_____ Warum? Warum geht es ihm schlecht im Paradies?

_____ Was, ein Student vom Paradies?!

_____ Er hat kein Geld und keine Kleider. Aber der Student geht übermorgen ins Paradies zurück und ich habe ihm für Hans ein großes Bündel Kleider und zehn Goldstücke mitgegeben.

_____ Ja, und denk dir nur, er kennt den Hans, und er hat mir erzählt, wie schlecht es ihm geht.

_____ Zehn Goldstücke! Oh, Frau!

_____ Glücklich? Warum?

Szene 5: Erzähler(in), Bauer, Student

Der Student war mit seinem Bündel schon weit gewandert. Da hörte er plötzlich ein Pferd galoppieren und rief:

___1___ Das ist bestimmt der Bauer! Also weg mit dem Bündel! Hier, hinter den großen Busch!

_____ Ja, das ist sicher der Mann, mit dem ich gerade gewandert bin. Als er Ihr Pferd hörte, ist er schnell in den Wald gerannt.

_____ Haben Sie vielleicht einen Studenten mit einem Bündel auf dem Rücken gesehen?

_____ Aber gern. Und viel Glück im Wald!

_____ Ich muss diesen Studenten fangen. Können Sie vielleicht so lange mein Pferd halten?

Szene 6: Erzähler(in), Bäuerin, Bauer

Der Bauer fand niemand im Wald, und als er wieder zurückkam, fand er auch den Studenten und das Pferd nicht mehr. Als er dann am Abend nach Hause kam, fragte seine Frau:

___1___ Warum bist du so schnell weggeritten, Hermann?

_____ Ich habe es dem Studenten gegeben. Mit dem Pferd kommt er schneller ins Paradies.

_____ Ja, das habe ich.

_____ Hast du ihn gefunden und hast du mein schönes Bündel gesehen?

_____ Aber sag mal, warum kommst du zu Fuß zurück? Wo ist denn dein Pferd?

_____ Ich wollte mit dem Studenten sprechen.

WWW Peruse the **Gutenberg-Bibel** at www.prenhall.com/treffpunkt
→ Kapitel 10 → Web Resources
→ Kultur

KULTUR
Der Beginn des Informationszeitalters

Wenn wir heute vom Informationszeitalter[1] sprechen, denken wir an Fernsehen, Computer, Internet und Satelliten, und wir vergessen, dass dieses Zeitalter eigentlich vor etwa 550 Jahren mit Johannes Gutenberg, dem Erfinder[2] des Buchdrucks,[3] begonnen hat. Vor Gutenberg brauchte ein Schreiber zwei volle Jahre, um eine einzige Bibel zu kopieren. Nach Gutenberg gab es bald Tausende von Druckereien[4] in Europa, die Millionen von Büchern und anderen Schriften[5] produzierten.

Genauso wichtig wie die Erfindung des Buchdrucks war für die deutschsprachigen Länder Martin Luthers Bibelübersetzung. Die deutschen Dialekte waren so verschieden, dass die Menschen aus dem Norden ihre Nachbarn im Süden oft nicht verstanden. Die wenigen Gebildeten[6] schrieben und sprachen damals Latein. Luther übersetzte nun die Bibel in ein Deutsch, das auch einfache[7] Menschen in allen deutschsprachigen Ländern verstehen konnten. Seine Übersetzungstechnik beschreibt er so: „… man muss die Mutter im Haus, die Kinder auf der Straße und den gemeinen[8] Mann auf dem Markt fragen und ihnen auf den Mund sehen, wie sie reden, und danach[9] übersetzen …"

Durch Gutenbergs Erfindung des Buchdrucks und Luthers Bibelübersetzung konnten immer mehr Menschen die Bibel und viele andere Schriften lesen, und manche[10] von ihnen begannen sogar, selbst zu schreiben. So schrieb der Schuhmacher Hans Sachs aus Nürnberg in seiner Freizeit Tausende von Gedichten[11] und Dramen. In *Der farend Schüler im Paradeiß* zeigte er mit viel Humor, was passieren kann, wenn man so schlecht informiert ist, dass man noch nie etwas von Paris gehört hat und deshalb Paradies versteht.

[1]*information age*   [2]*inventor*   [3]*printing*   [4]*print shops*
[5]*writings*   [6]*educated people*   [7]*ordinary*   [8]*common*
[9]*accordingly*   [10]*some*   [11]*poems*

10-4 Wo steht das im Text? Finden Sie die Antworten zu den folgenden Fragen und *underline* unterstreichen° Sie sie.

1. Wann hat das Informationszeitalter begonnen?
2. Wie lange brauchte man vor Gutenberg, um eine einzige Bibel zu kopieren?
3. Welche Sprache schrieben und sprachen die Gebildeten damals?
4. In was für ein Deutsch übersetzte Luther die Bibel?
5. Was war Hans Sachs von Beruf?
6. Wann schrieb Hans Sachs seine vielen tausend Gedichte und Dramen?

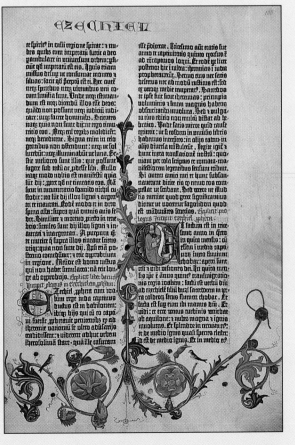

The illustration shows a page from Gutenberg's 42-line Latin Bible, so called because each page has 42 lines. The font he used was an accurate imitation of the best manuscript style of the period. After the printing process was completed, hand decoration was done by rubricators and illuminators. Rubricators emphasized holy names and words in red, illuminators decorated the printed text with magnificent initial letters and colorful foliage.

Nomen

das Informationszeitalter	information age
der Erfinder, -	inventor
die Erfinderin, -nen	
der Erzähler, -	narrator
die Erzählerin, -nen	
das Gedicht, -e	poem
der Sketch, -es	skit
die Übersetzung, -en	translation

der Bauer, -n, -n	farmer	**Bauer:** What identifies this word as an **n**-noun?
die Bäuerin, -nen		
das Pferd, -e	horse	
der Stall, ⁒e	stable	

die Angst	fear
das Glück	luck
das Jahrhundert, -e	century
die Kirche, -n	church

Verben

an·halten (hält an), hielt an, angehalten	to stop	**Verben:** Starting in this chapter, irregular verbs are listed with their principal parts. See p. 345 for more about principal parts.
drucken	to print	
fangen (fängt), fing, gefangen	to catch	
frieren, fror, gefroren	to be cold	
grüßen	to greet; to say hello	
lügen, log, gelogen	to lie	
reiten, ritt, ist geritten	to ride (a horse)	
rufen, rief, gerufen	to call	

stecken	to stick (put); to be	
stehen bleiben, blieb stehen, ist stehen geblieben	to stop (walking)	Why does **stehen bleiben** form the perfect with **sein**?
steigen, stieg, ist gestiegen	to climb	
unterstreichen, unterstrich, unterstrichen	to underline	
verstecken	to hide	
weinen	to cry	What English word is related to **weinen**?

Andere Wörter

mancher, manches, manche	many a; (pl) some	**mancher:** Like **dieser, jeder, welcher,** this is a **der**-word.
einfach	simple; ordinary	
fromm	pious	
gekleidet	dressed	
schlau	crafty, clever	
als	when (conj)	
damals	back then; at that time	
kürzlich	a short time ago, recently	

Ausdrücke

Angst kriegen	to get scared
Viel Glück!	Good luck!

Das Gegenteil

die Lüge, -n ≠ die Wahrheit	lie ≠ truth
einfach ≠ kompliziert	simple ≠ complicated

Leicht zu verstehen

die Bibel, -n	der Satellit, -en	
das Bündel, -	der Schuhmacher, -	
der Busch, ⁒e	die Schuhmacherin, -nen	
der Dialekt, -e	galoppieren	Which words in this list are stressed on a different syllable than their English equivalents?
das Drama, Dramen	kopieren	
das Internet	satteln	
das Paradies	hungrig	

▌ Sprachnotiz

The past perfect tense

Like the English past perfect, the German past perfect is used to refer to an event that precedes another event in the past. It is formed with the simple past of the auxiliaries **haben** or **sein** and the past participle.

Der Student war sehr hungrig, denn er **war** weit **gewandert** und **hatte** noch nichts **gegessen**.

*The student was very hungry, because he **had walked** a long way and **had not eaten** anything yet.*

Wörter im Kontext

10-5 Was passt?

1. Leute, _____, grüßen einander.
2. Katzen, _____, fangen keine Mäuse.
3. Ein Mann, _____, ist ein Bauer.
4. Ein Mensch, _____, ist ein Lügner.
5. Frauen, _____, sind Autorinnen.
6. Ein Mensch, _____, ist fromm.
7. Ein Mensch, _____, ist ein Erfinder.

a. der im Stall und auf dem Feld arbeitet
b. der sehr religiös ist
c. der nicht die Wahrheit sagt
d. die nicht hungrig sind
e. der sich etwas ganz Neues ausdenkt
f. die sich kennen
g. die Romane, Dramen und Gedichte schreiben

BERLINER GEDENKTAFEL

In diesem Hause wohnte und arbeitete von 1893 bis 1894

RUDOLF DIESEL
18.3.1858 – 29.9.1913
Ingenieur und Erfinder des Diesel-Motors

10-6 Mit anderen Worten. Welche zwei Sätze in jeder Gruppe bedeuten etwa dasselbe?

1. Mir ist kalt.
   Ich friere.
   Heute ist es kalt.

2. Warum stecken Sie die Fotos nicht ins Album?
   Warum stecken die Fotos nicht im Album?
   Warum sind die Fotos nicht im Album?

3. Warum bleibst du stehen?
   Warum bleibst du nicht stehen?
   Warum gehst du nicht weiter?

4. Er sagt immer die Wahrheit.
   Er sagt nie die Wahrheit.
   Er lügt immer.

10-6, #2. stecken: Like **legen**, **stellen**, and **hängen**, **stecken** can express *to put*. Like **liegen**, **stehen**, and **hängen**, **stecken** can also express *to be*. When **stecken** is followed by a two-case preposition, the case is determined by the same criteria as for the other verbs. **Wohin?:** Ich habe den Brief *in meine* Tasche gesteckt. **Wo?:** Der Brief steckt *in meiner* Tasche.

10-7 Was passt in jeder Gruppe zusammen?

1. die Erzählerin
2. die Kirche
3. das Jahrhundert
4. das Pferd

a. der Reiter
b. der Christ
c. die Zeit
d. die Geschichte

9. der Stall
10. das Drama
11. der Bauer
12. der Dialekt

i. die Szene
j. die Sprache
k. das Pferd
l. das Feld

5. fangen
6. galoppieren
7. frieren
8. drucken

e. der Winter
f. der Ball
g. das Buch
h. das Pferd

10-8 Assoziationen. Was passt wo?

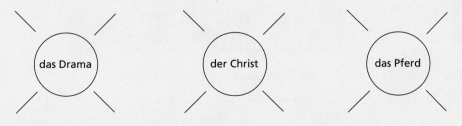

das Drama   der Christ   das Pferd

Sketch: This word is pronounced as in English. The German equivalent of English *sketch (drawing)* is **die Skizze.**

die Kirche / die Szene / reiten / die Autorin / satteln / die Bibel / der Sketch / der Stall / das Paradies / die Rolle / fromm / galoppieren

❶ Narrating past events

The simple past tense

Remember that conversational situations can include writing letters and diary entries.

In *Kapitel 6* you learned that in German you use the perfect tense to talk about past events in conversational situations.

ANN: Was **habt** ihr an Silvester **gemacht**?   *What did you do on New Year's Eve?*

TIM: Zuerst **haben** wir bei mir **gefeiert** und dann **sind** wir zum Brandenburger Tor **gefahren.**   *First we celebrated at my place and then we drove to the Brandenburg Gate.*

The simple past tense is used mainly in written German to narrate a series of connected events in the past. Sometimes called the narrative past, it is usually found in literary texts, newspaper reports, and newscasts. You will see that there are some similarities in the way the simple past is formed in German and English.

NEWSCAST:

Obwohl das Thermometer minus zehn **zeigte, kamen** über eine Million Menschen zum Brandenburger Tor und **feierten** dort Silvester.   *Although the thermometer read minus ten, over a million people came to the Brandenburg Gate and celebrated New Year's Eve there.*

The simple past of regular verbs

The simple past of regular verbs is formed by adding a past-tense marker to the verb stem (**-t-** in German and *-ed* in English).

German	English
lernen: ich lernte	*to learn: I learn**ed***
studieren: ich studierte	*to study: I studi**ed***

The **-t-** is inserted between the verb stem and the personal endings.

singular		plural	
ich	lernte	wir	lernten
du	lerntest	ihr	lerntet
er/es/sie	lernte	sie	lernten
	Sie	lernten	

The German simple past has more than one English equivalent.

ich lernte { *I learned* / *I did learn* / *I was learning* }

Verb stems that end in **-d, -t** (**lan*d*-en**, **arbei*t*-en**), or certain consonant combinations (**reg*n*-en**) add an **e** before the past tense marker **-t-**.

singular	plural
ich arbeitete	wir arbeiteten
du arbeitetest	ihr arbeitetet
er/es/sie arbeitete	sie arbeiteten
	Sie arbeiteten

10-9 Die arme Frau Tauber. Lesen Sie den folgenden Text und setzen Sie die fett gedruckten° Verben ins Präteritum°.

fett gedruckt: in boldface / simple past

Weil Frau Tauber nicht sehr viel **verdient, vermietet** sie ein Zimmer ihrer Wohnung an zwei Studenten. Die beiden **bezahlen** pünktlich ihre Miete, aber oft **kochen** sie nicht nur für sich in Frau Taubers Küche, sondern auch für ihre Freunde. Sie **machen** auch oft den Abwasch nicht, **leeren** fast nie den Mülleimer und manchmal **benutzen** sie sogar Frau Taubers Töpfe. Wenn sie Partys **feiern, übernachten** immer ein paar von ihren Freunden bei ihnen und morgens **duschen** und **baden** sich alle in Frau Taubers Bad. Und auch wenn die beiden Studenten mal keine Party **feiern, stören** sie die arme Frau die halbe Nacht mit ihrer lauten Musik. Nach drei Monaten **kündigt**° Frau Tauber den beiden und **sucht** sich nettere und ruhigere Mieter.

gives notice

The simple past of irregular verbs

In German as in English, the simple past of irregular verbs is signaled by a stem change.

You will find lists of the irregular verbs used in this text in the *Anhang* on pages A36 and A38.

German	English
kommen: ich k**am**	to come: I c**ame**
gehen: ich g**ing**	to go: I w**ent**
stehen: ich st**and**	to stand: I st**ood**

The simple past of German irregular verbs has no personal ending in the 1st and 3rd person singular.

singular	plural
ich kam	wir kamen
du kamst	ihr kamt
er/es/sie kam	sie kamen
	Sie kamen

BERLINER GEDENKTAFEL

In diesem Hause lebten von 1934 bis zu ihrem Tode

HANNING SCHRÖDER
4. 7. 1896 – 16. 10. 1987
Komponist

CORNELIA SCHRÖDER-AUERBACH
24. 8. 1900 – 21. 10. 1997
Musikwissenschaftlerin

Von Anfang 1944 bis zum März 1945 versteckten sie hier ein jüdisches Ehepaar und halfen ihm so die »Shoa« zu überleben

10-10 Die mysteriösen Euros. Lesen Sie den folgenden Text und setzen Sie die fett gedruckten Verben ins Präsens°.

Karin **saß** an einem der Tische vor einem kleinen Restaurant, **las** die Zeitung und **trank** einen Cappuccino. Da **hielt** auf der Straße ein roter BMW, der Fahrer **ging** zum Kellner, **sprach** kurz mit ihm, **gab** ihm einen Zettel° und ein Bündel Geldscheine und **stieg** wieder in seinen Wagen. Der Kellner **kam** zu Karin, **gab** ihr die Scheine und den Zettel und **lief**, ohne ein Wort zu sagen, schnell ins Restaurant. Auf dem Zettel **stand:** „Hier sind tausend Euro. Der Rest kommt, wenn die Sachen verkauft sind." Karin **verstand** von allem nichts und **rief** ein paarmal nach dem Kellner. Weil er aber nicht **kam, begann** sie, Angst zu kriegen, und **ging** mit dem vielen Geld schnell zur nächsten Polizeiwache°.

piece of paper

police station

The simple past of separable-prefix verbs

In the simple past, the prefix of separable-prefix verbs functions just as it does in the present tense.

In an independent clause, the prefix is separated and appears at the end of the clause.

Der Bauer sattelte sein Pferd und **galoppierte** dem Studenten **nach.**

In a dependent clause, the unseparated verb appears at the end of the clause.

Als der Bauer wieder **heimkam,** hatte er kein Pferd mehr.

state treasuries

irregular

10-11 Warum Staatskassen° immer leer sind. Lesen Sie die Geschichte und setzen Sie alle fett gedruckten Verben ins Präteritum. Das Präteritum der unregelmäßigen° Verben ist vor der Geschichte gegeben.

geben – gab	haben – hatte	lassen – ließ	sein – war
gehen – ging	kommen – kam	rufen – rief	sitzen – saß

one day

Obwohl der gute König Otto ein großes, reiches Land mit vielen fleißigen Menschen **hat, ist** seine Staatskasse immer leer. Deshalb **ruft** er eines Tages° seine Generäle und Minister zusammen, und als sie dann alle um den Tisch **herumsitzen, fragt** er sie: „Wo bleibt denn nur das ganze Geld?" Er **bekommt** aber keine Antwort. Die Generäle **schütteln**° nur den Kopf und die Minister **machen** ein dummes Gesicht.

shake

Da **sagt** der König: „Wenn ihr alle so dumm seid, dann muss ich wohl meinen Narren° rufen."

court jester

Der Narr **kommt** und der König **sagt:** „Narr, du weißt wohl auch nicht, wo das ganze Geld bleibt." „Doch", **antwortet** der Narr, „und wenn du es wirklich wissen willst, dann gib mir einen Klumpen° Butter."

lump

Der Narr **bekommt** die Butter und es **ist** ein großer Klumpen. Er **gibt** ihn dem Ministerpräsidenten in die Hand und **sagt:** „Geben Sie den Klumpen bitte weiter, Exzellenz!" Und so **geht** nun der Butterklumpen von Minister zu Minister und von General zu General um den ganzen Tisch herum. Als der Klumpen dann endlich wieder beim Narren **ankommt,** da **ist** das kein großer Klumpen mehr, sondern nur noch ein ganz miserables Klümpchen. Fast die ganze Butter **klebt**° an den großen, warmen Händen der Minister und der Generäle!

sticks

Da **sagt** der Narr zum guten König Otto: „Siehst du jetzt, wo dein Geld ist? – Es ist dort, wo auch die Butter ist."

■ Sprachnotiz ·······················

Contradicting negative statements or questions

Use **doch** to contradict a negative statement or a negative question.

EVA: Sven hat bestimmt noch keine Freundin.

I'm sure Sven doesn't have a girlfriend yet.

LILLI: **Doch,** sie heißt Leah und sie ist sehr nett.

Of course he does. Her name is Leah and she's very nice.

In this usage, **doch** has no direct English equivalent.

10-12 Fragen und Antworten. Ergänzen Sie **doch** oder **nein.**

1. Tim kann bestimmt nicht kochen. _____, er kocht sogar sehr gut.
2. Bist du noch nie geritten? _____, ich habe Angst vor Pferden.
3. Hast du denn keine besseren Schuhe? _____, sie sind nur gerade beim Schuhmacher.
4. Frierst du denn nicht? _____, aber ich habe kein Geld für einen warmen Wintermantel.
5. Ist das nicht wieder eine Lüge? _____, diesmal ist es die Wahrheit.
6. Du bist wohl nicht sehr fromm. _____, ich gehe nur nicht jeden Sonntag in die Kirche.

The simple past of mixed verbs

In the simple past, mixed verbs have the stem change of the irregular verbs, but the past-tense marker **-t-** and personal endings of the regular verbs.

bringen	**brachte**	nennen	**nannte**
denken	**dachte**	rennen	**rannte**
kennen	**kannte**	wissen	**wusste**

10-13 Mein erstes Semester. Ergänzen Sie die passenden Verben.

kannte / wussten / brachte / dachten / rannten / nannten

Anfang September _____ mein Vater mich zu meiner Uni. Obwohl ich dort keinen Menschen _____, hatte ich bald viele Freunde. Wir _____ von einer Party zur anderen, hatten viel Spaß, aber _____ nur selten an° unser Studium. Meine armen Eltern _____ bald nicht mehr, was sie mit mir tun sollten, und _____ mich einen richtigen Nichtsnutz°.

of

good-for-nothing

10-14 Die mysteriösen Rosen. Lesen Sie die Geschichte und setzen Sie alle fett gedruckten Verben ins Präteritum.

Am Morgen meines zwanzigsten Geburtstags **kommt** ein Mann vom Blumengeschäft und **bringt** mir fünf rote Rosen. „Sie können nur von Florian sein", **denke** ich. Aber die Karte, die in den Rosen **steckt, nennt** keinen Namen, und ich **kenne** auch die Handschrift° nicht. „Von wem sind denn diese Rosen?" **frage** ich den Mann, aber er **weiß** es auch nicht. Als ich dann später die Treppe **hinunterrenne, kommt** Florian zur Haustür herein und **bringt** mir fünf rote Rosen. Von wem die ersten fünf waren, weiß ich bis heute nicht.

handwriting

10-15 Manchmal sollte man gar nicht erst aufstehen.
Suchen Sie die passenden Sätze zu diesen Bildern und lesen Sie dann die Geschichte laut vor.

    1   Als Martin gestern aufwachte, schien ihm die Sonne ins Gesicht.

neither / nor _____ Da blieb zu nichts Zeit, weder° zum Duschen noch° zum Frühstück.

  _____ Es war schon halb zehn und um zehn hatte er eine wichtige Klausur!

hardly _____ Und als er auf seinen Wecker schaute, konnte er kaum° glauben, was er da sah.

  _____ Er sprang aus dem Bett und zog schnell Hemd und Hose an.

  _____ Aber er kam zu spät: der Bus fuhr gerade um die Ecke.

bus stop _____ Wie verrückt rannte er zur Bushaltestelle°.

finally _____ Schließlich° stoppte er ein Taxi.

  _____ „Was jetzt?" dachte Martin.

  _____ Er versuchte, ein Auto anzuhalten, aber niemand hielt.

  _____ Punkt zehn hielt das Taxi vor der Uni und der Fahrer sagte: „fünf Euro, bitte."

  _____ „Schnell zur Uni, bitte!" rief er, als er in das Taxi stieg.

Darn it! _____ „Verflixt!° Sie steckt zu Hause in meiner anderen Jacke!"

  _____ Aber da sah Martin auch schon die Lösung seines Problems: das war doch Claudia dort vor der Eingangstür!

raced _____ Und als das Taxi dann zur Uni raste°, wollte Martin seine Geldtasche aus der Jacke holen.

_____ Und Gott sei Dank hörte sie ihn und hatte auch fünf Euro bei sich.

_____ Aber obwohl es schon fünf nach zehn war, war der Hörsaal leer!

_____ Schnell steckte er den Kopf durchs Fenster und rief: „Claudia!"

_____ Und an der Tafel stand: Impressionismus: Klausur auf nächste Woche verschoben°.   *postponed*

_____ Dann rannten sie zusammen die Treppe zum Hörsaal hinauf.

② Expressing action in different time frames

A summary of verb tenses and principal parts

You have learned that in German as in English, all tenses of *regular* verbs derive from the stem of the infinitive. They are completely predictable in German.

infinitive	tenses		
	PRESENT	SIMPLE PAST	PERFECT
lernen	er **lern**t	er **lern**te	er hat ge**lern**t
to **learn**	he **learns**	he **learned**	he has **learn**ed

In both German and English, all tenses of *irregular* and *mixed* verbs are derived from a set of *principal parts*. These principal parts consist of the infinitive, the simple past, and the past participle, all forms you have already learned. Below are the principal parts of **gehen** and the tenses generated from them.

	infinitive	simple past	past participle
PRINCIPAL PARTS	**gehen**	**ging**	**gegangen**
	to go	*went*	*gone*
	present	simple past	perfect
TENSES	**er geht**	**er ging**	**er ist gegangen**
	he goes	*he went*	*he has gone*

German verbs that are irregular in the present tense have an additional principal part that reflects this irregularity.

infinitive	present-tense irregularity	simple past	past participle
geben	**gibt**	**gab**	**gegeben**
fahren	**fährt**	**fuhr**	**gefahren**

Remember that the present-tense irregularity is found in both the 2nd and 3rd person singular.

Remember that the past-tense forms of mixed verbs show the **-t-** marker of regular verbs *and* the stem change of irregular verbs.

infinitive		simple past	past participle
bringen		**brachte**	**gebracht**

The verb **werden** has characteristics of a mixed verb and an irregular verb.

infinitive	present-tense irregularity	simple past	past participle
werden	**wird**	**wurde**	**geworden**

The principal parts of the irregular and mixed verbs used in this book are in the *Anhang* on pages A36 and A38. Be sure to learn them.

❸ Expressing *when* in German

Wann, als, and wenn

Although **wann, als,** and **wenn** all correspond to English *when,* they are not interchangeable.

Wann is a question word that introduces direct and indirect questions.

Wann kriegt Nina ihren Führerschein?	*When is Nina getting her driver's license?*
Ich weiß nicht, **wann** Nina ihren Führerschein kriegt.	*I don't know when Nina is getting her driver's license.*

Als is a conjunction that introduces dependent clauses referring to a single event in the past or a block of time in the past. The verb in an **als**-clause is often in the simple past tense, even in conversation.

Als ich zur Tür hereinkam, klingelte das Telefon.	*When I walked in the door, the phone rang.*
Als wir in Bremen lebten, war ich sieben.	*When we lived in Bremen, I was seven.*

Wenn is a conjunction that introduces dependent clauses referring to events in the present or future or to *repeated* events in any time frame.

Ruf uns bitte gleich an, **wenn** du in Frankfurt ankommst.	*Please call us right away when you arrive in Frankfurt.*
Wenn Oma uns besuchte, brachte sie immer einen Kuchen mit.	*When (whenever) grandma visited us, she always brought a cake.*

Als Gott den Mann schuf hat sie bloß geübt

wann?	als	wenn
• questions	• single event in the past • block of time in the past	• events in the present or future • repeated events (all time frames)

Vorsicht!
Frei laufender Hund!

Wenn der Hund kommt, flach auf den Boden legen und auf Hilfe warten.

Wenn keine Hilfe kommt –

viel Glück!

10-16 Fragen und Antworten. Ergänzen Sie **als** oder **wenn**.

1. Wann hat Stephanie Peter kennen gelernt?
2. Wann macht Stephanie ihre tollen Pancakes?
3. Wann fährt Stephanie mit Peter zu seinen Eltern nach Berlin?
4. Wann fliegt Stephanie wieder nach Amerika zurück?
5. Wann haben sich Claudia und Martin kennen gelernt?
6. Wann wollen Martin und Claudia heiraten?

_____ sie nach München kam, um dort ein Jahr lang zu studieren.
Immer _____ Peter zum Frühstück kommt.
_____ das Wintersemester zu Ende ist.
_____ das Sommersemester zu Ende ist.
_____ sie vor zwei Jahren zum Skilaufen in Kitzbühel waren.
_____ sie mit dem Studium fertig sind.

10-17 Ein paar persönliche Fragen.

- Wann hast du Rad fahren gelernt? *Als ich …*
- Wann hast du schwimmen gelernt? *Als ich …*
- Wann hast du deinen Führerschein gekriegt? *Als ich …*
- Willst du mal nach Europa fliegen? Wann? *Wenn ich …*
- Willst du heiraten? Wann? *Wenn …*

10-18 Ein toller Reiter. Ergänzen Sie **als** oder **wenn**.

_____ ich zwölf war, lebten wir in Berlin. Im Sommer 1993 besuchten wir meinen Großvater in Schleswig-Holstein. Er war Bauer und hatte ein wunderschönes Pferd. Jeden Morgen, _____ wir im Stall fertig waren, durfte ich auf diesem Pferd reiten. Mein kleiner Bruder hatte Angst vor° Pferden. Jedes Mal _____ Großvater das Pferd aus dem Stall holte, rannte er ins Haus. Aber _____ wir wieder in Berlin waren, sagte er zu seinen Freunden: „_____ ich bei meinem Opa in Schleswig-Holstein war, habe ich sogar reiten gelernt."

hatte Angst vor: *was afraid of*

10-19 Aus meiner Kindheit. Schreiben Sie eine Geschichte im Präteritum.

Was machten Sie in den Sommerferien, als Sie klein waren?
Wohin reisten Sie mit Ihrer Familie?
Was spielten Sie mit den Nachbarskindern?

- Himmel und Hölle°
- Verstecken°
- Hockey
- Baseball
- mit Barbie-Puppen
- …

Schreibtipp: Writing about your childhood experiences is a good opportunity to use **als** (for single events) and **wenn** (for repeated events).

hopscotch
hide-and-seek

◀ Hören ···

Fantastische Angebote

announcement (over a PA system)

Sie hören eine Durchsage° im Kaufhaus Karstadt.

Stock: Floors in buildings are numbered differently in the German-speaking countries. **Das Erdgeschoss (das Parterre)** is equivalent to the ground or first floor. **Der erste Stock** is then equivalent to the second floor and so on.

Wühltisch: Wühlen means *to rummage.*

NEUE VOKABELN

das Angebot	*special offer*	**das Erdgeschoss**	*ground floor*
der Stock,	*floor; story*	**der Wühltisch**	*bargain table*
die Stockwerke		**modisch**	*fashionable*
die Auswahl	*selection*	**empfehlen**	*to recommend*
pflegeleicht	*easy to care for*	**(empfiehlt)**	
etwas Passendes	*something suitable*	**die Bohne**	*bean*

10-20 Erstes Verstehen. Haken Sie in jeder Kategorie ab, was Sie in der Durchsage hören.

1. Stockwerke

   _____ im Erdgeschoss   _____ im dritten Stock
   _____ im ersten Stock   _____ im vierten Stock
   _____ im zweiten Stock

2. Abteilungen

   _____ Damenabteilung   _____ Herrenabteilung
   _____ Kinderabteilung   _____ Sportabteilung

3. Kleidungsstücke

   _____ Hemden   _____ Hose
   _____ Blusen   _____ Handschuhe
   _____ Jacke   _____ Rock

4. Kombinationen mit dem Wort *Tennis*

   _____ Tennisbälle   _____ Tennisschuhe
   _____ Tennisschläger   _____ Tennisklub
   _____ Tennismatch   _____ Tennisspieler

5. Gemüse

   _____ Spinat   _____ Bohnen
   _____ Karotten   _____ Brokkoli

10-21 Detailverstehen. Hören Sie die Durchsage noch einmal und schreiben Sie Antworten zu den folgenden Fragen.

1. In welchem Stock ist die Damenabteilung?
2. Welche Kleidungsstücke für Damen gibt es heute zu stark reduzierten Preisen?
3. Wo ist die Sportabteilung?
4. Was gibt es auf den Wühltischen?
5. Von wann bis wann kann man im Gourmetrestaurant zu Mittag essen?
6. Was ist heute das Tagesmenü?
7. Wie viel kostet ein Seniorenteller?

10-22 Im Kaufhaus ist der Kunde König (?) Lesen Sie die Umfrage aus der Planitzer Zeitung über den Service in deutschen Kaufhäusern und ergänzen Sie dann die Tabelle.

Umfrage: Break this word into its two components to find a literal translation that helps you understand it.

 **Sarah Vogel, Lehrerin:** Letzte Woche war ich im Kaufhaus, um mich nach einem neuen Wintermantel umzuschauen. Wie immer, keine Hilfe! Die Verkäuferinnen unterhielten[1] sich über ihre Liebesprobleme und schauten mich nicht mal an. Deshalb kaufe ich lieber in kleinen Geschäften, auch wenn es dort ein bisschen mehr kostet.

 **Kirsten Ast, Schülerin:** Ich kaufe meine Klamotten nur im Kaufhaus. Gerade gestern war ich nach der Schule bei Karstadt, um ein Paar Jeans zu kaufen. Die Auswahl war fantastisch und die Jeans kosteten auch nicht die Welt.

 **Benedikt Frey, Student:** Vor etwa vierzehn Tagen wollte ich einen defekten Rasierapparat zurückbringen, den ich eine Woche zuvor[6] gekauft hatte. Was für ein Theater! Der Verkäufer versuchte sogar, mich zu beschuldigen[7]. Und da soll der Kunde König sein?!

Dieter Schnabel, Architekt: Als ich das letzte Mal[2] im Kaufhaus war, konnte ich mir in aller Ruhe[3] die Computer anschauen.  Kein Verkäufer störte mich und ich konnte mich anhand[4] der vielen Broschüren bestens informieren. Ich kam sehr zufrieden[5] nach Hause!

[1]*talked*   [2]*the last time*   [3]*in peace and quiet*
[4]*using*   [5]*satisfied*   [6]*before*   [7]*blame*

NAME	BERUF	ERFAHRUNG° IM KAUFHAUS	WAS WOLLTE SIE/ER KAUFEN ODER ZURÜCKBRINGEN?	
Kirsten Ast		gut		*experience*
			Rasierapparat	
	Architekt			
		schlecht		

✏️ **10-23 Meine Erfahrung im Kaufhaus.** Schreiben Sie im Stil der Umfrage aus der Planitzer Zeitung von einer guten oder schlechten Erfahrung im Kaufhaus.

Remember to use the simple past to write your narrative!

- Wie war die Verkäuferin/der Verkäufer? (freundlich, unfreundlich, hilfsbereit°, konnte keine Verkäuferin/keinen Verkäufer finden)   *helpful*
- Wie war die Auswahl? (gut, schlecht, fantastisch)
- Wollten Sie schon mal etwas Defektes zurückbringen? Was war das? Wie behandelte° man Sie?   *treated*

➍ Giving information about people, places, and things

The relative pronoun as object of a preposition

In *Kapitel 9* you learned that except for the dative plural **(denen)**, the forms of the relative pronoun and the definite article are identical.

forms of the relative pronoun				
	MASCULINE	NEUTER	FEMININE	PLURAL
NOMINATIVE	der	das	die	die
ACCUSATIVE	den	das	die	die
DATIVE	dem	dem	der	denen

You also learned that the relative pronoun has the same gender and number as its antecedent, but that its case is determined by its function within the relative clause.

		RELATIVE CLAUSE	
	ANTECEDENT	REL. PRON.	
Wie alt ist	**der Wagen,**	**den**	du gekauft hast?
How old is	*the car*	*that*	*you bought?*

When a relative pronoun is the object of a preposition, the gender and number of the relative pronoun are still determined by the antecedent, but the case is determined by the preposition.

			RELATIVE CLAUSE	
	ANTECEDENT	PREP.	REL. PRON.	
Das ist	**der Wagen,**	**für**	**den**	ich nur 3000 Euro bezahlt habe.
This is	*the car*	*for*	*which*	*I paid only 3,000 euros.*
Kennst du	**den Typ,**	**mit**	**dem**	Eva heute Abend ins Kino geht?
Do you know	*the guy*	*with*	*whom*	*Eva is going to the movies tonight?*

The English translation could also read *This is the car (that) I paid only 3,000 euros for.* Note that in German, the preposition always *precedes* the relative pronoun and the relative pronoun cannot be omitted.

Note: Relative pronouns never contract with prepositions.

Preposition + definite article:

Ich wohne **im** Studentenheim beim Sportplatz.

*I live **in the** dorm near the athletic field.*

Preposition + relative pronoun:

Das Studentenheim, **in dem** ich wohne, ist beim Sportplatz.

*The dorm **in which** I live is near the athletic field.*

10-24 Definitionen. Ergänzen Sie die Relativsätze.

▶ Was ist ein Hai?

Ein Hai ist ein Fisch, …

vor dem alle Schwimmer große Angst haben.

S1: Was ist ein Hai?

S2: Ein Hai ist ein Fisch, vor dem alle Schwimmer große Angst haben.

1. Was ist ein Lkw?

Ein Lkw ist ein Fahrzeug, …

3. Was sind Bienen?

Bienen sind Insekten, …

2. Was ist ein Bücherregal?

Ein Bücherregal ist ein Möbelstück, …

4. Was ist ein Spiegel?

Ein Spiegel ist ein Stück Glas, …

in das man seine Bücher stellt.	in dem man sich selbst sehen kann.
von denen wir Honig bekommen.	mit dem man schwere Sachen transportiert.

5. Was ist eine Waage?

Eine Waage ist ein Gerät, …

7. Was sind Pferde?

Pferde sind Tiere, …

6. Was ist eine Untertasse?

Eine Untertasse ist ein kleiner Teller, …

8. Was ist eine Säge?

Eine Säge ist ein Werkzeug, …

auf den man seine Tasse stellt.	auf denen man reiten kann.
mit dem man Bäume fällen kann.	mit dem man herausfindet, wie schwer etwas ist.

10-25 Weißt du das? **S1** stellt die Fragen und ergänzt die Relativpronomen. **S2** beginnt die Antworten mit „Er/Es/Sie heißt …".

1. Wie heißt der Fluss, an d__ Wien liegt?
2. Wie heißt der Ozean, über d__ man von Amerika nach Europa fliegt?
3. Wie heißt die Stadt, in d__ der Eiffelturm steht?
4. Wie heißt der Kontinent, auf d__ es Tausende von Kängurus gibt?
5. Wie heißt das Haus, in d__ der amerikanische Präsident wohnt?
6. Wie heißt der Kanal, durch d__ Schiffe vom Atlantik zum Pazifik fahren?
leaning 7. Wie heißt die Stadt, in d__ der berühmte schiefe° Turm steht?
sheep 8. Wie heißt die große Insel, auf d__ es mehr Schafe° als Menschen gibt?
toys 9. Wie heißt das Material, aus d__ das meiste Spielzeug° gemacht ist?
citizens 10. Wie heißt das kleine europäische Land, in d__ die meisten Bürger° drei Sprachen sprechen?

❺ A review of adjective endings

Lerntipp: To help you remember the endings, think of the five places with the adjective ending **-e** as forming the shape of a toothbrush. All of the other adjective endings are **-en**.

Adjectives preceded by *der*-words

Adjectives preceded by **der**-words take one of two endings: **-e** or **-en**.

	masculine	neuter	feminine	plural
NOMINATIVE	der jung**e** Mann	das klein**e** Kind	die jung**e** Frau	die klein**en** Kinder
ACCUSATIVE	den jung**en** Mann	das klein**e** Kind	die jung**e** Frau	die klein**en** Kinder
DATIVE	dem jung**en** Mann	dem klein**en** Kind	der jung**en** Frau	den klein**en** Kindern
GENITIVE	des jung**en** Mannes	des klein**en** Kindes	der jung**en** Frau	der klein**en** Kinder

10-26 Die reichen Müllers. Ergänzen Sie die Adjektivendungen.

1. Dieser reich__, alt__ Mann heißt Müller.

showy

2. Dieses groß__, protzig__° Haus gehört dem reich__, alt__ Müller.

3. Das ist die einzig__ Tochter dieses reich__, alt__ Mannes.

4. Diese beid__ weiß__ Pudel gehören der einzig__ Tochter des reich__, alt__ Müller.

5. Das ist der klein__ Sohn der einzig__ Tochter dieses reich__, alt__ Mannes.

6. Diese beid__ süß__ Hamster gehören dem klein__ Sohn der einzig__ Tochter des reich__, alt__ Müller.

7. Das ist der schön__, neu__ Käfig der beid__ süß__ Hamster des klein__ Sohnes der einzig__ Tochter dieses reich__, alt__ Mannes.

10-27 Was?! Du kennst die reichen Müllers nicht? Ergänzen Sie die Adjektivendungen.

1. JENS: Kennst du den alt__ Mann dort?
   ANN: Welchen alt__ Mann?
   JENS: Den alt__ Mann mit der groß__ Nase und der dick__ Zigarre.
   ANN: Ja klar, das ist doch der reich__, alt__ Müller.

2. JENS: Wem gehört denn das groß__ Haus dort?
   ANN: Welches groß__ Haus?
   JENS: Das groß__ Haus mit der protzig__ Fassade.
   ANN: Das gehört dem reich__, alt__ Müller.

3. JENS: Wer ist denn die jung__ Frau dort?
   ANN: Welche jung__ Frau?
   JENS: Die jung__ Frau mit der lang__ Nase und den kurz__ Haaren.
   ANN: Das ist die einzig__ Tochter des reich__, alt__ Müller.

4. JENS: Wem gehören denn die beid__ Pudel dort?
   ANN: Welche beid__ Pudel?
   JENS: Die beid__ weiß__ Pudel vor dem groß__, protzig__ Haus.
   ANN: Das sind die beid__ Pudel der einzig__ Tochter des reich__, alt__ Müller.

Adjectives preceded by *ein*-words

When an adjective is preceded by an **ein**-word that has no ending, the adjective shows the gender, number, and case of the noun by taking the appropriate **der**-word ending. This happens in only three instances.

	masculine	neuter
NOMINATIVE	ein jung**er** Mann	ein klein**es** Kind
ACCUSATIVE		ein klein**es** Kind

Lerntipp: Again, it may help you to picture the five places where the adjective endings are *not* **-en** as having the shape of a toothbrush.

All other adjective endings after **ein**-words are identical to those after **der**-words.

	masculine	neuter	feminine	plural
NOM.	ein jung**er** Mann	ein klein**es** Kind	eine jung**e** Frau	meine klein**en** Kinder
ACC.	einen jung**en** Mann	ein klein**es** Kind	eine jung**e** Frau	meine klein**en** Kinder
DAT.	einem jung**en** Mann	einem klein**en** Kind	einer jung**en** Frau	meinen klein**en** Kindern
GEN.	eines jung**en** Mannes	eines klein**en** Kindes	einer jung**en** Frau	meiner klein**en** Kinder

10-28 Lieschen Maiers Hund. Ergänzen Sie!

Lieschen Maier hatte einmal einen klein__, weiß__ Hund. Er war ein sehr schön__, weiß__ Hund und Lieschen liebte ihn sehr. Jeden Morgen gab sie ihm eine klein__ Dose Hundefutter und ging dann in die Schule. Wenn Lieschen nach der Schule mit ihrem klein__, weiß__ Hund im Park spazieren ging, hatte sie ihn immer an einer lang__ Leine. Und in Lieschens Schlafzimmer stand neben ihrem eigen__ Bett das Bettchen ihres klein__, weiß__ Hundes.

10-29 Fritzchen Müllers Katze.

Fritzchen Müller hatte einmal eine groß__, schwarz__ Katze. Sie war eine sehr schön__, schwarz__ Katze und Fritzchen liebte sie sehr. Jeden Morgen gab er ihr eine groß__ Dose Katzenfutter und ging dann in die Schule. Wenn Fritzchen nach der Schule mit seiner groß__, schwarz__ Katze im Park spazieren ging, hatte er sie immer an einer lang__ Leine. Und in Fritzchens Schlafzimmer stand neben seinem eigen__ Bett das Bettchen seiner groß__, schwarz__ Katze.

huge

10-30 Unser Krokodil.

Wir hatten einmal ein riesig__°, grün__ Krokodil. Es war ein sehr schön__, grün__ Krokodil und wir liebten es sehr. Jeden Morgen gaben wir ihm eine riesig__ Dose Krokodilfutter und gingen dann in die Schule. Wenn wir nach der Schule mit unserem riesig__, grün__ Krokodil im Park spazieren gingen, hatten wir es immer an einer lang__ Leine. Und in unserem Schlafzimmer stand neben unserem eigen__ Bett das Bettchen unseres riesig__, grün__ Krokodils.

What do you feel like having?

10-31 Worauf hast du Lust?°

Beschreiben Sie mit passenden Adjektiven, worauf Sie Lust haben.

LISA: Worauf hast du Lust, David?

juicy DAVID: Ich habe Lust auf einen großen, saftigen° Apfel.

DAVID: Und du, Tanja, worauf hast du Lust?

scoop TANJA: Ich habe Lust auf eine große Kugel° Schokoladeneis.

TANJA: Und du, …

groß / riesig / eiskalt / heiß / saftig / lecker…

	ZUM TRINKEN		ZUM ESSEN		ZUM NACHTISCH
bar	ein _____ Glas Orangensaft	einen _____ Teller Spaghetti		eine _____ Tafel° Schokolade
	ein _____ Glas Mineralwasser	eine _____ Portion Pommes		einen _____ Becher Fruchtjoghurt
	eine _____ Cola	frites		einen _____ Becher Vanilleeis
	ein _____ Bier	einen _____ Hamburger		ein _____ Stück Apfelkuchen
	…	ein _____ Steak		ein _____ Stück Schwarzwälder
		ein _____ Schnitzel		Kirschtorte
		ein _____ Stück Pizza		einen _____ Becher Softeis
		…		…

Unpreceded adjectives

When an adjective is not preceded by a **der**-word or an **ein**-word, the adjective shows the gender, number, and case of the noun by taking the appropriate **der**-word ending. The genitive forms are not listed here because they are less common.

	masculine	neuter	feminine	plural
NOMINATIVE	guter Kaffee	gutes Bier	gute Salami	gute Äpfel
ACCUSATIVE	guten Kaffee	gutes Bier	gute Salami	gute Äpfel
DATIVE	gutem Kaffee	gutem Bier	guter Salami	guten Äpfeln

10-32 Essen und Trinken. Ohne **der**-Wörter oder **ein**-Wörter, bitte!

▶ **Dieser** französische Käse ist sehr gut.

S: Französischer Käse ist sehr gut.

1. Mögen Sie **dieses** deutsche Bier?
2. Mit **einem** echten italienischen Mozzarella schmeckt die Pizza viel besser.
3. So **eine** gute Leberwurst habe ich noch nie gegessen.
4. Möchten Sie **den** kalifornischen Wein oder **den** französischen?
5. Mit **einem** trockenen Wein schmeckt **dieser** französische Camembert besonders gut.
6. **Diese** spanischen Mandarinen sind sehr süß.

10-33 Internationaler Geschmack. Erzählen Sie einander, was für ausländische° Produkte Sie besonders gern haben.   *foreign*

• Ich trinke gern …	amerikanisch	Bier (n)
• Ich esse gern …	deutsch	Wein (m)
• Ich fahre gern …	französisch	Brot (n)
• Ich sehe gern …	italienisch	Käse (m)
• Ich lese gern …	japanisch	Wurst (f)
	kanadisch	Autos (pl)
	polnisch	Motorräder (pl)
	spanisch	Filme (pl)
	mexikanisch	Literatur (f)
	…	…

A *Spiegel* edition has an average of
175 pages, while an edition of *Time*
has an average of 85 pages.

INFOBOX
Zeitungen und Zeitschriften

Im Durchschnitt[1] liest jeder Deutsche täglich eine halbe Stunde die
Zeitung. Das Boulevardblatt[2] *Bild* ist mit täglich 4 Millionen
Exemplaren[3] Deutschlands meistgelesene Zeitung. Weniger gelesen,
aber mit enormem Einfluss[4] sind überregionale Tageszeitungen wie die
Frankfurter Allgemeine (FAZ) und die *Süddeutsche Zeitung* und die
Wochenzeitung *Die Zeit*. Die Zeitschriften[5] *Der Spiegel, Focus* und *Stern*
erscheinen[6] wie *Time, Newsweek* und das kanadische *Maclean's*
wöchentlich. Besonders *Der Spiegel* berichtet aber viel detaillierter als die
nordamerikanischen Zeitschriften. *Der Spiegel* hat übrigens eine
deutschsprachige und auch eine englischsprachige Online-Version.

    In Österreich ist *Die Presse* die größte Tageszeitung. Die *Wiener Zeitung*,
die älteste Zeitung der Welt, gibt es seit dem 8. August 1703.

    Die größte Tageszeitung der Schweiz, die *Neue Zürcher Zeitung*,
erschien am 12. Januar 1780 zum ersten Mal und gehört zu den
international angesehensten[7] deutschsprachigen Zeitungen.

    Die größte luxemburgische Tageszeitung ist das dreisprachige
d'Wort. 82 Prozent sind darin auf Deutsch geschrieben, 16 Prozent auf
Französisch und 2 Prozent auf Lëtzebuergesch.

[1] *on average*   [2] *tabloid*   [3] *copies*   [4] *influence*   [5] *magazines*   [6] *appear*   [7] *most respected*

Zusammenschau

 Video-Treff ··············

Meine Lieblingslektüre

Kristina, Anja Szustak, André, Stefan Meister,
Maiga, Thomas und Stefan Kuhlmann
erzählen, was sie gern lesen.

Zum besseren Verstehen

10-34 Was ist das auf Englisch?

1. Ich lese englische Bücher, damit mein Englisch **am Leben bleibt.**
2. Das ist ein Mensch, der immer noch **auf der Suche** ist.
3. Ich lese Bücher, die mich **fesseln.**
4. Ich muss ja leider viel für die Uni lesen, und **das reicht mir.**
5. Hier geht es **größtenteils** um lokale Nachrichten.
6. Wenn ich **nicht gerade** Bücher lese, lese ich Zeitschriften.
7. Diese Zeitschrift gibt es **seit den 80er-Jahren.**

   a. searching
   b. largely
   c. grab
   d. not at the
      moment
   e. since the eighties
   f. stays alive
   g. that's enough
      for me

Schauen Sie jetzt das Video an und machen Sie die Übungen in
Video-Treff-Teil des *Student Activities Manual.*

◀)) ▶ Hören ···

Es allen recht machen°

Trying to please everybody

nach einer Fabel von Äsop

Die Personen in dieser Fabel sind ein Vater und sein Sohn mit ihrem Esel, ein Bäcker, ein Fleischer, ein Schneider° und ein Bauer. Die neun Bildchen illustrieren die Fabel.

tailor

Fables often contain a moral and frequently use animals as main characters. Many fables were attributed to Aesop. Legend has it that he lived in Greece in the 6th century B.C.

NEUE VOKABELN

sie trafen	*they met*	**sie banden**	*they tied*
kurz danach	*shortly afterwards*	**der Stock**	*stick*

10-35 Erstes Verstehen. Schauen Sie die Bildchen an und ergänzen Sie die folgende Tabelle. Erst danach sollten Sie die Fabel zum ersten Mal anhören.

	WER REITET?	WER GEHT ZU FUSS?		WER SPRICHT?
Bild 1:	*Der Vater.*		Bild 2:	
Bild 3:			Bild 4:	
Bild 5:			Bild 6:	
Bild 7:			Bild 8:	

10-36 Detailverstehen. Hören Sie die Fabel ein zweites Mal und schreiben Sie, wie Vater und Sohn auf die Kritik der vier Männer aus ihrem Dorf reagierten.

1. Der Bäcker sagte: „Ich finde es nicht recht, dass du reitest und dass dein kleiner Sohn zu Fuß geht. Du bist doch viel stärker als er." *Da stieg …*
2. Der Fleischer sagte: „Was, Junge, du reitest und lässt deinen Vater zu Fuß gehen? Das ist nicht recht!" *Da stieg …*
3. Der Schneider sagte: „Zwei Menschen auf einem kleinen Esel! Das ist nicht recht!" *Da stiegen …*
4. Der Bauer sagte: „Warum reitet denn nicht einer von euch?" *Weil nun aber nur der Esel noch nicht reiten durfte, banden …*

Schreibtipp (10-37): Use your imagination to make your story as creepy as possible. Don't forget to use the simple past tense to narrate your story. When your characters say something in direct speech, however, be sure to use the tense that suits what they are saying.

▉ Schreiben und Sprechen

creepy story   **10-37 Eine Gruselgeschichte°.** Schreiben Sie eine Gruselgeschichte. Beginnen Sie Ihre Geschichte mit den folgenden Worten:

strange / feeling *Es war eine kalte, stürmische Nacht. Ich hatte ein komisches° Gefühl°, aber ich wusste nicht warum. Plötzlich hörte ich …*

chain story
der Reihe nach: *in turn*

10-38 Wir erzählen eine Rundgeschichte°. Student 1 beginnt. Die anderen erzählen der Reihe nach° weiter.

S1: Es war eine kalte, stürmische Nacht.
S2: Plötzlich …
S3: …

▉ Lesen

Zum besseren Verstehen

10-39 Geschichten für Kinder.

1. Welche Geschichten haben Sie als Kind gehört oder gelesen?
2. Welche von diesen Geschichten haben Ihnen besonders gut gefallen und welche haben Ihnen nicht gefallen?
3. In welchen von diesen Geschichten haben Tiere eine Rolle gespielt? Was für Tiere waren das?
4. Die Illustration auf dieser Seite zeigt einen kleinen, dicken Igel und einen langen, dünnen Hasen. In Nordamerika gibt es den Igel nur im Zoo oder manchmal als Haustier. Wie nennt man ihn auf Englisch?

…as, „aver mienetwegen mach't sien, wenn du so …lt de Wett?" „En …Branwien", seggt …, spröök de Haas, …k los gahn." „Nä, …neen de Swinegel, …; eerst will ick to …röhstücken; inner …pp'n Platz."

…; denn de Haas …weges dachte de …s verlett sick up

10-40 Was ist das auf Englisch?

1. Ein Igel ist ein Tier, das kurze, **krumme** Beine hat.
2. Dass der Hase über seine kurzen, krummen Beine lachte, **ärgerte** den Igel.
3. Er wollte deshalb mit dem Hasen **einen Wettlauf machen.**
4. Ich **wette,** der Hase kann schneller laufen als der Igel.
5. Sie wollten vom **oberen** bis zum **unteren** Ende eines Feldes laufen.
6. Der Hase war **außer sich,** als der Igel vor ihm am unteren Ende des Feldes war.
7. Der Igel gewann die Wette und ging **vergnügt** nach Hause.

a. run a race
b. happily
c. crooked
d. made angry
e. beside himself
f. upper / lower
g. bet

Der Hase und der Igel

nach einem Märchen der Brüder Grimm

Es war an einem Sonntagmorgen zur Sommerzeit. Die Sonne schien hell vom blauen Himmel, der Morgenwind ging warm über die Felder und die Leute gingen in ihren Sonntagskleidern zur Kirche.

Der Igel aber stand vor seiner Tür und schaute in den schönen
5 Morgen hinaus. Als er so stand, dachte er: „Warum gehe ich nicht schnell aufs Feld und schaue meine Rüben[1] an, solange meine Frau die Kinder anzieht und das Frühstück macht."

Als der Igel zum Rübenfeld kam, traf er dort seinen Nachbarn, den Hasen, der auch einen Spaziergang machte. Der Igel sagte freundlich:
10 „Guten Morgen!" Aber der Hase grüßte nicht zurück, sondern sagte: „Wie kommt es denn, dass du hier am frühen Morgen auf dem Feld herumläufst?" „Ich gehe spazieren", sagte der Igel. „Spazieren?" lachte der Hase, „Du, mit deinen kurzen, krummen Beinen?"

Diese Antwort ärgerte den Igel sehr, denn für einen Igel hatte er
15 sehr schöne Beine, obwohl sie von Natur kurz und krumm waren. „Denkst du vielleicht", sagte er zum Hasen, „dass du mit deinen langen, dünnen Beinen schneller laufen kannst als ich?" „Das denke ich wohl", lachte der Hase, „willst du wetten?" „Ja, ein Goldstück und eine Flasche Schnaps", antwortete der Igel. „Gut", rief der Hase, „fangen wir an!"
20 „Nein, so große Eile[2] hat es nicht", sagte der Igel, „ich will erst noch nach Hause gehen und ein bisschen frühstücken. In einer halben Stunde bin ich wieder zurück."

Auf dem Heimweg dachte der Igel: „Diese Wette hast du verloren[3], lieber Hase, denn du hast zwar die langen Beine, aber ich habe den
25 klugen[4] Kopf." Als er zu Hause ankam, sagte er zu seiner Frau: „Frau, zieh schnell eine von meinen Hosen an, du musst mit mir aufs Feld."

[1]*turnips*   [2]*hurry*   [3]*lost*   [4]*clever*

„Eine von deinen Hosen? Ja, was ist denn los?" fragte seine Frau. „Ich habe mit dem Hasen um ein Goldstück und eine Flasche Schnaps gewettet. Ich will mit ihm einen Wettlauf machen und da brauche ich dich." „Oh, Mann", rief da die Frau ganz aufgeregt, „bist du nicht ganz recht im Kopf? Wie kannst du mit dem Hasen um die Wette laufen?" „Lass das mal meine Sache sein", sagte der Igel. „Zieh jetzt die Hose an und komm mit."

Unterwegs[1] sagte der Igel zu seiner Frau. „Nun pass mal auf, was ich dir sage. Siehst du, auf dem langen Feld dort wollen wir unseren Wettlauf machen. Der Hase läuft in der einen Furche[2] und ich in der anderen, und dort oben fangen wir an. Du aber sitzt hier unten in meiner Furche, und wenn der Hase hier ankommt, springst du auf und rufst: ‚Ich bin schon da.'"

Als der Igel am oberen Ende des Feldes ankam, wartete der Hase dort schon. „Können wir endlich anfangen?" fragte er. „Oder willst du nicht mehr?" „Doch", sagte der Igel. Dann ging jeder zu seiner Furche. Der Hase zählte: „Eins, zwei, drei" und rannte wie ein Sturmwind über das Feld. Der Igel aber blieb ruhig auf seinem Platz.

Als der Hase am unteren Ende des Feldes ankam, sprang die Frau des Igels auf und rief: „Ich bin schon da!" Der Hase konnte es kaum glauben. Aber weil die Frau des Igels genauso aussah wie ihr Mann, rief er: „Einmal ist nicht genug!" Und zurück raste er, dass ihm die Ohren am Kopf flogen. Die Frau des Igels aber blieb ruhig auf ihrem Platz. Als der Hase am oberen Ende des Feldes ankam, sprang der Igel auf und rief: „Ich bin schon da!" Der Hase war ganz außer sich und schrie[3]: „Noch einmal!" „Sooft du Lust hast", lachte der Igel. So lief der Hase noch dreiundsiebzigmal, und jedes Mal, wenn er oben oder unten ankam, riefen der Igel oder seine Frau: „Ich bin schon da!"

Das letzte Mal aber kam der Hase nicht mehr bis zum Ende, sondern stürzte[4] mitten auf dem Feld tot zur Erde[5]. Der Igel aber nahm das Goldstück und die Schnapsflasche, rief seine Frau, und beide gingen vergnügt nach Hause. Und wenn sie nicht gestorben sind, so leben sie noch heute.

[1]*on the way* [2]*furrow* [3]*screamed* [4]*fell* [5]*ground*

Arbeit mit dem Text

10-41 Wer war das? Sie hören zwölf Fragen zu *Der Hase und der Igel*. Haken Sie nach jeder Frage die richtige „Person" oder „Personen" ab.

	1.	2.	3.	4.	5.	6.	7.	8.	9.	10.	11.	12.
IGEL	___	___	___	___	___	___	___	___	___	___	___	___
FRAU IGEL	___	___	___	___	___	___	___	___	___	___	___	___
IGEL UND FRAU	___	___	___	___	___	___	___	___	___	___	___	___
HASE	___	___	___	___	___	___	___	___	___	___	___	___
HASE UND IGEL	___	___	___	___	___	___	___	___	___	___	___	___

INFOBOX

WWW Find out more about **Grimms Märchen** at www.prenhall.com/treffpunkt
→ Kapitel 10 → Web Resources
→ Kultur

Die Brüder Grimm

Im Jahr 1807 begannen die Brüder Jacob und Wilhelm Grimm, die uralten[1] Geschichten zu sammeln, die einfache Leute einander erzählten. Ihr Ziel[2] war, diese Geschichten aufzuschreiben, bevor sie für immer verloren gingen. Viele von den schönsten Geschichten hörten sie von Dorothea Viehmann, einer älteren Frau, die ihnen ein paar Mal in der Woche Lebensmittel ins Haus brachte. Den bezaubernden[3] Märchenstil verdanken[4] wir aber nicht dieser Erzählerin, sondern dem poetischen Talent von Wilhelm Grimm.

Wenn wir heute von Märchen sprechen, denken wir an wunderbare Erzählungen für Kinder. Die meisten von diesen Geschichten waren aber eigentlich für Erwachsene[5] gedacht, und viele Ausdrücke und Szenen waren für Kinder nicht geeignet[6]. „Deshalb haben wir", so schreibt Wilhelm Grimm, „jeden für das Kindesalter nicht passenden Ausdruck sorgfältig[7] gelöscht[8]." Trotzdem gibt es Kritiker, die manche Szenen in diesen Märchen immer noch zu grausam finden. Aber sind diese Szenen wirklich so grausam wie die Grausamkeiten, die wir heutzutage fast täglich auf dem Bildschirm sehen?

Die *Kinder- und Hausmärchen* der Brüder Grimm gibt es heute in über 160 Sprachen. Ein Grund[9], warum diese Märchensammlung in aller Welt so beliebt[10] geworden ist, ist wohl, dass ihre Themen oft auch in den Geschichten von vielen anderen Ländern und Kulturen erscheinen[11].

[1]*ancient*   [2]*goal*   [3]*enchanting*   [4]*owe*   [5]*adults*   [6]*suitable*
[7]*carefully*   [8]*deleted*   [9]*reason*   [10]*popular*   [11]*appear*

10-42 Richtig oder falsch?

1. _____ Aus Märchen für Kinder machten die Brüder Grimm Geschichten für Erwachsene.
2. _____ Die Geschichten von anderen Ländern und Kulturen haben oft dieselben Themen wie die Märchen der Brüder Grimm.
3. _____ Den bezaubernden Märchenstil haben wir Dorothea Viehmann zu verdanken.
4. _____ Was wir heutzutage auf dem Bildschirm sehen, ist oft grausamer als die grausamen Szenen in den Grimmschen Märchen.
5. _____ Die Brüder haben viele Ausdrücke, die für Kinder nicht geeignet waren, sorgfältig gelöscht.
6. _____ Es gibt immer noch Kritiker, denen manche Szenen in den Grimmschen Märchen zu grausam sind.

A second great undertaking of the Grimm brothers was their **Deutsches Wörterbuch,** an etymological dictionary that focuses on the historical development of words. They had only reached the letter "F" before their deaths. This is indicated on the postage stamp, where you can see a bit of their handwritten manuscript: All the words on the stamp are based on **Freiheit** *(freedom)*. It took generations of linguists to complete this monumental 32-volume work, which was finally finished in 1960. Jakob and Wilhelm Grimm are buried side by side in Berlin. To this day, fresh flowers adorn their graves.

Wort, Sinn und Klang

Wörter unter der Lupe

Words as chameleons: *als*

You have learned that **als** has a variety of meanings. Here is a summary.

- *as*   in expressions like **als Kind**   **Als** Kind konnte ich sehr schnell laufen.

- *than*   after the comparative form of an adjective or adverb   Mit meinen langen Beinen konnte ich schneller laufen **als** alle meine Freunde.

- *when*   as a conjunction   **Als** ich mit meinen Freunden mal einen Wettlauf machen wollte, hatten sie keine Lust.

- *but*   after **nichts**   Ich hatte auch später nichts **als** Probleme mit meinen langen Beinen.

10-43 Was bedeutet *als* hier? *Than, when, as, or but?*

1. Als Mensch ist Professor Huber sehr nett.
2. Professor Huber ist viel netter, als ich dachte.
3. Gestern habe ich den ganzen Tag nichts als gelesen.
4. Als Maria nach Hause kam, hatte ich das Buch gerade fertig gelesen.
5. Kathrin war schon als kleines Mädchen sehr sportlich.
6. In Hamburg hatten wir leider nichts als Regenwetter.
7. Als wir in Hamburg waren, regnete es fast jeden Tag.
8. Diesen Juni hat es in Hamburg mehr geregnet als letztes Jahr im ganzen Sommer.

Giving language color

Hundreds of colorful expressions make use of the names of animals. Here is a small sampling.

Da lachen ja die Hühner!	*What a joke!*
Da hast du Schwein gehabt!	*You were lucky!*
Ich habe einen Bärenhunger.	*I'm hungry as a bear.*
Es ist alles für die Katz.	*It's all for nothing.*
Da bringen mich keine zehn Pferde hin!	*Wild horses couldn't drag me there!*
Du musst dir Eselsbrücken bauen.	*You'll have to find some tricks to help you remember.*
Mein Name ist Hase, ich weiß von nichts.	*Don't ask me. I don't know anything about it.*

Eselsbrücke: This is also called a mnemonic device. It is often an aid to memory by association, like the suggestion that the five places in the adjective ending chart that don't take the ending **-en** have the shape of a toothbrush.

10-44 Was passt zusammen?

1. Gehst du mit zum Fußballspiel?
2. Günter denkt, er kriegt eine Eins in dieser Klausur.
3. Warum hörst du denn schon auf, zu lernen?
4. Wer hat denn die ganzen Bierflaschen ausgetrunken?
5. Wie soll ich denn alle diese Wörter lernen?
6. Sollen wir essen gehen?
7. Ich habe eine Eins in Physik!

a. Du musst dir Eselsbrücken bauen.
b. Mein Name ist Hase. Ich weiß von nichts.
c. Da hast du aber Schwein gehabt!
d. Der eine Eins?! Da lachen ja die Hühner!
e. Klar! Ich habe einen Bärenhunger.
f. Es ist ja doch alles für die Katz!
g. Bei dem Wetter bringen mich da keine zehn Pferde hin!

))) Zur Aussprache

German f, v, and w

In German the sound represented by the letter **f** is pronounced like English *f* and the sound represented by the letter **v** is generally also pronounced like English *f*.

10-45 Hören Sie gut zu und wiederholen Sie!

für	**vier**
Form	**vor**
folgen	**Volk**

Familie **F**eldmann **f**ährt in den **F**erien nach **F**innland.
Volkmars **V**orlesung ist um **V**iertel **v**or **v**ier vorbei°.
Volker ist **V**erkäufer **f**ür **F**arb**f**ernseher.

over

When the letter **v** appears in a word of foreign origin, it is pronounced like English *v*: **V**ase, **V**ideo, **V**ariation.

In German the sound represented by the letter **w** is always pronounced like English *v*: **w**ann, **w**ie, **w**o.

Felder und Wälder

10-46 Hören Sie gut zu und wiederholen Sie!

Wolfgang und **V**eronika **w**ohnen in einer **V**illa am **W**annsee.
Walter und David **w**aren im **N**ovember in **V**enedig.
Oliver ist **V**egetarier und **w**ill keine **W**urst.

In the following word pairs, distinguish clearly between German **f** and **w** sounds.

Vetter	**Wetter**	**Farm**	**warm**
vier	**wir**	**fein**	**Wein**
viel	**will**	**Fest**	**West**
voll	**Wolle**	**Felder**	**Wälder**

Nomen

das **E**rdgeschoss	ground floor
der St**o**ck, die St**o**ckwerke	floor; story

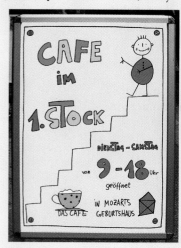

die B**u**shaltestelle, -n	bus stop
der F**ü**hrerschein, -e	driver's license
der L**k**w, -s (L**a**stkraftwagen)	truck
der L**a**stwagen, -	
der P**k**w, -s (Pers**o**nenkraftwagen)	car
der Pers**o**nenwagen, -	
der **E**influss, ⸚e	influence
die **E**rde	earth; ground
die Fr**ei**heit	freedom
das Gef**ü**hl, -e	feeling
der Gr**u**nd, ⸚e	reason
die K**i**ndheit	childhood
die **U**mfrage, -n	survey, poll
das Sp**ie**lzeug	toy; toys
das W**e**rkzeug, -e	tool
das Z**ie**l, -e	goal; aim

die Freiheit, Kindheit: Remember that all nouns with the suffix **-heit** are feminine.

Verben

empf**e**hlen (empf**ie**hlt), empf**a**hl, empf**o**hlen	to recommend
schr**ei**en, schr**ie**, geschr**ie**n	to scream; to shout
sich unterh**a**lten (unterh**ä**lt), unterh**ie**lt, unterh**a**lten	to talk; to converse
versch**ie**ben, versch**o**b, versch**o**ben	to postpone
w**e**tten	to bet

Andere Wörter

gr**au**sam	cruel
k**o**misch	strange; funny
kr**u**mm	crooked
m**o**disch	fashionable
s**a**ftig	juicy
s**o**rgfältig	careful(ly)
k**au**m	scarcely; hardly
unterw**e**gs	on the way
w**e**der … n**o**ch	neither . . . nor

grausam: Can you think of a English cognate for this word?

krumm: *Crummy* is a cognate.

Ausdrücke

Angst haben vor (+ *dat*)	to be afraid of
das l**e**tzte Mal	the last time
den K**o**pf schütteln	to shake one's head
eines T**a**ges	one day; some day
im D**u**rchschnitt	on average
im **E**rdgeschoss	on the ground floor
G**o**tt sei Dank!	Thank God!
Ich habe Lust auf eine Tafel Schokol**a**de.	I feel like having a chocolate bar.
Sie war **au**ßer sich.	She was beside herself.
Verfl**i**xt!	Darn it!

Durchschnitt: The noun **Schnitt** comes from **schneiden**. Break the word into its two components to find a literal translation that helps you understand it.

Das Gegenteil

der/die Erw**a**chsene, -n ≠ das K**i**nd, -er	adult ≠ child
gew**i**nnen, gew**a**nn, gew**o**nnen ≠ verl**ie**ren, verl**o**r, verl**o**ren	to win ≠ to lose
oben ≠ **u**nten	above ≠ below
r**ie**sig ≠ w**i**nzig	huge ≠ tiny
zufr**ie**den ≠ **u**nzufrieden	satisfied ≠ dissatisfied

zufrieden: Frieden means *peace*. If you give **zu** the same meaning as in **zu Hause,** what is the literal meaning of **zufrieden?**

Leicht zu verstehen

der Hamburger, -
das Insekt, -en
das Mikroskop, -e
das Produkt, -e
der Service

das Steak, -s
die Tabelle, -n
das Talent, -e
das Thema,
   Themen

Steak is pronounced as in English.

Which words in this list are stressed on a different syllable than their English equivalents?

Synonyme

die Erzählung, -en	=	die Geschichte, -n
kriegen	=	bekommen
beliebt	=	populär
defekt	=	kaputt
klug	=	intelligent
miserabel	=	schlecht
schließlich	=	endlich

Wörter im Kontext

10-47 Was passt zusammen?

1. Ein Lkw ist ein Fahrzeug,
2. Ein Pkw ist ein Fahrzeug,
3. Ein Führerschein ist ein Dokument,
4. Die Erde ist der Planet,
5. Erwachsene sind Menschen,

a. auf dem wir leben.
b. die keine Kinder mehr sind.
c. in dem nur wenige Personen Platz haben.
d. mit dem man schwere Sachen transportiert.
e. ohne das man weder einen Pkw noch einen Lkw fahren darf.

Führerschein: You already know the meaning of **Geldschein**, **Gutschein**, and **Schuldschein**. Can you guess the meaning of **Geburtsschein** and **Kassenschein?**

10-48 Was ist hier identisch? Welche zwei Sätze in jeder Gruppe bedeuten etwa dasselbe?

1. Stefan hat den Kopf geschüttelt.
   Stefan hat sich sehr aufgeregt.
   Stefan war außer sich.

2. Ann ist nicht hier, sondern in ihrem Zimmer.
   Ann ist weder hier noch in ihrem Zimmer.
   Ann ist nicht hier, und in ihrem Zimmer ist sie auch nicht.

3. Ich habe mich lang mit Kurt unterhalten.
   Mit Kurt habe ich nicht lang gesprochen.
   Ich habe lang mit Kurt gesprochen.

4. Jetzt habe ich Lust auf Tennis.
   Ich spiele sehr gern Tennis.
   Ich möchte jetzt am liebsten Tennis spielen.

10-49 Was passt wo?

riesiges / beliebter / winziges / unzufriedener / defektes / sorgfältige / modisches

1. Ein Professor, den alle Studenten gern haben, ist ein _____ Professor.
2. Ein Kleidungsstück, das vielen Leuten gefällt, ist ein _____ Kleidungsstück.
3. Ein Gerät, das nicht funktioniert, ist ein _____ Gerät.
4. Ein Insekt, das sehr klein ist, ist ein _____ Insekt.
5. Ein Gebäude, das hundert Stockwerke hat, ist ein _____ Gebäude.
6. Ein Mensch, dem nichts recht ist und der nie genug kriegen kann, ist ein _____ Mensch.
7. Eine Arbeit, die sehr gut und genau gemacht ist, ist eine _____ Arbeit.

Geschichte und Gegenwart

Die Westseite der Eastside Gallery

Kommunikationsziele

Talking about recent German history and current events

Making resolutions

Describing people, places, and things

Expressing feelings and emotions

Strukturen

The passive voice

Participles used as adjectives

Verb-preposition combinations

Wo-compounds

Kultur

Die Berliner Mauer

Kleine deutsche Chronik: 1918 bis 1990

Die Europäische Union

Video-Treff: **So war's in der DDR**

Lesen: **Mein Bruder hat grüne Haare**

Jana Hensel wurde 1976 in der DDR geboren und war 13, als die Mauer fiel und aus Ost- und Westdeutschland wieder ein Land wurde. Als sie 26 war, schrieb sie in Zonenkinder über ihre Kindheit, über den Kulturschock nach der Wiedervereinigung und über die Jahre der Anpassung an die neue Freiheit. In der zweiten Hälfte ihres Lebens wandeln sich ihre Gefühle vom „Sometimes you're better off dead" zum „we will start life new" aus den Liedern „West End Girls" und „Go West" der Pet Shop Boys.

Jana Hensel sieht sich jetzt als eine der „ersten Wessis aus Ostdeutschland", d.h. als eine der jungen Ostdeutschen, die ihre Zukunft nicht mehr dem Staat überlassen, sondern sie in die eigene Hand nehmen wollen.

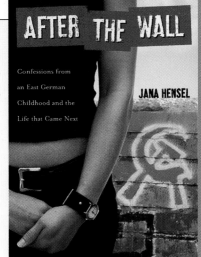

Die englische Ausgabe von Zonenkinder

Go West!

aus Zonenkinder *von Jana Hensel*

… Die ersten zehn Jahre in der Freiheit waren sehr ereignisreich. Viele Abschiede. Neue Bekannte. Die nächsten zehn Jahre werden ruhiger werden. Wir sind die ersten Wessis aus Ostdeutschland, und an Sprache, Verhalten und Aussehen ist unsere Herkunft nicht mehr
5   zu erkennen. Unsere Anpassung verlief erfolgreich, und wir wünschten, wir könnten dies ebenfalls von unseren Eltern und Familien behaupten. Es erschreckt uns, bemerken wir, dass wir in unserer Heimat nur kurz zu Gast gewesen sind. Die paar Jahre vor dem Fall der Mauer, die wir dort gelebt haben, machen zurzeit noch
10 die Hälfte unseres Lebens aus. Von nun an werden sie jedoch zahlenmäßig in die Minderheit geraten und die DDR wird für uns, als schauten wir in den Rückspiegel eines Autos, noch ferner, kleiner und immer märchenhafter werden.

Die Hand am Steuer des eigenen Wagens, heißt es daher,
15 Abschied von unserem Heimatland zu nehmen. Wir sind erwachsen geworden, und auf dem Armaturenbrett klebt kein Aufkleber „Die DDR ist tot, es lebe die DDR" mehr. Stattdessen habe ich kürzlich unter dem Beifahrersitz ein altes Tape von Jonathan wiedergefunden. Zu Beginn unserer Freundschaft in Leipzig hatte er es mir mit einem
20 Augenzwinkern in die Hand gedrückt und gemeint, hier würde ich viel lernen. Ich habe die Kassette damals nicht oft gehört und obendrein nie verstanden, was er mit dem Versprechen der Pet Shop Boys „Go West, Life is peaceful there" sagen wollte. Das Lied über die „West End Girls" und „East End Boys" mochte ich viel lieber.
25 Seit kurzem jedoch läuft sie unaufhörlich, wenn ich in Berlin unterwegs bin. Ich muss lachen, singen mir die beiden Engländer „we will fly so high, tell all our friends goodbye, we will start life new" ins Ohr, und wundere mich: Was es wohl daran einst nicht zu verstehen gab? …

11-1 Was ist das auf Englisch?

1. Für die jungen Ostdeutschen war die **Wiedervereinigung** ein Kulturschock.
2. Für Jana Hensel waren die ersten zehn Jahre in der Freiheit sehr **ereignisreich.**
3. Sie musste von ihrer Kindheit in der DDR **Abschied nehmen.**
4. Ihre **Anpassung an** das Leben in der Freiheit war erfolgreich.
5. Sie sah ihre Kindheit und die DDR wie im **Rückspiegel** eines Autos immer kleiner und märchenhafter werden.
6. In Ostdeutschland gab es nach der Wiedervereinigung den **Aufkleber** „Die DDR ist tot, es lebe die DDR".
7. Jana Hensel hat diesen Aufkleber von ihrem **Armaturenbrett** weggemacht.
8. Kürzlich fand sie unter dem **Beifahrersitz** ein altes Tape.
9. Ihr Freund Jonathan hatte es ihr vor ein paar Jahren in die Hand **gedrückt.**
10. Auf diesem Tape waren **Lieder** der Pet Shop Boys.
11. Das Lied „Go West" läuft jetzt **unaufhörlich,** wenn sie in Berlin unterwegs ist.
12. Sie **wundert sich,** dass sie dieses Lied früher nicht verstanden hat.

a. front passenger seat
b. eventful
c. constantly
d. adjustment to
e. dashboard
f. is surprised
g. sticker
h. rearview mirror
i. reunification
j. pressed
k. songs
l. bid farewell

11-2 Anders gesagt. Unterstreichen Sie in Jana Hensels Text die Sätze oder Satzteile, die etwa dasselbe bedeuten.

1. Im ersten Jahrzehnt nach der Wiedervereinigung ist sehr viel passiert.
2. Wir sind die ersten Ostdeutschen, die nicht mehr so sprechen, sich nicht mehr so benehmen und nicht mehr so aussehen, wie „typische Ossis".
3. … und es tut uns leid, dass wir dies nicht auch von unseren Vätern und Müttern und anderen Verwandten sagen können.

citizens
4. Wenn wir daran denken, dass wir nur wenige Jahre Bürger° der DDR waren, sind wir geschockt.
5. Von jetzt ab wird die Zahl der Jahre vor dem Fall der Mauer immer kleiner als die Zahl der Jahre danach …
6. Unser Leben selbst in die Hand nehmen bedeutet, dass wir nicht mehr so leben wollen wie in der DDR.
7. Wir sind keine Kinder mehr und wünschen uns ein Leben wie in der DDR nicht zurück.
8. Bald nachdem ich meinen Freund kennen gelernt hatte, gab er mir eine Kassette und sagte: „Was auf diesem Tape zu hören ist, ist bestimmt sehr interessant für dich."
9. Jetzt höre ich die Kassette mit dem Lied „Go West" aber die ganze Zeit, wenn …
10. … und ich bin überrascht, dass ich damals nicht verstanden habe, was mir dieses Lied sagen sollte.

11-3: Between September 1949 and August 1961, more than 2.5 million people out of a population of approximately 17 million fled from the GDR to West Germany.

divided

11-3 1949–1990: Das geteilte° Deutschland. Schauen Sie die Karte *Deutschland Bundesländer* am Anfang Ihres Buchs an. Mecklenburg-Vorpommern, Brandenburg, Sachsen-Anhalt, Thüringen und Sachsen waren von 1949 bis 1990 die Deutsche Demokratische Republik. Die Hauptstadt der DDR war Ostberlin.

Iron Curtain
an … grenzten: *bordered on*
Zeichnen Sie auf der Karte den „Eisernen Vorhang"° zwischen der BRD und der DDR ein. Wie heißen die Länder der BRD, die an die DDR grenzten°?

INFOBOX

Die Berliner Mauer

WWW Find out more about the **Berliner Mauer** at
www.prenhall.com/treffpunkt
→ Kapitel 11 → Web Resources
→ Kultur

Von 1949 bis 1990 lag Westberlin mitten in der DDR. Bis 1961 flohen[1] 1,6 Millionen Ostdeutsche über Westberlin in die BRD. Um diesen letzten Fluchtweg[2] zu schließen[3], baute die DDR 1961 die Mauer. Der Teil der Mauer, der mitten durch Berlin ging, war 43 km lang. Die restlichen 112 km trennten[4] Westberlin vom DDR-Umland[5].

Das Schaubild zeigt, warum nur wenige Ostdeutsche über Westberlin in die BRD fliehen konnten und warum über 160 Menschen hier ihr Leben verloren.

- Ostdeutsche, die nach Westberlin fliehen wollten, mussten zuerst durch den Kontaktzaun (9).

- Der Kontaktzaun aktivierte Signalgeräte (7), die Grenzpolizisten auf den Beobachtungstürmen (8) alarmierten.

- Am Führungsdraht der Hundelaufanlage (6) waren an langen Leinen Hunde, die durch ihr Bellen[6] die Grenzpolizisten alarmierten.

- Die Beleuchtungsanlage (4) ließ die Grenzpolizisten auch bei Nacht alles genau sehen.

- Der Kfz-Graben (5) stoppte Fahrzeuge, die versuchten, durch die Mauer zu kommen.

- Auf dem Kontrollstreifen (3) fuhren regelmäßig[7] Polizeipatrouillen.

- Auf der anderen Seite der Betonplattenwand (1) oder des Metallgitterzauns (2) – beide über vier Meter hoch – war Westberlin.

- Die Grenzpolizisten mussten auf jeden schießen[8], der versuchte, durch die Mauer zu fliehen.

[1]*fled* [2]*escape route* [3]*close* [4]*separated* [5]*the area of the GDR around it* [6]*barking* [7]*regularly* [8]*shoot*

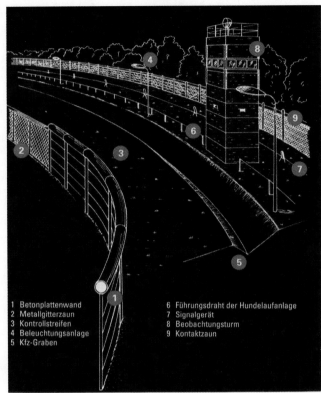

1 Betonplattenwand
2 Metallgitterzaun
3 Kontrollstreifen
4 Beleuchtungsanlage
5 Kfz-Graben

6 Führungsdraht der Hundelaufanlage
7 Signalgerät
8 Beobachtungsturm
9 Kontaktzaun

In West Berlin the Wall was covered in graffiti, many of which commented critically in writing and art on the division of East and West.

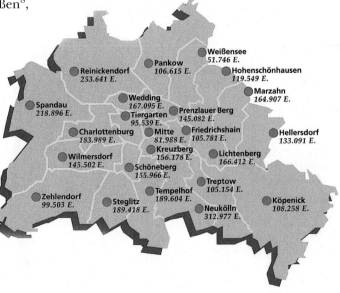

Weißensee 51.746 E.
Reinickendorf 253.641 E.
Pankow 106.615 E.
Hohenschönhausen 119.549 E.
Marzahn 164.907 E.
Spandau 218.896 E.
Wedding 167.095 E.
Tiergarten 95.539 E.
Prenzlauer Berg 145.082 E.
Charlottenburg 183.989 E.
Mitte 81.988 E.
Friedrichshain 105.781 E.
Hellersdorf 133.091 E.
Wilmersdorf 145.502 E.
Kreuzberg 156.178 E.
Lichtenberg 166.412 E.
Schöneberg 155.966 E.
Zehlendorf 99.503 E.
Tempelhof 189.604 E.
Treptow 105.154 E.
Steglitz 189.418 E.
Neukölln 312.977 E.
Köpenick 108.258 E.

11-4 Das geteilte Berlin. Von 1961 bis 1989 trennte die Mauer Westberlin von Ostberlin und von der DDR. Die Ostberliner Stadtteile, die an Westberlin grenzten, waren Köpenick, Treptow, Friedrichshain, Mitte, Prenzlauer Berg und Pankow. Zeichnen Sie die Mauer ein, die mitten durch die Stadt und um Westberlin herum ging.

Watch video clips of
Germany's history at
www.prenhall.com/treffpunkt
→ Kapitel 11 → Web Resources
→ Kultur

KULTUR

Kleine deutsche Chronik: 1918 bis 1990

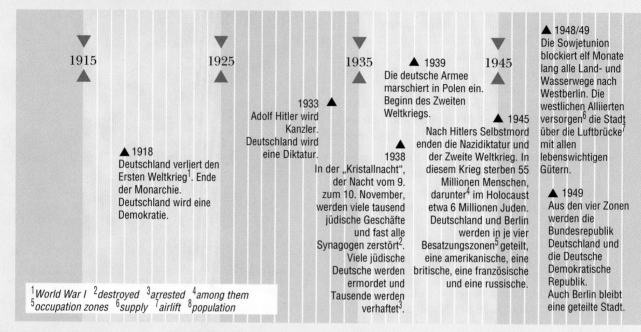

1915

1925

1935

▲ **1939**
Die deutsche Armee
marschiert in Polen ein.
Beginn des Zweiten
Weltkriegs.

1945

▲ **1948/49**
Die Sowjetunion
blockiert elf Monate
lang alle Land- und
Wasserwege nach
Westberlin. Die
westlichen Alliierten
versorgen[6] die Stadt
über die Luftbrücke[7]
mit allen
lebenswichtigen
Gütern.

1933 ▲
Adolf Hitler wird
Kanzler.
Deutschland wird
eine Diktatur.

▲ **1945**
Nach Hitlers Selbstmord
enden die Nazidiktatur und
der Zweite Weltkrieg. In
diesem Krieg sterben 55
Millionen Menschen,
darunter[4] im Holocaust
etwa 6 Millionen Juden.
Deutschland und Berlin
werden in je vier
Besatzungszonen[5] geteilt,
eine amerikanische, eine
britische, eine französische
und eine russische.

▲ **1918**
Deutschland verliert den
Ersten Weltkrieg[1]. Ende
der Monarchie.
Deutschland wird eine
Demokratie.

1938
In der „Kristallnacht",
der Nacht vom 9.
zum 10. November,
werden viele tausend
jüdische Geschäfte
und fast alle
Synagogen zerstört[2].
Viele jüdische
Deutsche werden
ermordet und
Tausende werden
verhaftet[3].

▲ **1949**
Aus den vier Zonen
werden die
Bundesrepublik
Deutschland und
die Deutsche
Demokratische
Republik.
Auch Berlin bleibt
eine geteilte Stadt.

[1]World War I [2]destroyed [3]arrested [4]among them
[5]occupation zones [6]supply [7]airlift [8]population

Berlin Airlift background information: In 1945 Berlin, like the rest of Germany, was divided into four occupation zones. The city was situated within the Soviet zone and access from West Germany was possible only via special transit routes. Beginning shortly after 1945, the Soviets constantly tried to gain control of the entire city. In June 1948 the Berlin conflict reached a climax. In an attempt to starve out the 2.2 million residents of West Berlin and thereby drive out the American, British, and French occupation forces, the Soviets blockaded all roads, rail lines, and waterways from West Germany to Berlin. But just 24 hours after the blockade began, the first American transport planes landed in West Berlin, and the largest air transport operation of all time, the Berlin Airlift or *Operation Vittles*, as the Americans called it, was initiated. The Soviets finally reopened the transit routes to Berlin in May 1949. The Airlift cost not only astronomical sums of money, but also the lives of 40 Britons, 31 Americans, and 5 Germans.

11-5, #4. vH: Note that **Prozent** is sometimes expressed as **vom Hundert.**

11-5 Die Berliner Luftbrücke. Beantworten Sie die Fragen zur Grafik.

1. Wie heißen die drei Flugplätze, auf denen die alliierten Transportflugzeuge landeten?
2. Wie viele Transportflugzeuge landeten dort von Juli 1948 bis Mai 1949?
3. In welchem Monat wurden die meisten Lebensmittel und in welchem die meiste Kohle nach Berlin geflogen?
4. Wie viel Prozent (vH) aller Luftbrückengüter waren Kohle?

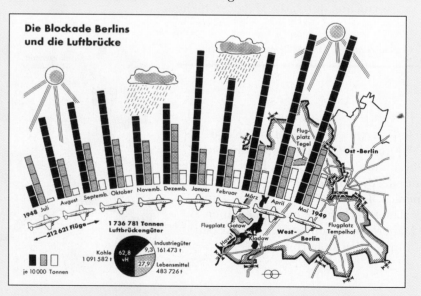

Die Blockade Berlins und die Luftbrücke

1948 Juli, August, Septemb. Oktober, Novemb. Dezemb. Januar, Februar, März, April, Mai 1949

212 621 Flüge
1 736 781 Tonnen Luftbrückengüter
je 10 000 Tonnen
Kohle 1 091 582 t 62,8 vH
Industriegüter 161 473 t 9,3
Lebensmittel 483 726 t 27,9

Flugplatz Tegel
Ost-Berlin
Flugplatz Gatow
West-Berlin
Flugplatz Tempelhof
Havel
Kladow

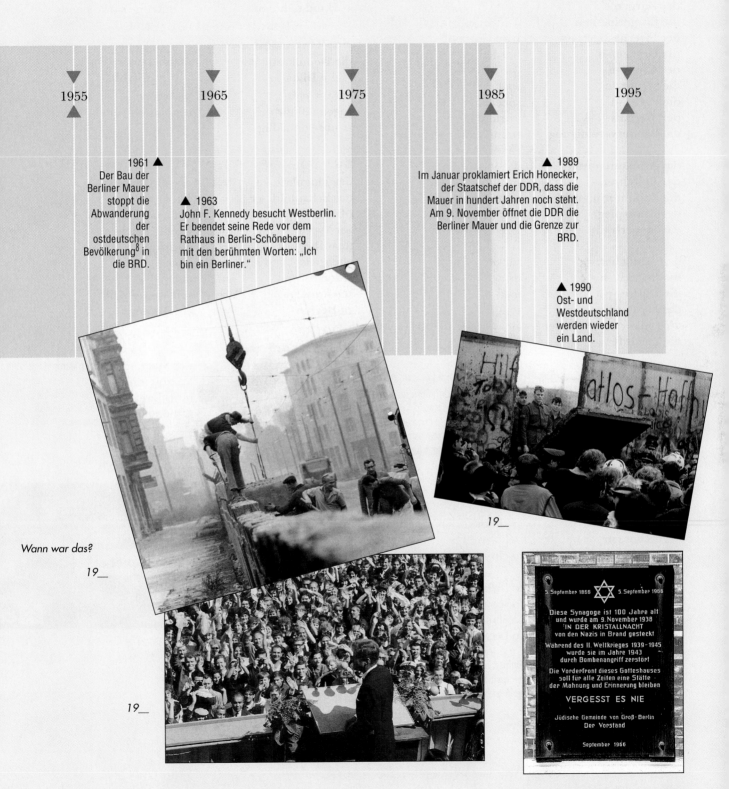

1955   1965   1975   1985   1995

1961 ▲
Der Bau der
Berliner Mauer
stoppt die
Abwanderung
der
ostdeutschen
Bevölkerung[8] in
die BRD.

▲ 1963
John F. Kennedy besucht Westberlin.
Er beendet seine Rede vor dem
Rathaus in Berlin-Schöneberg
mit den berühmten Worten: „Ich
bin ein Berliner."

▲ 1989
Im Januar proklamiert Erich Honecker,
der Staatschef der DDR, dass die
Mauer in hundert Jahren noch steht.
Am 9. November öffnet die DDR die
Berliner Mauer und die Grenze zur
BRD.

▲ 1990
Ost- und
Westdeutschland
werden wieder
ein Land.

19__

Wann war das?

19__

19__

5. September 1866   5. September 1966

Diese Synagoge ist 100 Jahre alt
und wurde am 9. November 1938
'IN DER KRISTALLNACHT'
von den Nazis in Brand gesteckt.

Während des II. Weltkrieges 1939-1945
wurde sie im Jahre 1943
durch Bombenangriff zerstört.

Die Vorderfront dieses Gotteshauses
soll für alle Zeiten eine Stätte
der Mahnung und Erinnerung bleiben

VERGESST ES NIE

Jüdische Gemeinde von Groß-Berlin
Der Vorstand

September 1966

Nomen

die Alliierten (pl)	the Allies
der Bürger, -	} citizen
die Bürgerin, -nen	
der Eiserne Vorhang	Iron Curtain
die Grenze, -n	border
der Krieg, -e	war
die Mauer, -n	wall
die Rede, -n	speech; talk
der Weltkrieg, -e	world war
die Wiedervereinigung	reunification

das Armaturenbrett	dashboard
der Beifahrer, -	} front-seat passenger
die Beifahrerin, -nen	(in a car)
der Rückspiegel, -	rearview mirror
das Steuer(rad)	steering wheel

der Aufkleber, -	sticker
die Brücke, -n	bridge
die Hälfte, -n	half
das Lied, -er	song
die Luft	air
die Zukunft	future

Verben

behaupten	to claim
bellen	to bark
ermorden	to murder
fliehen, floh, ist geflohen	to flee
meinen	to mean; to think, to be of or voice an opinion
schießen, schoss, geschossen	to shoot
schließen, schloss, geschlossen	to close
teilen	to divide
trennen	to separate
verhaften	to arrest
sich wundern	to be surprised

fliehen, schießen, schließen: Note that the principal parts of these three verbs show the same stem vowel changes (**ie-o-o**).

Ausdrücke

etwas in die eigene Hand nehmen	to take something into one's own hands

Das Gegenteil

die Demokratie ≠ die Diktatur	democracy ≠ dictatorship
fern ≠ nah	far ≠ near
regelmäßig ≠ unregelmäßig	regular ≠ irregular

Synonyme

der Flugplatz, ̈e	=	der Flughafen, ̈
das Schaubild, -er	=	die Grafik, -en
öffnen	=	auf·machen
zerstören	=	kaputt·machen
unaufhörlich	=	nonstop
ebenfalls	=	auch
jedoch	=	aber
seit kurzem	=	seit kurzer Zeit
zu Beginn	=	am Anfang

Leicht zu verstehen

die Blockade, -n	der Staat, -en	Which words in this list are stressed on a different syllable than their English equivalents?
die Monarchie, -n	alarmieren	
die Republik, -en	blockieren	
der Kulturschock	proklamieren	

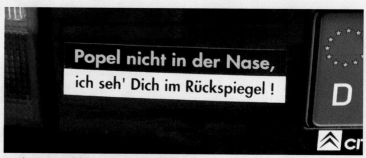

Ein lustiger Aufkleber

Popel nicht in der Nase, ich seh' Dich im Rückspiegel !

meinen: You know **bedeuten** *to mean*. **Meinen** *to mean* expresses intention or resolve: **Sie meint es gut. Ich meine, was ich sage. Bedeuten** expresses the idea of signifying: **Was bedeutet dieses Wort?**

Photo: From the context you should be able to guess what the verb **popeln** means.

The future tense

You can use the present tense to express that something is going to happen in the future, as long as the context refers to future time.

Nächstes Jahr **schreibe** ich ein Buch über meine Kindheit.	*Next year **I'm going to write** a book about my childhood.*

You can also use the future tense to express the same idea. The future tense consists of the auxiliary verb **werden** and an infinitive. The position of the auxiliary and infinitive follows the patterns you already know.

Nächstes Jahr **werde** ich ein Buch über meine Kindheit **schreiben.**	*Next year **I'm going to write** a book about my childhood.*

Wörter im Kontext

11-6 Was passt wo?

geteiltes / schießen / zerstört / Diktaturen / flohen / blockierten / Demokratien / ermordet / geschlossen / Alliierten / Wiedervereinigung / Mauer

1. In der Kristallnacht wurden in Deutschland viele jüdische Deutsche _____ und fast alle Synagogen _____.
2. Von 1949 bis zur _____ im Jahr 1990 war Deutschland ein _____ Land.
3. 1948 _____ die Sowjets alle Land- und Wasserwege nach Westberlin.
4. Die _____ brachten deshalb fast ein Jahr lang alle lebenswichtigen Güter über eine Luftbrücke nach Berlin.
5. Bis 1961 _____ 1,6 Millionen Ostdeutsche über Westberlin in die BRD.
6. 1961 baute die DDR um ganz Westberlin eine _____. Damit war die Grenze zwischen der DDR und Westberlin _____.
7. Die Grenzpolizisten mussten auf Menschen _____, die durch die Mauer nach Westberlin fliehen wollten.
8. Die Staaten hinter dem Eisernen Vorhang waren keine _____, sondern _____.

11-7 Zusammengesetzte Nomen. Kombinieren Sie in jeder der zwei Gruppen die passenden Nomen.

Remember that the gender of compound nouns is determined by the last element.

▶ die Luft + der Krieg = der Luftkrieg

1. die Schau	a. der Sitz	5. die Kultur	e. die Brücke
2. die Rede	b. das Bild	6. die Mauer	f. der Schock
3. der Beifahrer	c. der Krieg	7. der Flug	g. der Fall
4. die Welt	d. die Freiheit	8. die Luft	h. der Hafen

In diesem Bereich werden die Getränke serviert !
Speisen –
Selbstbedienung!
vom
Grill und Buffet

❶ Focusing on the receiver of an action

The passive voice

In grammatical terms, the doer of an action is usually the subject of the sentence. Such a sentence is said to be in the *active voice.*

> **Peter** holt mich um sieben ab.   *Peter is picking me up at seven.*

However, when you find it unnecessary or unimportant to mention the doer of the action, you can make the *receiver* of the action the subject of the sentence. Such a sentence is said to be in the *passive voice.*

> **Ich** *werde* um sieben **abgeholt.**   *I'm being picked up at seven.*

Note that in the passive voice

- the receiver of the action appears in the nominative case.
- the verb appears as a past participle with a form of **werden** as auxiliary.

The most commonly used tenses in the passive voice are the present and the simple past. The tense is indicated by the auxiliary **werden.**

PRESENT	ich **werde** abgeholt	*I'm being picked up*
SIMPLE PAST	ich **wurde** abgeholt	*I was picked up*

Use of the passive voice

In the passive voice, attention is focused on the receiver of the action and on the action itself. You may have been taught to avoid the passive in English, but in German it is used fairly frequently. In the examples below, the active sentences give unnecessary or unimportant information. This is particularly obvious in the second example. For the police, arresting people is routine; for Mr. Müller, being arrested is momentous. Here the passive voice is the more natural mode of expression, because what happens to the receiver of the action is more important than who does it.

passive	active
Mein Wagen **wird repariert.** *My car **is being repaired.***	Der Automechaniker **repariert** meinen Wagen. *The car mechanic **is repairing** my car.*
Herr Müller **wurde verhaftet.** *Mr. Müller **was arrested.***	Die Polizei **hat** Herrn Müller **verhaftet.** *The police **arrested** Mr. Müller.*

11-8 Was wird hier gemacht?

ein Haus / gebaut

S1: Was wird hier gemacht?　　　**S2:** Hier wird ein Haus gebaut.

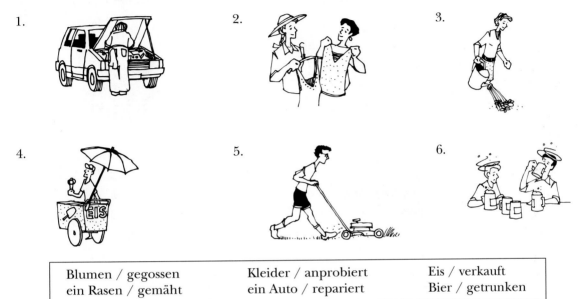

1.

2.

3.

4.

5.

6.

| Blumen / gegossen | Kleider / anprobiert | Eis / verkauft |
| ein Rasen / gemäht | ein Auto / repariert | Bier / getrunken |

 11-9 Was weißt du von Mario und Ann? Die Information für **S2** ist im
Anhang auf Seite A13.

S1: Warum ist Mario denn
so sauer°?

S2: Weil er nie nach seiner
Meinung° gefragt wird.

annoyed / opinion

MARIO		ANN	
Warum ist Mario denn so sauer?		Warum arbeitet Ann schon so lange bei IBM?	
	Weil seine Wohnung renoviert wird.		Weil dort ein neuer Teppich gelegt wird.
	Damit sein Mercedes nicht gestohlen wird.	Warum ist Ann heute mit dem Bus gekommen?	
Warum ist Mario so wenig zu Hause?			Weil sie gleich abgeholt wird.

11-10 Was wurde hier gemacht?

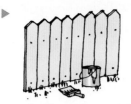

ein Zaun / gestrichen

S1: Was wurde hier gemacht?   **S2:** Hier wurde ein Zaun gestrichen.

1.

3.

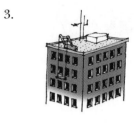

2.

4.

Äpfel / gepflückt	Schnee / geschaufelt
Fenster (pl) / geputzt	Bier / getrunken

5.

7.

6.

8.

wood

ein Baum / gefällt	Brot / gebacken
ein Feld / gepflügt	Holz° / gespalten

11-11 Gute Vorsätze. Sie sind auf einer Neujahrsparty und es ist kurz vor Mitternacht. Schreiben Sie drei gute Vorsätze, d.h. drei Dinge, die Sie im neuen Jahr anders machen wollen. Lesen Sie Ihre Vorsätze dann vor.

Von heute ab wird	regelmäßig Sport	geraucht.
	viel mehr Obst und Gemüse	gelernt.
	viel weniger Schokolade	ausgegeben.
	viel weniger Bier	gemacht.
	viel weniger Kaffee	erzählt.
	einmal täglich der Abwasch	gegessen.
	nicht mehr so viel Geld	angeschaut.
	keine einzige Zigarette mehr	getrunken.
Von heute ab werden	keine blöden Witze° mehr	…
	keine doofen Seifenopern mehr	*jokes*
	jeden Tag ein paar deutsche Vokabeln	
	…	

Mentioning the agent in a passive sentence

In most passive sentences, the agent (the doer of the action) is omitted. However, if the agent is mentioned, it appears in the dative case after the preposition **von.**

> 1923 wurde Adolf Hitlers Münchner Putschversuch **von Regierungstruppen** niedergeschlagen.

> *In 1923 Adolf Hitler's coup attempt in Munich was put down **by government forces.***

Photo: ADAC = Allgemeiner Deutscher Automobil-Club

Dieses Parkhaus wird vom ADAC empfohlen
ADAC

11-12 Ein bisschen deutsche Geschichte. Ergänzen Sie das Agens.

▶ Am 30. Januar 1933 wurde Adolf Hitler _____ zum Kanzler ernannt. (der Reichspräsident)
Am 30. Januar 1933 wurde Adolf Hitler vom Reichspräsidenten zum Kanzler ernannt.

1. In der Nacht vom 9. zum 10. November 1938 wurden _____ fast alle deutschen Synagogen zerstört. (die Nazis)
2. Am 1. September 1939 wurde Polen _____ überfallen°. (deutsche Truppen)
3. In den folgenden vier Jahren wurden fast ganz Europa und große Teile der Sowjetunion _____ besetzt°. (Nazideutschland)
4. Im Frühjahr 1945 wurde Berlin _____ erobert°. (die Rote Armee)
5. Im Juni 1945 wurden Deutschland und Berlin _____ in je vier Besatzungszonen geteilt. (die Alliierten)
6. Von Juni 1948 bis Mai 1949 wurden alle Land- und Wasserwege nach Westberlin _____ blockiert. (die Sowjetunion)
7. Elf Monate lang wurde die Millionenstadt _____ mit Lebensmitteln und Kohle versorgt°. (amerikanische und britische Transportflugzeuge)
8. 1961 wurde _____ der Bau der Berliner Mauer angeordnet°. (die Regierung° der DDR)
9. Am 9. November 1989 wurde die Mauer _____ geöffnet. (die Grenzpolizei der DDR)

invaded

occupied
conquered

Historical events like those desribed in these sentences are often expressed in the passive, even though the agent is mentioned. English does this also, e.g., *He was rejected by the Senate Judicial Committee.*

supplied
ordered
government

❷ Describing people, places, and things

The past participle used as an adjective

In your reading you have frequently seen past participles used as adjectives. Before a noun, the past participle takes the same endings as other adjectives.

Ich habe einen gut **bezahlten** Job.   *I have a well-**paid** job.*

11-13 Was ist das?

▶
eine elegant _____ Dame
gekleidet

Das ist eine elegant gekleidete Dame.

1. frisch _____ Hemden

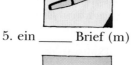

2. ein frisch _____ Brot (n)

3. ein schlecht _____ Mann

4. ein _____ Pferd (n)

5. ein _____ Brief (m)

6. eine _____ Jacke

7. ein gut _____ junger Mann

8. frisch _____ Äpfel

9. zwei _____ Koffer

gebaut	vergessen	gepackt
gewaschen	gebacken	gepflückt
gesattelt	angefangen	rasiert

11-14 Modenschau im Deutschkurs. Beschreiben Sie, was Ihre Mitstudentinnen und Mitstudenten tragen.

S: Lisa trägt einen langen, geschlitzten Rock.
David trägt ein sportliches, blau und weiß gestreiftes Polohemd.

interessant	braun	geblümt *(flowered)*	einen Pullover
cool	blau	gestreift *(striped)*	ein T-Shirt
sportlich	gelb	handgestrickt *(hand-knit)*	ein Sweatshirt
praktisch	grün	kariert *(plaid, checked)*	Jeans
toll	rot	geschlitzt *(slit)*	eine Jacke
…	…	…	…

Hören ···

Eine Radtour in den neuen Bundesländern

Es ist Mitte Juli, und Stephanie, Claudia, Martin und Peter sitzen bei einem Glas Bier im Englischen Garten. Hören Sie was die vier Freunde miteinander sprechen.

Since reunification, the term **die neuen Bundesländer** is frequently used for the states that were formerly **DDR** territory.

NEUE VOKABELN

überhaupt nicht	*not at all*	**der Schlafsack, ⁺e**	*sleeping bag*
die Gegend	*area*	**sich um·schauen nach**	*to look around for*
nördlich von	*north of*	**der Radwanderführer**	*cycling tour*
jederzeit	*anytime*		*guidebook*

11-15 Erstes Verstehen. Wer sagt das? Schreiben Sie C (Claudia), S (Stephanie), M (Martin) oder P (Peter).

_____ Ja, und ich kenne außer München, Berlin, Hamburg und Köln immer noch sehr wenig von Deutschland.

_____ Brandenburg und Mecklenburg-Vorpommern sind für eine Radtour absolut ideal.

_____ Wenn's uns da mal zu heiß wird, können wir jederzeit baden gehen.

_____ Sie möchten Stephanie sowieso noch mal sehen.

_____ Aber planen müssen wir gleich jetzt.

_____ Und dann setzen wir uns zusammen und schauen, was es dort oben alles zu tun und zu sehen gibt.

11-16 Detailverstehen.

1. Wie lange ist Stephanie noch in Deutschland?
2. Welchen Teil von Deutschland kennt Stephanie überhaupt nicht?
3. Warum findet Claudia Brandenburg und Mecklenburg-Vorpommern so ideal für eine Radtour?
4. Was war auf den schönen Bildern, die Stephanie gesehen hat?
5. Wer bekommt die folgenden Aufgaben?
   a. Im Internet nach einer preisgünstigen Gruppenreise schauen.
   b. Einen Radwanderführer und eine gute Karte von Nordostdeutschland kaufen.
   c. Sich nach Zelten umschauen.
   d. Berlin anrufen.

Cycling is very popular in the German-speaking countries and there are **Radwanderführer** for every region in Germany, Austria, and Switzerland. The railway has special cars for transporting bicycles.

11-17 Aus dem Radwanderführer für Mecklenburg-Vorpommern.

Schauen Sie die Karte und den Begleittext° an und ergänzen Sie zu jedem
Ortsnamen° die passende Lage° und Attraktion.

See: Note that **die See** is *sea* **(die Ostsee)**, but **der See** is *lake* **(der Conventer See).**

Lage:	An der Ostseeküste. (3x)	3 km südlich von Kühlungsborn.
	Östlich von Heiligendamm.	3 km südlich vom Conventer See.
Attraktion:	Hundert Jahre alte Kleinbahn.	Zugvögel.
	Herrlicher Buchenwald.	Weiße Häuser und Gebäude.
	4 km langer Sandstrand.	Wunderbare Aussicht.

ORTSNAME	LAGE	ATTRAKTION
Kühlungsborn	*An der Ostseeküste.*	*4 km langer Sandstrand.*
Diedrichshäger Berg		
Heiligendamm		
Conventer See		
Nienhägener Holz		
Bad Doberan		

1. Kühlungsborn mit seinem vier Kilometer langen Sandstrand ist der größte Badeort an der mecklenburgischen Ostseeküste. Drei Kilometer südlich davon liegt der Diedrichshäger Berg, von dem man eine wunderbare Aussicht[1] über die Küste und die mecklenburgische Landschaft hat.

2. Heiligendamm mit seinen weißen Häusern und Gebäuden wird oft „die weiße Stadt am Meer[2]" genannt. Das Hinterland liegt hier tiefer[3] als die Ostsee, und ein hoher Damm verhindert, dass es überflutet wird.

3. Am Conventer See machen Tausende von Zugvögeln[4] Rast[5], wenn sie im Herbst nach Süden fliegen und im Frühjahr wieder nach Skandinavien zurückkehren. Von diesem See ist es nicht weit zum Nienhägener Holz, einem herrlichen Buchenwald[6], der direkt hinter dem Strand beginnt.

4. In Bad Doberan ist die Hauptattraktion die über hundert Jahre alte Kleinbahn „Molli" mit ihrer Dampflokomotive. Eine Fahrt von hier nach Kühlungsborn dauert nur 40 Minuten und für ein paar Euro transportiert die Bahn auch Fahrräder.

[1]*view* [2]*by the sea* [3]*lower* [4]*migrating birds*
[5]*rest* [6]*beech forest*

11-18 Ein paar Fragen zum Begleittext.

1. Von wo aus hat man eine wunderbare Aussicht über die Ostseeküste?
2. Warum wird Heiligendamm oft „die weiße Stadt am Meer" genannt?
3. Warum ist bei Heiligendamm ein hoher Damm?
4. Wie nennt man Vögel, die den Sommer im Norden verbringen und im Winter nach Süden fliegen?
5. Wie alt ist die Doberaner Kleinbahn und was für eine Lokomotive hat sie?

Die Kleinbahn Molli

11-19 Ein paar Fragen zur Radwanderkarte.

1. Wo ist die Jugendherberge von Bad Doberan?
2. Wie hoch ist der Diedrichshäger Berg?
3. Wie viele Kirchen können Sie finden?
4. Wie viele Campingplätze gibt es?
5. Wie lang ist die Fahrradroute 2?

1	2	3
27 km	23 km	55 km

11-20 Ferienerlebnisse. Beschreiben Sie in drei kurzen Absätzen (*paragraphs*)

- wann, wo und mit wem Sie mal eine Radtour oder Fußwanderung gemacht haben oder campen gegangen sind.
- was Sie alles gesehen und erlebt° haben.
- was Sie besonders schön, interessant oder aufregend° fanden.

Ferienerlebnisse: You have learned another term for *experience* in the compound noun **Arbeitserfahrung** (*work experience*). **Erlebnis** is used for an exciting or unforgettable experience.

experienced
exciting

Heiligendamm: Die weiße Stadt am Meer

Denk dran
30

❸ Expanding the meaning of some verbs

Special verb-preposition combinations

Many English and German verbs are used in combination with prepositions. In the examples below, the prepositions used in both languages are direct equivalents.

Beverly Harper arbeitet **für** eine amerikanische Zeitung.

Sie arbeitet gerade **an** einem wichtigen Artikel über Polen.

*Beverly Harper works **for** an American newspaper.*

*She's currently working **on** an important article about Poland.*

In most instances, however, the prepositions used in German verb-preposition combinations do not correspond to those used in English.

Beverly interessiert sich **für** europäische Politik.

Sie wartet **auf** eine E-Mail aus Warschau.

*Beverly is interested **in** European politics.*

*She's waiting **for** an e-mail from Warsaw.*

Below and on the next page are two groups of commonly used verb-preposition combinations. Note that for the two-case prepositions, the test of **wohin/wo** does not apply, and the correct case is therefore given in parentheses.

arbeiten an *(+ dative)*	*to work on*
denken an *(+ accusative)*	*to think of, about*
erzählen von	*to tell about*
wissen von	*to know about*
warten auf *(+ accusative)*	*to wait for*
Angst haben vor *(+ dative)*	*to be afraid of*

11-21 Was passt zusammen? Ergänzen Sie die passenden Präpositionen.

S1:

1. Was weißt du _____ der ehemaligen° DDR?
2. Wann erzählst du uns _____ deiner Reise durch die neuen Bundesländer?
3. Wie lange hast du _____ diesem Referat gearbeitet?
4. Ich habe Angst _____ dieser Klausur.
5. Wo soll ich _____ dich warten, Peter?
6. _____ wen denkst du, Martin?

former

lot

S2:

a. An Claudia.
b. Ich auch.
c. Morgen Abend.
d. Eine ganze Woche.
e. Eine ganze Menge°.
f. Vor der Bibliothek.

11-22 Was machen diese Leute? Ergänzen Sie die Präpositionen und die passenden Objekte.

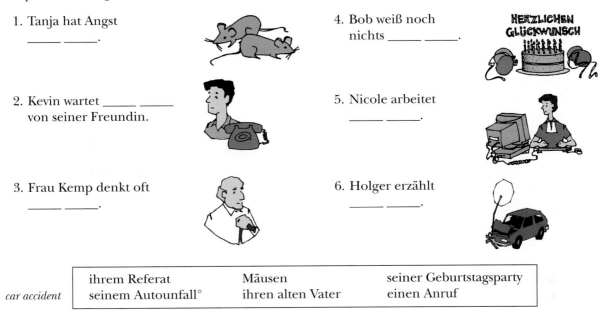

1. Tanja hat Angst
   _____ _____.

2. Kevin wartet _____ _____
   von seiner Freundin.

3. Frau Kemp denkt oft
   _____ _____.

4. Bob weiß noch
   nichts _____ _____.

5. Nicole arbeitet
   _____ _____.

6. Holger erzählt
   _____ _____.

car accident	ihrem Referat	Mäusen	seiner Geburtstagsparty
	seinem Autounfall°	ihren alten Vater	einen Anruf

Verbs that occur in verb-preposition combinations are often reflexive.

sich ärgern über (+ *accusative*)	*to be annoyed with, about*
sich auf·regen über (+ *accusative*)	*to get upset about; to get worked up about*
sich freuen über (+ *accusative*)	*to be happy about; to be pleased with*
sich freuen auf (+ *accusative*)	*to look forward to*
sich interessieren für	*to be interested in*
sich verlieben in (+ *accusative*)	*to fall in love with*

11-23 Was passt zusammen? Ergänzen Sie die passenden Präpositionen.

S1:

1. Warum interessiert sich Sabine so _____ die Geschichte der DDR?
2. Warum hat sich Herr Merz _____ den Fall der Mauer so gefreut?
3. Warum hat sich Frau Beck _____ die Rede des Bundeskanzlers so aufgeregt?
4. Warum freust du dich denn nicht _____ die Semesterferien?
5. Warum ärgerst du dich denn so _____ Müllers Hund?
6. Warum hat sich Maria denn _____ so einen komischen Typ verliebt?

S2:

a. Weil er jetzt auch in westliche Länder reisen konnte.
b. Weil er immer verspricht, was er nicht halten kann.
c. Weil ihre Familie aus der DDR kommt.
d. Weil er die ganze Nacht bellt.
e. Weil sie ihn nett findet.
f. Weil ich arbeiten und Geld verdienen muss.

Wir freuen uns auf ein Wiedersehen in Bad Buchau!

11-24 Was machen diese Leute? Ergänzen Sie die Präpositionen und die passenden Objekte.

1. Anna freut sich
   _____ _____.

2. Frau Klein ärgert sich _____ _____.

3. Maria freut sich
   _____ _____.

4. Heike regt sich
   _____ _____ auf.

5. Claudia interessiert sich _____ _____.

6. Peter hat sich
   _____ _____ verliebt.

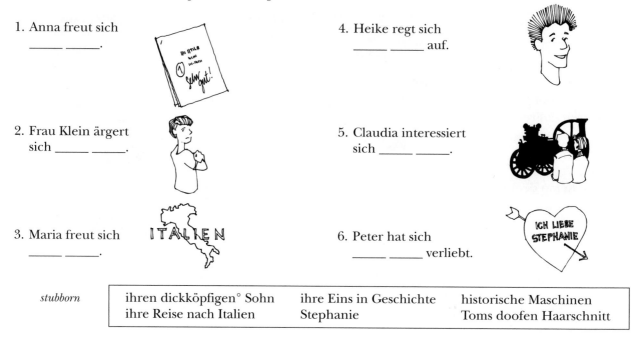

| *stubborn* | ihren dickköpfigen° Sohn | ihre Eins in Geschichte | historische Maschinen |
| | ihre Reise nach Italien | Stephanie | Toms doofen Haarschnitt |

❹ Asking questions about people or things

Wo-compounds

The question words **wem** and **wen** refer to persons. If a preposition is involved, it precedes the question word.

| **Vor wem** hast du Angst? | *Who* are you afraid *of?* |
| **An wen** denkst du? | *Who* are you thinking *of?* |

The question word **was** refers to things or ideas. If a preposition is involved, a **wo**-compound is used.

| **Wovor** hast du Angst? | *What* are you afraid *of?* |
| **Woran** denkst du? | *What* are you thinking *of?* |

Note that an **r** is added to **wo** if the preposition begins with a vowel: **woran, worauf, worüber,** etc.

11-25 Was für Leute sind Karin und Bernd? Die Information für **S2** ist im *Anhang* auf Seite A13.

S1: Wofür interessiert sich Karin am meisten?

S2: Für Politik und Geschichte.

	KARIN	BERND
Wofür interessiert sich Karin/Bernd am meisten?		Für Computer und das Internet.
Woran arbeitet sie/er gerade so intensiv?		An einer Website für die Firma seines Vaters.
Worüber hat sie/er sich gestern so aufgeregt?		Über einen defekten Scanner.
Worauf wartet sie/er denn so sehr?		Auf eine E-Mail von seiner Freundin.
Worüber freut sie/er sich am meisten?		Über tolle, neue Software.
Wovor hat sie/er manchmal Angst?		Vor einem besonders cleveren Virus.

11-26 Klatsch°. Erzählen Sie einander den neuesten Klatsch über Günter.   *gossip*

▶ Günter war gestern mit Bernds Freundin im Kino.
  Weißt du, _____ Günter gestern im Kino war?   _____ denn?
  Mit _____.

S1: Weißt du, mit wem Günter gestern im Kino war?   **S2:** Mit wem denn?
  Mit Bernds Freundin.

1. Für sein Studium interessiert sich Günter sehr wenig.
   Weißt du, _____ sich Günter sehr wenig interessiert?   _____ denn?
   Für _____.

2. Auf seine Zensuren freut sich Günter gar nicht.
   Weißt du, _____ sich Günter gar nicht freut?   _____ denn?
   Auf _____.

3. Die schlechteste Zensur bekommt er von Professor Rau.
   Weißt du, _____ er die schlechteste Zensur bekommt?   _____ denn?
   Von _____.

4. Vor der Klausur in Geschichte hat er am meisten Angst.
   Weißt du, _____ er am meisten Angst hat?   _____ denn?
   Vor _____.

5. Ich weiß das alles von Helga.
   Weißt du, _____ ich das alles weiß?   _____ denn?
   Von _____.

11-27 Ein paar persönliche Fragen.

- An wen oder woran denkst du im Moment?
- Wofür interessierst du dich ganz besonders?
- Hast du manchmal Angst? Wovor?
- Ärgerst du dich manchmal? Worüber oder über wen? Warum?
- Worauf freust du dich im Moment am meisten? Warum?

The 23 official languages of the EU are Bulgarian, Czech, Danish, Dutch, English, Estonian, Finnish, French, German, Greek, Hungarian, Irish, Italian, Latvian, Lithuanian, Maltese, Polish, Portuguese, Romanian, Slovak, Slovenian, Spanish, and Swedish. 24% of the EU population speak German as their first language. This makes German the most common mother tongue in the EU.

Bulgaria and Romania joined the EU in 2007. Accession negotiations with Croatia and Turkey were opened in 2005. At present, the euro is the official currency in 13 of the 27 EU countries. Denmark, Great Britain, Sweden, and 11 of the 12 countries that joined the EU since 2004 still use their national currencies.

INFOBOX

Die Europäische Union

Die Europäische Union nahm ihren Anfang im Jahr 1957, als Belgien, Deutschland, Frankreich, Italien, Luxemburg und die Niederlande die Europäische Wirtschaftsgemeinschaft[1] gründeten[2]. Heute ist die EU ein Gebiet[3] von 27 Staaten mit 500 Millionen Einwohnern, 23 offiziellen Sprachen und dem größten Bruttosozialprodukt[4] der Welt. Jedes EU-Mitglied[5] hat sein eigenes Parlament, schickt aber auch Abgeordnete[6] ins Europäische Parlament in Straßburg. Das Symbol der EU ist ein Kreis von 12 goldenen Sternen auf blauem Hintergrund, und die Europa-Hymne[7] ist die *Ode an die Freude* aus Beethovens Neunter Sinfonie.

[1]*European Economic Community*   [2]*founded*   [3]*area*   [4]*GNP*   [5]*member*   [6]*representatives*
[7]*anthem*

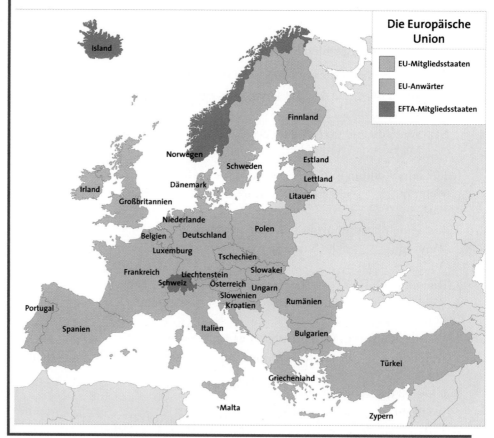

www Learn more about the **EU** at
www.prenhall.com/treffpunkt
→ Kapitel 11 → Web Resources → Kultur

The verb *lassen; der, das,* and *die* used as pronouns

When the verb **lassen** is used with the infinitive of another verb, it expresses *to have something done.*

> Ich **lasse** mir die Haare **färben.**   *I **have** my hair **dyed.***

When used in this way, **lassen** does not take the regular perfect participle in the perfect tense.

> Ich **habe** mir die Haare **färben lassen.**   *I **had** my hair **dyed.***

In colloquial German the definite articles **der, das,** and **die** are frequently used as pronouns. In this function they often appear at the beginning of a sentence.

> Der Junge ist alt genug. **Der** muss schon wissen, was er tut.   *The boy is old enough. **He** must know what he's doing.*

Zusammenschau

■ Video-Treff ....

So war's in der DDR

Thomas, Ines und Susann erzählen von ihrem Leben in der DDR.

Zum besseren Verstehen

11-28 Was ist das auf Englisch?

1. Wo wir jetzt stehen war früher **Niemandsland.**
2. Die Mauer sieht erst seit **Anfang der 90er-Jahre** so aus.
3. Früher war die Mauer nicht **bemalt.**
4. Auf der Mauer sind Bilder **zum Thema** Ost- und West-Berlin und zur Trennung der Stadt.
5. Für mich wurde die Mauer erst real nach **der Wende,** also Anfang der 90er-Jahre.
6. Man konnte dann die Mauer **anfassen** und kleine Steine aus der Mauer nehmen.
7. Wir haben beide **Erinnerungen an** die DDR.
8. Meine Eltern haben dort **im Gefängnis** gesessen.
9. Sie **haben** die Meinung des DDR-Regimes **nicht vertreten.**

a. touch
b. in prison
c. painted
d. did not agree with
e. no man's land
f. on the topic of
g. memories of
h. the turning point (i.e., the fall of the Wall)
i. the beginning of the nineties

Schauen Sie jetzt das Video an und machen Sie die Übungen im *Video-Treff*-Teil des *Student Activities Manual.*

Lesen ···

Zum besseren Verstehen 1

imagine **11-29 Ich habe grüne Haare.** Stellen Sie sich vor°, Sie haben sich beim Friseur die Haare grün färben lassen und kommen dann nach Hause. Wie reagiert Ihre Familie wohl?

11-30 Was ist das auf Englisch?

1. Mein Bruder Johannes hat sich eine **Haarsträhne** grün färben lassen.
2. Als er dann vor der Familie **erschienen ist,** gab es eine ziemliche Szene.
3. Tante Vera wurde immer **wütender.**
4. Sie fing richtig an, zu **kreischen.**
5. „Ihr wisst **vor lauter Wohlstand** nicht mehr", schrie sie, „was ihr noch machen sollt."
6. „Als ich fünfzehn war, war Krieg, und wir waren so hungrig, dass wir bei Bauern um ein paar Rüben **gebettelt haben.**"
7. „Und nachts haben wir dann im **Luftschutzkeller** gesessen."

a. with all your affluence
b. begged
c. scream
d. strand of hair
e. more furious
f. air-raid shelter
g. appeared

Mein Bruder hat grüne Haare

von Monika Seck-Agthe

Teil I

Gestern hat sich mein Bruder Johannes eine Haarsträhne grün färben lassen. Die restlichen Haare hat er mit Baby-Öl eingeschmiert, dann hat er sich ganz schwarz angezogen und sich an den Kaffeetisch gesetzt. Mein Bruder ist fünfzehn, und ich bin dreizehn. Er sagt, er ist jetzt *ein*
5 *Punk.* Wenn ich ihn frage, was das ist, weiß er das selbst nicht genau.

Jedenfalls[1] gab's einen ziemlichen Krach,[2] als er vor der versammelten[3] Familie erschienen ist. Meine Eltern haben sich noch nicht mal aufgeregt, aber dann war da noch meine Tante Vera. Und die ist fast vom Stuhl gefallen, als der Johannes in dem Aufzug[4] reingekommen ist.

10 „Bist du eigentlich übergeschnappt[5]? Ihr seid ja wohl heute alle total verrückt geworden!" hat sie sich aufgeregt. Der Johannes ist ganz ruhig geblieben, hat einfach nichts gesagt und angefangen, Kuchen zu essen. Das hat meine Tante natürlich nur noch wütender gemacht. Sie fing richtig an zu kreischen: „Kannst du nicht wenigstens deinen Schnabel[6]
15 aufmachen, wenn man dich was fragt? – Ich versteh euch aber auch nicht!" Sie funkelte[7] meine Eltern an. „Lasst ihr die Kinder denn alles machen, was ihnen in den Kopf kommt?" Mein Vater sagte bloß[8]: „Der

Junge ist doch alt genug! Der muss schon wissen, was er tut." – „Alt
genug? Fünfzehn Jahre ist der alt! Ein ganz grünes Bürschchen[9]!" Als
20 Tante Vera das Wort *grün* sagte, mussten wir alle auf die grüne
Haarsträhne gucken[10] und lachen. Nur eben Tante Vera, die musste
nicht lachen. Sie hat auch gar nicht kapiert[11], dass wir über die Haare
gelacht haben, sondern dachte natürlich, wir lachen über sie und
ärgerte sich schrecklich[12]. „Die wissen doch vor lauter Wohlstand nicht
25 mehr, was sie noch machen sollen! Wisst ihr eigentlich, was wir mit
fünfzehn gemacht haben? Mitten im Krieg! Wir sind bei Bauern betteln
gegangen! Um ein paar Rüben! Weil wir gehungert haben!"

„Lass das doch, Vera! Die Kinder leben doch heute in einer ganz
anderen Welt als wir damals." Meine Mutter stand auf und räumte die
30 Kaffeetassen weg.

Aber Tante Vera war in Fahrt[13]. „Im Luftschutzkeller haben wir
gesessen! Und wussten nicht, ob wir da je wieder lebendig
rauskommen! Und ihr färbt euch die Haare grün! Und schmiert euch
Öl auf den Kopf! Guckt mal lieber in eure Schulbücher!"

[1]*at any rate* [2]*Szene* [3]*ganzen* [4]*Kostüm* [5]*verrückt* [6]*Mund* [7]*lit into* [8]*nur*
[9]**grünes Bürschchen:** *greenhorn* [10]*schauen* [11]*verstanden* [12]*terribly* [13]*in full swing*

■ Sprachnotiz ....

The flavoring particles *eigentlich* and *überhaupt*

In *Kapitel 6* you learned that **eigentlich** means *actually,* and in this chapter
you have encountered **überhaupt** in the expression **überhaupt nicht** as
meaning *at all.*

Die Berliner Mauer war **eigentlich** viel mehr als nur eine Mauer.	*The Berlin Wall was **actually** much more than just a wall.*
Ich kenne Berlin **überhaupt** nicht.	*I don't know Berlin **at all**.*

Eigentlich and **überhaupt** can also be used as flavoring particles. Like **denn,**
they can express curiosity in questions, but in a somewhat impatient and
unfriendly tone. There are no direct English equivalents.

If you discover a three-year-old child in your yard, you might ask:

Was machst *du* **denn** hier?

However, if you discover a suspicious-looking stranger in your yard, you
would more likely ask:

Wer *sind* Sie **eigentlich** und was *machen* Sie hier **überhaupt?**

Zum besseren Verstehen 2

11-31 Was ist das auf Englisch?

1. Johannes sagte: „Deine blöden Kriegsgeschichten **hängen mir zum Hals heraus,** Tante Vera."
2. Dann tat er, **als müsste er** auf seinen Teller **kotzen.**
3. Johannes tat ganz cool, aber seine Hände **haben** ganz schön **gezittert,** und dann ist er einfach rausgegangen.
4. Ich bin auch rausgegangen, habe aber noch gehört, wie Tante Vera meinen Bruder einen **Rotzlümmel** nannte.
5. Aus Johannes' Zimmer **dröhnte** laute Rockmusik.
6. Ich **habe** seine Tür **zugepfeffert** und bin in mein Zimmer gegangen.
7. Abends im Bett war ich sehr glücklich, dass wir jetzt **Frieden** haben.

a. were shaking
b. slammed shut
c. I'm so sick of
d. was booming
e. peace
f. as if he had to puke
g. snotty-nosed brat

Kotzen is just as crude a word as *to puke*. More socially acceptable forms of this verb are **sich übergeben** or **sich erbrechen.**

Teil II

„Hör doch bloß auf mit deinen blöden Kriegsgeschichten. Die hängen mir absolut zum Hals heraus, Mensch!" Johannes tat, als müsste er auf seinen Teller kotzen. Dann sagte er noch: „Versuch doch einfach mal einigermaßen[1] cool zu bleiben, Vera."

5 Das war zu viel für meine Tante. „Seit wann nennst du mich Vera? Bin ich irgendein[2] Pipimädchen[3], das neben dir die Schulbank drückt[4]? Das ist doch unerhört[5]! Blöde Kriegsgeschichten hat er gesagt! Euch geht's doch einfach zu gut! Euch ist das doch gar nicht bewusst,[6] was das heißt, im Frieden zu leben! Begreift[7] ihr überhaupt, was das ist?"

10 Johannes tat weiter ganz cool. Aber ich hab gesehen, dass seine Hände ganz schön zitterten. Dann ist er aufgestanden und hat gesagt: „Vom Frieden hast du wohl selbst nicht allzuviel kapiert[8]. Sonst würdest[9] du hier nämlich nicht so einen Tanz machen." Dann ging er einfach raus.

Tante Vera kriegte einen knallroten[10] Kopf und fing an zu heulen[11].
15 Mein Vater holte die Kognakflasche aus dem Schrank. Meine Mutter sagte zu mir: „Du, geh mal für 'n Moment in dein Zimmer, ja?" Mir war alles plötzlich richtig peinlich[12]. Im Flur hab ich Tante Vera noch weiter heulen gehört. Die konnte kaum noch reden. „Wie wir damals gelitten[13] haben! Was wir durchgemacht[14] haben! Und da sagt dieser
20 Rotzlümmel ‚blöde Kriegsgeschichten'!"

Ich bin raufgegangen. Aus Johannes' Zimmer dröhnte knalllaute Musik. Mit einem Mal[15] hab ich eine Riesenwut[16] gekriegt auf den, bin in sein Zimmer gerannt und hab gebrüllt[17]: „Setz dir wenigstens deine Kopfhörer auf, wenn du schon so 'ne Scheißmusik hörst!"

25 Johannes hat mich groß angeguckt und gesagt: „Jetzt fängst du auch noch an auszurasten[18]! Was ist hier überhaupt los? Der totale Krieg oder was?" Mir war's zu blöd, ich hab die Tür zugepfeffert und mich in mein Zimmer verzogen[19].

Abends im Bett musste ich noch mal über alles nachdenken. Auch über
30 das, was Tante Vera gesagt hatte. Über die Luftschutzkeller und dass sie
Angst gehabt hat und so. Und dass sie meint, wir würden nicht
begreifen, was das ist: Frieden. So richtig im Frieden leben wir, glaub
ich, auch gar nicht. Aber natürlich auch nicht richtig im Krieg. Wir
können schon eine Menge machen, was die damals nicht konnten.
35 Und vieles, was die machen und aushalten[20] mussten, das passiert uns
eben nicht, dass wir zum Beispiel hungern müssen oder Angst haben,
ob wir den nächsten Tag noch erleben. Da bin ich eigentlich auch
unheimlich[21] froh[22] darüber. Aber trotzdem: bloß weil kein Krieg ist, ist
noch lange kein richtiger Frieden. Dazu gehört, glaub ich, noch eine
40 Menge mehr.

[1]ein bisschen   [2]some . . . or other   [3]dummes kleines Mädchen   [4]in der Schule sitzt
[5]unglaublich   [6]ihr wisst doch gar nicht   [7]versteht   [8]verstanden   [9]would
[10]sehr roten   [11]laut zu weinen   [12]embarrassing   [13]suffered   [14]went through
[15]plötzlich   [16]terrible rage   [17]laut geschrien   [18]verrückt zu werden
[19]gegangen   [20]endure   [21]sehr   [22]glücklich

Arbeit mit dem Text

11-32 Was passt zusammen?

1. Als Johannes mit seinen grünen Haaren ins Zimmer kam,
2. Als Tante Vera den Johannes ein ganz grünes Bürschchen nannte,
3. Als Tante Vera mit ihren Kriegsgeschichten anfing,
4. Als Tante Vera anfing, zu heulen,
5. Als Johannes' Schwester in ihr Zimmer raufging,
6. Als Johannes' Schwester abends im Bett lag,

a. mussten alle auf die grüne Haarsträhne gucken und lachen.
b. tat Johannes, als müsste er auf seinen Teller kotzen.
c. dröhnte aus dem Zimmer ihres Bruders knalllaute Musik.
d. fiel Tante Vera fast vom Stuhl.
e. dachte sie: bloß weil kein Krieg ist, ist noch lange kein richtiger Frieden.
f. holte der Vater die Kognakflasche aus dem Schrank.

▉ Schreiben und Sprechen ·······················

11-33 Krieg im Frieden. Seit dem 11. September 2001 ist in der Welt vieles anders geworden. Beschreiben Sie Ihre Erinnerungen° und Ihr Leben nach dieser Katastrophe.

memories

- Wo waren Sie im Moment der Katastrophe und wie erfuhren° Sie davon?
- Was machten Sie dann?
- Was fühlten und dachten Sie damals?
- Was ist in Ihrem Leben seit diesem Tag anders geworden?
- …

found out

Schreibtipp: This assignment covers two time frames. When you narrate your immediate reactions to the events of September 11, you will use the simple past tense. However, when you write about how your life has changed, you move into the here and now and will use the present tense.

11-34 Der 11. September. Sprechen Sie miteinander über den 11. September. Was ist in der Welt und in Ihrem persönlichen Leben seither anders geworden?

Wort, Sinn und Klang

Wörter unter der Lupe

Words as chameleons: *gleich*

As an adjective, **gleich** means *same*.

> Monika und ich wurden im
> **gleichen** Jahr geboren.

Monika and I were born in
*the **same** year.*

As an adverb, **gleich** has three meanings:

a. Expressing the idea of sameness, **gleich** means *equally.*

> Monika und ich sind beide **gleich**
> intelligent.

*Monika and I are both **equally***
intelligent.

b. Expressing time, **gleich** means *right (away), immediately.*

> Ich komme **gleich** nach dem
> Mittagessen.

*I'm coming **right** after lunch.*

> Ich komme **gleich.**

*I'm coming **right away (immediately).***
*I'll be **right** there.*

c. Expressing location, **gleich** means *right, directly.*

> Die Bank ist **gleich** neben dem
> Postamt.

*The bank is **right** beside the post office.*

11-35 Was bedeutet *gleich?* *Same, equally, right (right away), or right (directly)?*

1. Der Tennisplatz ist gleich hinter dem Studentenheim.
2. Die Jeans waren so billig, dass ich gleich zwei Paar gekauft habe.
3. Du hast ja genau das gleiche Kleid an wie ich!
4. Ich wohne gleich neben der Bäckerei Biehlmaier.
5. Steh gleich auf, Holger! Es ist schon zehn nach zehn.
6. Meine Schwester und ich spielen gleich gut Klavier.
7. Meine Freundin hat für den gleichen Pulli fünfzehn Euro mehr bezahlt als ich.
8. Möchtest du die fünfzig Euro gleich jetzt?
9. Sind die beiden Hotels gleich teuer?
mistakes 10. Mach doch nicht immer die gleichen Fehler°!

Rauchen
oder Gesundheit

Wähle Gesundheit

Predicting gender

All nouns with the suffixes **-heit** and **-keit** are *feminine* and most are derived from adjectives. The plural forms always end in **-en**. The suffix **-keit** is used whenever an adjective ends in **-lich** or **-ig**. Both suffixes frequently correspond to the English suffix *-ness.*

krank	*ill, sick*	**die** Krank**heit**	*illness, sickness*
freundlich	*friendly*	**die** Freundlich**keit**	*friendliness*
richtig	*right, correct*	**die** Richtig**keit**	*rightness, correctness*

Note that the German suffixes **-heit** and **-keit** do not always correspond to the English suffix *-ness*.

| wichtig | *important* | **die** Wichtig**keit** | *importance* |
| schön | *beautiful* | **die** Schön**heit** | *beauty* |

Some adjectives are extended with **-ig** before the suffix **-keit** is added.

| arbeitslos | *unemployed* | **die** Arbeitslos**igkeit** | *unemployment* |

11-36 Was ist das? Form nouns from the following adjectives and give their English meanings. Adjectives marked with an asterisk must be extended with **-ig** before adding the suffix **-keit**.

1. dunkel	6. klug
2. hell*	7. dumm
3. gesund	8. schnell*
4. klar	9. wirklich
5. frei	10. genau*

▶ Zur Aussprache

The consonant clusters *pf* and *kn*

In the German consonant clusters **pf** and **kn,** both consonants are pronounced.

11-37 Hören Sie gut zu und wiederholen Sie.

Was für ein süßer Zopf

Bäckerei Lang · Konditorei

zum Bäcker Lang lohnt jeder Gang

Pfanne	A**pf**el	Dam**pf**	
Pfennig	im**pf**en°	Ko**pf**	*to vaccinate*
Pfeffer	klo**pf**en	To**pf**	
Pflaume	tro**pf**en°	Zo**pf**°	*to drip / braid*
Pfund	Schnu**pf**en°	Strum**pf**°	*sniffles / stocking*

Nimm diese Tro**pf**en für deinen Schnu**pf**en.
A**pf**el**pf**annkuchen mit **Pf**efferminztee? **Pf**ui!

Knast°	**kn**abbern°	**Kn**äckebrot°	*jail / to nibble / crisp bread*
Kneipe	**kn**ipsen°	**Kn**oblauch°	*to snap a photo / garlic*
Knödel	**kn**utschen°	**Kn**ackwurst	*to smooch*

Herr **Kn**opf sitzt im **Kn**ast und **kn**abbert **Kn**äckebrot.
Knusper, **kn**usper **kn**äuschen. Wer **kn**uspert an meinem Häuschen?

Knusper, knusper, knäuschen:
This rhyming phrase is said by the witch in the fairy tale *Hänsel und Gretel* when she finds the children nibbling on her house. Do you remember what she says in the English version?

Nomen

die <u>Au</u>ssicht, -en	view
die G<u>e</u>gend, -en	area
die K<u>ü</u>ste, -n	coast

der (B<u>u</u>ndes)kanzler ⎫	
die (B<u>u</u>ndes)kanzlerin ⎭	(federal) chancellor
das Erl<u>e</u>bnis, -se	experience
der F<u>e</u>hler, -	mistake; error
der Kl<u>a</u>tsch	gossip
die K<u>o</u>pfhörer (pl)	headphones
die M<u>ei</u>nung, -en	opinion
das M<u>i</u>tglied, -er	member
der Schl<u>a</u>fsack, ⸚e	sleeping bag
der V<u>o</u>gel, ⸚	bird
der W<u>i</u>tz, -e	joke

Mitglied: Note that this word is neuter.

Verben

begr<u>ei</u>fen, begr<u>i</u>ff, begr<u>i</u>ffen	to understand, to grasp
erl<u>e</u>ben	to experience
erf<u>a</u>hren, erf<u>u</u>hr, erf<u>a</u>hren	to find out
reag<u>ie</u>ren	to react
sich etwas v<u>o</u>r·stellen	to imagine something
<u>a</u>rbeiten an (+ dat)	to work on
sich <u>ä</u>rgern über (+ acc)	to be annoyed with, about
sich <u>au</u>f·regen über (+ acc)	to get upset about; to get worked up about
d<u>e</u>nken an (+ acc)	to think of, about
sich fr<u>eu</u>en auf (+ acc)	to look forward to
sich fr<u>eu</u>en über (+ acc)	to be happy about; to be pleased with
sich interess<u>ie</u>ren für	to be interested in
sich verl<u>ie</u>ben in (+ acc)	to fall in love with
w<u>a</u>rten auf (+ acc)	to wait for
w<u>i</u>ssen von	to know about

Andere Wörter

<u>au</u>fregend	exciting
d<u>i</u>ckköpfig	stubborn
<u>e</u>hemalig	former
p<u>ei</u>nlich	embarrassing
schr<u>e</u>cklich	terrible; terribly
w<u>ü</u>tend	furious
j<u>e</u>denfalls	at any rate
j<u>e</u>derzeit	(at) any time

Ausdrücke

Es hängt mir zum H<u>a</u>ls heraus!	I'm totally sick of it!

Das Gegenteil

der Kr<u>ie</u>g ≠ der Fr<u>ie</u>den	war ≠ peace
hoch ≠ tief	high ≠ low; deep
lebendig ≠ tot	alive ≠ dead

Synonyme

die S<u>ee</u>, -n	=	das M<u>ee</u>r, -e	=	der <u>O</u>zean, -e
begr<u>ei</u>fen	=	verst<u>e</u>hen	=	kap<u>ie</u>ren
br<u>ü</u>llen	=	schr<u>ei</u>en		
h<u>eu</u>len	=	w<u>ei</u>nen		
froh	=	gl<u>ü</u>cklich		
h<u>e</u>rrlich	=	w<u>u</u>nderbar		
übergeschnappt	=	verr<u>ü</u>ckt		
bl<u>o</u>ß	=	nur		
überh<u>au</u>pt nicht(s)	=	gar nicht(s)		
eine M<u>e</u>nge	=	v<u>ie</u>l		

Leicht zu verstehen

die Attrakti<u>o</u>n, -en	die W<u>e</u>bsite, -s
die Katastr<u>o</u>phe, -n	cl<u>e</u>ver
die M<u>i</u>tternacht	kommun<u>i</u>stisch
die S<u>o</u>ftware	offizi<u>e</u>ll
der V<u>i</u>rus, V<u>i</u>ren	

Website and **Software** are pronounced as in English.

Wörter im Kontext

11-38 Was passt zusammen?

1. Wenn man nicht lebendig ist,
2. Wenn man immer nur das macht, was man selbst will,
3. Wenn man in einer Klausur eine gute Zensur bekommt,
4. Wenn man in einer Klausur eine Menge dumme Fehler gemacht hat,

a. ist man wütend auf sich.
b. ist man froh.
c. ist man tot.
d. ist man dickköpfig.

11-39 Optimist. Was passt zusammen?

1. Für meinen Deutschkurs
2. Vor den Klausuren in diesem Kurs
3. Über die lieben Mails von zu Hause
4. In meinen deutschen Freund
5. Auf seinen Besuch im Sommer

a. habe ich eigentlich nie Angst.
b. freue ich mich immer schrecklich.
c. interessiere ich mich sehr.
d. freue ich mich schon jetzt.
e. habe ich mich beim Chatten im Internet verliebt.

11-40 Pessimist. Was passt zusammen?

1. Das Leben im Studentenheim
2. Über die laute Musik im Nachbarzimmer
3. Die vielen verrückten Partys
4. Oft muss ich bis nach Mitternacht
5. Und auf das Geld von meinen Eltern

a. an einem blöden Referat arbeiten.
b. habe ich mir ganz anders vorgestellt.
c. ärgere ich mich manchmal sehr.
d. muss ich auch oft viel zu lang warten.
e. hängen mir schon jetzt zum Hals heraus.

11-41 Was passt in jeder Gruppe zusammen?

1. die Küste   a. die Aussicht   5. der Vogel   e. der Weltkrieg
2. der Berg   b. das Meer   6. das Mitglied   f. der Computer
3. der Schlafsack   c. die Musik   7. die Katastrophe g. die Luft
4. die Kopfhörer   d. das Zelt   8. der Virus   h. die Organisation

11-42 Florian hat grüne Haare. Ergänzen Sie die passenden Wörter.

wütend / peinlich / Frieden / brüllte / aufregt / übergeschnappt / begreifen

Mein Bruder Florian hat sich letzte Woche die Haare grün färben lassen. Als er nach Hause kam, war Vater schrecklich _____ und _____: „Du bist wohl _____, Florian!" Mir war diese Szene sehr _____, weil mein neuer Freund gerade bei uns war. Ich kann einfach nicht _____, warum sich Vater so _____, und möchte bloß, dass in unserem Haus bald wieder _____ ist.

You have learned various expressions meaning *You're crazy!* **(Du spinnst! Du bist verrückt! Du bist übergeschnappt! Du hast nicht alle Tassen im Schrank!)** Here is another: **Du hast einen Vogel!**

So ist das Leben

Eine Hochzeit

Kommunikationsziele

Talking about . . .

- relationships
- equal rights for women and men
- careers and family obligations
- your dreams for the future

Expressing feelings

Expressing wishes, regrets, and polite requests and questions

Asking for and giving advice

Strukturen

Present-time subjunctive

The subjunctive in wishes and polite requests

Past-time subjunctive

Genitive prepositions

Kultur

Frauen im 21. Jahrhundert

Video-Treff: **Wenn ich im Lotto gewinnen würde, …**

Lesen: **Meine Zukunft**

> Die Erzählerin ist mit ihrem Freund in der Disco. Im folgenden Monolog berichtet sie, was sie denkt, als ihr Freund und Kirsten miteinander flirten.

Eifersucht

von Tanja Zimmermann

Diese Tussi! Denkt wohl, sie wäre die Schönste. Juhu, die Dauerwelle wächst schon raus. Und die Stiefelchen von ihr sind auch zu
5 albern. Außerdem hat sie sowieso keine Ahnung. Von nix und wieder nix hat die 'ne Ahnung.

Immer, wenn sie ihn sieht, schmeißt sie die Haare zurück wie 'ne Filmdiva. Das sieht doch ein
10 Blinder, was die für 'ne Show abzieht.

Ja, O.K., sie kann ganz gut tanzen. Besser als ich. Zugegeben. Hat auch 'ne ganz gute Stimme, schöne Augen, aber dieses ständige Getue. Die geht einem ja schon nach fünf Minuten auf die Nerven.

Und der redet mit der – stundenlang. Extra nicht hingucken. Nee, jetzt
15 legt er auch noch den Arm um die. Ich will hier weg! Aber aufstehen und gehen, das könnte der so passen. Damit die ihren Triumph hat.

Auf dem Klo sehe ich in den Spiegel, finde meine Augen widerlich, und auch sonst, ich könnte kotzen. Genau, ich müsste jetzt in Ohnmacht fallen, dann wird ihm das schon leid tun, sich
20 stundenlang mit der zu unterhalten.

Als ich aus dem Klo komme, steht er da: „Sollen wir gehen?" Ich versuche es betont gleichgültig mit einem Wenn-du-willst, kann gar nicht sagen, wie froh ich bin. An der Tür frage ich, was denn mit Kirsten ist. „O Gott, eine Nervtante, nee, vielen Dank!" –

25 „Och, ich find die ganz nett, eigentlich", murmle ich.

12-1 Was ist das auf Englisch?

1. Diese **Tussi** flirtet schon wieder mit meinem Freund.
2. Was sie für eine Show **abzieht!**
3. Sie hat ja schöne Augen und eine gute **Stimme.**
4. Aber dieses **ständige Getue.**
5. Sie ist eine richtige **Nervtante.**
6. Wenn ich in den Spiegel schaue, könnte ich **kotzen.**
7. Ich finde mich und meine Augen **widerlich.**

a. voice
b. puke
c. constant carrying-on
d. very ugly
e. is putting on
f. hussy
g. pain in the neck

12-2 Anders gesagt. Unterstreichen Sie in Tanja Zimmermanns *Eifersucht* die Aussagen, die etwa dasselbe bedeuten.

1. Kirsten glaubt, dass sie schöner ist als alle anderen.
2. Und die Schuhe, die sie trägt, sind ganz unmöglich.
3. Ich tanze nicht so gut wie sie.
4. Er spricht sehr lang mit ihr.
5. Ich möchte jetzt gehen.
6. Wenn ich aufstehe und gehe, freut sie sich nur.
7. Meine Augen sind so hässlich.
8. Beim Hinausgehen frage ich nach Kirsten.

envious **12-3 Warum sind alle so neidisch° auf Maria und Paul?** Die Information für **S2** ist im *Anhang* auf Seite A14.

S1: Warum ist Stefan so neidisch auf Maria?

S2: Weil Maria immer so gute Zensuren bekommt.

	MARIA	PAUL
Stefan		Paul hat so ein tolles Motorrad.
Ann		
Florian	Marias Eltern schicken ihr so viel Geld.	Paul hat so viele Freundinnen.
Laura	Maria hat so einen netten Freund.	
Daniel		Paul ist so groß und sieht so gut aus.
Sophia	Maria wird zu so vielen Feten eingeladen.	

honest **12-4 Bist du manchmal neidisch?** Wenn wir ehrlich° sind, müssen wir *admit* zugeben°, dass wir alle manchmal auf andere Leute neidisch sind. Erzählen Sie einander, auf wen Sie manchmal neidisch sind und warum.

S1: Auf wen bist du manchmal neidisch? Warum?

S2: Auf meine Schwester.

Weil sie so einen tollen Wagen hat.

S2: Auf wen …?

S3: Auf …

meinen Bruder	spielt so gut Gitarre
meine Kusine	(Squash, Tennis usw.)
meinen Vetter	hat so eine tolle Figur
meine Freundin	bekommt immer eine Eins
meinen Freund	für ihre/seine Referate
meine Mitbewohnerin	verdient eine Menge Geld
meinen Mitbewohner	hat so einen interessanten Job
…	…

WWW Browse resources for working women in Germany at
www.prenhall.com/treffpunkt
→ Kapitel 12 → Web Resources
→ Kultur

KULTUR

Frauen im 21. Jahrhundert

Angela Merkel, Deutschlands erste Bundeskanzlerin

Frauen und Männer sind nach[1] den Verfassungen[2] der deutschsprachigen Länder gleichberechtigt[3], und Frauen haben deshalb auch Anspruch auf[4] gleichen Lohn[5] für gleichwertige[6] Arbeit. Die Statistik zeigt aber immer noch einen ziemlichen Unterschied[7] in der Bezahlung von Männern und Frauen. Ein Grund dafür ist, dass viele ältere Frauen keine so gute Ausbildung[8] haben und für besser bezahlte Berufe nicht qualifiziert sind. Aber auch jüngere und besser ausgebildete Frauen haben selten höhere Positionen. Wenn sie dann auch noch Mütter werden, unterbrechen[9] Geburt und Betreuung[10] der Kinder ihre Karriere, und danach beginnen sie meist dort, wo sie aufgehört haben. Sie haben in den stressigen Jahren, in denen sie für Familie und Kinder sorgten[11], vieles gelernt, was in höheren Positionen oft wichtig ist, aber viele Arbeitgeber[12] haben das noch nicht begriffen.

Viele Frauen möchten beides, Beruf und Familie, aber solange sie die meisten Aufgaben in Haushalt und Familie übernehmen[13], bleibt Gleichberechtigung im Beruf Utopie.

Zum Glück[14] spielen Frauen in der Politik eine immer größere Rolle. Anfang 2006 waren in Deutschland 30% der Abgeordneten[15] im Parlament Frauen, in Österreich 32% und in der Schweiz 25%. Im deutschen Kabinett waren 5 von 15 Mitgliedern Frauen, im österreichischen 6 von 11 und in der Schweiz 1 von 7. Und im November 2005 wurde Angela Merkel Deutschlands erste Bundeskanzlerin.

[1] according to [2] constitutions [3] **sind … gleichberechtigt:** have equal rights [4] **Anspruch auf:** the right to [5] pay [6] of equal value [7] difference [8] education [9] interrupt [10] care [11] cared [12] employers [13] take on [14] fortunately [15] representatives

---

Grundgesetz der Bundesrepublik Deutschland, Artikel 3

(1) Alle Menschen sind vor dem Gesetz gleich.

(2) Männer und Frauen sind gleichberechtigt. Der Staat fördert[1] die tatsächliche[2] Durchsetzung[3] der Gleichberechtigung von Frauen und Männern und wirkt[4] auf die Beseitigung[5] bestehender[6] Nachteile hin.

[1] promotes [2] actual [3] implementation [4] **wirkt hin auf:** works towards [5] removal [6] existing

---

Grundgesetz (Basic Law): The constitution of West Germany was drawn up in 1949, four years after the end of World War II. **Grundgesetz** was chosen as a provisional title, which was to serve until the two Germanies were reunited. It was generally thought that this would be achieved in a very short time. When reunification finally took place 41 years later, changes were made to the document itself, but the title remained the same.

Verfassung der Republik Österreich, Artikel 7

(1) Alle Bundesbürger sind vor dem Gesetz gleich. Vorrechte[1] der Geburt, des Geschlechtes[2], des Standes[3], der Klasse und des Bekenntnisses[4] sind ausgeschlossen[5]…

[1] privileges [2] gender [3] social status [4] religious affiliation [5] precluded

---

Bundesverfassung der Schweiz, Artikel 8

(3) Mann und Frau sind gleichberechtigt. Das Gesetz sorgt für ihre rechtliche[1] und tatsächliche Gleichstellung[2], vor allem in Familie, Ausbildung und Arbeit. Mann und Frau haben Anspruch auf gleichen Lohn für gleichwertige Arbeit.

[1] legal [2] equality

As of January 2007, 16% of the 535 seats in the U.S. Congress and 23% of the seats in Canada's Parliament were held by women. 4 of the 21 members of the U.S. Cabinet and 6 of the 27 ministers of the Canadian Cabinet were women.

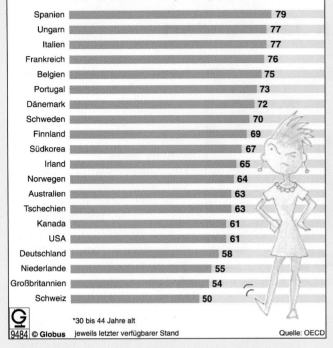

Der „kleine Unterschied"

Durchschnitt der Jahresgehälter von jüngeren Frauen*
in Prozent der Gehälter von gleichaltrigen Männern

Land	Prozent
Spanien	79
Ungarn	77
Italien	77
Frankreich	76
Belgien	75
Portugal	73
Dänemark	72
Schweden	70
Finnland	69
Südkorea	67
Irland	65
Norwegen	64
Australien	63
Tschechien	63
Kanada	61
USA	61
Deutschland	58
Niederlande	55
Großbritannien	54
Schweiz	50

G
9484 © Globus
*30 bis 44 Jahre alt
jeweils letzter verfügbarer Stand
Quelle: OECD

12-5 Der „kleine Unterschied". Männer und Frauen werden immer noch sehr unterschiedlich bezahlt. Die Zahlen in diesem Schaubild zeigen in Prozent, wie viel Gehalt[1] Frauen im Vergleich[2] zu Männern bekommen. (Gehalt von Männern = 100%)

1. In welchem Land werden Frauen im Vergleich zu Männern am schlechtesten bezahlt?
2. Wo verdienen Frauen im Vergleich zu Männern mehr, in den USA oder in Deutschland?
3. In welchen beiden Mitgliedstaaten der EU ist der Unterschied beim Jahresgehalt von Frauen und Männern gleich groß?
4. Finden Sie ein europäisches und ein außereuropäisches Land, wo der Unterschied beim Jahresgehalt von Frauen und Männern ebenfalls gleich groß ist.

[1]*pay*   [2]*comparison*

minutes per day x 365 = minutes per year ÷ 60 = hours per year ÷ 8 = 8-hour-days per year.

WOHIN GEHT DER TREND?
Tätigkeiten im Haushalt pro Tag in Minuten

	Frauen 1991/92	Frauen 2001/02	Männer 1991/92	Männer 2001/02
Kochen	85	66	24	23
Waschen	39	27	3	2
Putzen	47	40	14	16
Einkaufen	22	26	13	19
Summe	193	159	54	60

Quelle: Statistisches Bundesamt (BRD)

12-6 Wohin geht der Trend? Das zweite Schaubild zeigt, wie viele Minuten pro Tag deutsche Frauen und Männer 1991/92 und 2001/02 für Tätigkeiten[1] im Haushalt verwendeten.

1. Wie viele Minuten weniger pro Tag mussten Frauen 2001/02 im Haushalt arbeiten als zehn Jahre vorher? Wie viele 8-Stunden-Tage sind das pro Jahr? (Nehmen Sie Ihren Taschenrechner und verwenden Sie die folgende Formel: Minuten pro Tag x 365 ÷ 60 ÷ 8 = Tage.)
2. Wie viel mehr Haushaltsarbeit pro Tag haben Männer 2001/02 übernommen[2] als 10 Jahre vorher? Wie viele 8-Stunden-Tage sind das pro Jahr?
3. Wie viele Minuten weniger pro Tag verwendeten Frauen 2001/02 fürs Waschen als 1991/92? Und Männer?
4. Was könnten die Gründe sein, warum Frauen (und übrigens auch Männer) 2001/02 weniger Zeit fürs Waschen verwenden mussten?
5. Wofür verwendeten Frauen und Männer mehr Zeit als zehn Jahre vorher? Was könnten die Gründe dafür sein?
6. Was könnten die Gründe sein, warum Frauen (und übrigens auch Männer) 2001/02 weniger Zeit fürs Kochen verwenden mussten?

[1]*activities*   [2]*did . . . take on*

Nomen

der Arbeitgeber, - die Arbeitgeberin, -nen } employer	What are the literal meanings of **Arbeitgeber** and **Arbeitnehmer?**
der Arbeitnehmer,- die Arbeitnehmerin, -nen } employee	

die Aufgabe, -n	assignment; task
die Ausbildung	education; job training
die Geburt, -en	birth
das Geschlecht, -er	gender
das Gesetz, -e	law
die Gleichberechtigung	equal rights; equality
die Stimme, -n	voice; vote
der Unterschied, -e	difference
die Verfassung, -en	constitution

die Dauerwelle	perm
die Eifersucht	jealousy
die Figur	figure, physique
der Haushalt	household; housekeeping
der Stiefel, -	boot

Verben

murmeln	to mumble; to murmur
sorgen für	to care for
übernehmen (übernimmt), übernahm, übernommen	to take on (*a duty*) When **über-** and **unter-** are prefixed to verbs, they are usually inseparable.
unterbrechen (unterbricht), unterbrach, unterbrochen	to interrupt
wachsen (wächst), wuchs, ist gewachsen	to grow **wachsen:** Why does this verb use **sein** as auxiliary in the perfect tense?
zu·geben (gibt zu), gab zu, zugegeben	to admit

Andere Wörter

ständig	constant(ly)
tatsächlich	actual(ly)
widerlich	disgusting; repulsive
solange	as long as

Ausdrücke

eifersüchtig auf (+ acc)	jealous of
neidisch auf (+ acc)	envious of
gleichberechtigt sein	to have equal rights
im Vergleich zu	in comparison with

in Ohnmacht fallen	to faint
Karriere machen	to get ahead in one's career
zum Glück	fortunately, luckily
Sie hat keine Ahnung.	She doesn't have a clue. She has no idea.

Das Gegenteil

ehrlich ≠ unehrlich	honest ≠ dishonest
unterschiedlich ≠ gleich	different ≠ same; equal(ly)

Synonyme

der Lohn, ⸚e =	das Gehalt, ⸚er =	die Bezahlung
gucken =	schauen =	sehen
albern =	dumm =	doof = blöd
Sie ist eine = Nervtante.	Sie nervt = mich.	Sie geht mir auf die Nerven.

Leicht zu verstehen

das Kabinett, -e	der Trend, -s	Which words in this list are stressed on a different syllable than their English equivalents?
die Karriere, -n	der Triumph, -e	
das Parlament, -e	die Utopie, -n	
die Position, -en	flirten	
das Prozent, -e	blind	
die Statistik, -en	qualifiziert	

20 JAHRE
FRAUENSTIMMRECHT
2004: ANTEIL FRAUEN IM LANDTAG:

2001:	12%
1997:	4%
1993:	8%
1993:	4%
1989:	4%
1986:	6,7%

12%

Ein Plakat (*placard*) **aus Liechtenstein:** There are 25 Members of Parliament in Liechtenstein. In 1997, there was one woman in the Parliament, which constituted 4% of the total. How many female members were there in 2004? In 2005, there were six female members. What percentage is that?

Wörter im Kontext

Photo: Schrittgeschwindigkeit = *walking speed*

If **Macht** means *power*, what is the literal meaning of **Ohnmacht**?

Dauerwelle: This compound noun is made up of **dauern** *(to last)* and **die Welle** *(wave)*. For comparison, think about what *perm* is short for.

Eifersucht, eifersüchtig: The suffixes **-sucht** *(addiction)* and **-süchtig** *(addicted)* are added to many words. Try to guess the English equivalents of **Drogensucht, Esssucht, Kaufsucht, Spielsucht, alkoholsüchtig, nikotinsüchtig, magersüchtig** (**mager** = *thin*).

Haushalt can also mean *budget*. What is **ein Haushaltsdefizit**?

column

12-7 Mit anderen Worten. Ergänzen Sie die Sätze in der rechten Spalte° so, dass sie etwa dasselbe bedeuten wie die Sätze in der linken Spalte.

Aufgabe / gleichberechtigt / Karriere / unterbrichst / qualifiziert / ständig

1. Warum lässt du mich denn nie fertig reden?	Warum _____ du mich denn immer?
2. Sag doch nicht immer dasselbe!	Sag doch nicht _____ dasselbe!
3. Was soll ich tun?	Was ist meine _____?
4. Gina hat eine sehr gute Ausbildung.	Gina ist hoch _____.
5. Gina bekommt sicher mal eine hohe Position.	Gina macht bestimmt mal _____.
6. Im Grundgesetz steht, dass Frauen und Männer dieselben Rechte haben.	Im Grundgesetz steht, dass Frauen und Männer _____ sind.

12-8 Was passt zusammen?

1. Wenn Lisas Freund mit einer anderen Studentin flirtet,
2. Wenn Lisas Freundin bessere Zensuren bekommt als sie,
3. Wenn Lisas Freund sich albern benimmt,
4. Wenn Lisas Dauerwelle anfängt rauszuwachsen,
5. Wenn Lisas Mutter zu viel zu tun hat,
6. Wenn im Winter viel Schnee liegt,
7. Wenn Lisa einen Fehler gemacht hat,
8. Wenn Lisa Blut sieht,

a. wird Lisa neidisch.
b. übernimmt Lisa den Haushalt.
c. wird Lisa eifersüchtig.
d. fällt sie in Ohnmacht.
e. geht er ihr auf die Nerven.
f. gibt sie es zu.
g. zieht Lisa Stiefel an.
h. geht sie zum Friseur.

12-9 Mit anderen Worten. Ergänzen Sie die Sätze in der rechten Spalte so, dass sie etwa dasselbe bedeuten wie die Sätze in der linken Spalte.

Ahnung / Haushalt / Stimme / gewachsen / Arbeitgeber / widerlich

1. Robert ist viel größer geworden.	Robert ist sehr _____.
2. Maria singt sehr gut.	Maria hat eine sehr schöne _____.
3. Eva weiß nicht, dass ich komme.	Eva hat keine _____, dass ich komme.
4. Ich mag Paul gar nicht.	Ich finde Paul _____.
5. Laura arbeitet bei BMW.	BMW ist Lauras _____.
6. Wer kocht und putzt bei euch?	Wer macht bei euch den _____?

Kommunikation und Formen

① Talking about contrary-to-fact situations (1)

Present-time subjunctive

In English, when you talk about something that is contrary to the facts, you often use a different verb form than you do for factual statements.

FACT

*I **have** only fifty dollars.*

CONTRARY-TO-FACT

*If only **I had** a million dollars!*

The form *had* in the contrary-to-fact example is not the simple past and does not refer to past time. It is a subjunctive form of the verb *to have* and it refers to the present. By using subjunctive forms you indicate that what you are saying is contrary-to-fact.

*I don't **have** a car.*	*If only **I had** a car!*
*David **isn't** here.*	*If only David **were** here!*
*David **has to** work and **can't** pick me up.*	*If David **didn't have to** work, he **could** pick me up.*
*I don't **know** where the nearest bus stop is.*	*If only **I knew** where the nearest bus stop was.*

In German, you also use subjunctive forms to talk about contrary-to-fact situations. As in English, these subjunctive forms are very similar in form to the simple past, but they refer to present time.

Ich **habe** keinen Wagen.	Wenn ich nur einen Wagen **hätte!**
David **ist** nicht hier.	Wenn David nur hier **wäre!**
David **muss** arbeiten und **kann** mich nicht abholen.	Wenn David nicht arbeiten **müsste, könnte** er mich abholen.
Ich **weiß** nicht, wo die nächste Bushaltestelle ist.	Wenn ich nur **wüsste,** wo die nächste Bushaltestelle ist!

Man muss gut überlegen, was man sich wünscht. Es könnte passieren, dass man es bekommt

überlegen = *think about*

Fahr vorsichtig

Es könnte auch Dein Kind sein

The forms of the present-time subjunctive are derived from the simple past. Below are the subjunctive forms of **haben, sein, werden, wissen,** and the modals. Except for **sollte** and **wollte,** these forms are all umlauted.

infinitive	simple past	subjunctive
haben	hatte	**hätte**
sein	war	**wäre**
werden	wurde	**würde**
wissen	wusste	**wüsste**
dürfen	durfte	**dürfte**
können	konnte	**könnte**
mögen	mochte	**möchte**
müssen	musste	**müsste**
sollen	sollte	**sollte**
wollen	wollte	**wollte**

In the subjunctive, all verbs have the following set of personal endings.

singular		plural	
ich	hätte	wir	hätten
du	hättest	ihr	hättet
er/es/sie	hätte	sie	hätten
	Sie	hätten	

For **sein,** the e in **du wärest** and **ihr wäret** is often omitted: **du wärst, ihr wärt.**

English equivalents for these forms often include the auxiliary verb *would.*

Wenn du nicht so eifersüchtig **wärst,**
hätten wir eine bessere Beziehung.
Du **könntest** doch versuchen, nicht
immer so eifersüchtig zu sein.

*If you **weren't** so jealous, we **would**
have a better relationship.
You **could** really try not to be so
jealous all the time.*

12-10 Was passt zusammen?

1. Wenn ich besser qualifiziert wäre,
2. Wenn Frau Kuhn keine so wichtige Position hätte,
3. Wenn ich krank würde,
4. Wenn du kein so hohes Fieber hättest,
5. Wenn ich Pauls E-Mail-Adresse wüsste,
6. Wenn Beate kein Baby hätte,
7. Wenn Moritz nicht so albern wäre,

a. müsste ich die Klausur nicht schreiben.
b. hätte er bestimmt mehr Freunde.
c. könnte ich viel schneller Karriere machen.
d. könnte ich ihm schreiben.
e. wollte sie gern noch mehr Kinder.
f. dürftest du aufstehen.
g. müsste sie ihre Karriere nicht unterbrechen.

12-11 Wenn das Leben nur nicht so kompliziert wäre! Ergänzen Sie Konjunktivformen.

1. Holger **hat** kein Fahrrad und **will** deshalb immer mein Fahrrad leihen. Ich mag das gar nicht, aber ich **kann** nicht nein sagen.

   Wenn Holger nur ein Fahrrad _____!
   Wenn Holger nur nicht immer mein Fahrrad leihen _____!
   Wenn ich nur nein sagen _____!

2. Es ist Winter und es **wird** schon um fünf dunkel. Ich **habe** bis halb sechs Vorlesungen und **muss** zu Fuß nach Hause.

   Wenn es nur nicht so früh dunkel _____!
   Wenn ich nur nicht bis halb sechs Vorlesungen _____!
   Wenn ich nur nicht zu Fuß nach Hause _____!

3. Es **ist** sehr heiß, aber weil ich erkältet **bin, darf** ich nicht schwimmen gehen.

   Wenn es nur nicht so heiß _____!
   Wenn ich nur nicht erkältet _____!
   Wenn ich nur schwimmen gehen _____!

4. Ich **werde** immer so schnell müde. Ich möchte gern **wissen,** was mit mir los ist,° aber ich **habe** keine Zeit, zum Arzt zu gehen.

   Wenn ich nur nicht immer so schnell müde _____!
   Wenn ich nur _____, was mit mir los ist!
   Wenn ich nur Zeit _____, zum Arzt zu gehen!

   was … ist: *what's the matter with me*

12-12 Unglückliche Liebe! Ergänzen Sie Konjunktivformen.

1. TILMANN DENKT: Schade°, dass ich Nicoles Telefonnummer nicht weiß!

   too bad

   Wenn ich ihre Nummer _____, _____ ich sie anrufen. (wissen / können)
   Wenn sie viel Hausaufgaben _____, _____ ich ihr helfen. (haben / können)
   Wenn wir die Hausaufgaben dann fertig _____, _____ wir zusammen fernsehen und eine Pizza essen. (haben / können)

2. NICOLE DENKT: Gut, dass Tilmann meine Telefonnummer nicht weiß!

   Wenn er meine Nummer _____, _____ er mich anrufen. (wissen / können)
   Wenn er dann kommen _____, _____ ich lügen und sagen, ich _____ zu viel Hausaufgaben. (wollen / müssen / haben)
   Und was _____ ich sagen, wenn er mir bei den Hausaufgaben helfen _____? (können / wollen)

Würde + infinitive

To talk about a contrary-to-fact situation, you use the subjunctive forms for **haben, sein, werden, wissen,** and the modals. For all other verbs you usually use a construction that is parallel to English *would + infinitive:* **würde** + *infinitive*.

Was **würdest** du **tun,** wenn dein Freund ständig eifersüchtig wäre?	*What **would** you **do** if your boyfriend were constantly jealous?*
Ich **würde** mir einen anderen Freund **suchen.**	*I **would look for** another boyfriend.*

singular		plural	
ich **würde** suchen		wir **würden** suchen	
du **würdest** suchen		ihr **würdet** suchen	
er/es/sie **würde** suchen		sie **würden** suchen	
	Sie **würden** suchen		

 12-13 Wenn es nur wahr wäre! Die Information für **S2** ist im *Anhang* auf Seite A14.

S1: Was würde Claudia tun, wenn sie eine Million Euro gewinnen würde?

S2: Sie würde ihr Studium unterbrechen und eine Weltreise machen.

Claudia	
Martin	Er würde sich einen Porsche kaufen.
Stephanie und Peter	Sie würden heiraten und sich ein schönes Haus kaufen.
Herr und Frau Ziegler	
Robert	

12-14 Was würdest du mit all dem Geld tun?

S1: Was würdest du tun, wenn du eine Million Dollar gewinnen würdest?

S2: Ich würde …

12-15 Um Rat° fragen. *advice*

▶ Ich bin immer so müde. zum Arzt gehen

S1: Ich bin immer so müde. Was würdest du tun, wenn du immer so müde wärst?

S2: Ich würde zum Arzt gehen.

1. Ich kann nachts nicht schlafen.
2. Ich weiß, dass meine Schwester magersüchtig° ist. *anorexic*
3. Ich habe kein Geld mehr.
4. Ich will nicht auf Davids Party gehen.

advise

mir einen Job suchen	eine Schlaftablette nehmen
ihr raten°, sofort eine Therapie zu machen	ihm sagen, dass ich ein Referat fertig schreiben muss

5. Ich darf in meinem Zimmer keine laute Musik spielen.
6. Ich bin immer so nervös.
7. Ich kann kein Zimmer finden.
8. Ich habe Halsschmerzen.

mit Salzwasser gurgeln	eine Anzeige in die Zeitung setzen
weniger Kaffee trinken	mir gute Kopfhörer kaufen

12-16 Was würdest du tun, wenn ...? Stellen Sie Ihren Mitstudenten diese oder ähnliche Fragen.

Was würdest du tun, wenn jemand ...

- in der Vorlesung plötzlich in Ohnmacht fallen würde?
- dich ständig unterbrechen würde?
- nie zugeben könnte, dass sie/er nicht recht hat?

- dir ständig auf die Nerven gehen würde?
- immer alberne Witze machen würde?
- statt deutlich° zu sprechen, immer nur murmeln würde?   *distinctly*

❷ Expressing wishes, polite requests, and polite questions

The subjunctive in wishes and polite requests

In *Kapitel 4* you learned that **ich möchte** expresses wishes or requests more politely than **ich will,** and you have since used the **möchte**-forms without necessarily realizing that they are subjunctive forms.

Ich **will** ein Glas Bier.	*I **want** a glass of beer.*
Ich **möchte** ein Glas Bier.	*I **would like** a glass of beer.*

You can also express wishes or requests by using phrases like **hätte gern, wäre gern,** or **wüsste gern.**

Ich **hätte gern** ein Glas Bier.	*I **would like to have** a glass of beer.*
Ich **wäre** jetzt **gern** in Hawaii.	*I **would like to be** in Hawaii now.*
Wir **wüssten gern,** was wir für dieses Quiz lernen müssen.	*We **would like to know** what we have to study for this quiz.*

12-17 Wünsche°. Die Information für **S2** ist im *Anhang* auf Seite A14.   *wishes*

S1: Was hätte Laura gern?

S2: Sie hätte gern so eine tolle Figur wie ihre Freundin Eva.

	WAS HÄTTE ... GERN?	WO WÄRE ... JETZT GERN?	WAS WÜSSTE ... GERN?
Laura			
Lisa	einen Freund, der nicht eifersüchtig ist	auf einer sonnigen Südseeinsel	warum Maria so neidisch auf sie ist
Paul	eine Frau, die den ganzen Haushalt macht	mit Frau und Kindern in der Karibik	warum seine Frau ihn ständig kritisiert
Bernd			

12-18 Was sind deine Wünsche?

S1: Was hättest du gern?
Wo wärst du jetzt gern?
Was wüsstest du gern?

S2: Ich hätte gern …
Ich wäre jetzt gern …
Ich wüsste gern, …

The subjunctive in polite questions

You can also formulate questions more politely by using **haben, sein, werden, wissen,** and the modal verbs in present-time subjunctive.

Könnten Sie mir bitte sagen, wo die Apotheke ist?

__Could__ you please tell me where the pharmacy is?

12-19 Höfliche Fragen.
In jeder der folgenden fünf Gruppen sind zwei Fragen und zwei Antworten. **S1** drückt die beiden Fragen höflicher aus. **S2** wählt die passenden Anworten.

S1:

1. Wissen Sie vielleicht, ob es hier ein Fitnessstudio für Frauen gibt? Und wo ist das?

2. Darf ich Ihnen noch ein Stück Kuchen anbieten°? Kann ich dann wenigstens Ihr Glas noch mal füllen?

3. Haben Sie vielleicht ein gutes Buch über Berlin? Kann ich es mir ein bisschen genauer anschauen?

4. Darf ich fragen, wie viel Zinsen° ich auf dem Sparkonto° bekomme? Und was muss ich tun, um ein bisschen mehr zu bekommen?

5. Hast du Lust, am Sonntag mit uns nach Schwerin zu fahren? Du musst dann aber schon um halb sieben bei uns sein.

S2:

Gleich um die nächste Ecke, in der Schillerstraße.
Ja, hier gibt es sogar ein ganz tolles.

Ja, bitte. Dieser Wein ist wirklich sehr gut.
Danke, nein. Ich kann wirklich nichts mehr essen.

Ja, dieses hier kann ich Ihnen besonders empfehlen.
Aber sicher, lassen Sie sich nur Zeit.°

Sie dürften nie weniger als 5000 Euro auf dem Konto haben.
Normalerweise bekommen Sie zwei Prozent.

Klar! Da fahre ich gern mit.
Kein Problem. Ich bin sowieso Frühaufsteher.

offer

lassen Sie sich Zeit: *take your time*

interest
savings account

„Wie würden Sie sich fühlen, wenn Sie jung und knackig in die Mülltonne kämen?"

■ Sprachnotiz ···

Kommen and *gehen* in present-time subjunctive

Instead of **würde** + infinitive you will also commonly read and hear present-time subjunctive forms of verbs other than **haben, sein, werden, wissen,** and the modals. The most frequent are:

ich **käme** = ich würde kommen   ich **ginge** = ich würde gehen

Hören ···

Karrieren

Julia und Dieter leben in Köln. Julia hat eine gute Stelle bei einer Exportfirma und Dieter ist Motorenkonstrukteur bei Ford. Sein Traum ist aber, bei Porsche zu arbeiten. Weil Dieter heute vor Julia zu Hause ist, kocht er gerade das Abendessen.

NEUE VOKABELN

die Stelle	*job; position*	**an·bieten**	*to offer*
der Traum	*dream*	**träumen von**	*to dream about*
riechen	*to smell*	**die Abteilungsleiterin**	*department*
Champignons	*mushrooms*		*manager*

12-20 Erstes Verstehen. Haken Sie die richtigen Antworten ab.

	JULIA	DIETER
1. Wer hat nächste Woche Geburtstag?	_____	_____
2. Wer hat gut verkauft?	_____	_____
3. Wer hat Kerzen auf den Tisch gestellt?	_____	_____

	IN KÖLN	IN STUTTGART
4. Wo möchte Dieter arbeiten?	_____	_____
5. Wo könnte Julia bald Abteilungsleiterin werden?	_____	_____
6. Wo müsste Julia wieder von unten anfangen?	_____	_____

12-21 Detailverstehen.

1. Warum würde ein Glas Wein Julia so gut tun?
2. Wann hat Julia Geburtstag?
3. Was findet Julia so romantisch?
4. Warum bietet Porsche Dieter eine Stelle an?
5. Warum will Julia nicht nach Stuttgart?
6. Warum will Dieter jetzt nicht mehr weiterdiskutieren?

12-22 Ein ernster° Konflikt. Ben und Klara und ihre siebenjährige Tochter Ella leben in Hamburg. Ben hat eine gut bezahlte Stelle und auch Klara verdient gut, hat aber nicht dieselben Aufstiegsmöglichkeiten°. Bens Mutter lebt ebenfalls in Hamburg und sie hat immer Zeit, auf Ella aufzupassen°. Weil Ben in Hamburg zur Schule gegangen ist, haben er und Klara hier auch viele gute Freunde. – Da bekommt Klara aus Atlanta, vom Hauptsitz ihrer Firma, ein tolles Angebot. Es ist *die* Chance ihres Lebens und weil sie sehr ehrgeizig° ist, möchte sie diese Stelle annehmen. Übernehmen Sie die Rollen von Klara und Ben und sprechen Sie über die Vor- und Nachteile, die ein Umzug° für Sie, Ella und Bens Mutter mit sich bringen würde.

serious

chances for promotion

to take care of

ambitious

move

❸ Talking about contrary-to-fact situations (2)

Past-time subjunctive

To talk about past-time contrary-to-fact situations, you use the past participle of the verb with the appropriate auxiliary in the subjunctive (i.e., a form of **wäre** or **hätte**).

FACT	CONTRARY-TO-FACT
Ich **bin** zu schnell **gefahren.**	Wenn ich nur nicht zu schnell **gefahren wäre!**
I was driving too fast.	*If only I hadn't been driving too fast!*
Ich **habe** einen Strafzettel **bekommen.**	Wenn ich nur keinen Strafzettel **bekommen hätte!**
I got a ticket.	*If only I hadn't gotten a ticket!*

Note that in past-time subjunctive, German never uses **würde.**

Meine Eltern **wären** nicht zu schnell **gefahren.**	*My parents **wouldn't have driven** too fast.*
Sie **hätten** keinen Strafzettel **bekommen.**	*They **wouldn't have gotten** a ticket.*

12-23 Wenn wir nur nicht so dumm gewesen wären! Ergänzen Sie die passenden Partizipien und **hätte(n)** oder **wäre(n).**

1. Gestern **sind** wir nicht in unsere Vorlesungen **gegangen,** sondern **haben** Günter **angerufen** und **haben** den ganzen Tag mit ihm Karten **gespielt.**

   Wenn wir nur in unsere Vorlesungen _____ _____ !
   Wenn wir nur Günter nicht _____ _____!
   Wenn wir nur nicht den ganzen Tag mit Günter Karten _____ _____!

2. Gestern Abend **bin** ich mit Stefan **ausgegangen, habe** die halbe Nacht mit ihm Billard **gespielt,** aber meine Hausaufgaben **habe** ich nicht **gemacht.**

   Wenn ich nur nicht mit Stefan _____ _____!
   Wenn ich nur nicht die halbe Nacht Billard _____ _____!
   Wenn ich nur meine Hausaufgaben _____ _____!

3. Gestern **sind** wir nicht um sieben **aufgestanden,** sondern **sind** bis zehn im Bett **geblieben.** Wir **sind** deshalb leider nicht joggen **gegangen.**

   Wenn wir nur um sieben _____ _____!
   Wenn wir nur nicht bis zehn im Bett _____ _____!
   Wenn wir nur joggen _____ _____!

4. Gestern Nachmittag **habe** ich mich auf die Couch **gelegt** und **bin** gleich **eingeschlafen.** Deshalb **habe** ich mein Referat nicht fertig **geschrieben.**

   Wenn ich mich nur nicht auf die Couch _____ _____!
   Wenn ich nur nicht _____ _____!
   Wenn ich nur mein Referat fertig _____ _____!

12-24 Wenn ich das nur getan oder nicht getan hätte! Jeder Mensch tut manchmal Dinge, die er später bereut°. Erzählen Sie Ihren Mitstudenten ein paar Dinge, die Sie bereuen.

regrets

S1: Wenn ich nur meine Hausaufgaben gemacht hätte!
S2: Wenn ich nur gestern Nacht nicht so lange aufgeblieben wäre!
S3: …

12-25 Was hättest du getan, wenn …?

▶ Jemand hat meinen Wagen gestohlen.

… sofort zur Polizei gegangen.

S1: Was hättest du getan, wenn jemand deinen Wagen gestohlen hätte?

S2: Ich wäre sofort zur Polizei gegangen.

1. Ich habe eine Geldtasche mit 300 Euro gefunden.
2. Meine Professorin hat mir eine viel zu schlechte Zensur gegeben.
3. Die Verkäuferin hat mir zehn Euro zu viel herausgegeben.
4. Mir ist in Europa das Geld ausgegangen.
5. Ich habe in Europa meinen Pass verloren.

… mit ihr darüber gesprochen.	… meine Eltern angerufen.
… sofort zum nächsten Konsulat gegangen.	… sie ihr sofort zurückgegeben.
	… damit zur Polizei gegangen.

Wenn ich nur nicht so lange Beachvolleyball gespielt hätte!

Haben and *sein* in past-time subjunctive

In *Kapitel 5* you learned that most speakers of German use the simple past of **haben** and **sein** instead of the perfect tense to refer to past events.

> Weil ich heute eine Klausur **hatte,** war ich gestern nicht auf Lauras Fete.

> *Because I **had** a test today, I **wasn't** at Laura's party yesterday.*

However, when **haben** and **sein** are the main verbs in past-time contrary-to-fact situations, you need to use the past participles of these verbs.

> Wenn ich heute keine Klausur **gehabt hätte, wäre** ich gestern auf Lauras Fete **gewesen.**

> *If I **hadn't had** a test today, I **would have been** at Laura's party yesterday.*

12-26 Was hättest du gemacht, wenn ...? Ergänzen Sie **wäre, hätte** oder **hättest.**

▶ ..., wenn es gestern nicht so heiß gewesen _____?

Ich _____ Tennis gespielt.

S1: Was hättest du gemacht, wenn es gestern nicht so heiß gewesen wäre?   **S2:** Ich hätte Tennis gespielt.

1. ..., wenn wir letzten Winter mehr Schnee gehabt _____?

2. ..., wenn du letztes Wochenende mehr Geld gehabt _____?

flat tire 3. ..., wenn es letzten Sonntag nicht so kalt gewesen _____?

4. ..., wenn dein Drucker gestern Nacht plötzlich nicht mehr genug Toner gehabt _____?

5. ..., wenn das Konzert gestern Abend nicht gut gewesen _____?

6. ..., wenn dein Wagen heute früh einen Platten° gehabt _____?

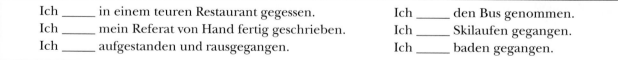

Ich _____ in einem teuren Restaurant gegessen.
Ich _____ mein Referat von Hand fertig geschrieben.
Ich _____ aufgestanden und rausgegangen.

Ich _____ den Bus genommen.
Ich _____ Skilaufen gegangen.
Ich _____ baden gegangen.

④ Expressing cause, opposition, alternatives, and simultaneity

Genitive prepositions

The following prepositions require an object in the genitive case.

wegen	*because of*	**Wegen des Schneesturms** waren gestern keine Vorlesungen.
trotz	*in spite of*	Lisa ist **trotz des Schneesturms** in die Bibliothek gegangen.
statt	*instead of*	Sie hat aber **statt einer Jacke** einen dicken Wintermantel angezogen.
während	*during*	Lisa war **während des ganzen Sturms** in der Bibliothek.

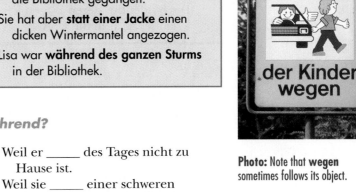

Photo: Note that **wegen** sometimes follows its object.

12-27 *Wegen, trotz, statt* oder *während?*

1. Warum rufst du Bernd nicht an?
2. Warum war Eva heute nicht in der Vorlesung?
3. Warum ist Laura denn in Ohnmacht gefallen?
4. Fährt Ralf immer noch seinen alten VW?
5. Warum spielst du dienstags nie mit uns Tennis?
6. Isst du oft Fertiggerichte°?
7. Warum kaufst du deine Milch in Flaschen statt in Kartons?
8. Warum seid ihr denn so nass?

Weil er _____ des Tages nicht zu Hause ist.

Weil sie _____ einer schweren Erkältung° im Bett bleiben musste.   *cold*

Weil sie _____ ihres hohen Fiebers tanzen gegangen ist.

Nein, er hat jetzt ein Motorrad _____ eines Wagens.

Weil ich _____ der Woche zu viel zu tun habe.

Nein, ich esse lieber Selbstgekochtes _____ Fertiggerichte.   *convenience foods*

_____ der Umwelt.°   *environment*

Weil wir _____ des Regens zu Fuß zur Uni gegangen sind.

12-28 Ergänzen Sie!

Wegen d__ schlecht__ Wetter__ (n) und ein__ schwer__ Erkältung (f) bin ich während d__ letzt__ zwei Tage zu Hause geblieben. Ich habe aber trotz mein__ bös__ Halsschmerzen (pl) und ein__ leicht__ Fieber__ (n) nicht die ganze Zeit im Bett gelegen. Weißt du, was ich gemacht habe? Ich habe gekocht! Und statt d__ ständig__ Fertiggerichte (pl), die ich sonst während d__ ganz__ Woche (f) esse, habe ich während dies__ zwei Tage meine selbstgemachte Gourmet-Hühnernudelsuppe gegessen.

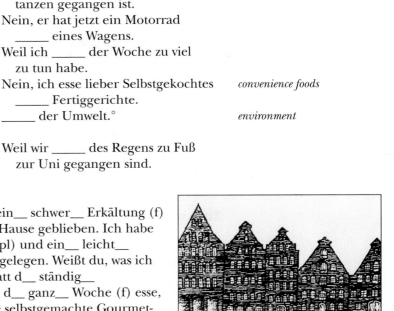

Nur für Kunden während des Einkaufs.
Chip für die Ausfahrt an der Kasse.
◀ TICKET ZIEHEN   **P**

Wann darf man hier parken?

■ Sprachnotiz ···

The relative pronoun in the genitive case

You know that in German the interrogative pronoun *whose* is **wessen**.

Wessen Fahrrad ist das?   *Whose bicycle is this?*

Whose can also be a relative pronoun. In this function it has two German equivalents: **dessen** if the antecedent is masculine or neuter, and **deren** if it is feminine or plural.

Der Student, **dessen** Wagen ich   *The student **whose** car I'm buying is*
kaufe, zieht in die USA.   *moving to the U.S.*
Die Studentin, **deren** Wagen ich   *The student **whose** car I'm buying is*
kaufe, zieht in die USA.   *moving to the U.S.*

12-29 *Dessen* oder *deren?*

1. Ein Witwer ist ein Mann, _____ Frau gestorben ist.
2. Eine Witwe ist eine Frau, _____ Mann gestorben ist.
3. Ein Waisenkind ist ein Kind, _____ Eltern gestorben sind.
4. Zwillinge sind Menschen, _____ Bruder oder Schwester kurz vor oder kurz nach ihnen geboren ist.
5. Eine Nervtante ist eine Person, _____ albernes Benehmen anderen Menschen auf die Nerven geht.
6. Ein Blindenhund ist ein Hund, _____ Aufgabe es ist, blinden Menschen den Weg zu zeigen.

Zusammenschau

 ## ■ Video-Treff ·····················

Wenn ich im Lotto gewinnen würde, ...

Anja Szustak und Kristina, Anja Peter, Øcsi, Stefan Meister und Stefan Kuhlmann erzählen, was sie mit ihrem Lottogewinn tun würden.

Zum besseren Verstehen

12-30 Anders gesagt.

1. Ich würde meinen Eltern einen Urlaub **spendieren**.   a. mitfliegen
2. Ich würde einfach so **Kleinigkeiten** kaufen.   b. sehen
3. Ich würde einkaufen gehen, ohne aufs Geld zu **gucken**.   c. absolut
4. Ich würde 'n Job suchen, den ich **unbedingt** machen möchte.   d. bezahlen
5. Ich würde von den Zinsen leben, wenn es **richtig** viel Geld ist.   e. kleine Sachen
6. Dann würde ich beim nächsten Flug ins All **mitmachen**.   f. sehr

Schauen Sie jetzt das Video an und machen Sie die Übungen im *Video-Treff*-Teil des *Student Activities Manual*.

Lesen ···

Zum besseren Verstehen

12-31 Meine Zukunft. Wie könnte Ihr Leben in zehn Jahren aussehen? Was wären Sie dann gern von Beruf und was hätten Sie gern alles?

12-32 Versicherungen°. Was passt wo?   *insurances*

Lebensversicherung / Rentenversicherung / Vollkaskoversicherung / Zusatz°-Krankenversicherung   *supplementary*

1. Wenn ich Geld haben will, um im Krankenhaus für ein Privatzimmer bezahlen zu können, brauche ich eine _____.
2. Wenn ich will, dass meine Familie genug Geld hat, wenn ich sterbe, brauche ich eine _____.
3. Wenn ich will, dass mein Auto auch dann voll versichert ist, wenn ich es selbst kaputt fahre, brauche ich eine _____.
4. Wenn ich als Rentner° genug Geld haben will, brauche ich eine _____.   *pensioner*

Meine Zukunft

von Nina Achminow

Ein Schulabschluss[1]
ein paar wilde Jahre
ein Haufen[2] Idealismus
ein Beruf
5   eine Hochzeit[3]
eine Wohnung
ein paar Jahre weiterarbeiten
eine Wohnzimmergarnitur[4]
ein Kind
10 eine wunderbare komfortable Einbauküche
noch 'n Kind
ein Mittelklassewagen[5]
ein Bausparvertrag[6]
ein Farbfernseher
15 noch 'n Kind
ein eigenes Haus
eine Lebensversicherung
eine Rentenversicherung
eine Zusatz-Krankenversicherung
20 ein Zweitwagen mit Vollkaskoversicherung
und so weiter …
und so weiter …
Hoffentlich bin ich stark genug,
meiner Zukunft zu entgehen[7]!

[1]z.B. das Abitur   [2]eine Menge   [3]Heirat   [4]Wohnzimmermöbel
[5]mittelgroßer Wagen   [6]*home savings plan*   [7]*escape*

Arbeit mit dem Text

line **12-33 Anders gesagt.** Welche Zeile° oder Zeilen in Nina Achminows Gedicht *Meine Zukunft* sagen etwa dasselbe?

8, 10, 14 Man macht es sich schön in der Wohnung.

_____ Man heiratet und mietet eine Wohnung.

_____ Man will die Welt verbessern.

_____ Man macht das Abitur.

_____ Man ist rebellisch.

old age _____ Man beginnt, ans Alter° zu denken.

_____ Man hat Kinder.

_____ Man findet einen Job.

_____ Man beginnt, an ein eigenes Haus zu denken.

_____ Man kauft einen Wagen, in dem auch die ersten beiden Kinder Platz haben.

_____ Man kauft noch einen Wagen und versichert ihn so gut wie möglich.

_____ Man möchte im Krankenhaus ein Privatzimmer haben.

_____ Man baut oder kauft ein Einfamilienhaus.

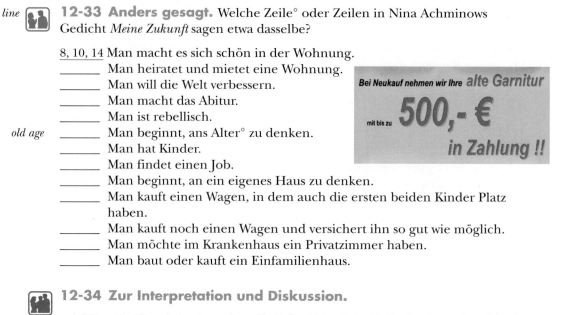

Bei Neukauf nehmen wir Ihre alte Garnitur mit bis zu 500,- € in Zahlung !!

12-34 Zur Interpretation und Diskussion.

1. Wie gibt Nina Achminow dem Gedicht *Meine Zukunft* die Struktur einer Liste?
2. Warum verwendet Nina Achminow diese Struktur? Was will sie vielleicht damit ausdrücken?
3. Finden Sie die Zukunft, die Nina Achminow beschreibt, auch so negativ wie die Autorin selbst? Warum oder warum nicht?

■ Schreiben und Sprechen ·······················

Schreibtipp: When writing a poem in a particular style, it helps to study the style and imitate it carefully while infusing it with your own personal meaning through the words you choose. Before you begin writing, look at Achminow's poem again. Note its structure and patterns (such as repeating words or lines), and use them as a model when composing your poem.

12-35 Meine Zukunft. Wie sehen Sie Ihre Zukunft? Schreiben Sie dazu ein Gedicht im Stil des Gedichts von Nina Achminow.

12-36 Traumberufe der deutschen Jugend. Studieren Sie das Schaubild auf der nächsten Seite und beantworten Sie die Fragen. Schreiben Sie die Antworten zu Fragen eins bis vier in die Tabelle.

NEUE VOKABELN

die Flugbegleiterin, -nen	*flight attendant*
die Bürokauffrau, -en	*office administrator*
die Bankkauffrau, -en	*office administrator at a bank*
die Rechtsanwältin, -nen	*lawyer*
der Softwareentwickler, -	*software developer*
der Informatiker, -	*computer specialist*
der EDV-Fachmann,	*data processing specialist*
die EDV-Fachleute	
der Kfz-Mechaniker, -	*car mechanic*
der Maschinenbaumechaniker, -	*machinist*

1. Wie viele der Traumberufe der Mädchen sind technisch orientiert?
2. Wie viele der Traumberufe der Jungen sind technisch orientiert?
3. Bei wie vielen der Traumberufe der Mädchen spielen menschliche Kontakte eine besonders wichtige Rolle?
4. Bei wie vielen der Traumberufe der Jungen spielen menschliche Kontakte eine besonders wichtige Rolle?
5. Welche von den Berufen in diesem Schaubild sind Ihrer Meinung nach° besonders kreativ?
6. Welche von diesen besonders kreativen Berufen sind Ihrer Meinung nach mehr künstlerisch kreativ und welche sind mehr mathematisch-technisch kreativ?

Ihrer Meinung nach: *in your opinion*

Traumberufe der Jugend

IT-Jobs locken die männliche Jugend
Welcher Beruf interessiert dich?

Mädchen | Angaben in Prozent | Jungen

Designerin	35	33	Softwareentwickler
Ärztin	27	30	Informatiker
Journalistin	25	24	EDV-Fachmann
Flugbegleiterin	22	23	Kfz-Mechaniker
Architektin	15	21	Ingenieur
Sozialarbeiterin	15	21	Maschinenbaumechaniker
Bürokauffrau	14	13	Polizist
Bankkauffrau	13	13	Elektroinstallateur
Lehrerin	13	12	Journalist
Rechtsanwältin	12	11	Architekt

Stand: Sommer 2000
Mehrfachnennungen möglich

Quelle: Institut für Demoskopie Allensbach
www.cartomedia.de

IT = Informationstechnologie.

Mehrfachnennungen möglich means that those polled may have responded in more than one category. This explains why the total of the percentages on each side adds up to more than 100%.

	MÄDCHEN	JUNGEN
Zahl der technisch orientierten Traumberufe		
Zahl der kontaktorientierten Traumberufe		

12-37 Unsere Traumberufe. Finden Sie die Traumberufe Ihrer Mitstudenten heraus und zeichnen Sie ein ähnliches Schaubild.

Wort, Sinn und Klang

Wörter unter der Lupe

The adjective suffix *-los*

Many German adjectives with the suffix **-los** have English equivalents ending in *-less*. With the knowledge of and feeling for the German language that you now have, you will have no trouble figuring out the English equivalents of the adjectives in the following activity.

12-38 Was ist das auf Englisch?

baumlos	fleischlos	hoffnungslos	selbstlos
bedeutungslos	geschmacklos	klassenlos	schlaflos
danklos	harmlos	leblos	sprachlos
endlos	herzlos	kinderlos	taktlos
farblos	hilflos	schamlos	zahnlos

However, not all English equivalents of the suffix **-los** are *-less*. Sometimes the English equivalents end in *-free* or begin with *un-*, as in the words in the activity below.

12-39 Was ist das auf English?

fehlerlos	arbeitslos	gefühllos
kostenlos	disziplinlos	interesselos
risikolos	erfolglos	skrupellos
sorglos	fantasielos	talentlos

The adjective suffix *-bar*

By attaching the suffix **-bar** to verb stems, German creates hundreds of adjectives. The English equivalents of **-bar** are often *-able* and *-ible*. These suffixes usually convey the idea that the action expressed by the verb can be done.

machen	**machbar**	*to do*	*doable*

In contrast to German, English sometimes attaches the suffix not to the Germanic verb stem, but to its Latin-based counterpart.

hören	**hörbar**	*to hear*	*audible*

To show that the action expressed by the verb can *not* be done, German attaches the prefix **un-** to the adjective. The English equivalents of this prefix are *un-* or *in-*.

bewohnen	**unbewohnbar**	*to inhabit*	*uninhabitable*

Kostenlos parken in der Altstadt!

1 Std 🅿 St.-Peters-Weg

½ Std 🅿 Tiefgarage am Theater

und jetzt auch

1 Std 🅿 Dachauplatz

FASZINATION ALTSTADT REGENSBURG

12-40 Man kann es oder man kann es nicht. Write the German adjectives and their English equivalents.

	DEUTSCH	ENGLISCH
1. Man kann es trinken.	_____	_____
2. Man kann es essen.	_____	_____
3. Man kann es erklären.	_____	_____
4. Man kann es verwenden.	_____	_____
5. Man kann es waschen.	_____	_____
6. Man kann es abwischen°.	_____	_____
7. Man kann es nicht denken.	_____	_____
8. Man kann es nicht definieren.	_____	_____
9. Man kann es nicht kontrollieren.	_____	_____
10. Man kann es nicht übersetzen.	_____	_____

wipe

Zur Aussprache

The glottal stop

In order to distinguish *an ice boat* from *a nice boat* in pronunciation, you use a glottal stop, i.e., you momentarily stop and then restart the flow of air to your voice box before saying the word *ice*. The glottal stop is much more frequent in German than in English. It occurs before words and syllables that begin with a vowel.

12-41 Hören Sie gut zu und wiederholen Sie!

1. Onkel _Alfred _ist _ein _alter _Esel!
2. Tante _Emma will _uns _alle _ent_erben°!
3. Be_eilt _euch! _Esst _euer _Eis _auf!
4. Lebt _ihr _in _Ober_ammergau _oder _in _Unter_ammergau?

enterben: *disinherit*

Nomen

die Beziehung, -en	relationship
die Erkältung, -en	cold
der Strafzettel, -	(traffic) ticket
der Umzug, ⸚e	move (change of residence)
die Umwelt	environment
die Versicherung, -en	insurance
die Witwe, -n	widow
der Witwer, -	widower
der Zwilling, -e	twin
der Traum, ⸚e	dream
der Wunsch, ⸚e	wish
das Sparkonto, Sparkonten	savings account
die Zinsen (pl)	(bank) interest

Beziehung, Erkältung, Versicherung: Remember that nouns ending in **-ung** are always feminine.

Note that **Zwilling** is always masculine, even when it refers to a female.

Verben

an·bieten, bot an, angeboten	to offer
bereuen	to regret
raten, (rät), riet, geraten (+ dat)	to advise
riechen, roch, gerochen	to smell
träumen	to dream

riechen: Can you guess the English cognate?

Andere Wörter

ehrgeizig	ambitious
magersüchtig	anorexic
stark	strong
statt (+ gen)	instead of
trotz (+ gen)	in spite of
während (+ gen)	during
wegen (+ gen)	because of

Ausdrücke

einen Platten haben	to have a flat tire
eine schwere Erkältung	a bad cold
erkältet sein	to have a cold
Lassen Sie sich Zeit.	Take your time.
meiner Meinung nach	in my opinion
Schade!	Too bad!
Was ist denn los mit dir?	What's the matter with you?

Synonyme

ein Haufen = eine Menge = viel
die Heirat, -en = die Hochzeit, -en
die Rente, -n = die Pension, -en
die Stelle, -n = die Position, -en = der Job, -s

What is the literal meaning of **Hochzeit**?

Leicht zu verstehen

der Idealismus	der Sturm, ⸚e
das Konsulat, -e	die Tablette, -n
der Kontakt, -e	die Therapie, -n
die Polizei	wild

Which words in this list are stressed on a different syllable than their English equivalents?

ab 4,35%
jetzt 30 jahre zinsen sichern

NÄHERE INFORMATIONEN ERHALTEN SIE IN JEDER FILIALE

Wörter im Kontext

12-42 Was passt wo?

Stelle / magersüchtig / Strafzettel / Zinsen / Rente

1. Wenn man zu schnell fährt, bekommt man einen _____.
2. Wenn man Geld auf dem Sparkonto hat, bekommt man _____.
3. Wenn man ständig zu wenig isst, könnte man _____ werden.
4. Wenn man eine gute Ausbildung hat, bekommt man hoffentlich auch eine gute _____.
5. Wenn man ein Leben lang gearbeitet hat, bekommt man eine _____.

12-43 Was sind die richtigen Antworten?

1. Warum denkst du, wir sind Zwillinge?
2. Warum gehst du denn zum Arzt?
3. Warum bist du mit dem Bus gekommen?
4. Was ist denn los mit dir?
5. Wann gehst du einkaufen?
6. Warum warst du gestern nicht in der Vorlesung?
7. Wie stellst du dir deine Zukunft vor?

a. Gar nichts. Ich habe nur einen Haufen Arbeit und weiß nicht, wo ich anfangen soll.
b. Wegen des Schneesturms.
c. Weil ihr einander so ähnlich seht.
d. Weil mein Fahrrad einen Platten hat.
e. Ich möchte bei der Polizei arbeiten.
f. Weil ich so erkältet bin.
g. Während der Mittagspause.

12-44 Was sind die richtigen Antworten?

1. Hätten Sie lieber Tee statt Kaffee?
2. Warum lernt Beate jedes Wochenende, statt mit uns mal auszugehen?
3. Was riecht denn hier so gut?
4. Bist du wieder so oft aufgewacht?
5. Sind Sie Witwer?
6. Warum kaufst du keinen Wagen?
7. Ich kann leider nicht zu deiner Fete kommen.

a. Das ist sicher Omas Rhabarberkuchen.
b. Schade.
c. Ja, meine Frau ist letztes Jahr gestorben.
d. Weil sie so ehrgeizig ist.
e. Ja, trotz der Schlaftabletten.
f. Ja, aber bitte keinen so starken.
g. Weil die Versicherung so teuer ist.

12-45 Was ist hier identisch? Welche zwei Sätze in jeder Gruppe bedeuten etwa dasselbe?

1. Wie viel Zinsen bezahlen Sie?
   Wie hoch ist Ihr Lohn?
   Wie viel verdienen Sie?

2. Wir haben eine gute Beziehung.
   Wir verstehen uns gut.
   Wir sind sehr ehrgeizig.

3. Wann war eure Hochzeit?
   Seit wann seid ihr verheiratet?
   Wann heiratet ihr?

4. Es tut ihm leid.
   Er bereut es.
   Er tut es leider nicht.

Anhang

Information Gap Activities

Erste Kontakte

E-14 Adressen. You (**S2**) and a friend (**S1**) are students in Berlin and are updating your address books. Your information is on this page.

S1: Ist Lillis Adresse immer noch° Albrechtstraße 17?

S2: Nein, die Adresse ist jetzt Bismarckstraße 25.

still

S1: Wie bitte?° Wie schreibt man das?°

S2: B-i-s-m-a-r-c-k

Pardon? / How do you spell that?

S1: Und die neue Telefonnummer?

S2: Die neue Telefonnummer ist 27 30 81 15.

S1: Oh, und was ist die Postleitzahl?

S2: Die Postleitzahl ist jetzt 12169.

NAME	POSTLEITZAHL	ADRESSE	TELEFON
LILLI SIEGER	12169 ~~12167~~	BISMARCKSTR. 25 ~~ALBRECHTSTR. 17~~	27 30 81 15 ~~35 41 56 03~~
ASHA SINGH	12207	BAHNHOFSTR. 28	68 94 26 38
DANIEL SOMMER	10825 ~~14167~~	MERANERSTR. 73 ~~SCHREBERSTR. 57~~	21 43 75 99 ~~77 46 33 84~~
HEATHER SMITH	10405	RAABESTR. 6	56 45 32 69

Kapitel 1

 1-32 Wie ist die Uni? You and your partner know different things about a university you've visited. Find out what your partner knows, and tell her/him what you know.

S1: Ist die Uni gut?
S2: Sind die Computer up to date?
...

S2: Ja, sie ist sehr gut.
S1: Nein, sie sind nicht alle up to date.
...

	Ja, ____ ist sehr gut.
Sind die Computer up to date?	
	Nein, ____ ist nicht sehr groß, aber ____ ist sehr schön.
	Ja, ____ sind fast alle sehr interessant.
Ist das Sportprogramm gut?	
Ist das Footballteam gut?	
	Ja, ____ sind fast alle sehr fair.
	Nein, ____ ist nicht sehr populär, aber ____ ist sehr gut.
Sind die Studenten intelligent?	
	Nein, ____ ist nicht sehr groß, aber ____ ist sehr gut.
Sind die Studentenheime modern?	
	Ja, ____ ist sehr gut.

Kapitel 2

 2-18 Günters Stundenplan. With a partner, complete Günter's schedule. Take turns asking your questions.

math lab

S1: Was hat Günter montags von acht bis zehn?
S2: Was hat Günter montags von fünfzehn bis achtzehn Uhr?

S2: Da hat er eine Matheübung.°
S1: ...

Note that the indefinite article **eine** will only be used when the response contains the word **-übung.**

2. Was hat Günter montags von fünfzehn bis achtzehn Uhr?
4. Was hat Günter mittwochs von neun bis elf?
6. Was hat Günter donnerstags von acht bis zehn?
8. Was hat Günter freitags von acht bis zehn?
10. Was macht Günter freitags von zwölf bis vierzehn Uhr?
12. Was macht Günter samstags?
14. Wie viele Freundinnen hat Günter?

	Mo	Di	Mi	Do	Fr	Sa	So
8.00	Mathe-übung						
9.00							
10.00		Botanik					bei Tina
11.00			mit Helga Tennis		Mathe		
12.00							
13.00			Zoologie				
14.00							
15.00				Botanik-übung			
16.00							
17.00							

2-21 Was machen diese Leute gern?

S1: Was für Sport macht Anna gern?　　**S2:** Sie geht gern schwimmen.
S2: Was für Musik hört Anna gern?　　**S1:** Sie hört gern …
S1: Was für Spiele spielt Anna gern?　　**S2:** Sie spielt gern …

…　　　　　　　　　　　　　　　　　…

	SPORT	MUSIK	SPIELE
Anna	schwimmen		Scrabble
Peter	Fußball	klassische Musik	
Maria			Billard
Moritz		Rock	

2-39 Wir spielen Trivial Pursuit. In each response, use the appropriate form of the indefinite article.

S1: Wer ist Johnny Depp?　　　　**S2:** Johnny Depp ist ein amerikanischer Filmstar.

…　　　　　　　　　　　　　　　　…

LEUTE (WER?)		GETRÄNKE (WAS?)		GEOGRAFIE (WAS?)	
Johnny Depp	amerikanischer Filmstar	Löwenbräu		Angola	
Margaret Atwood	kanadische Autorin	Chianti	italienischer Rotwein	Linz	österreichische Stadt
Tony Blair		Fanta	deutscher Softdrink	die Wolga	
Maria Callas	griechische Opernsängerin	Budweiser		Brandenburg	deutsches Bundesland
Felix Mendelssohn		Benedictine	französischer Likör	der Vesuv	

Kapitel 3

 3-12 Karstadt oder C&A? Frau Ziegler needs the items listed, but wants to save money. You know C&A's prices and your partner knows Karstadt's prices. Compare the prices for each item listed and decide where Frau Ziegler will get the better buy.

S1: Wie viel kostet der Rock bei C&A?

S2: Wie viel kostet der Rock bei Karstadt?

S2: Wo kauft Frau Ziegler den Rock?

S2: Wie viel kostet das Kleid …

S2: Bei C&A kostet der Rock 90 Euro.

S1: Bei Karstadt kostet der Rock 80 Euro.

S1: Frau Ziegler kauft den Rock bei Karstadt.

KLEIDUNGSSTÜCK	PREIS BEI KARSTADT	WAS KAUFT FRAU ZIEGLER WO?
der Rock		den Rock bei _____
das Kleid		das Kleid bei _____
die Jacke		die Jacke bei _____
die Bluse		die Bluse bei _____
der Mantel		den Mantel bei _____
das Sweatshirt		das Sweatshirt bei _____
die Schuhe		die Schuhe bei _____
der Gürtel		den Gürtel bei _____
die Socken		die Socken bei _____

3-42 Was machen diese Leute gern? Was machen sie lieber?

S1: Isst Maria gern Spaghetti?
S2: Isst Thomas gern Nudeln?
S1: Essen Tina und Lisa gern Hotdogs?

S2: Nein, sie isst lieber Makkaroni.
S1: Ja, er isst sehr gern Nudeln.
S2: Nein, sie essen lieber Pizza.

	MARIA	THOMAS	TINA UND LISA
ESSEN		Nudeln?	
	Nein, … Makkaroni.		Nein, … Pizza.
LESEN	Comics?		Sciencefiction?
		Nein, … Magazine.	
SEHEN	Horrorfilme?		
		Ja, …	Nein, … Talkshows.
SPRECHEN		Deutsch?	
	Ja, …		Ja, …
FAHREN	Rad?		Inlineskates?
		Nein, … Motorrad.	
TRAGEN		Pullover?	Bermudashorts?
	Nein, … lange Röcke.		

Kapitel 4

4-23 Verkehrszeichen. Ask each other what these German traffic signs mean.

S1: Was bedeutet Verkehrszeichen Nummer 1?

S2: Hier kommt gleich eine scharfe Rechtskurve.

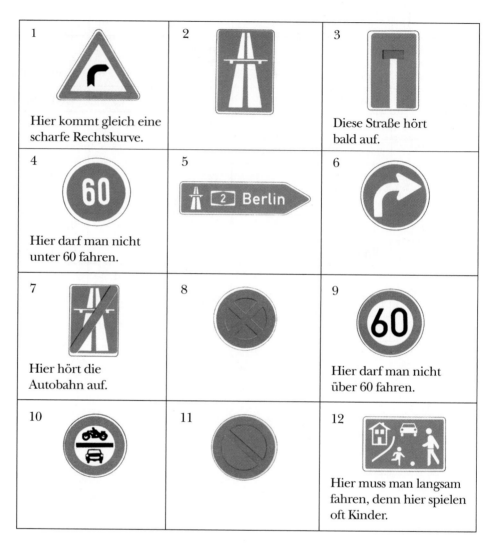

1 Hier kommt gleich eine scharfe Rechtskurve.

2

3 Diese Straße hört bald auf.

4 Hier darf man nicht unter 60 fahren.

5 Berlin

6

7 Hier hört die Autobahn auf.

8

9 Hier darf man nicht über 60 fahren.

10

11

12 Hier muss man langsam fahren, denn hier spielen oft Kinder.

4-37 Fragen, Fragen, Fragen. You and your partner are sharing information about Kathrin, Florian, and Frau Özal. Begin the responses to your partner's requests for information with the conjunctions provided.

S1: Warum geht Florian nicht ins Kino?

S2: Warum geht Kathrin nicht ins Kino?

S2: Weil er ein Referat schreiben muss.

S1: Weil …

		KATHRIN	FLORIAN	FRAU ÖZAL
Warum geht … nicht ins Kino?	weil		Er muss ein Referat schreiben.	
Geht … heute schwimmen?	wenn	Es regnet nicht.		Sie muss nicht arbeiten.
Wann geht … nach Hause?	sobald			Sie hat ihre Arbeit fertig.
Wie lange schläft … sonntags?	bis	Es ist Zeit zum Mittagessen.	Seine Freundin ruft an.	
Wann sieht … gern fern?	bevor		Er isst zu Abend.	Sie geht ins Bett.
Warum arbeitet …?	damit			Ihre Familie hat genug Geld.

Kapitel 5

5-17 Weißt du das? You and your partner are sharing general knowledge. Use comparative forms for the adjectives given.

S1: Ist der Rhein länger als die Donau?

S2: Nein, der Rhein ist kürzer als die Donau.

FRAGEN	ANTWORTEN	
	kurz: Nein, der Rhein ist _____ als die Donau.	
kalt: Ist es in Island _____ als in Grönland?		
	klein: Nein, Deutschland ist _____ als Kalifornien.	
	viel: Nein, in Deutschland leben _____ Menschen° als in Kalifornien.	*people*
hell: Ist der Mars _____ als die Venus?		
weit: Ist es zum Mars _____ als zum Jupiter?		

Kapitel 6

 6-5 Was steht in Lauras Pass? You want to know what Thomas and Bettina look like and your partner wants information about Laura and Philipp.

S2: Ist Thomas groß oder klein?
Was für eine Form hat sein Gesicht?
Was für Augen hat er?
Was für Haar hat er?

S1: Er ist …
Er hat ein _____es Gesicht.
Er hat _____e Augen.
Er hat _____es, _____es Haar.

	LAURA	THOMAS	BETTINA	PHILIPP
Größe	mittelgroß			nicht sehr groß
Gesichtsform	oval			oval
Augen	graugrün			schwarz
Haar	lang, rotbraun			schwarz, glatt

 6-12 Was haben Yusuf, Maria und Jennifer gestern gemacht?

S1: Was hat Yusuf gestern Vormittag gemacht?

S2: Gestern Vormittag hat er seinen Wagen repariert.

	MARIA	YUSUF	JENNIFER
gestern Vormittag		seinen Wagen repariert	
gestern Nachmittag	ihren Stammbaum gezeichnet	stundenlang gebloggt	
gestern Abend			Reisebroschüren studiert

 6-15 Was haben Julia, Moritz und Lisa gestern gemacht?

S1: Was hat Julia gestern Vormittag gemacht?

S2: Gestern Vormittag hat sie eine Torte gebacken.

	JULIA	MORITZ	LISA
gestern Vormittag	eine Torte gebacken	bis zwölf im Bett gelegen und geschlafen	
gestern Nachmittag			mit Professor Weber gesprochen
gestern Abend	stundenlang vor dem Fernseher gesessen	seine Wäsche gewaschen	

Kapitel 7

7-14 Geschenke.

S1: Was schenkt Laura ihren Eltern?

S2: Was schenkt Florian seinen Eltern?

S2: Laura schenkt ihren Eltern ein schönes Bild.

S1: Florian schenkt seinen Eltern eine neue Kaffeemaschine.

	LAURA	FLORIAN
ihren/seinen Eltern	ein schönes Bild	
ihrer/seiner Schwester	einen schicken Pulli	
ihrem/seinem Bruder		die neueste CD von Coldplay
ihrer/seiner Freundin		ein teures Parfüm

7-17 Geschenke.

S1: Weißt du, was Sophia ihren Eltern schenkt?

S2: Weißt du, was Daniel seinen Eltern schenkt?

S2: Ich glaube, sie schenkt ihnen einen neuen Toaster.

S1: Ich glaube, …

	SOPHIA	DANIEL
ihren/seinen Eltern	ihnen einen neuen Toaster	
ihrer/seiner Schwester		ihr ein Paar warme Skisocken
ihrem/seinem Bruder	ihm einen ganz lauten Wecker	

stellt Fragen: asks questions

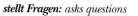 **7-32 Was weißt du von diesen Leuten?** Ihre Partnerin/Ihr Partner stellt Fragen° über Sabine und Osman, und Sie möchten Information über Wendy und Jan.

S2: Woher ist Wendy?
Wo arbeitet sie?

S1: Aus den USA.
...

	SABINE	WENDY	OSMAN	JAN
Woher ist __?	Aus der Schweiz.		Aus der Türkei.	
Wo arbeitet sie/er?	Bei der Bank.		Bei der Post.	
Seit wann arbeitet sie/er dort?	Seit einem Jahr.		Seit einem halben Jahr.	
Wie kommt sie/er zur Arbeit?	Mit dem Fahrrad.		Mit dem Bus.	
Wohin geht sie/er im nächsten Urlaub?	Zu ihrem Freund nach Zürich.		Zu seiner Familie nach Ankara.	
Woher weißt du das alles?	Von ihr selbst.		Von seinem Bruder.	

Kapitel 8

 8-2 Wo und wie wohnen diese Studenten?

S2: Wo wohnt Cindy?
Wie gefällt es ihr dort?

S1: Sie wohnt in einer WG.
...

	MAGDA	CINDY	PIETRO	KEVIN
Wo wohnt ____?	Sie wohnt im Studentenheim.		Er wohnt noch zu Hause.	
Wie gefällt es ihr/ihm dort?	Sie findet es ganz toll.		Es gefällt ihm gar nicht gut.	
Warum gefällt es ihr/ihm dort (nicht)?	Weil es da viele Partys gibt.		Weil er zu viel helfen muss.	
Wie kommt sie/er zur Uni?	Sie geht zu Fuß.		Er hat einen Wagen.	

8-27 In der WG.   Sie wohnen in einer WG und fragen einander, was Ihre
Mitbewohner mit diesen Geräten° machen wollen.   *appliances; utensils*

S1: Wozu° braucht Benedikt den   **S2:** Um in unserem Wohnzimmer   *what . . . for*
Staubsauger?   den Fußboden sauber° zu halten.   *clean*

		SABRINA	BENEDIKT
	der Staubsauger		in unserem Wohnzimmer den Fußboden sauber halten
	der Dosenöffner	eine Dose Tomatensuppe aufmachen°	
	das Bügeleisen	ihre Hemden bügeln	
	die Nähmaschine		das Loch in seiner Jacke flicken
	die Kaffeemaschine		für seine neue Freundin eine Tasse Kaffee machen
	der Korkenzieher	eine Flasche Wein aufmachen	
	die Waschmaschine	ihre vielen Jeans waschen	

to open

Kapitel 9

name plates
apartment building

9-10 Wer ist das? Was für Leute gehören zu den Namensschildern° an diesem Mietshaus°?

S1: Wer ist denn dieser Ergül Ertem?

S2: Wer sind denn diese Paul und Lisa Borg?

S2: Das ist der Mann, dem der Schnellimbiss beim Bahnhof gehört.

S1: Das sind die Leute, …

Ergül Ertem 🔔	dem der Schnellimbiss beim Bahnhof gehört
Paul u. Lisa Borg 🔔	
Maria Schulz 🔔	die im Café Mozart als Kellnerin arbeitet
Manuel Lima 🔔	

Monika Stroinska 🔔	
Hans Maier 🔔	den wir immer beim Einkaufen sehen
Karl u. Anna Weiler 🔔	
Teresa Venitelli 🔔	die im Supermarkt an der Kasse sitzt

9-19 Was macht Otilia um sieben Uhr zehn?

S1: Was macht Otilia um sieben Uhr zehn?

S2: Sie schminkt sich.

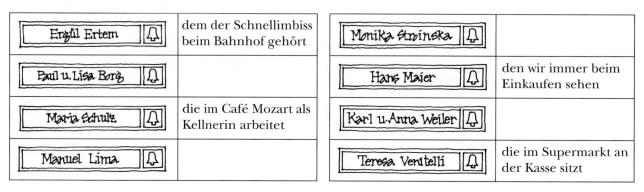

	OTILIA	BERND	MORITZ UND JENS
7.10	Sie schminkt sich.		Sie waschen sich.
7.25		Er rasiert sich.	
20.30		Er badet sich.	Sie ziehen sich aus.

Kapitel 11

11-9 Was weißt du von Mario und Ann?

S1: Warum ist Mario denn so sauer°?

S2: Weil er nie nach seiner Meinung° gefragt wird.

annoyed / opinion

	MARIO		ANN
	Weil er nie nach seiner Meinung gefragt wird.		Weil sie dort sehr gut bezahlt wird.
Warum wohnt Mario wieder zu Hause?		Warum ist Ann nicht in ihrem Büro?	
Wozu braucht Mario eine Alarmanlage?			Weil ihr Wagen repariert wird.
	Weil er immer auf Geschäftsreisen geschickt wird.	Warum zieht Ann schon ihren Mantel an?	

11-25 Was für Leute sind Karin und Bernd?

S2: Wofür interessiert sich Bernd am meisten?

S1: Für Computer und das Internet.

	KARIN	BERND
Wofür interessiert sich Karin/Bernd am meisten?	Für Politik und Geschichte.	
Woran arbeitet sie/er gerade so intensiv?	An einem Projekt über die ehemalige DDR.	
Worüber hat sie/er sich gestern so aufgeregt?	Über die laute Musik im Nachbarzimmer.	
Worauf wartet sie/er denn so sehr?	Auf einen Scheck von ihren Eltern.	
Worüber freut sie/er sich am meisten?	Über gute Zensuren.	
Wovor hat sie/er manchmal Angst?	Vor der Zeit nach dem Studium.	

Kapitel 12

envious **12-3 Warum sind alle so neidisch° auf Maria und Paul?**

S1: Warum ist Stefan so neidisch auf Maria?

S2: Weil Maria immer so gute Zensuren bekommt.

	MARIA	PAUL
Stefan	Maria bekommt immer so gute Zensuren.	
Ann	Maria hat so schöne Haare.	Paul hat so eine schöne Wohnung.
Florian		
Laura		Paul hat so einen guten Ferienjob gefunden.
Daniel	Maria spielt so gut Tennis.	
Sophia		Paul studiert nächstes Jahr in Innsbruck.

 12-13 Wenn es nur wahr wäre!

S1: Was würde Claudia tun, wenn sie eine Million Euro gewinnen würde?

S2: Sie würde ihr Studium unterbrechen und eine Weltreise machen.

Claudia	Sie würde ihr Studium unterbrechen und eine Weltreise machen.
Martin	
Stephanie und Peter	
Herr und Frau Ziegler	Sie würden erst mal ihre Schulden bezahlen.
Robert	Er würde seinen Eltern eine Villa an der Riviera kaufen.

wishes **12-17 Wünsche°.**

S1: Was hätte Laura gern?

S2: Sie hätte gern so eine tolle Figur wie ihre Freundin Eva.

	WAS HÄTTE … GERN?	WO WÄRE … JETZT GERN?	WAS WÜSSTE … GERN?
Laura	so eine tolle Figur wie ihre Freundin Eva	beim Skilaufen in den Alpen	was für eine Zensur sie für ihr Referat bekommt
Lisa			
Paul			
Bernd	eine höhere Position und mehr Lohn	zu Hause vor seinem Computer	wie viel sein Chef verdient

Expressions for the Classroom

As you progress in this course, you will want to ask your instructor questions in German and to understand and respond to her/his German instructions. The following expressions will help you do so.

What you might say or ask

I have a question. **Ich habe eine Frage.**
I don't understand that. **Ich verstehe das nicht.**
I don't know. **Ich weiß nicht.**
Pardon me? **Wie bitte?**
Could you speak more slowly, please? **Könnten Sie bitte langsamer sprechen?**
Could you please repeat that? **Könnten Sie das bitte wiederholen?**
What does . . . mean? **Was bedeutet …?**
How do you write (spell) . . .? **Wie schreibt (buchstabiert) man …?**
Is that correct? **Ist das richtig?**
What is . . . in German (in English)? **Was ist … auf Deutsch (auf Englisch)?**
What page is that on? **Auf welcher Seite ist das?**
Do we have to do that in writing? **Müssen wir das schriftlich machen?**
What homework do we have today? **Was haben wir heute für Hausaufgaben?**
When do we have to hand this in? **Wann müssen wir das abgeben?**
Will this be graded? **Wird das benotet?**
When are your office hours? **Wann sind Ihre Sprechstunden?**

What your instructor might say or ask

Auf Deutsch, bitte. In German, please.
Hören Sie bitte gut zu. Please listen carefully.
Wiederholen Sie das, bitte. Please repeat that.
Sprechen Sie das bitte nach. Please repeat after me.
Alle zusammen. All together.
Versuchen Sie es bitte noch einmal. Please try again.

Ausgezeichnet! Excellent!
Sprechen Sie bitte ein bisschen lauter (deutlicher). Please speak a bit louder (more clearly).
Schauen Sie bitte an die Tafel. Please look at the blackboard.
Gehen Sie bitte an die Tafel. Please go to the blackboard.
Bilden Sie bitte Zweiergruppen (Dreiergruppen, einen Kreis). Please form groups of two (groups of three, a circle).
Erzählen Sie einander (Ihren Mitstudenten), … Tell each other (your classmates) . . .
Fragen Sie einander, … Ask each other . . .
Stellen Sie einander die Fragen. Ask each other the questions.
Beschreiben Sie … Describe . . .
Berichten Sie … Report . . .
Machen Sie das bitte schriftlich (mündlich). Please do that in writing (orally).
Fangen Sie bitte an. Please begin.
Sind Sie fertig? Are you finished?
Schlagen Sie Ihre Bücher bitte auf Seite … auf. Please open your books to page . . .
Machen Sie Ihre Bücher bitte zu. Please close your books.
Finden Sie im Text … Find . . . in the text.
Wo steht das? Where does it say that?
Was fehlt hier? What is missing here?
Ergänzen Sie bitte die Endungen. Please supply the endings.
Ergänzen Sie bitte die Tabelle. Please complete the table.
Unterstreichen Sie bitte … Please underline . . .
Wer weiß die Antwort? Who knows the answer?
Lesen Sie den Satz vor. Read the sentence aloud.
Lesen Sie das bitte bis morgen. Please read that for tomorrow.
Legen Sie Ihre Hausaufgaben bitte auf meinen Schreibtisch. Please put your homework on my desk.
Wir schreiben (morgen) ein Quiz (eine Klausur). (Tomorrow) we're having a quiz (a test).
Hat jemand noch Fragen? Does anyone have any questions?

German Grammatical Terms

article	der Artikel, -
definite article	der bestimmte Artikel
indefinite article	der unbestimmte Artikel
der-word	das der-Wort, ⁼er
ein-word	das ein-Wort, ⁼er
noun	das Nomen, -
gender	das Genus, Genera
masculine, feminine, neuter	maskulin, feminin, neutral
singular	der Singular
plural	der Plural
case	der Fall, ⁼e; der Kasus, -
nominative	der Nominativ
accusative	der Akkusativ
dative	der Dativ
genitive	der Genitiv
subject	das Subjekt, -e
subject completion	der Prädikatsnominativ
object	das Objekt, -e
direct object	das direkte Objekt
indirect object	das indirekte Objekt
object of the preposition	das Objekt der Präposition
pronoun	das Pronomen, -
personal pronoun	das Personalpronomen
interrogative pronoun	das Fragepronomen
reflexive pronoun	das Reflexivpronomen
relative pronoun	das Relativpronomen
possessive adjective	das Possessivpronomen
verb	das Verb, -en
infinitive	der Infinitiv, -e
principal part	die Grundform, -en
regular verb	das regelmäßige Verb
irregular verb	das unregelmäßige Verb
mixed verb	das gemischte Verb
prefix	das Präfix, -e
separable-prefix verb	das trennbare Verb
inseparable-prefix verb	das untrennbare Verb
reflexive verb	das reflexive Verb
modal verb	das Modalverb
tense	die Zeitform, -en; das Tempus, Tempora

present tense	das Präsens
simple past tense	das Präteritum
perfect tense	das Perfekt
past perfect tense	das Plusquamperfekt
future tense	das Futur
auxiliary verb	das Hilfsverb, -en
past participle	das Partizip Perfekt
imperative	der Imperativ
passive voice	das Passiv
doer of the action	das Agens
receiver of the action	das Patiens
subjunctive	der Konjunktiv
subjunctive form	die Konjunktivform, -en
adjective	das Adjektiv, -e
adjective ending	die Adjektivendung, -en
comparative	der Komparativ
superlative	der Superlativ
adverb	das Adverb, -ien
preposition	die Präposition, -en
accusative preposition	die Akkusativpräposition
dative preposition	die Dativpräposition
two-case preposition	die Akkusativ-Dativ-Präposition
genitive preposition	die Genitivpräposition
contraction	die Kontraktion, -en
da-compound	die da-Form, -en
wo-compound	die wo-Form, -en
sentence	der Satz, ⁼e
independent clause	der Hauptsatz
dependent clause	der Nebensatz
object clause	der Objektsatz
infinitive phrase	der Infinitivsatz
relative clause	der Relativsatz
conjunction	die Konjunktion, -en
coordinating conjunction	die koordinierende Konjunktion
subordinating conjunction	die subordinierende Konjunktion
flavoring particle	die Modalpartikel, -n
word order	die Wortstellung
verb in (second) position	Verb (zweites) Element
time / manner / place	Zeit / Art und Weise / Ort

Useful Word Sets

These word sets provide convenient groupings of active vocabulary from the **Wortschatz** sections of each chapter as well as supplementary vocabulary relating to each topic.

Studienfächer

African studies	**Afrikanistik**
American studies	**Amerikanistik**
anthropology	**Anthropologie**
archaeology	**Archäologie**
architecture	**Architektur**
art	**Kunst**
art history	**Kunstgeschichte**
astronomy	**Astronomie**
biochemistry	**Biochemie**
biology	**Biologie**
botany	**Botanik**
business	**Betriebswirtschaftslehre (BWL)**
chemical engineering	**Chemotechnik**
chemistry	**Chemie**
Chinese language and literature	**Sinologie**
communications	**Kommunikationswissenschaft**
comparative literature	**Komparatistik**
computer science	**Informatik**
economics	**Volkswirtschaft**
education	**Erziehungswissenschaften**
electrical engineering	**Elektrotechnik**
English language and literature	**Anglistik**
exercise science	**Sportwissenschaft**
finance	**Finanzwirtschaft**
forestry	**Forstwissenschaft**
genetics	**Genetik**
geography	**Geographie**
geology	**Geologie**
German language and literature	**Germanistik**
history	**Geschichtswissenschaft**
humanities	**Geisteswissenschaften**
journalism	**Publizistik**
Latin American studies	**Lateinamerikanistik**
law	**Jura**
linguistics	**Linguistik**
mathematics	**Mathematik**
mechanical engineering	**Maschinenbau**
media studies	**Medienkunde**
medicine	**Medizin**
microbiology	**Mikrobiologie**
music	**Musik**
nursing	**Krankenpflege**
nutritional science	**Ernährungswissenschaft**
philosophy	**Philosophie**
physical education	**Sport**
physics	**Physik**
political science	**Politikwissenschaft**
psychology	**Psychologie**
religious studies	**Religionswissenschaft**
Romance languages and literatures	**Romanistik**
Slavic studies	**Slavistik**
sociology	**Soziologie**
theater	**Theaterwissenschaft**
women's studies	**Frauenstudien**
zoology	**Zoologie**

Jobs und Berufe

accountant	**Wirtschaftsprüfer/in**
actor	**Schauspieler/in**
archaeologist	**Archäologe/Archäologin**
architect	**Architekt/in**
artist	**Künstler/in**
athlete	**Athlet/in**
babysitter	**Babysitter/in**
baker	**Bäcker/in**
banker	**Bankkaufmann/ Bankkauffrau**
barber; hairdresser	**Friseur/in**
bookkeeper	**Buchhalter/in**
bus driver	**Busfahrer/in**
businessman/ businesswoman	**Kaufmann/Kauffrau**
butcher	**Fleischer/in**
chemist	**Chemiker/in**
computer programmer	**Programmierer/in**
computer specialist	**Informatiker/in**
construction worker	**Bauarbeiter/in**

cook; chef	Koch/Köchin
dancer	Tänzer/in
dentist	Zahnarzt/Zahnärztin
designer	Designer/in
detective	Detektiv/in
diplomat	Diplomat/in
DJ	DJ
doctor	Arzt/Ärztin
electrician	Elektriker/in
engineer	Ingenieur/in
event technician	Veranstaltungs-techniker/in
factory worker	Fabrikarbeiter/in
farmer	der Bauer/die Bäuerin
flight attendant	Flugbegleiter/in
gardener	Gärtner/in
housewife/househusband	Hausfrau/Hausmann
interpreter	Dolmetscher/in
journalist	Journalist/in
lawyer	Rechtsanwalt/Rechtsanwältin
letter carrier	Briefträger/in
librarian	Bibliothekar/in
lifeguard	Rettungsschwimmer/in
manager	Manager/in
mechanic	Mechaniker/in
model	Dressman/das Model
musician	Musiker/in
nurse	Krankenpfleger/in
office worker	Büroarbeiter/in
painter	Maler/in
pharmacist	Apotheker/in
physical therapist	Physiotherapeut/in
plumber	Klempner/in
police officer	Polizist/in
politician	Politiker/in
professor	Professor/in
psychiatrist	Psychiater/in
real estate agent	Immobilienmakler/in
salesperson	Verkäufer/in
server (in a restaurant)	Kellner/in
scientist	Wissenschaftler/in
secretary	Sekretär/in
social worker	Sozialarbeiter/in
software developer	Softwareentwickler/in
stockbroker	Börsenmakler/in
tax consultant	Steuerberater/in
teacher	Lehrer/in
tour guide	Fremdenführer/in
translator	Übersetzer/in
trucker (long distance)	Fernfahrer/in

veterinarian	Tierarzt/Tierärztin
waiter/waitress	Kellner/in
writer	Schriftsteller/in

Hobbys und Sport

to bake	backen
to blog	bloggen
to collect stamps (old comics, beer bottles)	Briefmarken (alte Comics, Bierflaschen) sammeln
to cook	kochen
to draw or sketch	zeichnen
to garden	im Garten arbeiten
to knit	stricken
to listen to music	Musik hören
to make videos	Videos machen
to paint	malen
to read	lesen
to sing	singen
to sew	nähen
to surf the Web	im Internet surfen
to take photos	fotografieren
to travel	reisen
to watch TV	fernsehen
to watch videos	Videos anschauen
to write (poetry, stories)	(Gedichte, Geschichten) schreiben
to do aerobics	Aerobics machen
to do bodybuilding	Bodybuilding machen
to do gymnastics	Gymnastik machen
to do weight lifting	Gewichtheben machen
to do weight training	Krafttraining machen
to work out	Fitnesstraining machen
to go biking	Rad fahren
to go bowling	kegeln gehen
to go camping	campen gehen
to go canoeing	Kanu fahren
to go dancing	tanzen gehen
to go fishing	angeln gehen
to go hang gliding	Drachenfliegen gehen
to go hiking	wandern gehen
to go hunting	jagen gehen
to go ice skating	Schlittschuhlaufen gehen
to go in-line skating	inlineskaten gehen
to go jogging	joggen gehen
to go kayaking	Kajak fahren
to go mountain biking	mountainbiken gehen
to go out with friends	mit Freunden ausgehen
to go rowing	rudern gehen

to go sailing	**segeln gehen**	the piano	**Klavier**
to go shopping	**einkaufen gehen**	the recorder	**Blockflöte**
to go skateboarding	**skateboarden gehen**	the saxophone	**Saxofon**
to go skiing	**Skilaufen gehen**	the trombone	**Posaune**
to go cross-country skiing	**Skilanglauf machen**	the trumpet	**Trompete**
to go downhill skiing	**Abfahrtslauf machen**	the viola	**Bratsche**
to go snowboarding	**snowboarden gehen**	the violin	**Geige, Violine**

to go surfing — **surfen gehen**
to go swimming — **schwimmen gehen**
to go to concerts — **ins Konzert gehen**
to go to museums — **ins Museum gehen**
to go to (the) movies — **ins Kino gehen**
to go to the theater — **ins Theater gehen**
to go windsurfing — **windsurfen gehen**

to play badminton — **Federball spielen**
to play baseball — **Baseball spielen**
to play basketball — **Basketball spielen**
to play cards — **Karten spielen**
to play chess — **Schach spielen**
to play computer games — **Computerspiele spielen**
to play football — **Football spielen**
to play golf — **Golf spielen**
to play hockey — **Eishockey spielen**
to play pool — **Billard spielen**
to play racquetball — **Racquetball spielen**
to play Scrabble — **Scrabble spielen**
to play soccer — **Fußball spielen**
to play softball — **Softball spielen**
to play squash — **Squash spielen**
to play table tennis (Ping-Pong) — **Tischtennis spielen**
to play tennis — **Tennis spielen**
to play video games — **Videospiele spielen**
to play volleyball — **Volleyball spielen**

Musikinstrumente

I play . . . — **Ich spiele …**
the accordion — **Akkordeon**
(the double) bass — **Bass, Kontrabass**
the cello — **Cello**
the clarinet — **Klarinette**
drums, percussion — **Schlagzeug**
the flute — **Flöte**
the guitar — **Gitarre**
the harmonica — **Mundharmonika**
the harp — **Harfe**
the keyboard — **Keyboard**
the organ — **Orgel**

Kleidungsstücke

I'm wearing . . . — **Ich trage …**
a baseball cap — **eine Baseballkappe**
a belt — **einen Gürtel**
a blazer — **einen Blazer**
a blouse — **eine Bluse**
boots — **Stiefel**
hiking boots — **Wanderstiefel**
clothes — **Kleider; Klamotten** (*colloq.*)
a coat — **einen Mantel**
a dress — **ein Kleid**
gloves — **Handschuhe**
a hat — **einen Hut**
a jacket — **eine Jacke**
a down jacket — **eine Daunenjacke**
a jeans jacket — **eine Jeansjacke**
a leather jacket — **eine Lederjacke**
jeans — **Jeans**
pants — **eine Hose**
a polo shirt — **ein Polohemd**
sandals — **Sandalen**
a scarf — **einen Schal**
a shirt — **ein Hemd**
shorts — **Shorts**
shoes — **Schuhe**
tennis shoes — **Tennisschuhe**
sneakers or running shoes — **Turnschuhe**
a skirt — **einen Rock**
slippers — **Hausschuhe**
socks — **Socken**
pantyhose — **eine Strumpfhose**
a suit (*men's*) — **einen Anzug**
a sweater — **einen Pullover**
a light sweater — **einen Pulli**
sweatpants — **eine Jogginghose**
a sweatshirt — **ein Sweatshirt**
a sweatsuit — **einen Jogginganzug**
a tie — **eine Krawatte**
tights — **Leggings**
a T-shirt — **ein T-Shirt**
a tuxedo — **einen Smoking**

Accessoires

I'm wearing . . .	**Ich trage …**
a bracelet	**ein Armband**
contact lenses	**Kontaktlinsen**
earrings	**Ohrringe**
an ear stud	**einen Ohrstecker**
glasses	**eine Brille** (*sing*)
sunglasses	**eine Sonnenbrille** (*sing*)
a nose stud	**einen Nasenstecker**
a necklace	**eine Halskette**
a ring	**einen Ring**
a wristwatch	**eine Armbanduhr**
I have . . .	**Ich habe …**
a beard	**einen Bart**
a mustache	**einen Schnurrbart**
a tattoo	**eine Tätowierung**

Essen und Trinken

I eat . . .	**Ich esse …**
for breakfast	**zum Frühstück**
bacon	**Speck**
bacon and eggs	**Eier mit Speck**
a bagel	**einen Bagel**
with cream cheese	**mit Frischkäse**
(a bowl of) cornflakes	**(eine Schüssel) Cornflakes**
an egg	**ein Ei**
eggs, sunny-side up	**Spiegeleier**
scrambled eggs	**Rührei**
granola, muesli	**Müsli**
a granola bar	**einen Müsliriegel**
a muffin	**einen Muffin**
(a slice of) bread	**(eine Scheibe) Brot**
(a slice of) toast	**(eine Scheibe) Toast**
with butter	**mit Butter**
with honey	**mit Honig**
with jam	**mit Marmelade**
with peanut butter	**mit Erdnussbutter**
(a container of) yogurt	**(einen Becher)**
with fruit	**Fruchtjoghurt**
a smoothie	**einen Smoothie**
for lunch	**zum Mittagessen**
for supper	**zum Abendessen**
a bowl of soup	**einen Teller Suppe**
bread	**Brot**
a burrito	**einen Burrito**
chicken	**Huhn**
chicken salad	**Geflügelsalat**
French fries	**Pommes frites, Pommes**
fish	**Fisch**
a hamburger	**einen Hamburger**

a hotdog	**ein Hotdog**
with ketchup	**mit Ketchup**
with mustard	**mit Senf**
with onions	**mit Zwiebeln**
with relish	**mit Relish**
meat	**Fleisch**
noodles	**Nudeln**
pickles	**Essiggurken**
a pizza	**eine Pizza**
porkchops	**Schweineschnitzel**
potatoes	**Kartoffeln**
potato salad	**Kartoffelsalat**
rice	**Reis**
rolls	**Brötchen**
a sandwich	**ein belegtes Brot**
a cheese sandwich	**ein Käsebrot**
a ham sandwich	**ein Schinkenbrot**
a sausage	**eine Wurst**
a steak	**ein Steak**
sushi	**Sushi**
a taco	**einen Taco**
tuna	**Thunfisch**
turkey	**Pute**
vegetables	**Gemüse**
asparagus	**Spargel**
beans	**Bohnen**
bell peppers	**Paprika**
broccoli	**Brokkoli**
carrots	**Karotten**
coleslaw	**Krautsalat**
cucumbers	**Gurken**
corn	**Zuckermais**
mushrooms	**Champignons**
peas	**Erbsen**
salad	**Salat**
sauerkraut	**Sauerkraut**
spinach	**Spinat**
tomatoes	**Tomaten**
snacks	**Snacks**
nuts	**Nüsse**
potato chips	**Kartoffelchips**
popcorn	**Popcorn**
pretzels	**Brezeln**
tortilla chips	**Tortillachips**
for dessert	**zum Nachtisch**
(a piece of) cake	**(ein Stück) Kuchen**
(a piece of) layer cake	**(ein Stück) Torte**
with whipped cream	**mit Schlagsahne**
a chocolate bar	**eine Tafel Schokolade**
cookies	**Kekse**
(a dish of) ice cream	**(einen Becher) Eis**

fruit	Obst
an apple	einen Apfel
a banana	eine Banane
blueberries	Heidelbeeren
cherries	Kirschen
a grapefruit	eine Grapefruit
grapes	Trauben
melon	Melone
an orange	eine Orange
a peach	einen Pfirsich
a pear	eine Birne
pineapple	Ananas
a plum	eine Pflaume
raspberries	Himbeeren
strawberries	Erdbeeren

I drink . . .	Ich trinke …
(a bottle of) beer	(eine Flasche) Bier
(a can of) cola	(eine Dose) Cola
(a cup of) coffee	(eine Tasse) Kaffee
(a cup of) tea	(eine Tasse) Tee
(a cup of) cocoa	(eine Tasse) Kakao
(a glass of) milk	(ein Glas) Milch
(a glass of) water	(ein Glas) Wasser
(a glass of) wine	(ein Glas) Wein
(a glass of) juice	(ein Glas) Saft
apple juice	Apfelsaft
grapefruit juice	Grapefruitsaft
orange juice	Orangensaft
tomato juice	Tomatensaft
a hot chocolate	eine heiße Schokolade
a soft drink	einen Softdrink

Länder und Sprachen

The names of most countries are neuter and are not preceded by an article. However, when the name of a country is masculine, feminine, or plural, the article must be used.

Ägypten	Finnland
Algerien	Frankreich
Argentinien	Griechenland
Australien	Indien
Belgien	der Irak
Brasilien	der Iran
Bulgarien	Irland
Chile	Israel
China	Italien
Dänemark	Japan
Deutschland	Kanada
England	Kolumbien
Estland	Korea

Kroatien	Russland
Kuba	Schottland
Lettland	Schweden
der Libanon	die Schweiz
Litauen	Serbien
Luxemburg	die Slowakei
Malta	Slowenien
Mexiko	Spanien
Neuseeland	Südafrika
die Niederlande *(pl)*	Tschechien
Nigeria	die Türkei
Nordirland	die Ukraine
Norwegen	Ungarn
Österreich	Venezuela
Pakistan	die Vereinigten Staaten,
Peru	die USA *(pl)*
Polen	Vietnam
Portugal	Wales
Rumänien	Zypern

Sie/Er spricht …	Lettisch
Arabisch	Litauisch
Chinesisch	Norwegisch
Dänisch	Polnisch
Deutsch	Portugiesisch
Englisch	Rumänisch
Estnisch	Russisch
Finnisch	Schwedisch
Französisch	Serbisch
Griechisch	Slovakisch
Hebräisch	Spanisch
Hindi	Tschechisch
Holländisch	Türkisch
Italienisch	Ukrainisch
Japanisch	Ungarisch
Koreanisch	Urdu
Kroatisch	Vietnamesisch

Persönliche Merkmale

ambitious	ehrgeizig
arrogant	arrogant
artistic	künstlerisch begabt
athletic	sportlich
attractive	attraktiv
(of) average height	mittelgroß
beautiful	schön
bilingual	zweisprachig
blond	blond
brilliant	genial
brunette	brünett

calm	ruhig	pessimistic	pessimistisch
chic	schick	plump	mollig
conservative	konservativ	polite	höflich
cool	cool	popular	populär
crazy	verrückt	practical	praktisch
creative	kreativ	pretty	hübsch
critical	kritisch	private	introvertiert
elegant	elegant	punctual	pünktlich
enchanting	bezaubernd	respectful	respektvoll
envious	neidisch	religious	fromm
exotic	exotisch	romantic	romantisch
extravagant	extravagant	selfless	selbstlos
fabulous	fabelhaft	sentimental	sentimental
fair	fair	serious	ernst
famous	berühmt	short	klein
fantastic	fantastisch	silly	albern
fashionably dressed	modisch gekleidet	slim	schlank
fit	fit	smart	klug
fun, funny	lustig	spontaneous	spontan
friendly	freundlich	strong	stark
generous	großzügig	stubborn	dickköpfig
great	spitze	successful	erfolgreich
happy	glücklich; vergnügt	sweet	süß
hard-working	fleißig	tactful	taktvoll
healthy	gesund	tall	groß
helpful	hilfsbereit	thrifty	sparsam
honest	ehrlich	tidy	ordentlich
humorous; having a sense of humor	humorvoll	tired	müde
		tolerant	tolerant
idealistic	idealistisch	witty	witzig
imaginative	fantasievoll		
informed	informiert		
in love	verliebt		

Höfliche Ausdrücke

innovative	innovativ
intelligent	intelligent; klug
interesting	interessant
lazy	faul
liberal	liberal
messy	unordentlich
modern	modern
mood: (always) in a good mood	(immer) guter Laune
moody	launisch
musical	musikalisch
nice	nett
natural	natürlich
nervous	nervös
optimistic	optimistisch
outgoing	aufgeschlossen

All the best!	Alles Gute!
Bless you!	Gesundheit!
Get well soon!	Gute Besserung!
Good luck!	Viel Glück!
Thanks a lot!	Vielen Dank!
Thanks a million!	Tausend Dank!
You're welcome.	Bitte schön.
Don't mention it.	Nichts zu danken.
No problem.	Kein Problem.
That's too bad.	Schade.
Excuse me; I'm sorry.	Entschuldigung; Es tut mir leid.
Have fun!	Viel Spaß!
Have a good weekend!	Schönes Wochenende!
Have a nice day!	Schönen Tag noch!

Note that these are not literal, word-for-word translations, but idiomatic English equivalents.

Erste Kontakte

Beim Studentenwerk *(At the student center)*

– Hi, my name is Christian, Christian Lohner.
– And I'm Asha Singh. Where are you from, Christian?
– I'm from Hamburg. And where are you from?
– I'm from Bombay.

Im Studentenheim *(In the dormitory)*

– Excuse me, are you Heike Fischer?
– Yes. And what's your name?
– I'm Yvonne Harris from Pittsburgh.
– Oh, hello, Yvonne!

Im Hörsaal *(In the lecture hall)*

MARTIN: *(to Claudia and Stephanie)* Hi, you two! How are you?
CLAUDIA: Super. Peter, this is Stephanie, my roommate.
PETER: Hi, Stephanie.
STEPHANIE: Hi, Peter.
MARTIN: Are you going to the cafeteria now too?
CLAUDIA: No, not yet.
MARTIN: Well then, so long, you two.
STEPHANIE: Bye!

Im Konferenzsaal *(In the conference hall)*

– Excuse me. My name is O'Brien. Are you Ms. Ziegler from Göttingen?
– Yes. – Oh, Mr. O'Brien from Dublin. Hello! How are you, Mr. O'Brien?
– Fine, thanks.

Kapitel 1

Semesterbeginn *(Beginning of the semester)*

Stephanie and Claudia are sitting together at breakfast.

CLAUDIA: Are you going to your lecture now, Stephanie?
STEPHANIE: Yes, and then to the foreign students office.
CLAUDIA: My lectures don't start until tomorrow.

STEPHANIE: And what are you doing today?
CLAUDIA: Not much. First I'll write a few postcards, and this afternoon I'm going to buy my books.
STEPHANIE: Well then, see you later.
CLAUDIA: So long, Stephanie.

Badewetter *(Swimming weather)*

Claudia and Martin are good friends. Stephanie and Peter also do a lot of things together.

MARTIN: Wow, is it ever hot!
PETER: Yes, almost thirty degrees (Celsius)! – Say, are you going swimming too?
MARTIN: Of course, right after Claudia's hydraulics lecture.
PETER: We're going right now. Stephanie's coming in five minutes.
MARTIN: Well then, see you later.

Der Tag beginnt *(The day begins)*

Ms. Ziegler is standing at the window. Mr. Ziegler is still in bed.

MR. ZIEGLER: What's the weather like?
MS. ZIEGLER: Not nice at all. The sky is gray and it's raining.
MR. ZIEGLER: Is it cold?
MS. ZIEGLER: The thermometer reads ten degrees (Celsius).
MR. ZIEGLER: Just ten degrees! What rotten weather!

Kapitel 2

Freundschaften *(Friendships)*

Nina Ziegler says: This is my boyfriend Alexander. He's tall and slim, dances really well, and has a fantastic motorcycle. Alex has lots of hobbies: he plays basketball and hockey very well, he likes to swim, he plays the guitar really well, he collects stamps, he also likes to cook, and he's good at it. By the way, Alex is also a very good student.

Robert Ziegler says: I think Alexander is a dope. He often talks on the phone with Nina for hours, and in the evenings he's often over at our place till ten or eleven and plays his dumb guitar. What does my sister think is so great about Alex? I just think his motorcycle is great.

Ms. Ziegler says: This is Beverly Harper. She's a journalist and my best friend. She works for American newspapers and writes articles about the political scene in Europe. Beverly is not only very intelligent, but also very athletic, and Mondays from 7 p.m. to 9 p.m. we always play tennis together. By the way, Beverly is also very elegant and likes to buy chic clothes.

Mr. Ziegler says: I don't like to play tennis with Beverly, because she plays much better than I do. But she is a good journalist and writes very interesting articles. We often have a glass of wine here at our house and have long discussions together.

Kapitel 3

Verwandte *(Relatives)*

Grandma Ziegler says: This is my daughter Bettina. She isn't married and she has no children, but she's a very good physical therapist. Bettina likes to buy expensive clothes, has a much too expensive car, and she often drives too fast, too. And why does Bettina travel so much all the time?

Nina says: Aunt Bettina is my favorite aunt. She has a really fantastic life: lots of money, chic clothes, big trips (also to North America, because she speaks English really well), and a red sport coupe.

Mr. Ziegler says: This is my brother Alfred. He's a bank manager, earns a lot of money, and drives a big, gray Mercedes. He likes to eat well, drinks expensive wines, and wears very expensive gray suits.

Robert says: Uncle Alfred is not my favorite uncle. He almost never laughs, and his suits are as gray and boring as his big, gray Mercedes. He sits at the computer all day or reads his stupid stock market reports.

Kapitel 4

So bin ich eben *(That's just the way I am)*

MARTIN:	*(gets up and yawns)* What?! You're up already? What time is it?
PETER:	Almost eight o'clock. I have to finish writing my report for Professor Weber. The seminar begins at eleven already.
MARTIN:	*(laughs)* Right, you and your reports: lots of stress, lots of coffee, no breakfast. Eat a slice of bread. And here's some butter, cold cuts, and cheese to go with it.
PETER:	I can't stop now, I have to finish writing the thing.
MARTIN:	You're really stupid, Peter. Why do you always start so late?
PETER:	I need the stress, Martin. That's just the way I am.

Morgen, morgen, nur nicht heute ... *(Why do today what you can put off until tomorrow . . .)*

STEPHANIE:	Our room looks like a pigsty! Can't you clean up a bit for a change, Claudia?
CLAUDIA:	Of course! But not today. Today I have way too much to do.
STEPHANIE:	That's what you always say, and then *I* have to clean up.
CLAUDIA:	You don't have to do that at all. Tomorrow I have lots of time.
STEPHANIE:	You always say that too.
CLAUDIA:	Yes, but this time it's true. Tomorrow I'll be home all morning, I'll get up early, and by twelve everything will be in tiptop shape here.
STEPHANIE:	Well, we'll see.

Stephanie schreibt eine E-Mail nach Hause *(Stephanie writes an e-mail home)*

Hi, everyone,
Everything here is still really super: the university, the city, and above all, my new friends. Claudia is still my best friend. By the way, she's a fabulous cook, and she makes really delicious dishes with lots of vegetables and salad, and not much meat. But she also likes my tomato sauce with noodles or spaghetti. By the way, they often eat cold cuts and cheese for breakfast here. But I usually eat a bowl of cornflakes, just like at home, and sometimes I also make my favorite breakfast, my pancakes. Peter, a friend of Claudia's boyfriend Martin, thinks they're really great. By the way, Peter is really nice. He comes over a lot and he also calls often.

Love,
Stephanie

Kapitel 5

Morgen haben wir keine Vorlesungen *(Tomorrow we don't have any lectures)*

Claudia tells Stephanie what she has planned for tomorrow.

STEPHANIE:	What are you doing tomorrow, Claudia?
CLAUDIA:	First I'm going to sleep until eleven or eleven-thirty and then I'll call Martin.
STEPHANIE:	And he'll pick you up and drag you to the *Alte Pinakothek* again.
CLAUDIA:	That's what you think! We've been there often enough now. Tomorrow we're doing what I want to do.
STEPHANIE:	And what's that?
CLAUDIA:	First we'll go eat veal sausages at the Donisl on the *Marienplatz* . . .
STEPHANIE:	Mmm, they're really delicious there.

CLAUDIA:	Then we'll go to the *Deutsche Museum* and look at historic machines.
STEPHANIE:	Poor Martin!
CLAUDIA:	And then we'll take the bus to the English Garden.
STEPHANIE:	Are you going to go swimming there?
CLAUDIA:	No, we're going for a walk. The *Eisbach* is still way too cold.
STEPHANIE:	And where are you going to have dinner?
CLAUDIA:	Tomorrow we're going to spend a lot of money for a change and go to Mövenpick.

Ferienpläne (*Vacation plans*)

Ms. Ziegler doesn't want to do what her children want to do, but Mr. Ziegler finds a good solution.

NINA:	Summer vacation begins in mid-July, Dad. Are we going to Grundl Lake again? The campground there was really great.
FATHER:	But you know that Mom isn't in favor of that. She didn't even want to go camping last year anymore.
ROBERT:	But we had so much fun there.
MOTHER:	Fun? With rain almost every day and everything in the tent wet. And that primitive cooking! You know, Robert, that's no vacation for me.
NINA:	But Robert and I had such good friends. They're sure to be there again this year.
MOTHER:	I know, I know, but I need a vacation too and would really prefer to stay in a hotel. And please, not in the cheapest one, Klaus.
FATHER:	Even if it's at Grundl Lake?
MOTHER:	If it's nice, I have nothing against it.
FATHER:	You see, I know a small but very nice hotel there, less than half a kilometer from the campground. Then the kids will have their friends, I can go to the lake to fish . . .
MOTHER:	And I can finally relax a bit too.

Kapitel 6

Ein bisschen Familiengeschichte (*A bit of family history*)

It's the beginning of October, Stephanie arrived in Munich yesterday, and Claudia wants to know why her American roommate has a German name.

CLAUDIA:	(*is writing and reads*) ". . . letter to follow soon. Love, Claudia" – There! The postcard is done! – Stephanie, have you written home yet?
STEPHANIE:	But Claudia, I haven't even unpacked my suitcases yet!
CLAUDIA:	A postcard with "Have arrived safely, letter to follow soon" doesn't even take five minutes.
STEPHANIE:	My parents don't want a postcard, but a long letter. They want to know where and how I live, my roommate's name, and how old she is, where she's from, and what she's like. And I don't even know a lot of that yet.
CLAUDIA:	No problem, Stephanie. You know my name is Claudia, Claudia Maria Berger. I'm from Hamburg and I'm very, very nice. – You know, you're actually much more interesting, Stephanie: an American from Chicago, young, pretty, intelligent . . .
STEPHANIE:	Oh, nonsense!
CLAUDIA:	And then that name, "Stephanie Braun!" (*laughs*) So typically American! – Tell me, is your father German? Did he emigrate?
STEPHANIE:	No, my father was born in America. But my grandfather is from Germany and emigrated to America in 1950.

Kapitel 7

Das Geburtstagsgeschenk (*The birthday present*)

NICOLE:	Hey, Maria, what should I give my little brother for his birthday?
MARIA:	Give him a watch. Or a CD. What does he like to listen to? Or buy him a computer game. Yes! Computer games are the thing to give a thirteen-year-old these days!
NICOLE:	David already has all of those things, and besides, a good computer game is much too expensive for me.
MARIA:	Then let's go to KaDeWe! When we see everything they've got, I'm sure we'll think of something.
NICOLE:	Good idea, Maria!

Beim KaDeWe (*At KaDeWe*)

At KaDeWe the winter sale has just begun and all prices have been drastically reduced. So the two friends take a quick detour to the women's department before they look for a gift for David. Maria buys a chic warm winter jacket there, and Nicole spends almost all of her money on an elegant black sweater. Then she looks a bit shamefacedly at the couple of euros in her wallet and says: "How am I supposed to buy my brother a birthday present with this?" But Maria has a good idea: "Buy him a funny birthday card, and with the card send him an IOU with the words: 'Dear David, I owe you a birthday present. You'll get it as soon as I have money again.'"

Kapitel 8

Die möblierte Wohnung (*The furnished apartment*)

Mrs. Wild is flying to her son's place in Texas for a year. Martin and Peter have rented her apartment and have just moved in. Claudia comes for a visit to see what her two friends' apartment is like.

MARTIN: Well, Claudia, how do you like the apartment? Completely furnished for only 450 euros a month!

CLAUDIA: Not bad, only – the furniture is all in the wrong place.

MARTIN: Sorry, but we promised not to rearrange it.

CLAUDIA: Hasn't Mrs. Wild's flight left already?

PETER: Yes, I think it left yesterday afternoon at two-thirty.

CLAUDIA: Well, then we can get started. You just mustn't forget where everything was.

PETER: No problem, I never forget anything.

CLAUDIA: Then take the floor lamp beside the armchair, Peter, and put it behind it. And Martin, you take the rug here, and put it in front of the couch! And that ugly old clock there on the desk, take it into the kitchen, Peter, and put it on the fridge. There, that looks a lot better already.

MARTIN: Come on, let's go out onto our balcony now, Claudia.

CLAUDIA: (*on the balcony*) Hey, those are gorgeous geraniums.

PETER: Yes, we have to water them every other day, too.

MARTIN: Hey, Peter, who is that woman down there? She almost looks like Mrs. Wild.

PETER: That can't be true! That *is* Mrs. Wild and she's coming up here! Quick, put the clock back on the desk and the floor lamp beside the armchair! And I'll put the rug back . . .

Kapitel 9

Im Gasthaus (*At the restaurant*)

Beverly Harper's niece Shauna is an exchange student and is staying with the Zieglers. Shauna and Nina are standing in front of a restaurant and studying the menu that's hanging outside in a small display case.

SHAUNA: I feel like having something typically German. Here, marinated roast beef with red cabbage and potato dumplings. That's what I'm going to order.

NINA: Good, then let's go inside!

SHAUNA: Hey, it's completely full. There isn't a single empty table left.

NINA: There are still two empty places by that couple with the little boy and the dog.

SHAUNA: Do you know those people?

NINA: No, but that doesn't matter. Come on, or someone else will sit there. – Excuse me, are these two places still free?

MAN: Yes, please have a seat here with us. Our dog won't hurt you.

WOMAN: And here's the menu, too. Then you can look for something good until the waiter comes.

Im Supermarkt (*At the supermarket*)

After the meal Nina and Shauna have to buy a few groceries.

NINA: Why don't you get one of the shopping carts that are standing over there. (*reads her shopping list*) Milk, potatoes, head lettuce, tomatoes.

SHAUNA: Why did you bring this shopping bag along, Nina?

NINA: Because I don't want to pay for a plastic bag.

SHAUNA: What?! You have to pay for plastic bags?

NINA: Of course. The plastic bags you get in the supermarket cost 15 cents a piece, and I can reuse this one again and again. – Here are the potatoes, the lettuce, and the tomatoes. There, now we just need two liters of milk.

SHAUNA: (*at the checkout*) Oh, your cashiers have it made, they're allowed to sit. – But why are you packing everything yourself? At home (in America) the cashier does that.

NINA: Different strokes for different folks.

■ Answer Key for *Wörter im Kontext*

Erste Kontakte (p. 11)

E-18
	your professor	*your fellow students*
9 a.m.	Guten Morgen!	Morgen!
3 p.m.	Guten Tag!	Tag!
7 p.m.	Guten Abend!	'n Abend!

E-19 1.c. 2.a. 3.d. 4.b.

E-20 1. Wie geht's; Super 2. Entschuldigung; Nein 3. Name; Wie bitte; Wie geht es Ihnen

Kapitel 1 (pp. 19 and 48-49)

1-6 1.e. 2.a. 3.d. 4.f. 5.c. 6.b.

1-7 1.d. 2.c. 3.b. 4.a. 5.f. 6.e.

1-8 1. braun 2. grün 3. weiß 4. gelb 5. schwarz 6. rot 7. blau 8. grau

1-9 1. Schweizerin 2. Österreicher 3. Deutsche 4. Amerikaner 5. Kanadierin

1-55 1. und 2. oder 3. sondern 4. aber 5. denn

1-56 1.e. 2.a. 3.d. 4.f. 5.b. 6.c.

1-57 1.c. 2.a. 3.e. 4.b. 5.f. 6.d.

1-58 1. die Kneipe 2. lernen 3. nichts

1-59 1. hell; dunkel 2. fragt; antwortet 3. viel; wenig 4. gut; schlecht

1-60 1. Dienstag 2. Sonntag 3. Mittwoch 4. Montag 5. Samstag

Kapitel 2 (pp. 55 and 81)

2-6 1. haben 2. Kochst 3. sagt 4. telefonierst 5. sammelt

2-7 1. stundenlang 2. Zeit 3. Uhr 4. Uhr 5. Stunde

2-8 1. Kaffee; Tee; Cola 2. Milch 3. Bier; Wein 4. Wasser

2-9 1. groß; klein 2. schlank 3. mollig 4. groß 5. klein

2-10 1.d. 2.g. 3.h. 4.i. 5.a. 6.f. 7.e. 8.b. 9.c.

2-52 1. die Hose 2. die Bluse *or* der Rock *(the only masculine noun)* 3. der Gürtel 4. die Schuhe

2-53 1. wohnen 2. leben 3. lebt; wohnt

2-54 1. die Wohnung 2. das Haus 3. die Straße 4. die Stadt 5. das Land

2-55 1. kurz; lang 2. billig; teuer 3. dick; dünn 4. immer; nie 5. Mann; Frau 6. sucht; findet

Kapitel 3 (pp. 89 and 117)

3-7 1. der Vetter *or* der Cousin 2. der Bruder 3. der Großvater 4. die Tante 5. die Oma 6. die Mutter 7. der Sohn 8. der Enkel 9. die Nichte

3-8 1. Wagen 2. Fahrräder; Motorräder 3. Zug 4. Fahrzeug

3-9 1.e. 2.g. 3.d. 4.a. 5.h. 6.c. 7.b. 8.f.

3-10 1. pessimistisch 2. optimistisch 3. Langsam 4. interessant; langweilig 5. schnell

3-55 1. von Beruf 2. gibt es 3. offen; niemand 4. Übermorgen; wird; nächste 5. Flugzeug; Flughafen; nimmt 6. bekommt

3-56 1.d. trägt 2.c. fährt 3.e. liest 4.f. isst 5.b. schläft 6.g. sieht 7.a. wäscht

3-57 1.a.c. 2.a.b. 3.a.b. 4.b.c. 5.a.c. 6.a.c.

Kapitel 4 (pp. 125 and 153)

4-5 1. der Orangensaft 2. der Nachtisch 3. die Scheibe 4. der Brokkoli

4-6 1. nach Hause 2. zu Hause 3. nach Hause 4. zu Hause 5. nach Hause 6. zu Hause 7. zu Hause

4-7 1. meistens; Manchmal; diesmal 2. Zum Nachtisch; Zum Frühstück; Zum Mittagessen 3. Joghurt, Käse, Butter; Pommes frites, Chips 4. ein Glas; eine Tasse; eine Scheibe; ein Stück; einen Becher

4-54 1. auf 2. weg; heim 3. vor 4. ein 5. aus; mit 6. fern 7. weiter 8. ab; an

4-55 1.b. 2.e. 3.h. 4.a. 5.g. 6.c. 7.d. 8.f.

4-56 1. besonders 2. genug 3. unordentlich 4. anders 5. endlich 6. in Ruhe 7. zu Fuß

4-57 1. gesund; ungesund 2. oft; selten 3. links; rechts 4. möglich; unmöglich

Kapitel 5 (pp. 161 and 191)

5-6 1.c. 2.d. 3.a. 4.e. 5.b. 6.j. 7.h. 8.i. 9.g. 10.f.

5-7 1.d. 2.g. 3.f. 4.a. 5.b. 6.c. 7.e.

5-8 1. Schloss; Berg; fließt; Tal; Dorf; Felder; Insel; baden; Strand; Wolken; Gebirge

5-51 1.e. 2.d. 3.g. 4.f. 5.a. 6.h. 7.b. 8.c.

5-52 1.b. 2.a. 3.f. 4.g. 5.d. 6.c. 7.e.

5-53 1.c. 2.d. 3.a. 4.b. 5.h. 6.g. 7.f. 8.e.

5-54 1. Durst; etwas; leider 2. wahr; trotzdem 3. wichtig; ziemlich

Kapitel 6 (pp. 199 and 227)

6-8 1. Familiengeschichte; Stammbaum; Vorfahren; väterlicherseits; ausgewandert; eigentlich

6-9 1. Emigrant; Emigrantin 2. Koffer 3. Geburtsort 4. Wohnort 5. Postkarte

6-10 1.b. 2.a. 3.d. 4.c. 5.f. 6.e. 7.j. 8.l. 9.k. 10.g. 11.i. 12.h.

6-11 1. Beruf 2. geboren; wohnt 3. Gesicht 4. Augen; Haar

6-49 1.e. 2.f. 3.d. 4.b. 5.c. 6.g. 7.a.

6-50 1. gewartet; gelegen; hereingerannt; passiert; erklärt; starten; warten; gerannt

6-51 1. Was bedeutet dieses Wort? Ich verstehe dieses Wort nicht. 2. Opa Ziegler lebt nicht mehr. Opa Ziegler ist gestorben. 3. Eva ist plötzlich arbeitslos geworden. Eva hat seit gestern keine Arbeit mehr. 4. Wie ist die Bezahlung? Wie viel verdienst du?

6-52 1. Tagebuch; sofort; mindestens; sparen; schwer; Hoffentlich

Kapitel 7 (pp. 235 and 265)

7-8 1. einkaufen 2. das Essen kochen 3. den Tisch decken 4. essen 5. den Abwasch machen

7-9 1.d. 2.a. 3.f. 4.b. 5.c. 6.e.

7-10 1.d. 2.e. 3.a. 4.c. 5.b.

7-11 1.e. 2.d. 3.c. 4.f. 5.b. 6.a.

7-12 1. feiert; Fest; gerade; lustig; Überraschung; geschenkt; außerdem

7-61 1.f. 2.g. 3.e. 4.a. 5.c. 6.h. 7.d. 8.b.

7-62 1.h. 2.d. 3.e. 4.a. 5.f. 6.g. 7.b. 8.c.

7-63 1.c. 2.g. 3.f. 4.b. 5.h. 6.d. 7.e. 8.a.

Kapitel 8 (pp. 273 and 299)

8-5 1. das Badezimmer 2. die Küche 3. das Wohnzimmer 4. das Schlafzimmer 5. der Flur 6. das Esszimmer

8-6 1.c. 2.d. 3.a. 4.b. 5.h. 6.g. 7.f. 8.e. 9. j. 10.i. 11.l. 12.k. 13.o. 14.p. 15.n. 16.m.

8-7 1. hässlich 2. möblierte 3. Geschirrspülmaschine; Spülbecken 4. Nachttisch 5. ruhig 6. Dusche 7. umgezogen; ausgezogen; eingezogen

8-43 1.b. 2.a. 3.d. 4.c. 5.g. 6.h. 7.e. 8.f.

8-44 1.d. 2.c. 3.b. 4.e. 5.a.

8-45 1.c. 2.e. 3.a. 4.f. 5.b. 6.d.

8-46 1.c. 2.f. 3.a. 4.g. 5.d. 6.b. 7.e.

Kapitel 9 (pp. 305 and 331)

9-6 1. eine Einkaufsliste 2. einen Einkaufswagen 3. eine Speisekarte 4. einen Löffel 5. ein Rezept 6. eine Pfanne 7. eine Schüssel 8. ein Messer und eine Gabel

9-7 1.c. 2.d. 3.a. 4.b. 5.f. 6.e. 7.h. 8.g.

9-8 1. Das mag ich. Das ist lecker. 2. Der Hund tut dir nichts. Der Hund beißt nicht. 3. Diese Jacke gehört jemand anders. Diese Jacke gehört mir nicht. 4. Kein einziger von meinen Freunden war da. Keiner von meinen Freunden war da.

9-44 1.f. 2.e. 3.g. 4.d. 5.b. 6.a. 7.c.

9-45 1. zieht man sich aus 2. zieht man sich wieder an 3. zieht man sich um 4. sich erkälten 5. sich beeilen 6. sich entschuldigen 7. sich nicht wohl fühlt

9-46 1. Diese Suppe schmeckt mir nicht. Ich mag diese Suppe nicht. 2. Das darfst du nicht. Das kommt nicht in Frage! 3. Ich fühle mich nicht wohl. Mir geht es nicht gut. 4. Kommt ja rechtzeitig! Verspätet euch nicht!

Kapitel 10 (pp. 339 and 365)

10-5 1.f. 2.d. 3.a. 4.c. 5.g. 6.b. 7.e.

10-6 1. Mir ist kalt. Ich friere. 2. Warum stecken die Fotos nicht im Album? Warum sind die Fotos nicht im Album? 3. Warum bleibst du stehen? Warum gehst du nicht weiter? 4. Er sagt nie die Wahrheit. Er lügt immer.

10-7 1.d. 2.b. 3.c. 4.a. 5.f. 6.h. 7.e. 8.g. 9.k. 10.i. 11.l. 12. j.

10-8 *das Drama*: die Szene, die Autorin, der Sketch, die Rolle. *der Christ*: die Kirche, die Bibel, das Paradies, fromm. *das Pferd*: reiten, satteln, der Stall, galoppieren

10-47 1.d. 2.c. 3.e. 4.a. 5.b.

10-48 1. Stefan hat sich sehr aufgeregt. Stefan war außer sich. 2. Ann ist weder hier noch in ihrem Zimmer. Ann ist nicht hier, und in ihrem Zimmer ist sie auch nicht. 3. Ich habe mich lang mit Kurt unterhalten. Ich habe lang mit Kurt gesprochen. 4. Jetzt habe ich Lust auf Tennis. Ich möchte jetzt am liebsten Tennis spielen.

10-49 1. beliebter 2. modisches 3. defektes 4. winziges 5. riesiges 6. unzufriedener 7. sorgfältige

Kapitel 11 (pp. 373 and 395)

11-6 1. ermordet; zerstört 2. Wiedervereinigung; geteiltes 3. blockierten 4. Alliierten 5. flohen 6. Mauer; geschlossen 7. schießen 8. Demokratien; Diktaturen

11-7 1. das Schaubild 2. die Redefreiheit 3. der Beifahrersitz 4. der Weltkrieg 5. der Kulturschock 6. der Mauerfall 7. der Flughafen 8. die Luftbrücke

11-38 1.c. 2.d. 3.b. 4.a.

11-39 1.c. 2.a. 3.b. 4.e. 5.d.

11-40 1.b. 2.c. 3.e. 4.a. 5.d.

11-41 1.b. 2.a. 3.d. 4.c. 5.g. 6.h. 7.e. 8.f.

11-42 wütend; brüllte; übergeschnappt; peinlich; begreifen; aufregt; Frieden

Kapitel 12 (pp. 402 and 421)

12-7 1. unterbrichst 2. ständig 3. Aufgabe 4. qualifiziert 5. Karriere 6. gleichberechtigt

12-8 1.c. 2.a. 3.e. 4.h. 5.b. 6.g. 7.f. 8.d.

12-9 1. gewachsen 2. Stimme 3. Ahnung 4. widerlich 5. Arbeitgeber 6. Haushalt

12-42 1. Strafzettel 2. Zinsen 3. magersüchtig 4. Stelle 5. Rente

12-43 1.c. 2.f. 3.d. 4.a. 5.g. 6.b. 7.e.

12-44 1.f. 2.d. 3.a. 4.e. 5.c. 6.g. 7.b.

12-45 1. Wie hoch ist Ihr Lohn? Wie viel verdienen Sie? 2. Wir haben eine gute Beziehung. Wir verstehen uns gut. 3. Wann war eure Hochzeit? Seit wann seid ihr verheiratet? 4. Es tut ihm leid. Er bereut es.

Grammatical Tables

1. *Der*-words

Common **der**-words are **der, das, die** *(the)*; **dieser** *(this)*; **jeder** *(each, every)*; and **welcher** *(which)*.

	masculine	neuter	feminine	plural
NOMINATIVE	der	das	die	die
	dieser	dieses	diese	diese
ACCUSATIVE	den	das	die	die
	diesen	dieses	diese	diese
DATIVE	dem	dem	der	den
	diesem	diesem	dieser	diesen
GENITIVE	des	des	der	der
	dieses	dieses	dieser	dieser

2. *Ein*-words

The **ein**-words are **ein** *(a, an)*, **kein** *(not a, not any, no)*, and the possessive adjectives **mein** *(my)*, **dein** *(your)*, **sein** *(his, its)*, **ihr** *(her, its)*, **unser** *(our)*, **euer** *(your)*, **ihr** *(their)*, **Ihr** *(your)*.

	masculine	neuter	feminine	plural
NOMINATIVE	ein	ein	eine	—
	mein	mein	meine	meine
ACCUSATIVE	einen	ein	eine	—
	meinen	mein	meine	meine
DATIVE	einem	einem	einer	—
	meinem	meinem	meiner	meinen
GENITIVE	eines	eines	einer	—
	meines	meines	meiner	meiner

3. Pronouns
a. Personal pronouns

nom.	subj.	acc.	dir. obj.	dat.	ind. obj.
ich	*I*	mich	*me*	mir	*me*
du	*you*	dich	*you*	dir	*you*
er	*he, it*	ihn	*him, it*	ihm	*him, it*
es	*it*	es	*it*	ihm	*it*
sie	*she, it*	sie	*her, it*	ihr	*her, it*
wir	*we*	uns	*us*	uns	*us*
ihr	*you*	euch	*you*	euch	*you*
sie	*they*	sie	*them*	ihnen	*them*
Sie	*you*	Sie	*you*	Ihnen	*you*

b. Reflexive pronouns

	acc.	dat.	dir. obj./ind. obj.
(ich)	mich	mir	*myself*
(du)	dich	dir	*yourself*
(er)	sich	sich	*himself, itself*
(es)	sich	sich	*itself*
(sie)	sich	sich	*herself, itself*
(wir)	uns	uns	*ourselves*
(ihr)	euch	euch	*yourselves*
(sie)	sich	sich	*themselves*
(Sie)	sich	sich	*yourself*
			yourselves

c. Interrogative pronouns

	for persons	for things
NOMINATIVE	wer	was
ACCUSATIVE	wen	was
DATIVE	wem	—
GENITIVE	wessen	—

d. Relative pronouns

	masculine	neuter	feminine	plural
NOMINATIVE	der	das	die	die
ACCUSATIVE	den	das	die	die
DATIVE	dem	dem	der	denen
GENITIVE	dessen	dessen	deren	deren

4. Adjective endings
a. After *der*-words

	masculine	neuter	feminine	plural
NOM.	der jung**e** Mann	das lieb**e** Kind	die jung**e** Frau	die lieb**en** Kinder
ACC.	den jung**en** Mann	das lieb**e** Kind	die jung**e** Frau	die lieb**en** Kinder
DAT.	dem jung**en** Mann	dem lieb**en** Kind	der jung**en** Frau	den lieb**en** Kindern
GEN.	des jung**en** Mannes	des lieb**en** Kindes	der jung**en** Frau	der lieb**en** Kinder

b. After *ein*-words

	masculine	neuter	feminine	plural
NOM.	ein jung**er** Mann	ein lieb**es** Kind	eine jung**e** Frau	keine lieb**en** Kinder
ACC.	einen jung**en** Mann	ein lieb**es** Kind	eine jung**e** Frau	keine lieb**en** Kinder
DAT.	einem jung**en** Mann	einem lieb**en** Kind	einer jung**en** Frau	keinen lieb**en** Kindern
GEN.	eines jung**en** Mannes	eines lieb**en** Kindes	einer jung**en** Frau	keiner lieb**en** Kinder

c. For unpreceded adjectives

	masculine	neuter	feminine	plural
NOM.	gut**er** Käse	gut**es** Brot	gut**e** Wurst	gut**e** Äpfel
ACC.	gut**en** Käse	gut**es** Brot	gut**e** Wurst	gut**e** Äpfel
DAT.	gut**em** Käse	gut**em** Brot	gut**er** Wurst	gut**en** Äpfeln

5. *N*-nouns

All **n**-nouns are masculine. They are listed in dictionaries as follows:
der Student, **-en**, **-en**.

	singular	plural
NOMINATIVE	der Student	die Studenten
ACCUSATIVE	den Studenten	die Studenten
DATIVE	dem Studenten	den Studenten
GENITIVE	des Studenten	der Studenten

6. Prepositions

with acc.	with dat.	with acc. or dat.	with gen.
durch	aus	an	statt
für	außer	auf	trotz
gegen	bei	hinter	während
ohne	mit	in	wegen
um	nach	neben	
	seit	über	
	von	unter	
	zu	vor	
		zwischen	

7. Adjectives and adverbs with irregular comparatives and superlatives

BASE FORM	gern	gut	groß	hoch	nah	viel
COMPARATIVE	lieber	besser	größer	höher	näher	mehr
SUPERLATIVE	liebst-	best-	größt-	höchst-	nächst-	meist-

8. Verbs

a. Indicative (to express facts)

Present tense

	lernen[1]	arbeiten[2]	reisen[3]	geben[4]	tragen[5]	laufen[6]	weg·gehen[7]
ich	lerne	arbeite	reise	gebe	trage	laufe	gehe … weg
du	lernst	arbeitest	reist	gibst	trägst	läufst	gehst … weg
er/es/sie	lernt	arbeitet	reist	gibt	trägt	läuft	geht … weg
wir	lernen	arbeiten	reisen	geben	tragen	laufen	gehen … weg
ihr	lernt	arbeitet	reist	gebt	tragt	lauft	geht … weg
sie	lernen	arbeiten	reisen	geben	tragen	laufen	gehen … weg
Sie	lernen	arbeiten	reisen	geben	tragen	laufen	gehen … weg

[1]Regular verbs

[2]Verbs with expanded endings (e.g., **arbeiten, finden, regnen, öffnen**)

[3]Verbs with contracted endings (e.g., **reisen, heißen, sitzen**)

[4]Irregular verbs with stem-vowel change **e** to **i (ie)**

[5]Irregular verbs with stem-vowel change **a** to **ä**

[6]Irregular verbs with stem-vowel change **au** to **äu**

[7]Separable-prefix verbs

Present tense of the auxiliaries *haben, sein, werden*

	haben	sein	werden
ich	habe	bin	werde
du	hast	bist	wirst
er/es/sie	hat	ist	wird
wir	haben	sind	werden
ihr	habt	seid	werdet
sie	haben	sind	werden
Sie	haben	sind	werden

Present tense of the modal verbs

	dürfen	können	mögen	(möcht-)	müssen	sollen	wollen
ich	darf	kann	mag	(möchte)	muss	soll	will
du	darfst	kannst	magst	(möchtest)	musst	sollst	willst
er/es/sie	darf	kann	mag	(möchte)	muss	soll	will
wir	dürfen	können	mögen	(möchten)	müssen	sollen	wollen
ihr	dürft	könnt	mögt	(möchtet)	müsst	sollt	wollt
sie	dürfen	können	mögen	(möchten)	müssen	sollen	wollen
Sie	dürfen	können	mögen	(möchten)	müssen	sollen	wollen

Simple past tense

	regular verbs		irregular verbs
ich	lernte	arbeitete	ging
du	lerntest	arbeitetest	gingst
er/es/sie	lernte	arbeitete	ging
wir	lernten	arbeiteten	gingen
ihr	lerntet	arbeitetet	gingt
sie	lernten	arbeiteten	gingen
Sie	lernten	arbeiteten	gingen

You will find the principal parts of the irregular verbs used in this text on pp. A36–A39.

Simple past tense of the auxiliaries *haben, sein, werden*

	haben	sein	werden
ich	hatte	war	wurde
du	hattest	warst	wurdest
er/es/sie	hatte	war	wurde
wir	hatten	waren	wurden
ihr	hattet	wart	wurdet
sie	hatten	waren	wurden
Sie	hatten	waren	wurden

Simple past tense of mixed verbs

	bringen	denken	kennen	nennen	rennen	wissen
ich	brachte	dachte	kannte	nannte	rannte	wusste
du	brachtest	dachtest	kanntest	nanntest	ranntest	wusstest
er/es/sie	brachte	dachte	kannte	nannte	rannte	wusste
wir	brachten	dachten	kannten	nannten	rannten	wussten
ihr	brachtet	dachtet	kanntet	nanntet	ranntet	wusstet
sie	brachten	dachten	kannten	nannten	rannten	wussten
Sie	brachten	dachten	kannten	nannten	rannten	wussten

Simple past tense of the modal verbs

	dürfen	können	mögen	müssen	sollen	wollen
ich	durfte	konnte	mochte	musste	sollte	wollte
du	durftest	konntest	mochtest	musstest	solltest	wolltest
er/es/sie	durfte	konnte	mochte	musste	sollte	wollte
wir	durften	konnten	mochten	mussten	sollten	wollten
ihr	durftet	konntet	mochtet	musstet	solltet	wolltet
sie	durften	konnten	mochten	mussten	sollten	wollten
Sie	durften	konnten	mochten	mussten	sollten	wollten

Perfect tense

	regular verbs				irregular verbs			
ich	habe	gelernt	bin	gereist	habe	gesungen	bin	gegangen
du	hast	gelernt	bist	gereist	hast	gesungen	bist	gegangen
er/es/sie	hat	gelernt	ist	gereist	hat	gesungen	ist	gegangen
wir	haben	gelernt	sind	gereist	haben	gesungen	sind	gegangen
ihr	habt	gelernt	seid	gereist	habt	gesungen	seid	gegangen
sie	haben	gelernt	sind	gereist	haben	gesungen	sind	gegangen
Sie	haben	gelernt	sind	gereist	haben	gesungen	sind	gegangen

You will find the principal parts of the irregular verbs used in this text on pp. A36–A39.

b. Imperative (to express commands or requests)

FAMILIAR SINGULAR	Lern(e)!	Gib!	Sei!
FAMILIAR PLURAL	Lernt!	Gebt!	Seid!
FORMAL	Lernen Sie!	Geben Sie!	Seien Sie!

c. Subjunctive (to express contrary-to-fact situations)

Present-time subjunctive

	haben	sein	können	wissen
ich	hätte	wäre	könnte	wüsste
du	hättest	wär(e)st	könntest	wüsstest
er/es/sie	hätte	wäre	könnte	wüsste
wir	hätten	wären	könnten	wüssten
ihr	hättet	wär(e)t	könntet	wüsstet
sie	hätten	wären	könnten	wüssten
Sie	hätten	wären	könnten	wüssten

For verbs other than **haben**, **sein**, **werden**, **wissen**, and the modals, use **würde** + infinitive.

ich	würde	lernen
du	würdest	lernen
er/es/sie	würde	lernen
wir	würden	lernen
ihr	würdet	lernen
sie	würden	lernen
Sie	würden	lernen

Past-time subjunctive

ich	hätte	gelernt	wäre	gegangen
du	hättest	gelernt	wär(e)st	gegangen
er/es/sie	hätte	gelernt	wäre	gegangen
wir	hätten	gelernt	wären	gegangen
ihr	hättet	gelernt	wär(e)t	gegangen
sie	hätten	gelernt	wären	gegangen
Sie	hätten	gelernt	wären	gegangen

d. Passive voice

	present tense		simple past tense	
ich	werde	abgeholt	wurde	abgeholt
du	wirst	abgeholt	wurdest	abgeholt
er/es/sie	wird	abgeholt	wurde	abgeholt
wir	werden	abgeholt	wurden	abgeholt
ihr	werdet	abgeholt	wurdet	abgeholt
sie	werden	abgeholt	wurden	abgeholt
Sie	werden	abgeholt	wurden	abgeholt

Principal Parts of Irregular and Mixed Verbs

The following list contains the principal parts of the irregular and mixed verbs in *Treffpunkt Deutsch*. With a few exceptions, the separable- and inseparable-prefix verbs are not included, since the stem changes are the same as for the basic verb (e.g., **ausgeben – geben, mitbringen – bringen, verstehen – stehen**).

INFINITIVE	IRR. PRESENT	SIMPLE PAST	PAST PARTICIPLE	
anfangen	(fängt an)	fing an	angefangen	*to begin*
backen	(bäckt)	backte	gebacken	*to bake*
beißen		biss	gebissen	*to bite*
beginnen		begann	begonnen	*to begin*
bekommen		bekam	bekommen	*to get; to receive*
beweisen		bewies	bewiesen	*to prove*
bieten		bot	geboten	*to offer*
bitten		bat	gebeten	*to ask*
bleiben		blieb	ist geblieben	*to stay; to remain*
bringen		brachte	gebracht	*to bring*
denken		dachte	gedacht	*to think*
einladen	(lädt ein)	lud ein	eingeladen	*to invite*
empfangen	(empfängt)	empfing	empfangen	*to welcome*
empfehlen	(empfiehlt)	empfahl	empfohlen	*to recommend*
entscheiden		entschied	entschieden	*to decide*
entwerfen	(entwirft)	entwarf	entworfen	*to design*
essen	(isst)	aß	gegessen	*to eat*
fahren	(fährt)	fuhr	ist gefahren	*to drive*
fallen	(fällt)	fiel	ist gefallen	*to fall*
fangen	(fängt)	fing	gefangen	*to catch*
finden		fand	gefunden	*to find*
fliegen		flog	ist geflogen	*to fly*
fliehen		floh	ist geflohen	*to flee*
fließen		floss	ist geflossen	*to flow*
fressen	(frisst)	fraß	gefressen	*to eat (of animals)*
frieren		fror	gefroren	*to be cold*
geben	(gibt)	gab	gegeben	*to give*
gehen		ging	ist gegangen	*to go*
gelten	(gilt)	galt	gegolten	*to be considered*
geschehen	(geschieht)	geschah	ist geschehen	*to happen*
gewinnen		gewann	gewonnen	*to win*
gießen		goss	gegossen	*to water*
haben	(hat)	hatte	gehabt	*to have*
halten	(hält)	hielt	gehalten	*to hold; to keep; to stop*
hängen		hing	gehangen	*to be hanging*
heißen		hieß	geheißen	*to be called*
helfen	(hilft)	half	geholfen	*to help*
kennen		kannte	gekannt	*to know (be acquainted with)*
kommen		kam	ist gekommen	*to come*
laden	(lädt)	lud	geladen	*to load*
lassen	(lässt)	ließ	gelassen	*to let; to leave*
laufen	(läuft)	lief	ist gelaufen	*to run*
leihen		lieh	geliehen	*to lend*
lesen	(liest)	las	gelesen	*to read*

INFINITIVE	IRR. PRESENT	SIMPLE PAST		PAST PARTICIPLE	
liegen		lag		gelegen	*to lie; to be situated*
lügen		log		gelogen	*to tell a lie*
nehmen	(nimmt)	nahm		genommen	*to take*
nennen		nannte		genannt	*to call; to name*
raten	(rät)	riet		geraten	*to guess; to advise*
reiten		ritt	ist	geritten	*to ride*
rennen		rannte	ist	gerannt	*to run*
riechen		roch		gerochen	*to smell*
rufen		rief		gerufen	*to call*
scheinen		schien		geschienen	*to shine; to seem*
schieben		schob		geschoben	*to push*
schlafen	(schläft)	schlief		geschlafen	*to sleep*
schießen		schoss		geschossen	*to shoot*
schließen		schloss		geschlossen	*to close*
schneiden		schnitt		geschnitten	*to cut*
schreiben		schrieb		geschrieben	*to write*
schreien		schrie		geschrien	*to shout*
schwimmen		schwamm	ist	geschwommen	*to swim*
sehen	(sieht)	sah		gesehen	*to see*
sein	(ist)	war	ist	gewesen	*to be*
singen		sang		gesungen	*to sing*
sinken		sank	ist	gesunken	*to sink*
sitzen		saß		gesessen	*to sit*
spinnen		spann		gesponnen	*to spin; to be crazy*
sprechen	(spricht)	sprach		gesprochen	*to speak*
springen		sprang	ist	gesprungen	*to jump*
stehen		stand		gestanden	*to stand*
stehlen	(stiehlt)	stahl		gestohlen	*to steal*
steigen		stieg	ist	gestiegen	*to climb*
sterben	(stirbt)	starb	ist	gestorben	*to die*
stinken		stank		gestunken	*to stink*
streichen		strich		gestrichen	*to paint*
tragen	(trägt)	trug		getragen	*to carry; to wear*
treffen	(trifft)	traf		getroffen	*to meet*
trinken		trank		getrunken	*to drink*
tun		tat		getan	*to do*
verbieten		verbot		verboten	*to forbid*
verbinden		verband		verbunden	*to connect*
vergessen	(vergisst)	vergaß		vergessen	*to forget*
vergleichen		verglich		verglichen	*to compare*
verlieren		verlor		verloren	*to lose*
vermeiden		vermied		vermieden	*to avoid*
vorschlagen	(schlägt vor)	schlug vor		vorgeschlagen	*to suggest*
waschen	(wäscht)	wusch		gewaschen	*to wash*
werden	(wird)	wurde	ist	geworden	*to become*
wissen	(weiß)	wusste		gewusst	*to know (a fact)*
ziehen		zog		gezogen	*to pull*

Modal verbs

dürfen	(darf)	durfte	gedurft	*to be allowed to*
können	(kann)	konnte	gekonnt	*to be able to*
mögen	(mag)	mochte	gemocht	*to like*
müssen	(muss)	musste	gemusst	*to have to*
sollen	(soll)	sollte	gesollt	*to be supposed to*
wollen	(will)	wollte	gewollt	*to want to*

Principal Parts of Irregular Verbs in Ablaut Groups

Group 1 (ei → i or ie → i or ie)

beißen	biss	gebissen	*to bite*
beweisen	bewies	bewiesen	*to prove*
bleiben	blieb	ist geblieben	*to stay; to remain*
entscheiden	entschied	entschieden	*to decide*
leihen	lieh	geliehen	*to lend*
reiten	ritt	ist geritten	*to ride*
scheinen	schien	geschienen	*to shine; to seem*
schneiden	schnitt	geschnitten	*to cut*
schreiben	schrieb	geschrieben	*to write*
schreien	schrie	geschrien	*to shout*
steigen	stieg	ist gestiegen	*to climb*
streichen	strich	gestrichen	*to paint*
vergleichen	verglich	verglichen	*to compare*
vermeiden	vermied	vermieden	*to avoid*

Group 2 (i → a → u)

finden	fand	gefunden	*to find*
singen	sang	gesungen	*to sing*
sinken	sank	ist gesunken	*to sink*
springen	sprang	ist gesprungen	*to jump*
stinken	stank	gestunken	*to stink*
trinken	trank	getrunken	*to drink*
verbinden	verband	verbunden	*to connect*

Group 3 (i → a → o)

beginnen	begann	begonnen	*to begin*
gewinnen	gewann	gewonnen	*to win*
schwimmen	schwamm	ist geschwommen	*to swim*
spinnen	spann	gesponnen	*to spin; to be crazy*

Group 4 (ie or ü → o → o)

anbieten	bot an	angeboten	*to offer*
fliegen	flog	ist geflogen	*to fly*
fliehen	floh	ist geflohen	*to flee*
fließen	floss	ist geflossen	*to flow*
frieren	fror	gefroren	*to be cold*
gießen	goss	gegossen	*to water*
riechen	roch	gerochen	*to smell*
schieben	schob	geschoben	*to push*
schießen	schoss	geschossen	*to shoot*
schließen	schloss	geschlossen	*to close*
verbieten	verbot	verboten	*to forbid*
verlieren	verlor	verloren	*to lose*
ziehen	zog	gezogen	*to pull*
lügen	log	gelogen	*to tell a lie*

Group 5 (a or au → i or ie → a or au)

anfangen	(fängt an)	fing an		angefangen	*to begin*
empfangen	(empfängt)	empfing		empfangen	*to welcome*
fallen	(fällt)	fiel	ist	gefallen	*to fall*
fangen	(fängt)	fing		gefangen	*to catch*
halten	(hält)	hielt		gehalten	*to hold; to keep; to stop*
lassen	(lässt)	ließ		gelassen	*to let; to leave*
raten	(rät)	riet		geraten	*to guess; to advise*
schlafen	(schläft)	schlief		geschlafen	*to sleep*
laufen	(läuft)	lief	ist	gelaufen	*to run*

Group 6 (a → u → a)

einladen	(lädt ein)	lud ein		eingeladen	*to invite*
fahren	(fährt)	fuhr	ist	gefahren	*to drive*
laden	(lädt)	lud		geladen	*to load*
schlagen	(schlägt)	schlug		geschlagen	*to hit; to beat*
tragen	(trägt)	trug		getragen	*to carry; to wear*
vorschlagen	(schlägt vor)	schlug vor		vorgeschlagen	*to suggest*
waschen	(wäscht)	wusch		gewaschen	*to wash*

Group 7 (e → a → e)

essen	(isst)	aß		gegessen	*to eat*
fressen	(frisst)	fraß		gefressen	*to eat (of animals)*
geben	(gibt)	gab		gegeben	*to give*
geschehen	(geschieht)	geschah	ist	geschehen	*to happen*
lesen	(liest)	las		gelesen	*to read*
sehen	(sieht)	sah		gesehen	*to see*
vergessen	(vergisst)	vergaß		vergessen	*to forget*

Group 8 (e → a → o)

empfehlen	(empfiehlt)	empfahl		empfohlen	*to recommend*
entwerfen	(entwirft)	entwarf		entworfen	*to design*
gelten	(gilt)	galt		gegolten	*to be considered*
helfen	(hilft)	half		geholfen	*to help*
nehmen	(nimmt)	nahm		genommen	*to take*
sprechen	(spricht)	sprach		gesprochen	*to speak*
stehlen	(stiehlt)	stahl		gestohlen	*to steal*
sterben	(stirbt)	starb	ist	gestorben	*to die*
treffen	(trifft)	traf		getroffen	*to meet*

Not classifiable

backen	(bäckt)	backte		gebacken	*to bake*
bitten		bat		gebeten	*to ask*
liegen		lag		gelegen	*to lie; to be situated*
gehen		ging	ist	gegangen	*to go*
hängen		hing		gehangen	*to be hanging*
heißen		hieß		geheißen	*to be called*
kommen		kam	ist	gekommen	*to come*
bekommen		bekam		bekommen	*to get; to receive*
rufen		rief		gerufen	*to call*
sitzen		saß		gesessen	*to sit*
stehen		stand		gestanden	*to stand*
tun		tat		getan	*to do*
werden	(wird)	wurde	ist	geworden	*to become*

German-English Vocabulary

This German-English vocabulary includes all the words and expressions used in *Treffpunkt Deutsch* except numbers and names of countries. The latter are listed in the *Useful Word Sets* on page A21. Each item is followed by the number of the chapter (and E for *Erste Kontakte*) in which it first occurs. Chapter numbers followed by -1 or -2 (e.g., 1-1 or 1-2) refer to items listed in the first or second vocabulary list in each chapter *(Wortschatz 1* or *Wortschatz 2)*.

Nouns are listed with their plural forms: **die Studentin, -nen.** If no plural entry is given, the plural is rarely used or nonexistent. When two entries follow a noun, the first one indicates the genitive and the second the plural: **der Student, -en, -en.**

Irregular, mixed, and modal verbs are listed with their principal parts. Vowel changes in the present tense are noted in parentheses: **lesen (liest), las, gelesen.** Auxiliary verbs are given only for verbs conjugated with **sein: kommen, kam, ist gekommen; reisen, reiste, ist gereist.** Separable prefixes are indicated by a raised dot between the prefix and the verb stem: **an·fangen.**

The following abbreviations are used:

acc	accusative	*gen*	genitive
adj	adjective	*indef*	indefinite
adv	adverb	*neg*	negative
art	article	*pl*	plural
conj	conjunction	*prep*	preposition
coord	coordinating	*sing*	singular
dat	dative	*sub*	subordinating

A

ab: ab morgen from tomorrow on (7)

der **Abend, -e** evening

  Guten Abend! 'n Abend! Good evening! (E-1)

  heute Abend this evening, tonight (1)

  zu Abend essen to have supper (4-1)

das **Abendessen** supper; evening meal (4-1)

  zum Abendessen for supper; for dinner (4-1)

abends in the evening (2)

aber *(coord conj)* but (1-2)

ab·fahren (fährt ab), fuhr ab, ist abgefahren to leave, to depart (4-2)

der/die **Abgeordnete, -n** delegate, representative (11); elected member of parliament (12)

ab·haken to check off (7)

ab·holen to pick up (5-1)

das **Abitur** high school diploma (E)

die **Abkürzung, -en** abbreviation (E)

ab·lehnen to refuse (7)

ab·reisen to leave, to depart (6)

der **Absatz, ¨e** paragraph (11)

der **Abschied, -e** farewell (11)

Abschied nehmen (nimmt), nahm, genommen to bid farewell (11)

absolut absolute (9)

die **Abteilung, -en** department (7-1)

der **Abteilungsleiter, -/die Abteilungsleiterin, -nen** department manager (12)

die **Abwanderung** moving away; migration (11)

der **Abwasch** dirty dishes (7)

  den Abwasch machen to do the dishes (7-1)

ab·wischen to wipe off (12)

ADAC (Allgemeiner Deutscher Automobil-Club) German automobile club (E)

die **Adresse, -n** address (E)

der **Adventskalender, -** Advent calendar (7)

der **Affe, -n, -n** ape; monkey (2)

der **Agent, -en, -en/die Agentin, -nen** agent (5)

ähnlich similar (7, 9-2)

die **Ähnlichkeit, -en** similarity (9)

Ahnung: Sie hat keine Ahnung. She has no idea. She doesn't have a clue. (12-1)

die **Akademie, -n** academy (9)

aktivieren to activate (12)

die **Akzeptanz** *(sing)* acceptance (9)

alarmieren to alarm (11-1)

die **Alarmanlage, -n** (11)

albern silly (12-1)

das **Album, Alben** album (5)

der **Alkohol** alcohol (4-2)

alkoholsüchtig addicted to alcohol (12)

alle all (the) (1); everybody (7)

allein alone (7-2)

die **Allergie, -n** allergy (9)

alles everything; all (3-2)

  Alles in Ordnung? Is everything okay? (9-2)

Es ist alles für die Katz. It's all for nothing. (10)

vor allem above all (4-1)

die **Alliierten** (pl) the Allies (11-1)

das **Alltagsleben** everyday life (4)

die **Alltagsszene, -n** everyday scene (4)

die **Alpen** (pl) Alps (1)

als from (2); as (2); than (2); when (conj) (9, 10-1); but (10)

als Kind as a child (5-2)

anders als different from (2)

besser als better than (2-2)

nichts als Ärger nothing but trouble (10)

also well then (2)

alt old (1, 3-2)

die **Alte Pinakothek** art gallery in Munich (5)

das **Alter** age (4); old age (12)

altmodisch old-fashioned (5-2)

die **Altstadt** (sing) old city center (9)

(das) **Amerika** America (6)

der **Amerikaner, -/**die **Amerikanerin, -nen** American (person) (1-1)

amerikanisch (adj) American (2-1)

das **Amt, ⸚er** office, department (6)

an (prep + acc/dat) at; to; on (a vertical surface) (2)

an·bieten, bot an, angeboten to offer (7, 12-2)

ander different, other (1)

ändern to change (4)

anders different(ly) (2, 4-2)

anders als different from (2)

jemand anders somebody else (9-1)

der **Anfang, ⸚e** beginning (4-2)

am Anfang at the beginning (11-1)

Anfang Juli (at) the beginning of July (5-1)

an·fangen (fängt an), fing an, angefangen to begin; to start (4-1)

an·fassen to touch (11)

an·funkeln to light into (11)

das **Angebot, -e** offer (10)

angeln to fish (5-1)

angesehen respected (10)

der **Angler, -/**die **Anglerin, -nen** fisher (5-1)

die **Angst, ⸚e** fear (10-1)

Angst haben to be afraid (9-2)

Angst haben vor (+ dat) to be afraid of (10-2)

Angst kriegen to get scared (10-1)

Keine Angst! Don't worry! (6)

an·halten (hält an), hielt an, angehalten to stop (10-1)

anhand by means of, using (10)

der **Anhang, ⸚e** appendix

an·hören to listen to (4-2)

an·kommen, kam an, ist angekommen to arrive (4-2)

die **Anmeldung, -en** registration (6)

an·ordnen to order (11)

die **Anpassung an** (+ acc) adjustment to (11)

an·probieren to try on (4-2)

der **Anrufbeantworter, -** answering machine (9)

an·rufen, rief an, angerufen to call (on the telephone) (4-1)

an·schauen to look at (5-1); to watch (9)

sich etwas an·schauen to look at something; to watch something (9)

Anspruch auf (+ acc) the right to (12)

die **Anstalt des öffentlichen Rechts** public institution (6)

anstatt (prep + gen) instead of (8-2)

der **Anteil, -e** share (4)

die **Antike** antiquity (9)

die **Antwort, -en** answer (1-2)

antworten (+ dat) to answer (1-2)

die **Anzeige, -n** ad; announcement (7-2)

an·ziehen, zog an, angezogen to put on, to wear (7-2)

sich an·ziehen, zog an, angezogen to dress, to get dressed (9-2)

der **Anzug, ⸚e** (men's) suit (2-2)

der **Apfel, ⸚** apple (1)

Der Apfel fällt nicht weit vom Stamm. Like father, like son. (7)

der **Apfelkuchen, -** apple pie (4)

der **Apfelsaft** (sing) apple juice (4)

die **Apotheke, -n** pharmacy (9-2)

der **Apotheker, -/**die **Apothekerin, -nen** pharmacist (9)

der **Apparat, -e** apparatus, appliance (9)

der **Appetit** appetite (9)

Guten Appetit! Enjoy your meal! (9-1)

der **April** April (1-2)

das **Äquivalent, -e** equivalent (6)

die **Arbeit** work (2-2)

arbeiten to work (1-2)

arbeiten an (+ dat) to work on (11-2)

der **Arbeiter, -/**die **Arbeiterin, -nen** worker (5)

der **Arbeitgeber, -/**die **Arbeitgeberin, -nen** employer (12-1)

der **Arbeitnehmer, -/**die **Arbeitnehmerin, -nen** employee (12-1)

die **Arbeitserfahrung, -en** work experience (6-2)

der **Arbeitskollege, -n, -n/**die **Arbeitskollegin, -nen** colleague from work (2)

arbeitslos unemployed (6-2)

die **Arbeitslosigkeit** unemployment (11)

der **Arbeitsplatz** place of work (7)

der **Arbeitsraum, ⸚e** study (8)

der **Architekt, -en, -en/**die **Architektin, -nen** architect (8-2)

die **Architektur** architecture (1)

der **Ärger** annoyance, trouble (10)

nichts als Ärger nothing but trouble (10)

ärgern to annoy (10)

sich ärgern über (+ acc) to be annoyed with, about (11-2)

das **Argument, -e** argument (5-2)

arm poor (5-1)

der **Arm, -e** arm (1, 6-1)

das **Armaturenbrett** dashboard (11-1)

das **Armband, ⸚er** bracelet (3, 5-2)

die **Armbanduhr, -en** wristwatch (7-1)

die **Armee, -n** army (4)

der **Ärmel, -** sleeve (7)

arrogant arrogant (5-2)

der **Artikel, -** article (2-1)

der **Arzt, ⸚e/**die **Ärztin, -nen** physician (1, 5-2)

der **Assistent, -en, -en/**die **Assistentin, -nen** assistant (5)

der **Athlet, -en, -en/**die **Athletin, -nen** athlete (9-2)

die **ATM Karte, -n** ATM card (5-2)

die **Attraktion, -en** attraction (5, 11-2)

auch also (E, 1-1)

Claudia kommt auch nicht. Claudia isn't coming either. (1-2)

der **Audi, -s** Audi (car) (4)

auf (prep + acc/dat) up (4); on, onto (6); to; on (a horizontal surface) (8)

auf sein to be up (4)

auf·essen (isst auf), aß auf, aufgegessen to eat up (11)

die **Aufgabe, -n** assignment; task (11, 12-1)

aufgeregt excited (8-2)

auf·hören to end; to stop (4-1)

der **Aufkleber, -** sticker (11-1)

auf·legen to hang up (the receiver) (8)

auf·listen to list (10)

auf·machen to open (8-2)

auf·passen to pay attention (4-2); to take care of (12)

auf·räumen to clean up (4-1)

sich **auf·regen** to get worked up; to get upset (9-2)

sich **auf·regen über** (+ acc) to get upset about; to get worked up about (11-2)

aufregend exciting (11-2)

auf·runden to round up (9)

auf·setzen to put on (one's head) (11)

auf·stehen, stand auf, ist aufgestanden to get up; to stand up (4-1)

der **Auftrag, ⁻e** order (4)

auf·wachen to wake up (4-2)

der **Aufzug** costume, get-up (11)

das **Auge, -n** eye (2, 6-1)

kein **Auge zu tun** to not sleep a wink (6)

unter vier **Augen** in private (9)

der **August** August (1-2)

aus (prep + dat) from, out of (E-1); over (4)

aus·bilden to train; to educate (6)

die **Ausbildung, -en** job training; education (12-1)

die **Ausbildungsförderung** education grant (6)

der **Ausdruck, ⁻e** expression (1)

aus·drucken to print out (5)

aus·drücken to express (12)

die **Ausgabe, -n** edition (7)

aus·geben (gibt aus), gab aus, ausgegeben to spend (money) (5-1)

aus·gehen, ging aus, ist ausgegangen to go out (4-2)

ausgeschlossen precluded (12)

ausgezeichnet excellent (3-2)

aus·halten (hält aus), hielt aus, ausgehalten to endure (11)

aus·höhlen to hollow out (7)

der **Ausländer, -/**die **Ausländerin, -nen** foreigner (2)

ausländisch foreign (10)

das **Auslandsamt** foreign students office (1-1)

aus·machen to represent (11)

aus·packen to unpack (6-1)

aus·probieren to try out (4-2)

aus·rasten to go off the deep end (11)

die **Ausrede, -n** excuse (5-2)

die **Aussage, -n** statement (7)

das **Aussehen** (sing) looks, appearance (11)

aus·sehen (sieht aus), sah aus, ausgesehen to look like, to appear (4-1); to look (8)

außen outside (9-1)

außer (prep + dat) except for (7)

Sie war **außer** sich. She was beside herself. (10-2)

außerdem besides; in addition (7-1)

außerhalb von (+ dat) outside of (3)

die **Aussicht, -en** view (11-2)

aus·spannen to relax (5-1)

die **Aussprache** pronunciation (E)

aus·stellen to exhibit (6)

die **Ausstellung, -en** exhibition, exhibit (6, 8-2)

aus·suchen to choose; to pick out (9-1)

sich etwas **aus·suchen** to pick something out (9)

der **Austauschschüler, -/**
die **Austauschschülerin, -nen** exchange student (high school) (9-1)

australisch (adj) Australian (3)

die **Auswahl** selection, choice (10)

der **Auswanderer, -/**die **Auswanderin, -nen** emigrant (6-1)

aus·wandern, wanderte aus, ist ausgewandert to emigrate (6-1)

aus·ziehen, zog aus, ist ausgezogen to move out (8-1)

sich **aus·ziehen, zog aus, hat ausgezogen** to undress, to get undressed (9-2)

der/die **Auszubildende, -n** apprentice (6)

der **Auszug, ⁻e** excerpt (6)

das **Auto, -s** car (1, 3-1)

Auto fahren (fährt Auto), fuhr Auto, ist Auto gefahren to drive (4)

die **Autobahn, -en** freeway, expressway (4-2)

der **Automechaniker, -/**die **Automechanikerin, -nen** (car) mechanic (1)

der **Autor, -en/**die **Autorin, -nen** author (2-2)

die **Autorität, -en** authority (11)

der **Autounfall, ⁻e** car accident (11)

der/die **Azubi, -s** (abbr of) **Auszubildende** (6)

B

das **Baby, -s** baby (1)

das **Baby-Öl** baby oil (11)

der **Babysitter, -/**die **Babysitterin, -nen** babysitter (4)

backen (bäckt), backte, gebacken to bake (3-2)

der **Bäcker, - /**die **Bäckerin, -nen** baker (E)

die **Bäckerei, -en** bakery (7-2)

das **Bad, ⁻er** bath; bathroom (2, 8-1)

der **Badeanzug, ⁻e** bathing suit (4)

die **Bademöglichkeit, -en** (place to go) swimming; swimming facility (5-1)

baden to swim; to bathe (5-1)

(sich) **baden** to bathe, to take a bath (9-2)

die **Badewanne, -n** bathtub (8-1)

das **Badewetter** swimming weather (1)

das **Badezimmer, -** bathroom (3, 8-1)

der **Bagel, -s** bagel (4-1)

die **Bahn** (sing) railway (4)

die **Bahnfahrt, -en** train trip (6)

der **Bahnhof, ⁻e** train station (4-2)

bald soon (2-2)

so **bald** wie möglich as soon as possible (4)

der **Balkon, -e** balcony (8-1)

der **Ball, ⁻e** ball (1)

der **Balletttänzer, -/**die **Balletttänzerin, -nen** ballet dancer (2)

die **Banane, -n** banana (1, 4-1)

die **Band, -s** band (2)

die **Bank, -en** bank (3-1)

der **Bankdirektor, -en/**die **Bankdirektorin, -nen** bank manager (3)

der **Bankkaufmann, Bankkaufleute/**die **Bankkauffrau, -en** office administrator at a bank (12)

die **Banknote, -n** banknote (9)

bankrott bankrupt (7)

der **Bär, -en, -en** bear (7, 9-2)

einen **Bärenhunger** haben to be famished (10)

das **Bargeld** cash (9-2)

die **Bar-Mizwa** (sing) Bar Mitzvah (7)

das **Barometer, -** barometer (1)

der **Bart, ⁻e** beard (5-2)

die **Baseballkappe, -n** baseball cap (5-2)

der **Basketball, ⁻e** basketball (2-1)

der **Bastelladen, ⁻** crafts store (2)

basteln to do crafts (2)

das **Basteln** (sing) crafts (4)

der **Bau** construction (10)

der **Bauch, ⸚e** stomach; belly (6-1)
 sich *(dat)* die **Beine in den Bauch stehen** to stand until one is ready to drop (9)
die **Bauchschmerzen** *(pl)* stomachache (6)
bauen to build (5, 8-1)
 Auf ihn kannst du Häuser bauen. He's absolutely dependable. (8)
der **Bauer, -n, -n**/die **Bäuerin, -nen** farmer (9, 10-1)
der **Baum, ⸚e** tree (5-1)
baumlos treeless (12)
der **Bausparvertrag, ⸚e** home savings plan (12)
der **Baustil, -e** building style (9)
bayerisch *(adj)* Bavarian (5)
(das) Bayern Bavaria (5)
beantworten to answer (7)
 eine Frage beantworten to answer a question (7-1)
der **Becher, -** cup; container (4-1)
 ein Becher Joghurt a container of yogurt (4-1)
bedeckt cloudy (1)
bedeuten to mean (2-2)
die **Bedeutung, -en** meaning (12)
bedeutungslos meaningless (12)
bedienen to serve *(guests in a restaurant)* (9-1)
die **Bedienung** server *(in a restaurant)* (9)
das **Bedienungsgeld** service charge (9)
sich **beeilen** to hurry (9-2)
beeindrucken to impress (12-2)
befragen to ask (12)
der/die **Befragte, -n** person questioned (9)
der **Beginn** beginning (1)
 zu Beginn at the beginning (11-1)
beginnen, begann, begonnen to begin (1-1)
der **Begleittext, -e** accompanying text (11)
begreifen, begriff, begriffen to understand, to grasp (11-2)
behandeln to treat (10)
behaupten to claim (11-1)
beherrschen to know (5)
bei *(prep + dat)* at (E); for; near (7)
 bei uns, bei Zieglers at our house, at the Zieglers (2-1)
beide both; two (2-2)
der **Beifahrer, -**/die **Beifahrerin, -nen** front-seat passenger *(in a car)* (11-1)

das **Bein, -e** leg (6-1)
 Hals- und Beinbruch! Break a leg! Good luck! (6-2)
 sich *(dat)* die **Beine in den Bauch stehen** to stand until one is ready to drop (9)
das **Beisel, -n** *(Austrian)* pub (2)
das **Beispiel, -e** example (6-2)
 zum Beispiel (z.B.) for example (e.g.) (4, 6-2)
beißen, biss, gebissen to bite (7)
der **Beistelltisch, -e** end table (8)
beizen to stain wood (9)
der/die **Bekannte, -n** acquaintance (8-2)
das **Bekenntnis** *(sing)* religious affiliation (12)
bekommen, bekam, bekommen to get; to receive (3-2)
beladen loaded (11)
belgisch *(adj)* Belgian (7)
beliebt popular, well-loved (10-2)
bellen to bark (11-1)
bemalt painted (11)
bemerken to notice (11)
das **Benehmen** *(sing)* behavior (12)
sich **benehmen (benimmt), benahm, benommen** to behave (9-2)
das **Beneluxland, ⸚er** Benelux country (11)
benutzen to use (8-2)
beraten to advise (5)
die **Beratung** *(sing)* advice; counseling (6)
bereuen to regret (12-2)
der **Berg, -e** mountain (5-1)
die **Bergwelt** alpine world (5)
berichten to report (7-2)
die **Bermudashorts** *(pl)* Bermuda shorts (3)
der **Beruf, -e** profession, occupation (1)
 Er ist Koch von Beruf. He's a cook by trade. (3)
 Was sind Sie von Beruf? What's your occupation? (3-2)
die **Berufsschule, -n** vocational school (6)
berühmt famous (5-2)
die **Besatzungszone, -n** occupation zone (7)
der/die **Beschäftigte, -n** employee (9)
beschämt shamefacedly (7)
die **Bescherung** gift-giving *(at Christmas)* (7)

die **Beschränkung, -en** restriction (11)
beschreiben, beschrieb, beschrieben to describe (6-1)
die **Beschreibung, -en** description (3)
beschuldigen to blame (10)
die **Beseitigung** *(sing)* removal (12)
besetzen to occupy (11)
besonders especially (4-2); particularly (7)
besser better (1)
 besser als better than (2-2)
best best (2)
das **Besteck** silverware, cutlery (9-1)
bestehend existing (12)
bestellen to order (4, 9-1)
bestens very well (10)
bestimmt definite(ly); for sure (4, 5-1)
bestreuen to sprinkle (9)
der **Besuch, -e** visit (3)
 zu Besuch kommen to come to visit (8-1)
besuchen to visit (2-2); to attend (6)
der **Besucher, -** visitor (4)
betonen to stress (12)
 betont gleichgültig with studied indifference (12)
beträufeln to drizzle (9)
Betreff subject *(in e-mail or letter)* (4)
betreuen to care for (12)
die **Betreuung** care (12)
das **Bett, -en** bed (1, 8-1)
 ins Bett to bed (1-2)
betteln (um) to beg (for) (10)
das **Bettzeug** *(sing)* bedding (3)
die **Bevölkerung** population (11)
bevor before *(sub conj)* (4-2)
bewölkt cloudy (1)
bewundern to admire (8)
bewusst conscious
 euch ist nicht bewusst you don't realize (11)
bezahlen to pay (3-2)
die **Bezahlung** pay; wages (6-2)
bezaubernd enchanting (10)
die **Beziehung, -en** relationship (12-2)
die **Bibel, -n** bible (10-1)
die **Bibliothek, -en** library (1)
 in die Bibliothek to the library (1-2)
die **Biene, -n** bee (10)
das **Bier** beer (1, 2-1)
 Das ist nicht mein Bier! That's not my problem!
der **Bierbauch, ⸚e** beer belly (5)

der **Biergarten, ⸚** beer garden (5)

das **Bierglas, ⸚er** beer glass (1)

das **Bild, -er** picture (1, 5-2)

bilden to form (9)

der **Bildschirm, -e** monitor; (computer, TV) screen (3-1)

das **Billard** (*sing*) billiards (2)

billig cheap (2-2)

bin: Ich bin's. It's me. (5-2)

die **Biochemie** biochemistry (2)

die **Biologie** biology (1)

die **Birne, -n** pear (4)

bis until (*prep + acc*) (2-1); (*sub conj*) (4-2)

  Bis später! See you later! (1-1)

  von ... bis from . . . to (1-2)

bisschen: ein bisschen a bit (1-2)

bissig vicious (4)

bitte please (E, 1-1)

  Wie bitte? Pardon? (E-1)

  Bitte schön! You're welcome! (6-2); Here you are. (9)

der **Bizeps** biceps (9)

die **Blase, -n** bladder (6)

blau blue (1-1); drunk (3)

  in Blau in blue (3)

der **Blazer, -** blazer (2)

bleiben, blieb, ist geblieben to stay, to remain (3, 4-2)

der **Blick, -e** look (6)

blind blind (12-1)

der/die **Blinde, -n** blind person (12)

der **Blindenhund, -e** guide dog (12)

blitzen: es blitzt it's lightning (1)

die **Blockade, -n** blockade (11-1)

blockieren to block (11-1)

blöd stupid (2-1)

bloggen to blog (6-2)

blond blond (1, 3-2)

bloß just, only (11-2)

die **Blume, -n** flower (1, 6-2)

das **Blumengeschäft, -e** flower shop (7)

die **Blumenzwiebel, -n** (flower) bulb (7)

die **Bluse, -n** blouse (1, 2-2)

das **Blut** blood (1)

die **Bockwurst, ⸚e** smoked sausage (9)

der **Bodensee** Lake Constance (5)

die **Bohne, -n** bean (10)

das **Boot, -e** boat (1)

Bord: an Bord on board (6-2)

der **Börsenbericht, -e** stock market report (2)

die **Botanik** botany (2)

das **Boulevardblatt, ⸚er** tabloid (10)

brandneu brand-new (4-2)

der **Braten, -** roast (9-1)

die **Bratkartoffeln** (*pl*) fried potatoes (4-1)

brauchen to need (3-2); to take (*of time*) (4)

die **Brauerei, -en** brewery (7)

braun brown (1-1)

das **Brett, -er** board

  das Schwarze Brett bulletin board (8-2)

  am Schwarzen Brett steht ... on the bulletin board it says . . . (6-2)

die **Brezel, -n** pretzel (9)

der **Brief, -e** letter (E, 6-1)

die **Briefmarke, -n** stamp (2-1)

der **Briefträger, -/**die **Briefträgerin, -nen** letter carrier (7-2)

die **Brille, -n** (eye)glasses (5-2)

bringen, brachte, gebracht to bring (5, 6-2)

der **Brokkoli** broccoli (4-1)

die **Broschüre, -n** brochure (5-1)

das **Brot, -e** bread; sandwich (1, 4-1)

das **Brötchen, -** roll (4-1)

  ein belegtes Brötchen sandwich (2)

die **Brücke, -n** bridge (9, 11-1)

der **Bruder, ⸚** brother (1, 3-1)

brüllen to yell (11-2)

der **Brunch, -es** brunch (7-1)

brünett brunette (3-2)

die **Brust, ⸚e** breast; chest (6-1)

das **Bruttosozialprodukt** Gross National Product (11)

das **Buch, ⸚er** book (1-1)

der **Buchdruck** printing (10)

die **Buche, -n** beech tree (11)

buchen to book (5-2)

der **Buchenwald, ⸚er** beech forest (11)

die **Bücherei, -en** library (7)

das **Bücherregal, -e** bookcase (8-1)

der **Buchhalter, -/**die **Buchhalterin, -nen** bookkeeper (1)

buchstabieren to spell (4-1)

sich **buchstabieren: Das buchstabiert sich ...** That's spelled . . . (1)

das **Büfett, -s** buffet (8-1)

das **Bügeleisen, -** iron (*for clothes*) (8-2)

bügeln to iron (8-2)

der **Bulle, -n** bull (1)

das **Bündel, -** bundle (10-1)

der **Bundeskanzler, -/**die **Bundeskanzlerin, -nen** federal chancellor (11-2)

das **Bundesland, ⸚er** German state (E)

das **Bundesministerium, Bundesministerien** federal ministry (3)

die **Bundesrepublik Deutschland (die BRD)** the Federal Republic of Germany (the FRG) (1-1)

der **Bundestag** German parliament (7)

der **Bürger, -/**die **Bürgerin, -nen** citizen (10, 11-1)

das **Büro, -s** office (E)

der **Bürokaufmann, Bürokaufleute/**die **Bürokauffrau, -en** office administrator (12)

der **Bursche, -n** boy (11)

bürsten to brush (9)

der **Bus, -se** bus (E, 3-1)

der **Busch, ⸚e** bush (10-1)

buschig bushy (2)

die **Bushaltestelle, -n** bus stop (10-2)

die **Buslinie, -n** bus route (5)

die **Butter** butter (1, 4-1)

  Es ist alles in Butter. Everything's going smoothly. (7)

C

der **Camembert** Camembert (*cheese*) (10)

campen to camp (5-1)

  campen gehen to go camping (1)

das **Campen** camping (5-1)

der **Campingplatz, ⸚e** campground; campsite (5-1)

der **Campus, -** campus (1)

der **Cappuccino, -s** cappuccino (10)

die **CD, -s** compact disc, CD (3-2)

das **CD-ROM-Laufwerk, -e** CD-ROM drive (3-1)

der **CD-Spieler, -** CD player (3-2)

der **Cent, -** cent (6)

der **Champagner** champagne (7)

der **Champignon, -s** mushroom (12)

(die) **Chanukka** Hanukkah (7)

der **Charakter, -e** character (9)

charakterisieren to characterize (8)

der **Cheddar** cheddar (*cheese*) (7)

der **Chef, -s/**die **Chefin, -nen** boss (5-2)

chemiefrei chemical-free (9)

chinesisch (*adj*) Chinese (4)

der **Chor, ⸚e** choir (6)

die **Chorprobe, -n** choir practice (5)

die **Chronik** chronicle (11)

Ciao! Bye! (E-1)

die **City** city center (5)

clever smart, clever (11-2)

die **Cola, -s** cola (2-1)

das **College, -s** college (7)

die **Comics** comics (3)

der **Computer, -** computer (3-1)

das **Computerspiel, -e** computer game (4, 7-1)

cool cool (*excellent*) (2)

  echt cool really cool (2-2)

die **Couch, -es** couch (8-1)

der **Couchtisch, -e** coffee table (8-1)

die **Currywurst** curry sausage (9)

D

d.h., das heißt i.e., that is (9-2)

da then (1)

das **Dach, ¨er** roof (8-2)

  eins aufs Dach kriegen to be bawled out (8)

dafür for it (5-2)

dagegen against it (5-2); on the other hand (9)

damalig at the time, former (7)

damals back then; at that time (8, 10-1)

die **Dame, -n** lady (10)

die **Damenabteilung, -en** women's department (7-1)

damit so that (*sub conj*) (4-2)

der **Damm, ¨e** dam (11)

der **Dampf, ¨e** steam (11)

die **Dampflokomotive, -n** steam engine (11)

die **Dampfnudel, -n** dumpling (9)

danach accordingly (10)

dänisch (*adj*) Danish (2)

der **Dank** thanks

  Gott sei Dank! Thank God! (10-2)

  Vielen Dank! Many thanks! (6-2)

danke thank you (E-1)

  Danke, gut. Fine, thanks. (E-1)

  Danke schön! Thank you! (6-2)

danken (*+ dat*) to thank (2, 7-2)

danklos thankless (12)

dann then (E, 1-1)

das this; that (1)

dass that (*sub conj*) (5)

dasselbe the same (7, 9-2)

das **Datum, Daten** date; (*pl*) data (5)

dauernd constantly (8)

die **Dauerwelle, -n** perm (12-1)

der **Daumen, -** thumb (6-1)

  Ich drücke dir die Daumen. I'll keep my fingers crossed for you. (9)

dazuhin additionally (4)

die **Decke, -n** ceiling (8-1)

decken: den Tisch decken to set the table (7-1)

defekt defective (10-2)

dein, dein, deine your (2)

die **Demokratie, -n** democracy (1, 11-1)

denken, dachte, gedacht to think (2-2)

  denken an (*+ acc*) to think of, about (11-2)

  denkste that's what you think (5)

denn because, for (*coord conj*) (1-2)

die **Depression, -en** depression (11-2)

derselbe, dasselbe, dieselbe the same (7, 9-2)

deshalb therefore; that's why (2-2)

der **Designer, -/die Designerin, -nen** designer (8-2)

detailliert in detail (10)

der **Detektiv, -e** detective (8)

deutlich distinct (12)

deutsch (*adj*) German (1)

das **Deutsch** German (*language*) (1)

  auf Deutsch in German (4-1)

der/die **Deutsche, -n** German (*person*) (1-1)

der **Deutschkurs, -e** German course; German class (4)

(das) **Deutschland** Germany (1)

deutschsprachig German-speaking (2, 9-1)

die **Deutschstunde, -n** German class (6)

der **Dezember** December (1-2)

der **Dialekt, -e** dialect (10-1)

der **Dialog, -e** dialogue (4)

dick thick; fat (2-2)

dickköpfig stubborn (11-2)

der **Dienstag** Tuesday (1-2)

  am Dienstagabend on Tuesday evening (2)

  am Dienstagmorgen on Tuesday morning (2)

  am Dienstagnachmittag on Tuesday afternoon (2)

dienstags Tuesdays, on Tuesdays (2)

dieselbe the same (7, 9-2)

dieser, dieses, diese this (2)

diesmal this time (4-1)

die **Diktatur, -en** dictatorship (5, 11-1)

das **Ding, -e** thing (2, 3-1)

das **Diplom** diploma (1)

  das Diplom machen to do or take one's diploma (1)

direkt directly (6)

der **Direktor, -en/die Direktorin, -nen** director (3-1)

die **Disco, -s** disco (1)

  in die Disco to the disco (1-2)

die **Diskette, -n** disk (1)

die **Diskussion, -en** discussion (2-1)

diskutieren to discuss (2-1)

die **Diva, -s** diva (12)

disziplinlos undisciplined (12)

der **DJ, -s** DJ (2)

doch but; anyway (4); *used to contradict negative statement or question* (10)

das **Dokument, -e** document (5)

der **Dokumentarfilm, -e** documentary film (3)

der **Dollar, -s** dollar (6)

  fünfundzwanzig Dollar twenty-five dollars (6)

die **Donau** Danube (*river*) (1)

der **Donner** thunder (2)

donnern: es donnert it's thundering (1)

der **Donnerstag** Thursday (1-2) (*see also* **Dienstag**)

doof stupid (2-1)

doppelt double (3)

das **Dorf, ¨er** village (2, 5-1)

dort there (1-2)

  dort drüben over there (9-1)

die **Dose, -n** can (8-2)

der **Dosenöffner, -** can opener (7, 8-2)

downloaden to download (2)

die **Drachme, -n** drachma (*former Greek currency*) (9)

das **Drama, Dramen** drama (10-1)

dran: Jetzt bist du dran. Now it's your turn. (9-2)

draußen outside (9)

die **Dreiergruppe, -n** group of three (10)

dreisprachig trilingual (9)

das **Dreivierteljahr** nine months (7)

der **Dressman, Dressmen** male model (2)

die **Drogensucht** drug addiction (12)

die **Drogerie, -n** drugstore (9-2)

dröhnen to boom (11)

drucken to print (10-1)

drücken to press (11)

  die Schulbank drücken to sit in school (11)

  Ich drücke dir die Daumen. I'll keep my fingers crossed for you. (9)

der **Drucker, -** printer (3-1)
die **Druckerei** print shop (10)
dual dual (6)
dumm stupid (2-1)
der **Dummkopf, ⁼e** dummy (3)
dunkel dark (1-2)
dünn thin; skinny (2-1)
durch *(prep + acc)* through (2)
durch·lesen (liest durch), las durch, durchgelesen to read through (4-2)
durch·machen to go through (11)
die **Durchsage, -n** announcement (10)
der **Durchschnitt, -e** average (10)
  im Durchschnitt on average (10-2)
die **Durchsetzung** *(sing)* implementation (12)
dürfen (darf), durfte, gedurft to be allowed to, be permitted to, may (4)
der **Durst** thirst (5)
  Ich habe Durst. I'm thirsty. (5-2)
die **Dusche, -n** shower (4, 8-1)
  unter die Dusche gehen to have a shower (4)
sich **duschen** to take a shower (9-2)
das **DVD-Laufwerk, -e** DVD drive (3-1)
der **DVD-Spieler, -** DVD player (9)

E

eben: So bin ich eben. That's just the way I am. (4-1)
ebenfalls also (11-1)
echt real, really (2)
  echt cool really cool (2-2)
  echt spitze really great (2-2)
die **Ecke, -n** corner (5-2)
EDV = Elektronische Datenverarbeitung data processing (12)
der **EDV-Fachmann, EDV-Fachleute**/die **EDV-Fachfrau, -en** data processing specialist (12)
egal no matter, regardless (11)
  Das ist mir egal. I don't care. (7-2)
ehemalig former (11-2)
das **Ehepaar, -e** married couple (9-1)
ehrenamtlich on a voluntary basis (7)
ehrgeizig ambitious (12-2)
ehrlich honest (4, 12-1)
das **Ei, -er** egg (4-1)
  Er gleicht seinem Bruder wie ein Ei dem anderen. He and his brother are as alike as two peas in a pod. (7)
die **Eifersucht** jealousy (12-1)

eifersüchtig auf *(+ acc)* jealous of (12-1)
eigen own (8-2)
  etwas in die eigene Hand nehmen to take something into one's own hands (11-1)
eigentlich actually (6-1)
die **Eigentumswohnung, -en** condominium (8-2)
die **Eile** hurry (10)
  Es hat keine Eile. There's no rush. (10)
ein, ein, eine a; an; one (1)
einander each other, one another (E)
die **Einbauküche, -n** built-in kitchen (12)
eineinhalb one and a half (4)
einfach simple, simply (7-2); ordinary (10-1)
ein·fallen (fällt ein), fiel ein, ist eingefallen (7)
  Mir fällt nichts ein. I can't think of anything. (7-2)
das **Einfamilienhaus, ⁼er** single-family dwelling (8-2)
der **Einfluss, ⁼e** influence (10-2)
der **Eingang, ⁼e** entrance (10)
die **Einheit, -en** unity, whole (7)
einheitlich common (11)
das **Einhorn, ⁼er** unicorn (1)
einigermaßen somewhat; a bit (11)
die **Einkäufe** *(pl)* shopping, purchases (9)
ein·kaufen to shop, to go shopping (5-2)
das **Einkaufen** shopping (4)
die **Einkaufsgewohnheit, -en** shopping habit (9)
die **Einkaufsliste, -n** shopping list (9-1)
die **Einkaufsmöglichkeit, -en** shopping facility (5)
die **Einkaufstasche, -n** shopping bag (9-1)
der **Einkaufswagen, -** shopping cart (9-1)
ein·laden (lädt ein), lud ein, eingeladen to invite (4-2)
einmal once (7-2)
  noch (ein)mal once more; (over) again (7-2)
ein·marschieren to invade (11)
ein·packen to pack (4)
ein·schlafen (schläft ein), schlief ein, ist eingeschlafen to fall asleep (4-2)

ein·schlagen (schlägt ein), schlug ein, eingeschlagen to wrap (7)
ein·schmieren to rub in (11)
ein·tauchen to dip (9)
der **Einwanderer, -/**die **Einwanderin, -nen** immigrant (6-1)
ein·wandern, wanderte ein, ist eingewandert to immigrate (6-1)
die **Einwanderung** immigration (6)
der **Einwohner, -/**die **Einwohnerin, -nen** inhabitant (2)
das **Einzelkind, -er** only child (3-1)
ein·ziehen, zog ein, ist eingezogen to move in (8-1)
einzig single; only (9-1)
das **Eis** ice; ice cream (4-1)
der **Eiserne Vorhang** Iron Curtain (11-1)
(das) **Eishockey** (ice)hockey (1, 2-1)
eisig icy (2)
der **Elefant, -en, -en** elephant (9-2)
elegant elegant (2-2)
elektrisch electric (9)
der **Elektroinstallateur, -e/**die **Elektroinstallateurin, -nen** electrician (12)
das **Elektronikgeschäft, -e** electronics store (3)
das **Element, -e** element (5)
der **Ellbogen, -** elbow (1)
die **Eltern** *(pl)* parents (2, 3-1)
die **Elternzeit** parental leave (3)
die **E-Mail, -s** e-mail (3-1)
die **E-Mail-Adresse, -n** e-mail address (3-1)
der **Emigrant, -en, -en/**die **Emigrantin, -nen** emigrant (6-1)
emigrieren to emigrate (8)
empfehlen (empfiehlt), empfahl, empfohlen to recommend (10-2)
die **Empfehlung, -en** recommendation (6)
das **Ende, -n** end (1, 4-2)
  Ende Juli (at) the end of July (1-2)
  zu Ende sein to be over (2-2)
enden to end (11)
endlich finally, at last (4-2)
endlos endless (6)
die **Energie, -n** energy (3)
englisch *(adj)* English (7)
das **Englisch** English *(language)* (1)
  auf Englisch in English (1)
englischsprachig English-speaking (5)
der **Enkel, -** grandson, grandchild (3-1)

die **Enkelin, -nen** granddaughter (3-1)

enorm enormous (8-2)

die **Ente, -n** duck (3)

enterben to disinherit (12)

die **Entfernung, -en** distance (5)

entgehen, entging, ist entgangen to escape (12)

entlang along (11)

entlassen (entlässt), entließ, entlassen to fire, to let go (4)

die **Entscheidung, -en** decision (5)

sich **entschuldigen** to apologize (9-2)

Entschuldigung! Excuse me! (E-1)

entweder … oder either . . . or (4)

entwerfen (entwirft), entwarf, entworfen to design (8)

entwickeln to develop (4)

der **Entwurf, ˙-e** design (9)

die **Epoche, -n** epoch (9)

die **Erde** earth; ground (4, 10-2)

das **Erdgeschoss** ground floor (10-2)
  im Erdgeschoss on the ground floor (10-2)

ereignisreich eventful (11)

erfahren (erfährt), erfuhr, erfahren to find out (11)

die **Erfahrung, -en** experience (10)

erfassen to seize (7)

der **Erfinder, -/**die **Erfinderin, -nen** inventor (10-1)

der **Erfolg, -e** success (4-2)

erfolglos unsuccessful(ly) (12)

erfolgreich successful(ly) (4-2)

erfrieren, erfror, ist erfroren to freeze to death (11)

ergänzen to complete (1); to supply (7)

erhältlich available (3)

erhängen to kill by hanging (11)

die **Erinnerung, -en** memory (11)

sich **erkälten** to catch a cold (9-2)

erkältet sein to have a cold (12-2)

die **Erkältung, -en** cold (12-2)
  eine schwere Erkältung a bad cold (12-2)

erkennen, erkannte, erkannt to recognize (3-2)

erklärbar explicable (12)

erklären to explain; to declare (5, 6-2)

erklecklich a lot (4)

die **Erlaubnis** permission (9)

erlaubt permitted, allowed (12)

erleben to experience (11-2)

das **Erlebnis, -se** experience (11-2)

ermorden to murder (11-1)

ernähren to feed (12)

ernst serious (8)

erobern to conquer (7)

eröffnen to open up *(shop)* (4)

erraten (errät), erriet, erraten to guess (9)

erscheinen, erschien, ist erschienen to appear (10)

erschießen, erschoss, erschossen to shoot dead (11)

erschrecken to frighten, to shock (11)

ersetzen (durch) to replace (with) (11)

erst *(adv)* not until (1-1); first; only (2-2)

erst- first (1)
  zum ersten Mal for the first time (7-2)

erstklassig first-class (3)

die **Erstkommunion** *(sing)* First Communion (7)

ertrinken, ertrank, ist ertrunken to drown (6)

erwachsen werden (wird), wurde, ist geworden to grow up *(become adult)* (11)

der/die **Erwachsene, -n** adult (10-2)

erzählen to tell *(a story)* (2-2)
  erzählen von to tell about (11)

der **Erzähler, -/**die **Erzählerin, -nen** narrator (10-1)

die **Erzählung, -en** story, narrative (6, 10-2)

der **Erzbischof, ˙-e** archbishop (3)

der **Erziehungsurlaub** child-rearing leave (3)

der **Esel, -** donkey (3)

die **Eselsbrücke, -n** mnemonic device (10)

essbar edible (12)

essen (isst), aß, gegessen to eat (3-2)
  zu Mittag essen to have lunch (4-1)
  zu Abend essen to have supper (4-1)

das **Essen** meal, food (7)

der **Essig** vinegar (9-2)

der **Esslöffel, -** tablespoon (9-1)

die **Esssucht** compulsive eating disorder (12)

das **Esszimmer, -** dining room (8-1)

etwa approximately (E, 7-2)

etwas something (5-2)

euer, euer, eure your (2)

der **Euro, -s** euro *(common European currency)* (1, 2-2)

drei Euro das Stück three euros apiece (7)

(das) **Europa** Europe (1)

der **Europäer, -/**die **Europäerin, -nen** European *(person)* (9)

europäisch *(adj)* European (9)

die **Europäische Union (die EU)** the European Union (the EU) (3)

die **Europäische Wirtschaftsgemeinschaft (die EG)** the European Economic Community (the EEC) (11)

die **Europäische Zentralbank (die EZB)** European Central Bank (the ECB) (9)

der **Euroschein, -e** euro bill (7)

das **Exemplar, -e** copy *(of a book, etc.)* (10)

exotisch exotic (6-1)

die **Expedition, -en** expedition (4)

das **Experiment, -e** experiment (5-2)

der **Experte, -n, -n/**die **Expertin, -nen** expert (9)

der **Export, -e** export (4)

exportieren to export (4)

extravagant extravagant (5)

die **Extrawurst: eine Extrawurst wollen** to want special treatment (7)

F

die **Fabel, -n** fable (10)

fabelhaft fabulous (4-1)

die **Fabrik, -en** factory (7-2)

das **Fach, ˙-er** field of study, subject (2-2)

die **Fachhochschule, -n** technical college (6-2)

die **Fahne, -n** flag (7)

fahren (fährt), fuhr, ist gefahren to drive, to go (3-2)

der **Fahrer, -/**die **Fahrerin, -nen** driver (5)

der **Fahrplan, ˙-e** train or bus schedule (4-2)

das **Fahrrad, ˙-er** bicycle (3-1)

der **Fahrradhelm, -e** bicycle helmet (7-1)

der **Fahrradverleih, -e** bike rental (5-1)

die **Fahrt, -en** ride (6)
  in Fahrt sein to be in full swing (11)

das **Fahrzeug, -e** vehicle (3-1)

fair fair (1)

der **Fall, ⸚e** fall (11)
fallen (fällt), fiel, ist gefallen to fall (6)
 Der Apfel fällt nicht weit vom Stamm. Like father, like son. (7)
 Er ist nicht auf den Kopf gefallen. He's no fool. (6)
 in Ohnmacht fallen to faint (12-1)
 Mir fällt nichts ein. I can't think of anything. (7-2)
fällen to fell (6)
falsch wrong, incorrect, false (E, 1-1)
falls in case (8)
die **Familie, -n** family (E, 3-1)
das **Familienbrunch** family brunch (7)
der **Familienname, -ns, -n** last name (E, 3-2)
der **Fan, -s** fan (2)
fangen (fängt), fing, gefangen to catch (10-1)
die **Fantasie** imagination (3-1)
fantasielos unimaginative(ly) (12)
fantastisch fantastic (5-2)
die **Farbe, -n** color (1)
 Welche Farbe hat Lisas Bluse? What color is Lisa's blouse? (1)
färben to color (9)
 färben lassen to have colored (11)
der **Farbfernseher, -** color TV (10)
das **Farbfoto, -s** color photo (7)
farblos colorless (6)
die **Farm, -en** farm (6)
der **Farmer, -** farmer (6)
das **Fass, ⸚er** barrel (9)
die **Fassade** façade (10)
fast almost (1-1)
faul lazy (7-2)
das **Fax, -e** fax (10-1)
der **Februar** February (1-2)
die **Feder, -n** feather (2)
der **Federball** badminton; badminton bird (1)
 Federball spielen to play badminton (1)
fehlen to be missing (8)
der **Fehler, -** mistake, error (11-2)
fehlerlos error-free (12)
feiern to celebrate (7-1)
der **Feiertag, -e** holiday (7-1)
das **Feinkostgeschäft, -e** gourmet foods store (2, 3-2)
das **Feld, -er** field (5-1)
die **Felge, -n** (tire) rim (4)
das **Fenster, -** window (1, 8-1)
die **Ferien** (pl) vacation (generally of students) (5-1)

Ferien machen to go on vacation (5-1)
das **Ferienhaus, ⸚er** vacation home (7-2)
der **Ferienjob, -s** summer job (6-2)
die **Ferienzeit** holiday time (5)
fern far (away) (11-1)
der **Fernfahrer, -** long-distance trucker (4)
das **Ferngespräch, -e** long-distance call (4)
das **Fernglas, ⸚er** binoculars (4)
der **Fernkurs, -e** correspondence course (4)
Fernost (the) Far East (4)
fern·sehen (sieht fern), sah fern, ferngesehen to watch TV (4-2)
das **Fernsehen** TV (7)
der **Fernseher, -** television set (4-2)
 vor dem Fernseher in front of the TV (4-2)
das **Fernsehprogramm, -e** TV show (3)
fertig ready; finished (4-1); (with verbs) finish (4)
fertig lesen (liest fertig), las fertig, fertig gelesen to finish reading (7)
fertig schreiben, schrieb fertig, fertig geschrieben to finish writing (4)
fesseln to captivate, to grab (10)
das **Fest, -e** celebration; festival (7-1)
die **Festplatte, -n** hard drive (3-1)
die **Fete, -n** party (7-2)
das **Fett** fat (9)
fettig fatty (2)
fett gedruckt in boldface (10)
das **Fieber** fever (7-2)
fieberhaft feverishly (3)
die **Figur** (sing) figure; physique (12-1)
die **Filiale, -n** branch (of a business) (6)
der **Film, -e** film (1, 2-2)
der **Filmstar, -s** filmstar (male or female) (1)
die **Finanzen** (pl) finances (5)
der **Finanzier, -s** financier (5)
finanzieren to finance (5-2)
finden, fand, gefunden to find (1-2)
der **Finger, -** finger (1, 6-1)
der **Fingernagel, ⸚** fingernail (1)
die **Firma, Firmen** business, company (4-2)
der **Fisch, -e** fish (1, 4-1)
fischen to fish (2)

fit fit (4)
das **Fitnesscenter, -** fitness center (5-1)
das **Fitnessstudio, -s** fitness studio (12)
der **Fitnessfreak, -s** fitness freak (5)
Fitnesstraining machen to work out (2-1)
die **Flasche, -n** bottle (5-2)
das **Fleisch** (sing) meat (2, 4-1)
das **Fleischgericht, -e** meat dish (9)
der **Fleischer, -/die Fleischerin, -nen** butcher (9)
die **Fleischerei, -en** butcher shop (7)
fleischlos meatless (6)
fleißig hard-working (7-2)
flicken to mend (7-2)
fliegen, flog, ist geflogen to fly (1-2)
fliehen, floh, ist geflohen to flee (11-1)
fließen, floss, ist geflossen to flow (9)
flirten to flirt (12-1)
der **Flohmarkt, ⸚e** flea market (8)
die **Flöte, -n** flute (7)
die **Flötenstunde, -n** flute lesson (7)
der **Fluchtweg, -e** escape route (11)
der **Flug, ⸚e** flight (3-2)
der **Flugbegleiter, -/die Flugbegleiterin, -nen** flight attendant (12)
der **Flughafen, ⸚** airport (3-2)
die **Flugnummer, -n** flight number (3-2)
der **Flugplatz, ⸚e** airport (11-1)
das **Flugzeug, -e** airplane (3-2)
der **Flur, -e** hall (8-1)
der **Fluss, ⸚e** river (2, 5-1)
folgen, folgte, ist gefolgt (+ dat) to follow (6-1)
folgend following (6)
der **Föhn, -e** blow-dryer (9-2)
föhnen: sich (dat) **die Haare föhnen** to blow-dry one's hair (9-2)
das **Footballteam, -s** football team (1)
fördern to promote (12)
die **Form, -en** shape; form (6-1)
die **Formel, -n** formula (12-1)
fort away (7)
das **Foto, -s** photo (1, 4-2)
das **Fotogeschäft, -e** photo store (2)
die **Fotografie, -n** photograph (8)
fotografieren to photograph (2-1)
das **Fotomodell, -e** model (2)
der **Foxterrier, -** fox terrier (3)
die **Frage, -n** question (1-2)
 eine Frage beantworten to answer a question (7-1)

eine Frage stellen to ask a question (7-2)

Das kommt nicht in Frage! That's out of the question! (9-2)

fragen to ask (1-2)

fragen nach to ask about (10)

der **Franken, -** franc *(former French currency)* (9)

französisch *(adj)* French (7)

Frau Mrs., Ms. (E-1)

die **Frau, -en** woman; wife (1, 2-2)

(das) **Fräulein, -** Miss (5)

frei free (5-1)

Heute habe ich frei. Today I have a day off. (5)

die **Freiheit** *(sing)* freedom (10-2)

das **Freilandei, -er** free-range egg (7)

der **Freitag** Friday (1-2) *(see also Dienstag)*

die **Freizeit** leisure time (5-1)

fressen (frisst), fraß, gefressen to eat *(of animals)* (2)

die **Freude, -n** joy, happiness (11)

Du hast mir eine Freude gemacht. You have made me happy. (7-2)

sich **freuen auf** *(+ acc)* to look forward to (11-2)

sich **freuen über** *(+ acc)* to be happy about; to be pleased with (11-2)

der **Freund, -e** *(male)* friend, boyfriend (1-1)

der **Freundeskreis** circle of friends (7)

die **Freundin, -nen** *(female)* friend, girlfriend (1-1)

freundlich friendly (2, 3-1)

die **Freundlichkeit** friendliness (11)

die **Freundschaft, -en** friendship (2-1)

der **Frieden** peace (11-2)

frieren, fror, gefroren to be cold (10-1)

frisch fresh (1)

der **Frischkäse** *(sing)* cream cheese (4)

der **Friseur, -e**/die **Friseurin, -nen** barber; hair stylist; hairdresser (5-2)

die **Frisur, -en** hairdo; hair style (5-2)

froh happy (11-2)

fromm pious (10-1)

früh early (4-1)

morgen früh tomorrow morning (2-2)

das **Frühjahr** spring (7)

der **Frühling** spring (1-2)

das **Frühstück** breakfast (1, 4-1)

zum Frühstück for breakfast (4-1)

frühstücken to have breakfast (4-1)

der **Fuchs, ̈e** fox (1)

fühlen to feel (9-2)

sich **wohl fühlen** to feel well; to feel at home (9-2)

der **Führerschein, -e** driver's license (10-2)

füllen to fill (9-1)

für *(prep + acc)* for (1)

die **Furche, -n** furrow (10)

der **Fuß, ̈e** foot (1, 6-1)

Hand und Fuß haben to make sense (6)

zu Fuß gehen to go on foot, to walk (4-2)

der **Fußball, ̈e** soccer ball (1)

Fußball spielen to play soccer (1)

das **Fußballspiel, -e** soccer game (5)

das **Fußballstadion, -stadien** soccer stadium (5)

der **Fußboden, ̈** floor (8-1)

die **Fußgängerzone, -n** pedestrian zone (8-2)

füttern to feed (6-2)

G

die **Gabel, -n** fork (9-1)

gähnen to yawn (4)

galoppieren to gallop (10-1)

die **Gans, ̈e** goose (7)

ganz quite; very; all; whole (3); absolutely; completely (10)

die ganze Familie the whole family (3-2)

ganz kurz very short (3-2)

gar tender *(in cooking)* (9)

gar nicht not at all (1-1)

gar nichts nothing at all (6, 11-1)

die **Garage, -n** garage (8-1)

der **Garantieschein, -e** warranty (7)

die **Garderobe, -n** front hall closet (8-1)

der **Garten, ̈** garden (1, 5-1)

die **Gartenterrasse, -n** garden terrace, patio (8)

der **Gärtner, -**/die **Gärtnerin, -nen** gardener (E)

die **Gärtnerei, -en** nursery (7)

der **Gast, ̈e** guest; customer *(in a restaurant)* (3, 7-2)

das **Gasthaus, ̈er** restaurant (8, 9-1)

die **Gaststätte, -n** restaurant (9)

die **Gastronomie** gastronomy (9-1)

das **Gebäude, -** building (8-2)

geben (gibt), gab, gegeben to give (3-2)

es gibt *(+ acc)* there is, there are (3-2)

der/die **Gebildete, -n** educated person (10)

das **Gebirge** mountain range (5-1)

geblümt flowered (11)

geboren born (1)

Wann bist du geboren? When were you born? (6-1)

die **Geburt, -en** birth (12-1)

der **Geburtsort, -e** birthplace (6-1)

der **Geburtsschein, -e** birth certificate (10)

der **Geburtstag, -e** birthday (4-2)

Herzliche Glückwünsche zum Geburtstag! Happy Birthday! (7-1)

zum Geburtstag for one's birthday (6, 7-1)

zum Geburtstag gratulieren to wish a Happy Birthday (7-2)

das **Geburtstagsgeschenk, -e** birthday present (7)

die **Geburtstagskarte, -n** birthday card (7)

die **Gedenktafel, -n** commemorative plaque (10)

das **Gedicht, -e** poem (10-1)

geeignet suitable (10)

gefallen (gefällt), gefiel, gefallen *(+ dat)* to like (7)

gefallen an *(+ dat)* to like about (7)

Diese Jacke gefällt mir. I like this jacket. (7-2)

das **Gefängnis, -se** prison (11)

das **Gefühl, -e** feeling (10-2)

gefühllos unfeeling(ly) (12)

gegen *(prep + acc)* against; around *(time)* (5)

die **Gegend, -en** area (3, 11-2)

das **Gegenteil, -e** opposite (1)

gegenüber across (from) (8)

das **Gehalt, ̈er** pay, wages (12-1)

gehen, ging, ist gegangen to go (1-1)

Wie geht es Ihnen?/Wie geht's? How are you? (E-1)

zu Fuß gehen to go on foot, to walk (4-2)

gehören *(+ dat)* to belong to (7-2)

der **Geiger, -**/die **Geigerin, -nen** violinist (5)

gekleidet dressed (10-1)

gelb yellow (1-1)

das **Geld** money (1, 2-2)

Mir ist das Geld ausgegangen. I ran out of money. (12)

der **Geldschein, -e** banknote, (money) bill (9-2)

die **Geldtasche, -n** wallet (7-1)

geliebt beloved (5)

gelten (gilt), galt, gegolten to be considered (9)

gemein in common (9); common (10)

gemeinsam common (1)

das **Gemüse** (*sing*) vegetables (4-1)

genau exact(ly); careful(ly) (4-1)

genauso gut just as good (well) (9-2)

der **General, -e** general (10)

die **Generation, -en** generation (7)

die **Genetik** genetics (2)

genial brilliant (3)

genug enough (4-2)

der **Genuss, -e** (*culinary*) delight (10)

die **Geografie** geography (1)

geometrisch geometric (8)

gepflegt: gepflegte Biersorten excellent choice of beers (8)

gerade just, just now (7-1); currently (10)

die **Geranie, -n** geranium (8)

das **Gerät, -e** utensil; appliance (8-2)

das **Gericht, -e** dish (*food*) (4, 9-2)

die **Germanistik** (*sing*) German Studies (1)

gern (lieber, am liebsten) gladly (2)

  jemand (*acc*) **gern haben** to like somebody (2)

  Ich koche gern. I like to cook. (2-1)

die **Gesamtbevölkerung** total population (9)

das **Geschäft, -e** business; store (3-2)

der **Geschäftspartner, -/die Geschäftspartnerin, -nen** business partner (4)

das **Geschenk, -e** present, gift (7-1)

die **Geschichte, -n** history; story (6-1)

geschieden divorced (3-1)

das **Geschirr** (*sing*) dishes (9-1)

die **Geschirrspülmaschine, -n** dishwasher (8-1)

das **Geschlecht, -er** gender (12-1)

geschlitzt slit (11)

der **Geschmack** (*sing*) taste (5)

geschmacklos tasteless (5-2)

geschmackvoll tasteful (5-2)

die **Geschwister** (*pl*) sisters and brothers, siblings (3-1)

die **Gesellschaft, -en** company (5); society (9)

das **Gesicht, -er** face (6-1)

das **Gesetz, -e** law (12-1)

das **Gespräch, -e** conversation (1)

die **Gestalt** stature, build (6)

gestern yesterday (3-2)

  gestern Nacht last night (2)

gestreift striped (11)

gesund healthy (3-2)

das **Getränk, -e** beverage (2-1)

getrennt separate(ly); separated (2)

  getrennt leben to be separated (3)

das **Getue** carrying on (12)

gewinnen, gewann, gewonnen to win (10-2)

gießen, goss, gegossen to water (6-2)

die **Gießkanne, -n** watering can (7-2)

die **Giraffe, -n** giraffe (9)

die **Gitarre, -n** guitar (2-1)

das **Glas, -er** glass (1, 4-1)

  die Nase zu tief ins Glas stecken to drink too much (6)

  ein Glas Orangensaft a glass of orange juice (4-1)

  zwei Glas Milch two glasses of milk (4)

glatt straight (*of hair*); smooth (3-2)

glauben to believe, to think (1-2)

gleich immediately, right away; in a minute (1-1); same; the same; right, directly (8-1); equal(ly) (11, 12-1)

  gleich um die Ecke right around the corner (5)

gleichberechtigt sein to have equal rights (12-1)

die **Gleichberechtigung** equal rights; equality (12-1)

gleichgültig indifferent (12)

  betont gleichgültig with studied indifference (12)

die **Gleichstellung** (*sing*) equality (12)

gleichwertig of equal value (12)

das **Gleis, -e** (*train*) track (5)

glitzern to glitter (3)

das **Glück** luck (10-1)

  Viel Glück! Good luck!, Lots of luck! (10-1)

  zum Glück fortunately, luckily (12-1)

glücklich happy (7-2)

der **Glückwunsch, -e** congratulations, best wishes (*pl*) (7)

  Herzliche Glückwünsche zum Geburtstag! Happy Birthday! (7-1)

die **Glückwunschanzeige, -n** congratulatory announcement (7)

die **Glückwunschkarte, -n** (congratulatory) card (10)

das **Gold** gold (2)

golden gold (3)

der **Goldschmied, -e/ die Goldschmiedin, -nen** goldsmith (6)

(das) **Golf** golf (2-1)

der **Golfplatz, -e** golf course (4)

(der) **Gott** God (10)

  Gott sei Dank! Thank God! (8, 10-2)

der **Gourmet, -s** gourmet (7)

das **Grab, -er** grave (2)

der **Grabstein, -e** gravestone, tombstone (10)

der **Grad, -e** degree (E)

die **Grafik, -en** graphic (11-1)

das **Gramm** gram (9-1)

die **Grapefruit, -s** grapefruit (4-1)

der **Grapefruitsaft** (*sing*) grapefruit juice (4)

das **Gras, -er** grass (1)

gratulieren (+ *dat*) to congratulate (7-2)

  zum Geburtstag gratulieren to wish a Happy Birthday (7-2)

grau gray (1-1)

grausam cruel; gruesome (10-2)

die **Grausamkeit, -en** cruelty (10)

die **Grenze, -n** border (11-1)

grenzen an (+ *acc*) to border on (11)

der **Grieche, -n, -n/die Griechin, -nen** Greek (*person*) (9)

griechisch (*adj*) Greek (7)

groß big, tall (1, 2-1)

die **Größe, -n** height; size (5, 6-1)

die **Großeltern** (*pl*) grandparents (3-1)

das **Großherzogtum** grand duchy (9)

die **Großmutter, -** grandmother (3-1)

größtenteils for the most part, largely (10)

der **Großvater, -** grandfather (3-1)

Grüezi! Hello! (*Swiss dialect*) (E)

grün green (E, 1-1)

  ein grünes Bürschchen a greenhorn (11)

der **Grund, -e** reason (10-2)

gründen to found (4)

das **Grundgesetz** Basic Law (*constitution of Germany*) (12) die **Grundschule, -n** elementary school; primary school (6-2)

grunzen to grunt (3)

die **Gruppe, -n** group (4)

der **Gruß, ⸚e** greeting (6)

Herzliche Grüße Kind regards *(closing in a letter)* (7)

Liebe Grüße "Love" *(closing in a letter)* (6)

grüßen to greet; to say hello (10-1)

Grüß dich! Hello! Hi! (E-1)

Grüß Gott! Hello! *(in Southern Germany and Austria)* (E)

die **Grußformel, -n** greeting (E)

gucken to look (11, 12-1)

die **Gulaschsuppe** goulash soup (9)

der **Gulden, -** guilder *(former Dutch currency)* (9)

gurgeln to gargle (12)

der **Gürtel, -** belt (2-2)

gut good, well (E, 1-2)

Guten Appetit! Enjoy your meal! (9-1)

Guten Tag! Hello! Hi! (E-1)

Mach's gut! Take care! (1-2)

Schon gut. It's all right. (9)

die **Güter** *(pl)* goods (11)

der **Gutschein, -e** voucher (7-1)

das **Gymnasium, Gymnasien** *(academic)* high school (E, 6-2)

H

das **Haar, -e** hair (1, 6-1)

ein Haar in der Suppe finden to find fault with something (9)

die **Haarbürste, -n** hairbrush (9-2)

haarig hairy (2)

der **Haarschnitt, -e** haircut (5-2)

die **Haarsträhne, -n** strand of hair (11)

haben (hat), hatte, gehabt to have (1, 2-1)

jemand *(acc)* **gern haben** to like somebody (2)

der **Hafen, ⸚** harbor (9)

der **Hahn, ⸚e** rooster (4)

der **Hai, -e** shark (10)

halb half (2)

halb zwei half past one (2)

die **Hälfte, -n** half (11-1)

Hallo! Hello! Hi! (E-1)

(das) **Halloween** *(sing)* Halloween (6)

der **Hals, ⸚e** neck; throat (6-1)

Es hängt mir zum Hals heraus! I'm totally sick of it! (11-2)

Hals- und Beinbruch! Break a leg! Good luck! (6-2)

die **Halskette, -n** necklace (5-2)

die **Halsschmerzen** *(pl)* sore throat (6)

halten (hält), hielt, gehalten to hold; to stop; to keep (3-2)

der **Hamburger, -** hamburger (10-2)

der **Hammer, ⸚** hammer (1)

der **Hamster, -** hamster (10)

die **Hand, ⸚e** hand (1, 6-1)

etwas in die eigene Hand nehmen to take something into one's own hands (11-1)

Hand und Fuß haben to make sense (6)

der **Händler, -** dealer (4)

das **Handy, -s** cell phone (E, 3-2)

handgestrickt hand-knit (11)

die **Handschrift, -en** handwriting (10)

der **Handschuh, -e** glove (7-2)

das **Handtuch, ⸚er** towel (9-2)

der **Handwerker, -/** die **Handwerkerin, -nen** craftsperson, tradesperson (8)

hängen to hang *(put in a hanging position)* (8)

hängen, hing, gehangen to hang *(be in a hanging position)* (8)

Es hängt mir zum Hals heraus! I'm totally sick of it! (11-2)

die **Harfe, -n** harp (2)

harmlos harmless (6)

hart hard (1)

der **Harz** Harz Mountains *(pl)* (1)

der **Hase, -n, -n** rabbit (9)

Mein Name ist Hase, ich weiß von nichts. Don't ask me. I don't know anything about it. (10)

hassen to hate (3)

hässlich ugly (8-1)

hauen to hit (9)

jemand *(acc)* **übers Ohr hauen** to cheat someone (9)

der **Haufen, -** pile; a lot of (12-2)

häufig often (2)

der **Hauptbahnhof, ⸚e** main railway station (5)

das **Hauptfach, ⸚er** major (field of study) (5)

das **Hauptgericht** main course (9-2)

die **Hauptreisezeit, -en** peak time for travel (5)

die **Hauptschule, -n** vocational secondary school (6)

der **Hauptschulabschluss** vocational secondary school diploma (6)

die **Hauptstadt, ⸚e** capital city (1, 5-2)

die **Hauptstraße, -n** main street (4)

das **Haus, ⸚er** house (1, 2-2)

Auf ihn kannst du Häuser bauen. He's absolutely dependable. (8)

nach Hause gehen to go home (4-1)

zu Hause sein to be at home (2, 4-1)

der **Hausarzt, ⸚e/**die **Hausärztin, -nen** family doctor (8)

die **Hausaufgabe, -n** homework (assignment) (4-2)

Häuschen: aus dem Häuschen sein to be all excited (8)

die **Hausfrau, -en** housewife (3-2)

der **Haushalt, -e** household; housekeeping; budget (12-1)

den Haushalt machen to do household chores (12)

der **Hausmann, ⸚er** househusband (3-2)

der **Hausmeister, -** janitor (8)

die **Hausnummer, -n** house number (1)

der **Hausschuh, -e** slipper (7-2)

das **Haustier, -e** pet (3-1)

die **Hecke, -n** hedge (6-2)

die Hecke schneiden to clip the hedge (6)

der **Heilige Abend** Christmas Eve (7)

die **Heilsarmee** *(sing)* Salvation Army (8)

die **Heimat, -en** home (country) (8-2)

heim·kommen, kam heim, ist heimgekommen to come home (4-2)

der **Heimtrainer, -** exercise bike (7-1)

der **Heimweg, -e** way home (10)

die **Heirat, -en** marriage (12-2)

heiraten to marry (2, 3-2)

heiß hot (1-1)

heißen, hieß, geheißen to be called (E); to mean (11)

das heißt (d.h.) that is (i.e.) (9-2)

Ich heiße … My name is . . . (E-1)

Wie heißen Sie?/Wie heißt du? What's your name? (E-1)

heiter: es ist heiter it's sunny with some clouds (1)

heizen to heat (9)

helfen (hilft), half, geholfen *(+ dat)* to help (2, 7-2)

helfen bei to help with (7)

hell light; bright (1-2)

das **Hemd, -en** shirt (2-2)
der **Henkel, -** handle (9)
herauf·ziehen, zog herauf, heraufgezogen to pull up (6)
heraus·finden, fand heraus, herausgefunden to find out (9)
heraus·geben (gibt heraus), gab heraus, herausgegeben to give *(change)* (12)
heraus·kommen, kam heraus, ist herausgekommen to come out (6)
heraus·ziehen, zog heraus, herausgezogen to pull out (4)
der **Herbst** fall, autumn (1-2)
der **Herd, -e** stove (8-1)
Herein! Come in! (6)
herein·kommen, kam herein, ist hereingekommen to come in (6)
her·fahren (fährt her), fuhr her, ist hergefahren to come here, to get here; to drive here (6)
die **Herkunft, ̈e** origin (11)
Herr Mr. (E-1)
der **Herr, -n, -en** gentleman (9-2)
die **Herrenabteilung, -en** men's department (7-1)
herrlich wonderful (11-2)
her·stellen to make, produce (7)
die **Herstellung** *(sing)* production (7)
herüber·springen, sprang herüber, ist herübergesprungen to jump across (6)
herum·sitzen, saß herum, herumgesessen to sit around (10)
herum·tanzen: jemand *(dat)* **auf der Nase herumtanzen:** to walk all over someone (9)
herunter down (4)
herunter·fallen (fällt herunter), fiel herunter, ist heruntergefallen to fall down (6)
herzlich warm, hearty (11)
Herzliche Glückwünsche zum Geburtstag! Happy Birthday! (7-1)
herzlos heartless (12)
heulen to cry; to howl (11-2)
heute today (1-1)
heute Abend tonight (1)
heute Morgen this morning (2)
heute Nachmittag this afternoon (1-1)
heutzutage nowadays (7-1)
hier here (E, 1-2)
die **Hilfe** help (6, 7-2)
hilflos helpless (7)

hilfsbereit helpful (10)
der **Himmel** sky; heaven (1-1)
Himmel und Hölle hopscotch (10)
hinaus·gehen, ging hinaus, ist hinausgegangen to go out (6)
hinein·fahren (fährt hinein), fuhr hinein, ist hineingefahren to drive in (4)
hinein·gehen, ging hinein, ist hineingegangen to go in (6)
hin·fahren (fährt hin), fuhr hin, ist hingefahren to drive there (5)
hin·gucken to look (12)
sich **hin·setzen** to sit down (9)
hinter *(prep + acc/dat)* behind; *(as adj)* back (8)
der **Hintergrund** background (11)
der **Hinterhof, ̈e** courtyard (E)
hinterlassen (hinterlässt), hinterließ, hinterlassen to leave behind (7)
hinüber·springen, sprang hinüber, ist hinübergesprungen to jump across (6)
hinunter·fallen (fällt hinunter), fiel hinunter, ist hinuntergefallen to fall down (6)
hinunter·schauen to look down (8)
hin·wirken auf *(+ acc)* to work towards (12)
historisch historical (5-1)
die **Hitze** heat (3)
das **Hobby, -s** hobby (2-1)
hoch (hoh-) high (5-2)
das **Hochhaus, ̈er** high-rise (8-2)
die **Hochschule, -n** university (6-2)
die **Hochzeit, -en** wedding (12-2)
die **goldene Hochzeit** golden wedding anniversary (7)
der **Höcker, -** hump *(of a camel)* (9)
der **Hockeyschläger, -** hockey stick (7-2)
hoffen to hope (2, 5-2)
hoffentlich hopefully, I hope (so) (6-2)
hoffnungslos hopeless (12)
höflich polite (7-2)
holen to get; to fetch (5, 9-1); to summon (5)
holländisch *(adj)* Dutch (7)
der **Holocaust** holocaust (11)
höllisch hellish (2)
das **Holz** wood (11)
der **Holzfäller, -** lumberjack (6)
die **Homepage, -s** home page (2)
der **Honig** honey (4-1)
hörbar audible (12)

hören to hear (2-2); to listen to (1)
der **Hörer, -** receiver *(of a telephone)* (9)
der **Horrorfilm, -e** horror film (3)
der **Hörsaal, Hörsäle** lecture hall (E)
die **Hose, -n** pants (2-2)
das **Hotdog, -s** hotdog (3)
das **Hotel, -s** hotel (1, 5-1)
hübsch pretty (2-2)
das **Huhn, ̈er** hen (4)
Da lachen ja die Hühner! What a joke! (10)
human humane (7)
der **Humor** humor (3-1)
humorlos humorless (5)
humorvoll humorous (5)
der **Hund, -e** dog (3-1)
das **Hundefutter** dog food (6)
das **Hundewetter** rotten weather (1)
der **Hunger** hunger (5)
Ich habe Hunger. I'm hungry. (4, 5-2)
hungern to go hungry (10-1)
hungrig hungry (10-1)
der **Hut, ̈e** hat (7-2)
die **Hymne, -n** hymn (11)

I

der **ICE** InterCity Express (4)
ich: Ich bin's. It's me. (5-2)
ideal ideal (5-1)
der **Idealismus** (12-2)
die **Idee, -n** idea (7-1)
identisch identical (9)
der **Igel, -** hedgehog (10)
ihr, ihr, ihre her (1), their (2)
Ihr, Ihr, Ihre your (2)
die **Ikone, -n** icon (8)
die **Illustration, -en** illustration (6)
imaginär imaginary (9)
die **Imitation, -en** imitation (4)
immer always (2-1)
immer mehr more and more (5)
immer noch still (3)
immer wieder again and again (9-1)
der **Immigrant, -en, -en**/die **Immigrantin, -nen** immigrant (6-1)
der **Immobilienmakler, -**/die **Immobilienmaklerin, -nen** real estate agent (3)
impfen to vaccinate (11)
der **Import, -e** import (7)
in *(prep + acc/dat)* in (E, 8), into; to (1, 8)
der **Individualist, -en, -en**/die **Individualistin, -nen** individualist (8)

industrialisiert industrialized (9)

die **Industrie, -n** industry (3)

industriell industrial (4)

die **Infobox, -en** infobox (E)

der **Informatiker, -/**die **Informatikerin, -nen** computer specialist (12)

die **Information, -en** information (7)

das **Informationszeitalter** information age (10-1)

informiert informed (10)

der **Ingenieur, -e/**die **Ingenieurin, -nen** engineer (4)

inklusive inclusive of (9)

die **Inlineskates** in-line skates (3)

innen inside (9-1)

die **Innovation, -en** innovation (4)

innovativ innovative (4)

das **Insekt, -en** insect (2, 10-2)

die **Insel, -n** island (5-1)

der **Inspektor, -en/**die **Inspektorin, -nen** inspector (5)

das **Instrument, -e** instrument (2)

intelligent intelligent, smart (1, 2-1)

interessant interesting (1-2)

das **Interesse, -n** interest (2)

interesselos uninterested (12)

interessieren to interest (6)

sich **interessieren für** to be interested in (11-2)

interkulturell intercultural (2)

international international(ly) (9-1)

das **Internet** Internet (6, 10-1)

im Internet surfen to surf the Internet (6)

das **Interview, -s** interview (3-2)

investieren to invest (1)

der **iPod, -s** iPod (3)

irgendein, irgendein, irgendeine some . . . or other (11)

irgendwann sometime or other (8)

irisch *(adj)* Irish (2)

der **Israeli, -s/**die **Israeli, -s** Israeli *(person)* (3)

israelisch *(adj)* Israeli (7)

der **Italiener, -/**die **Italienerin, -nen** Italian *(person)* (9)

italienisch *(adj)* Italian (3)

J

ja yes (E-1)

die **Jacke, -n** jacket (1, 2-2)

der **Jäger, -/**die **Jägerin, -nen** hunter (7)

das **Jahr, -e** year (1-2)

auf ein Jahr for a year (8)

die **80er-Jahre** the eighties (10)

Ein gutes Neues Jahr! Happy New Year! (7-1)

letztes Jahr last year (5)

jahraus, jahrein year in, year out (1)

die **Jahreszeit, -en** season (1-2)

das **Jahrhundert, -e** century (3, 10-1)

jährlich yearly, annual(ly) (2)

das **Jahrzehnt, -e** decade (11)

der **Januar** January (1-2)

im Januar in January (1-2)

der **Japaner, -/**die **Japanerin, -nen** Japanese *(person)* (4)

der **Jazz** jazz (2)

die **Jeans, -** *(pl)* jeans (2-2)

jedenfalls at any rate (11-2)

jeder, jedes, jede each, every (1)

jederzeit (at) any time (11-2)

jedoch but (11-1)

jemand somebody, someone (3-2)

jemand anders somebody else (9-1)

jetzig present (4)

jetzt now (E, 1-1)

von jetzt ab from now on (6)

der **Job, -s** job (5-2)

jobben to work *(part-time or during vacation)* (1)

die **Jobliste, -n** list of jobs (6)

die **Jobvermittlung** *(sing)* employment agency (6)

der **Jockey, -s** jockey (2)

joggen to jog (2, 4-2)

joggen gehen to go jogging (2-1)

der **Jogginganzug, ⁻e** jogging suit (3)

die **Jogginghose, -n** jogging pants (3)

der **Joghurt** yogurt (4-1)

das **Jonglieren** *(sing)* juggling (4)

der **Journalist, -en, -en/**die **Journalistin, -nen** journalist (2-1)

der **Jude, -n, -n/**die **Jüdin, -nen** Jew (11)

jüdisch Jewish (11)

die **Jugend** *(sing)* youth (3, 5-2)

die **Jugendherberge, -n** youth hostel (5-1)

jugendlich youthful (4)

der **Juli** July (1-2)

jung young (1, 5-1)

der **Junge, -n, -n** boy (5-2)

der **Juni** June (1-2)

das **Junkfood** junk food (4)

die **Jury, -s** jury (9)

K

das **Kabinett, -e** cabinet (12-1)

der **Kaffee** coffee (1, 2-1)

die **Kaffeekanne, -n** coffeepot (1, 9-1)

die **Kaffeemaschine, -n** coffee maker (3-2)

der **Käfig, -e** cage (10)

der **Kaiser, -/**die **Kaiserin, -nen** emperor/empress (3)

der **Kajak, -s** kayak (5)

der **Kajaker, -/**die **Kajakerin, -nen** kayaker (5)

das **Kalb, ⁻er** calf (2)

der **Kalender, -** calendar (5-2)

(das) **Kalifornien** California (5)

kalt cold (1-1)

das **Kamel, -e** camel (9-2)

die **Kamera, -s** camera (3-2)

der **Kamm, ⁻e** comb (9-2)

sich **kämmen** to comb one's hair (9-2)

(das) **Kanada** Canada (1-1)

der **Kanadier, -/**die **Kanadierin, -nen** Canadian *(person)* (1-1)

kanadisch *(adj)* Canadian (3)

der **Kanal, ⁻e** channel (6); canal (10)

das **Känguru, -s** kangaroo (10)

das **Kännchen, -** little pot (9)

die **Kantate, -n** cantata (3)

der **Kanzler, -/**die **Kanzlerin, -nen** chancellor (11)

kapieren to understand (11-2)

kaputt broken (7, 10-2)

kaputt fahren (fährt kaputt), fuhr kaputt, kaputt gefahren to drive into the ground (12)

kaputt machen to break; to ruin (7-1)

der **Karfreitag** Good Friday (7)

kariert plaid (11)

die **Karikatur, -en** caricature (7)

der **Karneval** Mardi Gras (1)

die **Karotte, -n** carrot (1)

die **Karriere, -n** career (3, 12-1)

Karriere machen to get ahead in one's career (12-1)

die **Karte, -n** card (*also* playing card); postcard; map (1-1); ticket (2)

die **Kartoffel, -n** potato (4-1)

die **Kartoffelchips** potato chips (7-2)

der **Karton, -s** box, carton (8)

der **Käse,** cheese (E, 4-1)

Das ist alles Käse. That's all baloney. (7)

der **Käsekuchen, -** cheesecake (4)

die **Kasse, -n** checkout (9-1)

der **Kassenschein, -e** receipt (10)

der **Kassenzettel, -** sales slip (7)

die **Kassette, -n** cassette (1)

der **Kassettenrecorder, -** cassette recorder (3)

der **Kassierer, -**/die **Kassiererin, -nen** cashier (9-1)

das **Kassler Rippchen, -** (das **Kassler**) smoked pork chop (9)

der **Kasten, ⸚** box; case (9-1)

die **Katastrophe, -n** catastrophe (11-2)

die **Katze, -n** cat (1, 3-1)

  Es ist alles für die Katz. It's all for nothing. (10)

kaufen to buy (1-1)

der **Käufer, -**/die **Käuferin, -nen** buyer (9)

das **Kaufhaus, ⸚er** department store (3-2)

die **Kaufsucht** shopping addiction (12)

kaum scarcely; hardly (10-2)

der **Kaviar** caviar (3)

kein, kein, keine not a, not any, no (1)

der **Keller, -** cellar, basement (8-2)

der **Kellner, -**/die **Kellnerin, -nen** server, waiter/waitress (3, 9-1)

kennen, kannte, gekannt to know; to be acquainted with (3-1)

  kennen lernen to get to know (E, 4-2)

die **Kenntnisse** *(pl)* experience; knowledge (6)

der **Kerl, -e** guy (6)

die **Kerze, -n** candle (7-2)

der **Kessel, -** kettle (3)

das **Keyboard, -s** keyboard *(musical instrument)* (3)

der **Kfz-Mechaniker, -**/die **Kfz-Mechanikerin, -nen** car mechanic (12)

der **Kilometer, -** kilometer (1)

das **Kind, -er** child (1, 3-1)

  als Kind as a child (5-2)

die **Kinderabteilung, -en** children's department (10)

der **Kindergarten, ⸚** kindergarten; nursery school (1)

die **Kinderlähmung** polio (7)

kinderlos childless (12)

die **Kindheit** *(sing)* childhood (10-2)

kindisch childish (2)

kindlich childlike (2)

das **Kinn, -e** chin (6-1)

das **Kino, -s** movies (1)

  ins Kino to the movies (1-2)

die **Kirche, -n** church (10-1)

die **Klamotten** *(pl)* clothes (3-2)

der **Klang, ⸚e** sound (1)

Klar! Of course! (1-1)

die **Klarinette, -n** clarinet (3)

die **Klasse, -n** class (3-2)

klassenlos classless (12)

klassisch classical (3)

der **Klatsch** gossip (11-2)

die **Klausur, -en** test (5-2)

  eine Klausur schreiben to take a test; to have a test (5)

das **Klavier** piano (2)

  Klavier spielen to play the piano (2)

das **Klavierkonzert, -e** piano concerto (3)

der **Klavierlehrer, -**/die **Klavierlehrerin, -nen** piano teacher (7)

kleben to stick (10)

das **Kleid, -er** dress; *(pl)* clothes (2-2)

kleiden to dress (10)

das **Kleidergeschäft, -e** clothing store (3-2)

das **Kleidungsstück, -e** article of clothing (2-2)

klein little, small; short (1, 2-1)

die **Kleinbahn, -en** narrow-gauge railway (11)

klicken to click (3-1)

klingeln to ring (8-2)

das **Klischee, -s** cliché (1)

das **Klo, -s** toilet (8-1)

klopfen to knock (6)

der **Klub, -s** club (10)

klug smart, intelligent (10-2)

der **Klumpen, -** lump (10)

knabbern to nibble (11)

das **Knäckebrot** crispbread (11)

knackig crisp (12)

die **Knackwurst, ⸚e** knackwurst (5)

knalllaut very loud (11)

knallrot beet red (11)

der **Knast** jail (11)

die **Kneipe, -n** pub (1)

  in die Kneipe to a pub (1-2)

das **Knie, -** knee (1, 6-1)

knipsen to snap a photo (11)

der **Knoblauch** garlic (11)

der **Knödel, -** dumpling (9-1)

knutschen to smooch (11)

der **Koch, ⸚e**/die **Köchin, -nen** cook; chef (3)

das **Kochbuch, ⸚er** cookbook (7-1)

kochen to cook (2-1)

die **Kocherei** *(constant)* cooking (5)

der **Kochkurs, -e** cooking lessons (5)

die **Kochmöglichkeit, -en** cooking facilities (4)

das **Koffein** caffeine (2)

der **Koffer, -** suitcase (2, 6-1)

der **Kofferraum** trunk *(of a car)* (4)

der **Kognak** cognac (7)

die **Kohle, -n** coal (1)

der **Kollege, -en, -en**/die **Kollegin, -nen** colleague (2, 9-2)

(das) **Köln** Cologne (12)

kombinieren to combine (4)

komfortabel comfortable (4, 5-1)

komisch funny; strange (10-2)

kommen, kam, ist gekommen to come (E, 1-1)

  Das kommt nicht in Frage! That's out of the question! (9-2)

  Ich komme aus … I'm from . . . (E-1)

kommend coming (8)

  Woher kommen Sie/kommst du? Where are you from? (E-1)

  zu Besuch kommen to visit (8-1)

die **Kommode, -n** dresser (8-1)

die **Kommunikation, -en** communication (1)

kommunistisch communist (11-2)

die **Komödie, -n** comedy (3)

das **Kompliment, -e** compliment (5-2)

kompliziert complicated (10-1)

der **Komponist, -en, -en**/die **Komponistin, -nen** composer (2, 5-1)

die **Komposition, -en** composition (3)

der **Konditor, -en**/die **Konditorin, -nen** confectioner, pastry cook (6)

die **Konditorei, -en** shop selling cakes and pastries (7)

der **Konflikt, -e** conflict (12)

der **König, -e** king (1)

die **Königin, -nen** queen (9)

die **Konjunktion, -en** conjunction (4)

können (kann), konnte, gekonnt to be able to, can (4)

konservativ conservative (5-2)

das **Konsulat, -e** consulate (12-2)

der **Kontakt, -e** contact (E, 12-2)

die **Kontaktlinse, -n** contact lens (5-2)

kontaktorientiert contact-oriented (12)

der **Kontext, -e** context (1)

der **Kontinent, -e** continent (2)

der **Kontrollstreifen, -** patrolled strip of land (part of the Berlin Wall) (11)

das **Konzept, -e** concept (4)

das **Konzert, -e** concert (1, 2-2)

  ins Konzert to a concert, to concerts (1-2)

der **Kopf, ⸚e** head (6-1)

den **Kopf schütteln** to shake one's head (10-2)

Er ist nicht auf den Kopf gefallen. He's no fool. (6)

Mir raucht der Kopf. I can't think straight anymore. (9)

die **Kopfhörer** *(pl)* headphones (11-2)

der **Kopfsalat, -e** head lettuce (9)

die **Kopfschmerzen** *(pl)* headache (6)

kopieren to copy (10-1)

der **Kork, -en** cork (9)

der **Korkenzieher, -** corkscrew (8-2)

der **Körper, -** body (6-1)

kosten to cost (1-2)

kotzen to puke, to throw up (11)

krabbeln to crawl (8)

der **Krach** row, scene (11)

der **Krampf, ̈e** cramp (3)

krank sick (3-2)

das **Krankenhaus, ̈er** hospital (6-2)

die **Krankenversicherung, -en** health insurance (12)

die **Krankheit, -en** illness, sickness (7-2)

die **Krawatte, -n** tie (7-2)

kreativ creative (2-1)

die **Krebsvorsorge** *(sing)* cancer prevention (6)

der **Kredit, -e** credit; loan (11)

die **Kreditkarte, -n** credit card (5-2)

der **Kreis, -e** circle (11)

kreischen to screech (11)

das **Kreuz, -e** cross (1)

der **Krieg, -e** war (7, 11-1)

kriegen to get, to receive (8, 10-2)

Angst kriegen to get scared (10-1)

eins aufs Dach kriegen to be bawled out (8)

der **Krimi, -s** detective story (3)

die **Kritik** *(sing)* criticism (10)

der **Kritiker, -/**die **Kritikerin, -nen** critic (10)

kritisch critical (5)

kritisieren to criticize (3-2)

die **Krone, -n** crown (1)

krumm crooked, bent (10-2)

die **Küche, -n** kitchen (8-1); cuisine (9)

der **Kuchen, -** cake (3, 4-1)

ein Stück Kuchen a piece of cake (3)

die **Küchenbenutzung** *(sing)* kitchen privileges (8-2)

die **Kuckucksuhr, -en** cuckoo clock (2)

die **Kugel, -n** ball (3); scoop *(of ice cream)* (10)

der **Kugelschreiber, -** ballpoint pen (7-2)

die **Kuh, ̈e** cow (1)

kühl cool *(of weather)* (5-2)

der **Kühlschrank, ̈e** refrigerator (7, 8-1)

der **Kuli, -s** ballpoint pen (7)

die **Kultur, -en** culture (1)

der **Kulturschock** culture shock (11-1)

der **Kunde, -n, -n/**die **Kundin, -nen** customer (7, 9-2)

kündigen to give notice (10)

die **Kunst, ̈e** art (5-2)

der **Künstler, -/**die **Künstlerin, -nen** artist (8-2)

künstlerisch artistic(ally) (12)

der **Kürbis, -se** pumpkin (4)

das **Kürbisschnitzen** *(sing)* pumpkin carving (4)

der **Kurs, -e** course; class (5-2)

kurz short (2-2)

seit kurzem recently (11-1)

seit kurzer Zeit recently (11-1)

kürzlich a short time ago, recently (10-1)

kuschelig cuddly (7-2)

die **Kusine, -n** *(female)* cousin (3-1)

die **Küste, -n** coast (11-2)

die **Kutsche, -n** *(horse-drawn)* carriage (3)

L

lachen to laugh (3-1)

Da lachen ja die Hühner! What a joke! (10)

der **Lachs** salmon, lox (3)

der **Laden, ̈** store (3)

laden (lädt), lud, geladen to load (6)

die **Lage, -n** location (11)

lahm lame (2)

das **Lama, -s** llama (2)

das **Lamm, ̈er** lamb (1)

die **Lampe, -n** lamp (1, 8-1)

das **Land, ̈er** country (2-2); state (6-1)

landen, landete, ist gelandet to land *(of airplanes)* (6-2)

die **Landschaft, -en** landscape (5-1)

das **Landschaftsbild, -er** landscape painting (8)

die **Landung, -en** landing (6)

lang long (1, 2-2)

eine Stunde lang for an hour (4)

langsam slow(ly) (3-1)

langweilig boring (3-1)

die **Lasagne** lasagna (4)

lassen (lässt), ließ, gelassen to let; to leave (3-2); to have (something) done (11)

Lass mich in Ruhe! Stop bothering me! (4-2)

Lassen Sie sich Zeit. Take your time. (12-2)

der **Lastkraftwagen, -** truck (10-2)

der **Lastwagen, -** truck (10-2)

(das) **Latein** Latin *(language)* (6)

laufen (läuft), lief, ist gelaufen to run (3-2)

die **Laus, ̈e** louse (1)

lausig lousy (2)

laut loud (1, 3-2)

der **Lautsprecher, -** loudspeaker (5)

leben to live *(in a country or a city)* (2-2)

das **Leben, -** life (3-1)

lebendig alive (11-2)

das **Lebensjahr** year of *(one's)* life (3)

die **Lebensmittel** *(pl)* food; groceries (9-1)

das **Lebensmittelgeschäft, -e** grocery store (9)

der **Lebensstil, -e** lifestyle (4, 5-2)

die **Lebensversicherung, -en** life insurance (12)

der **Lebensunterhalt** living expenses (11)

lebenswichtig essential (11)

die **Leberwurst, ̈e** liver sausage (10)

leblos lifeless (12)

lecker delicious (4, 5-1)

das **Leder** leather (2)

ledig single (3-1)

leer empty (7-1)

leeren to empty (7-1)

legen to lay *(down)*, to put *(in a horizontal position)* (8-1)

die **Lehne, -n** back *(of a chair)* (9)

die **Lehre, -n** apprenticeship (6)

lehren to teach (11)

der **Lehrer, -/**die **Lehrerin, -nen** teacher, instructor (2-1)

der **Lehrling, -e** apprentice (6)

der **Lehrplan** curriculum (8)

leicht easy; light (6-2)

leid: Es tut mir leid. I'm sorry. (7-2)

leiden, litt, gelitten to suffer (11)

leider unfortunately (5-2)

leihen, lieh, geliehen to lend (7-2)

die **Leine, -n** leash (10)

leisten to achieve (7)

die **Lektüre** *(sing)* reading material (10)

lernen to learn; to study (1-2)
lesen (liest), las, gelesen to read (3-2)
letzt last (3-2)
  das letzte Mal the last time (10-2)
  in letzter Zeit recently (6-2)
  zum letzten Mal for the last time (7-2)
die **Leute** *(pl)* people (1)
das **Licht, -er** light (8)
lieb dear (4-1)
  Liebe Grüße "Love" *(closing in a letter)* (6-1)
die **Liebe** love (2)
lieben to love (2, 5-2)
lieber rather (2)
liebevoll loving (5)
der **Liebling, -e** darling; favorite (3-1)
das **Lieblingsbuch, ⁻er** favorite book (3-1)
die **Lieblings-CD, -s** favorite CD (5)
die **Lieblingsfarbe** favorite color (3-1)
der **Lieblingsonkel, -** favorite uncle (3)
das **Lieblingsprogramm, -e** favorite program (5)
der **Lieblingssport** favorite sport (5)
die **Lieblingstante, -n** favorite aunt (3)
lieblos loveless (5)
liebst: Wo machst du am liebsten Ferien? Where's your favorite vacation spot? (5-1)
das **Lied, -er** song (11-1)
liegen, lag, gelegen to lie, to be situated (6-2)
  es liegt daran the reason is (11)
der **Likör, -e** liqueur (2)
die **Lilie, -n** lily (1)
die **Linie, -n** line (8)
links left; to the left (4-2)
die **Lippe, -n** lip (1)
der **Lippenstift, -e** lipstick (3, 9-2)
die **Lira, Lire** lira *(former Italian currency)* (9)
lispeln to lisp (8)
die **Liste, -n** list (6)
der **Liter, -** liter (9-1)
die **Literatur, -en** literature (5-2)
der **Lkw, -s (Lastkraftwagen)** truck (10-2)
das **Loch, ⁻er** hole (7-2)
lockig curly (3-2)
der **Löffel, -** spoon (9-1)
der **Lohn, ⁻e** wages, pay (8, 12-1)
los
  Was ist denn los? What's up? (8-2)

Was ist denn los mit dir? What's the matter with you? (12-2)
löschen to delete; to extinguish (10)
lösen to solve (4); to pay (8)
die **Lösung, -en** solution (5-1)
der **Lottoschein, -e** lottery ticket (12)
die **Luft** air (4, 11-1)
die **Luftbrücke** airlift (11)
die **Luftbrückengüter** *(pl)* goods transported by airlift (11)
der **Luftschutzkeller, -** air-raid shelter (11)
die **Lüge, -n** lie (10-1)
lügen, log, gelogen to lie *(tell an untruth)* (10-1)
der **Lumpen, -** rag (10-1)
die **Lüneburger Heide** Lüneburg Heath (1)
die **Lupe, -n** magnifying glass (1)
die **Lust** enjoyment (8)
  Ich habe keine Lust … I don't feel like . . . (8-2)
  Ich habe Lust auf eine Tafel Schokolade. I feel like having a chocolate bar. (10-2)
lustig funny, humorous; happy (7-1)
der **Luxus** luxury (8-2)

M

machbar doable (12)
machen to make; to do (1-1)
  Das macht doch nichts. That doesn't matter. (9-1)
  Mach's gut! Take care! (1-2)
  Sport machen to do sports, to be active in sports (1-2)
das **Mädchen, -** girl (2, 5-2)
das **Magazin, -e** magazine (2-2)
magersüchtig anorexic (12-2)
mähen to mow (6-2)
der **Mai** May (1-2)
die **Mail, -s** e-mail (3-1)
die **Makkaroni** *(pl)* macaroni (3)
das **Mal, -e** *(occurrence)* time (7)
  das letzte Mal the last time (10-2)
  jedes Mal every time (10)
  mit einem Mal suddenly (11)
  zum ersten Mal for the first time (7-2)
  zum letzten Mal for the last time (7-2)
mal, einmal once; for a change (5)
  nicht mal not even (10)
  noch mal once more; (over) again (7-2)
malen to paint *(a picture)* (8)

das **Malen** *(sing)* drawing, painting *(as an activity)* (4)
der **Maler, -/**die **Malerin, -nen** painter; artist (6-2)
die **Malerei** painting *(as an activity)* (8)
man one, you (E, 4-1)
  Wie sagt man das? How does one say that? How do you say that? (4-1)
mancher, manches, manche many a; *(pl)* some (10-1)
manchmal sometimes (4-1)
die **Mandarine, -n** mandarin (orange) (1)
der **Mann, ⁻er** man; husband (1, 2-2)
der **Mantel, ⁻** coat (2-2)
das **Märchen, -** fairy tale (4, 5-2)
märchenhaft fairy-tale *(adj)*, fantastic (5-2)
der **Märchenkönig, -e** fairy-tale king (5)
die **Märchensammlung, -en** collection of fairy tales (10)
die **Märchenstadt, ⁻e** fairy-tale city (5)
die **Märchenwelt** wonderland (5)
der **Markt, ⁻e** market (4)
die **Marktforschung** market research (9)
der **Marktplatz, ⁻e** market square (4)
marktwirtschaftlich *(adj)* free enterprise (11)
die **Marmelade, -n** jam (4-1)
der **Mars** Mars (5)
marschieren to march (5)
der **März** March (1-2)
die **Maschine, -n** machine (5-1)
der **Maschinenbaumechaniker, -/** die **Maschinenbaumechanikerin, -nen** machinist (12)
das **Massenprodukt, -e** mass-produced product (4)
massiv heavy; solid (5)
die **Mathe** math (2)
die **Mathematik** mathematics (5)
die **Mauer, -n** wall (7, 11-1)
die **Maus, ⁻e** mouse (1, 3-1)
maximal a maximum of (8-2)
das **Medikament, -e** medicine (9)
das **Meer, -e** ocean, sea (5, 11-2)
das **Mehl** flour (9-1)
mehr more (3-2)
  immer mehr more and more (7-2)
  nicht mehr no longer, not any more (3-2)

die **Mehrzahl** majority (6)

mein, mein, meine my (E)

meinen to mean; to think, to be of or voice an opinion (3, 11-1)

die **Meinung, -en** opinion (11-2)
  meiner Meinung nach in my opinion (12-2)

meist most (5)

meistens most of the time, usually (4-1)

sich **melden** to apply (3); to register (8)

die **Menge, -n** lot, great deal (11-2)
  eine Menge a lot (11-2)

die **Mensa** university dining hall (E, 1-1)
  in die Mensa to the cafeteria (1-2)

der **Mensch, -en, -en** human being; person; *(pl)* people (5-2)
  Mensch! Wow! (1-1)

menschlich human (12)

der **Mercedes** Mercedes (3)

merken to realize; to notice (9)

das **Merkmal, -e** characteristic; trait (2)

die **Messe, -n** trade fair (1)
  auf die Messe to the trade fair (1)

das **Messer, -** knife (4, 9-1)

der **Messerschmied, -e**/die **Messerschmiedin, -nen** knifesmith (4)

die **Messerwerkstatt, ¨en** knifesmith's shop (4)

das **Metall, -e** metal (9)

der **Meter, -** meter (1)

der **Methodist, -en, -en**/die **Methodistin, -nen** Methodist (3)

die **Miete, -n** rent (2)

mieten to rent (6-2)

der **Mieter, -**/die **Mieterin, -nen** renter (10)

das **Mietshaus, ¨er** apartment building (2)

der **Mietwagen, -** rental car (5)

die **Mikrobiologie** microbiology (2)

das **Mikroskop, -e** microscope (1, 10-2)

die **Mikrowelle, -n** microwave (oven) (8-1)

die **Milch** milk (1, 2-1)

die **Milliarde, -n** billion (9)

die **Million, -en** million (4)

mindestens at least (6-2)

das **Mineralwasser** mineral water (3-2)

der **Minister, -**/ die **Ministerin, -nen** minister *(in government)* (5)

der **Ministerpräsident, -en, -en**/die **Ministerpräsidentin, -nen** prime minister (10)

die **Minute, -n** minute (1, 2-1)

miserabel miserable (10-2)

der **Mist** manure (6)

mit *(prep + dat)* with (1); *(as verb prefix)* along (4)

der **Mitarbeiter, -**/die **Mitarbeiterin, -nen** (fellow) employee (4)

der **Mitbewohner, -**/die **Mitbewohnerin, -nen** housemate; roommate (E, 1-2)

mit·bringen, brachte mit, mitgebracht to bring along (4)

das **Mitbringsel, -** small gift *(for a host)* (7-2)

der **Mitbürger, -**/die **Mitbürgerin, -nen** fellow citizen (9-2)

miteinander with each other; together (2-1)

mit·gehen, ging mit, ist mitgegangen to go along (4)

das **Mitglied, -er** member (11-2)

mit·kommen, kam mit, ist mitgekommen to come along (4-2)

mit·lesen (liest mit), las mit, mitgelesen to read along (4)

mit·machen to take part in (12)

mit·nehmen (nimmt mit), nahm mit, mitgenommen to take along (4)

mit·singen, sang mit, mitgesungen to sing along (4)

der **Mitstudent, -en, -en**/die **Mitstudentin, -nen** classmate; fellow student (7, 8-2)

der **Mittag** noon (10)
  zu Mittag essen to have lunch (4-1)

das **Mittagessen** lunch; noon meal (4-1)
  zum Mittagessen for lunch (4-1)

die **Mittagspause, -n** lunch break (8-2)

die **Mitte, -n** middle (2)
  Mitte Juli (in) mid-July (5-1)

mittel average; medium
  mittelgroß of average height (6)
  die mittlere Reife tenth grade diploma (6)

der **Mittelklassewagen, -** midsized car (12)

das **Mittelmeer** *(sing)* Mediterranean Sea (5)

mitten: mitten im Winter in the middle of winter (3)

(die) **Mitternacht** midnight (4, 11-2)
  nach Mitternacht after midnight (4-2)

der **Mittwoch** Wednesday (1-2) *(see also* **Dienstag***)*

die **Möbel** *(pl)* furniture (8-1)

das **Möbelstück, -e** piece of furniture (8)

möbliert furnished (8-1)

das **Modell, -e** model (4)

die **Modenschau** fashion show (11)

modern modern (1, 2-1)

modisch fashionable (10-2)

mögen (mag), mochte, gemocht to like (4)
  ich möchte I would like (3)

möglich possible (4-2)
  so bald wie möglich as soon as possible (4)
  so schnell wie möglich as quickly as possible (10)
  so viel wie möglich as much as possible (9)

die **Möglichkeit, -en** possibility (5)

möglichst viel as much as possible (11)

mollig plump (2-1)

der **Moment, -e** moment (7)
  im Moment at the moment (11-1)

die **Monarchie, -n** monarchy (11-1)

der **Monat, -e** month (1-2)

monatlich monthly (2)

der **Mond** moon (1)

der **Monolog, -e** monologue (12)

der **Montag** Monday (1-2) *(see also* **Dienstag***)*

morgen tomorrow (1-1)
  morgen früh tomorrow morning (2-2)
  morgen Nachmittag tomorrow afternoon (2)

der **Morgen, -** morning (E)
  Guten Morgen! Morgen! Good morning! (E-1)
  heute Morgen this morning (1-2)

morgens in the morning (2)

der **Moskito, -s** mosquito (2)

der **Most** cider (8)

das **Motiv, -e** motif (9)

der **Motor, -en** motor (3)

das **Motorboot, -e** motorboat (4)

der **Motorenkonstrukteur, -e** engine designer (12)

das **Motorrad, ¨er** motorcycle (2, 3-1)

das **Mountainbike, -s** mountain bike (3-2)

der **Mozzarella** mozzarella (*cheese*) (10)

müde tired (5-2)

der **Muffin, -s** muffin (4-1)

der **Mülleimer, -** garbage can (7-1)

die **Mülltonne, -n** garbage bin (11-1)

multikulturell multicultural (9)

(das) **München** Munich (5)

der **Mund, ⁝er** mouth (6-1)

  den Mund voll nehmen to talk big (6)

die **Münze, -n** coin (9-2)

murmeln to mumble; to murmur (12-1)

das **Museum, Museen** museum (5-1)

die **Musik** music (1)

musikalisch musical (2-1)

der **Musiker, -/**die **Musikerin, -nen** musician (3)

das **Müsli** (*sing*) muesli (*cold, whole-grain cereal with nuts and fruit*) (4-1)

  eine Schüssel Müsli a bowl of muesli (4-1)

der **Müsliriegel, -** granola bar (4-1)

müssen (muss), musste, gemusst to have to, must (4)

die **Mutter, ⁝** mother (E, 3-1)

mütterlich motherly (2)

mütterlicherseits maternal (3, 6-1)

der **Muttertag, -e** Mother's Day (7-2)

die **Mutti** mom (5)

mysteriös mysterious (5)

N

na well (E)

nach (*prep + dat*) after; to (1-2); according to (10)

  meiner Meinung nach in my opinion (12-2)

  nach Claudias Vorlesung after Claudia's lecture (1-2)

  nach Florida to Florida (1-2)

  nach Hause gehen to go home (4-1)

der **Nachbar, -n, -n/**die **Nachbarin, -nen** neighbor (2-2)

nach·bestellen to reorder (9)

nachdem after (*sub conj*) (9-2)

nach·füllen to refill (9)

nach·galoppieren to gallop after (10)

nachher after; afterwards (*adv*) (5, 6-1)

der **Nachmittag, -e** afternoon (1)

  heute Nachmittag this afternoon (1)

  morgen Nachmittag tomorrow afternoon (2)

nachmittags in the afternoon (2)

der **Nachmittagskaffee** afternoon coffee (4-1)

  zum Nachmittagskaffee for afternoon coffee (4-1)

die **Nachrichten** (*pl*) news (10)

nächst next (1)

  nächstes Jahr next year (1, 3-2)

die **Nacht, ⁝e** night (2)

  bei Nacht at night (2)

  gestern Nacht last night (2)

  Gute Nacht! Good night! (E)

der **Nachteil, -e** disadvantage (8-2)

der **Nachtisch, -e** dessert (3, 4-1)

  zum Nachtisch for dessert (3, 4-1)

der **Nachtmensch, -en, -en** night person (4)

nachts at night (2)

der **Nachttisch, -e** night table (8-1)

die **Nachttischlampe, -n** bedside lamp (8)

nah near (5-1)

die **Nähe** vicinity (8)

  in der Nähe der Uni near the university (8-2)

die **Nähmaschine, -n** sewing machine (8-2)

der **Name, -ns, -n** name (E-1)

das **Namensschild, -er** name plate (9)

nämlich you see (5)

der **Narr, -en, -en** jester (10)

die **Nase, -n** nose (6-1)

  die Nase zu tief ins Glas stecken to drink too much (6)

  jemand (*dat*) **auf der Nase herumtanzen** to walk all over someone (9)

der **Nasenstecker, -** nose stud (5-2)

nass wet (5-1)

national national (4)

der **Nationalfeiertag, -e** national holiday (7)

die **Nationalität, -en** nationality (1)

die **Natur** nature (9)

natürlich of course (5-2); natural (2)

neben (*prep + acc/dat*) in addition to (4); beside, next to (8)

das **Nebengericht, -e** side dish (9)

neblig foggy (1)

der **Neffe, -n, -n** nephew (3-1)

negativ negative (1)

nehmen (nimmt), nahm, genommen to take (3-2)

neidisch jealous, envious (12)

  neidisch auf (*+ acc*) envious of (12-1)

nein no (E-1)

die **Nelke, -n** carnation (6)

nennen, nannte, genannt to call, to name (4)

der **Nerv, -en** nerve (12)

  Sie geht mir auf die Nerven. She gets on my nerves. (12-1)

nerven to get on one's nerves (4, 8-2)

nervös nervous, on edge (4-2)

Nervtante: Sie ist eine Nervtante. She gets on my nerves. (12-1)

nett nice; pleasant (2-1)

das **Netz, -e** net (3)

neu new (3-2)

  Ein gutes neues Jahr! Happy New Year! (7-1)

die **Neue Pinakothek** *art gallery in Munich* (5)

(das) **Neujahr** New Year (6)

neuseeländisch (*adj*) New Zealand (7)

nicht not (1-1)

  gar nicht not at all (1-1)

  nicht mal not even (10)

  nicht mehr no longer, not any more (3-2)

  noch nicht not yet (E)

  überhaupt nicht not at all (11-2)

die **Nichte, -n** niece (3-1)

nichts nothing (1-2)

  Das macht doch nichts. That doesn't matter. (9-1)

  Er tut dir nichts. He won't hurt you. (9-1)

  gar nichts nothing at all (6, 11-2)

  überhaupt nichts nothing at all (11-2)

der **Nichtsnutz, -e** good-for-nothing (10)

nie never (2-2)

niemand nobody, no one (3-2)

nieseln: es nieselt it's drizzling (1)

nikotinsüchtig addicted to nicotine (12)

nix = nichts (12)

noch still (1-1)

  immer noch still (3)

  noch einmal (over) again, once more (7-2)

noch mal (over) again, once more (2, 7-2)

noch nicht not yet (E, 1-1)

das **Nomen, -** noun (1)

nonstop nonstop (11-1)

(das) **Nordamerika** North America (3)

nordamerikanisch *(adj)* North American (8)

(das) **Norddeutschland** Northern Germany (3)

der **Norden** north (6)

nördlich (von) north (of) (11)

der **Nordpol** North Pole (1)

die **Nordsee** North Sea (1)

normalerweise usually, normally (2, 4-1)

das **Notebook, -s** notebook *(computer)* (3-1)

die **Notiz, -en** note (E)

der **November** November (1-2)

die **Nudel, -n** noodle (2, 4-1)

die **Nummer, -n** number (E)

nun now (8)

nur only (1-1)

die **Nuss, ⁻e** nut (3)

O

ob whether *(sub conj)* (5)

oben above (10-2)

ober upper (10)

das **Obst** *(sing)* fruit (4-1)

obwohl although, even though *(sub conj)* (4-2)

der **Ochse, -n, -n** ox (1)

die **Ode, -n** ode (11)

oder *(coord conj)* or (1-2)

offen open (2, 3-2)

öffentlich public (1)

offiziell official (9, 11-2)

der **Offizier, -e** officer (4)

öffnen to open (1, 11-1)

oft often (1-1)

ohne *(prep + acc)* without (E, 5-2)

die **Ohnmacht: in Ohnmacht fallen** to faint (12-1)

das **Ohr, -en** ear (6-1)

jemand *(acc)* **übers Ohr hauen** to pull a fast one on someone (9)

die **Ohrenschmerzen** *(pl)* earache (6)

der **Ohrring, -e** earring (5-2)

der **Ohrstecker, -** ear stud (5-2)

der **Oktober** October (1-2)

das **Oktoberfest** Octoberfest (1)

das **Öl, -e** oil (9-2)

der **Oldtimer, -** vintage car (2)

die **Olive, -n** olive (2-2)

das **Olivenöl** olive oil (2-2)

die **Oma, -s** grandma (3-1)

der **Onkel, -** uncle (3-1)

der **Opa, -s** grandpa (3-1)

die **Oper, -n** opera (2-2)

die **Operette, -n** operetta (4)

der **Opernsänger, -/**
die **Opernsängerin, -nen** opera singer (2)

optimistisch optimistic (3-1)

die **Orange, -n** orange (1, 4-1)

der **Orangensaft** *(sing)* orange juice (4-1)

das **Orchester, -** orchestra (3)

ordentlich decent (2); neat, tidy (4-2)

die **Ordnung** order (9)

in Ordnung bringen, brachte, gebracht to tidy up (4)

Ist alles in Ordnung? Is everything okay? (9-2)

orientiert oriented (12)

das **Ornament, -e** ornament (5)

der **Ortsname, -ns, -n** place name (11)

der **Ossi, -s** citizen of former East Germany (11)

der/die **Ostdeutsche, -n** citizen of East Germany (11)

(das) **Ostdeutschland** East Germany (11)

der **Osten** east (8)

der **Osterhase, -n, -n** Easter bunny (7-1)

der **Ostermontag** Easter Monday (7)

Ostern Easter (7-1)

(das) **Österreich** Austria (1-1)

der **Österreicher, -/**
die **Österreicherin, -nen** Austrian *(person)* (1-1)

österreichisch *(adj)* Austrian (9)

der **Ostersonntag** Easter Sunday (7)

osteuropäisch *(adj)* Eastern European (11)

östlich (von) east (of) (11)

die **Ostsee** Baltic Sea (1)

der **Ozean, -e** ocean (10, 11-2)

P

das **Paar, -e** pair, couple (6)

paar: ein paar a couple of, a few (1-1)

packen to pack (4, 6-1)

die **Packung, -en** package (5)

das **Paket, -e** package, parcel (7-2)

das **Papier, -e** paper (9)

der **Papierkorb, ⁻e** wastepaper basket (8-1)

das **Paradies** paradise (10-1)

der **Paragraph, -en, -en** paragraph (11)

das **Parfüm, -s** perfume (7-2)

der **Park, -s** park (1)

die **Parkmöglichkeit, -en** parking facility (4)

der **Parkplatz, ⁻e** parking lot (4)

der **Parkschein, -e** parking pass (8)

das **Parlament, -e** parliament (11, 12-1)

die **Partei, -en** *(political)* party (E); party *(to an agreement)* (8)

der **Partner, -/**die **Partnerin, -nen** partner (2, 3-1)

die **Party, -s** party (7-2)

der **Pass, ⁻e** passport (5-2)

passen to fit (E); to suit (12)

passend appropriate (7)

etwas Passendes something suitable (10)

passieren, passierte, ist passiert to happen (6-2)

passioniert ardent (5-1)

der **Patient, -en, -en/**die **Patientin, -nen** patient (5, 9-2)

die **Patrouille, -n** patrol (11)

die **Pause, -n** break (12)

peinlich embarrassing (11-2)

der **Pendler, -** commuter (9)

die **Pension, -en** pension (12-2)

die **Person, -en** person, individual (3-2)

die **Personalabteilung, -en** personnel department (9)

der **Personalchef, -s/**
die **Personalchefin, -nen** personnel manager (6-2)

das **Personalpronomen, -** personal pronoun (7)

die **Personenbeschreibung, -en** description of a person (3)

der **Personenkraftwagen, - (Pkw)** car (10-2)

der **Personenwagen, -** car (10-2)

persönlich personal(ly) (5)

die **Peseta, Peseten** peseta *(former Spanish currency)* (9)

pessimistisch pessimistic (3-1)

der **Pfad, -e** path (3)

die **Pfanne, -n** pan (3, 9-1)

der **Pfeffer** pepper (1, 9-2)

der **Pfefferminztee** peppermint tea (11)

die **Pfeife, -n** pipe (3)

der **Pfennig, -e** penny (3)

das **Pferd, -e** horse (10-1)

Da bringen mich keine zehn Pferde hin. Wild horses couldn't drag me there. (10)

(das) **Pfingsten, -** Pentecost (7)

die **Pflanze, -n** plant (3)

das **Pflaster, -** Band-Aid (9)

die **Pflaume, -n** plum (11)

pflegeleicht easy to care for (10)

pflücken to pick (11)

pflügen to plough (11)

der **Pfosten, -** post (3)

die **Pfote, -n** paw (9)

das **Pfund, -e** pound (3)

Pfui! Yuck! (11)

die **Philharmonie** philharmonic orchestra (1)

die **Philosophie, -n** philosophy (3)

die **Physik** physics (1)

der **Physiotherapeut, -en, -en**/die **Physiotherapeutin, -nen** physical therapist (3)

der **Pianist, -en, -en**/die **Pianistin, -nen** pianist (3)

das **Picknick, -s** picnic (4)

das **Pipimädchen, -** stupid little girl (11)

die **Pistazie, -n** pistachio (2)

die **Pistole, -n** pistol (7)

die **Pizza, -s** pizza (3)

die **Pizzeria, -s** pizzeria (6)

der **Pkw, -s (Personenkraftwagen)** car (10-2)

der **Plan, ⁻e** plan (1, 5-1)

planen to plan (7, 8-1)

das **Plastik, -s** plastic (9-1)

die **Plastiktasche, -n** plastic bag (9)

Platte: einen Platten haben to have a flat tire (12-2)

der **Platz, ⁻e** place; seat (4, 9-1); city square (5)

die **Platzreservierung, -en** seat reservation (7)

plötzlich suddenly, all of a sudden (6-2)

poetisch poetic (10)

die **Politik** politics (5)

der **Politiker, -**/die **Politikerin, -nen** politician (2)

politisch political (2-1)

die **Polizei** police (4, 12-2)

die **Polizeiwache, -n** police station (10)

der **Polizist, -en, -en**/die **Polizistin, -nen** police officer (2, 9-2)

polnisch (adj) Polish (2)

das **Polohemd, -en** polo shirt (3)

die **Pommes**/die **Pommes frites** (pl) French fries (4-1)

popeln to pick one's nose (11)

populär popular (1, 10-2)

das **Porträt, -s** portrait (9)

die **Position, -en** position (12-1)

die **Post** post office; mail (8)

das **Postamt, ⁻er** post office (10)

das **Poster, -** poster (8-2)

die **Postkarte, -n** postcard (6-1)

die **Postleitzahl, -en** zip code, postal code (E)

praktisch practical (2-1)

das **Präsens** present tense (10)

der **Präsident, -en, -en**/die **Präsidentin, -nen** president (1, 9-2)

das **Präteritum** simple past tense (10)

der **Preis, -e** price (3-2)

preisgünstig inexpensive (3-2)

primitiv primitive (5-1)

privat private (11)

das **Privathaus, ⁻er** private home (8)

privatisieren to privatize (11-2)

das **Problem, -e** problem (3-1)

das **Produkt, -e** product (4, 10-2)

die **Produktion** production (4)

der **Professor, -en**/die **Professorin, -nen** professor (1)

der **Profi, -s** pro (4)

der **Programmierer, -**/die **Programmiererin, -nen** programmer (1)

das **Projekt, -e** project (5)

der **Projektor, -en** projector (5)

proklamieren to proclaim (11-1)

prominent prominent (8)

Prost! Prosit! Cheers! To your health! (7-2)

protzig swanky, showy (10)

die **Provinz, -en** province (5)

das **Prozent, -e** percent (1, 12-1)

prüfen to test (9)

der **Psychiater, -**/die **Psychiaterin, -nen** psychiatrist (9)

der **Pudding, -s** pudding (3, 4-1)

der **Pudel, -n** poodle (2)

der **Pulli, -s** sweater (2-2)

der **Pullover, -** sweater (1, 2-2)

der **Punk, -s** punk (11)

der **Punkt, -e** dot; period (4)

Punkt halb zwei at one-thirty on the dot (4, 5-2)

pünktlich punctual, on time (7)

die **Puppe, -n** doll (7)

die **Pute, -n** turkey (6)

das **Putenfleisch** (sing) turkey (meat) (9)

putzen to clean (4, 6-2)

Q

der **Quadratfuß** square foot (8)

der **Quadratmeter, -** square meter (5)

qualifiziert qualified (12-1)

Quatsch! Nonsense! (6-1)

das **Quiz, -** quiz (5-2)

R

das **Rad, ⁻er** bike; wheel (3-1)

Rad fahren (fährt Rad), fuhr Rad, ist Rad gefahren to ride a bike, to go cycling (4-2)

das **Radio, -s** radio (6)

die **Radtour, -en** bicycle trip (2-2)

eine Radtour machen to go on a bicycle trip (5)

der **Radwanderführer, -** cycling tour guidebook (11)

die **Radwanderkarte, -n** cycling tour map (11)

rasen to race (10)

der **Rasen, -** lawn (6-2)

der **Rasierapparat, -e** shaver (9-2)

(sich) **rasieren** to shave (9-2)

das **Rasierwasser** (sing) aftershave (9-2)

rasseln to rattle (3)

Rast machen to stop over (11)

die **Raststätte, -n** restaurant (on the freeway) (9)

der **Rat** (sing) advice (4)

um Rat fragen to ask for advice (12)

raten (rät), riet, geraten (+ dat) to advise (12-2); to guess (7)

das **Rathaus, ⁻er** town hall; city hall (8-2)

der **Ratschlag, ⁻e** piece of advice (5)

die **Ratte, -n** rat (1)

rauchen to smoke (4-2)

Mir raucht der Kopf. I can't think straight anymore. (9)

das **Rauchen** smoking (7)

der **Raum, ⁻e** room (8)

raus·gehen, ging raus, ist rausgegangen to go out (8)

raus·kommen, kam raus, ist rausgekommen to come out (6)

raus·wachsen (wächst raus), wuchs raus, ist rausgewachsen to grow out (12)

reagieren (auf) to react (to) (4, 11-2)

real real (9)

die Realschule, -n college track secondary school (6)

recherchieren to do research (6-2)

der Rechner, - computer (3)

die Rechnung, -en bill (9-1)

recht right (adj) (4)

du hast recht you're right (4-2)

es allen recht machen trying to please everybody (10)

Es ist nicht recht, dass … It's not right that . . . (10)

das Recht right

rechtlich legal (12)

rechts right; to the right (4-2)

der Rechtsanwalt, ⸚e/die Rechtsanwältin, -nen lawyer (12)

die Rechtskurve, -n right curve (4)

rechtzeitig on time (6-2)

die Rede, -n speech; talk (11-1)

reden to speak, to talk (4-2)

reduziert reduced (7)

das Referat, -e (oral) report; paper (4-2)

das Reformhaus, ⸚er health food store (8, 9-2)

das Regal, -e shelf (6)

regelmäßig regular (11-1)

der Regen rain (2, 5-1)

der Regenschirm, -e (5)

das Regenwetter rainy weather (1)

die Regierung, -en government (11)

die Region, -en region (6-1)

regnen to rain (1-1)

Es regnet. It's raining. (1)

reich rich (1, 5-1)

reichen: Das reicht mir. That's enough for me. (10)

der Reichspräsident, -en, -en German president (before World War II) (11)

reif ripe (2)

die Reihenfolge sequence (7)

rein·gehen, ging rein, ist reingegangen to go in (6)

der Reis rice (4-1)

die Reise, -n trip (2, 3-1)

eine Reise machen to go on a trip,

to take a trip (5-1)

der Reisebegleiter, -/die Reisebegleiterin, -nen travel guide (6)

die Reisebroschüre, -n travel brochure (5)

das Reisebüro, -s travel agency (5-2)

reisen, reiste, ist gereist to travel (1-2)

reiten, ritt, ist geritten to ride (a horse) (10-1)

der Reiter, - horseback rider (10)

die Reklametafel, -n billboard (8)

der Rekord, -e record (9)

die Relativitätstheorie theory of relativity (6)

die Religion, -en religion (11)

rennen, rannte, ist gerannt to run (6-2)

renovieren to renovate (11-2)

die Rente, -n pension (12-2)

die Rentenversicherung, -en pension plan (12)

der Rentner, -/die Rentnerin, -nen pensioner (12)

reparieren to repair (4)

die Republik, -en republic (11-1)

das Requiem, Requien requiem (3)

reservieren to reserve (4)

respektlos disrespectful (5)

respektvoll respectful (5)

das Restaurant, -s restaurant (1)

restlich rest of the, remaining (11)

das Rezept, -e recipe (9-1)

rezeptfrei prescription-free (drugs) (9)

rezeptpflichtig prescription (drugs) (9)

der Rhabarber (sing) rhubarb (7)

der Rhein Rhine (river) (1)

das Rheintal Rhine valley (1)

richtig right; true (1-1); correct (4); really (9)

die Richtigkeit rightness, correctness (11)

riechen, roch, gerochen to smell (5, 12-2)

riesig huge (8, 10-2)

das Rind (sing) beef (6)

der Ring, -e ring (1, 7-2)

der Ringfinger, - ring finger (6)

risikolos risk-free (12)

riskieren to risk (8)

der Rock (sing) rock music (2)

der Rock, ⸚e skirt (2-2)

das Rockfest, -e rock festival (1)

die Rockgruppe, -n rock group (1)

der Rockstar, -s rock star (2)

die Rolle, -n role (9)

der Rollstuhl, ⸚e wheelchair (7-2)

der Roman, -e novel (5-2)

romantisch romantic (5-2)

rosarot pink (1-1)

die Rose, -n rose (1, 7-2)

rostfrei stainless (4)

rostig rusty (2)

rot red (1-1)

das Rote Kreuz the Red Cross (4)

der Rotkohl red cabbage (9)

der Rotwein, -e red wine (3)

der Rotzlümmel, - snotty-nosed brat (11)

die Rübe, -n turnip (4)

der Rücken, - back (6-1)

die Rückenschmerzen (pl) backache (6)

der Rucksack, ⸚e backpack (7-1)

die Rückseite, -n back (9)

der Rückspiegel, - rearview mirror (11-1)

rufen, rief, gerufen to call (9, 10-1)

die Ruhe peace and quiet (8)

in aller Ruhe in peace and quiet (10)

Lass mich in Ruhe! Stop bothering me! (4-2)

Ruhetag: Dienstag Ruhetag closed all day Tuesday (1)

ruhig calm, quiet (8-1)

das Rührei (sing) scrambled eggs (4-1)

der Rum rum (9-1)

rund round (6)

rund um around (10)

der Rüssel, - trunk (of an elephant) (9)

russisch (adj) Russian (7)

der Rutsch: Einen guten Rutsch (ins Neue Jahr)! Happy New Year! (7-1)

S

der Saal, Säle hall (9)

die Sache, -n thing (4, 7-2)

säen to sow (4)

der Saft, ⸚e juice (4)

saftig juicy (10-2)

die Säge, -n saw (tool) (10)

sagen to say, to tell (2-1)

sag mal say, tell me (1)

Wie sagt man das auf Deutsch? How do you say that in German? (4-1)

die Salami, -s salami (2-2)

der **Salat, -e** salad (4-1)

das **Salz** salt (1, 9-2)

salzig salty (2)

sammeln to collect (2-1)

die **Sammlung, -en** collection (10)

der **Samstag** Saturday (1-2) *(see also* **Dienstag***)*

die **Sandale, -n** sandal (3-2)

sandig sandy (2)

der **Sänger, -**/die **Sängerin, -nen** singer (5)

der **Sankt Nikolaus** Saint Nicholas (7)

die **Sardine, -n** sardine (8)

der **Satellit, -en** satellite (10-1)

satt full, satiated (8)

Ich bin satt. I'm full. (8)

Ich habe es satt, … I'm sick of . . ., I'm fed up with . . . (8-2)

satteln to saddle (10-1)

der **Satz, ⸚e** sentence (3)

der **Satzteil, -e** part of a sentence (11)

sauber clean (8-2)

sauer sour (1); annoyed (11)

der **Sauerbraten** marinated roast beef (9)

das **Sauerkraut** sauerkraut (4-1)

die **Sauna, -s** sauna (5-1)

das **Sauwetter** rotten weather (9)

die **S-Bahn** *commuter train* (5)

der **Scanner, -** scanner (3-1)

Schade! Too bad! (12-2)

das **Schaf, -e** sheep (10)

der **Schal, -e** scarf (8)

schälen to peel (9)

schamlos shameless (12)

scharf sharp (2); spicy, hot (9)

schattig shady (2)

das **Schaubild, -er** diagram; graph (11-1)

schauen (auf) to look (at) (7-1)

schaufeln to shovel (11)

der **Schaukelstuhl, ⸚e** rocking chair (8-2)

die **Scheibe, -n** slice (4-1)

eine Scheibe Brot a slice of bread (4-1)

der **Schein, -e** banknote, bill *(money)* (9-2)

scheinen, schien, geschienen to shine (1-1)

die **Scheißmusik** shitty music (11)

schenken to give *(a gift)* (7-1)

die **Schere, -n** scissors (9)

schick chic (2-2)

schicken to send (6-2)

schief crooked; leaning (10)

schießen, schoss, geschossen to shoot (7, 11-1)

das **Schiff, -e** ship (2)

der **Schilling, -** shilling *(former Austrian currency)* (2)

die **Schinkenwurst** ham sausage (9)

schlafen (schläft), schlief, geschlafen to sleep (3-2)

schlaflos sleepless (12)

die **Schlafmöglichkeit, -en** place to sleep (4)

der **Schlafsack, ⸚e** sleeping bag (12-2)

die **Schlaftablette, -n** sleeping pill (4)

das **Schlafzimmer, -** bedroom (8-1)

schlagen (schlägt), schlug, geschlagen to hit; to beat (9)

schlank slim (2-1)

schlau crafty, clever (10-1)

schlecht bad (1-2)

schleimig slimy (2)

schleppen to drag (5-1)

schließen, schloss, geschlossen to close (1, 11-1)

schließlich finally (10-2)

Schlittschuhlaufen gehen to go (ice) skating (1)

das **Schloss, ⸚er** castle (5-1)

der **Schlosser, -** toolmaker (6)

schlüpfrig slippery (2)

schmal slim, narrow; *(face)* thin (6)

schmecken to taste; to taste good (9-2)

der **Schmerz, -en** pain (6-2)

das **Schminken** face painting (4)

(sich) schminken to put on make-up (9-2)

der **Schmuck** jewelry (7-2)

schmutzig dirty (8-2)

der **Schnabel, ⸚** mouth *(slang)* (11)

der **Schnaps, ⸚e** schnapps; hard liquor (10)

schnarchen to snore (4)

die **Schnecke, -n** snail (9)

der **Schnee** snow (4-2)

der **Schneesturm, ⸚e** snowstorm (12)

schneeweiß snow-white (11)

schneiden, schnitt, geschnitten to cut (6-2)

der **Schneider, -** tailor (7)

die **Schneiderin, -nen** seamstress (7)

schneien to snow (1, 4-2)

Es schneit. It's snowing. (1)

schnell fast, quick (E, 3-1)

der **Schnellimbiss, -e** fast-food stand (5-2)

das **Schnitzel, -** cutlet (7)

das Wiener Schnitzel breaded veal cutlet (7)

der **Schnupfen** cold (11)

der **Schnurrbart, ⸚e** mustache (5-2)

der **Schock** shock (11-2)

schockiert shocked (7-2)

die **Schokolade** chocolate (1, 2-2)

eine Tafel Schokolade a chocolate bar (10)

schon already (2-2)

schon gut it's all right (9)

schon wieder again (E)

schön nice; beautiful (E, 1-1)

die **Schönheit** beauty (11)

der **Schopf, ⸚e** top *(of a turnip)* (4)

der **Schoß, ⸚e** lap (9)

der **Schrank, ⸚e** closet (8-1)

nicht alle Tassen im Schrank haben to be crazy (8)

der **Schrebergarten, ⸚** garden plot at the edge of town (8)

schrecklich awful(ly), terrible; terribly (11-2)

schreiben, schrieb, geschrien to write (E, 1-1)

der **Schreiber, -** scribe (10)

der **Schreibtisch, -e** desk (8-1)

das **Schreibzeug, -e** writing utensil (3)

schreien, schrie, geschrien to scream; to shout (10-2)

die **Schrift, -en** writing (10)

schriftlich in writing; written (4-2)

die **Schrittgeschwindigkeit** *(sing)* walking speed (12)

der **Schuh, -e** shoe (1, 2-2)

das **Schuhgeschäft, -e** shoe store (2)

der **Schuhmacher, -**/die **Schuhmacherin, -nen** shoemaker (10-1)

der **Schulabschluss** high school graduation (12)

die **Schulbank: die Schulbank drücken** to sit in school (11)

der **Schulbeginn** beginning of school (1)

die **Schuld, -en** debt; blame (3-2)

schulden to owe (7-1)

der **Schuldschein, -e** IOU (7-1)

die **Schule, -n** school (1, 2-1)

der **Schüler, -**/die **Schülerin, -nen** pupil; student in a primary or secondary school (2-1)

die **Schulter, -n** shoulder (1, 6-1)

die **Schulzeit** schooldays *(pl)* (7)

die **Schüssel, -n** bowl (4-1)
  eine Schüssel Müsli a bowl of muesli (4-1)
schütteln to shake (10)
  den Kopf schütteln to shake one's head (10-2)
schütten to spill (9)
der **Schutz** (*sing*) protection (4)
schützen to protect (4)
schwach weak (6-2)
die **Schwäche, -n** weakness (6-2)
der **Schwan, -̈e** swan (1)
schwanger pregnant (6)
schwarz black (1-1)
  das **Schwarze Brett** bulletin board (6)
  am Schwarzen Brett on the bulletin board (6-2)
das **Schwarzbrot** rye bread (7)
der **Schwarzwald** Black Forest (1)
die **Schwarzwälder Kirschtorte** Black Forest cake (10)
schwedisch (*adj*) Swedish (2)
das **Schwein, -e** pig (10)
  Du hast Schwein gehabt. You were lucky. (10)
der **Schweinebraten** pork roast (9)
die **Schweinerei, -en** mess (7)
der **Schweinestall, -̈e** pigsty (4)
  Was für ein Schweinestall! What a pigsty! (4-1)
der **Schweiß** sweat (9)
die **Schweiz** Switzerland (1-1)
der **Schweizer, -/die Schweizerin, -nen** Swiss (*person*) (1-1)
schweizerisch (*adj*) Swiss (4)
schwer hard; heavy (6-2)
  eine schwere Erkältung a bad cold (12-2)
die **Schwester, -n** sister (1, 3-1)
schwimmen, schwamm, ist geschwommen to swim (1, 2-1)
  schwimmen gehen to go swimming (1, 2-1)
schwül humid (1)
das **Schwyzerdütsch** Swiss German (8)
(die) **Sciencefiction** science fiction (3)
das **Scrabble** Scrabble (2)
der **See, -n** lake (5-1)
die **See, -n** sea (11-2)
seekrank seasick (6)
das **Segelboot, -e** sailboat (3)
segeln to sail (1)
sehen (sieht), sah, gesehen to see (3-2); to look (12-1)

sehenswert worth seeing (11)
sehr very (1-2)
die **Seife, -n** soap (9-2)
die **Seifenoper, -n** soap opera (5-2)
sein, sein, seine his, its (2)
sein (ist), war, ist gewesen to be (E)
  Ich bin's. It's me. (5-2)
seit (*prep + dat*) since (2); for (7)
  seit kurzem recently (11-1)
  seit kurzer Zeit recently (11-1)
die **Seite, -n** page (7); side (8)
der **Sekretär, -e/die Sekretärin, -nen** secretary (5)
die **Sekunde, -n** second (1, 2-1)
selber myself; yourself; herself; etc. (3)
selbst myself, yourself, herself, etc. (2, 4-2)
  von selbst by oneself (7)
selbstgemacht homemade (7)
selbstlos selfless (12)
der **Selbstmord, -e** suicide (11)
selten seldom, rarely (2, 4-2)
seltsam strange (9)
das **Semester, -** semester (1-1)
die **Semesterferien** (*pl*) vacation (7)
das **Seminar, -e** seminar (4-2)
der **Senf** mustard (7, 9-2)
der **Senior, -en** senior citizen (3)
die **Sensation, -en** sensation (3)
sentimental sentimental (5-2)
der **September** September (1-2)
der **Service** service (10-2)
servieren to serve (*a dish*) (5, 9-1)
die **Serviette, -n** napkin, serviette (9-1)
Servus! Hello! Hi! Good-bye! So long! (*Austrian*) (E)
der **Sessel, -** armchair (8-1)
das **Set, -s** place mat (2)
setzen to set (3)
sich setzen to sit down (9-2)
das **Shampoo** shampoo (9-2)
der **Shootingstar, -s** suddenly successful person (2)
die **Shorts** (*pl*) shorts (2-2)
die **Show, -s** show (12)
  eine Show ab·ziehen to put on a show (12)
sicher sure, certainly; probably (5, 8-2)
die **Sicherheit** (*sing*) safety (6)
sichern to secure (12)
das **Siegel, -** seal (4)
die **Signatur, -en** signature (4)
signieren to sign (7)

das **Silber** silver (4)
silbern silver (3)
(der) **Silvester** New Year's Eve (7-1)
die **Sinfonie, -n** symphony (8)
das **Sinfonieorchester, -** symphony orchestra (3)
singen, sang, gesungen to sing (1)
der **Sinn** (*sing*) meaning (1); sense (4)
die **Sinologie** Chinese Studies (4)
die **Sitte, -n** custom (9)
der **Sitz, -e** seat (3)
sitzen, saß, gesessen to sit (1-2)
der **Sitzplatz, -̈e** seat (7)
(das) **Skandinavien** Scandinavia (11)
der **Skelettsatz, -̈e** skeleton sentence (8)
der **Sketch, -es** skit (10-1)
der **Ski, -er** ski (1)
Ski laufen (läuft Ski), lief Ski, ist Ski gelaufen to ski (3)
das **Skilaufen** (*sing*) skiing (1)
Skilaufen gehen to go skiing (1)
der **Skilehrer, -/die Skilehrerin, -nen** ski instructor (1)
die **Skizze, -n** sketch (*drawing*) (10)
skrupellos unscrupulous (12)
die **Skulptur, -en** sculpture (8-2)
der **Smoking, -s** tuxedo (2)
snowboarden gehen to go snowboarding (2-1)
so so, such (1)
so ein (ein, eine) such a (2)
so ... wie as . . . as (2-2)
sobald as soon as (*sub conj*) (4-2)
die **Socke, -n** sock (2-2)
das **Sofa, -s** sofa (3)
sofort immediately, right away; in a minute (6-2)
das **Softdrink, -s** soft drink (2, 9-1)
das **Softeis** soft ice cream (10)
die **Software** software (11-2)
der **Softwareentwickler, -/die Softwareentwicklerin, -nen** software developer (12)
sogar even (2, 7-2)
der **Sohn, -̈e** son (1, 3-1)
solange (*sub conj*) as long as (10, 12-1)
so lang(e) (*adv*) so long (2); in the meantime (5)
solcher, solches, solche such (7)
der **Soldat, -en, -en/die Soldatin, -nen** soldier (4)
sollen, sollte, gesollt to be supposed to, should (4)
der **Sommer, -** summer (1-2)

die **Sommerferien** *(pl)* summer holidays, summer vacation (5)

der **Sommerschlussverkauf**, ¨e summer clearance sale (7-1)

sondern *(coord conj)* but; (but) . . . instead; but rather (1-2)

der **Song**, **-s** song (3)

die **Sonne** sun (1-1)

die **Sonnenbrille**, **-n** sunglasses (7-1)

die **Sonnencreme**, **-s** suntan lotion (4)

sonnig sunny (2)

der **Sonntag**, **-e** Sunday (1-2) *(see also* **Dienstag**)

sonst apart from that (12); otherwise, or else (9)

  was ... sonst what else (8)

sooft *(sub conj)* as often as (10)

sorgen für to care for (12-1)

sorgfältig careful(ly) (10-2)

sorglos carefree (12)

die **Soße**, **-n** sauce (4, 9-1)

sowieso anyway (4, 8-1)

die **Sowjetunion** Soviet Union (11)

der **Sozialarbeiter**, **-**/die **Sozialarbeiterin**, **-nen** social worker (2)

der **Sozialfall**, ¨e welfare case (12)

die **Soziologie** sociology (9)

der **Spaceshuttle**, **-s** space shuttle (4)

die **Spaghetti** *(pl)* spaghetti (3)

die **Spalte**, **-n** column (12)

spalten to split (11)

das **Spanferkel** *(sing)* suckling pig (9)

(das) **Spanisch** Spanish *(language)* (4)

spanisch *(adj)* Spanish (2)

sparen to save (6-2)

das **Sparkonto**, **-s** savings account (12-2)

sparsam thrifty (5)

der **Spaß** fun, enjoyment (1)

  Es macht mir Spaß, ... I enjoy . . . (8-2)

  Spaß haben to have fun (5-1)

spät late (4-1)

  Wie spät ist es? What time is it? (2-2)

später: Bis später! See you later! (1-1)

der **Spaziergang**, ¨e walk (7)

  einen Spaziergang machen to go for a walk (7)

spazieren gehen, ging spazieren, ist spazieren gegangen to go for a walk (4-2)

der **Speck** *(sing)* bacon (4)

die **Speise(n)karte**, **-n** menu (9-1)

der **Speisesaal**, **Speisesäle** dining hall, refectory (1)

spekulieren to speculate (7)

die **Spende**, **-n** donation (9)

spenden to donate (4)

spendieren *(+ dat)* to buy *(for someone)* (12)

die **Spezialität**, **-en** specialty (3)

der **Spiegel**, **-** mirror (9-2)

das **Spiegelei**, **-er** fried egg (sunny-side up) (4-1)

spielen to play (1-2)

der **Spielraum** *(sing)* leeway (3)

die **Spielsucht** gambling addiction (12)

die **Spielwaren** *(pl)* toys (7)

die **Spielwarenfabrik**, **-en** toy factory (7)

das **Spielwarengeschäft**, **-e** toy store (7)

das **Spielzeug** toy (3, 10-2)

der **Spinat** spinach (10)

spinnen, spann, gesponnen to be crazy (8)

spitze great (2)

  echt spitze really great (2-2)

der **Sport** sport(s), athletics (1-2)

  Sport machen to do sports (1-2)

  Was für Sport machst du? What sports do you do? (1-2)

die **Sportabteilung**, **-en** sporting goods department (10)

das **Sportcoupé**, **-s** sport coupe (3)

das **Sportgeschäft**, **-e** sporting goods store (2)

sportlich athletic (1-2); sporty (2)

das **Sportprogramm**, **-e** sports program (1)

die **Sportreportage**, **-n** sports report (3)

die **Sprache**, **-n** language (3-2)

die **Sprachnotiz**, **-en** note on language *(usage)* (E)

sprechen (spricht), sprach, gesprochen to speak, to talk (2, 3-2)

springen, sprang, ist gesprungen to jump (8)

das **Spülbecken**, **-** sink (8-1)

das **Squash** squash *(sport)* (2)

der **Staat**, **-en** state (5, 11-1)

der **Staatschef**, **-s**/die **Staatschefin**, **-nen** head of state (11)

die **Staatskasse**, **-n** state treasury (10)

das **Stadion, Stadien** stadium (5)

die **Stadt**, ¨e city, town (1, 2-2)

  in die Stadt to town (3)

der **Stadtplan**, ¨e map of the city/town (8-2)

der **Stadtteil**, **-e** district, part of the city/town (8-2)

das **Stadtzentrum** city center (5)

der **Stahl** steel (4)

der **Stall**, ¨e stable (10-1)

der **Stamm**, ¨e tree trunk (7)

  Der Apfel fällt nicht weit vom Stamm. Like father, like son. (7)

der **Stammbaum**, ¨e family tree (6-1)

der **Stand** *(sing)* social status (12)

ständig constant(ly) (12-1)

stark strong (6-2)

  stark reduziert sharply reduced (7-1)

die **Stärke**, **-n** strength (6-2)

der **Starnberger See** *(lake south of Munich)* (4)

starten, startete, hat gestartet to start *(e.g., a motor)*

starten, startete, ist gestartet to start; to take off *(of airplanes)* (6-2)

die **Statistik**, **-en** statistic (12-1)

statt instead of (7, 8-2); *(+ gen)* (12-2)

der **Staubsauger**, **-** vacuum cleaner (8-2)

das **Steak**, **-s** steak (10-2)

stecken in to put in, to stick in (10-1)

  die Nase zu tief ins Glas stecken to drink too much (6)

stehen, stand, gestanden to stand; to be standing (1-2); to say (6-2)

  Diese Jacke steht dir. This jacket looks good on you. (7-2)

stehen bleiben, blieb stehen, ist stehen geblieben to stop *(walking)* (10-1)

die **Stehlampe**, **-n** floor lamp (8-1)

stehlen (stiehlt), stahl, gestohlen to steal (11)

steif stiff (9-1)

steigen, stieg, ist gestiegen to climb (10-1)

die **Stelle**, **-n** job, position (12-2); place (12)

stellen to put *(in an upright position)* (8-1)

  eine Frage stellen to ask a question (7-2)

sterben (stirbt), starb, ist gestorben to die (4, 6-2)

die **Stereoanlage**, **-n** stereo (8-1)

der **Stern**, **-e** star (11)

das **Steuer(rad)** steering wheel (11-1)

das **Stichwort, ⸚er** key word (12)

der **Stiefel, -** boot (12-1)

die **Stiefmutter, ⸚** stepmother (3-1)

der **Stiefvater, ⸚** stepfather (3-1)

der **Stil, -e** style (8)

die **Stimme, -n** voice; vote (12-1)

stimmen to be right (4)

  Das stimmt. That's right. (4-1)

stinkig stinky (2)

stinklangweilig deadly boring (3)

die **Stirn, -en** forehead (6-1)

der **Stocherkahn, ⸚e** punting boat (1)

der **Stock, ⸚e** stick (10)

der **Stock, Stockwerke** floor, story (8, 10-2)

  im ersten Stock on the second floor (10)

der **Stoffbär, -en, -en** stuffed bear (7)

das **Stofftier, -e** stuffed animal (7-2)

stoppen to stop (6-2)

stören to disturb (8-2)

der **Strafzettel, -** *(traffic)* ticket (12-2)

der **Strand, ⸚e** beach (1, 5-1)

die **Straße, -n** street (E, 2-2)

streichen, strich, gestrichen to paint *(e.g., a fence, a house)* (6-2)

der **Stress** stress (4-2)

stressig stressful (8)

strikt strict (8)

der **Strumpf, ⸚e** stocking (11)

das **Stück, -e** piece (3, 4-1)

  ein Stück Torte a piece of layer cake (3, 4-1)

  drei Stück Kuchen three pieces of cake (4)

  fünf Euro das Stück five euros apiece (7)

  Stück für Stück bit by bit (11)

der **Student, -en, -en**/die **Studentin, -nen** student (1-1)

der **Studentenausweis, -e** student ID (5-2)

der **Studentenchor, ⸚e** student choir (6)

das **Studentenheim, -e** dormitory, student residence (E, 2-2)

das **Studentenleben** student life (6)

das **Studentenwerk** student center (E, 6-2)

das **Studienfach, ⸚er** field of study; subject (2-2)

studieren to study *(i.e., to attend college or university)* (1-1)

das **Studium** *(sing)* studies (10)

der **Stuhl, ⸚e** chair (2, 8-1)

jemand *(dat)* **den Stuhl vor die Tür setzen** to throw somebody out (8)

die **Stunde, -n** hour (2-1)

  eine Stunde lang for an hour (4)

  pro Stunde per hour (6)

stundenlang for hours (2-1)

der **Stundenplan, ⸚e** schedule, timetable (2-2)

der **Sturm, ⸚e** storm (12-2)

stürmisch stormy (6)

stürzen to fall; to plunge (10)

stylen to style (2)

die **Suche: auf der Suche sein** to be searching (10)

suchen to look for (2-2)

süchtig addicted (12)

süddeutsch *(adj)* Southern German (7)

der **Süden** south (8)

südlich (von) south (of) (11)

der **Südpol** South Pole (1)

die **Südseeinsel, -n** South Sea island (9)

super super (E)

der **Superlativ, -e** superlative (5)

der **Supermarkt, ⸚e** supermarket (7-2)

supersüß very sweet (3)

die **Suppe, -n** soup (2)

  ein Haar in der Suppe finden to find fault with something (9)

das **Surfbrett, -er** surfboard (4)

surfen to surf (6)

  surfen gehen to go surfing (1)

süß sweet (10)

die **Süßigkeiten** *(pl)* candy; sweets (6, 7-2)

das **Sweatshirt, -s** sweatshirt (1, 2-2)

das **Symbol, -e** symbol (4)

die **Synagoge, -n** synagogue (11)

das **Synonym, -e** synonym (10)

das **System, -e** system (6-2)

die **Szene, -n** scene (2-1)

T

die **Tabelle, -n** chart, table (10-2)

die **Tablette, -n** pill, tablet (12-2)

die **Tafel, -n** (black)board (4-2)

  eine Tafel Schokolade a chocolate bar (10)

der **Tag, -e** day (E, 1-2)

  eines Tages one day; someday (10-2)

  Guten Tag! Tag! Hello! (E-1)

  Tag der Arbeit Labor Day (7)

  Tag der Deutschen Einheit Day of German Reunification (7)

Tag der Fahne Flag Day (7)

vierzehn Tage two weeks (1, 5-1)

das **Tagebuch, ⸚er** diary (6-2)

der **Tageshöchstsatz** maximum daily rate (8)

der **Tagesjob, -s** job for a day (6)

das **Tagesmenü, -s** special of the day (10)

die **Tageszeitung, -en** daily newspaper (10)

täglich daily (2)

taktlos tactless (5)

taktvoll tactful (5)

das **Tal, ⸚er** valley (5-1)

das **Talent, -e** talent (10-2)

talentlos untalented (12)

die **Talkshow, -s** talk show (4)

der **Tango, -s** tango (2)

die **Tante, -n** aunt (3-1)

tanzen to dance (1-2)

der **Tänzer, -**/die **Tänzerin, -nen** dancer (2)

die **Tasche, -n** bag; pocket (4-2)

das **Taschenmesser, -** pocket knife (4-2)

der **Taschenrechner, -** calculator (E)

die **Tasse, -n** cup (4-1)

  eine Tasse Kaffee a cup of coffee (4-1)

  nicht alle Tassen im Schrank haben to be crazy (8)

die **Tastatur, -en** *(computer)* keyboard (3-1)

die **Tätigkeit, -en** activity (12)

die **Tätowierung, -en** tattoo (5)

tatsächlich actual(ly) (12-1)

das **Tausend, -e** thousand (4)

der **Tausendfüßler, -** millipede (9)

das **Taxi, -s** taxi (4)

die **Technik** technology (8-2)

technisch technical (12)

der **Teddybär, -en, -en** teddy bear (2)

der **Tee** tea (2-1)

die **Teekanne, -n** teapot (1, 9-1)

der **Teekessel, -** tea kettle (1, 7-2)

der **Teelöffel, -** teaspoon (9-1)

der **Teenager, -** teenager (4)

der **Teig** batter; dough (9-1)

der **Teil, -e** part, area (8-2)

teilen to divide (11-1)

teil·nehmen (nimmt teil), nahm teil, teilgenommen (an + *dat)* to take part (in) (9)

das **Telefon, -e** telephone (E)

das **Telefonbuch, ⸚er** telephone book (E)

das **Telefongespräch, -e** telephone conversation (5)

telefonieren (mit) to talk on the phone (with) (2-1)

die **Telefonnummer, -n** telephone number (E)

das **Teleskop, -e** telescope (1)

der **Teller, -** plate (5, 9-1)

die **Temperatur, -en** temperature (5)

das **Tennis** tennis (1)

Tennis spielen to play tennis (2-1)

der **Tennisklub, -s** tennis club (10)

das **Tennismatch, -es** tennis match (10)

der **Tennisplatz, -̈e** tennis court (4)

der **Tennisschläger, -** tennis racquet (7-2)

der **Tennisschuh, -e** tennis shoe (3)

der **Tenor, -̈e** tenor (2)

der **Teppich, -e** carpet, rug (3, 8-1)

die **Terrasse, -n** terrace, patio (8-1)

teuer expensive (2-2)

der **Teufel, -** devil (8)

den Teufel an die Wand malen to tempt fate (8)

der **Text, -e** text (7)

das **Theater, -** theater (1)

ins Theater to the theater (1-2)

die **Theaterkarte, -n** theater ticket (4)

das **Theaterstück, -e** play (8)

das **Thema, Themen** topic (10-2)

die **Theorie, -n** theory (3)

die **Therapie, -n** therapy (12-2)

das **Thermometer, -** thermometer (1)

tief deep; low (11-2)

die Nase zu tief ins Glas stecken to drink too much (6)

das **Tier, -e** animal (4, 7-2)

der **Tipp, -s** tip (*helpful hint*) (10)

tipptopp tiptop (4)

der **Tisch, -e** table (5, 8-1)

den Tisch decken to set the table (7-1)

der **Titel, -** title (7-2)

der **Toast** toast (4-1)

der **Toaster, -** toaster (7)

die **Tochter, -̈** daughter (1, 3-1)

der **Tod** death (5)

die **Todesanzeige, -n** death announcement (10)

die **Toilette, -n** lavatory (8-1)

tolerieren to tolerate (11)

toll fantastic, neat (1-1)

Das ist echt toll. That's really fantastic. (3-1)

die **Tomate, -n** tomato (1)

die **Tomatensoße** tomato sauce (5)

der **Ton, -̈e** tone; sound; note (2)

der **Toner** toner (12)

der **Topf, -̈e** pot (9-1)

das **Tor, -e** gate (9)

die **Torte, -n** layer cake (4-1)

ein Stück Torte a piece of layer cake (4-1)

tot dead (3-2)

total completely (1)

der **Totenschein, -e** death certificate (7)

der **Tourist, -en, -en/die Touristin, -nen** tourist (2, 5-2)

die **Touristenattraktion, -en** tourist attraction (5)

tragen (trägt), trug, getragen to wear (3-2); to carry (8)

der **Traum, -̈e** dream (12-2)

der **Traumberuf, -e** job of one's dreams (12)

träumen to dream (12-2)

(sich) treffen (trifft), traf, getroffen to meet (9-2)

der **Trend, -s** trend (12-1)

trennen to separate (11-1)

die **Treppe, -n** staircase (8-1)

trinkbar drinkable (12)

trinken, trank, getrunken to drink (2-2)

das **Trinkgeld, -er** tip (*in a restaurant*) (9-1)

der **Triumph, -e** triumph (12-1)

trocken dry (5-1)

sich (*dat*) **die Haare trocknen** to dry one's hair (9-2)

die **Trompete, -n** trumpet (2)

tropfen to drip (11)

trotz (*prep + gen*) in spite of (12-2)

trotzdem anyway; nevertheless (4, 5-2)

das **T-Shirt, -s** T-shirt (2-2)

Tschüss! Good-bye! So long! (E-1)

die **Tulpe, -n** tulip (1)

der **Turm, -̈e** tower (9)

tun, tat, getan to do (1-2)

Er tut dir nichts. He won't hurt you. (9-1)

Es tut mir leid. I'm sorry. (7-2)

die **Tür, -en** door (8-1)

jemand (*dat*) **den Stuhl vor die Tür setzen** to throw someone out (8)

der **Türke, -n, -n/die Türkin, -nen** Turk (2)

türkisch (*adj*) Turkish (2)

die **Tussi, -s** hussy (12)

der **Typ, -en** guy (7-2)

typisch typical(ly) (4-2)

U

üben to practice (6-2)

über (*prep + acc/dat*) about (2); across (1); over, above (6); via (6)

überfallen (überfällt), überfiel, überfallen to attack; to invade (11)

überfluten to flood (11)

der **Übergang, -̈e** crossing (11)

übergeschnappt crazy (11-2)

überhaupt at all; anyway (11)

überhaupt nicht not at all (11-2)

überhaupt nichts nothing at all (11-2)

überlassen (überlässt), überließ, überlassen to leave to (11)

überleben to survive (10)

überlegen to think about (12)

übermorgen the day after tomorrow (3-2)

übernachten to spend the night; to stay overnight (5-2)

die **Übernachtung, -en** overnight accommodation (6)

übernehmen (übernimmt), übernahm, übernommen to assume (*a role*) (12); to take on (*a duty*) (12-1)

die **Überraschung, -en** surprise (7-1)

überreden to persuade (12)

überregional national, nationwide (10)

über·schnappen, ist übergeschnappt to go crazy (11-2)

übersetzen to translate (6-2)

der **Übersetzer, -/die Übersetzerin, -nen** translator (9)

die **Übersetzung, -en** translation (10-1)

überzeugen to convince (12)

übrigens by the way (1-2)

die **Übung, -en** exercise; seminar; lab (2-2)

die **Uhr, -en** clock; watch (2-1)

zehn Uhr ten o'clock (2-1)

um zehn Uhr at ten o'clock (2-1)

um wie viel Uhr? (at) what time? (2-2)

Wie viel Uhr ist es? What time is it? (2-2)

die **Uhrzeit, -en** time of day (7)

um (*prep + acc*) at (2); around (5)

um zehn at ten o'clock (2-2)

um die Ecke around the corner (5)

um ... zu in order to (8)

die **Umfrage, -n** survey, poll (5, 10-2)

das **Umland** *(sing)* surrounding area (11)

umliegend surrounding (8)

sich **um·schauen (nach)** to look around (for) (10)

um·steigen, stieg um, ist umgestiegen to change trains (4)

um·stellen to rearrange (8-1)

um·tauschen to exchange (7-2)

die **Umwelt** environment (12-2)

um·ziehen, zog um, ist umgezogen to move *(change residence)* (8-1)

sich **um·ziehen, zog um, hat umgezogen** to change *(one's clothes)* (9-2)

der **Umzug, ⁻e** move *(change of residence)* (12-2)

unaufhörlich constantly (11-1)

unbedingt really (12)

unbewohnbar uninhabitable (12)

und *(coord conj)* and (E, 1-2)

undankbar ungrateful (12)

undefinierbar indefinable (12)

uneben uneven (2)

unehrlich dishonest (12-1)

unerhört outrageous (11)

der **Unfall, ⁻e** accident (11)

unfreundlich (3)

ungesund unhealthy (4-2)

unglücklich unhappy (7-2)

unheimlich tremendously, immensely (11)

unhöflich impolite (7-2)

die **Uni, -s** university (1-1)
  zur Uni to the university (2-2)

der **Uni-Abschluss** graduation (7)

die **Universität, -en** university (1-1)

das **Universitätsleben** *(sing)* university life (2-2)

die **Universitätsstadt, ⁻e** university town (8)

unkontrollierbar uncontrollable (12)

das **Unkraut** weeds (6)

unkultiviert uncultivated (9)

unmöglich impossible (4-2)

unordentlich messy, sloppy (4-2)

unregelmäßig irregular (11-1)

unser, unser, unsere our (1)

unten below (8, 10-2)
  dort unten down there (8)
  hier unten down here (10)
  von unten from the bottom (12)

unter *(prep + acc/dat)* under, below (4); among (9)

unterbrechen (unterbricht), unterbrach, unterbrochen to interrupt (12-1)

sich **unterhalten (unterhält), unterhielt, unterhalten** to talk; to converse (10-2)

die **Unterkunft, ⁻e** (living) accommodation (8)

der **Unterschied, -e** difference (12-1)

unterschiedlich different (3, 12-1)

unterstreichen, unterstrich, unterstrichen to underline (7, 10-1)

die **Untertasse, -n** saucer (9-1)

unterwegs on the way (10-2)

unübersetzbar untranslatable (12)

unvorstellbar unimaginable (12)

unzufrieden dissatisfied (10-2)

up to date up-to-date (1)

uralt ancient (10)

die **Urgroßeltern** *(pl)* great-grandparents (6-1)

die **Urgroßmutter, ⁻** great-grandmother (6-1)

der **Urgroßvater, ⁻** great-grandfather (6-1)

der **Urlaub** vacation *(generally of people in the work force)* (5-1)
  Urlaub machen to go on vacation (5-1)

ursprünglich originally (10)

usw. (und so weiter) etc. (et cetera, and so on) (E, 8-2)

die **Utopie, -n** utopia (12-1)

die **UV-Strahlen** *(pl)* UV rays (7)

V

(der) **Valentinstag** Valentine's Day (7-2)

das **Vanilleeis** vanilla ice cream (9)

die **Vanillesoße** vanilla sauce (9)

die **Vase, -n** vase (1)

der **Vater, ⁻** father (E, 3-1)

der **Vatertag, -e** Father's Day (7-2)

väterlich fatherly (2)

väterlicherseits paternal (6-1)

der **Vati** dad (5)

der **Vegetarier, -/die Vegetarierin, -nen** vegetarian (4, 9-2)

vegetarisch vegetarian (9-2)

(das) **Venedig** Venice (10)

die **Venus** Venus (5)

der **Veranstaltungstechniker, -/die Veranstaltungstechnikerin, -nen** event technician (2)

das **Verb, -en** verb (1)

der **Verband, ⁻e** association (4)

verbessern to improve; to correct (6-2)

verbittert bitter, embittered (5)

verbringen, verbrachte, verbracht to spend *(time)* (7-1)

verdanken *(+ dat)* to owe (10)

verdienen to earn (3-1)

Vereinbarung: nach Vereinbarung by appointment (6)

die **Vereinigten Staaten (die USA)** the United States (the U.S.) (1-1)

die **Verfassung, -en** constitution (12-1)

Verflixt! Darn it! (10-2)

vergangen past (8)

vergessen (vergisst), vergaß, vergessen to forget (3, 4-2)

der **Vergleich, -e** comparison (5)
  im Vergleich zu in comparison with (12-1)

vergnügt happy, in a good mood (10)

verhaften to arrest (11-1)

das **Verhalten** *(sing)* behavior (11)

verheiratet married (3-1)

verhören to interrogate (8)

verkaufen to sell (3-2)

der **Verkäufer, -/die Verkäuferin, -nen** sales clerk, salesman/saleswoman (3-2)

das **Verkehrszeichen, -** traffic sign (4)

verlassen (verlässt), verließ, verlassen to leave (8)

verlaufen (verläuft), verlief, ist verlaufen to happen, to run (12)

sich **verlieben in** *(+ acc)* to fall in love with (5, 11-2)

verliebt in love (2)

verlieren, verlor, verloren to lose (10-2)

vermieten to rent (out) (8-2)

der **Vermieter, -/die Vermieterin, -nen** landlord/landlady (9)

verrecken to croak, to die (8)

verrückt crazy; insane (5-2)

versalzen too salty (9-2)

versammeln to gather (11)

verschieben, verschob, verschoben to postpone (10-2)

verschieden different (7-1); various (9)

verschwenderisch wasteful (5)

versichern to insure (12)

die **Versicherung, -en** insurance (12-2)

versorgen to supply (11)

sich **verspäten** to be late (9-2)

versprechen (verspricht), versprach, versprochen to promise (3-2)

das **Verständnis** *(sing)* understanding (4)

verstecken to hide (10-1)

(das) **Verstecken** hide-and-seek (10)

verstehen, verstand, verstanden to understand (3-1)

das **Verstehen** understanding (1)

verstümmelt crippled (6)

versuchen to try (5, 8-2)

vertreten to represent (6)

die **Verwaltung, -en** administration (6)

verwandt related (1)

der/die **Verwandte, -n** relative (3-1)

die **Verwandschaft** relatives *(as a group)* (12)

verwendbar usable (12)

verwenden to use (8, 9-1)

verwirrt confused (9)

verwundert astonished (6)

sich **verziehen, verzog, verzogen** to withdraw (11)

vespern to snack (9)

der **Vetter, -n** *(male)* cousin (3-1)

das **Video, -s** video (3)

die **Videokamera, -s** video camera (10)

der **Videokassettenrecorder, -** video cassette recorder (3)

viel much; a lot (E, 1-1)

viel zu viel far too much (3-1)

viele many (1)

vielleicht perhaps (2-2)

viert: wir kommen zu viert the four of us are coming (8)

das **Viertel** quarter (2)

Viertel nach elf quarter after eleven (2)

Viertel vor elf quarter to eleven (2)

die **Viertelstunde** quarter hour (8)

die **Villa, Villen** villa (10)

violett purple (1-1)

der **Violinist, -en, -en**/die **Violinistin, -nen** violinist (3)

der **Virus, Viren** virus (11-2)

das **Vitamin, -e** vitamin (4)

der **Vogel, ⁻** bird (2, 11-2)

die **Vokabeln** *(pl)* vocabulary (1)

voll full (1, 7-1)

den Mund voll nehmen to talk big (6)

der **Volleyball, ⁻e** volleyball (1)

die **Vollkaskoversicherung, -en** comprehensive auto insurance (12)

vollständig complete (8)

von *(prep + dat)* from (E); of (E)

von ... bis from . . . to (1-2)

von jetzt ab from now on (6)

von Montag ab from Monday on (4-2)

vor *(prep + acc/dat)* in front of; before (4); ago (7)

vor allem above all (4-1)

vor dem Fernseher in front of the TV (4-2)

vorbei sein to be over (10)

die **Vorderseite, -n** front (9)

der **Vorfahr, -en, -en** ancestor (6-1)

vor·geben (gibt vor), gab vor, vorgegeben to set *(in advance)* (9)

vorgestern the day before yesterday (3-2)

vor·haben (hat vor), hatte vor, vorgehabt to plan, to have planned (4-2)

der **Vorhang, ⁻e** curtain (11)

der **Eiserne Vorhang** the Iron Curtain (11)

vorher before *(adv)* (6-1)

vor·lesen (liest vor), las vor, vorgelesen to read aloud (10)

die **Vorlesung, -en** lecture (1-1)

in die Vorlesung to lectures (1-2)

der **Vormittag, -e** morning (4)

vormittags in the morning (2)

der **Vorname, -ns, -n** first name (3-2)

das **Vorrecht, -e** privilege (12)

der **Vorsatz, ⁻e** resolution (9)

die **Vorschau** preview (1)

der **Vorschlag, ⁻e** suggestion (7)

Vorsicht! Careful! (10)

die **Vorspeise, -n** hors d'œuvre (9-2)

sich (etwas) **vor·stellen** to imagine (something) (11-2)

der **Vorteil, -e** advantage (8-2)

die **Vorwahl** area code (E)

der **Vulkan, -e** volcano (2)

W

die **Waage, -n** scales *(for weighing)* (10)

wach sein to be awake (4)

das **Wachs** wax (5)

wachsen (wächst), wuchs, ist gewachsen to grow (12-1)

der **Wagen, -** car (3-1)

wählen to dial (5); to choose, select (9)

wahr true (5-2)

während *(prep + gen)* during (12-2); *(conj)* while (9)

die **Wahrheit, -en** truth (5-2)

die **Währung, -en** currency (11)

das **Waisenkind, -er** orphan (12)

der **Wald, ⁻er** forest; woods (5-1)

der **Walzer, -** waltz (1)

die **Wand, ⁻e** wall (8-1)

den Teufel an die Wand malen to temp fate (8)

sich **wandeln** to change (11)

wandern, wanderte, ist gewandert to hike (2-1); to wander, to roam (5)

wandern gehen to go hiking (2-1)

der **Wanderschuh, -e** hiking boot (5)

der **Wanderstiefel, -** hiking boot (12)

wann when (1)

die **Wanne, -n** bathtub (8)

die **Ware, -n** merchandise (11)

warm warm (1-2)

warnen to warn (6-2)

die **Warnung, -en** warning (6-2)

warten to wait (6-2)

warten auf *(+ acc)* to wait for (11-2)

warum why (1-2)

die **Warze, -n** wart (3)

was what (E, 1-2)

Was für ein Hundewetter! What rotten weather! (1)

Was für Sport machst du? What sports do you do? (1-2)

was ... sonst what else (8)

waschbar washable (12)

das **Waschbecken, -** (bathroom) sink (8-1)

die **Wäsche** wash, laundry (5, 6-2)

die **Wäsche waschen** to do the laundry (6-2)

waschen (wäscht), wusch, gewaschen to wash (3-2)

die **Wäscherei, -en** laundry *(place of business)* (7)

der **Waschlappen, -** washcloth (9-2)

die **Waschmaschine, -n** washer (4)

der **Waschsalon, -s** laundromat (6-2)

das **Wasser** water (1, 2-1)

wässerig watery (2)

das **WC, -s** toilet (8)

die **Website, -s** Web site (11-2)

wecken to wake *(someone)* up (9)

der **Wecker, -** alarm clock (7-1)

weder ... noch neither . . . nor (10-2)

weg away; gone (6)

der **Weg, -e** way (5); path (9)

wegen *(prep + gen)* because of (12-2)

weg·fahren (fährt weg), fuhr weg, ist weggefahren to drive away (4-2)

weg·fliegen, flog weg, ist weggeflogen to fly away (8)

weg·gehen, ging weg, ist weggegangen to go away (4)

weg·laufen (läuft weg), lief weg, ist weggelaufen to run away (4)

weg·nehmen (nimmt weg), nahm weg, weggenommen to take away (4)

weg·räumen to clear away (11)

weg·rennen, rannte weg, ist weggerannt to run away (6)

weg·sehen (sieht weg), sah weg, weggesehen to look away (4)

weg·schwimmen, schwamm weg, ist weggeschwommen to swim away (4)

Weihnachten Christmas (7-1)

Frohe Weihnachten! Merry Christmas! (7-1)

zu Weihnachten at, for Christmas (7-1)

der Weihnachtsbaum, ⸚e Christmas tree (7-1)

der Weihnachtsfeiertag Christmas Day (7)

die Weihnachtsferien *(pl)* Christmas vacation (5)

die Weihnachtsgans, ⸚e Christmas goose (7)

das Weihnachtsgeschenk, -e Christmas present (7)

der Weihnachtsmarkt, ⸚e Christmas market (7)

weil because *(sub conj)* (4-2)

der Wein, -e wine (1, 2-1)

weinen to cry (10-1)

das Weinglas, ⸚er wine glass (1)

der Weinkeller, - wine cellar (9)

der Weinkenner, - wine connoisseur (9)

weiß white (1-1)

das Weiße Haus White House (4)

der Weißwein, -e white wine (3)

die Weißwurst, ⸚e veal sausage (5)

weit far (4, 5-1)

weiter *(as verb prefix)* to continue (4)

weiter·arbeiten to keep on working (4)

weiter·essen (isst weiter), aß weiter, weitergegessen to continue eating (4)

weiter·fahren (fährt weiter), fuhr weiter, ist weitergefahren to keep on driving (4)

weiter·geben (gibt weiter), gab weiter, weitergegeben to pass along (10)

weiter·lesen (liest weiter), las weiter, weitergelesen to continue reading (4-2)

weiter·schlafen (schläft weiter), schlief weiter, weitergeschlafen to continue sleeping (4)

weiter·schreiben, schrieb weiter, weitergeschrieben to continue writing (4)

weiter·studieren to continue studying (4)

welcher, welches, welche which (1); *(pl)* some (7)

wellig wavy (3)

die Welt, -en world (4, 5-2)

die Weltfirma, -en worldwide company (7)

der Weltkrieg, -e world war (11-1)

das Weltkulturerbe world cultural heritage

die Weltreise, -n trip around the world (4)

die Wende turning point *(i.e., the fall of the Berlin Wall)*

wenig little (1-2)

wenigstens at least (8-2)

wenn when *(sub conj)*; if *(sub conj)* (4-2)

wer who (1-2)

werden (wird), wurde, ist geworden to become; to get; to be (3-2)

Er wird Koch. He's going to be a cook. (3)

Sie wird einundzwanzig. She's going to be twenty-one. (3-2)

das Werk, -e work (9)

die Werkstatt, ⸚en workshop (6)

das Werkzeug, -e tool (3, 10-2)

die Wespe, -n wasp (9)

der/die Wessi, -s citizen of former West Germany (11)

(das) Westdeutschland West Germany (11)

der Westen west (8)

westlich (von) west (of) (11)

der Wettbewerb, -e contest (9)

die Wette, -n bet (10)

um die Wette laufen to run a race (with someone) (10)

wetten to bet (10-2)

das Wetter weather (1-1)

Wie ist das Wetter? What's the weather like? (1)

die Wetterkarte, -n weather map (1)

der Wettlauf, ⸚e race (10)

einen Wettlauf machen to run a race (10)

die WG, -s die (Wohngemeinschaft, -en) shared housing (8-2)

wichtig important (4, 5-2)

die Wichtigkeit importance (11)

widerlich disgusting; repulsive (12-1)

wie how (E, 1-2); like (3)

so … wie as . . . as (2-2)

Wie bitte? Pardon? (E-1)

wie ein König like a king (3)

Wie geht es Ihnen?/Wie geht's? How are you? (E-1)

Wie heißen Sie?/Wie heißt du? What's your name? (E-1)

Wie ist das Wetter? What's the weather like? (1)

Wie ist Ihr Name und Ihre Adresse? What's your name and your address? (3)

Wie ist Ihre Wohnung? What's your apartment like? (3)

Wie spät ist es? What time is it? (2-2)

wie viel how much (E, 1-2)

Wie viel Uhr ist es? What time is it? (2-2)

wie viele how many (1-2)

wieder again (1-2)

immer wieder again and again (9-1)

wiederholen to repeat (E, 8-2)

Wiederhören! Auf Wiederhören! Good-bye! *(on the telephone)* (E-1)

wieder·sehen (sieht wieder), sah wieder, wiedergesehen to see again (E)

Auf Wiedersehen! Wiedersehen! Good-bye! (E-1)

die Wiedervereinigung reunification (11-1)

(das) Wien Vienna (1)

das Wiener Schnitzel breaded veal cutlet (7)

der Wievielte (6)

am Wievielten on what date (6)

Den Wievielten haben wir heute? What's the date today? (6-2)

Der Wievielte ist heute? What's the date today? (6-2)

wild wild (12-2)

windig windy (1-1)

windstill windless, calm (1)

windsurfen gehen to go windsurfing (2-1)

winken *(+ dat)* to wave to (9)

der **Winter, -** winter (1-2)

 im Winter in winter (1-2)

die **Winterjacke, -n** winter jacket (7)

der **Wintermantel, ¨** winter coat (10)

der **Winterschlussverkauf, ¨e** winter clearance sale (7-1)

winzig tiny (10-2)

wirklich really (6, 9-2)

die **Wirklichkeit** reality (11)

die **Wirtschaft** economy (9)

das **Wirtschaftswunder** economic miracle (2)

das **Wirtshaus, ¨er** restaurant (9)

wissen (weiß), wusste, gewusst to know (5-1)

 wissen von to know about (11-2)

die **Witwe, -n** widow (12-2)

der **Witwer, -** widower (12-2)

der **Witz, -e** joke (11-2)

witzig witty; funny (7-2)

wo where *(in what place)* (E, 1-2)

die **Woche, -n** week (1-2)

das **Wochenende, -n** weekend (2-2)

das **Wochenendhaus, ¨er** cottage (8)

der **Wochenmarkt, ¨e** open-air market (8-2)

der **Wochentag, -e** day of the week (1-2)

wöchentlich weekly (2)

die **Wochenzeitung, -en** weekly newspaper (10)

woher where . . . from (E-1)

wohin where *(to what place)* (1-2)

Wohl: zum Wohl! Cheers! To your health! (7-2)

wohl probably; perhaps (7-2)

 sich **wohl fühlen** to feel well (9-2); to feel at home (8)

der **Wohlstand** affluence (11)

 vor lauter Wohlstand for all (their) affluence (11)

wohnen to live *(in a building or on a street)* (1, 2-2)

die **Wohngemeinschaft, -en (die WG, -s)** shared housing (1, 8-2)

das **Wohnhaus, ¨er** residential building (8)

der **Wohnort, -e** place of residence (1, 6-1)

die **Wohnung, -en** apartment (2-2)

das **Wohnviertel, -** residential area (8)

das **Wohnzimmer, -** living room (8-1)

die **Wohnzimmergarnitur, -en** living room set (12)

wollen (will), wollte, gewollt to want to (4)

die **Wolke, -n** cloud (5-1)

die **Wolle** wool (10)

das **Wort, -e** word *(in a meaningful context)* (6)

das **Wort, ¨er** word *(lexical item)* (1, 7-1)

das **Wörterbuch, ¨er** dictionary (7-1)

der **Wortschatz, ¨e** vocabulary (1)

wozu what . . . for (8-2)

der **Wühltisch, -e** bargain table (10)

wunderbar wonderful (3-2)

das **Wunderkind, -er** child prodigy (3)

sich **wundern** to be surprised (11-1)

wunderschön very beautiful (3-2)

wundervoll marvelous (5)

der **Wunsch, ¨e** wish (12-2)

wünschen to wish (7-2)

 Sie wünschen? May I help you? (7-2)

der **Wurm, ¨er** worm (1)

wurmig wormy (2)

die **Wurst, ¨e** sausage; cold cuts (4-1)

 Das ist mir wurst. I couldn't care less. (7)

würzen to season (9)

die **Wut** anger, rage (11)

wütend angry, furious (11-2)

Z

z.B.; zum Beispiel e.g., for example (6-2)

die **Zahl, -en** number (7)

zählen to count (10)

der **Zahn, ¨e** tooth (6-1)

der **Zahnarzt, ¨e**/die **Zahnärztin, -nen** dentist (7-2)

die **Zahnbürste, -n** toothbrush (5, 9-2)

zahnlos toothless (12)

die **Zahnpasta** toothpaste (9-2)

die **Zahnschmerzen** *(pl)* toothache (6, 7-2)

der **Zaun, ¨e** fence (6-2)

die **Zehe, -n** toe (6-1)

zeichnen to draw; to draft (6-1)

die **Zeichnung, -en** drawing (9)

zeigen to show (1, 7-2)

 Das Thermometer zeigt zehn Grad. The thermometer reads ten degrees. (1-1)

die **Zeile, -n** line *(of text on a page)* (12)

die **Zeit, -en** time (2-1)

 in letzter Zeit recently (6-2)

 seit kurzer Zeit recently (11-1)

 Lassen Sie sich Zeit! Take your time! (12-2)

das **Zeitalter** age (9)

die **Zeitschrift, -en** magazine, periodical (10)

die **Zeitung, -en** newspaper (2-1)

das **Zelt, -e** tent (5-1)

zelten to camp *(in a tent)* (9)

die **Zensur, -en** grade (5-2)

zentral central(ly) (11)

das **Zentrum, Zentren** center (5)

zerfallen (zerfällt), zerfiel, ist zerfallen to disintegrate (11)

zerkochen to cook to a pulp (11)

zerschneiden, zerschnitt, zerschnitten to cut up (11)

zerstören to destroy (11-1)

das **Zeug** *(sing)* thing (3)

der **Zettel, -** piece of paper (10)

ziehen, zog, gezogen to pull (4); to move (10)

das **Ziel, -e** goal, aim; destination (10-2)

ziemlich quite; rather (5-2); considerable (12)

die **Zigarre, -n** cigar (10)

die **Zigarette, -n** cigarette (4-2)

das **Zimmer, -** room (1-2)

die **Zimmerpflanze, -n** house plant (6-2)

der **Zimmermann, Zimmerleute** carpenter (8)

der **Zimt** cinnamon (9)

die **Zinsen** *(pl)* (bank) interest (12-2)

zirka approximately (1)

zittern to tremble (11)

die **Zone, -n** zone (11)

die **Zoologie** zoology (2)

der **Zopf, ¨e** braid (11)

zu *(prep + dat)* to; too (1); for (7)

 zu Hause (at) home (2, 4-1)

 zu viel too much (1)

der **Zucker** *(sing)* sugar (4-1)

zu·decken to cover up (4)

zuerst first (1-1)

zufrieden satisfied (10-2)

der **Zug, ¨e** train (3-1)

zu·geben (gibt zu), gab zu, zugegeben to admit (12-1)

der **Zugvogel, ¨** migratory bird (11)

zu·hören to listen (E)

die **Zukunft** future (11-1)

zuletzt last; finally (4-2)

zum Beispiel (z.B.) for example (e.g.) (6-2)

zum Glück fortunately, luckily (12-1)

die **Zunge, -n** tongue (3)

zu·pfeffern to slam shut (11)

zurück back (4)

zurück·bringen, brachte zurück, zurückgebracht to bring back (4)

zurück·fahren (fährt zurück), fuhr zurück, ist zurückgefahren to drive back (4)

zurück·geben (gibt zurück), gab zurück, zurückgegeben to give back (4)

zurück·gehen, ging zurück, ist zurückgegangen to go back (4)

zurück·kommen, kam zurück, ist zurückgekommen to come back (4-2)

zurück·nehmen (nimmt zurück), nahm zurück, zurückgenommen to take back (4)

zurück·rufen, rief zurück, zurückgerufen to call back (4)

zurück·schmeißen, schmiss zurück, zurückgeschmissen to throw back (4)

zurück·zahlen to pay back (11)

zurzeit at the moment (7-2)

zusammen together (1-2)

zusammen·binden, band zusammen, zusammengebunden to tie together (10)

zusammen·passen to go together; to match (1)

zusammen·rufen, rief zusammen, zusammengerufen to call together (10)

die **Zusammenschau** summary (1)

der **Zusatz** supplement (12)

die **Zusatz-Krankenversicherung** supplementary medical insurance (12)

die **Zutat, -en** ingredient (9)

zuvor before(hand) (10)

zwar … aber it's true . . . but (10)

zweieinhalb two and a half (9)

zweimal twice (5, 6-2)

der **Zweite Weltkrieg** Second World War (4)

der **Zweitwagen, -** second car (12)

der **Zwetschgenkuchen, -** plum cake (10)

der **Zwilling, -e** twin (12-2)

zwischen (*prep + acc/dat*) between (8)

die **Zwischenprüfung, -en** exam after two years of university (1)

das **Zwischenspiel, -e** interlude (1)

English-German Vocabulary

For classroom expressions and grammatical terms, see pages A15 and A16. For vocabulary referring to fields of study, jobs and professions, hobbies and sports, musical instruments, articles of clothing, accessories, food and drink, countries and languages, personal characteristics, and courteous expressions, see the *Useful Word Sets* beginning on page A17.

A

a lot (of) viel; eine Menge; ein Haufen

able: to be able to können (kann), konnte, gekonnt

about *(prep)* über *(+ acc)*; *(approximately)* etwa

above *(prep)* über *(+ acc/dat)*; *(adv)* oben

  above all vor allem

absolute(ly) absolut; ganz

accident der Unfall, ⸚e

acquaintance der/die Bekannte, -n

acquainted: to be acquainted with kennen, kannte, gekannt

across (from) gegenüber

active(ly) aktiv

  to be active in sports Sport machen

actually eigentlich

ad die Anzeige, -n

addition: in addition außerdem

additional weiter

address die Adresse, -n

  What's your address? Was (Wie) ist Ihre Adresse?

to admire bewundern

to admit zu·geben (gibt zu), gab zu, zugegeben

adult der/die Erwachsene, -n

advantage der Vorteil, -e

advice der Rat

  to ask for advice um Rat fragen

to advise raten (rät), riet, geraten

afraid: to be afraid (of) Angst haben (vor + *dat*)

African-American der Afro-Amerikaner, -/die Afro-Amerikanerin, -nen

after *(prep)* nach *(+ dat)*; *(conj)* nachdem; *(adv)* nachher

afternoon der Nachmittag, -e

  in the afternoon nachmittags

  this afternoon heute Nachmittag

afterwards nachher

again wieder; schon wieder

  again and again immer wieder

  (over) again noch einmal; noch mal

against *(prep)* gegen *(+ acc)*

age das Alter

ago vor *(+ dat)*

aim das Ziel, -e

air die Luft

airplane das Flugzeug, -e

airport *(international)* der Flughafen, ⸚; *(regional)* der Flugplatz, ⸚e

alarm clock der Wecker, -

alcohol der Alkohol

all (the) alle

  above all vor allem

  at all überhaupt

Allies die Alliierten *(pl)*

allowed: to be allowed to dürfen (darf), durfte, gedurft

almost fast

alone allein

along *(as prefix)* mit

Alps die Alpen *(pl)*

already schon

also auch

although *(sub conj)* obwohl

always immer

America (das) Amerika

American *(adj)* amerikanisch

American *(person)* der Amerikaner, -/die Amerikanerin, -nen

among *(prep)* unter *(+ acc/dat)*

ancestor der Vorfahr, -en, -en

and *(coord conj)* und

angry wütend

animal das Tier, -e

to annoy ärgern

annoyed sauer

  to be (get) annoyed (with, about) sich ärgern (über + *acc*)

anorexic magersüchtig

another *(different)* ander; *(in addition)* noch ein

answer die Antwort, -en

to answer *(someone)* antworten *(+ dat)*

  to answer a question eine Frage beantworten

answering machine der Anrufbeantworter, -

anyway sowieso; trotzdem; doch

apartment die Wohnung, -en

apiece: three euros apiece drei Euro das Stück

to apologize sich entschuldigen

to appear erscheinen, erschien, ist erschienen

appetite der Appetit

apple der Apfel, ⸚

  apple pie der Apfelkuchen, -

appliance der Apparat, -e; das Gerät, -e

apprentice der/die Auszubildende, -n; *(abbr)* der/die Azubi, -s

approximately etwa

April der April

area das Gebiet, -e; die Gegend, -en; *(of a city)* der Stadtteil, -e

area code die Vorwahl

to argue argumentieren

argument das Argument, -e

arm der Arm, -e

armchair der Sessel, -

around *(place)* um, rund um *(+ acc)*; *(time)* gegen *(+ acc)*

  around five o'clock gegen fünf

to arrive an·kommen, kam an, ist angekommen

arrogant(ly) arrogant

art die Kunst, ⸚e

article der Artikel, -

  article of clothing das Kleidungsstück, -e

artist der Künstler, -/die Künstlerin, -nen

artistic(ally) künstlerisch

as
  as a child als Kind
  as . . . as so … wie
  as long as *(sub conj)* solange
  as often as *(sub conj)* sooft
  as soon as *(sub conj)* sobald

to **ask** *(a question)* fragen
  to **ask a question** eine Frage stellen

assistant der Assistent, -en, -en/die Assistentin, -nen

astonished verwundert

at *(prep)* bei *(+ dat); (time)* um *(+ acc); (a vertical surface)* an *(+ acc/dat)*
  at all überhaupt
  at our house bei uns
  at the Zieglers bei Zieglers
  not at all gar nicht, überhaupt nicht

athlete der Athlet, -en, -en/die Athletin, -nen

athletic sportlich

athletics der Sport

to **attend** besuchen

attraction die Attraktion, -en

August der August

aunt die Tante, -n

Australian *(adj)* australisch

Austria (das) Österreich

Austrian *(adj)* österreichisch

Austrian *(person)* der Österreicher, -/die Österreicherin, -nen

author der Autor, -en/die Autorin, -nen

autumn der Herbst

average der Durchschnitt, -e
  of average height mittelgroß
  on average im Durchschnitt

away fort; weg

awful(ly) schrecklich

B

baby das Baby, -s

babysitter der Babysitter, -/die Babysitterin, -nen

back der Rücken, -; *(of a chair)* die Lehne, -n; *(adv)* zurück

back then damals

backache die Rückenschmerzen *(pl)*

backpack der Rucksack, ⁻e

bad('y) schlecht
  Too bad! Schade!

badminton: to play badminton Federball spielen

bag die Tasche, -n

to **bake** backen (bäckt), backte, gebacken

baker der Bäcker, -/die Bäckerin, -nen

bakery die Bäckerei, -en

balcony der Balkon, -e

ball der Ball, ⁻e

ballpoint pen der Kugelschreiber, -

banana die Banane, -n

band die Band, -s

Band-Aid das Pflaster, -

bank die Bank, -en

bank manager der Bankdirektor, -en/die Bankdirektorin, -nen

bankrupt bankrott

Bar Mitzvah die Bar Mizwa

barber der Friseur, -e/die Friseurin, -nen

to **bark** bellen

basement der Keller, -

bath das Bad, ⁻er

to **bathe,** to **have a bath** (sich) baden

bathing suit der Badeanzug, ⁻e

bathroom das Badezimmer, -; das Bad, ⁻er; das Klo, -s

bathroom sink das Waschbecken, -

bathtub die Badewanne, -n

batter der Teig

Bavaria (das) Bayern

Bavarian *(adj)* bayerisch

to **be** sein (ist), war, ist gewesen; *(become)* werden (wird), wurde, ist geworden
  He's going to be a cook. Er wird Koch.

beach der Strand, ⁻e

bean die Bohne, -n

bear der Bär, -en, -en

beard der Bart, ⁻e

beautiful(ly) schön
  very beautiful wunderschön

beauty die Schönheit, -en

because *(sub conj)* weil; *(coord conj)* denn

because of *(prep)* wegen *(+ gen)*

to **become** werden (wird), wurde, ist geworden

bed das Bett, -en
  to **go to bed** ins Bett gehen

bedroom das Schlafzimmer, -

beer das Bier
  beer belly der Bierbauch, ⁻e
  beer garden der Biergarten, ⁻

before *(prep)* vor *(+ acc/dat); (conj)* bevor; *(adv)* vorher

to **begin** an·fangen (fängt an), fing an, angefangen; beginnen, begann, begonnen

beginning der Anfang, ⁻e, der Beginn
  at the beginning zu Beginn
  (at) the beginning of Juli Anfang Juli
  beginning of school der Schulbeginn

to **behave** sich benehmen (benimmt), benahm, benommen

behind *(prep)* hinter *(+ acc/dat)*

Belgian *(adj)* belgisch

to **believe** glauben *(+ dat)*

belly der Bauch, ⁻e

to **belong to** gehören *(+ dat)*

beloved geliebt

below *(prep)* unter *(+ acc/dat); (adv)* unten

belt der Gürtel, -

bent krumm

beside *(prep)* neben *(+ acc/dat)*
  She was beside herself. Sie war außer sich.

besides außerdem

best best

to **bet** wetten

better besser
  better than besser als

between *(prep)* zwischen *(+ acc/dat)*

beverage das Getränk, -e

bicycle das Fahrrad, ⁻er
  bicycle helmet der Fahrradhelm, -e
  bicycle rental der Fahrradverleih, -e
  bicycle trip die Radtour, -en
  to **go on a bicycle trip** eine Radtour machen

big groß

bike das Rad, ⁻er

bike rental der Fahrradverleih, -e

biking: to go biking Rad fahren (fährt Rad), fuhr Rad, ist Rad gefahren

bill die Rechnung, -en; *(money)* der Schein, -e

billiards (das) Billard *(sing)*

bird der Vogel, ⁻

birth die Geburt, -en

birthday der Geburtstag, -e
  for one's birthday zum Geburtstag
  Happy Birthday! Herzliche Glückwünsche zum Geburtstag!
  to **wish a Happy Birthday** zum Geburtstag gratulieren

birthday card die Geburtstagskarte, -n

birthday present das Geburtstagsgeschenk, -e

birthplace der Geburtsort, -e

bit: a bit ein bisschen; einigermaßen

  bit by bit Stück für Stück

to **bite** beißen, biss, gebissen

black schwarz

  Black Forest der Schwarzwald

  Black Forest cake die Schwarzwälder Kirschtorte

blackboard die Tafel, -n, die Wandtafel, -n

blind blind

to **block** blockieren

blonde blond

blouse die Bluse, -n

to **blow-dry one's hair** sich *(dat)* die Haare föhnen

blow-dryer der Föhn, -e

blue blau

  in blue in Blau

board das Brett, -er

boat das Boot, -e

body der Körper, -

book das Buch, -er

to **book** buchen

bookcase das Bücherregal, -e

boot der Stiefel, -

border die Grenze, -n

to **border on** grenzen an *(+ acc)*

boring langweilig

  deadly boring stinklangweilig

born geboren

  When were you born? Wann bist du geboren?

boss der Chef, -s/die Chefin, -nen

both beide

bother: Stop bothering me! Lass mich in Ruhe!

bottle die Flasche, -n

bowl die Schüssel, -n

box der Karton, -s

boy der Junge, -n, -n

  Boy! Mensch!

boyfriend der Freund, -e

bracelet das Armband, -er

to **brag** an·geben (gibt an), gab an, angegeben

braid der Zopf, -e

brand-new brandneu

bread das Brot, -e

  a slice of bread eine Scheibe Brot

break die Pause, -n

to **break** kaputt machen

breakfast das Frühstück

  for breakfast zum Frühstück

to **have breakfast** frühstücken

breast die Brust, -e

bridge die Brücke, -n

bright(ly) hell

brilliant(ly) genial

to **bring** bringen, brachte, gebracht

to **bring along** mit·bringen, brachte mit, mitgebracht

broccoli der Brokkoli

brochure die Broschüre, -n

broken kaputt

brooch die Brosche, -n

brother der Bruder, -

brothers and sisters die Geschwister *(pl)*

brown braun

brunch der Brunch, -es

brunette brünett

to **brush** bürsten

buffet das Büfett, -s

to **build** bauen

building das Gebäude, -

bulletin board das Schwarze Brett

  on the bulletin board am Schwarzen Brett

bus der Bus, -se

bus route die Buslinie, -n

bus stop die Bushaltestelle, -n

bush der Busch, -e

business die Firma, Firmen; das Geschäft, -e

but *(coord conj)* aber; *(in the sense of* **but rather, (but) . . . instead***)* sondern

butcher der Fleischer, -/ die Fleischerin, -nin

butcher shop die Fleischerei, -en

butter die Butter

to **buy** kaufen

by: by then bis dahin

C

cafeteria *(for full meals)* die Mensa; *(for snacks)* die Cafeteria, -s

  to the cafeteria in die Mensa

caffeine das Koffein

cake der Kuchen, -

  a piece of cake ein Stück Kuchen

  layer cake die Torte, -n

calculator der Taschenrechner, -

calendar der Kalender, -

to **call** rufen, rief, gerufen; *(on the telephone)* an·rufen, rief an, angerufen; *(name)* nennen, nannte, genannt

called: to be called heißen, hieß, geheißen

calm ruhig; *(weather)* windstill

camera die Kamera, -s

to **camp** campen; *(in a tent)* zelten

campground der Campingplatz, -e

camping das Campen

  to go camping campen gehen

campsite der Campingplatz, -e

campus der Campus

can die Dose, -n

  can opener der Dosenöffner, -

can *(to be able to)* können (kann), konnte, gekonnt

Canadian *(adj)* kanadisch

Canadian *(person)* der Kanadier, -/ die Kanadierin, -nen

candle die Kerze, -n

candy die Süßigkeiten *(pl)*

capital city die Hauptstadt, -e

cappuccino der Cappuccino, -s

car das Auto, -s; der Wagen, -; der Personenwagen, -; der Pkw, -s (Personenkraftwagen)

car accident der Autounfall, -e

car mechanic der Automechaniker, - /die Automechanikerin, -nen

card die Karte, -n

  ATM card die ATM Karte

  credit card die Kreditkarte, -n

care

  I don't care. Das ist mir egal.

  I couldn't care less. Das ist mir wurst.

career die Karriere, -n

Careful! Vorsicht!

careful(ly) sorgfältig

carpet der Teppich, -e

carrot die Karotte, -n

to **carry** tragen (trägt), trug, getragen

carton der Karton, -s

cashier der Kassierer, -/die Kassiererin, -nen

cassette die Kassette, -n

cassette recorder der Kassettenrecorder, -

castle das Schloss, -er

cat die Katze, -n

to **catch** fangen (fängt), fing, gefangen

  to catch a cold sich erkälten

CD die CD, -s

CD player der CD-Spieler, -

CD-ROM drive das CD-ROM-Laufwerk, -e

ceiling die Decke, -n
to **celebrate** feiern
cell phone das Handy, -s
cellar der Keller, -
cent der Cent, -
center das Zentrum, Zentren
century das Jahrhundert, -e
certain(ly) sicher
chair der Stuhl, ⸚e
champagne der Champagner
change: for a change mal
to **change** ändern; *(one's clothes)* sich
  um·ziehen, zog um, umgezogen;
  (trains) um·steigen, stieg um, ist
  umgestiegen; *(a situation; one's
  behavior)* sich verändern
cheap billig
check der Scheck, -s
checkout die Kasse, -n
Cheers! Zum Wohl! Prosit!
cheese der Käse
cheesecake der Käsekuchen, -
chef der Koch, ⸚e/die Köchin, -nen
chest die Brust
chic schick
child das Kind, -er
  as a child als Kind
  only child das Einzelkind, -er
childhood die Kindheit
childish kindisch
childlike kindlich
chin das Kinn, -e
china das Geschirr *(sing)*
Chinese *(adj)* chinesisch
chocolate die Schokolade
  a chocolate bar eine Tafel
  Schokolade
choir der Chor, ⸚e
  choir practice die Chorprobe, -n
to **choose** aus·suchen; wählen
Christmas (das) Weihnachten
  at Christmas an (zu) Weihnachten
  for Christmas zu Weihnachten
  Merry Christmas! Frohe
  Weihnachten!
  Christmas Day der erste
  Weihnachtsfeiertag
  Christmas Eve der Heilige Abend,
  Heiliger Abend
  Christmas present das
  Weihnachtsgeschenk, -e
  Christmas tree der
  Weihnachtsbaum, ⸚e
church die Kirche, -n
cigarette die Zigarette, -n

circle der Kreis, -e
circle of friends
  der Freundeskreis, -e
city die Stadt, ⸚e
  city center die City; das
  Stadtzentrum
  city hall das Rathaus, ⸚er
  part of the city der Stadtteil, -e
class die Klasse, -n; der Kurs, -e;
  die Stunde, -n
  German class der Deutschkurs, -e;
  die Deutschstunde, -n
classmate der Mitstudent, -en,
  -en/die Mitstudentin, -nen
clean sauber
to **clean** putzen
to **clean up** auf·räumen
clever clever
to **climb** steigen, stieg, ist gestiegen
clock die Uhr, -en
to **close** zu·machen; schließen,
  schloss, geschlossen
closet der Schrank, ⸚e
  front hall closet die Garderobe, -n
clothes die Kleider *(pl)*, die
  Klamotten *(pl)*
clothing store das Kleidergeschäft, -e
cloud die Wolke, -n
  sunny with some clouds heiter
cloudy bedeckt; bewölkt
clue: She doesn't have a clue. Sie
  hat keine Ahnung.
coast die Küste, -n
coat der Mantel, ⸚
coffee der Kaffee
  coffee maker die Kaffeemaschine,
  -n
  coffeepot die Kaffeekanne, -n
  coffee table der Couchtisch, -e
cola die Cola, -s
cold kalt; *(illness)* die Erkältung, -en;
  der Schnupfen, -
  a bad cold eine schwere Erkältung
  cold cuts die Wurst *(sing)*
  to **be cold** frieren, fror, gefroren
  to **catch a cold** sich erkälten
  to **have a cold** erkältet sein
colleague der Kollege, -n, -n/die
  Kollegin, -nen; *(from work)* der
  Arbeitskollege, -n/die
  Arbeitskollegin, -nen
to **collect** sammeln
collection die Sammlung, -en
college das College, -s
color die Farbe, -n

What color is Lisa's blouse? Welche
  Farbe hat Lisas Bluse?
to **color** färben
color photo das Farbfoto, -s
color TV der Farbfernseher, -
colorless farblos
comb der Kamm, ⸚e
to **comb one's hair** sich kämmen
to **come** kommen, kam, ist
  gekommen
  to **come along** mit·kommen
  to **come back** zurück·kommen
  to **come in** herein·kommen
  to **come out** heraus·kommen
  to **come to visit** zu Besuch kommen
comfortable komfortabel
comics die Comics
compact disc die CD, -s
company die Firma, Firmen; die
  Gesellschaft, -en
to **compare** vergleichen, verglich,
  verglichen
complete(ly) total; ganz; vollständig
complicated kompliziert
compliment das Kompliment, -e
composer der Komponist, -en,
  -en/die Komponistin, -nen
computer der Computer, -,
  der Rechner, -
computer game das Computerspiel,
  -e
computer screen der Bildschirm, -e
concert das Konzert, -e
  to a concert, to concerts ins Konzert
condominium die
  Eigentumswohnung, -en
conflict der Konflikt, -e
confused verwirrt
to **congratulate** gratulieren *(+ dat)*
congratulations der Glückwunsch, ⸚e
  Congratulations! Herzliche
  Glückwünsche!
conservative konservativ
considered: to be considered gelten
  als (gilt), galt, gegolten
constant(ly) ständig
consulate das Konsulat, -e
contact der Kontakt, -e
contact lens die Kontaktlinse, -n
container: a container of yogurt ein
  Becher *(m)* Joghurt
contest der Wettbewerb, -e
continue *(as verb prefix)* weiter
  to **continue studying**
  weiter·studieren

to **converse** sich unterhalten (unterhält), unterhielt, unterhalten
conversation das Gespräch, -e
cook der Koch, ⸚e/die Köchin, -nen
to **cook** kochen
cookbook das Kochbuch, ⸚er
cooking lessons der Kochkurs, -e
cool (of weather) kühl; (excellent) cool
  really cool echt cool
to **copy** kopieren
corkscrew der Korkenzieher, -
corner die Ecke, -n
correct richtig
to **correct** verbessern
to **cost** kosten
cottage das Wochenendhaus, ⸚er; das Ferienhaus, ⸚er
couch die Couch, -es
to **count** zählen
countless zahllos
country das Land, ⸚er
couple (pair) das Paar, -e
  a couple of ein paar
  married couple das Ehepaar, -e
course der Kurs, -e
  main course (of a meal) das Hauptgericht
  Of course! Klar! Natürlich!
cousin (female) die Kusine, -n; (male) der Vetter, -n
crafty schlau
crazy verrückt; übergeschnappt
  to **be crazy** spinnen
  to **go crazy** über·schnappen
creative(ly) kreativ
credit card die Kreditkarte
critical(ly) kritisch
criticism die Kritik
to **criticize** kritisieren
crooked krumm; schief, kriminell
cruel grausam
to **cry** weinen; heulen
cuddly kuschelig
cup die Tasse, -n; der Becher, -
  a cup of coffee eine Tasse Kaffee
curly lockig
curtain der Vorhang, ⸚e
custom die Sitte, -n
customer der Kunde, -n, -n/ die Kundin, -nen; (in a restaurant) der Gast, ⸚e
to **cut** schneiden, schnitt, geschnitten
cutlery das Besteck

D

dad der Vati, -s; der Papa, -s
daily täglich
to **dance** tanzen
  to **go dancing** tanzen gehen
Danish (adj) dänisch
Danube (river) die Donau
dark dunkel
darling der Liebling, -e
Darn it! Verflixt!
data processing EDV (Elektronische Datenverarbeitung)
date das Datum, Daten
  on what date? am Wievielten?
  What's the date today? Den Wievielten haben wir heute? Der Wievielte ist heute?
daughter die Tochter, ⸚
day der Tag, -e
  day of the week der Wochentag, -e
  one day eines Tages
  the day after tomorrow übermorgen
  Today I have a day off. Heute habe ich frei.
dead tot
dear lieb
death der Tod
debt die Schuld, -en
December der Dezember
decent ordentlich
decision die Entscheidung, -en
deep tief
defective defekt
definite(ly) bestimmt
degree der Grad, -e
  ten degrees Celsius zehn Grad Celsius
delicious lecker
democracy die Demokratie
to **depart** ab·fahren (fährt ab), fuhr ab, ist abgefahren
department die Abteilung, -en
department manager der Abteilungsleiter, -/die Abteilungsleiterin, -nen
department store das Kaufhaus, ⸚er
depression die Depression, -en
to **describe** beschreiben, beschrieb, beschrieben
description die Beschreibung, -en
designer der Designer, -/die Designerin, -nen
desk der Schreibtisch, -e

dessert der Nachtisch, -e
  for dessert zum Nachtisch
destination das Ziel, -e
detective story der Krimi, -s
to **destroy** zerstören
diagram das Schaubild, -er; die Grafik, -en
dialect der Dialekt, -e
dialogue der Dialog, -e
diary das Tagebuch, ⸚er
dictatorship die Diktatur
dictionary das Wörterbuch, ⸚er
to **die** sterben (stirbt), starb, ist gestorben
difference der Unterschied, -e
different (adj) ander-; verschieden; (adv) anders
dining hall (at a university) die Mensa
dining room das Esszimmer, -
diploma das Diplom, -e
  to **do** or **take one's diploma** das Diplom machen
direct(ly) direkt
director der Direktor, -en/die Direktorin, -nen
dirty schmutzig
disadvantage der Nachteil, -e
disco die Disco, -s
  to the disco in die Disco
to **discuss** diskutieren
discussion die Diskussion, -en
disgusting widerlich
dish (food) das Gericht, -e
dishes das Geschirr (sing)
  dirty dishes der Abwasch (sing)
  to **do the dishes** den Abwasch machen
dishonest unehrlich
dishwasher die Geschirrspülmaschine, -n
disk die Diskette, -n
dissatisfied unzufrieden
distinct(ly) deutlich
district der Stadtteil, -e
to **disturb** stören
to **divide** teilen
divorced geschieden
to **do** machen; tun, tat, getan
  to **do sports** Sport machen
doable machbar
doctor der Arzt, ⸚e/die Ärztin, -nen
document das Dokument, -e
documentary film der Dokumentarfilm, -e
dog der Hund, -e

dog food das Hundefutter
doll die Puppe, -n
dollar der Dollar, -s
  twenty-five dollars fünfundzwanzig
    Dollar
door die Tür, -en
dormitory das Studentenheim, -e
dot: at eleven on the dot Punkt elf
double doppelt
to **drag** schleppen
drama das Drama, Dramen
to **draw** zeichnen
drawing die Zeichnung, -en
dream der Traum, ⸚e
to **dream** träumen
to **dress** sich an·ziehen, zog an,
    angezogen
dress das Kleid, -er
dressed gekleidet; angezogen
  to **get dressed** sich an·ziehen, zog
    an, angezogen
dresser die Kommode, -n
to **drink** trinken, trank, getrunken
to **drive** fahren (fährt), fuhr, ist
    gefahren; Auto fahren
  to **drive away** ab·fahren
driver der Fahrer, -/die Fahrerin,
    -nen
driver's license der Führerschein, -e
to **drizzle** *(rain)* nieseln
to **drown** ertrinken, ertrank, ist
    ertrunken
drugstore die Drogerie, -n
dry trocken
to **dry one's hair** sich *(dat)* die Haare
    trocknen
during *(prep)* während *(+ gen)*
Dutch *(adj)* holländisch
DVD drive das DVD-Laufwerk, -e

E

each jeder, jedes, jede
  each other einander
  with each other miteinander
ear das Ohr, -en
ear stud der Ohrstecker, -
early früh
to **earn** verdienen
earring der Ohrring, -e
earth die Erde
east der Osten
  east (of) östlich *(von + dat)*
Easter Ostern
Easter bunny der Osterhase, -n
easy leicht

easy to care for pflegeleicht
to **eat** essen (isst), aß, gegessen;
  (of animals) fressen (frisst), fraß,
  gefressen
to **eat up** auf·essen (isst auf), aß auf,
  aufgegessen
economy die Wirtschaft, -en
to **educate** aus·bilden
education die Ausbildung
egg das Ei, -er
either: Claudia isn't coming either.
  Claudia kommt auch nicht.
elbow der Ellbogen, -
electric elektrisch
electric kettle der Wasserkocher, -
elegant elegant
elementary school die Grundschule, -n
else
  or else sonst
  what else was … sonst
e-mail die E-Mail, -s, die Mail, -s
e-mail address die E-Mail-Adresse, -n
embarrassed beschämt
embarrassing peinlich
emigrant der Auswanderer, -/die
  Auswanderin, -nen; der Emigrant,
  -en, -en/ die Emigrantin, -nen
to **emigrate** aus·wandern; emigrieren
employee der Arbeitnehmer, -/
  die Arbeitnehmerin, -nen
employer der Arbeitgeber, -/
  die Arbeitgeberin, -nen
empty leer
to **empty** leeren
enchanting bezaubernd
end das Ende, -n
  (at) the end of January Ende Januar
end table der Beistelltisch, -e
to **end** auf·hören; enden; beenden
endless endlos
to **endure** aus·halten (hält aus), hielt
  aus, ausgehalten
English *(adj)* englisch
English *(language)* Englisch
  in English auf Englisch
enjoy
  Enjoy your meal! Guten Appetit!
  I enjoy it. Es macht mir Spaß.
enjoyment der Spaß; die Lust
enormous enorm
enough genug
entrance der Eingang, ⸚e
envious neidisch
  to **be envious of** neidisch sein auf
  (+ acc)

environment die Umwelt
equal(ly) gleich
equal rights; equality die
  Gleichberechtigung
  to **have equal rights**
    gleichberechtigt sein
error der Fehler, -
especially besonders
essay der Aufsatz, ⸚e
etc. (et cetera) usw. (und so weiter)
euro der Euro, -s
  five euros fünf Euro
Europe (das) Europa
European *(adj)* europäisch
even sogar
  even though *(sub conj)* obwohl
evening der Abend, -e
  evening meal das Abendessen, -
  Good evening! Guten Abend! 'n
    Abend!
  in the evening abends
  this evening heute Abend
ever jemals
every jeder, jedes, jede
  every time jedes Mal
everybody alle
everyday life das Alltagsleben
everything alles
exact(ly) genau
example das Beispiel, -e
  for example (e.g.) zum Beispiel
    (z.B.)
excellent ausgezeichnet
except for *(prep)* außer *(+ dat)*
exception die Ausnahme, -n
to **exchange** um·tauschen
exchange student der
  Austauschstudent, -en, -en/die
  Austauschstundentin, -nen; *(high*
  school) der Austauschschüler, -/die
  Austauschschülerin, -nen
excited aufgeregt
  to **get excited (about)** sich
    auf·regen (über + *acc*)
excuse die Ausrede, -n
  Excuse me! Entschuldigung!
exercise die Übung, -en
exercise bike der Heimtrainer, -
exhibition die Ausstellung, -en
exotic exotisch
expensive teuer
experience die Erfahrung, -en; das
  Erlebnis, -se; *(knowledge)* die
  Kenntnisse *(pl)*
to **experience** erleben

experiment das Experiment, -e
to **explain** erklären
to **express** aus·drücken
expressway die Autobahn, -en
eye das Auge, -n
eyeglasses die Brille, -n

F

fabulous fabelhaft
face das Gesicht, -er
factory die Fabrik, -en
to **faint** in Ohnmacht fallen
fair fair
fairy tale das Märchen, -
fall *(season)* der Herbst
  in the fall im Herbst
to **fall** fallen (fällt), fiel, ist gefallen
to **fall asleep** ein·schlafen
    (schläft ein), schlief ein, ist
    eingeschlafen
to **fall down** hinunter·fallen (fällt
    hinunter), fiel hinunter, ist
    hinuntergefallen
to **fall in love with** sich verlieben
    in *(+ acc)*
family die Familie, -n
family doctor der Hausarzt, ⸚e/die
    Hausärztin, -nen
family tree der Stammbaum, ⸚e
famished: to be famished einen
    Bärenhunger haben
famous berühmt
fantastic toll, fantastisch
  That's really fantastic. Das ist echt
    toll.
far weit
  far too much viel zu viel
farm die Farm, -en
farmer der Bauer, -n, -n/die Bäuerin,
    -nen; der Farmer, -
fashion show die Modenschau
fashionable modisch
fast schnell
fast-food stand der Schnellimbiss, -e
fat dick
father der Vater, ⸚
fatty fettig
fault *(blame)* die Schuld
favorite der Liebling, -e
  favorite CD die Lieblings-CD, -s
  favorite color die Lieblingsfarbe, -n
  favorite program
    das Lieblingsprogramm, -e
  favorite sport der Lieblingssport
fax das Fax, -e

fear die Angst, ⸚e
February der Februar
to **feed** füttern
to **feel** spüren, fühlen
  I don't feel like it. Ich habe keine
    Lust.
  I feel like having a chocolate bar.
    Ich habe Lust auf eine Tafel
    Schokolade.
to **feel well** sich wohl fühlen
fellow citizen der Mitbürger, -/
    die Mitbürgerin, -nen
fellow student der Mitstudent, -en,
    -en/die Mitstudentin, -nen
fence der Zaun, ⸚e
festival das Fest, -e
fever das Fieber
feverishly fieberhaft
few ein paar
field das Feld, -er
field of study das Fach, ⸚er,
    das Studienfach, ⸚er
figure die Figur *(sing)*
to **fill** füllen
film der Film, -e
finally endlich; schließlich; zuletzt
to **finance** finanzieren
finances die Finanzen *(pl)*
financial finanziell
to **find** finden, fand, gefunden
to **find out** heraus·finden, fand
    heraus, herausgefunden; erfahren
    (erfährt), erfuhr, erfahren
fine: Fine, thanks. Danke, gut.
finger der Finger, -
fingernail der Fingernagel, ⸚
to **finish reading** fertig lesen (liest
    fertig), las fertig, fertig gelesen
to **finish writing** fertig schreiben,
    schrieb fertig, fertig geschrieben
finished fertig
first *(adj)* erst; *(adv)* zuerst
  for the first time zum ersten Mal
first name der Vorname, -ns, -n
fish der Fisch, -e
to **fish** angeln; fischen
fit fit
to **fit** passen
  That coat doesn't fit you. Der
    Mantel passt dir nicht.
fitness center das Fitnesscenter, -
fitness freak der Fitnessfreak, -s
flag die Fahne, -n; die Flagge, -n
flat tire der Platte, -n, -n
  to **have a flat tire** einen Platten haben

to **flee** fliehen, floh, ist geflohen
flight der Flug, ⸚e
flight number die Flugnummer, -n
to **flirt** flirten
floor der Fußboden, ⸚; *(story)* der
    Stock, Stockwerke
  first (ground) floor das Erdgeschoss
  on the first floor im Erdgeschoss
  on the second floor im ersten
    Stock
floor lamp die Stehlampe, -n
flour das Mehl
to **flow** fließen, floss, ist geflossen
flower die Blume, -n
flower shop das Blumengeschäft, -e
flowered geblümt
to **fly** fliegen, flog, ist geflogen
foggy neblig
to **follow** folgen *(+ dat)*
food das Essen; die Lebensmittel *(pl)*
foot der Fuß, ⸚e
  to **go on foot** zu Fuß gehen
football team das Footballteam, -s
for *(prep)* für *(+ acc)*; *(prep)* seit *(+ dat)*;
    (coord conj) denn
  I've known him for years. Ich kenne
    ihn seit Jahren.
to **forbid** verbieten, verbot, verboten
forehead die Stirn, -en
foreign ausländisch
foreign students office das
    Auslandsamt
foreigner der Ausländer, -/
    die Ausländerin, -nen
forest der Wald, ⸚er
forever ewig
to **forget** vergessen (vergisst), vergaß,
    vergessen
fork die Gabel, -n
form die Form, -en
to **form** bilden
former ehemalig
free frei
freedom die Freiheit
freeway die Autobahn, -en
French *(adj)* französisch
French fries die Pommes frites *(pl)*
fresh frisch
Friday der Freitag, -e
  Fridays, on Fridays freitags
  on Friday afternoon am
    Freitagnachmittag
  on Friday evening am Freitagabend
  on Friday morning
    am Freitagmorgen

friend der Freund, -e/die Freundin, -nen

friendliness die Freundlichkeit

friendly freundlich

friendship die Freundschaft, -en

from *(prep)* *(a city, country)* aus (+ *dat*); *(an institution)* von (+ *dat*)

  from now on von jetzt ab

  from . . . to von … bis

front: in front of vor (+ *acc/dat*)

fruit das Obst *(sing)*

full voll

fun der Spaß

  That's fun. Das macht Spaß.

  to **have fun** Spaß haben

funny lustig; komisch; witzig

furious wütend

furnished möbliert

furniture die Möbel *(pl)*

future die Zukunft

G

to **gallop** galoppieren

garage die Garage, -n

garbage bin die Mülltonne, -n

garbage can der Mülleimer, -

garden der Garten, ⸚

garden terrace die Gartenterrasse, -n

gas das Benzin

generation die Generation, -en

generous großzügig

gentleman der Herr, -n, -en

German *(adj)* deutsch

German *(language)* Deutsch

  in German auf Deutsch

German class die Deutschstunde, -n, der Deutschkurs, -e

German parliament der Bundestag

German-speaking deutschsprachig

German state das Bundesland, ⸚er

Germany (das) Deutschland

to **get** *(fetch)* holen; *(receive)* bekommen, bekam, bekommen; kriegen

to **get dressed** sich an·ziehen, zog an, angezogen

to **get to know** kennen lernen

to **get undressed** sich aus·ziehen, zog aus, ausgezogen

to **get up** auf·stehen, stand auf, ist aufgestanden

gift-giving *(at Christmas)* die Bescherung

girl das Mädchen, -

girlfriend die Freundin, -nen

to **give** geben (gibt), gab, gegeben; *(a gift)* schenken; *(change)* heraus·geben (gibt heraus), gab heraus, herausgegeben

to **give back** zurück·geben (gibt zurück), gab zurück, zurückgegeben

to **give notice** kündigen

gladly gern (lieber, am liebsten)

glass das Glas, ⸚er

  a glass of orange juice ein Glas Orangensaft

  two glasses of milk zwei Glas Milch

glasses *(eye)* die Brille, -n

glove der Handschuh, -e

to **go** gehen, ging, ist gegangen; *(by car, bus, train)* fahren (fährt), fuhr, ist gefahren

  She's going to be twenty-one. Sie wird einundzwanzig.

to **go along** mit·gehen, ging mit, ist mitgegangen; mit·fahren (fährt mit), fuhr mit, ist mitgefahren

to **go away** weg·gehen, ging weg, ist weggegangen

to **go off the deep end** aus·rasten

to **go out** aus·gehen, ging aus, ist ausgegangen; hinaus·gehen

goal das Ziel, -e

God (der) Gott

  Thank God! Gott sei Dank!

gone weg

good gut

  Good evening! Guten Abend! 'n Abend!

  Good morning! Guten Morgen! Morgen!

  Good night! Gute Nacht!

  just as good genauso gut

Good-bye! Auf Wiedersehen! Wiedersehen! Tschüss!; *(on the telephone)* Auf Wiederhören!

good-for-nothing der Nichtsnutz, -e

gossip der Klatsch

grade die Zensur, -en

graduation der Uni-Abschluss

gram das Gramm

grandchild der Enkel, -

granddaughter die Enkelin, -nen

grandfather der Großvater, ⸚

grandma die Oma, -s

grandmother die Großmutter, ⸚

grandpa der Opa, -s

grandparents die Großeltern *(pl)*

grandson der Enkel, -

graph das Schaubild, -er

grass das Gras, ⸚er

gray grau

great spitze; toll

  really great echt spitze

great-grandfather der Urgroßvater, ⸚

great-grandmother die Urgroßmutter, ⸚

Greek *(adj)* griechisch

green grün

to **greet** grüßen

greeting der Gruß, ⸚e

groceries die Lebensmittel *(pl)*

ground die Erde

group die Gruppe, -n

group of three die Dreiergruppe, -n

to **grow** wachsen (wächst), wuchs, ist gewachsen

to **grow up** auf·wachsen (wächst auf), wuchs auf, ist aufgewachsen

gruesome grausam

to **guess** erraten (errät), erriet, erraten

guest der Gast, ⸚e

guide dog der Blindenhund, -e

guitarist der Gitarrist, -en, -en/die Gitarristin, -nen

guy der Typ, -en; der Kerl, -e

H

hair das Haar, -e

hairbrush die Haarbürste, -n

haircut der Haarschnitt, -e

hairdo die Frisur, -en

hairdresser der Friseur, -e/die Friseurin, -nen

half halb

  half past one halb zwei

hall, hallway der Flur, -e

Halloween (das) Halloween

hamburger der Hamburger, -

hamster der Hamster, -

hand die Hand, ⸚e

  on the other hand dagegen

handicapped behindert

hand-knit handgestrickt

handwriting die Handschrift, -en

to **hang** *(be in a hanging position)* hängen, hing, gehangen; *(put in a hanging position)* hängen

to **hang up** *(the receiver)* auf·legen

Hanukkah (die) Chanukka

to **happen** passieren, passierte, ist passiert

  What's happening? Was ist los?

happy glücklich; froh; vergnügt
  to **be happy (about)** sich freuen (über + *acc*)
  Happy Birthday! Herzliche Glückwünsche zum Geburtstag!
  Happy New Year! Einen guten Rutsch ins Neue Jahr!
hard hart; *(difficult)* schwer
hard disk die Festplatte, -n
hardly kaum
hard-working fleißig
harmless harmlos
hat der Hut, ⸚e
to **have** haben (hat), hatte, gehabt; *(something done)* etwas machen lassen
to **have to** müssen (muss), musste, gemusst
head der Kopf, ⸚e
head lettuce der Kopfsalat, -e
headache die Kopfschmerzen *(pl)*
headphone der Kopfhörer, -
health food store das Reformhaus, ⸚er
healthy gesund
to **hear** hören
hearty herzlich
heat die Hitze
heavy schwer
height die Größe, -n
  of average height mittelgroß
Hello! Hallo! Grüß dich! Guten Tag! Tag!
help die Hilfe
to **help** helfen (hilft), half, geholfen (+ *dat*)
  May I help you? *(to a customer)* Sie wünschen?
helpful hilfsbereit
her ihr, ihr, ihre
here hier
  down here hier unten
Hi! Grüß dich! Hallo! Guten Tag! Tag!
to **hide** verstecken
  hide-and-seek (das) Verstecken
high hoch (hoh-)
high school *(college track)* das Gymnasium, Gymnasien
high school diploma das Abitur
high-rise das Hochhaus, ⸚er
to **hike** wandern; wandern gehen
hiking boot die Wanderstiefel, -; der Wanderschuh, -e
his sein, sein, seine
historical historisch

history die Geschichte
to **hit** hauen; schlagen (schlägt), schlug, geschlagen
hobby das Hobby, -s
hockey das Eishockey
hockey stick der Hockeyschläger, -
to **hold** halten (hält), hielt, gehalten
hole das Loch, ⸚er
holiday der Feiertag, -e; das Fest, -e
home *(country)* die Heimat, -en
  at home zu Hause
  to **come home** nach Hause kommen; heim·kommen
  to **go home** nach Hause gehen
homework assignment die Hausaufgabe, -n
honest ehrlich
honey der Honig
hope die Hoffnung
to **hope** hoffen
  I hope hoffentlich
hopefully hoffentlich
hopeless hoffnungslos
hopscotch Himmel und Hölle
hors d'oeuvre die Vorspeise, -n
horse das Pferd, -e
hospital das Krankenhaus, ⸚er
hot heiß; *(taste)* scharf
hotdog das Hotdog, -s
hotel das Hotel, -s
hour die Stunde, -n
  for an hour eine Stunde lang
  for hours stundenlang
house das Haus, ⸚er
  at our house bei uns
house number die Hausnummer, -n
house plant die Zimmerpflanze, -n
household der Haushalt, -e
  to **do household chores** den Haushalt machen
househusband der Hausmann, ⸚er
housemate der Mitbewohner, -/die Mitbewohnerin, -nen
housewife die Hausfrau, -en
how wie
  How are you? Wie geht's?/Wie geht es Ihnen?
  how many wie viele
  how much wie viel
huge riesig
human being der Mensch, -en, -en
humid schwül
humor der Humor
humorous lustig; humorvoll
hunger der Hunger

hungry hungrig
  I'm hungry. Ich habe Hunger.
to **hurry** sich beeilen
hurt: He won't hurt you. Er tut dir nichts.
husband der Mann, ⸚er
hymn die Hymne, -n

I

i.e., that is d.h., das heißt
ice das Eis
ice cream das Eis
icy eisig
idea die Idee, -n
  She has no idea. Sie hat keine Ahnung.
ideal ideal
idealism der Idealismus
if *(sub conj)* wenn; *(whether)* *(sub conj)* ob
illness die Krankheit, -en
illustration die Illustration, -en
imagination die Fantasie
to **imagine (something)** sich (etwas) vor·stellen
immediately gleich; sofort
immigrant der Einwanderer, -/ die Einwanderin, -nen; der Immigrant, -en, -en/die Immigrantin, -nen
to **immigrate** ein·wandern
impolite unhöflich
importance die Wichtigkeit
important wichtig
impossible unmöglich
to **impress** beeindrucken
to **improve** verbessern
in, into *(prep)* in (+ *dat or acc*)
income das Einkommen
incorrect(ly) falsch
independent unabhängig
individual der Mensch, -en, -en; die Person, -en
inexpensive billig; preisgünstig
influence der Einfluss, ⸚e
information die Information, -en
informed informiert
inhabitant der Einwohner, - /die Einwohnerin, -nen
in-line skates die Inlineskates
insect das Insekt, -en
inside innen
instead of *(prep)* anstatt, statt *(+ gen)*
instructor der Lehrer, -/die Lehrerin, -nen
instrument das Instrument, -e

insurance die Versicherung, -en
intelligent intelligent, klug
interest *(bank)* die Zinsen *(pl)*
to **interest** interessieren
interested: to be interested in sich interessieren für *(+ acc)*
interesting interessant
international international
Internet das Internet
to **interrupt** unterbrechen (unterbricht), unterbrach, unterbrochen
interview das Interview, -s
invention die Erfindung, -en
inventor der Erfinder, -/ die Erfinderin, -nen
to **invest** investieren
to **invite** ein·laden (lädt ein), lud ein, eingeladen
Irish *(adj)* irisch
iron *(for clothes)* das Bügeleisen, -
to **iron** bügeln
irregular unregelmäßig
island die Insel, -n
Israeli *(adj)* israelisch
Italian *(adj)* italienisch
its sein, sein, seine; ihr, ihr, ihre

J

jacket die Jacke, -n
jam die Marmelade, -n
January der Januar
jazz der Jazz
jealous eifersüchtig
jealousy die Eifersucht
jeans die Jeans, - *(pl)*
jewelry der Schmuck
Jewish *(adj)* jüdisch
job die Stelle, -n; der Job, -s
  job for a day der Tagesjob, -s
to **jog** joggen
jogging pants die Jogginghose, -n
jogging suit der Jogginganzug, ⁼e
joke der Witz, -e
journalist der Journalist, -en, -en/die Journalistin, -nen
joy die Freude, -n
juice der Saft, ⁼e
juicy saftig
July der Juli
to **jump** springen, sprang, ist gesprungen
June der Juni
junk food das Junkfood
just nur; bloß; *(time)* gerade

just as good (well) genauso gut
just now gerade

K

keyboard *(instrument)* das Keyboard, -s; *(computer)* die Tastatur, -en
kilometer der Kilometer, -
kind: What kind of music do you like to listen to? Was für Musik hörst du gern?
kindergarten der Kindergarten, ⁼
king der König, -e
kitchen die Küche, -n
kitchen privileges die Küchenbenutzung *(sing)*
knee das Knie, -
knife das Messer, -
to **knock** klopfen
to **know** *(a fact)* wissen (weiß), wusste, gewusst; *(be acquainted with)* kennen, kannte, gekannt
to **know about** wissen von *(+ dat)*

L

lab die Übung, -en
lady die Dame, -n
lake der See, -n
Lake Constance der Bodensee
lamp die Lampe, -n
to **land** landen
landlord/landlady der Vermieter, - /die Vermieterin, -nen
landscape die Landschaft, -en
language die Sprache, -n
lasagna die Lasagne
to **last** *(take time)* dauern
last letzt; zuletzt
  at last endlich
late spät
  to **be late** sich verspäten
to **laugh** lachen
laundromat der Waschsalon, -s
laundry die Wäsche
lavatory die Toilette, -n
lawn der Rasen, -
to **lay** *(down)* legen
lazy faul
to **learn** lernen
least: at least wenigstens; mindestens
to **leave** *(depart)* ab·fahren (fährt ab), fuhr ab, ist abgefahren; *(let)* lassen (lässt), ließ, gelassen
lecture die Vorlesung, -en
  to a lecture, to lectures in die Vorlesung

lecture hall der Hörsaal, Hörsäle
left; to the left links
leg das Bein, -e
  Break a leg! Hals- und Beinbruch!
leisure time die Freizeit
to **lend** leihen, lieh, geliehen
to **let** lassen (lässt), ließ, gelassen
letter der Brief, -e
letter carrier der Briefträger, -/ die Briefträgerin, -nen
library die Bibliothek, -en
  to the library in die Bibliothek
lie die Lüge, -n
to **lie** *(tell a lie)* lügen, log, gelogen; *(be situated)* liegen, lag, gelegen
life das Leben, -
lifestyle der Lebensstil, -e
light das Licht, -er
light hell; *(weight)* leicht
lightning der Blitz, -e
  it's lightning es blitzt
  with lightning speed blitzartig
like wie
  like a king wie ein König
  What's your apartment like? Wie ist Ihre Wohnung?
to **like** mögen (mag), mochte, gemocht; gefallen (gefällt), gefiel, gefallen *(+ dat)*
  to **like about** gefallen an *(+ dat)*
  to **like somebody** jemand *(acc)* gern haben
  I like this jacket. Diese Jacke gefällt mir.
  I like to cook. Ich koche gern.
  I would like . . . Ich möchte …
lip die Lippe, -n
lipstick der Lippenstift, -e
list die Liste, -n
to **listen** zu·hören
to **listen to** hören; an·hören
liter der Liter, -
literature die Literatur, -en
little *(size)* klein; *(amount)* wenig
to **live** *(in a country or a city)* leben; *(in a street or building)* wohnen
living: What do you do for a living? Was sind Sie von Beruf?
living accommodation die Unterkunft, ⁼e
living expenses der Lebensunterhalt
living room das Wohnzimmer, -
to **load** laden (lädt), lud, geladen
location die Lage, -n
long lang

to **look** schauen; *(appear)* aus·sehen (sieht aus), sah aus, ausgesehen
to **look at** an·schauen; schauen auf *(+ acc)*
to **look for** suchen
to **look forward to** sich freuen auf *(+ acc)*
to **lose** verlieren, verlor, verloren
lot die Menge, -n
  a lot viel; eine Menge
loud laut
loudspeaker der Lautsprecher, -
love die Liebe; *(as closing of a letter)* Herzliche Grüße, Liebe Grüße
  to **fall in love with** sich verlieben in *(+ acc)*
  to **love** lieben
lox der Lachs
luck das Glück
  Good luck! Hals- und Beinbruch!; Viel Glück!
lunch das Mittagessen
  for lunch zum Mittagessen
  to **have lunch** zu Mittag essen
  lunch break die Mittagspause, -n
luxury der Luxus

M

macaroni die Makkaroni *(pl)*
machine die Maschine, -n
magazine das Magazin, -e; die Zeitschrift, -en
mail die Post
main course das Hauptgericht, -e
majority die Mehrzahl
to **make** machen
make-up: to put on make-up (sich) schminken
man der Mann, -er
many viele
many a mancher, manches, manche
map die Karte, -n
  map of the city der Stadtplan, -e
March der März
mark *(grade)* die Zensur, -en
market der Markt, -e; der Wochenmarkt, -e
marriage die Ehe, -n; die Heirat, -en
married verheiratet
to **marry** heiraten
maternal mütterlicherseits
math die Mathe
matter
  no matter egal

That doesn't matter! Das macht doch nichts!
What's the matter with you? Was ist los mit dir?
May der Mai
may: to be allowed to dürfen (darf), durfte, gedurft
  May I help you? *(to a customer)* Sie wünschen?
meal das Essen
  Enjoy your meal! Guten Appetit!
to **mean** meinen; bedeuten; heißen, hieß, geheißen
meaning die Bedeutung, -en; der Sinn *(sing)*
meantime: in the meantime inzwischen
meat das Fleisch
medicine das Medikament, -e
to **meet** (sich) treffen (trifft), traf, getroffen
member das Mitglied, -er
to **memorize** auswendig lernen
men's department die Herrenabteilung, -en
to **mend** flicken
menu die Speisekarte, -n
messy unordentlich
meter der Meter, -
microwave (oven) die Mikrowelle, -n
middle die Mitte, -n
  in the middle of mitten in
  (in) the middle of July Mitte Juli
midnight (die) Mitternacht
milk die Milch
mineral water das Mineralwasser
minute die Minute, -n
  in a minute gleich; sofort
mirror der Spiegel, -
miserable miserabel
mistake der Fehler, -
modern modern
modest bescheiden
mom die Mutti, -s, die Mama, -s
moment der Moment, -e
Monday der Montag, -e *(see also **Friday**)*
money das Geld
monitor der Bildschirm, -e
month der Monat, -e
monthly monatlich
mood: in a good mood vergnügt
moon der Mond
more mehr
  more and more immer mehr
  not any more nicht mehr

once more noch einmal; noch mal
morning der Morgen, -; der Vormittag, -e
  Good morning! Guten Morgen! Morgen!
  in the morning morgens; vormittags
  this morning heute Morgen
  tomorrow morning morgen früh
mosquito der Moskito, -s
most meist
mostly meistens
mother die Mutter, -
  on one's mother's side mütterlicherseits
  Mother's Day der Muttertag, -e
motherly mütterlich
motor der Motor, -en
motorboat das Motorboot, -e
motorcycle das Motorrad, -er
mountain der Berg, -e
mountain bike das Mountainbike, -s
mountain biking: to go mountain biking Mountainbiking gehen
mountain range das Gebirge
mouse *(also computer)* die Maus, -e
mustache der Schnurrbart, -e
mouth der Mund, -er
to **move** *(change residence)* um·ziehen, zog um, ist umgezogen
to **move in** ein·ziehen, zog ein, ist eingezogen
to **move out** aus·ziehen, zog aus, ist ausgezogen
movies das Kino, -s
  to the movies ins Kino
to **mow** mähen
Mr. Herr
Mrs., Ms. Frau
much viel
  far too much viel zu viel
  too much zu viel
muesli das Müsli
  a bowl of muesli eine Schüssel Müsli
Munich (das) München
to **murder** ermorden
museum das Museum, Museen
mushroom der Champignon, -s
music die Musik
musical musikalisch
must: to have to müssen (muss), musste, gemusst
mustard der Senf, -e
my mein, mein, meine
myself, yourself, herself, etc. selbst

N

name der Name, -ns, -n
  first name der Vorname, -ns, -n
  last name der Familienname, -ns, -n
  My name is . . . Ich heiße …
  What's your name? Wie heißen
    Sie?/Wie heißt du? Wie ist Ihr
    Name?
to **name** nennen, nannte, genannt
napkin die Serviette, -n
narrator der Erzähler, -/die
  Erzählerin, -nen
narrow schmal
nationality die Nationalität, -en
natural(ly) natürlich
nature die Natur
near bei; nah
  near the university in der Nähe der
    Uni
neat *(tidy)* ordentlich; *(excellent)* cool;
  toll
neck der Hals, ¨e
necklace die Halskette, -n
to **need** brauchen
negative negativ
neighbor der Nachbar, -n, -n/die
  Nachbarin, -nen
neither . . . nor weder … noch
nephew der Neffe, -n, -n
nerves: She gets on my nerves. Sie
  geht mir auf die Nerven. Sie nervt
  mich. Sie ist eine Nervtante.
nervous nervös
never nie; niemals
nevertheless trotzdem
new neu
New Year das Neujahr
  Happy New Year! Einen guten
    Rutsch ins neue Jahr!
New Year's Eve der Silvesterabend, -e,
  (der) Silvester
news die Nachrichten *(pl)*
newspaper die Zeitung, -en
newspaper ad die Anzeige, -n
next nächst
  next to neben *(+ acc/dat)*
  next year nächstes Jahr
nice *(pleasant)* nett; *(beautiful)* schön
niece die Nichte, -n
night die Nacht, ¨e
  at night bei Nacht; nachts
  Good night! Gute Nacht!
  last night gestern Nacht
  night table der Nachttisch, -e

no nein; *(neg indef art)* kein, kein,
  keine
  no longer nicht mehr
no one niemand
nobody niemand
Nonsense! Quatsch!
noodle die Nudel, -n
noon der Mittag
normally normalerweise
north der Norden
  north (of) nördlich (von + *dat*)
North America (das) Nordamerika
North American *(adj)*
  nordamerikanisch
nose die Nase, -n
not nicht
  not any more nicht mehr
  not at all gar nicht; überhaupt nicht
  not even nicht mal
  not until erst
  not yet noch nicht
not a, not any, no kein, kein, keine
note die Notiz, -en
notebook *(computer)* das Notebook, -s
nothing nichts
  nothing at all gar nichts; überhaupt
    nichts
  nothing but trouble nichts als Ärger
to **notice** merken
novel der Roman, -e
November der November
now jetzt
  from now on von jetzt ab
nowadays heutzutage
number die Nummer, -n; die Zahl,
  -en
nut die Nuss, ¨e

O

ocean das Meer, -e; der Ozean, -e
occupation der Beruf, -e
  What's your occupation? Was sind
    Sie von Beruf?
o'clock: at one o'clock um ein Uhr;
  um eins
October der Oktober
of *(prep)* von *(+ dat)*
  Of course! Natürlich! Klar!
offer das Angebot, -e
to **offer** an·bieten, bot an, angeboten
office das Büro, -s
office help die Bürohilfe
often oft
oil das Öl, -e
OK in Ordnung

old alt
old-fashioned altmodisch
old age das Alter
olive die Olive, -n
on, onto *(prep)* *(a vertical surface)* an
  (+ acc/dat); *(a horizontal surface)* auf
  (+ acc/dat)
once einmal
  once more noch einmal, noch mal
one *(you)* man
  one and a half eineinhalb
  one another einander
only bloß; nur; erst; *(single)* einzig
only child das Einzelkind, -er
to **open** auf·machen; öffnen
opera die Oper, -n
opinion die Meinung, -en
  in my opinion meiner Meinung
    nach
optimistic optimistisch
or *(coord conj)* oder
  or else sonst
orange die Orange, -n
orange juice der Orangensaft
orchestra das Orchester, -
order die Ordnung
  in order to um … zu
to **order** bestellen
ordinary einfach
originally ursprünglich
other ander-
otherwise sonst
our unser, unser, unsere
out of *(prep)* aus *(+ dat)*
outfit das Outfit, -s
outside außen
over über *(+ acc/dat)*
  to **be over** zu Ende sein;
    vorbei sein
overnight
  overnight accommodation die
    Übernachtung, -en
  to **stay overnight** übernachten
oversalted versalzen
to **owe** schulden
own eigen

P

to **pack** packen; ein·packen
package die Packung, -en
page die Seite, -n
pain der Schmerz, -en
to **paint** *(a picture)* malen; *(a house)*
  streichen, strich, gestrichen
painter der Maler, -/die Malerin, -nen

pair das Paar, -e
a pair of shoes ein Paar Schuhe
pan die Pfanne, -n
pants die Hose, -n
paper das Papier, -e; *(report)* das Referat, -e
  piece of paper der Zettel, -
paragraph der Absatz, ⸚e; der Paragraph, -en, -en
parcel das Paket, -e
Pardon? I beg your pardon? Wie bitte?
parents die Eltern *(pl)*
park der Park, -s
to park parken
parking lot der Parkplatz, ⸚e
parking space der Parkplatz, ⸚e
part der Teil, -e
partially teilweise
particularly besonders
partner der Partner, -/die Partnerin, -nen
party die Party, -s; die Fete, -n; *(political)* die Partei, -en
passport der Pass, ⸚e
paternal väterlicherseits
patio die Terrasse, -n
pay die Bezahlung; der Lohn, ⸚e
to pay bezahlen
to pay attention auf·passen
peace der Frieden; die Ruhe
  in peace and quiet in aller Ruhe
pedestrian area die Fußgängerzone, -n
penny der Pfennig, -e
people die Leute *(pl)*; die Menschen *(pl)*
pepper der Pfeffer
percent das Prozent, -e
perfume das Parfüm, -s
perhaps vielleicht; wohl
perm die Dauerwelle, -n
permission die Erlaubnis
permitted: to be permitted dürfen (darf), durfte, gedurft
person der Mensch, -en, -en; die Person, -en
personal persönlich
personnel manager der Personalchef, -s/die Personalchefin, -nen
to persuade überreden
pessimistic pessimistisch
pet das Haustier, -e
pharmacy die Apotheke, -n
photo das Foto, -s; die Fotografie, -n

photo store das Fotogeschäft, -e
to photograph fotografieren
physique die Figur
to pick out something sich *(dat)* etwas aus·suchen
to pick up ab·holen
picnic das Picknick, -s
picture das Bild, -er
piece das Stück, -e
  a piece of cake ein Stück Kuchen
  piece of furniture das Möbelstück
pig das Schwein, -e
pigsty der Schweinestall, ⸚e
  What a pigsty! Was für ein Schweinestall!
pile der Haufen, -
pill die Tablette, -n
pink rosarot
pizza die Pizza, -s
pizzeria die Pizzeria, -s
place der Ort, -e; der Platz, ⸚e
  place of residence der Wohnort, -e
  place of work der Arbeitsplatz, ⸚e
plaid kariert
plan der Plan, ⸚e
to plan planen
to plan, to have planned vor·haben (hat vor), hatte vor, vorgehabt
plant die Pflanze, -n
plastic das Plastik, -s
plastic bag die Plastiktasche, -n
plate der Teller, -
play das Theaterstück, -e
to play spielen
pleasant nett
please bitte
pleased: to be pleased (with) sich freuen (über + *acc*)
plump mollig
pocket die Tasche, -n
pocket knife das Taschenmesser, -
poem das Gedicht, -e
police die Polizei *(sing)*
police station die Polizeiwache, -n
Polish *(adj)* polnisch
polite höflich
political politisch
politics die Politik
poll die Umfrage, -n
poor arm
popular beliebt; populär
population die Bevölkerung
position die Position, -en
possibility die Möglichkeit, -en
possible möglich

as much (quickly, soon) as possible so viel (schnell, bald) wie möglich
post office die Post; das Postamt, ⸚er
postal code die Postleitzahl, -en
postcard die Postkarte, -n
poster das Poster, -
to postpone verschieben, verschob, verschoben
pot der Topf, ⸚e
potato die Kartoffel, -n
potato chips die Kartoffelchips *(pl)*
pound das Pfund, -e
practical praktisch
to practice üben
present das Geschenk, -e
president der Präsident, -en, -en/die Präsidentin, -nen
pretty hübsch
pretzel die Brezel, -n
price der Preis, -e
primitive primitiv
to print drucken
printer der Drucker, -
private privat
private home das Privathaus, ⸚er
pro der Profi, -s
probably wohl; sicher
problem das Problem, -e
to produce produzieren
product das Produkt, -e
profession der Beruf, -e
professionally beruflich
project das Projekt, -e
to promise versprechen (verspricht), versprach, versprochen
pronunciation die Aussprache
province die Provinz, -en
pub die Kneipe, -n; *(Austria)* das Beisel, -
  to a pub in die Kneipe
pudding der Pudding, -s
to pull ziehen, zog, gezogen
punctual pünktlich
punk der Punk, -s
purple violett
to put *(in an upright position)* stellen; *(stick)* stecken; *(in a horizontal position)* legen
to put on an·ziehen, zog an, angezogen; *(one's head)* auf·setzen
to put on make-up sich schminken

Q

qualified qualifiziert
quarter das Viertel, -

quarter after eleven Viertel nach elf
quarter to eleven Viertel vor elf
queen die Königin, -nen
question die Frage, -n
  to **ask (answer) a question** eine
    Frage stellen (beantworten)
  That's out of the question! Das
    kommt gar nicht in Frage!
quick(ly) schnell
quiet ruhig
quite ganz; ziemlich

R

to **race** rasen
radio das Radio, -s
rag der Lumpen, -
rage die Wut
railway die Bahn
rain der Regen
to **rain** regnen
rainy weather das Regenwetter
rare selten
rate: at any rate jedenfalls
rather ziemlich
to **reach** erreichen
to **react (to)** reagieren (auf + *acc*)
to **read** lesen (liest), las, gelesen
  The thermometer reads ten
    degrees. Das Thermometer zeigt
    zehn Grad.
to **read aloud** vor·lesen (liest vor), las
  vor, vorgelesen
to **read through** durch·lesen (liest
  durch), las durch, durchgelesen
ready fertig
real echt
reality die Wirklichkeit
to **realize** merken
really wirklich; echt
  That's really fantastic. Das ist echt
    toll.
to **rearrange** um·stellen
reason der Grund, ⁼e
reasonable *(price)* preisgünstig
to **receive** bekommen, bekam,
  bekommen; kriegen
receiver *(of a telephone)* der Hörer, -
recently in letzter Zeit
recipe das Rezept, -e
to **recognize** erkennen, erkannte,
  erkannt
to **recommend** empfehlen
  (empfiehlt), empfahl, empfohlen
red rot
red wine der Rotwein, -e

reduced reduziert
  sharply reduced stark reduziert
refrigerator der Kühlschrank, ⁼e
regardless egal
to **regret** bereuen
regular(ly) regelmäßig
related verwandt
relative der/die Verwandte, -en;
  relatives *(as a group)* die
    Verwandschaft
to **relax** aus·spannen
to **renovate** renovieren
rent die Miete, -n
to **rent** mieten
to **rent out** vermieten
to **repair** reparieren
to **repeat** wiederholen
to **replace (with)** ersetzen (durch
  + *acc*)
report das Referat, -e
to **report** berichten
to **reserve** reservieren
residence *(place of)* der Wohnort, -e;
  (student) das Studentenheim, -e
resolution der Vorsatz, ⁼e
restaurant das Gasthaus, ⁼er; das
  Restaurant, -s
reunification die Wiedervereinigung
Rhine *(river)* der Rhein
rhubarb der Rhabarber
rice der Reis
rich reich
ride die Fahrt, -en
to **ride** *(a bike)* Rad fahren (fährt
  Rad), fuhr Rad, ist Rad gefahren
to **ride** *(a horse)* reiten, ritt, ist geritten
right richtig; das Recht, -e
  It's not right that . . . Es ist nicht
    recht, dass …
  right around the corner gleich um
    die Ecke
  right away gleich; sofort
  That's right. Das stimmt.
  to **be right** stimmen
  You're right. Du hast recht.
right, to the right rechts
ring der Ring, -e
to **ring** klingeln
ripe reif
to **risk** riskieren
river der Fluss, ⁼e
roast der Braten, -
rock festival das Rockfest, -e
rock group die Rockgruppe, -n
rock music der Rock

rock star der Rockstar, -s
rocking chair der Schaukelstuhl, ⁼e
role die Rolle, -n
roll das Brötchen, -
romantic romantisch
roof das Dach, ⁼er
room das Zimmer, -
roommate der Mitbewohner, -/die
  Mitbewohnerin, -nen
rose die Rose, -n
round rund
rug der Teppich, -e
to **ruin** kaputt·machen
to **run** rennen, rannte, ist gerannt;
  laufen (läuft), lief, ist gelaufen
  I ran out of money. Mir ist das Geld
    ausgegangen.
rush: There's no rush. Es hat keine
  Eile.
Russian *(adj)* russisch
rye bread das Schwarzbrot

S

to **saddle** satteln
to **sail** segeln
sailboat das Segelboot, -e
salad der Salat, -e
salami die Salami, -s
sales slip der Kassenzettel, -
salesperson der Verkäufer, -/die
  Verkäuferin, -nen
salt das Salz
salty salzig
  too salty versalzen
same gleich; derselbe, dasselbe,
  dieselbe
sandal die Sandale, -n
sandwich das Brot, -e
satisfied zufrieden
Saturday der Samstag, -e *(see also*
  Friday)
sauce die Soße, -n
saucer die Untertasse, -n
sauerkraut das Sauerkraut
sauna die Sauna, -s
sausage die Wurst, ⁼e
to **save** sparen
to **say** sagen
  Say . . . Sag mal …
scanner der Scanner, -
scarcely kaum
scared
  to **be scared (of)** Angst haben
    (vor + *dat*)
  to **get scared** Angst kriegen

scarf der Schal, -e
scene die Szene, -n
schedule *(train or bus)* der Fahrplan, ⸚e
school die Schule, -n
schooldays die Schulzeit
science fiction die Sciencefiction
Scrabble das Scrabble
to scream schreien, schrie, geschrien
scoop *(ice cream)* die Kugel, -n
sea das Meer, -e; die See, -n
seasick seekrank
season die Jahreszeit, -en
seat der Sitz, -e; der (Sitz)platz, ⸚e
second die Sekunde, -n; *(ordinal)* zweit
secretary der Sekretär, -e / die Sekretärin, -nen
to see sehen (sieht), sah, gesehen
  See you later! Bis später!
to see again wieder·sehen (sieht wieder), sah wieder, wiedergesehen
seldom selten
selection die Auswahl
to sell verkaufen
semester das Semester, -
seminar das Seminar, -e; die Übung, -en
to send schicken
senior citizens' home das Seniorenheim, -e
sense der Sinn
sentimental sentimental
separate getrennt
to separate trennen
September der September
serious ernst
to serve servieren; *(guests in a restaurant)* bedienen
server der Kellner, - / die Kellnerin, -nen; die Bedienung
service der Service
serviette die Serviette, -n
to set setzen
to set the table den Tisch decken
sewing machine die Nähmaschine, -n
to shake schütteln
  to shake one's head den Kopf schütteln
shampoo das Shampoo, -s
shape die Form, -en
shared housing die Wohngemeinschaft, -en; die WG, -s
sharp scharf

to shave (sich) rasieren
shaver der Rasierapparat, -e
to shine scheinen, schien, geschienen
ship das Schiff, -e
shirt das Hemd, -en
shock der Schock
to shock schockieren
shoe der Schuh, -e
shoe store das Schuhgeschäft, -e
shopping das Einkaufen
  to go shopping ein·kaufen gehen
shopping bag die Einkaufstasche, -n
shopping cart der Einkaufswagen, -
shopping list die Einkaufsliste, -n
short kurz; *(stature)* klein
shorts die Shorts *(pl)*
should *(to be supposed to)* sollen, sollte, gesollt
shoulder die Schulter, -n
to shout schreien, schrie, geschrien
to show zeigen
shower die Dusche, -n
to shower sich duschen
showy protzig
siblings die Geschwister *(pl)*
sick krank
  I'm sick of it. Ich habe es satt.
  I'm totally sick of it! Das hängt mir zum Hals heraus!
sickness die Krankheit, -en
side die Seite, -n
silly albern
silver das Silber
silverware das Besteck *(sing)*
similar ähnlich
simple einfach
since *(prep)* seit *(+ dat)*
  since then seither
to sing singen, sang, gesungen
single einzig; *(unmarried)* ledig
  single-family dwelling das Einfamilienhaus, ⸚er
sink das Spülbecken, -; *(bathroom)* das Waschbecken, -
to sink sinken, sank, ist gesunken
sister die Schwester, -n
sisters and brothers die Geschwister *(pl)*
to sit sitzen, saß, gesessen
to sit down sich setzen; sich hin·setzen
size die Größe, -n
skate (ice) der Schlittschuh, -e
  to go (ice) skating Schlittschuhlaufen gehen

ski der Ski, -er
  to go skiing Skilaufen gehen
skirt der Rock, ⸚e
skit der Sketch, -es
sky der Himmel
to sleep schlafen (schläft), schlief, geschlafen
sleeping bag der Schlafsack, ⸚e
sleeping pill die Schlaftablette, -n
sleeve der Ärmel, -
slice die Scheibe, -n
  a slice of bread eine Scheibe Brot
slim schlank; schmal
slipper der Hausschuh, -e
slit *(adj)* geschlitzt
slow(ly) langsam
small klein
smart klug; intelligent; clever
to smell riechen, roch, gerochen
to smoke rauchen
smooth(ly) glatt
to snore schnarchen
snow der Schnee
to snow schneien
snowstorm der Schneesturm, ⸚e
so so
  So long! Auf Wiedersehen! Tschüss!
  so that *(sub conj)* damit
  so-called so genannt
soap die Seife, -n
soap opera die Seifenoper, -n
soccer: to play soccer Fußball spielen
soccer ball der Fußball, ⸚e
soccer game das Fußballspiel, -e
soccer stadium das Fußballstadion, -stadien
sock die Socke, -n
soft drink der Softdrink, -s
soft ice cream das Softeis
software die Software
solution die Lösung, -en
to solve lösen
some manche
  some . . . or other irgendein, irgendein, irgendeine
somebody, someone jemand
  somebody else jemand anders
something etwas
sometimes manchmal
somewhat einigermaßen
son der Sohn, ⸚e
song das Lied, -er; der Song, -s
soon bald
  as soon as possible so bald wie möglich

sore throat die Halsschmerzen (pl)
sorry: I'm sorry. Es tut mir leid.
soup die Suppe, -n
sour sauer
south der Süden
  south (of) südlich (von + dat)
spaghetti die Spaghetti (pl)
Spanish (adj) spanisch
to **speak** sprechen (spricht), sprach, gesprochen; reden
special
  special day das Fest, -e
  special of the day das Tagesmenü, -s
speech die Rede, -n
  to **give a speech** eine Rede halten
to **spell** buchstabieren
to **spend** (money) aus·geben (gibt aus), gab aus, ausgegeben; (time) verbringen, verbrachte, verbracht; (the night) übernachten
spicy scharf
spinach der Spinat
spite: in spite of (prep) trotz (+ gen)
spoon der Löffel, -
sport coupe das Sportcoupé, -s
sport(s) der Sport
  What sport(s) do you do? Was für Sport machst du?
sporting goods store das Sportgeschäft, -e
sports program das Sportprogramm, -e
spotless tipptopp
spring der Frühling; das Frühjahr
  in spring im Frühling (Frühjahr)
square foot der Quadratfuß
  ten square feet zehn Quadratfuß
squash (sport) das Squash
stable der Stall, ¨e
stadium das Stadion, Stadien
staircase die Treppe, -n
stamp die Briefmarke, -n
to **stand** stehen, stand, gestanden; (put in an upright position) stellen; (endure) aus·halten (hält aus), hielt aus, ausgehalten
to **stand up** auf·stehen, stand auf, ist aufgestanden
star der Stern, -e
to **start** an·fangen (fängt an), fing an, angefangen; beginnen, begann, begonnen; starten
state der Staat, -en; das Land, ¨er
statement die Aussage, -n
statistic die Statistik, -en

to **stay** bleiben, blieb, ist geblieben
to **stay overnight** übernachten
steak das Steak, -s
to **steal** stehlen (stiehlt), stahl, gestohlen
stepfather der Stiefvater, ¨
stepmother die Stiefmutter, ¨
stereo die Stereoanlage, -n
to **stick** stecken
stiff steif
still noch; immer noch
stocking der Strumpf, ¨e
stomach der Bauch, ¨e
stomachache die Bauchschmerzen (pl)
stool der Hocker, -
to **stop** halten (hält), hielt, gehalten; an·halten (hält an), hielt an, angehalten; stoppen; (doing something) auf·hören; (walking) stehen bleiben, blieb stehen, ist stehen geblieben
  Stop bothering me! Lass mich in Ruhe!
store das Geschäft, -e
  clothing store das Kleidergeschäft, -e
  department store das Kaufhaus, ¨er
  electronics store das Elektronikgeschäft, -e
  gourmet foods store das Feinkostgeschäft, -e
storm der Sturm, ¨e
stormy stürmisch
story die Geschichte, -n; die Erzählung, -en; (in a building) der Stock, Stockwerke
stove der Herd, -e
straight (of hair) glatt
street die Straße, -n
stress der Stress
to **stress** betonen
stressful stressig
striped gestreift
strong(ly) stark
stubborn dickköpfig
student (university) der Student, -en, -en/die Studentin, -nen; (elem. or high school) der Schüler, -/ die Schülerin, -nen
student choir der Studentenchor, ¨e
student center das Studentenwerk
student ID der Studentenausweis, -e
student residence das Studentenheim, -e
studies das Studium (sing)

to **study** (i.e., to attend college or university) studieren; (to spend time studying) lernen
stuffed toy animal das Stofftier, -e
stupid dumm; doof; blöd; bescheuert
stylish flott
subject (of study) das Fach, ¨er, das Studienfach, ¨er
success der Erfolg, -e
such solcher, solches, solche
  such a so ein
suddenly plötzlich; mit einem Mal; auf einmal
sugar der Zucker
suit (men's) der Anzug, ¨e
  jogging suit der Jogginganzug, ¨e
to **suit** passen; stehen
  That doesn't suit me at all. Das passt mir gar nicht.
suitable geeignet; passend
  something suitable etwas Passendes
suitcase der Koffer, -
summer der Sommer, -
  in summer im Sommer
summer cottage das Ferienhaus, ¨er
summer holidays, summer vacation die Sommerferien (pl)
summer job der Ferienjob, -s
summer sale der Sommerschlussverkauf, ¨e
sun die Sonne
Sunday der Sonntag, -e (see also **Friday**)
sunglasses die Sonnenbrille, -n
sunny sonnig
  sunny with some clouds heiter
suntan lotion die Sonnencreme, -s
super super
supermarket der Supermarkt, ¨e
supper das Abendessen, -
  for supper zum Abendessen
  to **have supper** zu Abend essen
supposed: to be supposed to sollen, sollte, gesollt
sure, surely sicher
  for sure bestimmt
surfboard das Surfbrett, -er
surfing: to go surfing surfen gehen
surprise die Überraschung, -en
survey die Umfrage, -n
swanky protzig
sweater der Pulli, -s; der Pullover, -
sweatshirt das Sweatshirt, -s
sweet (adj) süß; (candy) die Süßigkeit, -en

to **swim** schwimmen, schwamm, ist
  geschwommen
swimming: to go swimming baden
  gehen; schwimmen gehen
swimming weather (das) Badewetter
Swiss *(adj)* schweizerisch
Switzerland die Schweiz
symphony die Sinfonie, -n
synagogue die Synagoge, -n
system das System, -e

T

T-shirt das T-Shirt, -s
table der Tisch, -e
  to **set the table** den Tisch decken
tablet die Tablette, -n
tablespoon der Esslöffel, -
tactless taktlos
to **take** nehmen (nimmt), nahm,
  genommen; *(time)* dauern,
  brauchen
  Take care! Mach's gut!
to **take along** mit·nehmen (nimmt
  mit), nahm mit, mitgenommen
to **take off** *(airplane)* starten
to **take on** *(a duty)* übernehmen
  (übernimmt), übernahm,
  übernommen
to **take part (in)** teil·nehmen (nimmt
  teil), nahm teil, teilgenommen
  (an + *dat*)
talent das Talent, -e
talk die Rede, -n
  talk show die Talkshow, -s
to **talk** sprechen (spricht), sprach,
  gesprochen; reden; *(converse)* sich
  unterhalten (unterhält),
  unterhielt, unterhalten
  to **talk on the phone (with)**
  telefonieren (mit)
tall groß
tango der Tango, -s
task die Aufgabe, -n
taste der Geschmack
to **taste, to taste good** schmecken
tasteful geschmackvoll
tasteless geschmacklos
taxi das Taxi, -s
tea der Tee
tea kettle der Teekessel, -;
  der Wasserkocher, -
to **teach** lehren; unterrichten
teacher der Lehrer, -/die Lehrerin,
  -nen
teapot die Teekanne, -n

teaspoon der Teelöffel, -
technical college die
  Fachhochschule, -n
teddy bear der Teddybär, -en, -en
teenager der Teenager, -
telephone das Telefon, -e
telephone number die
  Telefonnummer, -n
television der Fernseher, -; *(TV
  broadcasting)* das Fernsehen
  to **watch television** fern·sehen
  (sieht fern), sah fern, ferngesehen
television set der Fernseher, -
to **tell** sagen; *(a story)* erzählen
  Tell me . . . Sag mal …
  to **tell about** erzählen von
tender *(cooking)* gar
tennis: to play Tennis Tennis spielen
tennis court der Tennisplatz, ̈-e
tennis racquet der Tennisschläger, -
tent das Zelt, -e
terrible schrecklich
test die Klausur, -en
textbook das Unterrichtsbuch, ̈-er;
  das Lehrbuch, ̈-er
than als
  better than besser als
to **thank** danken (+ *dat*)
  Thank God! Gott sei Dank!
  thank you danke; danke schön
thanks der Dank *(sing)*
  Fine, thanks. Danke, gut.
that *(sub conj)* dass
that is (i.e.) das heißt (d.h.)
theater das Theater, -
  to the theater ins Theater
their ihr, ihr, ihre
then dann; da; *(at that time)* damals
  since then seither
therapy die Therapie, -n
there dort; da
  down there dort unten
  over there dort drüben
there is, there are es gibt *(+ acc)*
therefore deshalb
thermometer das Thermometer, -
  The thermometer reads ten degrees.
  Das Thermometer zeigt zehn Grad.
thick dick
thin dünn; *(face)* schmal
thing das Ding, -e; die Sache, -n
to **think** denken, dachte, gedacht;
  glauben; meinen
  I can't think of anything. Mir fällt
  nichts ein.

  that's what you think denkste
to **think of (about)** denken (an
  + *acc*)
thirst der Durst
  I'm thirsty. Ich habe Durst.
this dieser, dieses, diese
  this afternoon (evening, morning)
  heute Nachmittag (Abend,
  Morgen)
thrifty sparsam
through *(prep)* durch *(+ acc)*
to **throw** werfen (wirft), warf,
  geworfen
thumb der Daumen, -
thunder der Donner
to **thunder** donnern
Thursday der Donnerstag, -e *(see also*
  Friday)
ticket die Karte, -n; *(traffic)*
  der Strafzettel, -
tie die Krawatte, -n
time die Zeit, -en; *(occurrence)*
  das Mal, -e
  (at) any time jederzeit
  at that time damals
  (at) what time um wie viel Uhr
  every time jedes Mal
  for the first time zum ersten Mal
  on time rechtzeitig; pünktlich
  the last time das letzte Mal
  this time diesmal
  What time is it? Wie spät ist es? Wie
  viel Uhr ist es?
time of day die Uhrzeit
timetable der Stundenplan, ̈-e
tiny winzig
tip das Trinkgeld, -er
tired müde
title der Titel, -
to *(prep)* zu; *(a city or country)* nach;
  (an institution) auf *(+ acc/dat)*;
  (a vertical surface) an *(+ acc/dat)*;
  in *(+ acc/dat)*
toast der Toast
toaster der Toaster, -
today heute
toe die Zehe, -n
together zusammen
  to **go together** *(match)*
  zusammen·passen
toilet das Klo, -s; das WC, -s
tomato die Tomate, -n
tomorrow morgen
  the day after tomorrow
  übermorgen

tomorrow afternoon morgen Nachmittag

tomorrow morning morgen früh

toner der Toner

tongue die Zunge, -n

tonight heute Abend

too *(also)* auch; zu

tool das Werkzeug, -e

tooth der Zahn, ⸚e

toothache die Zahnschmerzen *(pl)*

toothbrush die Zahnbürste, -n

toothpaste die Zahnpasta

topic das Thema, Themen

tourist der Tourist, -en, -en/die Touristin, -nen

towel das Handtuch, ⸚er

town die Stadt, ⸚e

  to town in die Stadt

trade: He's a cook by trade. Er ist Koch von Beruf.

train der Zug, ⸚e

  train trip die Bahnfahrt, -en

  train station der Bahnhof, ⸚e

to train aus·bilden

training die Ausbildung

to translate übersetzen

translation die Übersetzung, -en

to travel reisen

travel agency das Reisebüro, -s

travel brochure die Reisebroschüre, -n

to treat behandeln

tree der Baum, ⸚e

trip die Reise, -n

  to go on a trip eine Reise machen

trouble der Ärger

  nothing but trouble nichts als Ärger

truck der Lastwagen, -; der Lastkraftwagen, -; der Lkw, -s

true wahr; richtig

trunk *(of a car)* der Kofferraum

truth die Wahrheit, -en

to try versuchen

to try on an·probieren

to try out aus·probieren

T-shirt das T-Shirt, -s

Tuesday der Dienstag, -e *(see also* **Friday***)*

Turkish *(adj)* türkisch

turn: Now it's your turn. Jetzt bist du dran.

TV der Fernseher, -; *(TV broadcasting)* das Fernsehen

  to watch TV fern·sehen (sieht fern), sah fern, ferngesehen

TV screen der Bildschirm, -e

TV set der Fernseher, -

TV show das Fernsehprogramm, -e

twice zweimal

twin der Zwilling, -e

two zwei; beide

typical(ly) typisch

U

ugly hässlich

umbrella der Regenschirm, -e

uncle der Onkel, -

under *(prep)* unter *(+ acc/dat)*

to underline unterstreichen, unterstrich, unterstrichen

to understand verstehen, verstand, verstanden; begreifen, begriff, begriffen; kapieren

to undress sich aus·ziehen, zog sich aus, sich ausgezogen

unemployed arbeitslos

unemployment die Arbeitslosigkeit

unfortunately leider

unhappy unglücklich

unhealthy ungesund

university die Universität, -en; die Uni, -s; die Hochschule, -n

  to the university zur Uni

university dining hall die Mensa

university town die Universitätsstadt, ⸚e

to unpack aus·packen

until *(prep)* bis *(+ acc)*

  not until erst

up

  to be up auf sein

  What's up? Was ist denn los?

upset: to get upset (about) sich auf·regen *(über + acc)*

up-to-date up to date

to use benutzen; verwenden

used: to get used to sich gewöhnen an *(+ acc)*

usually meistens; normalerweise

V

vacation *(generally of students)* die Ferien *(pl)*; die Semesterferien *(pl)*; *(generally of people in the work force)* der Urlaub

  to go on vacation Ferien (Urlaub) machen

vacuum cleaner der Staubsauger, -

Valentine's Day der Valentinstag

valid: to be valid gelten (gilt), galt, gegolten

valley das Tal, ⸚er

vase die Vase, -n

vegetables das Gemüse *(sing)*

vegetarian der Vegetarier, -/die Vegetarierin, -nen; *(adj)* vegetarisch

vehicle das Fahrzeug, -e

very sehr

  very short ganz kurz

via *(prep)* über *(+ acc/dat)*

vicinity die Nähe

  in the vicinity of in der Nähe von *(+ dat)*

video das Video, -s

video camera die Videokamera, -s

Vienna (das) Wien

view die Aussicht, -en

village das Dorf, ⸚er

vinegar der Essig

violinist der Geiger, -/die Geigerin, -nen; der Violinist, -en, -en/die Violinistin, -nen

visit der Besuch, -e

  to come to visit zu Besuch kommen

to visit besuchen

visitor der Besucher, -

vitamin das Vitamin, -e

vocabulary die Vokabeln *(pl)*; der Wortschatz, ⸚e

voice die Stimme, -n

volleyball der Volleyball, ⸚e

vote die Stimme, -en

voucher der Gutschein, -e

W

wages die Bezahlung; der Lohn, ⸚e; der Verdienst, -e

to wait (for) warten *(auf + acc)*

waiter der Kellner, -

  Waiter! Bedienung!

waitress die Kellnerin, -nen

to wake up auf·wachen

to wake up *(someone)* wecken

walk der Spaziergang, ⸚e

  to go for a walk spazieren gehen, ging spazieren, ist spazieren gegangen; einen Spaziergang machen

to walk gehen, ging, ist gegangen; zu Fuß gehen

wall die Mauer, -n; *(of a room)* die Wand, ⸚e

wallet die Geldtasche, -n

to want to wollen (will), wollte, gewollt

war der Krieg, -e
  world war der Weltkrieg, -e
warm warm; herzlich
to warn warnen
warning die Warnung, -en
wash die Wäsche
to wash waschen (wäscht), wusch, gewaschen
washcloth der Waschlappen, -
washer die Waschmaschine, -n
wastepaper basket der Papierkorb, ̈e
watch die Armbanduhr, -en; die Uhr, -en
to watch TV fern·sehen (sieht fern), sah fern, ferngesehen
water das Wasser
to water gießen, goss, gegossen
watering can die Gießkanne, -n
way der Weg, -e
  by the way übrigens
  in this way auf diese Weise
  on the way unterwegs
  That's just the way I am. So bin ich eben.
weak schwach
to wear tragen (trägt), trug, getragen; (put on) an·ziehen, zog an, angezogen
weather das Wetter
  What rotten weather! Was für ein Hundewetter!
  What's the weather like? Wie ist das Wetter?
weather map die Wetterkarte, -n
Web site die Website, -s
wedding die Hochzeit, -en
Wednesday der Mittwoch, -e (see also Friday)
week die Woche, -n
  day of the week der Wochentag, -e
  two weeks vierzehn Tage
weekend das Wochenende, -n
weekly wöchentlich
weekly newspaper die Wochenzeitung, -en
Welcome! Willkommen!
  You're welcome. Bitte schön!
well gut
  to feel well sich wohl fühlen
well-known bekannt
well-loved beliebt
west der Westen
  west (of) westlich (von + dat)

wet nass
what was
  what . . . for wozu
  what else was ... sonst
wheel das Rad, ̈er
wheelchair der Rollstuhl, ̈e
when (sub conj) wenn; (sub conj) als; (question word) wann
where (to what place) wohin; (in what place) wo
where . . . from woher
whether (sub conj) ob
which welcher, welches, welche
while (sub conj; prep + gen) während
white weiß
white wine der Weißwein, -e
who wer
whole ganz
why warum
  that's why deshalb
widow die Witwe, -n
widower der Witwer, -
wife die Frau, -en
wild wild
to win gewinnen, gewann, gewonnen
wind der Wind, -e
windless windstill
window das Fenster, -
windsurfing: to go windsurfing windsurfen gehen
windy windig
wine der Wein, -e
wine glass das Weinglas, ̈er
winter der Winter, -
  in winter im Winter
winter jacket die Winterjacke, -n
winter sale der Winterschlussverkauf, ̈e
wish der Wunsch, ̈e
to wish wünschen
  to wish a Happy Birthday zum Geburtstag gratulieren
with (prep) mit (+ dat)
without (prep) ohne (+ acc)
witty witzig
woman die Frau, -en
women's advocate die Frauenbeauftragte, -n
women's department die Damenabteilung, -en
wonderful wunderbar; herrlich
wood das Holz
woods der Wald, ̈er

wool die Wolle
word (in a meaningful context) das Wort, -e; (individual vocabulary item) das Wort, ̈er
work die Arbeit
work experience die Arbeitserfahrung, -en
to work arbeiten; (part-time or during vacation) jobben
to work on arbeiten an (+ dat)
worked up aufgeregt
  to get worked up (about) sich auf·regen (über + acc)
worker der Arbeiter, -/die Arbeiterin, -nen
world die Welt, -en
worry: Don't worry! Keine Angst!
Wow! Mensch!
wristwatch die Armbanduhr, -en
to write schreiben, schrieb, geschrieben
writing die Schrift, -en
  in writing schriftlich
wrong falsch

Y

to yawn gähnen
year das Jahr, -e
  for a year auf ein Jahr
  last year letztes Jahr
  year in, year out jahraus, jahrein
yearly jährlich
to yell brüllen
yellow gelb
yes ja
yesterday gestern
  yesterday night gestern Nacht
  the day before yesterday vorgestern
yet: not yet noch nicht
yogurt der Joghurt
you (one, people) man
young jung
your dein, dein, deine; Ihr, Ihr, Ihre; euer, euer, eure
youth die Jugend
youth hostel die Jugendherberge, -n
youthful jugendlich
Yuck! Pfui!

Z

zip code die Postleitzahl, -en

Index

At the end of the index under **Kultur** you will find a list of the cultural topics explored in *Treffpunkt Deutsch.* This is followed by **Wörter in Sinngruppen,** which refers you to pages where vocabulary on particular themes appears.

discourse strategies
Sag mal, 14
Und dann? 174
doch
as flavoring particle, 138, 157, 176
to contradict negative statements and
questions, 343
du / Sie / ihr, 4

E

each other, reflexive pronouns to
express, 319
eigentlich as flavoring particle, 389
ein, ein, eine, 23
ein-words, 68, 94
erst, meanings of, 77
es gibt, 105
Eszett, 3, 10

F

false friends, 45, 78
flavoring particles, 14
aber, 244
denn, 51, 150
doch, 138, 157, 176
eigentlich, 389
ja, 14, 138
mal, 138, 157, 176
überhaupt, 389
forms of address, 4
future time
present tense to express, 39
future tense to express, 373

G

ganz, meanings of, 189
gender
of names of countries, 19
of nouns, 20, 21, 54, 88, 188, 224,
262, 296, 328, 392f.
of pronouns, 34
genitive case, 288
adjective endings in, 291
interrogative pronoun in, 288
n-nouns in, 309f.
prepositions with, 413
relative pronoun in, 414
von + dative instead of, 291
gern, 61
comparative of, 61
gern haben, 62
gleich, meanings of, 392

H

haben
as auxiliary of perfect tense, 200
in past-time subjunctive, 412
perfect tense of, 207

present tense of, 59
simple past tense of, 182
versus **sein,** 96
hin and **her,** 217, 219

I

ihr / Sie / du, 4
immer + comparative, 167
imperative, 137ff.
du-imperative, 137
ihr-imperative, 139
Sie-imperative, 139
in
and English *to,* 281
in time phrases, 284
indefinite article, 23
accusative forms of, 91
dative forms of, 236
genitive forms of, 288
negative forms of, 23
nominative forms of, 63
omission of, 96
indirect object, 236, 241
indirect questions, 177
infinitive
(an)statt + **zu**-infinitive, 287
definition of, 37
modals with, 126
of inseparable-prefix verbs, 213
of separable-prefix verbs, 130
ohne + **zu**-infinitive, 287
omission of, after modals, 129
phrases, 285ff.
um + **zu**-infinitive, 286
used as a noun, 262
würde with, 405f.
zu-infinitive, 285
inseparable-prefix verbs, 213
interrogative pronouns
accusative case of, 93
dative case of, 237
genitive case of, 288
nominative case of, 64

J

ja as flavoring particle, 14, 138

K

kein, kein, keine, 23, 63
kennen versus **wissen,** 179

L

lassen, 387
leben versus **wohnen,** 81
lernen versus **studieren,** 49
letter-writing conventions, 216
lieber, 61
Lieblings-, 85
loan words, 10, 78

M

mal as flavoring particle, 138, 157, 176
man, 121
manner, expressions of, 249
mixed verbs
perfect tense of, 214
simple past tense of, 343
modal verbs, 126ff.
in dependent clauses, 142
meaning of, 126
möchte versus **mögen,** 128
omission of infinitive after, 129
position of, 126
position of **nicht** with, 129
present tense of, 126f.
simple past tense of, 182
with separable-prefix verbs, 132
with verb-verb combinations, 134

N

n-nouns, 309f.
nach versus **zu,** 253
nach Hause versus **zu Hause,** 125
negation
with **kein,** 23
with **nicht,** 30
nicht, position of, 30, 103, 129, 132,
134, 202
nominative case, 63
adjective endings in, 70ff.
as subject, 63
as subject completion, 63
der-words in, 67
ein-words in, 68
interrogative pronouns in, 64
personal pronouns in, 34
relative pronouns in, 306f.
nouns
agent, 188, 328
as units of measure, 124
capitalization of, 3
compound, 296
gender of, 20, 21, 54, 88, 188, 224,
262, 296, 328, 392f.
infinitives used as, 262
n-nouns, 309f.
plural forms of, 21f.
suffixes determining gender of, 188,
224, 328, 392f.
that function like separable prefixes,
133
numbers
cardinal, 5f.
ordinal, 215
phone, 6

O

object clauses, 176ff.
after **dass,** 176

DHL, 39
Diesel, Rudolf, 339
Döner Kebab, 76
Drogerie versus Apotheke, 322
du, ihr, and Sie and their social
    implications, 4
Einstein, Albert, 196
Elsener, Karl, 148f.
English and German, 10, 45, 78
ethnic diversity in Germany, 76
Euro, 326f.
Europäische Union, 19, 86, 325, 386
Fachhochschule, 211
Fahrenheit and Celsius scales, 6
fairy tales, 361
families, government support for, 109
fast food, 313
floors in buildings, 348
Fußball, 136, 145
German Democratic Republic (GDR),
    210, 230, 367–371
German language in North America, 208
grades, 49
Grimm, Jakob und Wilhelm, 361
Gropius, Walter, 294, 295
Gropius house, 294
Gutenberg, Johannes, 337
Gymnasium, 2, 211
Hauptschule, 211
Hensel, Jana, 367
Hindemith, Paul, 196
history of Germany, 1918–1990, 370f.
holidays in the German-speaking
    countries, 232f.
housing, 270
immigrants in Germany, 76
immigration to North America, 196f.,
    222f.
Internationale Rote Kreuz, das, 122
Jandl, Ernst, 87
Jugendstil, 86
Jugendherbergen, 158
Kaffee und Kuchen, 246
Kalina, Robert, 326f.
Kiel, 97
landscapes of the German-speaking
    countries, 16
letter-writing conventions, 216
Liechtenstein, 67
Ludwig II. von Bayern, 186f.
Luftbrücke, die Berliner, 370
Luther, Martin, 337
Luxemburg, 325
Mann, Thomas, 196
Mauer, die Berliner, 230, 369, 371
Mecklenburg-Vorpommern, 380f.
Mensa, 2
Merkel, Angela, 399

metric measure, 42
Mitbringsel, 246
Mitfahrzentrale, 41
Mozart, Wolfgang Amadeus, 112f.
Munich, 156
newspapers and magazines, 356
Oktoberfest, 156
paid vacation, 171
parental leave in Germany, 109
phone etiquette, 6
postal adresses, 6
railway system, 135
Realschule, 211
recipes in German, 303
Reichstag, 230
Reformhaus, 322
restaurant customs, 301, 303, 311, 312
Sachs, Hans, 337
Sachsen, 210
Schoenberg, Arnold, 196
school systems of German-speaking
    countries, 211
Schrebergärten, 270
Schüler versus Student, 54
Schurz, Carl, 196
Schwarzfahren, 135
shopping, 301, 322, 323, 324
similarities between German and
    English, 10, 45
Sommersemester, 41
South Tyrol, 184
Steiff, Margarete, 260f.
Strandkörbe, 16
Student versus Schüler, 54
student housing, 268
Swiss Army Knife, 148f.
Switzerland, 122f.
table etiquette, 303
Teddybär, 260f.
topography of the German-speaking
    countries, 16
traffic signs, 133
train travel, 135
tuition fees in Germany, 2
universities, 2, 23, 211
Urlaub, 171
van der Rohe, Mies, 196, 295
vocational training, 211
Walser, Robert, 123
Wilder, Billy, 196
Wintersemester, 41
Wirtschaftswunder, 76
Wohngemeinschaft (WG), 268
women's issues, 399f.
women in government, 399, 401
youth hostels, 158
Zwischenprüfung, 23

Wörter in Sinngruppen

academic subjects, A17
accessories, 163, 190, A20
body, parts of, 198
    expressions with, 224, 328
characteristics and personal traits,
    52, 195, A21f.
classroom expressions, A15
clothing, 80, A19
colors 18, 35
computer, 88
congratulations and good wishes,
    247, 258
countries, 19, A21
eating utensils, 304
days of the week, 48
family, 20, 84, 88, 195
fields of study, A17
food and drink, 124, A20f.
    beverages 54, A21
    breakfast, 121, 124, A20
    expressions with, 263
    dishes and utensils, 304
    lunch, 124, A20
    supper, 124, A20
furnishings, 272
geographical features, 16, 160
grammatical terms, A16
greetings and farewells, 4f., 11
hobbies, 52, A18f.
holidays and celebrations, 234
house and home, 272, 273, 298
household chores, 231
idiomatic expressions, 224, 263, 297,
    328, 362
jobs, 416f., A17f.
languages, A21
months and seasons, 48
musical instruments, A19
nationalities, 19
numbers, 5
personal traits and characteristics,
    52, 195, A21f.
personal grooming, 163, 190,
    315, 330
polite expressions, A22
professions, 416f., A17f.
question words, 25
restaurant, 304, 311f.
rooms of a house, 272
sports, 54, A18f.
time, 54, 57f., 80
university life, 18, 80
vacationing, 160, 161
vehicles, 88
weather, 14, 28, 32

Credits

Text Material

p. 87: "harte vögel für hitchcock" by Ernst Jandl. In Ernst Jandl, poetische Werke, ed. Klaus Siblewski, © 1997 by Luchterhand Literaturverlag, Munich, a publisher of the Random House Publishing Group. **p. 123:** Excerpt from "Schneien" by Robert Walser. *Das Gesamtwerk*, Band 2, *Kleine Dichtungen*. © 1978 by Suhrkamp Verlag, Frankfurt am Main. **p. 367:** Excerpt from *Zonenkinder* by Jana Hensel. Copyright © 2002 by Rowohlt Verlag GmbH, Reinbek bei Hamburg. **p. 388:** "Mein Bruder hat grüne Haare" by Monika Seck-Agthe. © Monika Seck-Agthe. **p. 397:** "Eifersucht" by Tanja Zimmermann. In *Total Verknallt*, rotfuchs 356 © 1984 by Rowohlt Verlag GmbH, Reinbek. **p. 415:** "Meine Zukunkft" by Nina Achminow. In *Morgen beginnt heute. Jugendliche schreiben über die Zukunft*, ed. Biedermann/Boseke/Burkert. Beltz Verlag, Weinheim und Basel 1981.

Photos and realia

Photographs are by Fritz and Rosemarie Widmaier except for the following:

p. 8: Volkswagen Canada; BMW Canada; Allgemeiner Deutscher Automobil-Club e.V.; CDU-Bundesgeschäftsstelle. **p. 16:** (bottom left) German National Tourist Board / Andreas Kaster; (right) Baden-Württemberg, Tourismus Marketing GmbH. **p. 17:** (top left) Austrian Tourist Office; (lower left) Switzerland Tourism / swiss-image.ch, Christof Sonderegger; (right) German National Tourist Board. **p. 32:** (top) Schwäbische Zeitung, Leutkirch. **p. 44:** Rick Strange / Index Stoch Imagery, Inc. **p. 50:** Johannes Tauber. **p. 53:** Brunner Welt der Tausend Uhren, Titisee. **p. 57:** John Paul Heins. **p. 67:** LGT Group. **p. 75:** Granitsas / The Image Works. **p. 82:** Man–Helga Lade Fotoagentur / Peter Arnold, Inc. **p. 97:** Christian-Albrechts-Universität zu Kiel. **p. 98:** (left) Anne Sandhack-Grosser. **p. 108:** Sabine Grosser. **p. 109:** (top) Sabine Grosser. **p. 111:** David Simson / Stock Boston. **p. 113:** Painting, Baroque, 18th Century. Della Croce, Johann Nepomuk (18th), "The Mozart Family" (1780-1781). Oil on canvas. 140 + 186 cm. Mozart House, Salzburg, Austria. Erich Lessing / Art Resource, N.Y. **p. 118:** Switzerland Tourism / swiss-image.ch / Stephan Engler. **p. 122:** Switzerland Tourism New York. **p. 123:** (left) Switzerland Tourism / swiss-image.ch / Schweizer Alpenclub (SAC). **p. 134:** Deutsche Bahn AG. **p. 135:** (bottom) Switzerland Tourism / swiss-image.ch / Christof Sonderegger. **p. 136:** (top left) Fußballclub Bayern Sport-Werbe GmbH; (top right) Fußballclub Schalke 04. **p. 145:** John Gress / Corbis/Bettmann. **p. 148:** Victorinox. **p. 149:** (top and bottom) Victorinox. **p. 156:** Tourismusamt der Landeshauptstadt München, Film- und Fotoservice. **p. 158:** (top) Gerd Hermann; (bottom) Regionaler Fremdenverkehrsverband Erzgebirge e.V. **p. 159:** Regionaler Fremdenverkehrsverband Erzgebirge e.V. **p. 165:** (left) Erster Fußballsportverein Mainz 05; (right) Fußballclub Hansa Rostock. **p. 171:** (graph) Sabine Grosser. **p. 173:** (graph) Sabine Grosser. **p. 187:** (top) German National Tourist Board / Andrew Cowin. **p. 192:** Corbis/Bettmann. **p. 196:** (masthead) Deutsche Presse, Toronto. **p. 197:** (top) Ausländerbefragte des Senats Berlin. Graph: Dr. H.J.-Kämmer. **p. 208:** Amerika Woche. **p. 215:** Lang. **p. 228:** Switzerland Tourism / swiss-image.ch / Christof Sonderegger. **p. 230:** Per Eide / Edelpix. **p. 231:** Verlag Dominique GmbH. **p. 233:** (top) Residence Hotel, Potsdam. **p. 234:** (bottom left) German National Tourist Board. **p. 260:** (top) Margarete Steiff GmbH. **p. 283:** (map) Presse- und Informationsamt des Landes Berlin. **p. 294:** (top right) Karen Storz. **p. 295:** Bauhaus-Archiv, Berlin. **p. 303:** (top) Inter Nationes. **p. 317:** Christiane Morton. **p. 322:** Andrew Dexter. **p. 325:** (top) Gavin Hellier / Robert Harding World Imagery. **p. 325:** (bottom) SuperStock, Inc. **p. 327:** AP Wide World Photos. **p. 337:** Art Resource/Bildarchiv Preussischer Kulturbesitz. **p. 349:** (top right) Katharina Richter. **p. 356:** SPIEGEL-Verlag; Neue Zürcher Zeitung; Die Presse; Luxemburger Wort; Frankfurter Allgemeine Zeitung GmbH; Axel Springer Verlag GmbH; Gruner & Jahr. **p. 358:** Droemersche Verlagsanstalt. Th. Knaur Nachf. München. **p. 367:** PublicAffairs. **p. 369:** Presse- und Informationsamt des Landes Berlin. **p. 370:** Erich Schmidt Verlag, Berlin. **p. 371:** (lower left) Bettmann/Corbis. **p. 371:** (upper left) Norman Currie/UPI/Corbis-Bettmann. **p. 371:** (right) Agence France Presse/Getty Images. **p. 380:** Stadtverwaltung Bad Doberan. **p. 381:** (map) Fink, Kümmerley und Frey GmbH, Ostfildern. **p. 386:** Michael Widmaier. **p. 399:** Presse- und Informationsamt der Bundesregierung. **p. 400:** Globus Infografik GmbH; (bottom) Statistisches Bundesamt BRD; Graph: Sabine Grosser. **p. 411:** Per Eide / Edelpix. **p. 417:** Oliver Hauptstock, Infografik, www.cartomedia.de.

Cover 1: Marian Rene Menges / Bildagentur Hamburg. **Cover 2:** Christian Ohde / Bildagentur Hamburg.

Endpaper maps: CartoGraphics.